BORDERLINE PERSONALITY DISORDER

Primer on Series

Anxiety Disorders
Kerry J. Ressler, Daniel S. Pine, Barbara Olasov Rothbaum

Autism Spectrum Disorder
Christopher J. McDougle

Schizophrenia and Psychotic Spectrum Disorders
S. Charles Schulz, Michael F. Green, Katharine J. Nelson

Mental Health Practice and the Law
Ronald Schouten

BORDERLINE PERSONALITY DISORDER

Edited by

Barbara Stanley, PhD
Professor of Medical Psychology
Department of Psychiatry
Columbia University College of Physicians and Surgeons
Director, Suicide Prevention Training, Implementation and Evaluation
New York State Psychiatric Institute
New York, NY

Antonia S. New, MD
Associate Professor of Psychiatry
Director, Medical Student Education
Department of Psychiatry
Mount Sinai School of Medicine
New York, NY

OXFORD
UNIVERSITY PRESS

OXFORD

UNIVERSITY PRESS

Oxford University Press is a department of the University of Oxford. It furthers
the University's objective of excellence in research, scholarship, and education
by publishing worldwide. Oxford is a registered trade mark of Oxford University
Press in the UK and certain other countries.

Published in the United States of America by Oxford University Press
198 Madison Avenue, New York, NY 10016, United States of America.

CIP data is on file at the Library of Congress
ISBN 978–0–19–999751–0

This material is not intended to be, and should not be considered, a substitute for medical or other professional
advice. Treatment for the conditions described in this material is highly dependent on the individual
circumstances. And, while this material is designed to offer accurate information with respect to the subject
matter covered and to be current as of the time it was written, research and knowledge about medical and health
issues is constantly evolving and dose schedules for medications are being revised continually, with new side
effects recognized and accounted for regularly. Readers must therefore always check the product information
and clinical procedures with the most up-to-date published product information and data sheets provided by
the manufacturers and the most recent codes of conduct and safety regulation. The publisher and the authors
make no representations or warranties to readers, express or implied, as to the accuracy or completeness of this
material. Without limiting the foregoing, the publisher and the authors make no representations or warranties as
to the accuracy or efficacy of the drug dosages mentioned in the material. The authors and the publisher do not
accept, and expressly disclaim, any responsibility for any liability, loss or risk that may be claimed or incurred
as a consequence of the use and/or application of any of the contents of this material.

9 8 7 6 5 4 3 2 1

Printed by WebCom, Inc., Canada

This primer is dedicated to two leaders in our field, Dr. Larry J Siever and Dr. Kenneth Silk. Both have been very valued mentors and colleagues to the Editors of this volume as well as to many of the chapter authors. Dr. Siever has been a moving force in the reconceptualization of personality disorders by bringing the tools of neuroscience and genetics to the study of these illnesses. Neurobiological scrutiny has brought hope to patients through a better understanding, and better treatments, of their illnesses. Larry was also an inspiringly brilliant mentor to a generation of research scientists in the study of personality disorders. He has now retired due to an ongoing illness. Dr. Silk, who died in April of 2016, was a true leader in the development of treatments for personality disorders. He worked tirelessly to enhance the assessment, psychosocial and pharmacologic management of personality disorders. He was also a mentor to many of the authors in this primer and was known for his wonderful sense of humor, his warmth and his generosity to his mentees.

CONTENTS

CONTRIBUTORS

Margaret S. Andover, PhD
Department of Psychology
Fordham University
Bronx, New York

Ron B. Aviram, PhD
Ferkauf Graduate School
Yeshiva University
Private Practice
New York, New York

Beth S. Brodsky, PhD
Department of Psychiatry
Columbia University
New York State Psychiatric Institute
New York, New York

Adam Carmel, PhD
Department of Psychiatry
Harvard Medical School
Massachusetts Mental Health Center
Beth Israel Deaconess Medical Center
Boston, Massachusetts

Alexander L. Chapman, PhD
Department of Psychology
Simon Fraser University
Burnaby, British Columbia, Canada

Eunice Chen, PhD
Department of Psychology
Temple University
Philadelphia, Pennsylvania

Megan S. Chesin, PhD
Department of Psychology
William Paterson University
Wayne, New Jersey

Lois W. Choi-Kain, MD
Department of Psychiatry
Harvard Medical School
McLean Hospital
Belmont, Massachusetts

Katherine Anne Comtois, PhD, MPH
Department of Psychiatry and
    Behavioral Sciences
University of Washington
Harborview Medical Center
Seattle, Washington

Lindsey C. Conkey, MA
Psychological and Brain Sciences
University of Massachusetts
Amherst, Massachusetts

Kate M. Davidson, PhD
Institute of Health and Well Being
University of Glasgow
Glasgow, Scotland

Marleen H. M. de Moor, PhD
Department of Clinical Child and
    Family Studies
Vrije University
Amsterdam, the Netherlands

Jill C. Delaney, LCSW
Private Practice
New York, New York

Linda Dimeff, PhD
Portland DBT Institute
Portland, Oregon

Marijn A. Distel, PhD
Department of Psychiatry
Vrije University
Amsterdam, the Netherlands

Eric A. Fertuck, PhD
Graduate Center
City University of New York
Department of Psychology
City College of New York
New York, New York

David J. Hellerstein, MD
Department of Psychiatry
Columbia University
New York, New York

André Ivanoff, PhD
School of Social Work
Columbia University
New York, New York

Brian Johnston, MA
Graduate Center
City University of New York
Department of Psychology
City College of New York
New York, New York

Julia Knauber, MD
Department of Psychosomatic Medicine
Central Institute of Mental Health
  Mannheim
Medical Faculty Mannheim
Heidelberg University
Heidelberg, Germany

Annegret Krause-Utz, PhD
Department of Psychosomatic Medicine
Central Institute of Mental Health
  Mannheim
Medical Faculty Mannheim
Heidelberg University
Heidelberg, Germany
Institute of Psychology
Leiden University
Leiden Institute for Brain and Cognition
Leiden, the Netherlands

Blair W. Morris, PhD
Behavioral Health Integration Program
Montefiore Medical Center
Bronx, New York

Antonia S. New, MD
Department of Psychiatry
Mount Sinai School of Medicine
New York, New York

Inga Niedtfeld, MD
Department of Psychosomatic Medicine
Central Institute of Mental Health
  Mannheim
Medical Faculty Mannheim
Heidelberg University
Heidelberg, Germany

Joel Paris, MD
Department of Psychiatry
McGill University
Montreal, Canada

Paul A. Pilkonis, MD
Department of Psychiatry
University of Pittsburgh School of
    Medicine
Pittsburgh, Pennsylvania

Valerie Porr, MA
TARA4BPD
New York, New York

Shireen L. Rizvi, PhD
Graduate School of Applied and
    Professional Psychology
Rutgers University
New Brunswick, New Jersey

Kristen M. Roman, PsyD
Graduate School of Applied and
    Professional Psychology
Rutgers University
New Brunswick, New Jersey

Heather T. Schatten, PhD
Department of Psychiatry and Human
    Behavior
Butler Hospital
The Warren Alpert Medical School
Brown University
Providence, Rhode Island

Christian Schmahl, MD
Department of Psychosomatic Medicine
Central Institute of Mental Health
    Mannheim
Medical Faculty Mannheim
Heidelberg University
Heidlberg, Germany

Lori N. Scott, PhD
Department of Psychiatry
University of Pittsburgh School of
    Medicine
Pittsburgh, Pennsylvania

Larry Siever, MD
Department of Psychiatry
Mount School of Medicine
New York, New York

Kenneth R. Silk, MD (deceased)
Professor of Psychiatry
University of Michigan Health System
Department of Psychiatry
Ann Arbor, Michigan

Tanya Singh, MA
New York State Psychiatric Institute
New York, New York

Barbara Stanley, PhD
Department of Psychiatry
Columbia University College of
    Physicians and Surgeons
New York State Psychiatric Institute
New York, New York

Jeffrey Sung, MD
Department of Psychiatry and
    Behavioral Sciences
University of Washington
Harborview Medical Center
Seattle, Washington

Joseph Triebwasser, MHCC
Attending Physician
James J. Peters VA Medical Center
West Kingsbridge Road
Bronx, NY

Bea Tusiani
Author, Remnants of a Life on
   Paper: A Mother and Daughter's
   Struggle with Borderline Personality
   Disorder
New York, New York

Paula Tusiani-Eng, LMSW, MDiv
Emotions Matter, Inc.
Author, Remnants of a Life on Paper:
   A Mother and Daughter's Struggle
   with Borderline Personality Disorder
New York, New York

Frank E. Yeomans, MD, PhD
Department of Psychiatry
Cornell University Medical College
New York, New York

Mary C. Zanarini, EdD
Department of Psychiatry
Harvard Medical School
Laboratory for the Study of Adult
   Development
McLean Hospital
Belmont, MA

A History of Borderline Personality Disorder

ANTONIA S. NEW AND JOSEPH TRIEBWASSER

INTRODUCTION

Borderline personality disorder (BPD) is complex disorder, and the phenomenology of the disorder has been hard to define in straightforward terms. This has contributed to the persistence, in some, of the view that it is not a "real" disorder. Yet there has been increasingly powerful research that suggests that it is indeed "real" and that it can be a disabling condition with high morbidity and even mortality. A review of the history of the disorder may help to shed light on the possible confusion surrounding the diagnosis and also provide insight into what has been consistently observed through different iterations of the disorder.

The term "borderline personality disorder" has its origins in decades-old responses to a then bewildering, previously unrecognized patient population. We present here some of the history of the name "borderline personality disorder" as well as historical case descriptions of individuals with symptoms that currently would likely be classified as having BPD. We also consider the implications of the reclassification of "personality disorders" in the fifth edition of the *Diagnostic and Statistical Manual of Mental Health Disorders* (DSM-5) into "Section 2" alongside disorders that have to date been placed on Axis I (e.g., psychotic disorders, mood disorders, anxiety disorders).

In reviewing the history of the "borderline personality disorder" diagnosis, we will touch on those features that have contributed to the stigmatization of this disorder. It is abundantly clear that there is an enormous burden of stigma attached to the borderline diagnosis, which has risen to the level where calling a patient "borderline" has become a common way, even among mental health professionals, to refer disparagingly to any individual whom they find annoying. We will address historical contributions to the fundamental misconceptions about BPD that we believe have contributed to misunderstanding of this illness.

The first misconception relates directly to the name "borderline personality disorder." The name implies that this disease lies on the "border" between two states, a view that has its origins in early psychoanalytic conceptualizations of the disorder that are no longer widely viewed as informative; nonetheless, this way of construing the illness continues to confuse understanding of the disorder. A second misconception about the disorder is that since it is a "disorder of character," neurobiological studies attempting to elucidate a pathophysiology of the illness are misplaced. This view in part derives from the sharp distinction (made in the DSM-III and beyond) between Axis I and Axis II disorders, a distinction for which there was very little evidence and that has been eliminated from the DSM-5. Finally, we will address the historic misconception that BPD is the direct consequence of early life trauma rather than a phenotypic expression of a heritable vulnerability to symptoms and behaviors that then emerge in the context of past and present-day stressful life events.

HISTORY OF THE NAME: ON THE "BORDER" BETWEEN "PSYCHOSIS" AND "NEUROSIS"

The name "borderline personality disorder" arose because of theories in the early 20th century that the disorder was on the "border" between "neurosis" and "psychosis" (Stern, 1938) (see Table 1.1). This conceptualization was based on Freud's definition of these terms: "In neurosis the ego suppresses part of the id out of allegiance to reality, whereas in psychosis it lets itself be carried away by the id and detached from a part of reality" (Freud, 1953–74). This somewhat opaque psychoanalytic construct informed the thinking of Adolph Stern who coined the term "borderline" in 1938. He described a group of patients who "teetered" on the "borderline" between neuroses and psychoses. His initial paper coining the name was largely descriptive, and the patients he characterized resemble contemporarily described BPD (Stern, 1938). He described individuals who

> instead of a resilient reaction to a painful or traumatic experience . . . goes down
> in a heap. . .(with) inordinate hypersensitivity: patients are constantly being
> deeply insulted and injured by trifling remarks made by people with whom they
> come in contact. . . . (They have) negative therapeutic reactions . . . (such that)
> an enlightening interpretation throws them . . . into despondency. (Stern, 1945)

In a subsequent review of borderline disorders, Stern departed from clinical description and instead hypothesized an etiology. He stated, "It is not that these patients are exposed to specific experiences, sexual or otherwise, which are in themselves of a necessarily traumatic nature, but that their environment is . . . so traumatic that when they are exposed to such experiences they react to them as if they were traumatic." He went on to conjecture that this excessive sensitivity was the result

TABLE 1.1 Historical development of borderline personality disorder diagnosis

Author, Year	Diagnostic Criteria	Hypothesized Etiology	Evidence
Adolph Stern, 1938, 1945	Border between psychotic and neurotic: specific symptoms: 1. "Narcissism: These patients suffer from affective (narcissistic) malnutrition." 2. "Psychic bleeding: Instead of a resilient reaction to a painful or traumatic experience, the patient goes down in a heap, so to speak, and is at the point of death. There is immobility, lethargy instead of action, collapse instead of a rebound: a sort of playing 'possum.'" 3. "Inordinate hypersensitivity: patients are constantly being deeply insulted and injured by trifling remarks made by people with whom they come in contact." 4. "Psychic and body rigidity—The rigid personality' . . . shifting, watchful, alert eyes and the rigid picture of his body." 5. "Negative therapeutic reactions . . . an enlightening interpretation throws them, at least for the moment, into despondency." 6. "What looks like constitutionally rooted feelings of inferiority, deeply imbedded in the personality of the patient." 7. "Masochism: self-pity and self-commiseration, the presentation of a long suffering, helpless picture of the injured one, are regularly met; also what I call wound-licking, a tendency to indulge in self-pity."	"It is not that these patients are exposed to specific experiences, sexual or otherwise, which are in themselves of a necessarily traumatic nature, but that their environment is in itself so traumatic that when they are exposed to such experiences they react to them as if they were traumatic," which he ascribes to "unfavorable personality traits (neurotic, psychotic or psychopathic) of the child's father" and "a depriving, rejecting mother" with "moods and silences of long duration, the absence of gaiety, failure to play with the children, outright rejections and deprivations, severe criticism, rigidity of the personality with too little tenderness and show of maternal affection."	Case studies

(continued)

TABLE 1.1 Continued

Author, Year	Diagnostic Criteria	Hypothesized Etiology	Evidence
Gregory Zilboorg, 1941	Wanted to rename those referred to as borderline as ambulatory schizophrenia, emphasizing the odd thoughts, unstable relationships, and "dereistic thinking" (e.g., non sequitur)	As a schizophrenia spectrum disorder: no emphasis on etiology	Case studies
Helena Deutsch, 1942	"as if." "The apparently normal relationship to the world corresponds to a child's imitativeness and is the expression of identification with the environment, a mimicry which results in an ostensibly good adaptation to the world of reality despite the absence of object cathexis" with "suggestibility, narcissism and the poverty of object relationships."	"Whether the emotional disturbances described in this paper imply a 'schizophrenic disposition' or constitute rudimentary symptoms of schizophrenia is not clear to me.... They do not belong among the commonly accepted forms of neurosis, and they are too well adjusted to reality to be called psychotic." No presumption of cause.	Case studies
Robert Knight, 1952	No criteria laid out, but a "typical" patient has intact intelligence, but shows blocking of thought, peculiarities of word usage, obliviousness to obvious implications, contaminations of idioms, arbitrary inferences, inappropriate affect, and suspicion-laden behavior.	As a schizophrenia spectrum disorder: no emphasis on etiology	Case studies

Wolberg, 1952	No criteria laid out, but an occasional disturbed sensations of smell or taste, or may even show evidence of misinterpretation of sounds.	As a schizophrenia spectrum disorder: no emphasis on etiology	Case studies
Schmideberg, 1959	Patients "stable in their instability," resembling "schizophrenics in remission," often with "various offenses, sexual perversions, homosexuality and prostitution, alcoholism, drug addiction, hypochondriasis, eccentricities, peculiar behavior, querulousness, and vegetarianism."	As a schizophrenia spectrum disorder: no emphasis on etiology	Case studies
Otto Kernberg, 1966	Described borderline patients as having "nonspecific ego weakness"; i.e., multiple deficits in the psychological practices fostering adaptive functioning, including poor impulse control, low anxiety tolerance, and breakthroughs of "primary process" thinking; i.e., disordered thinking. As we shall see, many of these features are, empirically, descriptive of the types of patients he placed under the rubric of BPO.	Abnormal psychological defenses, with "structural" problem in intrapsychic function: borderline personality organization	Case studies
Roy R Grinker, 1968	Focused on importance of classification: (1) anger (2) "defect in affectional relationships" (3) "absence of a self-identity" (4) "depression"	Presumed no etiology, but an "adequate affectional system has probably not developed in the early years." He describes a lack of information to distinguish a constitutional cause or early deprivation as the etiology of this developmental failure.	Data collection: 51 systematically assessed patients

(continued)

TABLE 1.1 Continued

Author, Year	Diagnostic Criteria	Hypothesized Etiology	Evidence
DSM-I, 1952	"Emotionally unstable personality." "The individual reacts with excitability and ineffectiveness when confronted by minor stress. His judgment may be undependable under stress and his relationship to other people is continuously fraught with fluctuating emotional attitudes, because of strong and poorly controlled hostility, guilt and anxiety."	Presumed no specific etiology	Consensus meetings
DSM-II, 1968	Cyclothymic: "recurring and alternating periods of depression and elation . . . not readily attributable to external circumstances." Explosive: gross outbursts of rage or of verbal or physical aggressiveness . . . strikingly different from the patient's usual behavior. "These patients are generally considered excitable, aggressive and over-responsive to environmental pressures."	Presumed no specific etiology	Consensus meetings
DSM-III: John Gunderson, 1980	Five (or more) of the following: 1. Impulsivity or unpredictability 2. Unstable and intense interpersonal relationships	Presumed no specific etiology	Case studies/ early empirical studies with diagnostic instruments

3. Inappropriate, intense anger or lack of control of anger
4. Identity disturbance
5. Affective instability
6. Intolerance of being alone
7. Physically self-damaging acts
8. Chronic feelings of emptiness or boredom

DSM-III-R, 1987	Same as DSM-III except "intolerance of being alone" was replaced by "frantic efforts to avoid real or imagined abandonment."	Presumed no specific etiology	See Section "Core Symptoms of Borderline Personality Disorder"
DSM-IV and IV-TR, 1994	Same as DSM-III-R with the addition of a ninth possible criterion, "transient, stress-related paranoid ideation or severe dissociative symptoms"	Presumed no specific etiology	

of "unfavorable personality traits ... of the child's father" as well as the presence of "a depriving, rejecting mother" with "moods and silences of long duration, the absence of gaiety, failure to play with the children, outright rejections and deprivations, severe criticism ... with too little tenderness and show of maternal affection" (Stern, 1945).

Stern's formulation of BPD as existing between neurosis and psychosis was further developed by Helena Deutsch. She posited that these patients were on the border between psychosis and neurosis and lacked a consistent sense of identity. She created the term "as-if" personality because the patients completely identified with those on whom they were dependent and were highly suggestible (Deutsch, 1945). In 1941, Gregory Zilboorg explored the border between psychosis and neurosis, describing a group of patients with "ambulatory schizophrenia" who had "odd thoughts," "unstable relationships," and "dereistic thinking" ("thinking that does not follow one thing after another"; e.g., non sequiturs, which might be described now as a mild thought disorder) (Zilboorg, 1941). A more contemporary diagnosis given to this group of patients would be schizotypal personality disorder, a disorder empirically shown to be in the schizophrenia spectrum (Gunderson & Siever, 1985).

Psychiatrists in the 1950s struggled with the complexity of this diagnosis, leading Robert Knight to write that "the label 'borderline state' conveys more information about the uncertainty and indecision of the psychiatrist than it does about the condition of the patient." However, Knight remained unable to give a clinical description about what borderline state is, rather than what it is not (e.g., neurosis or psychosis). He gave a brief description of a "typical" patient as one who, despite intact intelligence, "shows blocking of thought, peculiarities of word usage, obliviousness to obvious implications, contaminations of idioms, arbitrary inferences, inappropriate affect and suspicion-laden behavior" (Knight, 1954). This description better describes the mild formal thought disorder seen in schizotypal patients than contemporarily diagnosed BPD. Similarly, Arlene Robbins Wolberg in 1952 described a group of patients who also conform to the contemporarily diagnosed schizotypal group, lying "between neurotic difficulties and the psychoses," with "occasional disturbed sensations of smell or taste, or ... misinterpretation of sounds" (Wolberg, 1952). Melitta Schmideberg built on this conceptualization of the "borderline state" as characterizing patients "stable in their instability," who resemble "schizophrenics in remission." Her clinical description offered a complex grab-bag of associated symptoms, stating that borderline patients frequently show "various offenses, sexual perversions, homosexuality and prostitution, alcoholism, drug addiction, hypochondriasis, eccentricities, peculiar behavior, querulousness, and vegetarianism" (Schmideberg, 1959).

In 1967, Otto Kernberg attempted to draw clarity out of the confusion surrounding this diagnosis by defining "borderline personality organization," which he asserted was "a stable character pathology." He was struck that, although it was not difficult to distinguish borderline personality disorder from psychosis, it was more difficult to distinguish it from "the neuroses." He viewed no specific symptom

as pathognomonic, but rather that patients with borderline personality organization exhibit a variety of symptoms including anxiety, "polymorphous perverse sex-
uality," "impulse neuroses" and addiction, phobias, hypochondriasis, dissociation,
paranoias, and conversion reactions. He asserted, however, that what patients with
borderline personality organization have in common is "low level character neuroses," as manifested by the presence of (1) "ego weakness," manifest in poor impulse
control and anxiety tolerance; (2) a shift to "primary process thinking," in the use of
dissociation and ego instability; and (3) primitive psychological defense mechanisms
such as "splitting," "primitive idealization," "projective identification," "denial," and
"omnipotence and devaluation" (Kernberg, 1966).

An alternative path of development in conceptualizing BPD followed the behaviorally descriptive track laid out in Stern's early descriptions (Stern, 1938). The first
and second editions of the DSM (DSM-I and DSM-II) did not include the diagnosis
of BPD. In DSM-I, a patient who had symptoms resembling the current DSM-IV
diagnosis of BPD would have been given the diagnosis of "emotionally unstable
personality" (an individual reacting with "excitability and ineffectiveness when confronted by minor stress ... his relationship to other people is continuously fraught
with fluctuating emotional attitudes because of strong and poorly controlled hostility, guilt and anxiety") or "cyclothymic personality" (an individual with "frequent
alternating moods of elation and sadness, stimulated apparently by internal factors
rather than by external events" (American Psychiatric Association [APA], 1952).
DSM-II, which came out in 1968, retains the diagnosis of "cyclothymic personality";
however, it eliminates "emotionally unstable personality" and adds "explosive personality," characterized by "gross outbursts of rage or of verbal or physical aggressiveness" for which the individual often feels "repentant," and it is the "intensity of
the outbursts and the individual's inability to control them which distinguishes this
group" (APA, 1968). These early descriptions suggest that the symptom domains of
fluctuating moods are seen in a different group of patients from those of behavioral
disinhibition. Contemporary views of BPD, on the other hand, include individuals
with symptoms in both of these domains.

Roy Grinker, a neurologist and psychiatrist, made the first efforts to define BPD
through descriptive empirical investigation. He assessed 51 nonpsychotic, non–
substance abusing adult inpatients diagnosed with BPD and attempted to identify the
core features of the disorder through a systematic assessment of symptoms. A factor analysis yielded four core features: (1) anger, (2) a defect in "affectional relationships," (3) absence of a "consistent self-identity," and (4) depression (Grinker,
Werble, & Drye, 1968).

The modern era of empirical investigation of BPD, however, really began
with John Gunderson. In 1981, Gunderson published the Diagnostic Interview for
Borderline Personality Disorder (Gunderson, Kolb, & Austin, 1981), which was
the first diagnostic instrument to operationalize the diagnosis of BPD. This diagnostic instrument closely adhered to the definition of the disorder delineated under
Gunderson's leadership in DSM-III, which included a behaviorally characterized

diagnosis of BPD based on a systematic description of observable clinical characteristics (APA, 1980). While the DSM definitions have varied somewhat since DSM-III, the fundamental diagnostic criteria have remained largely unchanged. The most important alteration was the inclusion of "transient, stress-related paranoid ideation or severe dissociative symptoms" in DSM-IV (APA, 1987) and DSM-IV-TR (APA, 2000), but not in DSM-III (APA, 1980) or DSM-III-R (APA, 1987).

Grinker and Gunderson did the groundbreaking work that provided empirical evidence for the existence of a set of symptoms that run together in individuals and constitute a psychiatric disorder. Unfortunately, they retained the name "borderline personality disorder," which harkens back to the psychoanalytic description of an illness on the border between two states. The evidence-based work of Grinker and Gunderson in no way relies on the Freudian view of a disorder teetering between "neurosis" and "psychosis," but the misleading name remains in use. The name further poses an obstacle for descriptive or biological psychiatrists to take scientific work on this disorder seriously because it alludes to an era of empirically ill-grounded psychiatric theory.

Some have argued that the name should be changed to *emotion regulation disorder*. Although this name may capture a component of the symptoms of BPD, it does not adequately distinguish it from mood disorders, especially bipolar disorder. A more apt name might be *interpersonal emotion dysregulation disorder* (IEDD). Unlike "borderline personality disorder," which conveys nothing to clinicians or patients about the illness's signs, symptoms, or pathophysiology, this designation would capture the element of emotion dysregulation that is the hallmark of the disorder; in addition, it brings attention to the salience of symptoms that arise in the context of interpersonal conflict. We are not here arguing for changing the name. Although a name change might permit a shedding of the baggage of concepts that have led to stigma in BPD, we also acknowledge that changing the name of a disorder may sow confusion and runs the risk of losing the thread of developing neuroscience and evidence-based treatment for the disorder.

WHAT IS THE EVIDENCE FOR A DISTINCTION BETWEEN AXIS I AND AXIS II?

The distinction between Axis I and Axis II disorders in the DSM system prior to DSM-5 was grounded in little empirical investigation. This distinction initially stemmed from an assumption that Axis I disorders arise out of "biological" predispositions, whereas Axis II disorders arise out of "environmental" conditions (Siever & Davis, 1991). The distinction between Axis I and II remained encoded in the DSM from DSM-III through DSM-IV-TR. The problematic definition of a personality disorder as "an enduring pattern of inner experience and behavior that deviates markedly from the expectations of the individual's culture, is pervasive and inflexible, has an onset in adolescence or early adulthood, is stable over time and leads to distress or impairment" persists even in DSM-5. This definition, meant to distinguish Axis II from

Axis I, is problematic in many ways that go beyond the scope of this chapter. Briefly, however, many Axis I disorders meet these criteria. For example, schizophrenia also confers pervasive and enduring patterns of behavior that are inflexible, typically with onset of symptoms in adolescence that become chronic in nature. However, we do not view schizophrenia as a disorder of "character." Clearly, if schizophrenia fits the DSM definition of a personality disorder, the definition is incomplete. Simply stating that a character disorder is not better accounted for by an Axis I disorder begs the question of setting personality disorders apart from Axis I disorders.

Another feature that has been used to distinguish personality disorders from other psychiatric illnesses is that personality disorders have been traditionally conceptualized as being the result of environmental factors, whereas Axis I disorders have been viewed as having a "biological basis" (Siever & Davis, 1991). Twin and family studies show high heritability for BPD. One large study showed consistent heritability for BPD using the DSM-IV criteria across three European countries (0.42) (Distel et al., 2008). Another recent study that examined the heritability of BPD by using a derived convergent latent factor with information from both interview and self-report was 0.67 for BPD (Torgersen, Myers, Reichborn-Kjennerud, Røysamb, Kubarych, & Kendler, 2012). All studies show a substantial effect for genes contributing to a gene × environment interaction for risk of BPD, with a recent study positing heritability for likelihood of adverse life events themselves (Distel et al., 2011). Although environmental stresses clearly play a role in the development of BPD, this is the case with many Axis I disorders as well, including major depressive disorder (MDD), in which environmental stresses in conjunction with vulnerability genes appear to give rise to the disorder (Caspi et al., 2003). Thus, neither the presentation nor the etiology of BPD clearly differentiates it from disorders classified on Axis I.

Finally, traditionally, Axis II disorders have been thought to be best treated with psychotherapy whereas Axis I disorders are thought to be responsive to medications. This distinction also fails to hold up to careful scrutiny because many Axis I disorders are quite unresponsive to pharmacotherapy, including substance abuse disorders, post-traumatic stress disorder (PTSD), and delusional disorder. In addition, a number of Axis I disorders are actually quite responsive to psychotherapy, including MDD, panic disorder, and specific phobias. Thus, treatment implications also fail to distinguish adequately between Axis I and II.

With all these considerations in mind, the field has moved to abolish the distinction between Axis I and Axis II in the DSM-5. However, defining what precisely characterizes "a personality disorder" and, specifically, what the core feature of BPD might be, is still a point of controversy.

EARLY EXPERIENCES OF BORDERLINE PATIENTS: THE ROLE OF TRAUMA

Research into the childhood antecedents of BPD has also yielded controversial results. Although this topic is addressed more comprehensively in Chapter 5, the construal of BPD as a disorder in the trauma spectrum is part of the evolving history of the disorder. The idea of BPD as a trauma-related illness derived in part from an effort to destigmatize the disorder. The notion that the symptoms of BPD have their origins in childhood trauma was thought to suggest that the disorder was not the patient's "fault." However, the empirical grounding for the childhood trauma as the etiology of BPD is shaky (Table 1.2). This is not in any way to suggest that the symptoms *are* the patient's fault but rather to pay attention to the empirical data. Much of what is known about childhood trauma in BPD is based on data obtained retrospectively from adult patients with BPD, which is subject to the "negative halo" recall bias inevitable with already ill probands (Paris, 2000). Nevertheless, the published literature does provide some relevant findings about the early lives of patients who go on to develop BPD.

It is generally believed that adults with BPD tend to have had childhoods marked by some combination of trauma, neglect, and deficient parenting. Herman

TABLE 1.2 Borderline personality disorder (BPD) and trauma: Studies supporting and undercutting a traumatic etiology for BPD

Studies supporting trauma etiology for BPD	Studies undercutting trauma etiology for BPD
• Adults with BPD more likely than without BPD to report early physical and sexual abuse and witnessing domestic violence.	• 20–45% of BPD patients have no history of sexual abuse.
• Abuse history predicts adult BPD more than neglect.	• 80% of those with sexual abuse histories have no personality pathology.
• Adult BPD predicted by sexual abuse and/or emotional denial by male caretakers and inconsistent treatment by female caretakers.	• Longitudinal follow-up of children with documented abuse show a high rate of resilience.
• Childhood sexual abuse associated with later BPD.	• Meta-analysis of 21 studies yielded a small pooled effect size for BPD/child abuse association.
• Childhood abuse, neglect, environmental instability, and parental psychopathology increased the risk of adult BPD.	• Community samples of personality disorders and childhood physical and sexual abuse did not predict BPD.
• Childhood sexual abuse, separation from parents, and unfavorable parental rearing styles predicted adult BPD.	• Nonclinical sample: childhood physical and sexual abuse, lifetime Axis I disorders, parental mental illness independent predictors of BPD.
• Association of BPD with childhood abuse and neglect more than major depressive disorder, or schizotypal, avoidant, or obsessive-compulsive personality disorders.	• Familial neurotic spectrum disorders, childhood sexual abuse, separation from parents and unfavorable parental rearing styles independently predicted BPD.
	• 2-year longitudinal study of adult BPD showed childhood trauma and baseline severity of BPD symptoms contributed independently to predict worse outcome.

and colleagues reported that adults with BPD and, to a lesser extent, borderline traits, were more likely than those without BPD to give histories of early physical and sexual abuse and of witnessing domestic violence (Herman, Perry, & van der Kolk, 1989). Zanarini and colleagues found that a history of abuse was more strongly predictive of adult BPD than a history of neglect and that exposure to disturbed adult caretakers bestowed a greater risk than separation from these caretakers (Zanarini, Gunderson, Marino, Schwartz, & Frankenburg, 1989). Later research from the same laboratory found that the pathological childhood experiences most closely associated with adult BPD were sexual abuse and/or emotional denial by male caretakers and inconsistent treatment by female caretakers (Zanarini & Frankenburg, 1997). Paris and colleagues, analyzing data on men and women separately, found that, in both sexes, negative childhood experiences, especially childhood sexual abuse (CSA), were associated with later BPD (Paris, Sweig-Frank, & Guzder, 1994a, 1994b).

Although evidence does suggest that patients with BPD appear to have higher rates of child abuse than population averages, it is important to note that this is not a universal feature of the disorder (Goodman & Yehuda, 2002). CSA in particular has been implicated in BPD, and yet it is not an inevitable prerequisite of BPD. An estimated 20–45% of patients with BPD have a history of sexual abuse (Goodman & Yehuda, 2002), and 80% of those with sexual abuse have no personality pathology (Gunderson et al., 1981). Although CSA is common in BPD, it is also common in obsessive-compulsive personality disorder (OPD) in a hospitalized sample, and, in fact, Zanarini et al. concluded that whereas CSA may be an important etiological factor, it is neither necessary nor sufficient for development of BPD. Childhood abuse rather may be part of a larger context of family neglect/chaos (Zanarini et al., 1997). Meta-analysis of 21 studies looking at BPD and CSA with more than 2,000 subjects (Fossati, Madeddu, & Maffei, 1999) yielded a pooled effect size of only $r = .28$, which is a modest effect size. Finally, a prospective study of children with confirmed childhood sexual and/or physical abuse showed that while some did develop BPD, many other diagnoses were even more prevalent. These include PTSD, depression, and substance abuse disorders (Spatz-Widom, 2012).

TOWARD A NEW MODEL FOR BPD

We have reviewed studies that show a latent unitary construct that underlies BPD and yet it has been hard to define. If we turn to early descriptions of BPD, they do shed some light. Setting aside those descriptions of BPD that would now more appropriately describe schizotypal PD (Knight, 1954; Wolberg, 1952; Schmideberg, 1959), what is in common in the clinical descriptions is hypersensitivity especially to interpersonal stimuli. Stern described the patient who "goes down in a heap ... [with] inordinate hypersensitivity," and the DSM-I describes a patient who is "excitable" when confronted with a minor stress and whose "relationships to other people [are] continuously fraught with fluctuating emotional attitudes." Perhaps it is the fact that the symptoms of BPD are evident only in particular contexts that has made this disorder so difficult to pin down in empirical studies.

We, like others, see that interpersonal symptoms are at the center of borderline pathology (New & Stanley, 2010; Gunderson, 2007). Clearly, individuals with BPD have affective instability, but it is also clear that the sort of instability seen in BPD is highly contextual and is especially prevalent in the context of interpersonal triggers. People with BPD react intensely and can become emotionally dysregulated during interactions, especially with people to whom they are close. The fact that symptoms of emotional instability are prominent only in specific social contexts is one of the reasons that BPD has been so hard to characterize reliably in research studies. There are other mental illnesses that have at their heart a disruption in social interactions. Individuals with autism, for example, have a relatively constant difficulty with perceiving social cues, and people with schizophrenia often have a constant diminution in social interest. Thus, when individuals with these illnesses present for empirical research studies, they consistently show the social deficits. People with BPD, in contrast, can show minimal emotional instability when they are not activated or triggered. The contextual nature of the symptoms of BPD may also underlie a second problem with the development of pharmacologic targets for BPD. If the symptoms of BPD arise in the context specifically of close relationships, then the outcome measures typically used to assess pharmacologic treatment response (brief cross-sectional assessments of an individual in a clinical research laboratory) are inadequate to detect response. BPD patients may appear asymptomatic or highly symptomatic at the particular moment they are assessed in the lab depending on the immediate antecedent interpersonal interaction or on the relationship developed with the specific research staff member assessing them. Alternative approaches that track symptoms outside of a clinical assessment may be necessary to detect a clinically relevant treatment response in BPD. Viewing BPD as fundamentally a disorder of social interaction and not merely of "emotion" or "affective instability" may also help to explain the absence of highly effective somatic treatments to date. Although much is known about the neuroscience of emotion, the field of social neuroscience is in its infancy and so has not yet yielded biological targets for effective pharmacology. The field of BPD treatment, therefore, has much to gain by the rapid progress being made in this nascent field.

REFERENCES

American Psychiatric Association. (1952). *Diagnostic and statistical manual of mental disorders*. Washington DC: American Psychiatric Association.

American Psychiatric Association. (1968). *Diagnostic and statistical manual of mental disorders* (2nd Edition, DSM-II). Washington DC: American Psychiatric Association.

American Psychiatric Association. (1980). *Diagnostic and statistical manual of mental disorders* (3rd Edition, DSM-III). Washington DC: American Psychiatric Association.

American Psychiatric Association. (1987). *Diagnostic and statistical manual of mental disorders* (3rd Edition-Revised, DSM-III-R). Washington DC: American Psychiatric Association.

American Psychiatric Association (2000). *Diagnostic and statistical manual of mental disorders* (4th Edition, Text Revision). Washington DC: American Psychiatric Association.

Caspi, A., Sugden, K., Moffitt, T. E., Taylor, A., Craig, I. W., Harrington, H., . . . Poulton, R. (2003). Influence of life stress on depression: Moderation by a polymorphism in the 5-HTT gene. *Science, 301*(5631), 386–389.

Deutsch, H. (1945). Some forms of emotional disturbance and their relationship to schizophrenia. *Psychoanalytic Quarterly, 11*, 301–321.

Distel, M. A., Middeldorp, C. M., Trull, T. J., Derom, C. A., Willemsen, G., & Boomsma, D. I. (2011). Life events and borderline personality features: The influence of gene-environment interaction and gene-environment correlation. *Psycholological Medicine, 41*(4), 849–860.

Distel, M. A., Trull, T. J., Derom, C. A., Thiery, E. W., Grimmer, M. A., Martin, N. G., . . . Boomsma, D. I. (2008). Heritability of borderline personality disorder features is similar across three countries. *Psychological Medicine, 38*(9), 1219–1229.

Fossati, A., Madeddu, F., & Maffei, C. (1999). Borderline personality disorder and childhood sexual abuse: A meta-analytic study. *Journal of Personality Disorders, 13*(3), 268–280.

Freud, S. (1953–74). *The Standard Edition of the Complete Psychological Works of Sigmund Freud.* London: Hogarth.

Goodman, M., & Yehuda, R. (2002). The relationship between psychological trauma and borderline personality disorder. *Psychiatric Annals, 32*(6), 337–346.

Grinker, R., Werble, B., & Drye, R. (1968). *The borderline syndrome: A behavioral study of ego-function.* New York: Basic Books.

Gunderson, J. G. (2007). Disturbed relationships as a phenotype for borderline personality disorder. *American Journal of Psychiatry, 164*(11), 1637–1640.

Gunderson, J. G., Kolb, J. E., & Austin, V. (1981). The diagnostic interview for borderline patients. *American Journal of Psychiatry, 138*(7), 896–903.

Gunderson, J. G., & Siever, L. J. (1985). Relatedness of schizotypal to schizophrenic disorders: editors' introduction. *Schizophrenia Bulletin, 11*(4), 532–537.

Herman, J. L., Perry, J. C., & van der Kolk, B. A. (1989). Childhood trauma in borderline personality disorder. *American Journal of Psychiatry, 146*(4), 490–495.

Kernberg, O. (1966). Structural derivatives of object relationships. *International Journal of Psychoanalysis, 47*(2), 236–253.

Knight, R. (1954). Borderline states. In R. P. Knight & C. R. Friedman (Eds.), *Psychoanalytic Psychiatry and Psychology* (pp. 203–215). New York: International Universities Press.

New, A. S., & Stanley, B. (2010). An opioid deficit in borderline personality disorder: Self-cutting, substance abuse, and social dysfunction. *American Journal of Psychiatry, 167*(8), 882–885.

Paris, J. (2000). Childhood precursors of borderline personality disorder. *Psychiatric Clinics of North America, 23*(1), 77–88, vii.

Paris, J., Zweig-Frank, H., & Guzder, J. (1994a). Psychological risk factors for borderline personality disorder in female patients. *Comprehensive Psychiatry, 35*, 301–305.

Paris, J., Zweig-Frank, H., & Guzder, J. (1994b). Risk factors for borderline personality in male outpatients. *Journal of Nervous and Mental Disease, 182*, 375–380.

Schmideberg, M. (1959). The borderline patient. In S. Arieti (Ed.), *American Handbook of Psychiatry* (vol. I., pp. 398–416). New York: Basic Books.

Siever, L. J., & Davis, K. L. (1991). A psychobiologic perspective on the personality disorders. *American Journal of Psychiatry, 148*, 1647–1658.

Spatz-Widom, C. (2012). *Trauma, psychopathology, and violence: Causes, consequences, or correlates?* New York: Oxford University Press.

Stern, A. (1938). Psychoanalytic investigation of and therapy in the borderline group of neuroses. *Psychoanalytic Quarterly, 7*, 467–489.

Stern, A. (1945). Psychoanalytic therapy in the borderline neuroses. *Psychoanalytic Quarterly*, *14*, 190–198.

Torgersen, S., Myers, J., Reichborn-Kjennerud, T., Røysamb, E., Kubarych, T. S., & Kendler, K. S. (2012). The heritability of Cluster B personality disorders assessed both by personal interview and questionnaire. *Journal of Personality Disorders*, *26*(6), 848–866.

Wolberg, A. R. (1952). The borderline patient. *American Journal of Psychotherapy*, *6*(4), 694–710.

Zanarini, M. C., & Frankenburg, F. R. (1997). Pathways to the development of borderline personality disorder. *Journal of Personality Disorders*, *11*(1), 93–104.

Zanarini, M. C., Gunderson, J. G., Marino, M. F., Schwartz, E. O., & Frankenburg, F. R. (1989). Childhood experiences of borderline patients. *Comprehensive Psychiatry*, *30*(1), 18–25.

Zanarini, M. C., Williams, A. A., Lewis, R. E., Bradford Reich, R., Vera, S. C, . . . Frankenburg, F. R. (1997). Reported pathological childhood experiences associated with the development of borderline personality disorder. *American Journal of Psychiatry*, *154*(8), 1101–1106.

Zilboorg, G. (1941). The sense of reality. *Psychoanalytic Quarterly*, *10*, 183–210.

/// 2 /// Diagnosis of Borderline Personality Disorder

BARBARA STANLEY AND TANYA SINGH

INTRODUCTION

Borderline personality disorder (BPD) is characterized by instability on several domains: affect regulation, impulse control, interpersonal relationships, and self-image (Lieb, Zanarini, Schmahl, Linehan, & Bohus, 2004). BPD affects about 1–2% of the general population—up to 10% of psychiatric outpatients and 20% of inpatients (Hampton, 1997; Widiger & Weissman, 1991; Zimmerman, Rothschild, & Chelminski, 2005). About 1–3% of nonclinical samples (Lenzenweger, Lane, Loranger, & Kessler, 2007; Tomko, Trull, Wood, & Sher, 2014; Trull, Jahng, Tomko, Wood, & Sher, 2010) are diagnosed with BPD. With respect to gender, in clinical samples, women comprise about 70% of the population (American Psychiatric Association, 2013; J. G. Gunderson, 2009; Widiger & Weissman, 1991). The difference in rates between clinical and population samples are likely due to women's greater help seeking. However, in studies of the general population, men and women meet the diagnostic criteria at almost equal rates (Lenzenweger et al., 2007; Tomko et al., 2014).

According to the *Diagnostic and Statistical Manual of Mental Disorders* (DSM-V) (American Psychiatric Association, 2013) the diagnosis of BPD is made by determining if an individual meets at least five of the following nine criteria:

- Inappropriate intense anger or difficulty controlling anger
- Chronic feelings of emptiness
- Affective instability due to a marked reactivity of mood (e.g., intense sadness, irritability, or anxiety usually lasting a few hours to a few days)
- Transient stress-related paranoid ideation or severe dissociative symptoms

- Identity disturbance: striking and persistent unstable self-image or sense of self
- Recurrent suicidal behavior, gestures, or threats, or nonsuicidal self-injurious behavior
- Impulsivity in at least two areas that are potentially self-damaging that do not include suicidal or self-injuring behavior
- Frantic efforts to avoid real or imagined abandonment
- A pattern of unstable and intense interpersonal relationships characterized by alternating between extremes of idealization and devaluation

In addition to meeting five of these nine BPD criteria, BPD, like all personality disorders, is characterized by a pervasive and persistent pattern of behavior that begins in early childhood and is stable across contexts (American Psychiatric Association, 2013). Affective dysregulation (inappropriate, intense anger or difficulty controlling anger; affective instability due to a marked reactivity of mood)is one of the core domains associated with BPD (APA, 2013) and is characterized by erratic, easily aroused mood changes and disproportionate emotional responses. Affect dysregulation differs in BPD and mood disorders because in BPD it can shift rapidly and is affected by environmental triggers (Koenigsberg, Harvey, Mitropoulou, & New, 2001) Furthermore, individuals with BPD have more intense emotions that are worsened by their difficulty in controlling their emotions (Henry et al., 2001; Koenigsberg et al., 2001) and consequently may display inappropriate, intense, and difficult-to-control anger. Individuals with BPD also suffer from self-image difficulties that are sometimes characterized as self-other representational disturbances (Skodol, 2007). BPD patients may suffer from separation insecurity, that is, they fear rejection or separation from their significant others. Thus, they may make attempts to avoid real or imagined separation (American Psychiatric Association, 2013)). Additionally, there can be dramatic fluctuations between idealization and devaluation of individuals with whom they are in relationships based on how they are feeling in the moment (Skodol, 2007). Similarly, their sense of self and their self-image can fluctuate (American Psychiatric Association, 2013). Another manifestation of self–other representational disturbance is a chronic feeling of emptiness (American Psychiatric Association, 2013). This experience is subjective and thus hard to define compared with other diagnostic criteria (Johansen, Karterud, Pedersen, Gude, & Falkum, 2004). It overlaps with hopelessness, isolation, and loneliness, along with symptoms of depression and is described by patients as if "something is missing" (Klonsky, 2008).

BPD is also characterized by impulsivity (American Psychiatric Association, 2013). Moeller et al. (2001) define impulsivity as a biopsychosocial construct that includes decreased sensitivity to negative and long-term consequences of one's behavior and impetuous actions to immediate stimuli without much forethought. BPD patients often score high on all aspects of impulsivity as measured by standard self-report scales such as the Barratt Impulsivity Scale (Links, Heselgrave, & van Reekum, 1998). Impulsive spectrum disorders such as substance use disorders or antisocial personality are most frequently found in the first-degree relatives of patients with BPD (White, Gunderson, Zanarini, & Hudson, 2003).

Impulsivity can also include self-harming behaviors in response to emotional distress. Recurrent suicidal behavior is a very common feature of the disorder (Black, Blum, Pfohl, & Hale, 2004; Forman, Berk, Henriques, Brown, & Beck, 2004). Patients with BPD regularly engage in cutting or overdosing in response to stressful events as a means of regulating their emotions. Regular visit to the emergency department due to suicidality is suggestive of the diagnosis (Bongar, Peterson, Golann, & Hardiman, 1990;; Forman et al., 2004). Conversely, having the diagnosis of the disorder is considered a risk factor for death by suicide (Kjellander, Bongar, & King, 1998). It is important to remember, however, that suicidal behaviors are not necessarily impulsive and can often be planned in advance, even in BPD (Chaudhury et al., 2016). Unfortunately, because patients with BPD attempt suicide so often, their suicidal intents are often underestimated by clinicians (Brodsky & Stanley, 2013; Cowdry, Pickar, & Davies, 1986).

At the least half of patients with BPD also show cognitive disturbances, such as paranoid (but not psychotic) thoughts, usually interpersonal in nature (being purposely excluded) or dissociative experiences (Yee, Korner, McSwiggan, Meares, & Stevenson, 2005; Zanarini, Gunderson, Frankenburg, & Chauncey, 1989). Also noteworthy is the unique quality of physical pain in self-harm. Self-harm in BPD may be devoid of any pain (Gerson & Stanley, 2002); conversely, when physical pain is present it may be a way to demonstrate the individual's emotional distress and make it feel more "real."

MAKING THE DIAGNOSIS

Making the diagnosis of BPD can be difficult for a number of reasons. In the past, it has been argued that the disorder does not exist (Charland, 2007) and that it can best be explained as a form of atypical depression(Akiskal et al., 1985), and that treating other Axis I disorders (e.g., major depression, bipolar illness) would resolve symptoms of BPD so that personality would be "within normal limits". Furthermore, there is a reluctance to label adolescents as having BPD because what may seem like a disorder in adolescence may no longer be present in adulthood (American Psychological Association, 2000; Bleiberg, 1994). Additionally, clinicians have been disinclined to label patients as having BPD for fear that the diagnosis will be perceived as stigmatizing because of the reputation individuals with BPD have for "being difficult" or "manipulative"; as well, patients often react to the notion that their personality is "disordered" (Gerson & Stanley, 2002; Rumpza, 2015). Often, more socially acceptable diagnoses of depression or bipolar disorder are given, and, indeed, these disorders have a high comorbidity with BPD. However, a diagnosis of depression or bipolar disorder does not adequately describe the symptom picture and lived experience of individuals with BPD, and there is a danger in omitting the BPD diagnosis even when other Axis I diagnoses are provided because the treatments for comorbid depression or bipolar illness and BPD differ from those without comorbidity. Patients describe years of seeking the right diagnosis and right treatment for their disorder (Silk, 2010).

BPD AS A DISTINCT DISORDER

BPD has significant overlapping symptoms with other personality disorders (Costa & Widiger, 2001; Livesley, Jang, & Vernon, 1998). Paris (2005) postulates that the real problem in distinguishing BPD is our lack of understanding of the nature of pathology being observed. While personality disorders are categorized as being ego-syntonic, disorders such as major depression and bipolar disorder are ego-dystonic (Gerson & Stanley, 2002). Keeping this distinction in mind, BPD can be thought of as ego-dystonic because patients with BPD are often distressed about their symptoms and want to get better. This is not true of other personality disorders, such as obsessive-compulsive or antisocial personality disorder. Proponents of reclassifying BPD also suggest that doing so may help reduce the stigma attached with the disorder (Paris, 2005). Patients with BPD who are often seen as being difficult may then be seen as having a "chemical imbalance" rather than a problematic personality, thus reducing blame in the process (although reclassifying may not be the entire solution to this problem since patients may continue to be seen as "difficult" even under a different diagnostic label; Paris, 2005). Some researchers have also tried to find linkages between BPD and schizotypal personality because BPD can sometimes include psychotic symptoms (Spitzer et al., 1979). However, neither family studies nor biological markers have been able to provide support for this claim (White et al., 2003). These cognitive symptoms might prove to be a challenge for mental health professionals striving to make a differential diagnosis. One difference between the two disorders is that, in BPD, these symptoms are often stress-related and patients retain insight into their condition (Paris, 2007a).

The issue of overlapping symptoms has also led some to propose BPD to be a variant of other disorders, specifically unipolar depression (Akiskal et al., 1985) and bipolar disorder (Akiskal, 2002; Ghaemi, Ko, & Goodwin, 2002). The argument for BPD being a variant of unipolar depression is based on the number of patients with a family history of depression. In order to investigate whether BPD was in fact a variant of depression, attempts were made to discover the common biological markers between the two, but with poor results and the only consistent finding being a short rapid eye movement (REM) latency (Akiskal et al., 1985). The reformulation of BPD as a variant of bipolar disorder is also problematic since no common etiology between the two disorders has been found, and most people with BPD do not have bipolar disorder (Paris, 2004). According to family prevalence data, the first-degree relatives of patients with BPD are more likely to have an impulsive disorder rather than a mood disorder (White et al., 2003). Moreover, patients with BPD do not have the same response to mood stabilizers as do patients with bipolar disorder (Paris, 2005).

The robust association between a history of childhood abuse and post-traumatic stress disorder (PTSD) has also led some research to postulate that BPD may be a "complex" form PTSD (Herman & Kolk, 1987). The problem with the conceptualization is that it considers trauma to be the primary cause of BPD, whereas in reality it is one of the many risk factors.

DIFFERENTIAL DIAGNOSIS WITH MAJOR DEPRESSIVE DISORDER

Major depression is a common comorbidity in BPD, which makes differentiating the two a common diagnostic dilemma. Major depressive disorder (MDD) and dysthymia are the most commonly co-occurring disorders with BPD (Pepper et al., 1995; Pfohl, Stangl, & Zimmerman, 1984). Interestingly, even if patients with BPD do not meet the criteria for comorbid major depression, they may still display similar levels of depression on scored ratings (Silk, 2010). There are various ways in which a differential diagnosis can be made.

First, as previously discussed, mood changes in BPD tend be to swift and are typically in response to environmental factors. The moods of such a patient can vary tremendously during the course of a day, from sadness and anxiety to anger, elation, or even numbness (Akiskal et al., 1985). Moreover, BPD patients tend to have chronically lower moods rather than acute episodes. In fact, dysthymia is often a marker of BPD (Pepper et al., 1995). Unlike the mood swings of BPD, mood in major depression remains relatively stable over weeks and is not manipulated by external circumstances (Gunderson & Phillips, 1991). Westen and colleagues (1992) found that depression in BPD is characterized by feelings of emptiness, loneliness, and desperation related to the absence of a significant other. Furthermore, this depression was also more volatile, pervasive, and had a significant amount of negative affect related to it.

Patients with BPD also differ from patients with bipolar disorder in the characteristics of personality structure before the start of the depressive episode. Patients with BPD have severe dysthymic reactions in which in they often have symptoms of depression, but these never reach the intensity, consistency, or duration of that of major depression (Kernberg & Yeomans, 2013). Differential diagnosis can also be made by looking at the environmental triggers that predate the depression. Depression in the context of BPD is often triggered by disproportionate responses to minor environmental factors. Major depression does not typically show a direct relationship between environmental factors, although it can be triggered by the combination of an existing genetic disposition and environmental stressors.

Patients with BPD also display much higher levels of impulsivity compared to patients with unipolar depression (Zanarini, 1993). Additionally, BPD tends to have a more robust association with a history of childhood abuse compared to major depression (Zanarini, Frankenburg, Reich, Henned & Silk, 2005). Depression in BPD has been shown to be resistant to pharmacological treatments or electroconvulsive therapy (ECT) that may otherwise work for depression (Binks et al, 2006; Feske et al., 2004; Ingenhoven, Lafay, Rinner, Passchier, & Duivenvoorden, 2009; Nose, Cipriani, Biancosino, Grassi, & Barbui, 2006).

When BPD and MDD co-occur in patients, suicidality is found to be higher than in BPD or MDD alone (Soloff, 2000) (Soloff et al., 2000). It is also important to note that although the two may sometimes follow independent courses, research suggests that when BPD and MDD co-occur, prior improvements in BPD predict improvements in MDD (Gunderson et al., 2004). One study found depression in BPD to be of a more chronic form (Yoshimatsu & Palmer, 2014). These findings suggest that depression in the context of BPD is unlike other depression and thus may not respond as successfully to treatments that work for other forms of that disorder.

Patients with BPD and MDD are also said to differ on the construct of "mental pain." When an individual's basic needs are not met and no change is expected in the future, normal negative emotional experiences can turn into a chronic experience of intolerable mental pain (Orbach, Mikulincer, Sirota, & Gilboa-Schechtman, 2003). This experience is distinct from other negative affects such as depressed mood or anxiety. It includes both a negative chronic sense of self as well as negative affect. It has been suggested that both nonsuicidal self-injury and suicide attempts in BPD are made to cope with this mental pain (Zanarini & Frankenburg, 2007). In a study conducted by Fertuck and colleagues (Fertuck, Karan, & Stanley, 2016), researchers used the Orbach and Mikulincer Mental Pain Scale (OMMP) to test whether patients with BPD differed from patients with MDD in terms of mental pain. Researchers found that the two groups were comparable on 8 of the 9 subscales of the test. However, the two groups differed on the "narcissistic wounds" subscale that measures rejection and loss, along with devalued self-concept. This subscale was found to be associated with BPD status and severity independent of depression status and severity (Fertuck et al., 2016).

DIFFERENTIAL DIAGNOSIS WITH BIPOLAR DISORDER

Owing to some overlapping symptoms, patients with BPD are often misdiagnosed as having bipolar disorder. Zimmerman et al. (2010) reported that 24% of patients clinically diagnosed with bipolar disorder actually met criteria for BPD and not bipolar disorder. Affective instability, impulsivity, inappropriate anger, suicidal behavior, and unstable relationships are some of the characteristics shared by the two disorders (Paris & Black, 2015). Because the mania associated with bipolar I disorder is easily distinguishable from the mood changes in BPD, the confusion between BPD and bipolar II is more problematic (Fiedorowicz & Black, 2010). The milder mood changes in bipolar II more closely resemble the mood shifts of BPD.

It has been suggested that even though affective instability is a hallmark feature of both disorders, the patterns are entirely different. Whereas affective instability in the context of BPD is often triggered by interpersonal stressors (Russell, Moskowitz, Sookman, & Paris, 2007), affective instability in bipolar disorder is usually autonomous and not affected by environmental cues (Koenigsberg, 2010; Parker, 2011).

The mood changes in BPD often shift from euthymia to anger, whereas they change from depression to elation in bipolar disorder (Henry et al., 2001; Zimmerman et al., 2010). Moreover, whereas the mood changes in BPD are of short duration, those of bipolar disorder tend to be longer (Paris, 2004). For patients with BPD, mood changes can occur within a matter of minutes or hours and, with the exception of depression, are rarely sustained for days or weeks on end (Fiedorowicz & Black, 2010).

Patients with bipolar disorder and BPD also are distinguishable on their patterns of impulsivity, although this relationship is complicated. While impulsivity has been shown to be a relatively stable aspect of BPD, it is also the trait that is most likely to remit (Zanarini et al.,2005). Contrary to our expectations, some research shows that some aspects of impulsivity across bipolar II disorder are stable across both manic and euthymic episodes, rather than being episodic (Swann, Pazzaglia, Nicholls, Dougherty, & Moeller, 2003) In a study conducted by Wilson et al. (2007), researchers sought to investigate whether BPD, bipolar disorders, and MDD could be differentiated from each other: 173 participants were divided into four groups consisting of patients with comorbid MDD and BPD, MDD only, comorbid bipolar disorder II and BPD, and bipolar disorder II only. After conducting various assessments with the participants, researchers found a unique symptom and trait profile that could successfully distinguish BPD from other patients. Researchers found that BPD groups were distinguishable from the other two groups through high levels of impulsiveness and hostility. These findings are similar to those of other researchers who found that when bipolar and BPD patients were compared on Cloninger's (Cloninger, Przybeck, Svrakic, & Wetzel, 1994) personality dimensions, patients with BPD scored higher on harm avoidance and impulsivity (Atrevaidya & Hussain, 1999).

Wilson and colleagues (2007) also found that BPD patients differed from patients without it on anxiety-related symptoms and cognitive symptoms such as guilt, suicide ideation, obsessive thoughts, and depersonalization. Patients with bipolar disorder tend to have more episodic than pervasive impulsive behaviors (Zimmerman et al., 2010).

Psychosocial morbidity is another symptom shared by both disorders, although people with BPD usually show more deficits (Zimmerman & Morgan, 2013). As previously discussed, these problems include but are not limited to unstable interpersonal relationships, attachment and dependence issues, and fear of abandonment (Gunderson & Lyons-Ruth, 2008). Additionally, BPD is also marked by high neuroticism and low agreeableness (Zweig-Frank & Paris, 1995).

CATEGORICAL VERSUS DIMENSIONAL DIAGNOSTIC APPROACH TO BPD

Currently, BPD is a categorical diagnosis that an individual either meets or does not meet based on diagnostic criteria. In the most recent version of the DSM (DSM-V) (American Psychiatric Association, 2013), endorsement of five out of the nine criteria is the threshold cutoff for receiving the BPD diagnosis; those endorsing four criteria or less are not considered to have BPD. These criteria represent nine distinct symptom clusters characteristic of individuals with the disorder.

However, in the planning phases of the DSM-V, a dimensional mode of diagnosis was strongly considered as a replacement of the categorical diagnostic approach for personality disorders in general and BPD in particular (Samuel et al., 2012). This consideration reflects an ongoing controversy in the field regarding whether personality disorders are best understood as discrete entities comprised of distinct symptom clusters or whether they should be viewed as existing on a continuum of dimensional personality traits ranging from nondisordered levels to a more amplified expression of traits that leads to and underlies the symptoms of the disorder.

There are theoretical and pragmatic reasons why the diagnosis has been considered to be, and remains (at least for now), a categorical entity. Historically, Kernberg's (1993) "borderline personality organization" was proposed as a categorically distinct level of personality that distinguished between psychosis and neurosis, although he and Millon (1981) also proposed that this borderline level of personality organization cuts across various types of personality disorders (Kernberg, 1993; Millon, 1981). Gunderson (1982) argues that (1) the particular symptomatology of the DSM BPD diagnosis distinguishes it from other diagnoses and (2) the current diagnostic criteria describe BPD well and additionally clarify the aspects of the disorder that should be targeted in treatment, particularly suicidality, self-harm, and impulsive behaviors and affective dysregulation (Paris, 2007a) Relatedly, a categorical diagnosis is a clinically useful tool for easy communication among clinicians and for making treatment recommendations and decisions.

The rationale for considering a dimensional approach to diagnosing BPD includes the high prevalence of comorbidity with Axis I and other Axis II disorders among individuals diagnosed with BPD significant symptom overlap with other disorders, and limited evidence of the validity of the categorical diagnosis (Skodol et al., 2011). Difficulty knowing where one diagnosis ends and other begins (called "boundary disputes" among the developers of the DSM) may be the result of trying to impose arbitrary categorical dimensions on underlying domains of functioning (Trull, Widiger, & Guthrie, 1990). A dimensional approach can enhance diagnostic flexibility and retain more information when diagnosing someone with BPD (Trull et al., 1990). For example, using the current categorical system, someone meeting 3 or 4 criteria for BPD might have significant BPD pathology but might be simply classified as non-BPD; in other words, despite significant impairment, the patient would receive no diagnosis. In addition, the 5 out of 9 criteria standard for assigning the diagnosis account for a wide range of heterogeneity among individuals diagnosed with BPD. A more dimensional approach of recognizing underlying trait structures (that account for a number of symptoms) could lead to a more homogeneous diagnosis. Studies that have applied factor analytic methodology to identify possible trait structures have found evidence of underlying trait structures that account for and map onto the DSM criteria (using samples diagnosed with the DSM-III-R system, which only consisted of eight BPD criteria) (Trull et al., 1990). In a somewhat different approach, Clarkin, Widiger, Frances, Hurt, & Gilmore (1983) identified three core dimensions of BPD: disturbed relatedness, affective/emotional dysregulation, and behavioral dyscontrol.

Although the controversy remains, there is some agreement that, in addition to the DSM symptomatology, the BPD diagnosis can be understood as consisting of a number of underlying domains—affective, cognitive, behavioral, and interpersonal (Stanley & Siever, 2009), and that further work is needed to identify the genetic and neurobiological underpinnings of emotional dysregulation and impulsivity (Paris, 2007a; Skodol et al., 2002). Paris (2007a) recommends retaining but refining the categorical approach to diagnosing BPD. He argues that the five out of nine threshold is arbitrary and too broad, and that it should be dropped. It would be important, however, to maintain the description of the nine criteria since it is not clear how the dimensions alone could do justice to articulating the actual symptomatology of the BPD diagnosis.

DISCUSSING THE DIAGNOSIS WITH PATIENTS

Disclosing a diagnosis of BPD with patients can be difficult for a clinician (Hersh, 2008; Lequesne & Hersh, 2004; Sulzer, Muenchow, Potvin, Harris, & Gigot, 2016. McDonald-Scott et al. (McDonald-Scott, Machizawa, & Satoh, 1992) found that the rate of such disclosure was only 50%. Research suggests that diagnoses that are associated with more stigma are less likely to be disclosed (Rumpza, 2015) and that the stigma associated with BPD continues to hinder disclosure (Lequesne & Hersh, 2004; Rumpza, 2015). Clinicians sometimes choose to discuss other disorders comorbid with BPD, such as depression and anxiety, instead of disclosing BPD (Sulzer et al., 2016). They also sometimes use PTSD as an alternative label because they believe it is a less "blaming" way to discuss the diagnosis. There are several reasons why this may be the case. First, making a correct personality disorder requires specific expertise and training (Paris, 2005). The belief that these conditions may be untreatable may also compound the reluctance to disclose (Lewis & Appleby, 1988) despite evidence that some forms of psychotherapy are effective with BPD (Paris, 2007b).

Disclosure of the disorder is also influenced by the clinician's concerns for the patient and self, societal norms, sex of the professional, and the professional's frequency of working with patients diagnosed with BPD (Rumpza, 2015). Concerns about protecting the therapeutic relationship also hinder disclosure (Rumpza, 2015), although a recent study has found that patients believe that open communication is vital for a successful therapeutic relationship (Sulzer et al., 2016). Finally, stigma associated with the label of BPD is another major reason for not revealing the diagnosis (Paris, 2005b). Patients with BPD are often labeled "difficult" and "manipulative."

BPD in adolescents is common (Feenstra, Busschbach, Verheul, & Hutsebaut, 2011; Johnson et al., 2005) and thus there is sufficient indication for diagnosing adolescents with BPD (Gunderson, 2009; Miller, Muehlenkamp, & Jacobson, 2008; Paris, 2008; Silk, 2008). Studies have found that the reliability and validity of a BPD diagnosis in adolescent samples is adequate, suggesting that it may have a similar pattern regardless of age or developmental period (Miller et al., 2008). Although many adolescents meet the criteria for this disorder, they are diagnosed with more "benign" conditions such as depression. This leaves them in the unfortunate position of not receiving the treatment they need and possibly preventing years of suffering until the proper diagnosis and treatment is provided. Furthermore, they are at added risk for problems like suicidality, criminal misconduct, academic failure, and substance abuse (Kernberg, Weiner, & Bardenstein, 2000). If adolescents with BPD were to get appropriate psychological intervention at an early age, it could prevent such harmful behavior patterns from developing.

In a study conducted by Laurenssen at al. (2013), 567 psychologists participated in an online survey relating to personality disorders in adolescents. Respondents were asked whether they believed adolescents could be diagnosed with personality disorders, whether they themselves diagnosed adolescents with a personality disorder, and, if not, their reasons for not doing so. Finally, they were asked if they provided specific treatments for adolescents with personality disorders. It was found that even though more than half the psychologist acknowledged the presence of personality disorders in adolescence (57.8%), very few diagnosed it (8.7%). Even fewer (6.5%) offered specialized treatments for these disorders. A majority of the psychologists cited the transience of adolescent personality problems and the incapacity of the DSM-IV-TR to diagnose personality disorders as the primary reason for not giving the diagnosis. This finding is supported by previous research in which the transient nature of adolescent diagnoses prevented mental health workers from making a BPD diagnosis in adolescents (Johnson et al., 2000). Some researchers believe that doing so is a mistake because the diagnosis does not account for variability during adolescence (Shapiro, 1990). This argument is supported by some studies showing that diagnosis is not stable across the developmental period (Bernstein et al., 1993; Mattanah, Becker, Levy, Edell, & McGlashan, 1995). However, newer research shows that there is a subgroup of individuals for whom the diagnosis remains stable over time and another subgroup whose eligibility for the diagnosis fluctuates (Miller et al., 2008). Stigma attached to the label of BPD is another vital reason that prevents mental health professionals from making the diagnosis in this age group (Miller et al., 2008).

In clinical interviews conducted with doctors, nurses, and allied health professionals working with child and adolescent mental health services (CAMHS), reluctance to diagnose adolescents with BPD was consistently noted. The staff was concerned about the dangers of overdiagnosing and misdiagnosing. The clinicians utilized specific strategies, such as hedging, when discussing the diagnosis. Words like "emerging" and "traits" were used preceding or following the term "borderline personality disorder." They reportedly did so to make things more vague so that giving and receiving the diagnosis would be easier. Additionally, rather than using diagnostic language, clinicians tended to talk to their patients in terms of symptoms, behaviors, and problems. Many clinicians found the diagnosis problematic due to its inherent ambiguity and thus tried to eschew or reshape the term according to their own preference or the perceived need of the adolescent. The participants stated that their primary reasons for their reluctance for disclosure were the dissatisfaction they felt with the label as well as their wish to maintain hopefulness in their clients (Koehne, Hamilton, Sands, & Humphreys, 2013).

Even though many clinicians are reluctant to openly discuss this diagnosis, there is some clinical utility to disclosing the diagnosis of BPD. Arguments in favor of disclosure claim that there is no evidence for harm caused by a certain disclosure (McDonald-Scott et al., 1992). In fact, disclosure helps patients improve their understanding of their disorder and reduces the stigma surrounding the disease (Biskin & Paris, 2012; Gunderson, 2011). A diagnosis like BPD could account for a range of cognitive, affective, and impulsive symptoms for which no other alternative offered so far can do. It could also inform pharmacological treatment. Literature strongly suggests that depressed patients respond inefficiently and inconsistently to medications for depression in the presence of a personality disorder (Pepper et al., 1995). Additionally, patients with BPD have consistently been shown to have a good response to psychotherapy. Denying them the diagnosis may also deny them a successful treatment, thereby denying them the chance to get better.

It has been suggested that discussing the diagnostic criteria with the patient and explaining the reasoning for diagnosis could be helpful during disclosure (Biskin & Paris, 2012; Gunderson, 2011). Asking patients whether the criteria describes them may also be beneficial in their acceptance of the diagnosis (Gunderson, 2011). Clinicians are also encouraged to inform their patients about the increasing number of specific treatments and their effectiveness in gradually resolving symptoms because it may help alleviate the patient's anxiety about the diagnosis (Biskin & Paris, 2012). Discussing the stigma associated with the disease and strategies for focusing on effective treatment options rather than stereotypes can greatly benefit the patient (Sulzer et al., 2016).

INTERVIEW SCHEDULES AND SELF-REPORT MEASURES OF BPD

There are several structured and semi-structured tests and interviews to make the diagnosis of BPD. Clinician-administered diagnostic assessments include the Diagnostic Interview for Borderline Personality (DIB; Zanarini, Gunderson, Frankenburg, & Chauncey, 1989), Structured Interview for DSM-IV Personality (SIDP-IV; Pfohl, Blum, & Zimmerman, 1997), and the Structured Clinical Interview for DSM-IV Disorders—II (SCID-II; First, Spitzer, Gibbon, & Williams, 1995). The Personality Disorder Interview for DSM–IV (PDI–IV; Widiger, Mangine, Corbitt, Ellis, & Thomas, 1995) is another interview used for the assessment of BPD with strong interrater reliability and internal consistency. However, it has been noted that PDI-IV tends to overdiagnose BPD compared to SCID-II due to variations in diagnostic thresholds across the two interviews (Huprich, Paggeot, & Samuel, 2015). This finding suggests that the choice of interview measure could affect the prevalence and severity of the diagnosis.

Other tests for diagnosis include the Diagnostic Interview for Borderline–Revised (DIBR; Zanarini et al., 1989) and the McLean Screening Instrument for Borderline Personality Disorder (MSI-BPD; Zanarini et al., 2003). The MSI-BPD has been shown to have good specificity (.85) and sensitivity (.81) in nonpsychotic and nonmanic subjects. This measure is also useful for screening inpatient adolescents (Melartin et al., 2009). The DIBR is a frequently used tool in making the diagnosis, but it can take up to 30–60 minutes to administer.

All these interview measures have published reliability and validity. Although these interview tools are useful, their clinical utility is limited by the fact that they require a significant time to administer. Additionally, they require a skilled examiner for administration and scoring.

The interview-based Zanarini Rating Scale for BPD (ZAN-BPD) is probably the most widely used clinician rating scale commonly used in psychotherapy and medication outcome trials involving BPD patients (Zanarini, Weingeroff, Frankenburg, & Fitzmaurice, 2015). Apart from ZAN-BPD, Borderline Evaluation of Severity over Time (BEST), the Borderline Personality Disorder Severity Index (Arntz et al., 2003), and the Borderline Symptom List (Bohus et al., 2007) are used to measure severity and rate change in clinical trials. BEST has high internal consistency, good test–retest reliability, and high discriminant reliability (Pfohl et al., 2009).

There are also various self-report measures that have been developed to aid in the diagnosis. These measures include the BEST (Pfohl et al., 2009), the Personality Diagnostic Questionnaire (PDQ; Hyler, Skodol, Kellman, Oldham, & Rosnick, 1990), and the "the Mood Disorder Questionnaire," although the last is known to often misdiagnose BPD as bipolar disorder (Zimmerman et al., 2010). The PDQ is a 99-item self-report questionnaire used to measure personality disorder. It is known to have a high sensitivity (.98) and low specificity (.41), but it often misdiagnoses non-borderline patients as borderline (Hyler et al., 1990; Zimmerman & Coryell, 1990). Currently, a self-report version of ZAN-BPD is also available for use in clinical settings (Zanarini et al., 2015). This version is very similar to the interview-based version of ZAN-BPD in terms of organization and scoring. It was created due to ZAN-BPD's limited use in clinical practice owing to the amount of time it took to administer. As previously discussed, it has also been suggested that the "narcissistic wounds" subscale, one the nine subscales of the OMMP can predict BPD status and the severity of patient's symptoms (Fertuck et al., 2016). Even though there are various scales available to aid them in diagnosis, clinicians should be cautious about using these tools as the sole diagnostic measure and instead should use them to identify patients who need a more thorough evaluation.

REFERENCES

Akiskal, H. S., Chen, S. E., Davis, G. C., Puzantian, V., Kashgarian, M., & Bolinger, J. (1985). Borderline: An adjective in search of a noun. *Journal of Clinical Psychiatry*.

Akiskal, H. S. (2002). The bipolar spectrum—the shaping of a new paradigm in psychiatry. *Current Psychiatry Reports*, 4(1), 1–3.

American Psychiatric Association (APA). (2013). *Diagnostic and statistical manual of mental disorders* (5th ed.). Washington, DC.

American Psychological Association. (2000). *Diagnostic and statistical manual of mental disorders* (4th edn. rev. ed.). Washington, DC.

Arntz, A., van den Hoorn, M., Cornelis, J., Verheul, R., van den Bosch, W. M., de Bie, A. J. (2003). Reliability and validity of the borderline personality disorder severity Index. *Journal of Personality Disorders*, 17, 45–59.

Atre-Vaidya, N., & Hussain, S. M. (1999). Borderline personality disorder and bipolar mood disorder: two distinct disorders or a continuum? *The Journal of Nervous and Mental Disease*, 187(5), 313–315.

Bernstein, D. P., Cohen, P., Velez, C. N., Schwab-Stone, M., Siever, L. J., & Shinsato, L. (1993). Prevalence and stability of the DSM-III-R personality disorders in a community-based survey of adolescents. *American Journal of Psychiatry*, 150, 1237–1243.

Binks, C., Fenton, M., McCarthy, L., Lee, T., Adams, C. E., & Duggan, C. (2006). Pharmacological interventions for people with borderline personality disorder. *The Cochrane library*.

Biskin, R., & Paris, J. (2012). Diagnosing borderline personality disorder. *Canadian Medical Association*, 184(6), 1789–1794.

Black, D. W., Blum, N., Pfohl, B., & Hale, N. (2004). Suicidal behavior in borderline personality disorder: Prevalence, risk factors, prediction, and prevention. *Journal of Personality Disorders*, 18(3), 226–239.

Bleiberg, E. (1994). Borderline disorders in children and adolescents: The concept, the diagnosis, and the controversies. *Bulletin of the Menninger Clinic*, 58(2), 169.

Bohus, M., Limberger, M. F., Frank, U., Chapman, A., Kuhler, T., & Steiglitz, R. D. (2007). Psychometric properties of the borderline symptom list (BSL). *Psychopathology*, 40, 126–132.

Bongar, B., Peterson, L. G., Golann, S., & Hardiman, J. J. (1990). Self-mutilation and the chronically suicidal patient: An examination of the frequent visitor to the psychiatric emergency room. *Annals of Clinical Psychiatry*, 2(3), 217–222.

Brodsky, B. S., & Stanley, B. (2013). *The Dialectical Behavior Therapy Primer: How DBT Can Inform Clinical Practice*. John Wiley & Sons.

Charland, L. C. (2007). Does borderline personality disorder exist. *Canadian Psychiatry Aujourd'hui*, 3, 16.

Chaudhury, S. R., Singh, T., Burke, A., Stanley, B., Mann, J. J., Grunebaum, M., . . . & Oquendo, M. A. (2016). Clinical correlates of planned and unplanned suicide attempts. *The Journal of Nervous and Mental Disease*, 204(11), 806-811.

Clarkin, J., Widiger, T., Frances, A., Hurt, S., & Gilmore, M. (1983). Prototypic typology and the borderline personality disorder. *Journal of Abnormal Psychology*, 92(3), 263–275.

Cloninger, C., Przybeck, T., Svrakic, D., & Wetzel, R. (1994). TCI—The Temperament and Character Inventory: a guide to its development and use. *St Louis (MO): Center for Psychobiology of Personality, Washington University*.

Costa, P. T., and Widiger, T. A., Eds. (2001). *Personality disorders and the five-factor model of personality*, 2nd edition. Washington, DC: American Psychological Association.

Cowdry, R. W., Pickar, D., & Davies, R. (1986). Symptoms and EEG findings in the borderline syndrome. *Journal of Psychological Medicine*, 15, 201–211.

Feenstra, D. J., Busschbach, J. J. V., Verheul, R., & Hutsebaut, J. (2011). Prevalence and comorbidity of Axis I and Axis II disorders among treatment refractory adolescents admitted for specialized psychotherapy. Journal of Personality Disorders, 25, 842–850.

Fertuck, E. A., Karan, E., & Stanley, B. (2016). The specificity of mental pain in borderline personality disorder compared to depressive disorders and healthy controls. *Borderline Personality Disorder and Emotion Dysregulation, 3*(1), 1.

Feske, U., Mulsant, B. H., Pilkonis, P. A., Soloff, P., Dolata, D., Sackeim, H. A., & Haskett, R. F. (2004). Clinical outcome of ECT in patients with major depression and comorbid borderline personality disorder. *American Journal of Psychiatry, 161*(11), 2073–2080.

Fiedorowicz, J. G., & Black, D. W. (2010). Borderline, bipolar or both. *Current Psychiatry, 9*, 21–31.

First, M. B., Spitzer, R. L., Gibbon, M., & Williams, J. B. (1995). The structured clinical interview for DSM-III-R personality disorders (SCID-II). Part I: Description. *Journal of personality disorders, 9*(2), 83–91.

Forman, E. M., Berk, M. S., Henriques, G. R., Brown, G. K., & Beck, A. T. (2004). History of multiple suicide attempts as a behavioral marker of severe psychopathology. *American Journal of Psychiatry, 161*, 437–443.

Gerson, J., & Stanley, B. (2002). Suicidal and self-injurious behavior in personality disorder: controversies and treatment directions. *Current Psychiatry Reports, 4*(1), 30–38.

Ghaemi, S. N., Ko, J. Y., & Goodwin, F. K. (2002). "Cade's disease" and beyond: Misdiagnosis, antidepressant use, and a proposed definition for bipolar spectrum disorder. *Canadian Journal of Psychiatry, 47*, 125–134.

Gunderson, J. (1982). Empirical studies of the borderline diagnosis. *Psychiatry, 1*, 414–437.

Gunderson, J. G. (2009). *Borderline personality disorder: A clinical guide*: American Psychiatric Pub.

Gunderson, J. G. (2011). Borderline personality disorder. *New England Journal of Medicine, 364*(21), 2037–2042.

Gunderson, J. G., & Lyons-Ruth, K. (2008). BPD's interpersonal hypersensitivity phenotype: A gene-environment-developmental model. *Journal of personality disorders, 22*(1), 22.

Gunderson, J. G., Morey, L. C., Stout, R. L., Skodol, A. E., Shea, M. T., McGlashan, T. H., . . . Yen, S. (2004). Major depressive disorder and borderline personality disorder revisited: longitudinal interactions. *Journal of Clinical Psychiatry, 65*(8), 1049.

Gunderson, J. G., & Phillips, K. A. (1991). A current view of the interface between borderline personality disorder and depression. *Am J Psychiatry, 148*(8), 967–975.

Hampton, M. D. (1997). Dialectical behavior therapy in the treatment of persons with borderline personality disorder. *Archives of psychiatric nursing, 11*(2), 96–101.

Henry, C., Mitropoulou, V., New, A. S., Koenigsberg, H. W., Silverman, J., & Siever, L. J. (2001). Affective instability and impulsivity in borderline personality and bipolar II disorders: similarities and differences. *Journal of Psychiatric Research, 35*(6), 307–312.

Herman, J., & van der Kolk (1987). Traumatic antecedents of borderline personality disorder. In: B. van der Kolk (Ed.), *Psychological trauma*. Washington, DC: American Psychiatric Press.

Hersh, R. (2008). Confronting myths and stereotypes about borderline personality disorder. *Social Work in Mental Health, 6*(1/2), 13–32.

Huprich, S. K., Paggeot, A. V., & Samuel, D. B. (2015). Comparing the Personality Disorder Interview for DSM–IV (PDI–IV) and SCID–II Borderline Personality Disorder Scales: An item–response theory analysis. *Journal of Personality Assessment, 97*(1), 13–21.

Hyler, S. E., Skodol, A. E., Kellman, H. D., Oldham, J. M., & Rosnick, L. (1990). Validity of the Personality Diagnostic Questionnaire-Revised: Comparison with two semistructured interviews. *American Journal of Psychiatry, 147*(8), 1043–1048.

Ingenhoven, T., Lafay, P., Rinne, T., Passchier, J., & Duivenvoorden, H. (2009). Effectiveness of pharmacotherapy for severe personality disorders: Meta-analyses of randomized controlled trials. *Journal of Clinical Psychiatry, 71*(1), 14–25.

Johansen, M., Karterud, S., Pedersen, G., Gude, T., & Falkum, E. (2004). An investigation of the prototype validity of the borderline DSM-IV construct. *Acta Psychiatrica Scandinavica, 109*(4), 289–298.

Johnson, J. G., Cohen, P., Smailes, E., Kasen, S., Oldham, J. M., Skodol, A. E., et al. (2000). Adolescent personality disorders associated with violence and criminal behavior during adolescence and early adulthood. *American Journal of Psychiatry, 157*(9), 1406–1412.

Johnson, J. G., First, M. B., Cohen, P., Skodol, A. E., Kasen, S., & Brook, J. S. (2005). Adverse outcomes associated with personality disorder not otherwise specified in a community sample. *American Journal of Psychiatry, 162*, 1926–1932.

Kernberg, O. F. (1993). *Severe personality disorders: Psychotherapeutic strategies.* New Haven, CT: Yale University Press.

Kernberg, O. F., & Yeomans, F. E. (2013). Borderline personality disorder, bipolar disorder, depression, attention deficit/hyperactivity disorder, and narcissistic personality disorder: practical differential diagnosis. *Bulletin of the Menninger Clinic, 77*(1), 1.

Kernberg, P. F., Weiner, A. S., & Bardenstein, K. K. (2000). *Personality disorders in children and adolescents.* New York: Basic Books.

Kjellander, C., Bongar, B., & King, A. (1998). Suicidality in borderline personality disorder. Thorough summary of risk factors for suicidality or self-harm in borderline personality disorder. *Crisis, 19*(3), 125–135.

Klonsky, E. D. (2008). What is emptiness? Clarifying the 7th criterion for borderline personality disorder. *Journal of Personality Disorders, 22*, 418–426.

Koehne, K., Hamilton, B., Sands, N., & Humphreys, C. (2013). Working around a contested diagnosis: Borderline personality disorder in adolescence. *Health:, 17*(1), 37–56.

Koenigsberg, H. (2010). Affective instability: Toward an integration of neuroscience and psychological perspectives. *Journal of Personality Disorders, 24*(1), 60–82.

Koenigsberg, H. W., Harvey, P. D., Mitropoulou, V., & New, A. S. (2001). Are the interpersonal and identity disturbances in the borderline personality disorder criteria linked to the traits of affective instability and impulsivity? *Journal of personality disorders, 15*(4), 358.

Laurenssen, E. M. P., Hutsebaut, J., Feenstra, D. J., Van Busschbach, J. J., & Luyten, P. (2013). Diagnosis of personality disorders in adolescents: a study among psychologists. *Child and Adolescent Psychiatry and Mental Health, 7*(1), 1.

Lenzenweger, M. F., Lane, M. C., Loranger, A. W., & Kessler, R. C. (2007). DSM-IV personality disorders in the National Comorbidity Survey Replication. *Biological Psychiatry, 62*, 553–564.

Lequesne, E. R., & Hersh, R. G. (2004). Disclosure of a diagnosis of borderline personality disorder. *Journal of Psychiatric Practice, 10*(3), 170–176.

Lewis, L., & Appleby, L. (1988). Personality disorder: The patients psychiatrists dislike. *British Journal of Psychiatry, 153*, 44–49.

Lieb, K., Zanarini, M. C., Schmahl, C., Linehan, M. M., & Bohus, M. (2004). Borderline personality disorder. *The Lancet, 364*(9432), 453–461.

Links, P. S., Heselgrave, R., & van Reekum, R. (1998). Prospective follow-up study of borderline personality disorder: Prognosis, prediction of outcome, and Axis II comorbidity. *Canadian Journal of Psychiatry, 43*(3), 265–270.

Livesley, W. J., Jang, K. L., & Vernon, P. A. (1998). Phenotypic and genetic structure of traits delineating personality disorder. *Archives of General Psychiatry, 55*, 941–948.

Mattanah, J. J. F., Becker, D. F., Levy, K. N., Edell, W. S., & McGlashan, T. H. (1995). Diagnostic stability in adolescents followed up 2 years after hospitalization. *American Journal of Psychiatry, 152*(6), 889–894.

McDonald-Scott, P., Machizawa, S., & Satoh, H. (1992). Diagnostic disclosure: A tale in two cultures. *Psychological Medicine, 22*, 147–157.

Melartin, T., Häkkinen, M., Koivisto, M., Suominen, K., & Isometsä, E. (2009). Screening of psychiatric outpatients for borderline personality disorder with the McLean Screening Instrument for Borderline Personality Disorder (MSI-BPD). *Nordic Journal of Psychiatry, 63*(6), 475–479.

Miller, A. L., Muehlenkamp, J. J., & Jacobson, C. M. (2008). Fact or fiction: Diagnosing borderline personality disorder in adolescents. *Clinical Psychology Review, 28*(6), 969–981.

Millon, T. (1981). *Disorders of personality: DSM-III, axis II.* New York: Wiley.

Moeller, F. G., Barratt, E. S., Dougherty, D. M., Schmitz, J. M., & Swann, A. C. (2001). Psychiatric aspects of impulsivity. *American Journal of Psychiatry, 158,* 1783–1793.

Nose, M., Cipriani, A., Biancosino, B., Grassi, L., & Barbui, C. (2006). Efficacy of pharmacotherapy against core traits of borderline personality disorder: Meta-analysis of randomized controlled trials. *International Clinical Psychopharmacology, 21*(6), 345–353.

Orbach, I., Mikulincer, M., Sirota, P., & Gilboa-Schechtman, E. (2003). Mental pain: A multidimensional operationalization and definition. *Suicide and Life Threatening Behavior, 33*(3), 219–230.

Paris, J. (2004). Borderline or bipolar? Distinguishing borderline personality disorder from bipolar spectrum disorders. *Harvard Review of Psychiatry, 12*(3), 140–145.

Paris, J. (2005). The diagnosis of borderline personality disorder: Problematic but better than the alternatives. *Annals of Clinical Psychiatry, 17*(1), 41–46.

Paris, J. (2007a). The nature of borderline personality disorder: multiple dimensions, multiple symptoms, but one category. *Journal of personality disorders, 21*(5), 457.

Paris, J. (2007b). Why psychiatrists are reluctant to diagnose: borderline personality disorder. *Psychiatry.*

Paris, J. (2008). Commentary: Personality disorder in adolescence: The diagnosis that dare not speak its name. *Personality and Mental Health, 2*(1), 42–43.

Paris, J., & Black, D. W. (2015). Borderline personality disorder and bipolar disorder: what is the difference and why does it matter? *Journal of Nervous and Mental Disease, 203*(1), 3–7.

Parker, G. (2011). Clinical differentiation of bipolar II disorder from personality-based "emotional dysregulation" conditions. *Journal of Affective Disorders, 133,* 16–21.

Pepper, C. M., Klein, D. N., Anderson, R. L., Riso, L. P., Ouimette, P. C., & Lizardi, H. (1995). DSM-III-R Axis II comorbidity in dysthymia and major depression. *American Journal of Psychiatry, 152,* 239–247.

Pfohl, B., Blum, N., John, D. S., McCormick, B., Allen, J., & Black, D. W. (2009). Reliability and validity of the Borderline Evaluation of Severity Over Time (BEST): A self-rated scale to measure severity and change in persons with borderline personality disorder. *Journal of Personality Disorders, 23*(3), 281.

Pfohl, B., Blum, N., & Zimmerman, M. (1997). *Structured interview for dsm-iv personality: Sidp-iv*: American Psychiatric Pub.

Pfohl, B., Stangl, D., & Zimmerman, M. (1984). The implications of DSM-III personality disorders for patients with major depression. *Journal of Affective Disorders, 7*(3–4), 309–18.

Rumpza, L. M. (2015). Borderline Personality Disorder: The Frequency of Disclosure and the Choice to Disclose.

Russell-Archambault, J., Moskowitz, D., Sookman, D., & Paris, J. (2007). Affective instability in patients with borderline personality disorder. *Journal of Abnormal Psychology, 116,* 578–588.

Samuel, D. B., Miller, J. D., Widiger, T. A., Lynam, D. R., Pilkonis, P. A., & Ball, S. A. (2012). Conceptual changes to the definition of borderline personality disorder proposed for DSM-5. *Journal of abnormal psychology, 121*(2), 467.

Shapiro, T. (1990). Debate forum—resolved: Borderline personality disorder exists in children under twelve. *Journal of the American Academy of Child and Adolescent Psychiatry, 29,* 478–483.

Silk, K. (2008). Commentary: Personality disorder in adolescence: The diagnosis that dare not speak its name. *Personality and Mental Health, 2,* 46–48.

Silk, K. R. (2010). The quality of depression in borderline personality disorder and the diagnostic process. *Journal of Personality Disorders, 24*(1), 25.

Skodol, A. E. (2007). Borderline personality as a self-other representational disturbance. *Journal of personality disorders, 21*(5), 500.

Skodol, A. E., Bender, D. S., Morey, L. C., Clark, L. A., Oldham, J. M., Alarcon, R. D., . . . Siever, L. J. (2011). Personality disorder types proposed for DSM-5. *Journal of Personality Disorders*, *25*(2), 136–169.

Skodol, A. E., Gunderson, J. G., Pfohl, B., Widiger, T. A., Livesley, W. J., & Siever, L. J. (2002). The borderline diagnosis I: psychopathology, comorbidity, and personaltity structure. *Biological psychiatry*, *51*(12), 936–950.

Soloff, P. (2000). Psychopharmacological treatment of borderline personality disorder. *Psychiatric Clinics of North America*, *23*(1), 169–192.

Spitzer, R. L., Endicott, J., & Gibbon, M. (1979). Crossing the border into borderline personality and borderline schizophrenia: The development of criteria. *Archives of General Psychiatry*, *36*(1), 17–24.

Stanley, B., & Siever, L. J. (2009). The interpersonal dimension of borderline personality disorder: toward a neuropeptide model. *American Journal of Psychiatry*, *167*(1), 24–39.

Sulzer, S. H., Muenchow, E., Potvin, A., Harris, J., & Gigot, G. (2016). Improving patient-centered communication of the borderline personality disorder diagnosis. *Journal of Mental Health*, *25*(1), 5–9.

Swann, A. C., Pazzaglia, P., Nicholls, A., Dougherty, D. M., & Moeller, F. G. (2003). Impulsivity and phase of illness in bipolar disorder. *Journal of Affective Disorders*, *73*(1), 105–111.

Tomko, R. L., Trull, T. J., Wood, P. K., & Sher, K. J. (2014). Characteristics of borderline personality disorder in a community sample: Comorbidity, treatment utilization, and general functioning. Journal of Personality Disorders, *28*(5), 734.

Trull, T. J., Jahng, S., Tomko, R. L., Wood, P. K., & Sher, K. J. (2010). Revised NESARC personality disorder diagnoses: Gender, prevalence, and comorbidity with substance dependence disorders. *Journal of Personality Disorders*, *24*(4), 412.

Trull, T. J., Widiger, T. A., & Guthrie, P. (1990). Categorical versus dimensional status of borderline personality disorder. *Journal of Abnormal Psychology*, *99*(1), 40–48.

Westen, D., Moses, M. J., Silk, K. R., Lohr, N. E., Cohen, R., & Segal, H. (1992). Quality of depressive experience in borderline personality disorder and major depression: When depression is not just depression. *Journal of Personality Disorders*, *6*(4), 382.

White, C. N., Gunderson, J. G., Zanarini, M. C., & Hudson, J. I. (2003). Family studies of borderline personality disorder: A review. *Harvard Review of Psychiatry*, *11*(1), 8–19.

Widiger, T. A., Mangine, S., Corbitt, E. M., Ellis, C. G., & Thomas, G. V. (1995). *Personality Disorder Interview–IV*. Odessa, FL: Psychological Assessment Resources.

Widiger, T. A., & Weissman, M. M. (1991). Epidemiology of borderline personality disorder. *Hospital and Community Psychiatry*, *42*, 1015–1021.

Wilson, S. T., Stanley, B., Oquendo, M. A., Goldberg, P., Zalsman, G., & Mann, J. J. (2007). Comparing impulsiveness, hostility, and depression in borderline personality disorder and bipolar II disorder. *The Journal of clinical psychiatry*, *68*(10), 1533.

Yee, L., Korner, A. J., McSwiggan, S., Meares, R. A., & Stevenson, J. (2005). Persistent hallucinosis in borderline personality disorder. *Comprehensive Psychiatry*, *46*, 147–155.

Yoshimatsu, K., & Palmer, B. (2014). Depression in patients with borderline personality disorder. *Harvard Review of Psychiatry*, *22*(5), 266–273.

Zanarini, M. C. (1993). Borderline personality disorder as an impulse spectrum disorder. In: J. Paris (Ed.), Borderline Personality Disorder: Etiology and Treatment (pp. 67–86). Washington, D.C.: American Psychiatric Publishing, Inc.

Zanarini, M. C., & Frankenburg, F. R. (2007). The essential nature of borderline psychopathology. *Journal of personality disorders*, *21*(5), 518–535.

Zanarini, M. C., Frankenburg, F. R., Reich, D. B., Hennen, J., & Silk, K. R. (2005). Adult experiences of abuse reported by borderline patients and axis II comparison subjects over six years of prospective follow-up. *The Journal of nervous and mental disease*, *193*(6), 412–416.

Zanarini, M. C., Gunderson, J. G., Frankenburg, F. R., & Chauncey, D. L. (1989). The revised diagnostic interview for borderlines: discriminating BPD from other axis II disorders. *Journal of personality disorders*, *3*(1), 10–18.

Zanarini, M. C., Vujanovic, A. A., Parachini, E. A., Boulanger, J. L., Frankenburg, F. R., & Hennen, J. (2003). A screening measure for BPD: The McLean screening instrument for borderline personality disorder (MSI-BPD). *Journal of personality disorders*, *17*(6), 568–573.

Zanarini, M. C., Weingeroff, J. L., Frankenburg, F. R., & Fitzmaurice, G. M. (2015). Development of the self-report version of the Zanarini Rating Scale for Borderline Personality Disorder. *Personality and Mental Health*, *9*(4), 243–249.

Zimmerman, M., & Coryell, W. (1990). Diagnosing personality disorders in the community: a comparison of self-report and interview measures. *Archives of General Psychiatry*, *47*, 527–531.

Zimmerman, M., Galione, J. N., Ruggero, C. J., Chelminski, I., Young, D., Dalrymple, K., & McGlinchey, J. B. (2010). Screening for bipolar disorder and finding borderline personality disorder. *The Journal of clinical psychiatry*, *71*(9), 1212–1217.

Zimmerman, M., & Morgan, T. (2013). Problematic boundaries in the diagnosis of bipolar disorder: The interface with borderline personality disorder. *Current Psychiatry Reports*, *15*(12), 422–426.

Zimmerman, M., Rothschild, L., & Chelminski, I. (2005). The prevalence of DSM-IV personality disorders in psychiatric outpatients. *American Journal of Psychiatry*, *162*(10), 1911–1918.

Zweig-Frank, H., & Paris, J. (1995). The five-factor model of personality in borderline and nonborderline personality disorders. *Canadian Journal of Psychiatry*, *40*(9), 523–526.

Onset, Course, and Prognosis for Borderline Personality Disorder

MARY C. ZANARINI AND LINDSEY C. CONKEY[*]

Borderline personality disorder (BPD) is a common psychiatric disorder, with the best epidemiological evidence estimating that about 2% of American adults meet criteria from the *Diagnostic and Statistical Manual of Mental Disorders* (DSM-IV) for BPD (Lenzenweger, Lane, Loranger, & Kessler, 2007; Swartz, Blazer, George, & Winfield, 1990; Trull, Jahng, Tomko, Wood, & Sher, 2010). It has also been estimated that approximately 19% of psychiatric inpatients and approximately 11% of psychiatric outpatients meet criteria for BPD (Widiger & Frances, 1989). In addition, cross-sectional studies have found that BPD is associated with high levels of mental health service utilization (Bender et al., 2001; Skodol, Buckley, & Charles, 1983; Swartz et al., 1990) and a serious degree of psychosocial impairment (Skodol et al., 1983, 2002; Swartz et al., 1990). Taken together, these facts suggest that BPD is a serious public health problem, and yet, until recently, no large-scale, prospective study of the long-term course of BPD in adults had been conducted.

ONSET OF BPD

The course of BPD has received relatively little attention. Most studies have used adult samples (people age 18 or older). In addition, clinicians have been reluctant until very recently to diagnose adolescents or latency-aged children as meeting

---

[*] Supported by NIMH grants MH47588 and MH62169.

full-blown criteria for BPD. And the DSM-5 (American Psychiatric Association [APA], 2013) has added a new diagnosis that clinicians may decide to give to adolescents instead of BPD: disruptive mood dysregulation disorder (DMDD)—a disorder of childhood marked by frequent temper outbursts and chronic anger or irritability.

And yet studies of adult samples of borderline patients have found retrospective evidence of the existence of BPD in children and adolescents. In one study, 13 was the average age that those with BPD first began to feel psychiatrically ill (Zanarini, Frankenburg, Khera, & Bleichmar, 2001). In a related study, it was found that one-third of those with BPD began to deliberately harm themselves physically in latency (12 or younger), another third in adolescence (13–17), and the final third in adulthood (18 years of age or older) (Zanarini, Frankenburg, Ridolfi, Jager-Hyman, Hennen, & Gunderson, 2006). In an online-based retrospective study, parents reported that their adult sons (Goodman, Patel, Oakes, Matho, & Triebwasser, 2013) and daughters (Goodman et al., 2010) with rigorously diagnosed BPD began to exhibit symptoms of BPD early in life.

In addition, studies of adolescents have found that they meet full criteria for BPD. Some of these studies have been rigorous cross-sectional studies of adolescent outpatients (Chanen, Jovev, & Jackson, 2007) and inpatients (Grilo et al., 1998; Meijer, Goedhart, & Treffers, 1998). In both cases, fully developed BPD was found. In addition, two community studies of the prevalence of BPD in nonadult samples have been conducted (Bernstein et al., 1993; Zanarini et al., 2011). Both found that 3% of their subjects met DSM criteria for BPD. The first study had a mean age of 16 and the second had a mean age of 12—indicating that BPD is as common in the community for adolescents and late latency children as it is for adults.

EARLY STUDIES OF THE SHORT- AND LONG-TERM COURSE OF BPD

Starting in the 1960s, 11 small-scale, prospective studies of the short-term course and outcome of BPD in adult patients had been conducted (Akiskal et al., 1985; Barasch, Frances, Hurt, Clarkin, & Cohen, 1985; Grinker, Werble, & Drye, 1968; Gunderson, Carpenter, & Strauss, 1975; Links, Mitton, & Steiner, 1990; Mehlum et al., 1991; Modestin & Villiger, 1989; Nace, Saxon, & Shore, 1986; Perry & Cooper, 1985; Pope, Jonas, Hudson, Cohen, & Gunderson, 1983; Tucker, Bauer, Wagner, Harlam, & Sher, 1987). During the ensuing years, the results of six additional small-scale, prospective studies of the short-term course of BPD have been published (Antikainen, Hintikka, Lehtonen, Koponen, & Arstila, 1995; Linehan, Heard, & Armstrong, 1993; Najavits & Gunderson, 1995; Sandell et al., 1993; Senol, Dereboy, & Yuksel, 1997; Stevenson & Meares, 1992). In addition, four large-scale, follow-back studies of the long-term course and outcome of BPD in adult patients have been conducted (McGlashan, 1986; Paris, Brown, & Nowlis, 1987; Plakun, Burkhardt, & Muller, 1985; Stone, 1990).

The results of these 17 short-term, prospective studies have generally been interpreted to mean that most borderline patients are doing relatively poorly 1 to 7 years after their initial evaluation. In contrast, the results of these long-term, follow-back studies have generally been interpreted to mean that most borderline patients are doing reasonably well a mean of 14 to 16 years after their index admission.

Although all studies of the course of BPD provided useful information and many were considered state of the art at the time that they were conducted, they all suffered from one or more methodological problems that limited what could be generalized from their results. Chief among these limitations were the use of chart review or clinical interviews to diagnose BPD, no comparison group or the use of less than optimal comparison subjects, reliance on small-size samples with high attrition rates, only basic information collected at baseline and follow-up, typically only one post-baseline reassessment, non-blind post-baseline assessments, and variable number of years of follow-up in the same study. In addition, only one of the four long-term follow-back studies used a socioeconomically representative sample (Paris et al., 1987).

LARGE-SCALE, PROSPECTIVE STUDIES OF THE LONG-TERM COURSE OF BPD

Few large-scale prospective studies of the long-term course of BPD have been conducted. Of note, Zanarini and colleagues conducted the most extensive study of long-term course, the McLean Study of Adult Development (MSAD), and we will focus on these findings. We include other studies where they are available. The MSAD began 21 years ago. It is the first National Institute of Mental Health (NIMH)-funded prospective study of the course and outcome of BPD. Publications from this study have come in four waves: baseline data, information from the first three waves of follow-up, the first five waves of follow-up, and the first eight waves of follow-up (i.e., up to the 6-year wave, 10-year wave, and now the 16-year wave). Our 18-year and 20-year waves of data collection are almost complete, and our 22-year wave began in July 2015.

The Collaborative Longitudinal Personality Disorders Study (CLPS) began 4 years after MSAD and ended a number of years ago after collection of 10 years of prospective data. This NIMH-funded study did not publish in set waves of follow-up data. Due to this, we will focus on relevant papers regardless of the exact number of years of follow-up that they describe.

As noted, MSAD began more than two decades ago. We have completed eight waves of blind follow-up: 2-, 4-, 6-, 8-, 10-, 12-, 14-, and 16-year follow-up evaluations. In addition, we are more than 99% of the way through the 18- and 20-year follow-up waves. The trace rate in this series of patients has remained high. After eight waves of completed follow-up (on which some of the longitudinal findings presented here are based), 89% of the surviving borderline patients and 83% of the surviving Axis II comparison subjects were still participating.

TRAUMA HISTORY

Most of this sample of borderline patients reported coming from troubled backgrounds. More than 90% reported some type of abuse in childhood, and more than

90% reported some type of neglect (mostly emotional in nature) before the age of 18 (Zanarini et al., 1997). In terms of abuse, 62% reported a childhood history of sexual abuse, and 86% reported a childhood history of verbal, emotional, and/or physical abuse. Most of those reporting a childhood history of sexual abuse reported being severely sexually abused (i.e., more than 75% reported abuse that was ongoing and/or involved penetration) (Zanarini, Yong, et al., 2002). In addition, the severity of childhood sexual abuse, other forms of abuse, and neglect were all significantly correlated with both severity of borderline psychopathology and severity of psychosocial impairment.

High percentages of borderline patients also reported being abused and neglected by caretakers of both genders (Zanarini, Frankenburg, et al., 2000). More specifically, more than 50% reported a childhood history of biparental abuse, and more than 70% reported a childhood history of biparental neglect. In addition, the combination of female caretaker neglect and male caretaker abuse was found to be a risk factor for childhood sexual abuse by a non-caretaker for women with BPD.

It was also found that adult experiences of violence were common among borderline patients (Zanarini et al., 1999). More specifically, 46% of the borderline patients in the study reported being the victim of some type of adult violence. In terms of specific forms of violence, 33% reported having had a physically abusive partner, 31% reported that they had been raped, and 19% reported having both been physically assaulted and raped. Both childhood sexual abuse and emotional withdrawal by a caretaker were found to be risk factors for adult experiences of physical and/or sexual violence reported by women with BPD.

FAMILY HISTORY OF PSYCHIATRIC DISORDER

Family history of psychiatric disorder was also studied in this sample (Zanarini, Frankenburg, Yong et al., 2004). It was found that the first-degree relatives of borderline patients had a heightened prevalence of DSM-III-R and DSM-IV BPD. It was also found that they had a heightened prevalence of the symptoms of BPD, particularly inappropriate anger, affective instability, paranoia/dissociation, general impulsivity, and intense, unstable relationships. Not surprisingly, the symptoms of BPD were substantially more common among these relatives than BPD itself.

In another family history study, it was found that BPD co-aggregates with major depression, dysthymic disorder, bipolar I disorder, alcohol abuse/dependence, drug abuse/dependence, panic disorder, social phobia, obsessive-compulsive disorder, generalized anxiety disorder, post-traumatic stress disorder (PTSD), somatoform pain disorder, and all four Axis II disorders studied (antisocial, histrionic, narcissistic, and sadistic personality disorder) (Zanarini, Barison, Frankenburg, Reich, & Hudson, 2009).

CORE SYMPTOMS, COMORBID DISORDERS, AND TREATMENT HISTORY

Some aspects of the subsyndromal phenomenology of BPD were also studied at baseline. It was found that the subjective pain of borderline patients (i.e., dysphoric affective and cognitive inner states) was both more severe and more multifaceted than previously recognized (Zanarini, Frankenburg, DeLuca et al., 1998). For example, 75% of borderline patients reported feeling damaged beyond repair up to 90% of the time.

Dissociation was found to be heterogeneous in severity, with about a third of borderline patients reporting "normal" levels of dissociation, about 40% reporting moderate levels of dissociation, and about a quarter reporting high levels of dissociation typically associated with PTSD or dissociative identity disorder (DID) (Zanarini, Ruser, Frankenburg, & Hennen, 2000).

It was also found that borderline patients had elevated levels of absorption and amnesia (subtypes of dissociation) as well as depersonalization. In addition, childhood sexual abuse, inconsistent treatment by a caretaker, witnessing sexual violence as a child, and an adult rape history were found to be significant predictors of the level of dissociation (Zanarini, Ruser, Frankenburg, Hennen, & Gunderson, 2000).

Both Axis I and II disorders were found to be common among these borderline patients (Zanarini, Frankenburg, Dubo et al., 1998a). The most common lifetime Axis I disorders were unipolar mood disorders and anxiety disorders, particularly PTSD, panic disorder, and social phobia. Substance use disorders and eating disorders, particularly eating disorder not otherwise specified (NOS), were also common (Marino & Zanarini, 2001). In terms of personality disorders, paranoid personality disorder, avoidant personality disorder, dependent personality disorder, and self-defeating personality disorder were most common (Zanarini, Frankenburg, Dubo et al., 1998b).

By the time of their index admission, a high percentage of borderline patients had a history of psychiatric treatment (Zanarini et al., 2001). More than three-quarters had been in individual therapy, had previous psychiatric hospitalizations, and had been on standing medications. In addition, more than 50% had participated in self-help groups. About 35–45% had been in group therapy, couples/family therapy, day treatment, and residential treatment. Only electroconvulsive therapy (ECT) was rare among borderline patients (<10%).

Taken together, these baseline findings suggest that this sample of borderline patients had a high degree of morbidity. They also suggest that they commonly reported a childhood and adult history of adversity as well as familial psychopathology.

COURSE OF BORDERLINE PSYCHOPATHOLOGY: REMISSIONS AND RECURRENCES OF BPD

Remission was defined as no longer meeting either of our study criteria sets for BPD (DIB-R and DSM-III-R) (Zanarini, Gunderson, Frankenburg, & Chauncey, 1989; Zanarini, Frankenburg, & Vujanovic, 2002).) during at least one 2-year follow-up period. Recurrence was defined as meeting both criteria sets for BPD during at least one 2-year follow-up period after meeting study criteria for a remission in a previous follow-up period.

Several papers have dealt with rates of remission and recurrence of BPD. One detailed our findings at 6-year follow-up, another detailed our findings at 10-year follow-up, and the third detailed our findings at 16-year follow-up (Zanarini, Frankenburg, Hennen, & Silk, 2003; Zanarini, Frankenburg, Hennen, Reich, & Silk, 2006; Zanarini, Frankenburg, Reich, & Fitzmaurice, 2012). After 6 years of prospective follow-up, 76% of borderline patients had achieved at least a 2-year remission of BPD. The comparable figures for 10 and 16 years of follow-up were 91% and 99%. At 16-year follow-up, we also focused on sustained remissions and found that 95% of borderline patients had at least a 4-year remission, 90% had at least a 6-year remission, and 78% had at least an 8-year remission.

In terms of recurrences after 16 years of prospective follow-up, 36% of borderline patients had a recurrence after a 2-year remission, 25% after a 4-year remission, 19% after a 6-year remission, and 10% after an 8-year remission. These results suggest that the longer a borderline patient is in remission, the less likely he or she is to have a recurrence of full-blown BPD.

In terms of suicide, 13 borderline patients (4.5%) took their own lives during the first 16 years of prospective follow-up. Furthermore, one comparison subject with another personality disorder (1.4%) committed suicide during this same 16-year period. This rate of 4.5% is only about half the 9–10% found in the three long-term follow-back studies that assessed this most unfortunate outcome (McGlashan, 1986; Paris et al., 1987; Stone, 1990).

SUBSYNDROMAL PHENOMENOLOGY OF BPD

Three important findings concerning the subsyndromal phenomenology of BPD have also emerged over the first 16 years of follow-up (Zanarini et al., 2003). At 6-year follow-up, we found that the prevalence of all of the 24 symptoms that we studied declined significantly over time for all subjects considered together (borderline patients and Axis II comparison subjects) but remained significantly more common among borderline patients than those with other forms of personality disorders. (Twenty-two of these symptoms are from the DIB-R and two are DSM-III-R criteria not assessed by the DIB-R—mood lability and serious identity disturbance).

Careful examination of these results suggested that different sectors of borderline psychopathology resolve at different rates. Affective symptoms are the most stable, impulsive symptoms resolve the most rapidly, and cognitive and interpersonal symptoms occupy an intermediate position.

Careful examination of these results also suggested that some of the symptoms of BPD seem to be acute in nature and others seem to be temperamental in nature. Acute symptoms, which are akin to the positive symptoms of schizophrenia, resolve relatively quickly, are the best markers for the disorder (Zanarini, Gunderson, Frankenburg, & Chauncey, 1990) and are often the immediate reason for needing costly forms of treatment, such as psychiatric hospitalizations. Temperamental symptoms, which are akin to the negative symptoms of schizophrenia, resolve more slowly, are not specific to BPD, and are closely associated with ongoing psychosocial impairment.

Using 10 years of prospectively collected data and survival analyses, we found that 12 of the 24 symptoms we were studying seemed to be acute in nature and 12 seemed to be temperamental (Zanarini et al., 2007). The 12 acute symptoms are affective instability, quasi-psychotic thought, serious identity disturbance, substance abuse, promiscuity, self-mutilation, suicide threats and attempts, stormy relationships, manipulation/devaluation/sadism, demandingness/entitlement, serious treatment regressions, and countertransference problems/"special treatment relationships." The 12 temperamental symptoms are depression, helplessness/hopelessness/worthlessness, anger, anxiety, loneliness/emptiness, odd thinking/unusual perceptual experiences (e.g., overvalued ideas or experiences of depersonalization), nondelusional paranoia, other forms of impulsivity, intolerance of aloneness, abandonment/engulfment/annihilation concerns, counterdependency, and undue dependency/masochism.

As can be seen, some acute symptoms reflect areas of core impulsivity, such as self-mutilation and suicide attempts. Other acute symptoms, such as stormy relationships or problems with devaluation or demandingness, involve active attempts to manage interpersonal difficulties. Temperamental symptoms also tend to fall into two categories. The first group involves chronic feelings of dysphoria, such as anger or loneliness/emptiness. The second group involves interpersonal symptoms that reflect abandonment or dependency issues, such as intolerance of aloneness or counterdependency problems. Currently, there are no empirical data showing which type responds best to specific evidence-based therapies, and it is recommended that future research investigate such therapeutic outcomes.

Knowing that there are two types of symptoms of BPD with different courses and different areas of life that they impact negatively can help guide patients, their families, and the mental health professionals treating them about what to expect in the future. If treatment as usual does not help to alleviate the acute symptoms of BPD, one of the five comprehensive evidenced-based forms of psychotherapy for BPD may need to be considered: dialectical behavioral therapy (DBT; Linehan, Armstrong, Suarez, Almon, & Heard, 1991); mentalization-based treatment (MBT; Bateman & Fonagy, 1999); schema-focused therapy (SFT; Giesen-Bloo et al., 2006); transference-focused psychotherapy (TFP; Clarkin, Levy, Lenzenweger, & Kernberg, 2007); and general psychiatric management (GPM; McMain et al., 2009). Additionally, if the temperamental symptoms of BPD do not lessen in severity over time, a rehabilitation model of treatment might be needed (Zanarini et al., 2012).

COURSE OF CO-OCCURRING DISORDERS

After 6 years of prospective follow-up, it was found that a high percentage of borderline patients continue to suffer from episodes of Axis I disorders over time (Zanarini, Frankenburg, Hennen, Reich, & Silk, 2004). Even by the time of the third wave of follow-up, 75% of borderline patients met criteria for a mood disorder, 60% for an anxiety disorder, 34% for an eating disorder, and 19% for a substance use disorder (SUD). It was also found that the ongoing prevalence of Axis I disorders was strongly influenced by remission status from BPD. More specifically, the percentage of remitted borderline patients who met criteria for various Axis I disorders decreased over time, whereas the rates of all types of disorders studied remained relatively constant over time for nonremitted borderline patients, except for SUDs, which declined from a baseline high of 64% to 41% by the time of the 6-year follow-up.

In addition, it was found that the absence of a SUD was a stronger predictor of time-to-remission from BPD than the absence of any other type of disorder; looked at another way, SUDs were the disorders that most interfered with remission from BPD. This finding runs counter to clinical lore, which suggests that BPD is most affected by the course of mood disorders or PTSD. However, this finding makes clinical sense because abusing alcohol and/or drugs could easily lead to greater impairment in all four core sectors of borderline psychopathology: more intense feelings of depression and anger, heightened distrust, increased impulsivity, and even more turbulent relationships.

In terms of Axis II disorders over this 6-year period, most co-occurring personality disorders declined significantly over time (Zanarini, Frankenburg, Vujanovic et al., 2004). This substantial decline was noted in many cases for both remitted and nonremitted borderline patients. The three exceptions were avoidant, dependent, and self-defeating personality disorders—which remained common among nonremitted borderline patients. Even by the fifth to sixth year after their index admission, 59% of nonremitted borderline patients met criteria for avoidant personality disorder, 45% for dependent personality disorder, and 27% for self-defeating personality disorder. This contrasts with 16%, 8%, and 1%, respectively, for remitted borderline patients.

We also found that the absence of avoidant, dependent, and self-defeating personality disorders significantly reduced a borderline patient's time to remission or, looked at another way, significantly improved a borderline patient's chances of remitting. It might be that for nonremitted borderline patients these co-occurring disorders represent enduring aspects of their temperament, whereas for remitted borderline patients they were symptomatic manifestations secondary to their BPD. If so, once their borderline psychopathology was significantly diminished, their fear of embarrassment and rejection, dependency, and masochism may have also declined in severity. In other words, there may be subtypes of borderline patients, and those most likely to remit in the short- to midterm may be less temperamentally impaired than those whose borderline psychopathology remains relatively constant.

After 10 years of prospective follow-up, separable substudies of the course of SUDs, eating disorders, PTSD, and other anxiety disorders were published. In general, these disorders (except anorexia and bulimia nervosa) were significantly more common among borderline patients than Axis II comparison subjects. But a significant decline in prevalence was observed for those in both study groups.

We also studied time-to-remission, time-to-recurrence, and time-to-new-onsets for each of these disorders. In terms of SUDs, it was found that remissions were both common (>90% for both alcohol and drug abuse and dependence) and relatively stable (recurrences of 40% and 35%, respectively). It was also found that new onsets were less common than might be expected (23% for alcohol-related disorders and 21% for drug-related disorders).

Remissions lasting at least 2 years were also common (>90%) for the three eating disorders studied: anorexia nervosa, bulimia nervosa, and eating disorder not otherwise specified (EDNOS) (mostly binge eating disorder). By the time of the 10-year follow-up, more than 50% of borderline patients reporting a remission of EDNOS reported a recurrence of this disorder. However, less than 30% of borderline patients who reported a remission of either anorexia or bulimia later reported a recurrence of these disorders. For borderline patients who did not meet criteria for these disorders at baseline, only 4% reported a new onset of anorexia and only 11% reported a new onset of bulimia, but more than 40% reported a new onset of some form of EDNOS. It was also found that crossover or diagnostic migration was common, particularly for borderline patients with a diagnosis of anorexia (88%) or bulimia (71%) at baseline. However, diagnostic migration was less common among borderline patients with a diagnosis of EDNOS during their index admission (20%).

Remission from PTSD was also very common (87%). However, recurrences (40%) and new onsets (27%) over the decade of prospective follow-up were less common and relatively rare.

The course of anxiety disorders other than PTSD (panic disorder, agoraphobia, social phobia, simple phobia, obsessive-compulsive disorder, and generalized anxiety disorder) was also studied. By 10-year follow-up, the rates of remission for borderline patients who met criteria for these disorders at baseline were high (77–100%), whereas the rates of recurrences (30–65%) and new onsets (15–47%, $Mdn = 23.5\%$) were moderate, suggesting an intermittent course among those with BPD (Silverman, Frankenburg, Reich, Fitzmaurice, & Zanarini, 2012).

PSYCHIATRIC TREATMENT OVER TIME

Four main findings concerning psychiatric treatment have emerged from a 6-year study of the mental health services received by borderline patients and Axis II comparison subjects (Zanarini, Frankenburg, Hennen, & Silk, 2004). The first of these findings is that a significantly higher percentage of borderline patients reported being in 13 of the 17 treatment modalities studied (all but individual therapy, couples/family therapy, day treatment, and ECT).

The second of these findings is that only a declining minority of borderline patients used more intensive forms of treatment during each of the 2-year follow-up periods (i.e., psychiatric hospitalization, residential care, and/or day treatment). At baseline, for example, 79% of borderline patients had a history of prior hospitalization, 60% had been hospitalized multiple times, and an equal percentage had been hospitalized for 30 days or more. By the time of the 6-year follow-up, only 33% of borderline patients had been hospitalized for psychiatric reasons, only 23% had been hospitalized two or more times, and only 19% had spent a month or more in inpatient care. A similar pattern of declining participation was found for both day treatment and residential care (e.g., the percentage of borderline patients in day and/or residential treatment decreased over time from 55% at baseline to 22% 5 to 6 years after their index admission).

The third major finding concerning psychiatric treatment is that at least 70% of borderline patients were in psychotherapy and/or taking standing medications during all three follow-up periods. As a corollary, most of the borderline patients who participated in these two outpatient modalities did so in a sustained manner.

The fourth main finding is that high rates of intensive polypharmacy were reported by borderline patients in all three follow-up waves. More specifically, 40% of these patients reported taking three or more concurrent standing medications during each follow-up period, 20% reported taking four or more, and 10% reported taking five or more. This trend, which is commonly found in the treatment of many psychiatric disorders, has developed despite the fact that there is no empirical evidence of the effectiveness of polypharmacy in the treatment of BPD. In fact, the only controlled trial of polypharmacy in BPD found that olanzapine alone was as effective as the olanzapine-fluoxetine combination (Zanarini, Frankenburg, & Parachini, 2004). Perhaps most importantly, these high rates of polypharmacy are related to the high rates of obesity found in borderline patients at the 6-year follow-up period (about 30% had a body mass index of ≥30).

At 10-year follow-up, a study of three treatment modalities was conducted (Hörz, Zanarini, Frankenburg, Reich, & Fitzmaurice, 2010). In terms of prevalence rates, there was a significant decrease in the percentage of patients with BPD (and Axis II comparison subjects) participating in individual therapy, standing medication, and psychiatric hospitalization. In terms of time to cessation and resumption, 52% of patients with BPD stopped individual therapy, and 44% stopped taking standing medications for a period of 2 years or more. However, 85% of those who had stopped psychotherapy resumed it, and 67% of those who stopped taking standing medications later resumed taking them. In contrast, 88% had no hospitalizations for at least 2 years, but almost half of these patients were subsequently rehospitalized. Taken together, these results suggest that patients with BPD tend to use outpatient treatment without interruption over prolonged periods of time. They also suggest that inpatient treatment is used far more intermittently and by only a relatively small minority of those with BPD.

PSYCHOSOCIAL FUNCTIONING OVER THE YEARS OF FOLLOW-UP

The psychosocial functioning of borderline patients, while improving over time, was found to be significantly more impaired than that of Axis II comparison subjects over 6 years of prospective follow-up (Zanarini, Frankenburg, Reich, Hennen, &

Silk, 2005). In terms of specific realms of functioning, borderline patients and Axis II comparison subjects functioned about the same socially and in their meaningful use of leisure time. However, their vocational functioning was more impaired. More specifically, they were significantly less likely to go to work or school in a sustained manner. Additionally, they were less likely to perform well at work or school than Axis II comparison subjects. They were also about three times more likely to be receiving disability payments.

It was also found that the symptomatic status of borderline patients seems to have a strong impact on their psychosocial functioning over the 6-year time period. While the social and vocational functioning of ever-remitted borderline patients improved steadily over time, that of never-remitted borderline patients was relatively steady at a low level in most areas. In terms of overall functioning, more than 40% of ever-remitted borderline patients had a global assessment of functioning (GAF) score in the good range (≥ 61) by the time of the 6-year follow-up, and more than 65% had attained or maintained good overall psychosocial functioning (which, unlike the GAF, does not assess an admixture of symptoms and psychosocial impairment but rather is defined as having one emotionally sustaining relationship with a friend or romantic partner plus a good vocational performance that is also sustained over time). In contrast, no nonremitted borderline patient had a good GAF score at 6-year follow-up, and only about a quarter had attained or maintained good psychosocial functioning.

A 10-year study of the psychosocial functioning of borderline patients and Axis II comparison subjects was also conducted (Zanarini, Frankenburg, Reich, & Fitzmaurice, 2010). At baseline, 26% of borderline patients and 58% of Axis II comparison subjects had had good social and vocational functioning in the 2 years prior to their index admission. In this study, good psychosocial functioning was defined as in the 6-year study described except that full-time vocational engagement was now required. About 60% of borderline patients and 93% of Axis II comparison subjects who did not have good psychosocial functioning at baseline achieved this outcome by the time of the 10-year follow-up. In addition, more than 80% of those in both study groups who were high functioning psychosocially prior to their index admission lost this level of functioning over the decade of follow-up. However, only 40% of borderline patients and 30% of Axis II comparison subjects who lost this level of functioning regained it over the years of follow-up. Finally, more than 90% of the poor psychosocial functioning of borderline patients was due to poor vocational but not social performance.

All the figures just presented for both study groups would be quite different if we had defined good psychosocial functioning as including part-time work or school (rather than full-time vocational engagement). With only this one change to our definition, 82% of borderline patients and 94% of Axis II comparison subjects (rather than 60% and 93%) who did not have good psychosocial functioning in the 2 years prior to their index admission achieved this outcome over the years of follow-up. In a similar vein, 68% of borderline patients and 60% of Axis II comparison subjects (rather than 88% and 84%), who did have good psychosocial functioning at baseline lost it over time. Finally, 81% of borderline patients and 71% of Axis II comparison subjects (rather than 40% and 30%) who lost their initially good psychosocial functioning regained it over time.

RECOVERY FROM BPD OVER 16 YEARS OF PROSPECTIVE FOLLOW-UP

We selected a GAF score of 61 or higher as our measure of recovery because it offers a reasonable description of a good overall outcome (i.e., some mild symptoms or some difficulty in social, occupational, or school functioning, but generally functioning pretty well, has some meaningful interpersonal relationships). We operationalized this score to enhance its reliability and meaning. More specifically, to be given this score or higher, a subject typically had to be in remission from his or her primary Axis II diagnosis, have at least one emotionally sustaining relationship with a close friend or life partner/spouse, and be able to work or go to school consistently, competently, and on a full-time basis (which included being a housekeeper taking care of minor children).

In terms of recoveries, 60% of borderline patients achieved a 2-year recovery, 54% achieved a 4-year recovery, 44% achieved a 6-year recovery, and 40% achieved an 8-year recovery. Axis II comparison subjects had an easier time achieving this multifaceted outcome. More specifically, 85% achieved a 2-year recovery, 82% achieved a 4-year recovery, 80% achieved a 6-year recovery, and 75% achieved an 8-year recovery.

In terms of loss of recovery, 44% of borderline patients lost their 2-year recovery, 32% lost their 4-year recovery, 26% lost their 6-year recovery, and 20% lost their 8-year recovery. The recoveries achieved by Axis II comparison subjects were substantially more stable than those achieved by borderline patients. More specifically, 28% lost their 2-year recovery, 20% lost their 4-year recovery, 13% lost their 6-year recovery, and 9% lost their 8-year recovery.

MEDICAL CONDITIONS, HEALTH-RELATED LIFESTYLE CHOICES, AND COSTLY FORMS OF MEDICAL TREATMENT OVER TIME

At 6-year follow-up, remitted borderline patients were found to be significantly less likely than nonremitted borderline patients to have a history of a "syndrome-like" condition (i.e., chronic fatigue, fibromyalgia, or temporomandibular joint syndrome) (Frankenburg & Zanarini, 2004). They were also found to be significantly less likely to have a history of one or more of the following chronic medical conditions: obesity, osteoarthritis, diabetes, hypertension, back pain, and urinary incontinence. In addition, they were found to be significantly less likely to report pack-per-day smoking, daily consumption of alcohol, lack of regular exercise, daily use of sleep medications, and sustained use of pain medications. Finally, remitted borderline patients were significantly less likely than nonremitted borderline patients to have had at least one medically related emergency room visit and/or medical hospitalization.

In sum, the failure to remit from BPD seems to be associated with a heightened risk of suffering from poorly understood medical syndromes and chronic physical conditions, making poor health-related lifestyle choices, and using costly forms of medical services.

Obesity was found in 28% of the 264 borderline patients studied at 6-year follow-up (Frankenburg & Zanarini, 2006). Those who were obese were significantly more likely than the nonobese patients to report suffering from diabetes, hypertension, osteoarthritis, chronic back pain, carpal tunnel syndrome, urinary incontinence, gastroesophageal reflux disorder, gallstones, and asthma. Four significant risk factors for obesity were found: chronic PTSD, lack of exercise, a family history of obesity, and a recent history of psychotropic polypharmacy.

More recently, the 10-year course of these topics was studied (Keuroghlian, Frankenburg, & Zanarini, 2013). It was found that ever-recovered borderline patients had significantly better physical health, made significantly better health-related lifestyle choices, and used significantly less costly forms of medical treatment than never-recovered borderline patients.

OTHER DEATHS

The same number of borderline patients have died from natural causes or an accident ($N = 13$, 4.5%) as have died of suicide over the first 16 years of follow-up. In contrast, one Axis II comparison individual died by suicide and another died of natural causes.

SYMPTOMATIC COURSE OF BPD FOUND IN OTHER STUDIES

The borderline subjects in the CLPS study, who were inpatients, outpatients, and nonpatients applying for treatment at study entry, also had high levels of comorbidity at baseline (McGlashan et al., 2000). They also reported high levels of childhood adversity (Battle et al., 2004), psychosocial impairment (Skodol et al., 2002), and prior psychiatric treatment (Bender et al., 2001). Despite differences in study design, a 10-year study of the course of BPD found that remissions of BPD were very common and recurrences were relatively rare (Gunderson et al., 2011). In addition, the MSAD finding that there are two types of borderline symptoms was confirmed by another CLPS study (McGlashan et al., 2005). In this study, acute symptoms are called *symptomatic behaviors* and temperamental symptoms are called *traits*. Finally, ongoing psychosocial impairment was also found (Gunderson et al., 2011).

Three small-scale studies have assessed the 2–3 year stability of DSM BPD in adolescent samples (Chanen et al., 2004; Mattanah, Becker, Levy, Edell, & McGlashan, 1995; Meijer et al., 1998). Taken together, these studies found that only a minority of adolescents retained their BPD diagnosis over time. In addition, two of the three found that new onsets were relatively common (Chanen et al., 2004; Mattanah et al., 1995).

PROGNOSIS

The prognosis for adult borderline patients who were once hospitalized is mixed. The high rates of remission of BPD, relatively low rates of recurrence, and lower than expected suicide rate that have been found suggest that the symptomatic prognosis for BPD is substantially better than previously known. These findings have given hope to patients, their families, and the mental health professionals treating them, and, subsequently, BPD has begun to be seen as a good prognosis disorder.

Clearly, borderline patients have far more difficulty attaining a recovery than a remission from BPD. They also lose their recoveries more frequently than they experience symptomatic recurrences. This set of findings highlights the psychosocial impairment that many borderline patients exhibit, particularly in the vocational realm. It is also clear that Axis II comparison subjects do not share this impairment because they were more likely to attain and maintain high levels of recovery regardless of the length of recovery.

Poor physical health has also emerged as an area with a more guarded prognosis, particularly for those who are slow to remit and/or who do not achieve a recovery from BPD. The rising death rate from natural causes and accidents is another sobering finding.

Symptomatically, 99% achieve at least a 2-year remission of their BPD. However, only 60% of borderline patients (as opposed to 85% of Axis II comparison subjects) achieve both a symptomatic and psychosocial recovery lasting at least 2 years. Those who do not recover receive more psychiatric and medical care and have poorer vocational functioning and physical health than those who do.

It should be noted that the long-term course of adult borderline patients who have never been hospitalized has not been studied. In addition, the long-term course of BPD first diagnosed in adolescents is unknown.

Taken together, these results also suggested that the course of BPD is very different from that of mood disorders. While major depression (Mueller et al., 1999; Solomon et al., 1997) and bipolar disorder (Coryell et al., 1995; Tohen et al., 2000) are relatively quick to remit, recurrences are common. In contrast, BPD is relatively slow to remit, but recurrences are relatively rare.

This finding of a slow progression toward health also differs from the DSM definition of a personality disorder as a pattern of maladaptive functioning that is stable over time. This definition has led many clinicians and theoreticians to believe that BPD is a chronic condition with little chance of true symptomatic improvement. Our findings suggest that BPD is relatively stable over time compared to mood disorders, for example, but mutable over more sustained periods of time.

REFERENCES

Akiskal, H. S., Chen, S. E., Davis, G. C., Puzantian, V. R., Kashgarian, M., & Bolinger, J. M. (1985). Borderline: An adjective in search of a noun. *Journal of Clinical Psychiatry, 46*, 41–48.

American Psychiatric Association (APA). (2013). *Diagnostic and statistical manual of mental disorders* (5th ed.). Arlington, VA: American Psychiatric Publishing.

Antikainen, R., Hintikka, J., Lehtonen, J., Koponen, H., & Arstila, A. (1995). A prospective three-year follow-up study of borderline personality disorder inpatients. *Acta Psychiatrica Scandanavica, 92*, 327–335.

Barasch, A., Frances, A., Hurt, S., Clarkin, J., & Cohen, S. (1985). Stability and distinctness of borderline personality disorder. *American Journal of Psychiatry, 142*, 1484–1486.

Bateman, A., & Fonagy, P. (1999). Effectiveness of partial hospitalization in the treatment of borderline personality disorder: A randomized controlled trial. *American Journal of Psychiatry, 156*, 1563–1569.

Battle, C. L., Shea, M. T., Johnson, D. M., Yen, S., Zlotnick, C., Zanarini, M. C., . . . Morey, L. C. (2004). Childhood maltreatment associated with adult personality disorders: Findings from the Collaborative Longitudinal Personality Disorders Study. *Journal of Personality Disorders, 18*, 193–211.

Bender, D. S., Dolan, R. T., Skodol, A. E., Sanislow, C. A., Dyck, I. R., McGlashan, T. H., . . . Gunderson, J. G. (2001). Treatment utilization of patients with personality disorders. *American Journal of Psychiatry, 158*, 295–302.

Bernstein, D. P., Cohen, P., Velez, C. N., Schwab-Stone, M., Siever, L. J., & Shinsato, L. (1993). Prevalence and stability of the DSM-III-R personality disorders in a community-based sample of adolescents. *American Journal of Psychiatry, 150*, 1237–1243.

Chanen, A. M., Jackson, H. J., McGorry, P. D., Allot, K. A., Clarkson, V., & Yuen, H. P. (2004). Two-year stability of personality disorder in older adolescent outpatients. *Journal of Personality Disorders, 18*, 526–541.

Chanen, A. M., Jovev, M., & Jackson H. J. (2007). Adaptive functioning and psychiatric symptoms in adolescents with borderline personality disorder. *Journal of Clinical Psychiatry, 68*, 297–306.

Clarkin, J. F., Levy, K. N., Lenzenweger, M. F., & Kernberg, O. F. (2007). Evaluating three treatments for borderline personality: A multiwave study. *American Journal of Psychiatry, 164*, 922–928.

Coryell, W., Endicott, J., Maser, J. D., Mueller, T., Lavori, P., & Keller, M. (1995). The likelihood of recurrence in bipolar affective disorder: The importance of episode recency. *Journal of Affective Disorder, 14*, 201–206.

Frankenburg, F. R., & Zanarini, M. C. (2004). The association between borderline personality disorder and chronic medical illnesses, poor health-related life style choices, and costly forms of health care utilization. *Journal of Clinical Psychiatry, 65*, 1660–1665.

Frankenburg, F. R., & Zanarini, M. C. (2006). Obesity and obesity-related illnesses in borderline patients. *Journal of Personality Disorders, 20*, 71–80.

Giesen-Bloo, J., van Dyck, R., Spinhoven, P., van Tilburg, W., Dirksen, C., van Asselt, T., . . . Arntz, A. (2006). Outpatient psychotherapy for borderline personality disorder. *Archives of General Psychiatry, 63*, 649–658.

Goodman, M., Patel, U., Oakes, A., Matho, A., & Triebwasser, J. (2013). Developmental trajectories to male borderline personality disorder. *Journal of Personality Disorders, 27*(6), 764–782.

Goodman, M., Patel, U., Triebwasser, J., Diamond, E., Hiller, A., Hoffman, P.,. . . New, A. (2010). Parental viewpoints of trajectories to borderline personality disorder in female offspring. *Journal of Personality Disorders, 24*, 204–216.

Grilo, C. M., McGlashan T. H., Quinlan D. M., Walker M. L., Greenfield D., & Edell, W. S. (1998). Frequency of personality disorders in two age cohorts of psychiatric inpatients. *American Journal of Psychiatry, 155*, 140–142.

Grinker, R. R., Werble, W., & Drye, R. (1968). *The borderline syndrome*. New York: Basic Books.

Gunderson, J. G., Carpenter, W. T., & Strauss, J. S. (1975). Borderline and schizophrenic patients: A comparative study. *American Journal of Psychiatry, 132*, 1257–1264.

Gunderson, J. G., Stout, R. L., McGlashan, T. H., Shea, M. T., Morey, L. C., Grilo, C. M., . . . Ansell, E. (2011). Ten-year course of borderline personality disorder: Psychopathology and function from the Collaborative Longitudinal Personality Disorders study. *Archives of General Psychiatry, 68*(8), 827–837.

Hörz, S., Zanarini, M. C., Frankenburg, F. R., Reich, D. B., & Fitzmaurice, G. (2010). Ten-year use of mental health services by patients with borderline personality disorder and with other axis II disorders. *Psychiatric Service, 61*, 612–616.

Keuroghlian, A., Frankenburg, F. R., & Zanarini, M. C. (2013). The relationship of chronic medical illnesses, poor health-related lifestyle choices, and health care utilization to recovery status in borderline patients over a decade of prospective follow-up. *Journal of Psychiatric Research, 47*(10), 1499–1506.

Lenzenweger, M. F., Lane, M. C., Loranger, A. W., & Kessler, R. C. (2007). DSM-IV personality disorders in the national comorbidity survey replication. *Biological Psychiatry, 62*, 553–564.

Linehan, M. M., Armstrong, H. E., Suarez, A., Allmon, D., & Heard, H. L. (1991). Cognitive-behavioral treatment of chronically parasuicidal borderline patients. *Archives of General Psychiatry, 48*, 1060–1064.

Linehan, M. M., Heard, H. L., & Armstrong, H. F. (1993). Naturalistic follow-up of a behavioral treatment for chronically parasuicidal borderline patients. *Archives of General Psychiatry, 50*, 971–974.

Links, P. S., Mitton, J. E., & Steiner, M. (1990). Predicting outcome for borderline personality disorder. *Comprehensive Psychiatry, 31*, 490–498.

Marino, M. F., & Zanarini, M. C. (2001). Subtypes of eating disorder NOS comorbid with borderline personality disorder. *International Journal of Eating Disorders, 29*, 349–353.

Mattanah, J. F., Becker D. F., Levy K. N., Edell W. S., & McGlashan T. H. (1995). Diagnostic stability in adolescents followed up 2 years after hospitalization. *American Journal of Psychiatry, 152*, 889–894.

McGlashan, T. H. (1986). The Chestnut Lodge follow-up study. III. Long-term outcome of borderline personalities. *Archives of General Psychiatry, 43*, 20–30.

McGlashan, T. H., Grilo, C. M., Sanislow, C. A., Ralevski, E., Morey, L. C., Gunderson, J. G., . . . Pagano, M. (2005). Two-year prevalence and stability of individual criteria for schizotypal, borderline, avoidant, and obsessive-compulsive personality disorders. *American Journal of Psychiatry, 162*, 883–889.

McGlashan, T. H., Grilo, C. M., Skodol, A. E., Gunderson, J. G., Shea, M. T., Morey, L. C., . . . Stout, R. L. (2000). The collaborative longitudinal personality disorders study: Baseline axis I/II and II/II diagnostic co-occurrence. *Acta Psychiatrica Scandanavica, 102*, 256–264.

McMain, S. F., Links, P. S., Gnam, W. H., Guimond, T., Cardish, R. J., Korman, L., Streiner, D. L. (2009). A randomized trial of dialectical behavior therapy versus general psychiatric management for borderline personality disorder. *American Journal of Psychiatry, 166*, 1365–1374.

Mehlum, L., Friis, S., Irion, T., Johns, S., Karterud, S., Vaglum, P., Vaglum, S. (1991). Personality disorders 2–5 years after treatment: A prospective follow-up study. *Acta Psychiatrica Scandanavica, 84*, 72–77.

Meijer J., Goedhart A. W., & Treffers P. D. A. (1998). The persistence of borderline personality disorder in adolescence. *Journal of Personality Disorders, 12*, 13–22.

Modestin, J., & Villiger, C. (1989). Follow-up study on borderline versus nonborderline personality disorders. *Comprehensive Psychiatry, 30*, 236–244.

Mueller, T. I., Leon, A. C., Keller, M. B., Solomon, D. A., Endicott, J., Coryell, W., . . . Maser, J. D. (1999). Recurrence after recovery from major depressive disorder during 15 years of observational follow-up. *American Journal of Psychiatry, 156*, 1000–1006.

Nace, E. P., Saxon, J. J., & Shore, N. (1986). Borderline personality disorder and alcoholism treatment: A one-year follow-up study. *Journal of Studies on Alcohol, 47*, 196–200.

Najavits, L. M., & Gunderson, J. G. (1995). Better than expected: Improvements in borderline personality disorder in a 3-year prospective outcome study. *Comprehensive Psychiatry, 36,* 296–302.

Paris, J., Brown, R., & Nowlis, D. (1987). Long-term follow-up of borderline patients in a general hospital. *Comprehensive Psychiatry, 28,* 530–536.

Perry, J. C., & Cooper, S. H. (1985). Psychodynamics, symptoms, and outcome in borderline and antisocial personality disorders and bipolar type II affective disorder. In T. H. McGlashan (Ed.), *The borderline: Current empirical research* (pp. 19–41). Washington, DC: American Psychiatric Press.

Plakun, E. M., Burkhardt, P. E., & Muller, J. P. (1985). 14-year follow-up of borderline and schizotypal personality disorders. *Comprehensive Psychiatry, 26,* 448–455.

Pope, H. G., Jonas, J. M., Hudson, J. I., Cohen, B. M., & Gunderson, J. G. (1983). The validity of DSM-III borderline personality disorder. *Archives of General Psychiatry, 40,* 23–30.

Sandell, R., Alfredsson, E., Berg, M., Crafoord, K., Lagerlof, A., Arkel, I., . . . Rugolska, A. (1993). Clinical significance of outcome in long-term follow-up of borderline patients at a day hospital. *Acta Psychiatrica Scandanavica, 87,* 405–413.

Senol, S., Dereboy, C., & Yuksel N. (1997). Borderline disorder in Turkey: A 2- to 4-year follow-up. *Social Psychiatry and Psychiatric Epidemiology, 32,* 109–112.

Skodol, A. E., Buckley, P., & Charles, E. (1983). Is there a characteristic pattern to the treatment history of clinic outpatients with borderline personality? *Journal of Nervous and Mental Disease, 171,* 405–410.

Skodol, A. E., Gunderson, J. G., McGlashan, T. H., Dyck, I. R., Stout, R. L., Bender, D. S., . . . Oldham, J. M. (2002). Functional impairment in schizotypal, borderline, avoidant, and obsessive-compulsive personality disorders. *American Journal of Psychiatry, 159,* 276–283.

Silverman, M. H., Frankenburg, F. R., Reich, D. B., Fitzmaurice, G., & Zanarini, M. C. (2012). The course of anxiety disorders other than PTSD in patients with borderline personality disorder and Axis II comparison subjects: A 10-year follow-up study. *Journal of Personality Disorders, 26,* 804–814.

Solomon, D. A., Keller, M. B., Leon, A. C., Mueller, T. I., Shea, M. T., Warshaw, M., . . . Endicott, J. (1997). Recovery from major depression: A 10-year prospective follow-up across multiple episodes. *Archives of General Psychiatry, 54,* 989–991.

Stevenson, J., & Meares, R. (1992). An outcome study of psychotherapy for patients with borderline personality disorder. *American Journal of Psychiatry, 149,* 358–362.

Stone, M. H. (1990). *The fate of borderline patients.* New York: Guilford.

Swartz, M., Blazer, D., George, L., & Winfield, I. (1990). Estimating the prevalence of borderline personality disorder in the community. *Journal of Personality Disorders, 4,* 252–272.

Tohen, M., Hennen, J., Zarate, C. M., Baldessarini, R. J., Strakowski, S. M., Stoll, A. L., . . . Cohen, B. M. (2000). Two-year syndromal and functional recovery in 219 cases of first episode major affective disorder with psychotic features. *American Journal of Psychiatry, 157,* 220–228.

Trull, T. J., Jahng, S., Tomko, R. L., Wood, P. K., & Sher, K. J. (2010). Revised NESARC personality disorder diagnoses: Gender, prevalence, and comorbidity with substance dependence disorders. *Journal of Personality Disorders, 24,* 412–426.

Tucker, L., Bauer, S. F., Wagner, S., Harlam, D., & Sher, I. (1987). Long-term hospital treatment of borderline patients: A descriptive outcome study. *American Journal of Psychiatry, 144,* 1443–1448.

Widiger, T. A., & Frances, A. J. (1989). Epidemiology, diagnosis, and comorbidity of borderline personality disorder. In A. Tasman, R. E. Hales, & A. Frances (Eds.), *Review of psychiatry* (Vol. 8, pp. 8–24). Washington, DC: American Psychiatric Press.

Zanarini, M. C., Barison, L. K., Frankenburg, F. R., Reich, D. B., & Hudson, J. I. (2009). Family history study of the familial coaggregation of borderline personality disorder with axis I and nondramatic cluster axis II disorders. *Journal of Personality Disorders, 23,* 357–369.

Zanarini, M. C., Frankenburg, F. R., DeLuca, C. J., Hennen, J., Khera, G. S., & Gunderson, J. G. (1998). The pain of being borderline: Dysphoric states specific to borderline personality disorder. *Harvard Review of Psychiatry, 6,* 201–207.

Zanarini, M. C., Frankenburg, F. R., Dubo, E. D., Sickel, A. E., Trikha, A., Levin, A., & Reynolds, V. (1998a). The axis I comorbidity of borderline personality disorder. *American Journal of Psychiatry, 155*, 1733–1739.

Zanarini, M. C., Frankenburg, F. R., Dubo, E. D., Sickel, A. E., Trikha, A., Levin, A., & Reynolds, V. (1998b). The Axis II comorbidity of borderline personality disorder. *Comprehensive Psychiatry, 39*, 296–302.

Zanarini, M. C., Frankenburg, F. R., Hennen, J., Reich, D. B., & Silk, K. R. (2004). Axis I comorbidity of borderline personality disorder: Description of six-year course and prediction to time-to-remission. *American Journal of Psychiatry, 161*, 2108–2114.

Zanarini, M. C., Frankenburg, F. R., Hennen, J., Reich, D. B., & Silk, K. R. (2006). Prediction of the 10-year course of borderline personality disorder. *American Journal of Psychiatry, 163*, 827–832.

Zanarini, M. C., Frankenburg, F. R., Hennen, J., & Silk, K. R. (2003). The longitudinal course of borderline psychopathology: 6-year prospective follow-up of the phenomenology of borderline personality disorder. *American Journal of Psychiatry, 160*, 274–283.

Zanarini, M. C., Frankenburg, F. R., Hennen, J., & Silk, K. R. (2004). Mental health service utilization by borderline personality disorder patients and Axis II comparison subjects followed prospectively for 6 years. *Journal of Clinical Psychiatry, 65*, 28–36.

Zanarini, M. C., Frankenburg, F. R., Khera, G. S., & Bleichmar, J. (2001). Treatment histories of borderline inpatients. *Comprehensive Psychiatry, 42*, 144–150.

Zanarini, M. C., Frankenburg, F. R., Marino, M. F., Reich, D. B., Haynes, M. C., & Gunderson, J. G. (1999). Violence in the lives of adult borderline patients. *Journal of Nervous and Mental Disease, 187*, 65–71.

Zanarini, M. C., Frankenburg, F. R., & Parachini, E. A. (2004). A preliminary, randomized trial of fluoxetine, olanzapine, and the olanzapine-fluoxetine combination in women with borderline personality disorder. *Journal of Clinical Psychiatry, 65*, 903–907.

Zanarini, M. C., Frankenburg, F. R., Ridolfi, M. E., Jager-Hyman, S., Hennen, J., & Gunderson, J. G. (2006). Reported childhood onset of self-mutilation among borderline patients. *Journal of Personality Disorders, 20*(1), 9–15.

Zanarini, M. C., Frankenburg, F. R., Reich, D. B., & Fitzmaurice, G. (2012). Attainment and stability of sustained symptomatic remission and recovery among patients with borderline personality disorder and axis II comparison subjects: A 16-year prospective follow-up study. *American Journal of Psychiatry, 169*, 476–483.

Zanarini, M. C., Frankenburg, F. R., Reich, D. B., Hennen, J., & Silk, K. R. (2005). Psychosocial functioning of borderline patients and axis II comparison subjects followed prospectively for six years. *Journal of Personality Disorders, 19*, 19–29.

Zanarini, M. C., Frankenburg, F. R., Reich, D. B., Marino, M. F., Lewis, R. E., Williams, A. A., Khera, G. S. (2000). Biparental failure in the childhood experiences of borderline patients. *Journal of Personality Disorders, 14*, 264–273.

Zanarini, M. C., Frankenburg, F. R., Reich, D. B., Silk, K. R., Hudson, J. I., & McSweeney, L. B. (2007). The subsyndromal phenomenology of borderline personality disorder: A 10-year follow-up study. *American Journal of Psychiatry, 164*, 929–935.

Zanarini, M. C., Frankenburg, F. R., & Vujanovic, A. A. (2002). The interrater and test-retest reliability of the Revised Diagnostic Interview for Borderlines (DIB-R). *Journal of Personality Disorders, 16*, 270–276.

Zanarini, M. C., Frankenburg, F. R., Vujanovic, A. A., Hennen, J., Reich, D. B., & Silk, K. R. (2004). Axis II comorbidity of borderline personality disorder: Description of six-year course and prediction to time-to-remission. *Acta Psychiatrica Scandanavica, 110*, 416–420.

Zanarini, M. C., Frankenburg, F. R., Yong, L., Raviola, G., Reich, D. B., Hennen, J., . . . Gunderson, J. G. (2004). Borderline psychopathology in the first-degree relatives of borderline and axis II comparison probands. *Journal of Personality Disorders, 18*, 439–447.

Zanarini, M. C., Gunderson, J. G., Frankenburg, F. R., & Chauncey, D. L. (1989). The revised diagnostic interview for borderlines: Discriminating BPD from other Axis II disorders. *Journal of Personality Disorders, 3*, 10–18.

Zanarini, M. C., Gunderson, J. G., Frankenburg, F. R., & Chauncey, D. L. (1990). Discriminating borderline personality disorder from other Axis II disorders. *American Journal of Psychiatry, 147*, 161–167.

Zanarini, M. C., Frankenburg, F. R., Reich, D. B., & Fitzmaurice, G. (2010). The 10-year course of psychosocial functioning among patients with borderline personality disorder and axis II comparison subjects. *Acta Psychiatr Scand, 122*(2), 103–109.

Zanarini, M. C., Horwood, J., Wolke, D., Waylen, A., Fitzmaurice, G., & Grant, B. F. (2011). Prevalence of DSM-IV borderline personality disorder in two community samples: 6,330 English 11-year olds and 34,653 American adults. *Journal of Personality Disorders, 25*, 607–619.

Zanarini, M. C., Ruser, T., Frankenburg, F. R., & Hennen, J. (2000). The dissociative experiences of borderline patients. *Comprehensive Psychiatry, 41*, 223–227.

Zanarini, M. C., Ruser, T., Frankenburg, F. R., Hennen, J., & Gunderson, J. G. (2000). Risk factors associated with the dissociative experiences of borderline patients. *Journal of Nervous and Mental Disease, 188*, 26–30.

Zanarini, M. C., Williams, A. A., Lewis, R. E., Reich, D. B., Vera, S. C., Marino, M. F., . . . Frankenberg, F. R. (1997). Reported pathological childhood experiences associated with the development of borderline personality disorder. *American Journal of Psychiatry, 154*, 1101–1106.

Zanarini, M. C., Yong, L., Frankenburg, F. R., Hennen, J., Reich, D. B., & Marino, M. F. (2002). Severity of reported childhood sexual abuse and its relationship to severity of borderline psychopathology and psychosocial impairment. *Journal of Nervous and Mental Disease, 190*, 381–387.

/// 4 /// Clinical Phenomenology of Borderline Personality Disorder

LARRY SIEVER

This chapter will take an in-depth look at the clinical phenomenology of borderline personality disorder (BPD); the core, essential dimensions that are widely recognized as part of this personality disorder; and, essentially, what an individual with borderline personality disorder looks like.

CLINICAL PHENOMENOLOGY

Phenomenology can be understood as one's lived experience. Philosopher Edmund Husserl identified phenomenology as "a descriptive account of the essential structures of the directly given" (http://www.merriam-webster.com/dictionary/phenomenology), or, to describe it more simply, a study of things as they appear in our experience of them. As clinicians, we must gain an understanding of what it is like for those with BPD in order to be able to help them. We must gain insight into the ways they think, process information, and make decisions; into the ways they feel; and how all of these factors affect their relationships with other people. There has been controversy in the field as to whether to view personality disorders as discreet categories or as a set of symptom dimensions that converge in particular clusters. This controversy informed the newest edition of the *Diagnostic and Statistical Manual of Mental Disorders* (DSM-5) (APA,2013) and which approach to adopt. In its final version, the DSM-5 retained the categorical definitions but included a dimensional approach in a section for future research.

Over the past 25 years, the symptom domains that are seen to be central to BPD are affective instability, impulsivity, and interpersonal disruptions. Psychology and psychiatry have been utilizing a categorical approach to diagnosis that requires an individual meet at least 5 of the 9 criteria in order to receive a diagnosis of BPD (American Psychiatric Association [APA], 2013).

BPD has been widely regarded as a heterogeneous and complex disorder (Hopwood, Thomas, & Zanarini, 2012). Zanarini and Frankenburg (2007) developed a model to help understand the complexity of this disorder, one that includes both genetic and environmental factors. Their model identifies a combination of contributions leading to the eventual development of BPD that begins with a primarily genetic, "hyperbolic temperament." This temperament is marked by a proclivity toward a general negative mood and sensitivity marked by being easily offended. An additional contributing aspect is environmental factors that can range from normal life events to "kindling events" (Hopwood et al., 2012), which are more traumatic events involving heightened arousal and an increased need for support. An individual with BPD, they argue, then attempts to overcome these negative feelings and perceived slights by using several means including seeking constant attention from others to mitigate their significant inner pain. This cycle of inner pain and compensatory methods often utilized is important to keep in mind when conceptualizing, diagnosing, and treating those with BPD. This pattern of relating will be discussed further in subsequent sections of this chapter.

AFFECTIVE INSTABILITY

BPD is characterized by a pervasive pattern of instability in regulation of mood, impulse control, and relationships. In particular, there is a consistent pattern of affect dysregulation and instability that is distinctive of the personality disorder. Lability of affect is the fifth of the nine BPD criteria detailed in the DSM. Affective instability was originally defined in the DSM-III-R as "marked shifts from baseline mood [formerly "normal mood" in DSM-III] to depression, irritability, or anxiety, usually lasting a few hours and only rarely more than a few days" (DSM-III-R; APA, 1987; Skodol et al., 2002). Its definition was modified with the DSM-IV to include "marked *reactivity* of mood; e.g., intense episodic dysphoria, irritability, and anxiety" (DSM-IV; APA, 2000; emphasis added). More specifically, affective instability is marked by fluctuations in individuals' capacities to regulate their experiences of mood states throughout the dimensions of intensity, frequency, and stability (Goodman et al., 2003). Furthermore, excluding self-injurious behavior, affective instability is the BPD criterion most associated with suicidal behaviors (Yen et al., 2004). Therefore, affective instability is a critical, prominent, and yet complex aspect of the personality disorder, and its appearance in the DSM-IV is exclusive to the diagnostic criterion for BPD (DSM-IV; APA, 2000). The following is an examination of the concept of affective instability, the understanding of which may elucidate its broader implications for the appearance, diagnosis, and treatment of BPD.

Practical Phenomenological Implications of Affective Instability

Understanding in greater detail the nature of affective instability as it appears in cases of BPD is essential to the understanding of its overall clinical phenomenology. Central to this understanding is the recognition that the affective instability so paramount to BPD differs from that of its relative Axis I mood disorders (e.g., major affective disorders, post-traumatic stress disorder [PTSD]) and other Axis II personality disorders (i.e., other cluster B "dramatic" personality disorders). Henry et al. (2001) found that individuals with BPD scored significantly higher on the Affective Lability Scale (ALS; Harvey, Greenberg, & Serper, 1989) than did subjects without BPD, even those diagnosed with other mood disorders including bipolar disorder II. Persons with BPD were found to score significantly higher as well on ALS subscale measures including shifts to euthymia (normal, nondepressed mood) from anger and anxiety, impulsiveness, and aggressiveness.

The affective dysregulation so characteristic of BPD is often described as distinctive from that associated with Axis I mood disorders in that BPD is marked by affective states that are "disturbingly transient and often rapidly reversible... more responsive to stimuli in the environment—both inanimate and interpersonal" (Goodman et al., 2003, p. 764). For example, individuals with BPD have been found to experience moods that are significantly more variable both in a 2-week period and from morning to night than a cohort of individuals with major depressive disorder (MDD; Cowdry et al., 1991). Whereas the context of maladaptive regulation of affect is often intensely interpersonal, precipitants habitually include things like criticism, deviation of expectations, separation, threats of abandonment, and mistrust. The notion that transient affective shifting is associated with greater impulsivity in BPD than in bipolar disorder may lend itself to explain the fact that self-damaging impulsiveness and random, inappropriate, and/or uncontrolled anger appear more often than enduring dysphoria, as in the case with bipolar disorder (Henry et al., 2001; MacKinnon & Pies, 2006).

Similarly, compared with patients with BPD, those with BPD were found by Koenigsberg et al. (2002) to score significantly higher in measures of lability of anger, anxiety, and oscillation between depression and anxiety on ALS subscales even after controlling for subjective affective intensity. Oscillation between elation and depression, however, was not found to be significantly greater in the BPD group leading Koenigsberg and his colleagues (2002) to suggest that, although a prominent characteristic of BPD, high affective intensity is likely not the catalyst of affect dyscontrol. That said, the construct might better serve to elucidate the distinction between BPD and other mood spectrum disorders. Finally, Koenigsberg and his colleagues (2002) also found that labile anger alone was sufficient to discriminate the BPD group from the other personality disorder group with 72% accuracy. Therefore, affective instability was not found to be affect-specific but instead was most commonly associated with impulsive anger and fluctuations from depression and anxiety in those with BPD, which has compelling clinical implications.

Certain affective symptoms, such as depressive symptoms, have been found to be unique to BPD-only and comorbid BPD-MDD compared to MDD-only diagnostic groups (Westen et al., 1992). A direct relationship was found in both BPD and BPD-MDD patients who endorsed feelings of helpless dependency, emptiness, and aversive affective experiences resulting from fear of rejection and abandonment with severity of depression. Severity of depression in those with the MDD diagnosis only were, in fact, found to be inversely related to complaints of helpless dependency and disturbing affect experiences. Moreover, those with BPD and comorbid BPD-MDD were found more so than those with MDD to demonstrate "diffuse negative affectivity," including anger, loneliness, fear, and desperation as well as inconstant self-concept and self-esteem, dependency, and interpersonal concerns related to fear of abandonment (Westen et al., 2002, p. 388). That is, the interpersonal concerns and dysphoria that was found to be so connected to the depression of BPD patients was not found to be associated with the depressive experiences of a nonborderline MDD sample.

Finally, at the heart of affective instability lies the inability to regulate one's emotions at onset, which is a crucial component of the BPD phenomenon. According to Levine and her colleagues (Levine, Marziali, & Hood, 1997), impulsivity, rage, self-harm, and intolerance of being alone can be considered maladaptive responses to intolerable emotions. Affective lability has been found to be significantly correlated with negative-affect intensity, identity disturbance, chronic feelings of emptiness or boredom, inappropriate anger, and suicidality in BPD cohorts (Koenigsberg et al., 2001; Levine et al., 1997). Levine et al. presented data that demonstrated that individuals with BPD showed significantly lower levels of emotional awareness, a reduced capacity to coordinate and modulate feelings of mixed valence, shifting between opposing views of themselves and others, lower accuracy at recognizing facial expressions of emotion, and more intense reactions to negative emotions than nonborderline controls. Consistent with clinical observations of BPD and typical diagnostic criteria (i.e., intense anger, affect dysregulation, chronic emptiness), individuals with BPD were found to have lesser skills in the recognition, differentiation, and integration of intense and often oscillating emotions. The authors suggest that the limited range of these emotion integration skills produces an inability to decipher feelings and translate them into appropriate behavioral responses. Likewise, failure to properly identify facial emotions may be related to cognitive distortions that are precipitated by overwhelming negative affect states, emotionally salient memory encoding and retrieval processes (e.g., state-based learning and the propensity of self-referential emotional processing), and/or already-formed "global impressions" that supersede more flexible interpretations of social cues (Goodman et al., 2003; Levine et al., 1997).

The earlier writing on personality disorders incorporated psychodynamic concepts that emphasized the connections of affect to the development of representations of the self and others in order to account for their unstable presentation and identity diffusion. More recent research has attempted to understand the biological underpinnings of the disorders. Borderline personality organization has been characterized by Kernberg (1984) as an unstable sense of self and others, the employment of primitive and immature defense mechanisms, and temporary lapses in the ability to distinguish reality and illusion. Affective instability can be best described as the outcome of an interaction between both psychobiological predispositions (Siever & Davis, 1991) as well as environmental factors that ultimately serve to reinforce the emergence of rapidly shifting affective behavior (Goodman et al., 2003).

DEVELOPMENTAL AND OBJECT RELATIONAL PERSPECTIVES

The impact of early trauma may change the way that these genetic and neurological factors are expressed or may serve to solely contribute to the development of borderline personality organization. An infant who is temperamental, hard to soothe, or emotionally reactive, for example, will put a strain on parents and affect attachments, which will go on to affect, in turn, the child's future relationships and expectations of others (Berzoff, Flanagan, & Hertz, 2011). Zanarini (2000) found a 91% rate of abuse and a 92% rate of emotional or physical neglect within a cohort of BPD and that severity of neglect and sexual abuse were directly related to affective symptoms. Goodman et al. (2003), on the other hand, found evidence that suggested no direct relationship between affective lability and prior abuse of any kind (e.g., sexual, emotional), which they interpreted to suggest that nontrauma factors such as affective dyscontrol may be more relevant for the etiology of BPD than trauma factors.

Disruptions in early attachment and an accompanying pattern of maladaptive interactional responses to objects can contribute to an unstable sense of self and identity, diffusion, and tumultuous interpersonal relationships within the BPD personality (which, by way of reminder, have all been found to be correlated with affective instability; Koenigsberg et al., 2001). An individual with borderline personality organization, therefore, may be vulnerable to a vicious cycle of distress because he or she tends to be sensitive and highly reactive to incoming frustrations and/or separations. Their efforts to mitigate feelings of distress can range from clinging to tantrums, which may thus exacerbate difficulties upholding relationships (i.e., devaluation of a previously esteemed object; Gacono, Meloy, & Berg, 1992). Disruptions in both nature and nurture features that incite episodes of mood disturbance hereby serve to reinforce and exacerbate each other: Goodman and her colleagues (2003) describe this as "chronic, repetitive, and maladaptive interactional patterns with others," whereby defense responses that are aimed at self-protection actually compromise the ability to cope with and integrate incongruous affective states (p. 764). Unlike individuals with antisocial personality disorder (ASPD) and narcissistic personality disorder (NPD) who tend to demonstrate a similar egocentricity as BPDs, those with BPD lack the internalized object relation structure that serves to defend against anxiety and helplessness (Gacono et al., 1992).

Moreover, one's awareness of one's inability to regulate affect may lead to enduring feelings of guilt or shame that may also serve to exacerbate unstable moods, sense of self, and interpersonal difficulties:

> BPDs' need for continued object relatedness serves to regulate aggressive outbursts in such a manner that the object of the aggression is likely to become psychically devalued while physically spared.... The devaluation in BPDs ultimately results in feelings of dysphoria and images of the self as damaged. (Gacono et al., 1992, p. 34)

Therefore, the heightened need for object relatedness and the aggressive displays that may result from the failures thereof both result from and contribute to affective instability in an unremitting, self-fulfilling cycle (Goodman et al., 2003). This process of self-perpetuating affective instability has been thought by some to be regulated by primitive defense mechanisms such as splitting/idealization, suppression, and acting out (Kernberg, 1984; Koenigsberg et al., 2001). In fact, affective instability has been found to be significantly correlated with splitting, acting out, and projection (Koenigsberg et al., 2002). Impressionistic responses—the concentration of affect into rapid, diffuse, and nonspecific symbolization—has also been found to be a common defensive response of those with BPD, suggesting that their lability and their dynamic responsiveness may be so great that affective instability is heightened. This supports the concept that the instability associated with BPD may be a function of disturbed relatability and responses to their own dynamic affects (i.e., deficits in emotion control may be a result of unstable sense of self) rather than more pervasive structural and neurological deficits like those seen in schizophrenia (Gacono et al., 1992). Findings regarding the direct correlation between affective instability and the ability to uphold stable interpersonal relationships, however, have been variable (Koenigsberg et al., 2001).

IMPULSIVITY

The second major dimension germane to BPD is impulsivity. Impulsivity is described as "doing things suddenly. . .and without careful thought." (http://www.learnersdictionary.com/search/impulsive). The impulsivity associated with BPD can be subdivided into several more specific types and includes impulsive aggression. One subtype is intentional physical self-destructiveness, which includes self-mutilation, suicidal gestures, and suicide attempts. The other subtype is a more general impulsivity that includes things like shopping sprees, reckless sexual behaviors, binge eating, dangerous driving, and substance abuse (Jacob et al., 2013; Lieb, Zanarini, Schmahl, Linehan, & Bohus, 2004). However, one form of impulsivity, impulsive aggression, has been suggested to correlate with certain personality disorders (Siever & Davis, 1991). Koenigsberg and his colleagues (2001) found that unstable interpersonal relationships, a core dimension to be discussed later, was correlated with impulsive aggression. They surmised that this correlation exists despite the fact that unstable relationships did not correlate with affective instability, thus explaining that affective instability is an emotion directed inward whereas impulsive aggression is an emotion directed outward, thus tending toward a more physical expression of symptomatology. They found that this impulsivity predicted other criteria from DSM-III-R of impulsiveness and intense inappropriate anger.

Due to the heterogeneity of this disorder, it has been difficult to identify the exact neurobiological underpinnings of BPD. Much work has been done in an attempt to identify as much as possible the heritability of BPD (Lieb et al., 2004). Through monozygotic and dizygotic twin studies, it has been found that whereas personality disorders themselves are not heritable, there are several traits—in particular impulsive aggression—which are significantly heritable (Coccaro, Bergman, & McLean, 1993). Some neurobiological mechanisms of impulsive aggression have begun to be understood (Goodman & New, 2000; McCloskey et al., 2009).

In a study by McCloskey et al. (2009), using the Point-Subtraction Aggression Paradigm, a laboratory measure of aggression, those with BPD showed greater affective aggression when compared to healthy controls even after controlling for Axis I comorbidity. However, they did not differ from other personality disorders. Most interesting to note is the finding that self-report measures of both aggression and impulsivity did discriminate BPD from either healthy control or other personality disorder control groups. Interestingly, those with BPD have been referred to as "dramatic" (Linehan, 1993, pp. V, 44, 161). As described previously, BPD is categorized as a Cluster B personality disorder (DSM) that has been categorized as the "dramatic" cluster. This well-known penchant for drama associated with BPD is often seen in self-reports by those with BPD. Many studies have attempted to find specific neurobiological pathways associated with the impulsivity often seen in those with BPD (Goodman & New, 2000; McCloskey et al., 2009). While research is still under way to identify more specific neurobiological links to BPD, the serotonin system has been found to play a major role in the underlying dimensions of BPD. Siever and Davis (1991) have found that lower central serotonergic activity plays a role in the impulsivity seen in BPD. Many of the core symptoms seen in BPD, including rage, anger, and impulsivity, have been linked to particular areas of the brain. More specifically, the limbic system has been identified as having a key role in those areas (Dell'Osso, Berlin, Serati, & Altamura, 2010). In a study comparing BPD patients and patients with lesions on the orbitofrontal cortex, Berlin, Rolls, and Iversen (2005) found the two groups had similar psychiatric deficits but also found the BPD patients to have dissimilar deficits to nonorbitofrontal cortex–lesioned individuals.

Interesting research has recently examined impulsivity and anger, two constructs well known to be part of the BPD pathology. One such study has linked behavioral inhibition to activation of networks within the frontal and subthalamic regions during simple go/no-go impulsivity tasks after inducting anger through stories (Jacob et al., 2013).

Another core issue related to impulsivity in the BPD population is that of self-injury and suicide. Approximately 75% of those diagnosed with BPD (and a slightly higher percentage in those who have also been hospitalized) have been found to engage in parasuicidal acts, including cutting, burning, hitting themselves, and hair-pulling (Gunderson, 2011). Ten percent of those diagnosed with BPD ultimately complete suicide, with completion occurring most often after the age of 30 but commonly with multiple attempts in the early 20s (Paris, 2005). In a longitudinal study of BPD, Zanarini and her colleagues (2003) found that, at baseline, 81% of the study sample reported self-mutilation and suicidal efforts. At a 6-year follow-up, self-injury and suicide efforts had declined to 25%. Other impulsive acts like substance abuse and sexual promiscuity also significantly declined (from 49% to 25% and 26.9% to 11.7%, respectively). However, other forms of impulsivity, including binge eating, verbal outbursts, and spending, only declined from 93.9% at baseline to 65.6% at 6-year follow-up.

The suicidal gestures and attempts also contribute to the difficulty in treating this population, and often precludes this severely ill population from obtaining the treatment they need (Bornstein, Becker-Matero, Winarick, & Reichman, 2010; Salzer et al., 2013). Details on suicidal gestures and their effects on practitioners will be further discussed later.

INTERPERSONAL DISRUPTIONS

The final cluster or dimension of BPD to be discussed here is that of interpersonal disruptions. Whereas many, if not all, psychiatric illnesses affect those around the patient, few occur with more chronicity and severity than BPD (Salzer et al., 2013). Therefore, understanding the interpersonal relatedness of those with BPD is essential to anyone who plans to assess and/or treat an individual with BPD. Some argue that the true core of BPD is the inability to assess oneself and others (Fonagy & Bateman, 2008). This is a key component of BPD, accounting for two of the possible nine criteria that make up the disorder according to the DSM-IV-TR. The first is identity disturbance, which can be understood as an unstable self-image and feelings of emptiness. It cannot be stated enough that, as clinicians and aspiring clinicians, we must gain an understanding of how one comes to develop this type of interpersonal relatedness in order to see these styles of relating as coping mechanisms, as how individuals in a great deal of pain attempt to compensate for their anxiety and fear. The interpersonal style of patients with BPD has earned this group a strong negative reputation among clinicians (Aviram, Brodsky, & Stanley, 2006; Bornstein et al., 2010) due to a variety of behaviors including frequent emergency calls with suicidal ideations, gestures, and/or attempts; idealizing and devaluing their clinicians; splitting; and repeated boundary testing (Occhiogrosso & Auchincloss, 2012).

As previously stated, whereas a clear, definite cause of BPD has not yet been identified, neurobiological systems have been implicated (Stanley & Siever, 2010), as well as environmental factors, including early maternal attachments (Steele &

Siever, 2010). It seems most appropriate to delve into a discussion of attachments here, in the interpersonal disruptions section. Specifically, Steele and Siever reported that a 1-month or longer separation from the mother within an infant's first 5 years is an early risk factor for later development of BPD. They found that mothers with BPD were often withdrawn or exhibited fear when interacting with their infants, leading the infants to experience a disorganized interaction pattern with their mothers. These infants exhibited increased sensitivity to stress, appearing fearful during assessments when their mothers would leave them alone in a room with a stranger (Ainsworth's Strange Situation). Further evidence of the role of early separation in infants is the 2009 study conducted by Crawford and colleagues (Crawford, Cohen, Chen, Anglin, & Ehrensaft, 2009) that found children with separations had more BPD symptoms than did children without separations. They also found that the BPD symptoms seen in most of the children declined naturally over time. This slower decline in symptoms seen in the separation group implies a slower development process for those children. Separation from mothers for substantial periods of time can have long-term and significant effects on the development of a child.

Object relations theorists argue that those with BPD have not yet achieved object constancy, a concept with roots from early infancy (Berzoff et al., 2011). An infant whose mother is present and supportive for periods of time and then withdraws may find it difficult to have the sense that his or her mother will always be there when needed. This could potentially lead to a lack of object constancy attributable to a lack of attunement from primary caregivers, thus making it difficult for the child to form internal representations of caregivers and thus preventing them from developing the ability to self-soothe or form a stable sense of themselves (Ruggiero, 2012). For an infant who yearns for its mother only to find she is not there or is lacking in the necessary attunement, the struggle to feel worthy of love is paramount. As this child grows and interacts with people over the course of his early life, he may develop a pattern of relating that is similar to the relatedness seen in the BPD population, one marked with instability, a fear of abandonment, and a sense of being unloved. He may then act in ways that attempt to prevent those fears from actualizing.

BPD is characterized by intense relationships, often fluctuating between need for attachment and distance. This prototypical idealizing and devaluing of others is difficult for those around the patient to understand and often leads to the abandonment that the person with BPD fears most. Due to a lack of an integrated sense of self and a need to prevent perceived abandonment by others, the individual with BPD ultimately pushes others, away thus confirming his or her worst fears. They also struggle to realize that the people they are pushing away are the very same people they previously loved and admired (Berzoff et al., 2011). This pattern often leads individuals with BPD to become hypervigilant, looking for cues that someone might leave them. This hyperfocus often prevents them from integrating the entirety of an interaction and leads the individual to remain solely focused on the perceived slights and perceived or real abandonments. For instance, if a romantic partner says he has to stay late at work and miss a previously arranged dinner with an individual with BPD, that individual might only hear, "He doesn't love me enough to have dinner with me, he's thinking about leaving me." The patient likely doesn't hear that this is a mandatory work situation over which the partner has no control.

Berzoff et al. (2011) described the case of the patient with BPD who, having not internalized maternal objects, was unable to picture the therapist's face, hear the therapist's voice, or recall the soothing things the patient had been told by the therapist, unless the therapist was right in front of the patient. Anecdotally, many therapists have described similar situations where they have gone on vacation or taken too long to respond to a patient with BPD only to find the patient furious with them, hurt, or sometimes self-injured as a way to display their pain and frustration with the therapist for not being there in exactly the way the patient needed. Again, this contributes to the difficulty in treating this population because these actions can often feel like manipulations; this is why understanding where these patterns of relating come from is of the utmost importance.

Another feature related to the interpersonal disruptions experienced by and with those with BPD is a marked reactivity to perceived or real rejection. Several theories attempt to understand the factors underlying this tendency, including the emotional dysregulation well known to the BPD population (Gratz, Dixon-Gordon, Breetz, & Tull, 2013). This parallels Koenigsberg and colleagues' (2001) theory that emotional dysregulation gives rise to other BPD constructs, including the interpersonal difficulties described here. Emotional dysregulation is a multifaceted construct that has significant effects on one's interpersonal relationships. If we consider the combination of fear of rejection, hypervigilance for that rejection, and the sharp reactivity of mood common in individuals with BPD, we can just begin to understand the near-constant raw feelings of negative emotions familiar to this population. In their laboratory study on emotional dysregulation, Gratz et al. compared the reactions of those with BPD and without BPD to social rejection. They found that after experiencing social rejection, those with BPD compared to non-BPD participants reported higher levels of threats to four fundamental social needs: the need to belong, the need for self-esteem, the need for perceived control over one's environment, and the need for a meaningful existence.

In an attempt to control the fear of being abandoned, those with BPD will often frantically attempt to prevent being left. These individuals often act out with rage, sexual promiscuity, self-destructive threats and behaviors, self-harm, and threats of suicide in order to create a situation they believe will prevent them from being left by others. It is not simply a fear of being lonely, but fear of an empty void that cannot be filled. Those with BPD can become terrorized and paralyzed with fear that they will be abandoned. They will act out in impulsive, self-harming, dangerous ways to reduce the pain and attempt to re-engage the other person. Eventually, others in their lives are depleted and may leave, thus confirming the worst fears of the person with BPD. This cycle of continuously needing to be intensely close and then also needing to push others away creates a pattern of relating that often marks many of the dysfunctional relationships central to those with BPD (Berzoff et al., 2011).

Recent research has pointed to subtypes of interpersonal relatedness within the BPD population (Salzer et al., 2013) and has implications for not only understanding underlying patterns of relating but also as it relates to the relationships individuals with BPD have with their clinicians. In their work, Salzer et al. utilized the Inventory of Interpersonal Problems (IIP-C) to identify clusters of interpersonal problems on a dual axis leading to a blend of dominant and nurturant problems. They found that differing clusters related to varying levels of interpersonal distress, with patients from the "nonassertive" cluster experiencing the highest level of interpersonal distress and global severity in symptoms. Those patients clustered in the "socially avoidant" subtype reported only average levels of interpersonal distress and also strong global severity of symptoms. Of interest are the results found from the therapists' assessment of the therapeutic alliance depending on BPD subtype. Clinicians experienced those in the "socially avoidant" subtype as having the lowest therapeutic alliance. Interestingly, the patients themselves did not seem aware of the lack of alliance. This disconnect between patient and therapist has significant implications for the prognosis of treatment and may speak to the patient with BPD's lack of awareness of self, as previously discussed.

In understanding the dynamics of relating commonly associated with those with BPD, it is important to discuss primitive defense mechanisms and the concept of identity diffusion. Both are common among individuals with BPD and both affect the way one relates to another person (Lenzenweger, McClough, Clarkin, & Kernberg, 2012). Object relations theorists explain that those with BPD have not been able to create internal objects, necessary to learn how to relate to others and how to self-soothe (Berzoff et al., 2011).

Having reviewed the three essential dimensions underlying BPD, the presentation here will hopefully bring to life some of the concepts previously discussed. It is our hope that this case allows you to see the patient with BPD as a person in great need of help and for whom help is possible.

CASE STUDY: CLINICAL PRESENTATION OF BPD

Sabrina is a 25-year-old Caucasian woman who contacted me via phone stating that she was depressed and "terrified" because she thought her fiancé was going to leave her. She sounded frantic on the phone and reported that she had just "fired" her previous therapist after their last session yesterday because, "just like the rest of you, she didn't understand me."

When Sabrina walked into her first therapy session, she threw herself down on the couch, sighed, and said, "I wonder how long it'll take before you leave me too?" Sabrina reported feeling like an "emotional roller coaster," flipping moods constantly. She stated that she can wake up feeling fine and then she almost immediately feels a sense of "impending doom or emptiness" that she attempts to fill by cutting herself with a razor. She stated she has been doing this for the past year and often feels guilty and depressed afterward. She described a long history of impulsivity involving excessive shopping, putting herself in credit card debt three times in the past 5 years. She also reported engaging in promiscuous sexual experiences, "whenever I feel empty, which is all the time." She stated that she has been in therapy for the past 5 years, "on and off," leaving each therapist when she felt they could no longer handle her.

Sabrina reported three psychiatric hospitalizations beginning at age 14 when she overdosed on her mother's antianxiety medication and her father's vodka. The precipitating event to her first suicide attempt was her parents' week-long vacation, during which time her uncle supervised her. Sabrina's uncle was reported to have begun sexually abusing Sabrina when she was 8 years old. When Sabrina reported this abuse to her mother, she was told to keep quiet about it because her mother did not want "trouble" within the family. Sabrina had trouble keeping female friends, always reporting that they were selfish and were never there for her when she needed them. She began abusing alcohol as a way to calm her rages.

Sabrina's mother has been psychiatrically hospitalized several times over the course of her life for suicide attempts, depression, and anxiety. She was given a diagnosis of BPD after her last hospitalization but does not receive treatment currently.

It is important to rule out Axis I mood disorders including bipolar disorder I and II and MDD. The key distinguishing features to determine the BPD diagnosis in this case are the long-standing, chronic conditions that do not seem episodic, as in MDD; the disruptions in interpersonal relationships; and the intense fear of being abandoned, with compensatory self-injurious behaviors including suicide attempts. Also of note is the importance of gaining an understanding of the underlying reasons driving some of the symptoms seen in BPD. For instance, many individuals with BPD will report having few close friends. This lack of close relationships can be seen in a number of different mental illnesses including MDD, social phobia, panic disorder, schizotypal personality disorder, and avoidant personality disorder. Upon a more detailed interview into the driving forces behind this lack of close friends in a BPD, one might find that such individuals have been told they are too clingy, too needy, or too angry, or the individual with BPD himself may report he cannot tolerate the possibility of being left so he keeps himself isolated.

It is important to remember that in the DSM-V one only needs to meet five of the possible nine criteria to meet for a full diagnosis. Also, not everyone who has BPD displays the more sensationalized symptoms like cutting, impulsive and reckless sexual behaviors, or multiple hospitalizations. One patient known to our research group was a particularly observant woman who strictly adhered to the laws and customs of her religious group. Due to this overarching boundary placed on and chosen by her, she had only one romantic relationship, and she didn't drink or gamble or shop excessively. She refused psychiatric hospitalizations because of the stigma placed on mental illness in her community. However, she did still engage in impulsive behaviors like binge eating with compensatory behaviors and cutting herself. It is important to get a full, detailed clinical history, always keeping an open mind about what patients tell you while trying to gain an understanding of what it is like for them and how each person has come to develop their own coping mechanisms and personality.

CONCLUSION

Although this chapter on the clinical phenomenology of BPD has been divided into three major dimensions of BPD—affective instability, impulsiveness, and interpersonal disruptions—the three are not mutually exclusive. Each one relates to another, and all correlate to the underlying pathology of BPD. Regarding prognosis, in longitudinal studies, symptoms of impulsivity have been found to resolve most quickly, followed by cognitive and interpersonal symptoms, and last, affective instability (Zanarini, Frankenburg, Hennen, & Silk, 2003). This faster decline noted in impulsivity and slower decline in affective symptoms might suggest that, as individuals age, they gain a better sense of control over their outward actions yet still suffer with the underlying issues that led them to act out previously.

Although research on mental illness is moving toward a more neurobiological approach to understanding illness as we learn more about the brain and the ways in which it affects us, we must maintain awareness of the clinical phenomenology. The importance of learning the biological components of mental illness cannot be underscored enough; yet, while we learn what parts of the brain are activated during various mental activities, we need to be able to understand patients' clinical manifestations of a disorder and the ways in which it directly affects their lives and the lives of those around them.

REFERENCES

http://www.merriam-webster.com/dictionary/phenomenology

American Psychiatric Association (APA). (2013). *Diagnostic and statistical manual of mental disorders* (5th ed.). Arlington, VA: American Psychiatric Publishing.

Aviram, R. B., Brodsky, B. S., & Stanley, B. (2006). Borderline personality disorder, stigma, and treatment implications. *Harvard Review Psychiatry, 14*(5), 249–256.

Berlin, H. A., Rolls, E. T., & Iversen, S. D. (2005). Borderline personality disorder, impulsivity, and the orbitofrontal cortex. *American Journal of Psychiatry, 162*(12), 2360–2373.

Berzoff, J., Flanagan, L. M., & Hertz, P. (2011). *Inside out and outside in: Psychodynamic clinical theory and psychopathology.* London: Rowman and Littlefield.

Bornstein, R. F., Becker-Matero, N., Winarick, D. J., & Reichman, A. L. (2010). Interpersonal dependency in borderline personality disorder: Clinical context and empirical evidence. *Journal of Personality Disorders, 24*(1), 109–127.

Coccaro E., Bergman, C. S., & McLean, G. E. (1993). Heritability of irritable impulsiveness: A study of twins reared together and apart. *Psychiatry Research, 48*, 229–242.

Cowdry, R. W., Gardner, D. L., O'Leary, K. M., Leibenluft, E., & Rubinow, D. R. (1991). Mood variability: a study of four groups. *American Journal of Psychiatry, 148*(11), 1505–1511.

Crawford, T. N., Cohen, P. R., Chen, H., Anglin D. M., & Ehrensaft, M. (2009). Early maternal separation and the trajectory of borderline personality disorder symptoms. *Development and Psychopathology, 21*,1013–1030.

Dell'Osso, B., Berlin, H. A., Serati, M., & Altamura, A. C. (2010). Neuropsychobiological aspects, comorbidity patterns and dimensional models in borderline personality disorder. *Neuropsychobiology 61*(4), 169–179.

Fonagy, P., & Bateman, A. (2008). The development of the borderline personality disorder: A mentalizing model. *Journal of Personality Disorders, 22*, 4–21.

Gacono, C. B., Meloy, J. R., & Berg, J. L. (1992). Object relations, defensive operations, and affective states in narcissistic, borderline, and antisocial personality disorder. *Journal of Personality Assessment, 59*(1), 32–49.

Goodman, M., & New, A. (2000). Impulsive aggression in borderline personality disorder. *Current Psychiatry Reports, 2*, 56–61.

Goodman, M., Weiss, D. S., Koenigsberg, H., Kotlyarevsky, V., New, A. S., Mitropoulou, V. . . . Siever, L. J. (2003). The role of childhood trauma in differences in affective instability in those with personality disorders. *CNS Spectrums, 8*(10), 763–770.

Gratz, K. L., Dixon-Gordon, K. L., Breetz, A., & Tull, M. (2013). A laboratory-based examination of responses to social rejection in borderline personality disorder: The mediating role of emotion dysregulation. *Journal of Personality Disorders, 27*(2), 157–171.

Gunderson, J. G. (2011). A BPD brief: An introduction to borderline personality disorder, diagnoses, origins, course, and treatment. Retrieved from http://www.borderlinepersonalitydisorder.com/understading-bpd/a-bpd-brief

Harvey, P. D., Greenberg, B. R., & Serper, M. R. (1989). The affective lability scales: Development, reliability and validity. *Journal of Clinical Psychology, 45*, 786–793.

Henry, C., Mitropoulou, V., New, A. S., Koenigsberg, H. W., Silverman, J., & Siever, L. J. (2001). Affective instability and impulsivity in borderline personality and bipolar II disorders: Similarities and differences. *Journal of Psychiatric Research, 35*, 307–312.

Hopwood, C. J., Thomas, K. M., & Zanarini, N. C. (2012). Hyperbolic temperament and borderline personality disorder. *Personality and Mental Health, 6*, 22–32.

Jacob, G. A., Zvonik, K., Kamphausen, S., Sebastian, A., Maier, S., Philipsen, A., . . . Tuscher, O. (2013). Emotional modulation of motor response inhibition in women with borderline personality disorder: An fMRI study. *Journal of Psychiatry and Neuroscience, 38*(3), 164–172.

Kernberg, O. F. (1984). *Object relations theory and clinical psychoanalysis.* Lanham, MD: Rowman & Littlefield.

Koenigsberg, H. W., Harvey, P. D., Mitropoulou, V., Schmeidler, J., New, A. S., Goodman, M., Silverman, J. M. . . . Siever, L. J. (2001). Are the interpersonal and identity disturbances in the borderline personality disorder criteria linked to the traits of affective instability and impulsivity? *Journal of Personality Disorder, 15*(4), 358–370.

Koenigsberg, H. W., Harvey, P. D., Mitropoulou, V., Schmeidler, J., New, A. S., Goodman, M., Silverman, J. M. . . . & Siever, L. J. (2002). Characterizing affective instability in borderline personality disorder. *American Journal of Psychiatry, 159*, 784–788.

Lenzenweger, M. F., McClough, J. F., Clarkin, J. F., & Kernbeg, O. F. (2012). Exploring the interface of neurobehaviorally linked personality dimensions and personality organization in borderline personality disorder: The multidimensional personality questionnaire and inventory of personality organization. *Journal of Personality Disorders, 26*(6), 902–918.

Levine, D., Marziali, E., & Hood, J. (1997). Emotion processing in borderline personality disorders. *Journal of Nervous and Mental Disease, 185*(4), 240–246.

Lieb, K., Zanarini, M. C., Schmahl, C., Linehan, M., & Bohus, M. (2004). Borderline personality disorder. *Lancet, 364*, 453–461.

Linehan, M. (1993). *Cognitive-behavioral treatment of borderline personality disorder.* New York: Guilford.

McCloskey, M. S., New, A. S., Siever, L. J., Goodman, M., Koenigsberg, H. W., Flory, J. D., & Coccaro, E. F. (2009). Evaluation of behavioral impulsivity and aggression tasks as endophenotypes for borderline personality disorder. *Journal of Psychiatric Research, 43*, 1036–1048.

MacKinnon, D. F., & Pies, R. (2006). Affective instability as rapid cycling: Theoretical and clinical implications for borderline personality and bipolar spectrum disorders. *Bipolar Disorders, 8*, 1–14.

Occhiogrosso, M., & Auchincloss, E. L. (2012). The challenge of treating (and supervising) patients with borderline pathology in a residents' clinic. *Psychodynamic Psychiatry, 40*(3), 451–468.

Paris, J. (2005). Borderline personality disorder. *Canadian Medical Association Journal, 172*(12), 1579–1583.

Ruggiero, I. (2012). The unreachable object? Difficulties and paradoxes in the analytical relationship with borderline patients. *International Journal of Psychoanalysis, 93*, 341–362.

Salzer, S., Streeck, R., Jaeger, U., Masuhr, O., Warwas, J., Leichsenring, R., & Leibing, E. (2013). Patterns of interpersonal problems in borderline personality disorder. *Journal of Nervous and Mental Disease, 201*(2), 94–98.

Siever, L. J., & Davis, K. L. (1991). A psychobiological perspective on the personality disorders. *American Journal of Psychiatry, 148*, 1647–1658.

Stanley, B., & Siever, L. (2010). The interpersonal dimension of borderline personality disorder: toward a neuropeptide model. *American Journal of Psychiatry, 167*(1), 24–39.

Skodol, A. E., Gunderson, J. G., Pfohl, V., Widiger, T. A., Lively, W. J., & Siever, L. J. (2002). The borderline diagnosis I: Psychopathology, comorbidity, and personality structure. *Society of Biological Psychiatry, 51*, 936–950.

Steele, H., & Siever, L. (2010). An attachment perspective on borderline personality disorder: Advances in gene-environment considerations. *Current Psychiatry Reports, 12*, 61–67.

Westen, D., Moses, J., Silk, K. R., Lohr, N. E., Cohen, R., & Segal, H. (1992). Quality of depressive experience in borderline personality disorder and major depression: When depression is not just depression. *Journal of Personality Disorders, 6*(4), 382–393.

Yen, S., Shea, M. T., Sanislow, C. A., Griol, C. M., Skodol, A. E., Gunderson, J. G., McGlashan, T. H. . . . Morey, L. C. (2004). Borderline personality disorder criteria associated with prospectively observed suicidal behavior. *American Journal of Psychiatry, 161*, 1296–1298.

Zanarini, M. (2000). Childhood experiences associated with the development of borderline personality disorder. *Psychiatric Clinics of North America, 23*, 89–101.

Zanarini, M. C., & Frankenburg, F. R. (2007). The essential nature of borderline psychopathology. *Journal of Personality Disorders, 21*, 518–535.

Zanarini, M. C., Frankenburg, F. R., Hennen, J., & Silk, K. R. (2003). The longitudinal course of borderline psychopathology: 6-year prospective follow-up of the phenomenology of borderline personality disorder. *American Journal of Psychiatry, 160*, 274–283.

/// 5 /// The Relationship Between Childhood Adversity and Borderline Personality Disorder

JOEL PARIS

CHILDHOOD ADVERSITY: LONG-TERM EFFECTS

Adverse events in childhood take many forms, but surveys around the world confirm that they increase the overall risk for adult psychopathology (Kessler, McLaughlin, & Green, 2010; McLaughlin, Green, Sampson, Zaslavsky, & Kessler, 2010). We need to assess the size of these effects and determine to what extent they are mediated by other risk factors.

Parental loss is a stressor for children, but research on its long-term effects (Luecken & Roubinov, 2012) shows that the circumstances following a death are more important than the loss itself. Similarly, whereas research on the long-term effects of divorce shows an increased risk for psychopathology in adulthood, the circumstances around family breakdown are much more important as predictors of outcome (Amato & Booth, 1997).

The most researched area of childhood adversity is sexual and physical abuse and neglect, and a large body of research has assessed their long-term effects. But the term "abuse" needs to be carefully defined. The term *childhood sexual abuse* (CSA) should be limited to sexual activity carried out by adults with children and to acts that involve physical contact (Fergusson & Mullen, 1999). Even using this narrower definition, one should exclude events that are formally illegal but not abusive, such as sexual relations between a 16-year-old girl and an 18-year-old boy.

There is a vast body of research on CSA. It is a risk factor for a wide range of adult mental disorders, but it does not, by itself, consistently predict their development, and long-term outcome depends on the nature of the abuse as defined by a number of parameters (Brown & Finkelhor, 1986; Fergusson & Mullen, 1999). The relationship of the victim to the perpetrator is the most crucial parameter; others relate to severity (i.e., the nature of the sexual act and duration of abuse). Thus, a single incident of molestation by a nonfamily member during childhood is unlikely to account for an adult mental disorder. In contrast, father–daughter incest, experienced as a profound betrayal, has frequent long-term consequences.

Another issue that emerges from research on CSA is that although this risk factor has an independent effect on adult psychopathology, outcomes can often be accounted for by the family dysfunction accompanying CSA (Fergusson et al., 2013). Children from dysfunctional families are more likely to be abused and to lack support from their family when they are abused. Therefore, it is important that clinicians avoid explaining current symptoms exclusively on the basis of a history of CSA since doing so oversimplifies the complex pathways to mental disorder.

Physical abuse (PA) in childhood has been researched less extensively. The term should only be used when abuse occurs inside a family, not for bullying by peers. Research on PA yields findings similar to CSA: it is a risk factor for the development of mental disorders, but long-term outcome depends on severity and circumstance (Malinovsky-Rummell & Hansen, 1993). As with CSA, many of the effects of PA can be attributed to family dysfunction (Fergusson et al., 2013).

The term *emotional abuse* (EA) refers to consistently demeaning and hurtful comments from parents about children, and EA is one of the variables measured in a widely used interview for child abuse (Fink, Bernstein, Handelsman, Foote, & Lovejoy, 1995). Although not thoroughly researched, EA is a risk factor for many adult mental disorders (Finzi-Dottan & Karu, 2006).

Neglect can refer to either physical neglect (failure to provide minimal care in the protection of children) or to the more subtle risk factor of emotional neglect (failure of parents to approve of and/or provide emotional support). Emotional neglect has been widely studied as a risk factor for mental disorders (Young, Lennie, & Minnie, 2011), but it is difficult to measure given the limitations of self-report measures (Hernandez, Arntz, & Gaviria, 2012).

Overall, it is important to keep in mind the principle that *family dysfunction* underlies all forms of abuse and neglect. Families with high levels of conflict and low levels of positive interaction are more likely to mistreat and/or fail to respond appropriately to children.

COMPLEXITY OF PATHWAYS IN DEVELOPMENT OF PSYCHOPATHOLOGY

Resilience is a key concept for understanding the outcome of childhood adversity. The majority of children who suffer single adversities do not grow up to develop mental disorders but instead become normal adults (Rutter, 2012). However, multiple adversities and a temperamental vulnerability to adversity carries a much higher risk (Rutter, 2007). Thus, the mechanisms behind resilience are partly genetic, partly environmental, and reflect gene–environment interactions. For example, children with positive personality traits can find alternative attachment figures to buffer the effect of adversities, but children who are more sensitive, neurotic, and introverted will have a difficult time doing so (Rutter, 2012).

Since resilience is ubiquitous, one cannot assume that mental disorders will be accompanied by specific adversities or that specific adversities will predictably lead to any form of mental disorder. For each type of abuse and neglect, adversities increase the risk but do not directly cause disorders. By and large, even the most traumatic events do not lead to illness unless there are multiple risk factors with cumulative effects or a "double hit" in which a vulnerable temperament produces gene–environment interactions (Rutter, 2007).

Although these principles are well known to researchers, clinicians who are not trained in research may mistakenly assume that unique causes produce unique effects. Even in medicine, univariate models do not often explain illness, and multivariate models are usually required. Cicchetti and Rogosch (1996) described the complexity of pathways in developmental psychopathology as reflecting both *equifinality* (different risk factors leading to the same outcome) and *multifinality* (the same risk factors leading to different outcomes).

In spite of these complexities, clinical assessment of patients should include an exploration of childhood adversity. This information can almost always be elicited by tactful questioning. Such a history is easier to obtain if one spends less time on symptom checklists and more on life history. Whether or not adversity is directly or indirectly related to current symptoms, knowing about early experience helps therapists to understand their patients.

CHILDHOOD ADVERSITY IN BPD

Adult BPD patients report a particularly high frequency of childhood adversity. This relationship has been consistently found in retrospective studies (Zanarini, 2000) and can be readily confirmed by interviewing family members (Laporte & Guttman, 1996; Laporte et al., 2012). These relationships have been further supported by longitudinal studies of children in the community (Johnson, Cohen, Brown, Smailes, & Bernstein, 1999) that show a relationship between adversity and BPD symptoms. They have also been confirmed by long-term follow-up of children who had been involved in the judicial system because they were abused (Widom, Cjaza, & Paris, 2009).

When these findings first became widely known about 25 years ago, some clinicians concluded that abuse and neglect are the main *cause* of BPD. This idea is still widely held, but it is mistaken. For example, the claim that CSA fulfills criteria for causality established in the medical literature (Ball & Links, 2009) is incorrect, given that it is only one risk factor among many and because it correlates with many other risks (Fergusson et al., 1999). Also, BPD is not a form of post-traumatic stress disorder (PTSD; Lewis & Grenyer, 2009) nor, as has sometimes been claimed, "complex PTSD" (Herman & van der Kolk, 1987). Not all BPD patients experience childhood adversity, and many events that have been considered by researchers as examples of CSA in this clinical population are relatively nontraumatic (Paris, Zweig-Frank, & Guzder, 1994*a*, 1994*b*). Thus, BPD demonstrates equifinality, and child abuse is an example of multifinality.

It is also not true that patients with BPD who do not have histories of abuse must have forgotten or "repressed" these experiences (McNally, 2003). While supporters of traumatic causation of BPD (Herman & van der Kolk, 1987) have made this claim, it is not consistent with a large body of research on human memory (McNally, 2003).

Another complication involves determining the precise frequency of child abuse in BPD patients. These numbers depend on how abuse is defined. Earlier claims that 70% of all patients report CSA were misleading because they included a very wide variety of events and failed to examine the parameters of abuse such as involved family member, nature, frequency, and severity of abuse. Our research (Paris et al., 1994*a*, 1994*b*) in a sample large enough to conduct multivariate analyses supported the findings of community studies showing that CSA is most likely to be a risk factor when a caretaker is involved and when incidents are severe and multiple. Our study, as well as that of Zanarini (2000) and later confirmed by Laporte et al. (Laporte, Paris, Russell, Guttman, & Correa, 2013), found that about 25% of BPD patients have been sexually abused by a caretaker (such as a step-parent). We also found that whereas about a third of BPD patients reported serious CSA, another third only reported single events (almost always molestation by a nonfamily member), while another third reported no abuse at all. These conclusions have been supported by meta-analysis (Fossati, Madeddu, & Maffei, 1999).

However, CSA is associated with more severe forms of BPD (Soloff, Lynch, & Kelly, 2002). And because frequency depends on sampling, inpatients and patients attending tertiary care centers will tend to have a higher rate.

In summary, CSA is an important risk factor for BPD, but it has more impact when it occurs within a family, when it lasts for years, and when sexual acts are more severe.

The relationship between PA and BPD is weaker, as one might expect from its inconsistent effect in community studies. Because PA is more common in boys, we conducted a study of men with BPD (Paris et al., 1994*b*). What we found was a relationship between BPD and CSA, not between BPD and PA.

There is also a relationship in women between EA and BPD (Laporte et al., 2013). In a nonclinical sample, Goodman et al. (Goodman, Fertuck, Chesin, Lichenstein, & Stanley, 2014) found that EA, when interacting with a trait vulnerability (rejection sensitivity), is related to BPD symptoms. Thus, this adversity, like CSA and PA, has different effects in different individuals and is best seen as a marker for broader family dysfunction.

As for emotional neglect, many studies have found this adversity to be reported by BPD patients more frequently than by patients with other personality disorders (Zanarini, 2000) or with common mental disorders (Paris, 2008). Linehan (1993) has suggested a theory that might help to explain this relationship. Children at risk for BPD have an abnormal temperament and need more emotional support to manage emotional dysregulation. It is possible that emotional neglect, a subtle and less dramatic adversity compared to CSA or PA, is a risk factor in the large number of patients who have not been abused or who report only single episodes of abuse. Still, measurement of emotional neglect is tricky because its experience is relative, not absolute.

Some of the research on trauma in BPD had proposed that CSA is related to specific symptoms of dissociation or self-harm (Herman & van der Kolk, 1987). Our research group examined this question and found that these phenomena were related to having a diagnosis of BPD, not to trauma (Zweig-Frank, Paris, & Guzder, 1994). Thus symptoms were just as common in patients without abuse and in those who had been abused. In a meta-analysis of community studies, Klonsky and Meyer (2008) found no direct relationship between CSA and self-harm.

There is a need for prospective research on childhood adversities to determine what relation they have to BPD as an outcome. The longest study of this kind is the Children in the Community Study (Cohen, Crawford, Johnson, & Kasen, 2005), which has followed its cohort for several decades. While the results suggest that child abuse is related to symptoms of BPD, there were not enough clinical cases in the cohort, and the dependent variable was a symptom count, not a diagnosis (Johnson et al., 1999).

In recent years, several research groups have followed cohorts of children longitudinally to examine these relationships. However, since BPD is very rare before puberty, researchers have had to measure features of the disorder rather than identify formal diagnoses. One of these cohorts (Bornovalova, Hicks, Iacono, & McGue, 2009) consisted of twin pairs, allowing the researchers to control for temperamental effects. Four other studies include (1) a birth cohort in the United Kingdom representative of the general population (Belsky et al., 2012) that has followed children up to age 12; (2) a cohort of girls in England and the United States (Zanarini et al., 2011; Wolke et al., 2012), in which follow-up has thus far been conducted to age 11; and (3) a cohort of girls growing up in a large American city (Hipwell, Chung, Stepp, & McTeague, 2010) followed to age 10–13. All these studies point to a consistent relationship between early adversity and BPD-like symptoms just prior to puberty. As results become available in adolescence and young adulthood, when clinical cases become apparent, these relationships will become clearer.

Another approach involves research on children who show clinical features that resemble adult BPD. Along with other research groups, we conducted such a study and showed that adverse experiences in this population were similar to those found in adult cases (Guzder, Paris, Zelkowitz, & Marchessault, 1996). However, when we followed-up these patients, who were mostly boys, into adolescence, they developed general features of a personality disorder but not BPD (Zelkowitz, Guzder, Paris, Feldman, & Roy, 2004).

What can clinicians conclude from all this research? About half of BPD patients can be expected to report a serious child adversity of some kind. Clearly, abuse and neglect are major risk factors for this disorder. Also, the other half of patients, those who do not report serious abuse and neglect, will not necessarily have experienced adequate parenting. Parents who are "good enough" for the average child may not be good enough for those who are vulnerable to the disorder who require more sensitive attunement.

INTERACTIONS BETWEEN TEMPERAMENT AND CHILDHOOD ADVERSITY IN BPD

The main reason why the traumatic theory of BPD is misleading is that it does not apply a stress-diathesis model, failing to take into account interactions between temperament and experience. While childhood trauma is a frequent risk factor for the development of BPD, adverse experiences have a different impact on different children, depending on their personality traits.

It is difficult to demonstrate gene–environment interactions empirically (Carpenter, Tomko, Trull, & Moomsma, 2013; Wilson et al., 2012). However, it has been shown that many of the environmental risk factors in BPD have a strong genetic component due to the risky choices these patients make (Distel et al., 2011). Another mechanism concerns genetic differences in sensitivity to environmental adversities, as reflected in personality traits.

Our research group conducted a study in which we compared 56 female probands diagnosed with BPD to their biological sisters (Laporte, Paris, Russell, & Guttman, 2011). We found that only 3 of the sisters also had BPD, and that none of the others had serious current psychopathology. When we designed the study, we had anticipated that we would find that BPD patients would have suffered more trauma and that sisters free of mental disorder would have suffered less. But that is not what we found. Both probands and sisters described similar experiences in childhood, with only a few measures of severity higher in those with BPD. The most important difference was in personality. BPD patients had an abnormal personality trait profile, with elevations on almost every scale. The most likely explanation is that the sisters who developed the disorder processed traumatic experience in a different way, creating negative feedback loops that led to serious psychopathology.

In BPD, behavior genetic studies show that at least 40% of variance in outcome is due to heritable influences (Torgersen et al., 2000). That still leaves another half of the variance related to the environment. However, the environmental factors in BPD, as is the case for most mental disorders, are "unshared": siblings brought up by the same parents do not share the risk. While one can look outside the family for social risk factors (Millon, 1993), the most useful concept derives from interactions between temperament and adversity.

Behavior genetics sheds light on the relationship between trauma and BPD. The longitudinal twin study of children by Bornovalova et al. (2012) found that the association between childhood abuse and BPD traits stemmed from common genetic influences that also overlap with heritable vulnerabilities to internalizing and externalizing disorders. While this study was not conducted on adult patients, it is consistent with a larger body of research on the pathways that lead to BPD.

The mechanisms behind a temperamental predisposition to BPD are not well understood. They could parallel the mixture of internalizing symptoms (associated with emotion dysregulation) and externalizing symptoms (associated with impulsive behaviors) seen in adult patients (Crowell, Beauchaine, & Linehan, 2009). Children with such characteristics are more prone to be distressed, to remain distressed, and to act impulsively when distressed (Paris, 2008). They are more sensitive to adverse events, are affected by them more deeply, and react in ways that can make their situation worse. However, there is also evidence that temperamental risks for mental disorders are based on a broader concept of sensitivity to both positive and negative aspects of the environment (Ellis & Boyce, 2008).

Interactions between temperament and life adversities have a broad significance for abnormal psychology. Almost all mental disorders have a genetic component rooted in temperament, even conditions often considered as environmental, such as PTSD (True et al., 1993). BPD is an excellent example. These temperamental vulnerabilities can be associated with increased sensitivity to the environment (Belsky & Pluess, 2009), so that the pathways to disorder are marked by a "double hit."

CLINICAL IMPLICATIONS

It is difficult to think multivariately. On the one hand, biological reductionism in contemporary psychiatry has led to a downgrading or dismissal of the psychosocial factors that are so important in shaping mental disorders and to an overreliance on inconsistently effective biological interventions (Bracken, Thomas, & Timimi, 2012). On the other hand, traditional views about the primacy of early experience and childhood adversity for psychopathology have sometimes been used to support rather ineffective forms of psychotherapy (Paris, 2000). These models have not been well supported by evidence, and the treatments based on them can do harm. BPD patients can be suggestible and vulnerable to therapeutic methods that encourage false memories. Moreover, current psychopathology drives perceptions of the past (McNally, 2003). Thus, clinical practice in BPD, like the patients themselves, has had a tendency to go to extremes.

It is now well established that many patients with BPD benefit from structured psychotherapies specifically developed for the disorder. But none of these methods promotes a strong focus on childhood adversity. While it is important to validate childhood experiences, effective treatments, such as dialectical behavior therapy (Linehan, 1993), mentalization-based treatment (Bateman & Fonagy, 2004), or systems training for emotional predictability and problem-solving (Blum, St. John, & Pfohl, 2008) apply cognitive models that focus on current problems, particularly the management of emotion dysregulation, the reduction of impulsivity, and an ability to understand interpersonal encounters.

CASE STUDY: CHILDHOOD ADVERSITY

The following is a case in which childhood adversity played a major role:

Sharon was a 25-year-old telemarketer who presented following a series of overdoses. She had been cutting herself for several years and had experimented with a wide range of street drugs. Sharon described her emotional life as a "roller coaster," and her relationships, particularly with men, were unstable and impulsive.

Sharon's parents, who never married, separated when she was a baby, and she never saw her father again. Her mother, left with the task of raising both Sharon and an older daughter, was overwhelmed and provided little emotional support. Moreover, a series of partners came into the mother's life, some of whom were criminals. Sharon had been sexually abused by one of these men from age 8 to 12, but could not tell her mother about it. Years later, she found that this man had also abused her older sister. However, the sister did not develop BPD and even played a supportive role in Sharon's life.

What follows is a case in which the effects of childhood adversity were subtle:

Georgina was a 20-year-old university student who was hospitalized after a serious suicide attempt. She had a long psychiatric history, with chronic suicidality since puberty, unstable intimate relationships, and repeated angry outbursts in which she would become physically aggressive.

Georgina grew up in a comfortable middle-class family and was the middle of three daughters. Her parents were busy with their professional lives, and, although they provided a comfortable life for their children and encouraged their education, they had little time to spend on their emotional needs. Georgina remembered her mother coming home exhausted and taking long hot baths while the children waited outside for her to relax. Georgina was a sensitive but lonely child who became easily upset about rejection by her peers. Although Georgina had been in therapy on and off since the age of 13, neither of her sisters had required treatment for a mental disorder.

These two cases demonstrate the principle of equifinality in BPD. Similar symptoms can arise from dramatic psychological trauma or from a failure to manage needs effectively in children who are emotionally vulnerable.

CONCLUSION

The missing piece in research on adversity and BPD is longitudinal data. This could involve research in community samples, but the frequency of BPD as an outcome is not high enough to make that strategy effective. Instead, a high-risk strategy is called for, in which children identified as suffering from abuse and neglect are followed well into adulthood. These investigations will need to be multivariate and to take temperament into account.

REFERENCES

Amato, P. R., & Booth, A. (1997). *A generation at risk: Growing up in an era of family upheaval.* Cambridge MA: Harvard University Press.

Ball, J. S., & Links, P. S. (2009). Borderline personality disorder and childhood trauma: Evidence for a causal relationship. *Current Psychiatry Reports, 11,* 63–68.

Bateman, A., & Fonagy, P. (2004). *Psychotherapy for borderline personality disorder: Mentalization based treatment.* Oxford: Oxford University Press.

Belsky, J., Caspi, A., Arsenault, L., Bleidorn, W., Fonagy, P., Goodman, M., & Houts, R. (2012). Etiological features of borderline personality related characteristics in a birth cohort of 12-year-old children. *Development and Psychopathology, 24,* 251–265.

Belsky, J., & Pluess, M. (2009). Beyond diathesis stress: Differential susceptibility to environmental influences. *Psychological Bulletin, 135,* 885–908.

Blum, N., St. John, D., & Pfohl, B. (2008). Systems Training for Emotional Predictability and Problem Solving (STEPPS) for outpatients with borderline personality disorder: A randomized controlled trial and 1-year follow-up. *American Journal of Psychiatry, 165,* 468–478.

Bornovalova, M. A., Hicks, B. M., Iacono, I., & McGue, M. (2009). Stability, change, and heritability of borderline personality disorder traits from adolescence to adulthood: A longitudinal twin study. *Development and Psychopathology, 21,* 1335–1353.

Bornovalova, M. A., Huibregtse, B. M., Hicks, B. M., Keyes, M., McGue, M., & Iacono, W. (2012). Tests of a direct effect of childhood abuse on adult borderline personality disorder traits: A longitudinal discordant twin design. *Journal of Abnormal Psychology.* doi: 10.1037/a0028328

Bracken, P., Thomas, P., & Timimi, S. (2012). Psychiatry beyond the current paradigm. *British Journal of Psychiatry, 201,* 430–434.

Browne, A., & Finkelhor, D. (1986). Impact of child sexual abuse: A review of the research. *Psychological Bulletin, 99*(1), 66–77.

Carpenter, R. W., Tomko, R. L., Trull, T. J., & Boomsma, D. I. (2013). Gene-environment studies and borderline personality disorder: A review. *Current Psychiatry Reports, 15,* 336.

Cicchetti, D., & Rogosch, F. A. (1996). Equifinality and multifinality in developmental psychopathology. *Development and Psychopathology, 8,* 597–600.

Cohen, P., Crawford, T. N., Johnson, J. G., & Kasen, S. (2005). The children in the community study of developmental course of personality disorder. *Journal of Personality Disorders, 19,* 466–486.

Crowell, S. E., Beauchaine, T., & Linehan, M. M. (2009). A biosocial developmental model of borderline personality: Elaborating and extending Linehan's theory. *Psychological Bulletin, 135,* 495–510.

Distel, M. A., Middeldorp, C. M., Trull, T. J., Derom, C. A., Willemsen, G., & Boomsma, D. I. (2011). Life events and borderline personality features: The influence of gene–environment interaction and gene–environment correlation *Psychological Medicine, 41,* 849–860.

Ellis, B. J., & Boyce, W. T. (2008). Biological sensitivity to context. *Current Directions in Psychological Science, 17,*183–86.

Fergusson, D. M., & Mullen, P. E. (1999). *Childhood sexual abuse: An evidence based perspective.* Thousand Oaks, California: Sage Publications.

Fergusson, D. M., McLeod, G. F., Horwood, L. J. (2013). Childhood sexual abuse and adult developmental outcomes: findings from a 30-year longitudinal study in New Zealand. *Child Abuse Neglect, 37*(9), 664–674.

Fink, L. A., Bernstein, D., Handelsman, L., Foote, J., & Lovejoy, M. (1995). Initial reliability and validity of the Childhood Trauma Interview: A new multidimensional measure of childhood interpersonal trauma. *American Journal of Psychiatry, 152,* 1329–1335.

Finzi-Dottan, R., & Karu, T. (2006). From emotional abuse in childhood to psychopathology in adult-hood: A path mediated by immature defense mechanisms and self-esteem. *Journal of Nervous and Mental Disease, 194*, 616–621.

Fossati, A., Madeddu, F., & Maffei, C. (1999). Borderline personality disorder and childhood sexual abuse: A metanalytic study. *Journal of Personality Disorders, 13*, 268–280.

Goodman, J., Fertuck, E., Chesin, M., Lichenstein, S., & Stanley, B. (2014). The moderating role of rejection sensitivity in the relationship between emotional maltreatment and borderline symptoms. *Personality and Individual Differences, 71*, 146–165.

Guzder, J., Paris, J., Zelkowitz, P., & Marchessault, K. (1996). Risk factors for borderline pathology in children. *Journal of the American Academy of Child & Adolescent Psychiatry, 35*, 26–33.

Herman, J., & van der Kolk, B. (1987). Traumatic antecedents of borderline personality disorder. In B. van der Kolk (Ed.), *Psychological trauma* (pp. 111–126). Washington, DC: American Psychiatric Press.

Hernandez, A., Arntz, A., & Gaviria, A. M. (2012). Relationships between childhood maltreatment, parenting style, and borderline personality disorder criteria. *Journal of Personality Disorders, 26*, 727–736.

Hipwell, A., Chung, T., Stepp, S., & McTeague, K. (2010). The Pittsburgh Girls Study: Overview and initial findings. *Journal of Clinical Child & Adolescent Psychology, 39*, 506–521.

Johnson, J. J., Cohen, P., Brown, J., Smailes, E. M., & Bernstein, D. P. (1999). Childhood maltreatment increases risk for personality disorders during early adulthood. *Archives of General Psychiatry, 56*, 600–606.

Kessler, R. C., McLaughlin, K. S., & Green, J. G. (2010). Childhood adversities and adult psychopathology in the WHO World Mental Health Surveys. *British Journal of Psychiatry, 197*, 378–385.

Klonsky, E. D., & Meyer, A. (2008). Childhood sexual abuse and non-suicidal self-injury: Meta-analysis. *British Journal of Psychiatry 192*, 166–170.

Laporte, L., & Guttman, H. (1996). Traumatic childhood experiences as risk factors for borderline and other personality disorders. *Journal of Personality Disorders, 10*, 247–259.

Laporte, L., Paris, J., Russell, J., & Guttman, H. (2011). Psychopathology, trauma, and personality traits in patients with borderline personality disorder and their sisters. *Journal of Personality Disorders, 25*, 448–462.

Laporte, L., Paris, J., Russell, J., Guttman, H., & Correa, J. (2012). Childhood trauma in patients with borderline personality disorder and their sisters. *Child Maltreatment, 17*(4), 318–329.

Lewis, K. L., & Grenyer, B. F. S. (2009). Borderline personality or complex posttraumatic stress disorder? An update on the controversy. *Harvard Review of Psychiatry, 17*, 322–328.

Linehan, M. M. (1993). *Dialectical behavior therapy for borderline personality disorder.* New York: Guilford.

Luecken, L. J., & Roubinov, D. S. (2012). Health following childhood parental death. *Social and Personality Psychology Compass, 6*, 243–257.

Malinovsky-Rummell, R., & Hansen, D. J. (1993). Long-term consequences of physical abuse. *Psychological Bulletin, 114*, 68–79.

McLaughlin, K. A., Green, M. J., Sampson, N. A., Zaslavsky, A. M., & Kessler, R. C. (2010). Childhood adversities and adult psychopathology in the National Comorbidity Survey Replication (NCS-R) III: Associations with functional impairment related to DSM-IV disorders. *Psychological Medicine, 40*, 857–859.

McNally, R. J. (2003). *Remembering trauma.* Cambridge, MA: Belknap/Harvard University Press.

Millon, T. (1993). Borderline personality disorder: A psychosocial epidemic. In J. Paris (Ed.), *Borderline personality disorder: Etiology and treatment* (pp. 197–210). Washington, DC: American Psychiatric Press.

Paris, J. (2000). *Myths of childhood.* Philadelphia: Brunner/Mazel.

Paris, J. (2008). *Treatment of Borderline Personality Disorder: A guide to evidence-based practice.* New York: Guilford.

Paris, J., Zweig-Frank, H., & Guzder, J. (1994*a*). Risk factors for borderline personality in male outpatients. *Journal of Nervous and Mental Disease, 182*, 375–380.

Paris, J., Zweig-Frank, H., & Guzder, J. (1994*b*). Psychological risk factors for borderline personality disorder in female patients. *Comprehensive Psychiatry, 35*, 301–305.

Rutter, M. (2007). Gene-environment interdependence. *Development Science, 10*(1), 12–18.

Rutter, M. (2012). Resilience as a dynamic concept. *Development and Psychopathology, 24*(2), 335–344.

Soloff, P. H., Lynch, K. G., & Kelly, T. M. (2002). Childhood abuse as a risk factor for suicidal behavior in borderline personality disorder. *Journal of Personality Disorders, 16*, 201–214.

Stepp, S. D., Whalen, D. J., Pilkonis, P. A., Hipwell, A. E., & Levine, M. D. (2012). Children of mothers with borderline personality disorder: Identifying parenting behaviors as potential targets for intervention. *Personality Disorders: Theory, Research, and Treatment, 3*, 76–91.

Torgersen, S., Lygren, S., Oien, P. A., Skre, I., Onstad, S., Edvardsen, J., . . . Kringlen, E. (2000). A twin study of personality disorders. *Comprehensive Psychiatry, 41*, 416–425.

True, W. R., Rice, J., Eisen, S. A., Heath, A. C., Goldberg, J., & Lyons, M. J. (1993). A twin study of genetic and environmental contributions to liability for post traumatic stress symptoms. *Archives of General Psychiatry, 50*, 257–264.

Widom, C., Cjaza, C., & Paris, J. (2009). A prospective investigation of borderline personality disorder in abused and neglected children followed up into adulthood. *Journal of Personality Disorders, 23*, 433–446.

Wilson, S. T., Stanley, B., Brent, D. A., Oquendo, M. A., Huang, Y., Haghighi, F., . . . Mann, J. J. (2012). Interaction between tryptophan hydroxylase I polymorphisms and childhood abuse is associated with increased risk for borderline personality disorder in adulthood. *Psychiatric Genetics, 22*, 15–24.

Wolke, D., Schreier, A., Zanarini, M. C., & Winsper, C. (2012). Bullied by peers in childhood and borderline personality symptoms at 11 years of age: A prospective study. *Journal of Child Psychology and Psychiatry, 53*, 846–855.

Young, R., Lennie, S., & Minnie, H. (2011). Children's perceptions of parental emotional neglect and control and psychopathology. *Journal of Child Psychology and Psychiatry, 52*, 889–897.

Zanarini, M. C. (2000). Childhood experiences associated with the development of borderline personality disorder. *Psychiatric Clinics of North America, 23*, 89–101.

Zanarini, M. C., Horwood, J., Wolke, D., Waylen, A., Fitzmaurice, G., & Grant, B. F. (2011). Prevalence of DSM-IV borderline personality disorder in two community samples: 6,330 English 11-year-olds and 34,653 American adults. *Journal of Personality Disorders, 25*, 607–619.

Zelkowitz, P., Guzder, J., Paris, J., Feldman, R., & Roy, C. (2004). Follow-up of children with and without borderline pathology. *Journal of Personality Disorders, 13*, 58–61.

Zweig-Frank, H., Paris, J., & Guzder, J. (1994). Psychological risk factors for dissociation and self-mutilation in female patients with personality disorders. *Canadian Journal of Psychiatry, 39*, 259–265.

/// 6 /// Neurobiology of Borderline Personality Disorder

ANNEGRET KRAUSE-UTZ, INGA NIEDTFELD, JULIA KNAUBER, AND CHRISTIAN SCHMAHL

INTRODUCTION

According to current conceptualizations, the psychopathology of borderline personality disorder (BPD) is related to the three core domains: (1) disturbed emotion processing and emotion dysregulation, (2) behavioral dysregulation and impulsivity, and (3) interpersonal disturbances (Leichsenring, Leibing, Kruse, New, & Leweke, 2011; Lieb, Zanarini, Schmahl, Linehan, & Bohus, 2004). Previous research in individuals with BPD points to an interaction between dysfunctional affective and cognitive appraisal processes, maladaptive behavior patterns, and neurobiological alterations such as an imbalanced network of frontolimbic brain regions (Leichsenring et al., 2011; Lis, Greenfield, Henry, Guile, & Dougherty, 2007; O'Neill & Frodl, 2012). Thus, experimental approaches investigating BPD psychopathology on the subjective, behavioral, and neurobiological levels have become increasingly important for an improved understanding of BPD.

Over the past decades, neuroimaging has become one of the most important tools in clinical neurobiology. Neuroimaging includes a broad spectrum of methods such as positron emission tomography (PET), structural and functional magnetic resonance imaging (fMRI), MR spectroscopy, and diffusion tensor imaging (DTI). Structural MRI and DTI investigate structural and volumetric abnormalities in specific brain regions. MR spectroscopy measures the concentration of neurochemical metabolites such as glutamate, N-acetylaspartate (NAA), lactate, or choline in the brain. By detecting cerebral blood flow (glucose metabolism and hemodynamic response), (18)fluorodeoxyglucose (FDG⁻) PET and functional MRI can be used to assess brain activation during resting states as well as during experimental challenges. In combination with pharmacologic challenge, PET can further be used to investigate the function of neurotransmitter systems. Finally, fMRI has been applied in numerous studies in BPD patients to investigate the activity of specific brain regions in response to standardized emotional material (e.g., emotional pictures, autobiographical scripts), cognitive tasks, or sensory stimuli (e.g., heat stimuli). These studies have already provided valuable insight into potential neurobiological underpinnings of BPD.

In this chapter, neuroimaging findings in BPD are discussed referring to the three core domains of BPD psychopathology: disturbed emotion processing and emotion dysregulation (including dissociation and altered pain processing), behavioral dysregulation and impulsivity, and interpersonal disturbances.

DISTURBED EMOTION PROCESSING AND EMOTION DYSREGULATION

Disturbed emotion processing, characterized by a hypersensitivity to emotional stimuli, affective instability, and deficits in emotion regulation, is a hallmark symptom of BPD (Carpenter & Trull, 2013; Herpertz et al., 1997; Levine, Marziali, & Hood, 1997; Rosenthal et al., 2008). Not only is affective instability the most common and consistently found diagnostic criterion of BPD (Glenn & Klonsky, 2009; Gunderson et al., 2011; Lieb et al., 2004), but it also represents one of the most detrimental characteristics of the disorder because it is closely linked to suicidal behavior, extreme anger, and pervasive feelings of emptiness (Stiglmayr et al., 2005). Although a precise characterization of the neurobiology underlying disturbed emotion processing in BPD remains elusive, a growing number of converging findings provides evidence for a limbic hyperreactivity (e.g., excessive activity of subcortical brain regions including the amygdala and insula) combined with dysfunctional prefrontal regulation processes (Johnson, Hurley, Benkelfat, Herpertz, & Taber, 2003; Leichsenring et al., 2011; McCloskey, Phan, & Coccaro, 2005; New, Goodman, Triebwasser, & Siever, 2008).

Disturbed Emotion Processing

A growing number of studies have used fMRI during emotional challenge (e.g., presentation of emotionally arousing pictures or facial expressions) to investigate the neural correlates of emotional responding in individuals with BPD compared to healthy individuals: the majority of fMRI studies have observed a hyperreactivity of the amygdala in response to negative emotional stimuli in BPD patients compared to healthy controls (Donegan et al., 2003; Herpertz et al., 2001; Koenigsberg et al., 2009; Krause-Utz et al., 2012; Minzenberg, Fan, New, Tang, & Siever, 2007; Niedtfeld et al., 2010; Schulze et al., 2011). The amygdala has been critically implicated in the generation and processing of emotions, such as the initiating of stress and fear responses (Ochsner & Gross, 2007). In addition to an exaggerated amygdala response to emotional pictures, several studies in BPD patients found increased amygdala activation in response to pictures that have been rated as neutral in the general population (e.g., Donegan et al., 2003; Koenigsberg et al., 2009; Krause-Utz et al., 2012; Niedtfeld et al., 2010). Patients with BPD also showed prolonged amygdala activation, suggesting a failure to habituate, during repeated presentation of negative pictures (Hazlett et al., 2012), an instructed fear task (Kamphausen et al., 2012), and during aversive fear conditioning (Krause-Utz et al., 2016).

Findings of increased and prolonged amygdala activation are in line with the well-documented clinical feature of high sensitivity to emotional stimuli with intense and long-lasting reactions in patients with BPD (Crowell, Beauchaine, & Linehan, 2009; Gilbert et al., 2009; Kamphausen et al., 2012). Contradictory findings have also been reported: a first meta-analysis even suggested decreased amygdala activity during processing of negative emotions relative to neutral conditions in patients with BPD compared to healthy controls (Ruocco, Amirthavasagam, Choi-Kain, & McMain, 2013). However, meta-analyses always include the possibility of selection biases (e.g., concerning the studies selected and the inclusion of different numbers of contrasts into the analysis). The most recent meta-analysis on emotion processing in BPD (Schulze, Schmahl, & Niedtfeld, 2016), however, confirmed increased amygdala activation. Most interestingly, medication-free samples were characterized by limbic hyperactivity, whereas no such group differences were found in patients currently taking psychotropic medication.

In addition to amygdala hyperreactivity, increased activation in the insula has been observed in emotional challenge studies in BPD patients compared to healthy controls, thus emphasizing the role of this brain area in disturbed emotion processing in BPD (Beblo et al., 2006; Krause-Utz et al., 2012; Niedtfeld et al., 2010; Ruocco et al., 2013; Schulze et al., 2011). In numerous studies in healthy individuals, the insula has been associated with the encoding of unpleasant feelings, interoceptive awareness (awareness of one's own bodily experiences), perceived social exclusion, and pain perception (Damasio et al., 2000; Menon & Uddin, 2010).

Many neuroimaging studies revealed frontal hypoactivation (Leichsenring et al., 2011; Lis et al., 2007; O'Neill & Frodl, 2012), especially blunted responses of the bilateral dorsolateral prefrontal cortex (Schulze et al., 2016) in response to emotionally arousing stimuli. For example, in the study by Minzenberg and colleagues (2007), BPD patients not only showed hyperreactivity of the amygdala, but also decreased activation of frontal areas including the anterior cingulate cortex (ACC) in response to fearful faces. The ACC has been associated with up- and downregulation of negative emotions (Ochsner & Gross 2007). Schmahl and colleagues (2003) presented individualized auditory scripts of abandonment situations to their participants and found increased activation in dorsolateral prefrontal cortex (DLPFC) and decreased activation in the medial prefrontal cortex (Schmahl, Elzinga, et al., 2003). Furthermore, when patients were confronted with their self-reported traumatic memories, they did not exhibit increased activity in ACC or orbital frontal cortex (OFC) and DLPFC as did healthy controls. Instead, they showed unaltered or diminished activity (Schmahl, Vermetten, Elzinga, & Bremner, 2004). The OFC and DLPFC are thought to be implicated in a top-down appraisal system that modulates activation in limbic and subcortical brain areas (Ochsner & Gross, 2007). Hence, it is conceivable that the pattern of hypoactivation observed in frontal brain regions during emotional challenge in BPD might represent a neural correlate of altered processing of negative autobiographical memories and negative emotions. Taken together, the heightened activity of amygdala and insula, together with the lower activity of prefrontal brain areas that modulate lower brain regions, raises the possibility of an imbalance of control such that the lower brain regions generating emotion are untethered from prefrontal control areas. This model may not be specific to BPD because it is also seen in anxiety disorders (Killgore et al., 2014). In order to directly investigate the interaction between frontal and limbic brain regions in BPD, fMRI studies have increasingly examined the functional connectivity between these brain regions both during resting states (i.e., in the absence of experimental conditions) and during experimental challenge. An early PET study measuring baseline metabolic activity in BPD patients pointed to diminished functional connectivity between prefrontal and limbic structures (New et al., 2007).

In fMRI studies, BPD patients showed a stronger positive functional connectivity between amygdala and ACC (Cullen et al., 2011) and between amygdala and ventromedial PFC (Kamphausen et al., 2012) during experimentally induced fear conditions. Krause-Utz, Elzinga, Oei, Paret, Niedtfeld, Spinhoven, Bohus, and Schmahl (2014) found a stronger coupling between the amygdala and hippocampus as well as dorsomedial PFC in BPD patients with interpersonal trauma history when viewing disturbing interpersonal pictures. An increased information exchange between the amygdala and brain regions involved in self-referential processing (e.g., retrieval of autobiographical memories) might underlie hypervigilance to social cues in BPD.

Koenigsberg, Denny, Fan, Liu, Guerreri, Mayson, Rimsky, New, Goodman, and Siever (2014) observed a lack of an increase in the dorsal ACC along with smaller increases in insula-amygdala functional connectivity in BPD patients while they were viewing repeatedly presented (vs. novel) negative pictures. These findings suggest a failure to effectively engage emotional habituation processes, which might contribute to affective instability in individuals with BPD (Koenigsberg et al., 2014).

In other fMRI studies, individuals with BPD already showed altered functional connectivity during rest. More specifically, they showed altered resting-state functional connectivity within the "default mode network," which is associated with self-referential processes (e.g., daydreaming, rumination, autobiographical memory) as well as within the "salience network," which has been associated with attentional processes (Doll et al., 2013; Krause-Utz, Veer, et al., 2014; Wolf et al., 2011). In the study by Krause-Utz and colleagues (2014), individials with BPD further showed a stronger coupling of the amygdala with insula and orbitofrontal cortex during rest.

Turning to studies of brain structures (e.g., brain volume) in patients with BPD compared to healthy controls, several studies have shown reduced volume in limbic(-related) brain regions, most prominently in the amygdala, hippocampus, ACC, and insula in BPD (Brambilla et al., 2004; Driessen et al., 2000; Goodman et al.,

2011; Hazlett et al., 2005; Irle, Lange, & Sachsse, 2005; Minzenberg, Fan, New, Tang, & Siever, 2008; Rüsch et al., 2003; Schmahl et al., 2009; Schmahl, Vermetten, Elzinga, & Bremner, 2003; Soloff, Nutche, Goradia, & Diwadkar, 2008; Soloff et al., 2012; Tebartz van Elst et al., 2003; Zetzsche et al., 2006). A meta-analysis (Nunes et al., 2009) even proposed that reduced volumes of amygdala and hippocampus may be regarded as "biological markers" or endophenotypes of BPD. It is nonetheless controversial whether the observed alterations may rather stem from experience of abuse in childhood (Stein, Koverola, Hanna, Torchia, & McClarty, 1997; Wilson et al., 2012) or might even be a substrate of comorbid post-traumatic stress disorder (PTSD), both of which are highly prevalent conditions in BPD (Krause-Utz & Schmahl, 2010; Lieb et al., 2004). Structural imaging research in PTSD patients has indeed shown smaller volumes in hippocampus and amygdala (Karl et al., 2006) although, in a more recent meta-analysis, this has been associated with trauma history rather than a PTSD diagnosis per se (Woon & Hedges, 2009). In BPD, another meta-analysis concluded that BPD patients with a comorbid diagnosis of PTSD show reduced volumes in the amygdala and hippocampus that are more pronounced than in BPD patients without comorbid PTSD (Rodrigues et al., 2011). To more clearly disentangle characteristics of BPD as compared to the effects of traumatic experiences for structural alterations in BPD, studies that precede traumatic experiences and follow patients after those experiences would be required.

Although early structural studies examined predominantly limbic regions (e.g., amygdala), recent studies have turned to whole-brain analyses (Soloff et al., 2008). Several studies observed volume alterations in various regions of the parietal and temporal lobes in patients with BPD (Irle et al., 2005; Irle, Lange, Weniger, & Sachsse, 2007; Soloff et al., 2008, 2012; Völlm et al., 2009). An early MRI study suggested a reduction of frontal lobe volume in BPD (Lyoo, Han, & Cho, 1998). Although the former result should be interpreted cautiously due to limitations of this study (Lis et al., 2007), a series of subsequent investigations also found reduced gray matter volume in the OFC (Soloff et al., 2012; Tebartz van Elst et al., 2003; Völlm et al., 2009), DLPFC (Brunner et al., 2010; Sala et al., 2011), and ventromedial PFC (Bertsch et al., 2013) as well as reduced gray and increased white matter volume in the ACC (Goodman et al., 2011; Hazlett et al., 2005; Soloff et al., 2008) in patients with BPD. Kuhlmann and colleagues (Kuhlmann, Bertsch, Schmidinger, Thomann, & Herpertz, 2013) further detected a reduced volume of the hypothalamus, which extends previous findings of alterations in the hypothalamic-pituitary-adrenal-axis in BPD (Wingenfeld, Spitzer, Rullkötter, & Löwe, 2010, Wingenfeld & Wolf, 2014).

Reduced volumes of the OFC (Chanen et al., 2008) and ACC (Whittle et al., 2009) could already be detected in adolescents with first presentation of BPD, whereas amygdala and hippocampal volumes were not altered in teenagers with BPD (Chanen et al., 2008). It has been proposed that volumetric changes in frontal structures possibly represent neural correlates of altered regulatory or inhibitory mechanisms in BPD (Goodman et al., 2011; Hazlett et al., 2005; Soloff et al., 2008, 2012; Tebartz van Elst et al., 2003; Völlm et al., 2009), whereas altered volume in limbic structures may more closely relate to life experiences such as trauma (as discussed later).

In providing further evidence for a disturbed frontolimbic circuitry on the structural level, studies investigating structural connectivity with DTI found reduced white matter connections in frontal and temporal cortices (Carrasco et al., 2012; Grant et al., 2007; Maier-Hein et al., 2014; New et al., 2013; Rüsch, Bracht, et al., 2010; Rüsch et al., 2007).

Taken together, these findings suggest that there may be structural abnormalities in frontal and limbic brain regions in patients with BPD. However, interpretation of these findings is complicated due to methodological aspects such as small sample sizes, treatment with psychotropic medication, trauma history, and comorbid PTSD (Krause-Utz & Schmahl, 2010; O'Neill & Frodl, 2012; Schmahl & Bremner, 2006). Comparing patients with BPD and comorbid PTSD to patients with BPD and without PTSD, a voxel-based morphometry study revealed more gray matter volume in superior temporal gyrus and DLPFC in patients with BPD + PTSD (Niedtfeld et al., 2013). In this study, BPD symptom severity predicted lower volume in amygdala and dorsal ACC, whereas grey matter volume in middle temporal gyrus was correlated with self-reported dissociation.

Emotion Dysregulation

This research has led to a current conceptualization of BPD suggesting that emotion dysregulation may stem from deficient "top-down" frontal control mechanisms involved in regulating activation in hyperactive "bottom-up" emotion-generating limbic structures. To investigate neural correlates of voluntary emotion regulation processes more directly, experimental research in BPD has used reappraisal paradigms from general emotion regulation research (Ochsner, Bunge, Gross, & Gabrieli, 2002). During explicit emotion regulation tasks, subjects are instructed to change their affective response to emotional pictures by predetermined cognitive reappraisal strategies. At present, three studies provide evidence for abnormalities in the voluntary regulation of negative emotions through reappraisal in BPD, which were presumably mediated by a reduced recruitment of prefrontal networks (Koenigsberg et al., 2009; Lang et al., 2012; Schulze et al., 2011). More specifically, the study by Koenigsberg and colleagues (2009) found diminished activity in DLPFC and ventrolateral prefrontal cortices when patients with BPD tried to cognitively distance themselves from negative stimuli. Similarly, cognitive reappraisal yielded decreased recruitment of the left OFC and increased activation of the insula in patients with BPD relative to healthy participants (Schulze et al., 2011).

In an attempt to clarify the role of trauma history on downregulation of emotional responses in BPD patients, Lang, Kotchoubey, Frick, Spitzer, Grabe, and Barnow (2012) compared trauma-exposed BPD patients to trauma-exposed healthy subjects without PTSD and nontraumatized healthy subjects. In this study, BPD patients as well as healthy individuals with trauma history recruited brain regions associated with up- and downregulation of negative emotions (e.g., ACC) to a lesser extent, which might reflect compensatory changes associated with trauma exposure.

Findings of these studies are in line with the assumption that diminished emotion regulation abilities in BPD are associated with a failure to activate prefrontal control regions. However, it is interesting to note that individuals with BPD did not differ from healthy controls on behavioral measures of reappraisal success (Koenigsberg et al., 2009; Lang et al., 2012; Schulze et al., 2011). This raises the possibility that individuals with BPD are less able than healthy controls to self-monitor and make assessments of their regulatory abilities and perhaps of their own emotional states. Indeed, individuals with BPD have been shown to score very highly on measures of alexithymia (New et al., 2013). This is consistent with both neuroimaging (Gilbert et al., 2009; Herpertz et al., 2001) and psychophysiological startle studies (Hazlett et al., 2007) demonstrating discrepancies between the subjective experience of emotion and the physiological response in BPD.

Interestingly, preliminary studies investigating the influence of dialectical behavior therapy (DBT), which involves teaching emotion regulation skills, on neural correlates of emotion dysregulation show normalization of limbic hyperactivity with effective treatment (Goodman et al., 2014; Schnell & Herpertz, 2007). Although these findings have to be regarded with caution due to limited sample size, successful psychotherapy was indeed associated with significant neural changes.

Dissociation

During negative affective states, individuals with BPD frequently report dissociative experiences (Korzekwa, Dell, Links, Thabane, & Fougere, 2009; Stiglmayr et al., 2005, 2008). Moreover, dissociation in BPD is not only accompanied by emotional distress, but also by elevated pain thresholds (analgesia) in individuals with BPD (Bohus et al., 2000; Ludäscher, Bohus, Lieb, Philipsen, & Schmahl, 2007; Ludäscher et al., 2010). Terminating aversive states of dissociation (e.g., numbing) was reported to be one of the major motives for self-injury in patients with BPD (Kemperman, Russ, & Shearin, 1997; Kleindienst et al., 2008).

In general, dissociation involves disruptions of usually integrated functions such as consciousness, memory, attention, pain perception, and perception of the self and environment. Accordingly, dissociative experiences include amnesia, analgesia, derealization, and depersonalization (American Psychiatric Association [APA], 2000). Lanius and colleagues (2010) proposed that dissociative experiences can be conceptualized as a specific subtype of emotion modulation characterized by symptoms of emotion *overmodulation* (e.g., numbing, feelings of being detached from others and the environment) and prefrontal inhibition of the amygdala and insula (Lanius et al., 2010). Although the neurobiological underpinnings of dissociation are not yet completely understood, there is growing evidence supporting theoretical assumptions (Lanius et al., 2010; Sierra & Berrios, 1998; Wolf et al., 2011). Compared to the extensive body of research in dissociative patients with PTSD (Lanius, Brand,

Vermetten, Frewen, & Spiegel, 2012; Lanius et al., 2010), relatively few studies have to date investigated the neurobiological correlates of dissociation in patients with BPD. One study used script-driven imagery to induce dissociative states in BPD (Ludaescher et al., 2010): patients with BPD showed significantly increased activation in the left inferior frontal gyrus during exposure to the dissociation-inducing script. Self-reported dissociative experiences predicted activation in the left superior frontal gyrus and were negatively associated with activation in the right middle and inferior temporal gyrus. Findings of this pilot study resemble findings in dissociative patients with PTSD, suggesting increased frontal activation and decreased limbic activation during dissociative states. In line with findings by Ludaescher and colleagues (2010), Winter, Krause-Utz, Lis, Chiu, Lanius, Schriner, Bohus, and Schmahl (2015) recently found increased activity in the left inferior frontal gyrus in response to negative versus neutral words during an emotional Stroop task in BPD patients after dissociation induction (with script-driven imagery). Wolf and colleagues assessed resting-state fMRI in patients with BPD, who showed altered patterns of resting-state functional connectivity in brain regions within the default mode network (a part of the brain typically active under situations of low external stimulation). Interestingly, resting-state functional connectivity in the insula was positively correlated with self-reported state dissociation (Wolf et al., 2011).

Krause-Utz and colleagues (2012) investigated amygdala activation during emotional distraction. While viewing distracting negative pictures, patients with BPD showed stronger amygdala and insula activation compared to healthy participants, and activation in the amygdala and insula was negatively correlated with self-reported dissociation (Krause-Utz et al., 2012).

In sum, there is growing evidence for an involvement of frontolimbic brain regions in dissociative states in individuals with BPD: dissociation seems to be associated with *dampened* amygdala activation and *increased* activation in frontal brain regions that play an important role in inhibitory control and attention (Lanius et al., 2010; Sierra & Berrios, 1998). From this view, dissociation can be regarded as a regulatory strategy to cope with overwhelming affective arousal during stressful situations and shows findings opposite to those seen in BPD during emotional provocation without dissociation.

Self-Injury and Altered Pain Processing

A very common dysfunctional behavior, one closely linked to emotion dysregulation in BPD, is self-injurious behavior (also referred to as *deliberate self-harm, self-injury,* or *nonsuicidal self-injury*) (Welch, Linehan, Sylvers, Chittams, & Rizvi, 2008). Interestingly, many BPD patients report analgesic phenomena during self-injury (Shearer, 1994). Since pain appears to have an important emotion-regulating effect in BPD (Klonsky, 2007), it is crucial to explore the effects of pain on emotions at the neurobiological level.

A large body of experimental research investigating pain perception in individuals with BPD points to reduced sensitivity in BPD patients (Bohus et al., 2000; Cardenas-Morales et al., 2011; Ludäscher et al., 2007; McCown, Galina, Johnson, de Simone, & Posa, 1993; Russ et al., 1992; Schmahl et al., 2004, 2006, 2010). To investigate analgesic states in BPD, Schmahl et al. applied laser-evoked pain and a spatial discrimination task to test both pain perception and thresholds in a study gathering subjective ratings and electroencephalography (EEG) (Schmahl et al., 2004). Schmahl and his colleagues showed that self-reported pain ratings were *lower* in BPD patients and that pain thresholds were altered. Interestingly, no differences where observed in discrimination task performance of laser-evoked brain potentials, which showed that the analgesic state in BPD is not explained by an impairment of the sensory-discriminative component of pain (Schmahl et al., 2004). Aiming to explore neural correlates of reduced pain sensitivity in BPD, several studies used fMRI to assess brain activation in response to painful stimulation. In a first study by Schmahl et al. (2006), patients with BPD and self-injurious behavior underwent an fMRI scan while heat stimuli were applied to their hands. While BPD patients showed increased pain thresholds and smaller overall activation in response to *standardized* temperature stimuli (compared to healthy controls), the overall activation was similar in response to *individually adjusted* heat stimuli. However, BPD patients showed increased DLPFC activation along with decreased activations of the posterior parietal cortex. Moreover, painful heat stimulation evoked neural deactivation in the amygdala and the perigenual ACC in participants with BPD (Schmahl et al., 2006). The observed interaction between increased pain-induced response in the DLPFC coupled with deactivations in the ACC and the amygdala could be interpreted as an antinociceptive mechanism in BPD (Schmahl et al., 2006). While sensory discrimination processes remain intact, this mechanism may modulate pain circuits primarily by an increased top-down regulation of emotional components of pain or an altered affective appraisal of pain (Schmahl et al., 2006).

Based on these initial findings of altered pain processing in BPD, Kraus and colleagues (Kraus et al., 2009) investigated whether the observed antinociceptive mechanisms distinguished BPD patients with comorbid PTSD from those without such a comorbid diagnosis. While no differences in reported pain sensitivity were found between the two patient groups, fMRI results revealed that deactivation in the right amygdala was less pronounced in BPD patients without comorbid PTSD compared to those with PTSD. The authors speculated that the degree of amygdala deactivation during pain processing is modulated by comorbid PTSD in BPD patients. To further explore neural processing of self-injurious behavior in patients with BPD, Kraus et al. (2009) used script-driven imagery of self-injury. Patients showed an increased activation of dorsolateral prefrontal cortex, a brain region associated with emotion regulation.

Examining the neural mechanisms underlying the role of self-inflicted pain as a means of affect regulation in BPD more directly, Niedtfeld and colleagues (2010) conducted an fMRI study using pictures to elicit negative affect and thermal stimuli to induce heat pain. Although the authors found an attenuation of activation in limbic areas (amygdala, insula) in response to sensory stimulation, it was neither specific to patients with BPD nor to painful stimulation. The authors argue that possible mechanisms underlying this deactivation could include an attentional shift caused by sensory stimuli per se (Pessoa, McKenna, Gutierrez, & Ungerleider, 2002), the automatic use of cognitive regulation strategies or (re-) appraisal (Ochsner et al., 2004), or habituation processes (Breiter et al., 1996). To identify brain mechanisms underlying the limbic deactivation observed (Niedtfeld et al., 2010), the authors measured functional connectivity between those regions that had been identified to be involved in emotional processing; namely, the amygdala, the insula, and ACC (Niedtfeld et al., 2012). Results of their analyses indicated that painful sensory stimuli, as opposed to warmth perception, resulted in enhanced negative coupling between (para-) limbic and prefrontal structures in BPD thus indicating inhibition of limbic arousal (Niedtfeld et al., 2012). Increased coupling between amygdala and medial frontal gyrus (Broca's areas [BA]8 and BA9) may point to attentional distraction processes (see McRae et al., 2010). Additionally, in the patient group, the DLPFC showed enhanced coupling to the posterior insula, a brain region known to play a critical role in pain processing (Rainville, 2002) and the affective appraisal of pain perception (Treede, Apkarian, Bromm, Greenspan, & Lenz, 2000). Hence, one could speculate that the connectivity between DLPFC and posterior insula in BPD may imply an altered, possibly positive, appraisal of pain.

Additional evidence for an altered appraisal mechanism of pain in patients with BPD stems from a recent fMRI study of functional connectivity during pain processing that showed that patients with BPD exhibited less connectivity between the posterior cingulate cortex and DLPFC when exposed to painful heat rather than neutral temperature stimulation (Kluetsch et al., 2012). The authors discuss their findings as a possible indicator for a cognitive and affective appraisal of pain in patients with BPD that is less self-relevant and aversive.

To test the direct effect of tissue damage, two recent studies induced stress with the Montreal Imaging Stress Task, followed by either an incision into the forearm (tissue damage) or a sham condition (Reitz et al., 2012; Reitz et al., 2015), The incision resulted in a decrease in tension and heart rate in the BPD group, in contrast to a short-term increase in aversive tension in the healthy control group (Reitz et al., 2012). A resting state fMRI scan after the incision pointed to a decrease in amygdala activity, together with normalized functional connectivity of amygdala and superior frontal gyrus after incision in the BPD group (Reitz et al., in press). These results may point to a stress-reducing effect of tissue damage that affects subjective experience, psychophysiological reactions, and brain function in BPD.

In sum, the overall reported results on pain processing in BPD suggest that self-injurious behavior may be interpreted as an attempt to compensate for a deficient emotion regulation mechanism in BPD patients. More specifically, the reported findings implicate that the soothing effect of pain in BPD seems to be mediated by different emotion regulation processes (attentional shift and altered appraisal of pain).

Interim Summary

To sum up, results of neuroimaging studies argue for a strong correspondence across methods implying limbic hyperreactivity in BPD. In addition, individuals with BPD showed a diminished recruitment of frontal brain regions involved in the downregulation of emotional arousal. Thus, emotion dysregulation in BPD seems to be related to disturbed top-down prefrontal regulation of hyperreactive limbic regions. Moreover, patients with BPD showed structural alterations of brain regions involved in emotion processing, such as the amygdala, hippocampus, ACC, and insula. Which brain imaging findings in BPD are accounted for by trauma exposure is not yet clear: a recent study demonstrated structural and functional alterations in healthy subjects with childhood maltreatment that were strikingly similar to some findings in BPD research (Dannlowski et al., 2012). Alterations in limbic brain regions could be interpreted as mediators between adverse events in childhood and the development of psychiatric disorders like BPD, PTSD, or depression (Gilbert et al., 2009). Nonetheless, Crowell and colleagues (2009) argued that the co-occurrence of early childhood abuse along with a lowered ability to regulate affect, heightened impulsivity, and interpersonal disturbances might be more specific for the development of BPD.

BEHAVIORAL DYSREGULATION AND IMPULSIVITY

Another key feature of BPD is the common occurrence of impulsive behavior patterns that are often harmful to patients themselves or to others. For example, typical expressions of impulsivity in patients with BPD are substance abuse, binge eating, high-risk behavior, aggressive outbursts, or sudden relationship breakups (APA, 2000).

On the neurochemical level, neurotransmitters such as serotonin, dopamine, norepinephrine, glutamate, and γ-aminobutyric acid (GABA) modulate premotor behavioral responses and contribute to the initiation of impulsive behavior (Yanowitch & Coccaro, 2011). On the cortical level, frontal brain regions such as the OFC and ACC and corticostriatal pathways play an important role in regulating impulsive urges and inhibiting motor responses (Bush, Luu, & Posner, 2000; Coccaro, Sripada, Yanowitch, & Phan, 2011; Fineberg et al., 2010; Schoenbaum, Roesch, Stalnaker, & Takahashi, 2009).

In patients with BPD, numerous FDG-PET studies investigated neuroendocrine responses to serotonergic agents such as fenfluramine or meta-chlorophenylpiperazine (New et al., 2008; Schmahl & Bremner, 2006). In an early PET study, Siever and colleagues (1999) investigated patients with impulsive aggression who did not show enhanced prefrontal activity after fenfluramine challenge compared to the placebo condition, which was seen in healthy controls (Siever et al., 1999). In line with these findings, Soloff and colleagues (Soloff, Meltzer, Greer, Constantine, & Kelly, 2000) observed blunted metabolism in prefrontal and temporal areas in response to fenfluramine challenge. Furthermore, FDG-PET studies investigating cerebral blood flow during resting states revealed blunted baseline metabolism in premotor and pre-frontal brain areas (including the OFC and DLPFC) in patients with BPD (de la Fuente et al., 1997; Juengling et al., 2003; Lange, Kracht, Herholz, Sachsse, & Irle, 2005; Salavert et al., 2011; Soloff et al., 2000).

New and colleagues (2002) used meta-chlorophenylpiperazine (m-CPP)— another serotonergic agent—to investigate metabolic responses in impulsive-aggressive individuals. Whereas healthy participants showed increased activation in the left anteromedial OFC and ACC in response to m-CPP, this was not observed in impulsive-aggressive patients. In contrast to healthy controls, who showed a deacti-vation of the posterior cingulate gyrus, patients with impulsive aggression showed an increased activation in this region (New et al., 2002). Using FDG-PET, New and col-leagues (2004) further explored the influence of selective serotonin reuptake inhibi-tor (SSRI) treatment (fluoxetine) on activation in cortical areas in patients with BPD (New et al., 2004). BPD patients showed normalization of metabolic rates. In sum, findings of pharmacologic challenge studies with fenfluramine and m-PCC point to a serotonergic dysfunction in the prefrontal cortex and ACC in individuals with BPD. New and colleagues (New et al., 2007) examined relative glucose metabolic rates in the amygdala and PFC during resting state and after m-CPP in a larger sample of patients with BPD and found no differences in amygdala metabolism in response to m-CPP. Moreover, as already mentioned, they found a tight coupling of meta-bolic activity between ventral amygdala—which has been associated with emotion processing—and right OFC—which plays an important role in inhibitory control—during serotonergic challenge in healthy subjects but not in impulsive aggressive patients with BPD.

Blunted metabolism in frontal brain areas (implicated in inhibitory control) during resting states and in response to serotonin agents might be associated with impulsive-aggressive behavior in BPD. Yet there seem to be important differences in central serotonergic function between male BPD patients and female BPD patients, who constitute the majority of BPD patients in the psychiatric setting (New et al., 2003). For example, Soloff and colleagues (2003) assessed several self-reports of impul-sivity and impulsive aggression as well as prolactin responses to D,L-fenfluramine in female and male BPD patients. Prolactin responses were significantly dimin-ished in male but not in female patients with BPD compared to healthy participants. Self-reports of impulsivity and aggression were inversely related to peak prolactin responses and to δ-prolactin among male patients but not among women with BPD (Soloff, 2003). In another study by Soloff and colleagues (Soloff, Meltzer, Becker, Greer, & Constantine, 2005), male (but not female) BPD patients exhibited signif-icantly decreased glucose uptake in the temporal lobe in response to fenfluramine (relative to placebo). Interestingly, gender differences in responses to placebo or fenfluramine were rendered nonsignificant when covarying for self-reports of impul-sive aggression. Thus, gender differences in central serotonergic function might be related to variations in behavioral expression of impulsive aggression in individuals with BPD (Soloff et al., 2005).

It should be pointed out that serotonin is not the only neurotransmitter thought to be involved in impulsivity in BPD (Skodol et al., 2002). One study using MR spectroscopy showed that, compared to healthy women, levels of glutamate in the ACC were higher in (female) patients with BPD. Notably, significant positive correlations between glutamate concentrations and the behavioral inhibition system (BIS) total score as well as the BIS subscale of Cognitive Impulsiveness were observed in both healthy women and women with BPD (Hoerst et al., 2010a). These findings may have been confirmed recently in a MR spectroscopy study by Ende and colleagues (2016) that also demonstrated a relation of aggression scores with reduced GABA levels in ACC.

To investigate brain metabolic correlates of aggression, New and colleagues (New et al., 2009) employed a task to provoke aggressive behavior (Point Subtraction Aggression Paradigm [PSAP]) in a large sample of BPD patients with intermittent explosive disorder. In this FDG-PET study, patients showed increased relative glucose metabolic rate in OFC and amygdala when provoked (compared to a nonprovocation version of the PSAP), whereas healthy control participants showed decreased relative glucose metabolic rate in these areas. In healthy participants, provocation led to a stronger increase of glucose metabolism in DLPFC than in the patient group. In an additional data analysis that specifically focused on the striatum—a brain region closely connected with medial frontal cortices and one that has been associated with processing of rewarding stimuli—differences in metabolic activity between provoked and nonprovoked versions of the PSAP were examined separately in male and female BPD patients with intermittent explosive disorder (Perez-Rodriguez et al., 2012). In male patients, significantly lower striatal relative glucose metabolic rates were observed than in female patients and healthy controls. Results of this analysis are in line with previous studies suggesting an involvement of frontal-striatal circuits (Leyton et al., 2001) and an important effect of gender on glucose metabolic activity (New et al., 2003; Soloff, 2003; Soloff et al., 2005) in impulsive-aggressive patients with BPD.

More recent studies in BPD patients have applied fMRI to investigate brain activity during the performance of behavioral tasks that assess different aspects of impulsivity (for a more detailed overview, see Sebastian et al., 2014). For example, Völlm and colleagues (Völlm et al., 2004) investigated neuronal networks that might be involved in response inhibition in eight patients with impulsivity-related cluster B personality disorders (BPD or antisocial personality disorder) compared to healthy participants. In this study, participants performed a go/no-go task during fMRI. While healthy controls primarily activated areas of the prefrontal cortex, specifically in the right DLPFC and left OFC, patients showed a more bilateral and extended pattern of activation across the medial, superior, and inferior frontal gyri during successful response inhibition. The authors conclude that patients might engage a more widespread activity than healthy controls to attain the same level of impulse control (Völlm et al., 2004).

Taken together, these studies suggest that impulsivity might be related to frontal hypoactivation, serotonergic dysfunction, and abnormalities in event-related brain potentials. Further evidence for a dysregulation of serotonergic function in BPD stems from a study showing increased hippocampal $5HT_{2A}$ receptor binding in patients with BPD (Soloff et al., 2007). Other researchers found a link between aggression in BPD and a haplotype of the serotonergic gene tryptophan-hydroxylase 2 (Perez-Rodriguez et al., 2010). On this empirical basis, it has been argued that deficient serotonergic function related to impulsive-aggressive behavior and deficient inhibitory control might serve as an endophenotype of BPD (Goodman, New, Triebwasser, Collins, & Siever, 2010; Mak & Lam, 2013; McCloskey et al., 2009). Identifying endophenotypes of BPD would help to develop specific interventions for subgroups of BPD patients that could be characterized by specific genetic aberrations (Goodman et al., 2010; McCloskey et al., 2009). However, further studies comparing BPD patients to patients with other psychiatric disorders (e.g., major depression) are needed to clarify whether serotonergic dysfunction is specific to BPD. Moreover, other neurotransmitters in addition to serotonin—such as glutamate or GABA—might be involved in impulsivity in BPD (Skodol et al., 2002).

In addition, impulsivity in individuals with BPD might be related to negative affective states (Sebastian, Jacob, Lieb, & Tuscher, 2013; Sebastian et al., 2014). For example, Silbersweig and colleagues (2007) investigated the interaction between response inhibition and negative emotions applying an emotional version of a go/no-go task during fMRI. In a "negative no-go condition," patients with BPD showed significantly more "impulsive" commission and omission errors, which were associated with decreased activation in the medial OFC and subgenual ACC (Silbersweig et al., 2007). Moreover, BPD patients showed increased activation in the insula, dorsal ACC, and lateral orbitofrontal areas. Activation in the extended amygdala and ventral striatum during the negative no-go condition was correlated with self-reported emotional states in BPD patients. In another recent fMRI study (Jacob et al., 2013), participants performed go/no-go tasks after induction of a neutral mood, joy, or anger by vocally presented short stories. Patients with BPD showed stronger activation in the left amygdala and decreased activation in the subgenual ACC during anger induction compared to healthy controls. While healthy participants showed increased activation in the left inferior frontal cortex during response inhibition following anger induction, this was not observed in women with BPD. Findings of this study provide further evidence for a disturbed amygdala-prefrontal network as a potential neurobiological underpinning of emotion dysregulation and impulsivity in patients with BPD.

In the above-mentioned fMRI study, Krause-Utz and colleagues (2012) investigated the influence of task-irrelevant emotional stimuli on working memory performance. Participants performed a modified Sternberg item recognition task that measures working memory performance. During the short delay interval between encoding and retrieval of task-relevant information, distracting neutral versus emotionally arousing International Affective Pictures System (IAPS) pictures were presented (Krause-Utz et al., 2012). Patients with BPD showed significantly stronger amygdala activation and impaired behavioral performance both during emotional distraction and while viewing neutral pictures compared to healthy participants. Findings of this study are in line with the assumption of increased susceptibility to emotional cues and impaired inhibitory control in the presence of emotional stimuli in individuals with BPD. Likewise, Prehn et al. (2013) presented emotional IAPS pictures during an *n*-back task to investigate susceptibility to emotional distraction in male patients with BPD and antisocial personality disorder. Compared to healthy participants, patients showed delayed reaction times and enhanced activation in the left amygdala during the presence of emotionally high-salient pictures. Similarly, Holtmann et al. (2013) applied a modified flanker task to investigate susceptibility to distraction by fearful faces. Patients with BPD showed increased ACC activation during distraction by fearful faces compared to neutral faces. During an incongruent (i.e., more difficult) condition (but not during the congruent condition), patients with BPD additionally showed increased amygdala activation.

All in all, there is growing evidence for impaired inhibitory functioning that may be related to deficits in impulse control, particularly in the presence of negative emotional stimuli (Baer, Peters, Eisenlohr-Moul, Geiger, & Sauer, 2012; Fertuck, Lenzenweger, Clarkin, Hoermann, & Stanley, 2006) and during experimentally induced stress (Cackowski et al., 2014) in individuals with BPD. Administration of cortisol appears to have an effect on response inhibition in BPD as well (Carvalho Fernando et al., 2013).

On a neurobiological level, this seems to be reflected in altered activation in frontolimbic brain regions, including an increased limbic activation and decreased activation in brain areas associated with impulse control (Pessoa, Padmala, Kenzer, & Bauer, 2012). It remains an interesting topic for future research to discover to what extent impulsivity is related to emotion dysregulation in BPD.

INTERPERSONAL DISTURBANCES

In the past few years, research has increasingly focused on social cognition in BPD (Lis & Bohus, 2013). Conversely, neurobiological studies in this domain are relatively sparse. In response to social stimuli, the amygdala and other limbic regions were found to show heightened activity in BPD compared to healthy controls, thus corroborating the findings of heightened affective sensitivity (Donegan et al., 2003; Frick et al., 2012; Holtmann et al., 2013; Mier et al., 2013; Minzenberg et al., 2007; Prehn et al., 2013). In the study by Minzenberg and colleagues (2007), patients with BPD showed less activation in subgenual ACC during the presentation of fearful facial expressions. In response to angry faces, a heightened activity of the subgenual ACC and less activation in the bilateral amygdala was observed (Minzenberg et al., 2007). Additionally, pictures of emotional facial expressions led to higher activation in temporal cortical areas, cingulate cortex, and the hippocampus as well as lower activation in the DLPFC and inferior frontal gyrus in patients with BPD compared to healthy controls (Guitart-Masip et al., 2009; Holtmann et al., 2013; Mier et al., 2012; Radaelli et al., 2012). When patients had to infer mental states in theory of mind/empathy tasks (e.g., from affective eye gazes), they showed hypoactivation of right superior temporal sulcus and BA45 than did controls (Dziobek et al., 2011; Frick et al., 2012; Mier et al., 2012). Additionally, a higher activation in medial frontal gyrus, the left temporal pole, and the middle temporal gyrus was observed (Frick et al., 2012). The authors conclude that emotional interference might have a negative impact on cognitive processing of complex social stimuli in patients with BPD.

In addition to studies investigating the perception of social stimuli, some research focused on potentially problematic social interactions in BPD (i.e., social exclusion and cooperation). Findings on the behavioral level point to a heightened rejection sensitivity in BPD (Staebler, Helbing, Rosenbach, & Renneberg, 2010), indicating that individuals with BPD more readily expect and perceive rejection in social situations and that they react more strongly to social exclusion (Staebler et al., 2011). Examining functional brain correlates of social exclusion with near-infrared spectroscopy, Ruocco and colleagues (2010) found more activity in medial prefrontal cortex in BPD patients compared to healthy controls. Furthermore, this activation was correlated to general rejection sensitivity and fear of abandonment (Ruocco et al., 2010). A recent study investigated social inclusion and exclusion in BPD and healthy controls (Domsalla et al., 2014) and found that BPD subjects felt more excluded than did healthy controls during the inclusion condition, whereas both groups felt similarly excluded during the exclusion condition. In all conditions, BPD patients showed a stronger engagement of the dorsal anterior cingulate and medial prefrontal cortex, thus supporting the idea of increased sensitivity in a "neural alarm system" relevant for the detection of social exclusion.

When patients with BPD played a trust game with healthy partners (King-Casas et al., 2008), cooperation tended to decrease over time, whereas it was more stable in healthy dyads. Interestingly, the authors show a differential activation of the insula in healthy controls depending on the fairness of the transaction. Conversely, in BPD patients, insula activity was high during the whole experiment. The authors conclude that patients with BPD might have difficulty perceiving the violation of social norms (King-Casas et al., 2008). Apart from different experimental designs, the insula seems to play an important role in the processing of social information in BPD. More specifically, it was argued that high insula activity corresponds to a diminished ability to differentiate between fair and unfair interactions in the context of social interaction (King-Casas et al., 2008; Meyer-Lindenberg, 2008). In addition, difficulty in empathy has been found to correspond to heightened activity in the middle and posterior insula in BPD (Dziobek et al., 2011). Since the insula possibly plays a key role in the detection of unfairness (Sanfey, Rilling, Aronson,

Nystrom, & Cohen, 2003), insula hyperreactivity in BPD may not only be related to affective instability (as discussed in Chapter 1), but also to difficulties in social interaction.

CONCLUSION

Taken together, individuals with BPD show functional and structural abnormalities in frontolimbic brain regions, including limbic hyperreactivity (e.g., in the amygdala and insula) and diminished recruitment of frontal brain regions (e.g., the ACC, OFC, and DLPFC) that are involved in inhibitory and regulatory process. This imbalanced frontolimbic network has been linked to emotion dysregulation, but also to aspects of impulsivity and interpersonal disturbances, suggesting that central features of BPD are closely linked to each other. For example, inhibitory control processes (including response inhibition and cognitive inhibition) are not only an important aspect of impulse control, but are also crucial for social interaction competencies and emotion regulation (Bjorklund & Harnishfeger, 1995; Rueda, Posner, & Rothbart, 2005). Moreover, one could argue that limbic hyperreactivity yields a connection between the symptoms of emotion dysregulation and interpersonal disturbances in BPD: hyperreactivity in the amygdala and insula could lead to disturbed emotion processing and to a bias toward the perception of potential threatening stimuli. For example, one could hypothesize that an attentional bias toward negative information could heighten emotional vulnerability (MacLeod, Rutherford, Campbell, Ebsworthy, & Holker, 2002) and, therefore, limbic hyperreactivity. It remains an interesting topic for future research to reveal links among emotion dysregulation, impulsivity, and interpersonal disturbances in BPD on both behavioral and neurobiological levels.

REFERENCES

American Psychiatric Association (APA). (2000). *Diagnostic and statistical manual of mental disorders* (4th ed., text rev.). Washington, DC: Author.

Baer, R. A., Peters, J. R., Eisenlohr-Moul, T. A., Geiger, P. J., & Sauer, S. E. (2012). Emotion-related cognitive processes in borderline personality disorder: A review of the empirical literature. *Clinical Psychology Review, 32*(5), 359–369.

Beblo, T., Driessen, M., Mertens, M., Wingenfeld, K., Piefke, M., Rullkoetter, N., . . . Woermann, F. G. (2006). Functional MRI correlates of the recall of unresolved life events in borderline personality disorder. *Psychological Medicine, 36*(6), 845–856.

Bertsch, K., Grothe, M., Prehn, K., Vohs, K., Berger, C., Hauenstein, K., . . . Herpertz, S. C. (2013). Brain volumes differ between diagnostic groups of violent criminal offenders. *European Archives of Psychiatry and Clinical Neuroscience, 263*(7), 593–606.

Bjorklund, D. F., & Harnishfeger, K. K. (1995). The role of inhibition mechanisms in the evolution of human cognition and behavior. In F. N. Dempster & C. J. Brainerd (Eds.), *New perspectives on interference and inhibition in cognition* (pp. 141–173). New York: Academic Press.

Bohus, M., Limberger, M., Ebner, U., Glocker, F. X., Schwarz, B., Wernz, M., & Lieb, K. (2000). Pain perception during self-reported distress and calmness in patients with borderline personality disorder and self-mutilating behavior. *Psychiatry Research, 95*(3), 251–260.

Brambilla, P., Soloff, P. H., Sala, M., Nicoletti, M. A., Keshavan, M. S., & Soares, J. C. (2004). Anatomical MRI study of borderline personality disorder patients. [Research Support, U.S. Gov't, P.H.S.]. *Psychiatry Research, 131*(2), 125–133.

Breiter, H. C., Etcoff, N. L., Whalen, P. J., Kennedy, W. A., Rauch, S. L., Buckner, R. L., . . . Rosen, B. R. (1996). Response and habituation of the human amygdala during visual processing of facial expression. *Neuron, 17*(5), 875–887.

Brunner, R., Henze, R., Parzer, P., Kramer, J., Feigl, N., Lutz, K., . . . Stieltjes, B. (2010). Reduced prefrontal and orbitofrontal gray matter in female adolescents with borderline personality disorder: Is it disorder specific? *NeuroImage, 49*(1), 114–120.

Bush, G., Luu, P., & Posner, M. I. (2000). Cognitive and emotional influences in anterior cingulate cortex. *Trends in Cognitive Science, 4*(6), 215–222.

Cackowski, S., Reitz, A. C., Ende, G., Kleindienst, N., Bohus, M., Schmahl, C., & Krause-Utz, A. (2014). Impact of stress on different components of impulsivity in borderline personality disorder. *Psychological Medicine, 44*(15), 3329–3340.

Cardenas-Morales, L., Fladung, A. K., Kammer, T., Schmahl, C., Plener, P. L., Connemann, B. J., & Schonfeldt-Lecuona, C. (2011). Exploring the affective component of pain perception during aversive stimulation in borderline personality disorder. *Psychiatry Research, 186*(2-3), 458–460.

Carpenter, R. W., & Trull, T. J. (2013). Components of emotion dysregulation in borderline personality disorder: A review. *Current Psychiatry Reports, 15*(1), 335.

Carrasco, J. L., Tajima-Pozo, K., Diaz-Marsa, M., Casado, A., Lopez-Ibor, J. J., Arrazola, J., & Yus, M. (2012). Microstructural white matter damage at orbitofrontal areas in borderline personality disorder. *Journal of Affective Disorders, 139*(2), 149–153.

Carvalho Fernando, S., Beblo, T., Schlosser, N., Terfehr, K., Wolf, O. T., Otte, C., . . . Wingenfeld, K. (2013). Acute glucocorticoid effects on response inhibition in borderline personality disorder. *Psychoneuroendocrinology, 38*(11), 2780–2788.

Chanen, A. M., Velakoulis, D., Carison, K., Gaunson, K., Wood, S. J., Yuen, H. P., . . . Pantelis, C. (2008). Orbitofrontal, amygdala and hippocampal volumes in teenagers with first-presentation borderline personality disorder. *Psychiatry Research, 163*(2), 116–125.

Coccaro, E. F., Sripada, C. S., Yanowitch, R. N., & Phan, K. L. (2011). Corticolimbic function in impulsive aggressive behavior. *Biological Psychiatry, 69*(12), 1153–1159.

Crowell, S. E., Beauchaine, T. P., & Linehan, M. M. (2009). A biosocial developmental model of borderline personality: Elaborating and extending Linehan's theory. *Psychological Bulletin, 135*(3), 495–510.

Cullen, K. R., Vizueta, N., Thomas, K. M., Han, G. J., Lim, K. O., Camchong, J., . . . Schulz, S. C. (2011). Amygdala functional connectivity in young women with borderline personality disorder. *Brain Connect, 1*(1), 61–71.

Damasio, A. R., Grabowski, T. J., Bechara, A., Damasio, H., Ponto, L. L. B., Parvizi, J., & Hichwa, R. D. (2000). Subcortical and cortical brain activity during the feeling of self-generated emotions. *Nature Neuroscience, 3*(10), 1049–1056.

Dannlowski, U., Stuhrmann, A., Beutelmann, V., Zwanzger, P., Lenzen, T., Grotegerd, D., . . . Kugel, H. (2012). Limbic scars: Long-term consequences of childhood maltreatment revealed by functional and structural magnetic resonance imaging. *Biological Psychiatry, 71*(4), 286–293.

de la Fuente, J. M., Goldman, S., Stanus, E., Vizuete, C., Morlán, I., Bobes, J., & Mendlewicz, J. (1997). Brain glucose metabolism in borderline personality disorder. *Journal of Psychiatric Research, 31*(5), 531–541.

Doll, A., Sorg, C., Manoliu, A., Woller, A., Meng, C., Forstl, H., . . . Riedl, V. (2013). Shifted intrinsic connectivity of central executive and salience network in borderline personality disorder. *Frontiers in Human Neuroscience, 7*, 727. doi: 10.3389/fnhum.2013.00727

Domsalla, M., Koppe, G., Niedtfeld, I., Vollstadt-Klein, S., Schmahl, C., Bohus, M., & Lis, S. (2014). Cerebral processing of social rejection in patients with borderline personality disorder. *Social Cognitive and Affective Neuroscience, 9*(11), 1789–1797.

Donegan, N. H., Sanislow, C. A., Blumberg, H. P., Fulbright, R. K., Lacadie, C., Skudlarski, P., . . . Wexler, B. E. (2003). Amygdala hyperreactivity in borderline personality disorder: Implications for emotional dysregulation. *Biological Psychiatry, 54*(11), 1284–1293.

Driessen, M., Herrmann, J., Stahl, K., Zwaan, M., Meier, S., Hill, A., . . . Petersen, D. (2000). Magnetic resonance imaging volumes of the hippocampus and the amygdala in women with borderline personality disorder and early traumatization. *Archives of General Psychiatry, 57*(12), 1115–1122.

Dziobek, I., Preissler, S., Grozdanovic, Z., Heuser, I., Heekeren, H. R., & Roepke, S. (2011). Neuronal correlates of altered empathy and social cognition in borderline personality disorder. *Neuroimage, 57*(2), 539–548.

Ende, G., Cackowski, S., VanEijk, J., Sack, M., Bohus, M., Sobanski, E., . . . Schmahl, C. (2016). Impulsivity and aggression are associated with anterior cingulate glutamate and GABA concentrations in BPD and ADHD. *Neuropsychopharmacology, 41*(2), 410–418.

Fertuck, E. A., Lenzenweger, M. F., Clarkin, J. F., Hoermann, S., & Stanley, B. (2006). Executive neurocognition, memory systems, and borderline personality disorder. *Clinical Psychology Review, 26*(3), 346–375.

Fineberg, N. A., Potenza, M. N., Chamberlain, S. R., Berlin, H. A., Menzies, L., Bechara, A., . . . Hollander, E. (2010). Probing compulsive and impulsive behaviors, from animal models to endophenotypes: A narrative review. *Neuropsychopharmacology, 35*(3), 591–604.

Frick, C., Lang, S., Kotchoubey, B., Sieswerda, S., Dinu-Biringer, R., Berger, M., . . . Barnow, S. (2012). Hypersensitivity in borderline personality disorder during mindreading. *PLoS One, 7*(8), e41650.

Gilbert, R., Widom, C. S., Browne, K., Fergusson, D., Webb, E., & Janson, S. (2009). Burden and consequences of child maltreatment in high-income countries. *Lancet, 373*(9657), 68–81.

Glenn, C. R., & Klonsky, E. D. (2009). Emotion dysregulation as a core feature of borderline personality disorder. *Journal of Personality Disorders, 23*(1), 20–28.

Goodman, M., Carpenter, D., Tang, C. Y., Goldstein, K. E., Avedon, J., Fernandez, N., . . . Hazlett, E. A. (2014). Dialectical behavior therapy alters emotion regulation and amygdala activity inpatients with borderline personality disorder. *Journal of Psychiatric Research, 57*, 108–116.

Goodman, M., Hazlett, E. A., Avedon, J. B., Siever, D. R., Chu, K. W., & New, A. S. (2011). Anterior cingulate volume reduction in adolescents with borderline personality disorder and co-morbid major depression. *Journal of Psychiatric Research, 45*(6), 803–807.

Goodman, M., New, A. S., Triebwasser, J., Collins, K. A., & Siever, L. (2010). Phenotype, endophenotype, and genotype comparisons between borderline personality disorder and major depressive disorder. *Journal of Personality Disorders, 24*(1), 38–59.

Grant, J. E., Correia, S., Brennan-Krohn, T., Malloy, P. F., Laidlaw, D. H., & Schulz, S. C. (2007). Frontal white matter integrity in borderline personality disorder with self-injurious behavior. *Journal of Neuropsychiatry and Clinical Neurosciences, 19*(4), 383–390.

Guitart-Masip, M., Pascual, J. C., Carmona, S., Hoekzema, E., Berge, D., Perez, V., . . . Vilarroya, O. (2009). Neural correlates of impaired emotional discrimination in borderline personality disorder: An fMRI study. *Progress in Neuropsychopharmacology and Biological Psychiatry, 33*(8), 1537–1545.

Gunderson, J. G., Stout, R. L., McGlashan, T. H., Shea, M. T., Morey, L. C., Grilo, C. M., . . . Skodol, A. E. (2011). Ten-year course of borderline personality disorder: Psychopathology and function from the Collaborative Longitudinal Personality Disorders Study. *Archives of General Psychiatry.* doi: 10.1001/archgenpsychiatry.2011.37

Hazlett, E. A., New, A. S., Newmark, R., Haznedar, M. M., Lo, J. N., Speiser, L. J., . . . Buchsbaum, M. S. (2005). Reduced anterior and posterior cingulate gray matter in borderline personality disorder. *Biological Psychiatry, 58*(8), 614–623.

Hazlett, E. A., Speiser, L. J., Goodman, M., Roy, M., Carrizal, M., Wynn, J. K., . . . New, A. S. (2007). Exaggerated affect-modulated startle during unpleasant stimuli in borderline personality disorder. *Biological Psychiatry, 62*(3), 250–255.

Hazlett, E. A., Zhang, J., New, A. S., Zelmanova, Y., Goldstein, K. E., Haznedar, M. M., . . . Chu, K. W. (2012). Potentiated amygdala response to repeated emotional pictures in borderline personality disorder. *Biological Psychiatry, 72*(6), 448–456.

Herpertz, S., Gretzer, A., Steinmeyer, E. M., Muehlbauer, V., Schuerkens, A., & Sass, H. (1997). Affective instability and impulsivity in personality disorder. Results of an experimental study. *Journal of Affective Disorders, 44*(1), 31–37.

Herpertz, S. C., Dietrich, T. M., Wenning, B., Krings, T., Erberich, S. G., Willmes, K., . . . Sass, H. (2001). Evidence of abnormal amygdala functioning in borderline personality disorder: A functional MRI study. *Biological Psychiatry, 50*(4), 292–298.

Hoerst, M., Weber-Fahr, W., Tunc-Skarka, N., Ruf, M., Bohus, M., Schmahl, C., & Ende, G. (2010a). Metabolic alterations in the amygdala in borderline personality disorder: A proton magnetic resonance spectroscopy study. *Biological Psychiatry, 67*(5), 399–405.

Holtmann, J., Herbort, M. C., Wustenberg, T., Soch, J., Richter, S., Walter, H., . . . Schott, B. H. (2013). Trait anxiety modulates fronto-limbic processing of emotional interference in borderline personality disorder. *Frontiers in Human Neuroscience, 7*, 54. doi: 10.3389/fnhum.2013.00054

Irle, E., Lange, C., & Sachsse, U. (2005). Reduced size and abnormal asymmetry of parietal cortex in women with borderline personality disorder. *Biological Psychiatry, 57*(2), 173–182.

Irle, E., Lange, C., Weniger, G., & Sachsse, U. (2007). Size abnormalities of the superior parietal cortices are related to dissociation in borderline personality disorder. *Psychiatry Research, 156*(2), 139–149.

Jacob, G. A., Zvonik, K., Kamphausen, S., Sebastian, A., Maier, S., Philipsen, A., . . . Tuscher, O. (2013). Emotional modulation of motor response inhibition in women with borderline personality disorder: An fMRI study. *Journal of Psychiatry and Neuroscience, 38*(3), 164–172.

Johnson, P. A., Hurley, R. A., Benkelfat, C., Herpertz, S. C., & Taber, K. H. (2003). Understanding emotion regulation in borderline personality disorder: Contributions of neuroimaging. *Journal of Neuropsychiatry & Clinical Neurosciences, 15*(4), 397–402.

Juengling, F. D., Schmahl, C., Hesslinger, B., Ebert, D., Bremner, J. D., Gostomzyk, J., . . . Lieb, K. (2003). Positron emission tomography in female patients with borderline personality disorder. *Journal of Psychiatric Research, 37*(2), 109–115.

Kamphausen, S., Schroder, P., Maier, S., Bader, K., Feige, B., Kaller, C. P., . . . Tuscher, O. (2012). Medial prefrontal dysfunction and prolonged amygdala response during instructed fear processing in borderline personality disorder. *World Journal of Biological Psychiatry*. doi: 10.3109/15622975.2012.665174

Karl, A., Schaefer, M., Malta, L. S., Dorfel, D., Rohleder, N., & Werner, A. (2006). A meta-analysis of structural brain abnormalities in PTSD. *Neuroscience and Biobehavioral Reviews, 30*(7), 1004–1031.

Kemperman, I., Russ, M. J., & Shearin, E. N. (1997). Self-injurious behavior and mood regulation in borderline patients. *Journal of Personality Disorders, 11*(2), 146–157.

Killgore, W. D., Britton, J. C., Schwab, Z. J., Price, L. M., Weiner, M. R., Gold, A. L., . . . Rauch, S. L. (2014). Cortico-limbic responses to masked affective faces across PTSD, panic disorder, and specific phobia. *Depression and Anxiety, 31*(2), 150–159.

King-Casas, B., Sharp, C., Lomax-Bream, L., Lohrenz, T., Fonagy, P., & Montague, P. R. (2008). The rupture and repair of cooperation in borderline personality disorder. *Science, 321*(5890), 806–810.

Kleindienst, N., Bohus, M., Ludascher, P., Limberger, M. F., Kuenkele, K., Ebner-Priemer, U. W., . . . Schmahl, C. (2008). Motives for nonsuicidal self-injury among women with borderline personality disorder. *Journal of Nervous and Mental Disease, 196*(3), 230–236.

Klonsky, E. D. (2007). The functions of deliberate self-injury: A review of the evidence. *Clinical Psychology Review, 27*(2), 226–239.

Kluetsch, R. C., Schmahl, C., Niedtfeld, I., Densmore, M., Calhoun, V. D., Daniels, J., . . . Lanius, R. A. (2012). Alterations in default mode network connectivity during pain processing in borderline personality disorder. *Archives of General Psychiatry, 9*(10), 993–1002.

Koenigsberg, H. W., Denny, B. T., Fan, J., Liu, X., Guerreri, S., Mayson, S. J., . . . Siever, L. J. (2014). The neural correlates of anomalous habituation to negative emotional pictures in borderline and avoidant personality disorder patients. *American Journal of Psychiatry, 171*(1), 82–90.

Koenigsberg, H. W., Fan, J., Ochsner, K. N., Liu, X., Guise, K. G., Pizzarello, S., . . . Siever, L. J. (2009). Neural correlates of the use of psychological distancing to regulate responses to negative social cues: A study of patients with borderline personality disorder. *Biological Psychiatry, 66*(9), 854–863.

Korzekwa, M. I., Dell, P. F., Links, P. S., Thabane, L., & Fougere, P. (2009). Dissociation in borderline personality disorder: A detailed look. *Journal of Trauma and Dissociation, 10*(3), 346–367.

Kraus, A., Esposito, F., Seifritz, E., Di Salle, F., Ruf, M., Valerius, G., . . . Schmahl, C. (2009). Amygdala deactivation as a neural correlate of pain processing in patients with borderline personality disorder and co-occurrent posttraumatic stress disorder. *Biological Psychiatry, 65*(9), 819–822.

Krause-Utz, A., Elzinga, B. M., Oei, N. Y. L., Paret, C., Niedtfeld, I., Spinhoven, P., . . . Schmahl, C. (2014). Amygdala and dorsal anterior cingulate connectivity during an emotional working memory task in borderline personality disorder patients with interpersonal trauma history. *Frontiers in Human Neuroscience, 8*, 848. doi: 10.3389/fnhum.2014.00848

Krause-Utz, A., Keibel-Mauchnik, J., Ebner-Priemer, U., Bohus, M., . . . Schmahl, C. (2016). Classical conditioning in borderline personality disorder: An fMRI study. *European Archives of Psychiatry and Clinical Neuroscience, 266*(4), 291–305. Krause-Utz, A., Oei, N. Y., Niedtfeld, I., Bohus, M., Spinhoven, P., Schmahl, C., & Elzinga, B. M. (2012). Influence of emotional distraction on working memory performance in borderline personality disorder. *Psychological Medicine, 42*(10), 2181–2192.

Krause-Utz, A., & Schmahl, C. (2010). Neurobiological differentiation between borderline patients with and without post-traumatic stress disorder. *European Psychiatric Review, 3*(2), 63–68.

Krause-Utz, A., Veer, I. M., Rombouts, S. A. R. B., Bohus, M., Schmahl, C., & Elzinga, B. M. (2014). Amygdala and anterior cingulate resting-state functional connectivity in borderline personality disorder patients with a history of interpersonal trauma. *Psychological Medicine, 44*(13), 2889–2901.

Kuhlmann, A., Bertsch, K., Schmidinger, I., Thomann, P. A., & Herpertz, S. C. (2013). Morphometric differences in central stress-regulating structures between women with and without borderline personality disorder. *Journal of Psychiatry and Neuroscience, 38*(2), 129–137.

Lang, S., Kotchoubey, B., Frick, C., Spitzer, C., Grabe, H. J., & Barnow, S. (2012). Cognitive reappraisal in trauma-exposed women with borderline personality disorder. *Neuroimage, 59*(2), 1727–1734.

Lange, C., Kracht, L., Herholz, K., Sachsse, U., & Irle, E. (2005). Reduced glucose metabolism in temporo-parietal cortices of women with borderline personality disorder. *Psychiatry Research, 139*(2), 115–126.

Lanius, R. A., Brand, B., Vermetten, E., Frewen, P. A., & Spiegel, D. (2012). The dissociative subtype of posttraumatic stress disorder: Rationale, clinical and neurobiological evidence, and implications. [Review]. *Depression and Anxiety, 29*(8), 701–708.

Lanius, R. A., Vermetten, E., Loewenstein, R. J., Brand, B., Schmahl, C., Bremner, J. D., & Spiegel, D. (2010). Emotion modulation in PTSD: Clinical and neurobiological evidence for a dissociative subtype. *American Journal of Psychiatry, 167*(6), 640–647.

Leichsenring, F., Leibing, E., Kruse, J., New, A. S., & Leweke, F. (2011). Borderline personality disorder. *Lancet, 377*(9759), 74–84.

Levine, D., Marziali, E., & Hood, J. (1997). Emotion processing in borderline personality disorders. *Journal of Nervous and Mental Disease, 185*(4), 240–246.

Leyton, M., Okazawa, H., Diksic, M., Paris, J., Rosa, P., Mzengeza, S., ... Benkelfat, C. (2001). Brain regional alpha-[11C]methyl-L-tryptophan trapping in impulsive subjects with borderline personality disorder. *American Journal of Psychiatry, 158*(5), 775–782.

Lieb, K., Rexhausen, J. E., Kahl, K. G., Schweiger, U., Philipsen, A., Hellhammer, D. H., & Bohus, M. (2004). Increased diurnal salivary cortisol in women with borderline personality disorder. *Journal of Psychiatric Research, 38*(6), 559–565.

Lieb, K., Zanarini, M. C., Schmahl, C., Linehan, M. M., & Bohus, M. (2004). Borderline personality disorder. *Lancet, 364*(9432), 453–461. doi: 10.1016/s0140-6736(04)16770-6

Lis, E., Greenfield, B., Henry, M., Guile, J. M., & Dougherty, G. (2007). Neuroimaging and genetics of borderline personality disorder: A review. *Journal of Psychiatry and Neuroscience, 32*(3), 162–173.

Lis, S., & Bohus, M. (2013). Social interaction in borderline personality disorder. *Current Psychiatry Reports, 15*(2), 338. doi: 10.1007/s11920-012-0338-z

Ludaescher, P., Bohus, M., Lieb, K., Philipsen, A., & Schmahl, C. (2007). Elevated pain thresholds correlate with dissociation and aversive arousal in patients with borderline personality disorder. *Psychiatry Research, 149*(1-3), 291–296.

Ludaescher, P., Valerius, G., Stiglmayr, C., Mauchnik, J., Lanius, R., Bohus, M., & Schmahl, C. (2010). Pain sensitivity and neural processing during dissociative states in patients with borderline personality disorder with and without comorbid PTSD—a pilot study. *Journal of Psychiatry and Neuroscience, 35*(3), 177–184.

Lyoo, I. K., Han, M. H., & Cho, D. Y. (1998). A brain MRI study in subjects with borderline personality disorder. *Journal of Affective Disorders, 50*(2-3), 235–243.

MacLeod, C., Rutherford, E., Campbell, L., Ebsworthy, G., & Holker, L. (2002). Selective attention and emotional vulnerability: Assessing the causal basis of their association through the experimental manipulation of attentional bias. *Journal of Abnormal Psychology, 111*(1), 107–123.

Maier-Hein, K. H., Brunner, R., Lutz, K., Henze, R., Parzer, P., Feigl, N., ... Stieltjes, B. (2014). Disorder-specific white matter alterations in adolescent borderline personality disorder. *Biological Psychiatry, 75*(1), 81–88.

Mak, A. D., & Lam, L. C. (2013). Neurocognitive profiles of people with borderline personality disorder. *Current Opinion in Psychiatry, 26*(1), 90–96.

McCloskey, M. S., New, A. S., Siever, L. J., Goodman, M., Koenigsberg, H. W., Flory, J. D., & Coccaro, E. F. (2009). Evaluation of behavioral impulsivity and aggression tasks as endophenotypes for borderline personality disorder. *Journal of Psychiatric Research, 43*(12), 1036–1048.

McCloskey, M. S., Phan, K. L., & Coccaro, E. F. (2005). Neuroimaging and personality disorders. *Current Psychiatry Reports, 7*(1), 65–72.

McCown, W., Galina, H., Johnson, J., de Simone, P. A., & Posa, J. (1993). Borderline personality disorder and laboratory-induced cold pressor pain: Evidence of stress-induced analgesia. *Journal of Psychopathology and Behavioral Assessment, 15*(2), 87–95.

McRae, K., Hughes, B., Chopra, S., Gabrieli, J. D., Gross, J. J., & Ochsner, K. N. (2010). The neural bases of distraction and reappraisal. *Journal of Cognitive Neuroscience, 22*(2), 248–262.

Menon, V., & Uddin, L. Q. (2010). Saliency, switching, attention and control: A network model of insula function. *Brain Structure and Function, 214*(5-6), 655–667.

Meyer-Lindenberg, A. (2008). Psychology. Trust me on this. *Science, 321*(5890), 778–780.

Mier, D., Lis, S., Esslinger, C., Sauer, C., Hagenhoff, M., Ulferts, J., ... Kirsch, P. (2013). Neuronal correlates of social cognition in borderline personality disorder. *Social Cognitive and Affective Neuroscience, 8*(5), 531–537.

Minzenberg, M. J., Fan, J., New, A. S., Tang, C. Y., & Siever, L. J. (2007). Fronto-limbic dysfunction in response to facial emotion in borderline personality disorder: An event-related fMRI study. *Psychiatry Research, 155*(3), 231–243.

Minzenberg, M. J., Fan, J., New, A. S., Tang, C. Y., & Siever, L. J. (2008). Frontolimbic structural changes in borderline personality disorder. *Journal of Psychiatric Research, 42*(9), 727–733.

New, A. S., Buchsbaum, M. S., Hazlett, E. A., Goodman, M., Koenigsberg, H. W., Lo, J., . . . Siever, L. J. (2004). Fluoxetine increases relative metabolic rate in prefrontal cortex in impulsive aggression. *Psychopharmacology (Berlin), 176*(3-4), 451–458.

New, A. S., Goodman, M., Triebwasser, J., & Siever, L. J. (2008). Recent advances in the biological study of personality disorders. *Psychiatric Clinics of North America, 31*(3), 441–461.

New, A. S., Hazlett, E. A., Buchsbaum, M. S., Goodman, M., Koenigsberg, H. W., Iskander, L., . . . Siever, L. J. (2003). M-CPP PET and impulsive aggression in borderline personality disorder. *Biological Psychiatry,* 53, 104.

New, A. S., Hazlett, E. A., Buchsbaum, M. S., Goodman, M., Mitelman, S. A., Newmark, R., . . . Siever, L. J. (2007). Amygdala-prefrontal disconnection in borderline personality disorder. *Neuropsychopharmacology, 32*(7), 1629–1640.

New, A. S., Hazlett, E. A., Buchsbaum, M. S., Goodman, M., Reynolds, D. A., Mitropoulou, V., . . . Siever, L. J. (2002). Blunted prefrontal cortical 18fluorodeoxyglucose positron emission tomography response to meta-chlorophenylpiperazine in impulsive aggression. *Archives of General Psychiatry, 59*(7), 621–629.

New, A. S., Hazlett, E. A., Newmark, R. E., Zhang, J., Triebwasser, J., Meyerson, D., . . . Buchsbaum, M. S. (2009). Laboratory induced aggression: A positron emission tomography study of aggressive individuals with borderline personality disorder. *Biological Psychiatry, 66*(12), 1107–1114.

New, A. S., Carpenter, D. M., Perez-Rodriguez, M. M., Ripoll, L. H., Avedon, J., Patil, U., . . . Goodman, M. (2013). Developmental differences in diffusion tensor imaging parameters in borderline personality disorder. *Journal of Psychiatric Research, 47*(8), 1101–1109.

Niedtfeld, I., Kirsch, P., Schulze, L., Herpertz, S. C., Bohus, M., & Schmahl, C. (2012). Functional connectivity of pain-mediated affect regulation in borderline personality disorder. *PloS One, 7*(3), e33293.

Niedtfeld, I., Schulze, L., Kirsch, P., Herpertz, S. C., Bohus, M., & Schmahl, C. (2010). Affect regulation and pain in borderline personality disorder: A possible link to the understanding of self-injury. *Biological Psychiatry, 68*(4), 383–391.

Niedtfeld, I., Schulze, L., Krause-Utz, A., Demirakca, T., Bohus, M., & Schmahl, C. (2013). Voxel-based morphometry in women with borderline personality disorder with and without comorbid posttraumatic stress disorder. *PloS One, 8*(6), e65824. doi: 10.1371/journal.pone.0065824

Nunes, P. M., Wenzel, A., Borges, K. T., Porto, C. R., Caminha, R. M., & de Oliveira, I. R. (2009). Volumes of the hippocampus and amygdala in patients with borderline personality disorder: A meta-analysis. *Journal of Personality Disorders, 23*(4), 333–345.

Ochsner, K. N., Bunge, S. A., Gross, J. J., & Gabrieli, J. D. (2002). Rethinking feelings: An FMRI study of the cognitive regulation of emotion. *Journal of Cognitive Neuroscience, 14*(8), 1215–1229.

Ochsner, K. N., & Gross, J. J. (2008). Cognitive Emotion Regulation: Insights from Social Cognitive and Affective Neuroscience. *Current Directions in Psychological Science, 17*(2), 153–158.

Ochsner, K. N., Ray, R. D., Cooper, J. C., Robertson, E. R., Chopra, S., Gabrieli, J. D., & Gross, J. J. (2004). For better or for worse: Neural systems supporting the cognitive down- and up-regulation of negative emotion. *NeuroImage, 23*(2), 483–499.

O'Neill, A., & Frodl, T. (2012). Brain structure and function in borderline personality disorder. *Brain Structure and Function, 217*(4), 767–782.

Perez-Rodriguez, M. M., Hazlett, E. A., Rich, E. L., Ripoll, L. H., Weiner, D. M., Spence, N., . . . New, A. S. (2012). Striatal activity in borderline personality disorder with comorbid intermittent explosive disorder: Sex differences. *Journal of Psychiatric Research, 46*(6), 797–804.

Perez-Rodriguez, M. M., Weinstein, S., New, A. S., Bevilacqua, L., Yuan, Q., Zhou, Z., . . . Siever, L. J. (2010). Tryptophan-hydroxylase 2 haplotype association with borderline personality disorder and aggression in a sample of patients with personality disorders and healthy controls. *Journal of Psychiatric Research, 44*(15), 1075–1081.

Pessoa, L., McKenna, M., Gutierrez, E., & Ungerleider, L. G. (2002). Neural processing of emotional faces requires attention. *Proceedings of the National Academy of Science USA, 99*(17), 11458–11463.

Pessoa, L., Padmala, S., Kenzer, A., & Bauer, A. (2012). Interactions between cognition and emotion during response inhibition. *Emotion, 12*(1), 192–197.

Prehn, K., Schulze, L., Rossmann, S., Berger, C., Vohs, K., Fleischer, M., . . . Herpertz, S. C. (2013). Effects of emotional stimuli on working memory processes in male criminal offenders with borderline and antisocial personality disorder. *World Journal of Biological PsychiatryBiological Psychiatry, 14*(1), 71–78.

Radaelli, D., Poletti, S., Dallaspezia, S., Colombo, C., Smeraldi, E., & Benedetti, F. (2012). Neural responses to emotional stimuli in comorbid borderline personality disorder and bipolar depression. *Psychiatry Research, 203*(1), 61–66.

Rainville, P. (2002). Brain mechanisms of pain affect and pain modulation. *Current Opinion in Neurobiology, 12*(2), 195–204.

Reitz, S., Kluetsch, R., Niedtfeld, I., Knorz, T., Lis, S., Paret, C., . . . Schmahl, C. (2015). Incision and stress regulation in borderline personality disorder: Neurobiological mechanisms of self-injurious behaviour. *British Journal of Psychiatry, 207*(2), 165–172.

Reitz, S., Krause-Utz, A., Pogatzki-Zahn, E. M., Ebner-Priemer, U., Bohus, M., & Schmahl, C. (2012). Stress regulation and incision in borderline personality disorder—a pilot study modeling cutting behavior. *Journal of Personality Disorders, 26*, 605–615.

Rodrigues, E., Wenzel, A., Ribeiro, M. P., Quarantini, L. C., Miranda-Scippa, A., de Sena, E. P., & de Oliveira, I. R. (2011). Hippocampal volume in borderline personality disorder with and without comorbid posttraumatic stress disorder: A meta-analysis. *European Psychiatry, 26*(7), 452–456.

Rosenthal, M. Z., Gratz, K. L., Kosson, D. S., Cheavens, J. S., Lejuez, C. W., & Lynch, T. R. (2008). Borderline personality disorder and emotional responding: A review of the research literature. *Clinical Psychology Review, 28*(1), 75–91.

Rueda, M. R., Posner, M. I., & Rothbart, M. K. (2005). The development of executive attention: Contributions to the emergence of self-regulation. *Developmental Neuropsychology, 28*(2), 573–594.

Ruocco, A. C., Amirthavasagam, S., Choi-Kain, L. W., & McMain, S. F. (2013). Neural correlates of negative emotionality in borderline personality disorder: An activation-likelihood-estimation meta-analysis. *Biological Psychiatry, 73*(2), 153–160.

Ruocco, A. C., Medaglia, J. D., Tinker, J. R., Ayaz, H., Forman, E. M., Newman, C. F., . . . Chute, D. L. (2010). Medial prefrontal cortex hyperactivation during social exclusion in borderline personality disorder. *Psychiatry Research, 181*(3), 233–236.

Rüsch, N., Bracht, T., Kreher, B. W., Schnell, S., Glauche, V., Il'yasov, K. A., . . . van Elst, L. T. (2010). Reduced interhemispheric structural connectivity between anterior cingulate cortices in borderline personality disorder. *Psychiatry Research, 181*(2), 151–154.

Rüsch, N., van Elst, L. T., Ludaescher, P., Wilke, M., Huppertz, H. J., Thiel, T., . . . Ebert, D. (2003). A voxel-based morphometric MRI study in female patients with borderline personality disorder. *NeuroImage, 20*(1), 385–392.

Rüsch, N., Weber, M., Il'yasov, K. A., Lieb, K., Ebert, D., Hennig, J., & van Elst, L. T. (2007). Inferior frontal white matter microstructure and patterns of psychopathology in women with borderline personality disorder and comorbid attention-deficit hyperactivity disorder. *NeuroImage, 35*(2), 738–747.

Russ, M. J., Roth, S. D., Lerman, A., Kakuma, T., Harrison, K., Shindledecker, R. D., . . . Mattis, S. (1992). Pain perception in self-injurious patients with borderline personality disorder. *Biological Psychiatry, 32*(6), 501–511.

Sala, M., Caverzasi, E., Lazzaretti, M., Morandotti, N., De Vidovich, G., Marraffini, E., . . . Brambilla, P. (2011). Dorsolateral prefrontal cortex and hippocampus sustain impulsivity and aggressiveness in borderline personality disorder. *Journal of Affective Disorders, 131*(1-3), 417–421.

Salavert, J., Gasol, M., Vieta, E., Cervantes, A., Trampal, C., & Gispert, J. D. (2011). Fronto-limbic dysfunction in borderline personality disorder: A 18F-FDG positron emission tomography study. *Journal of Affective Disorders, 131*(1-3), 260–267.

Sanfey, A. G., Rilling, J. K., Aronson, J. A., Nystrom, L. E., & Cohen, J. D. (2003). The neural basis of economic decision-making in the Ultimatum Game. *Science, 300*(5626), 1755–1758.

Schmahl, C., Berne, K., Krause, A., Kleindienst, N., Valerius, G., Vermetten, E., & Bohus, M. (2009). Hippocampus and amygdala volumes in patients with borderline personality disorder with or without posttraumatic stress disorder. *Journal of Psychiatry and Neuroscience, 34*(4), 289–295.

Schmahl, C., Bohus, M., Esposito, F., Treede, R. D., Di Salle, F., Greffrath, W., . . . Seifritz, E. (2006). Neural correlates of antinociception in borderline personality disorder. *Archives of General Psychiatry, 63*(6), 659–667.

Schmahl, C., & Bremner, J. D. (2006). Neuroimaging in borderline personality disorder. *Journal of Psychiatric Research, 40*(5), 419–427.

Schmahl, C., Greffrath, W., Baumgartner, U., Schlereth, T., Magerl, W., Philipsen, A., . . . Treede, R. D. (2004). Differential nociceptive deficits in patients with borderline personality disorder and self-injurious behavior: Laser-evoked potentials, spatial discrimination of noxious stimuli, and pain ratings. *Pain, 110*(1–2), 470–479.

Schmahl, C., Meinzer, M., Zeuch, A., Fichter, M., Cebulla, M., Kleindienst, N., . . . Bohus, M. (2010). Pain sensitivity is reduced in borderline personality disorder, but not in posttraumatic stress disorder and bulimia nervosa. *World Journal of Biological Psychiatry, 11*(2 Pt 2), 364–371.

Schmahl, C. G., Elzinga, B. M., Vermetten, E., Sanislow, C., McGlashan, T. H., & Bremner, J. D. (2003). Neural correlates of memories of abandonment in women with and without borderline personality disorder. *Biological Psychiatry, 54*(2), 142–151.

Schmahl, C. G., Vermetten, E., Elzinga, B. M., & Bremner, J. D. (2003). Magnetic resonance imaging of hippocampal and amygdala volume in women with childhood abuse and borderline personality disorder. *Psychiatry Research, 122*(3), 193–198.

Schmahl, C. G., Vermetten, E., Elzinga, B. M., & Bremner, J. D. (2004). A positron emission tomography study of memories of childhood abuse in borderline personality disorder. *Biological Psychiatry, 55*(7), 759–765.

Schnell, K., & Herpertz, S. C. (2007). Effects of dialectic-behavioral-therapy on the neural correlates of affective hyperarousal in borderline personality disorder. *Journal of Psychiatric Research, 41*(10), 837–847.

Schoenbaum, G., Roesch, M. R., Stalnaker, T. A., & Takahashi, Y. K. (2009). A new perspective on the role of the orbitofrontal cortex in adaptive behaviour. *Nature Reviews Neuroscience, 10*(12), 885–892.

Schulze, L., Domes, G., Kruger, A., Berger, C., Fleischer, M., Prehn, K., . . . Herpertz, S. C. (2011). Neuronal correlates of cognitive reappraisal in borderline patients with affective instability. *Biological Psychiatry, 69*(6), 564–573.

Schulze, L., Schmahl, C., & Niedtfeld, I. (2016). Neural correlates of disturbed emotion processing in borderline personality disorder: A multimodal meta-analysis. *Biological Psychiatry, 79*(2), 97–106.

Sebastian, A., Jacob, G., Lieb, K., & Tuscher, O. (2013). Impulsivity in borderline personality disorder: A matter of disturbed impulse control or a facet of emotional dysregulation?. *Current Psychiatry Reports, 15*(2), 339.

Sebastian, A., Jung, P., Krause-Utz, A., Lieb, K., Schmahl, C., & Tüscher, O. (2014). Frontal dysfunctions of impulse control—a systematic review in borderline personality disorder and attention-deficit/hyperactivity disorder. *Frontiers in Human Neuroscience, 8*, 698. doi: 10.3389/fnhum.2014.00698

Shearer, S. L. (1994). Phenomenology of self-injury among inpatient women with borderline personality disorder. *Journal of Nervous and Mental Disease, 182*(9), 524–526.

Sierra, M., & Berrios, G. E. (1998). Depersonalization: Neurobiological perspectives. *Biological Psychiatry, 44*(9), 898–908.

Siever, L. J., Buchsbaum, M. S., New, A. S., Spiegel-Cohen, J., Wei, T., Hazlett, E. A., . . . Mitropoulou, V. (1999). d,l-fenfluramine response in impulsive personality disorder assessed with [18F]fluorodeoxyglucose positron emission tomography. *Neuropsychopharmacology, 20*(5), 413–423.

Silbersweig, D., Clarkin, J. F., Goldstein, M., Kernberg, O. F., Tuescher, O., Levy, K. N., . . . Stern, E. (2007). Failure of frontolimbic inhibitory function in the context of negative emotion in borderline personality disorder. *American Journal of Psychiatry, 164*(12), 1832–1841.

Skodol, A. E., Siever, L. J., Livesley, W. J., Gunderson, J. G., Pfohl, B., & Widiger, T. A. (2002). The borderline diagnosis II: Biology, genetics, and clinical course. *Biological Psychiatry, 51*(12), 951–963.

Soloff, P. (2003). Impulsivity, gender, and response to fenfluramine challenge in borderline personality disorder. *Psychiatry Research, 119*(1-2), 11–24.

Soloff, P., Nutche, J., Goradia, D., & Diwadkar, V. (2008). Structural brain abnormalities in borderline personality disorder: A voxel-based morphometry study. *Psychiatry Research, 164*(3), 223–236.

Soloff, P. H., Meltzer, C. C., Becker, C., Greer, P. J., & Constantine, D. (2005). Gender differences in a fenfluramine-activated FDG PET study of borderline personality disorder. *Psychiatry Research, 138*(3), 183–195.

Soloff, P. H., Meltzer, C. C., Becker, C., Greer, P. J., Kelly, T. M., & Constantine, D. (2003). Impulsivity and prefrontal hypometabolism in borderline personality disorder. *Psychiatry Research, 123*(3), 153–163.

Soloff, P. H., Meltzer, C. C., Greer, P. J., Constantine, D., & Kelly, T. M. (2000). A fenfluramine-activated FDG-PET study of borderline personality disorder. *Biological Psychiatry, 47*(6), 540–547.

Soloff, P. H., Price, J. C., Meltzer, C. C., Fabio, A., Frank, G. K., & Kaye, W. H. (2007). 5HT2A receptor binding is increased in borderline personality disorder. *Biological Psychiatry, 62*(6), 580–587.

Soloff, P. H., Pruitt, P., Sharma, M., Radwan, J., White, R., & Diwadkar, V. A. (2012). Structural brain abnormalities and suicidal behavior in borderline personality disorder. *Journal of Psychiatric Research, 46*(4), 516–525.

Staebler, K., Helbing, E., Rosenbach, C., & Renneberg, B. (2010). Rejection sensitivity and borderline personality disorder. *Clinical Psychology and Psychotherapy, 18*(4), 275–283.

Staebler, K., Renneberg, B., Stopsack, M., Fiedler, P., Weiler, M., & Roepke, S. (2011). Facial emotional expression in reaction to social exclusion in borderline personality disorder. *Psychological Medicine, 41*(9), 1929–1938.

Stein, M. B., Koverola, C., Hanna, C., Torchia, M. G., & McClarty, B. (1997). Hippocampal volume in women victimized by childhood sexual abuse. *Psychological Medicine, 27*(4), 951–959.

Stiglmayr, C. E., Ebner-Priemer, U. W., Bretz, J., Behm, R., Mohse, M., Lammers, C. H., . . . Bohus, M. (2008). Dissociative symptoms are positively related to stress in borderline personality disorder. *Acta Psychiatrica Scandinavica, 117*(2), 139–147.

Stiglmayr, C. E., Grathwol, T., Linehan, M. M., Ihorst, G., Fahrenberg, J., & Bohus, M. (2005). Aversive tension in patients with borderline personality disorder: A computer-based controlled field study. *Acta Psychiatrica Scandinavica, 111*(5), 372–379.

Tebartz van Elst, L., Hesslinger, B., Thiel, T., Geiger, E., Haegele, K., Lemieux, L., . . . Ebert, D. (2003). Frontolimbic brain abnormalities in patients with borderline personality disorder: A volumetric magnetic resonance imaging study. *Biological Psychiatry, 54*(2), 163–171.

Treede, R. -D., Apkarian, A. V., Bromm, B., Greenspan, J. D., & Lenz, F. A. (2000). Cortical representation of pain: Functional characterization of nociceptive areas near the lateral sulcus. *Pain, 87*(2), 113–119.

Vollm, B., Richardson, P., Stirling, J., Elliott, R., Dolan, M., Chaudhry, I., . . . Deakin, B. (2004). Neurobiological substrates of antisocial and borderline personality disorder: Preliminary results of a functional fMRI study. *Criminal Behavior and Mental Health, 14*(1), 39–54.

Vollm, B. A., Zhao, L., Richardson, P., Clark, L., Deakin, J. F., Williams, S., & Dolan, M. C. (2009). A voxel-based morphometric MRI study in men with borderline personality disorder: Preliminary findings. *Criminal Behavior and Mental Health, 19*(1), 64–72.

Welch, S. S., Linehan, M. M., Sylvers, P., Chittams, J., & Rizvi, S. L. (2008). Emotional responses to self-injury imagery among adults with borderline personality disorder. *Journal of Consulting and Clinical Psychology, 76*(1), 45–51.

Whittle, S., Chanen, A. M., Fornito, A., McGorry, P. D., Pantelis, C., & Yucel, M. (2009). Anterior cingulate volume in adolescents with first-presentation borderline personality disorder. *Psychiatry Research, 172*(2), 155–160.

Wilson, S. T., Stanley, B., Brent, D. A., Oquendo, M. A., Huang, Y. Y., Haghighi, F., . . . Mann, J. J. (2012). Interaction between tryptophan hydroxylase I polymorphisms and childhood abuse is associated with increased risk for borderline personality disorder in adulthood. *Psychiatric Genetics, 22*(1), 15–24.

Wingenfeld, K., Spitzer, C., Rullkötter, N., & Löwe, B. (2010). Borderline personality disorder: Hypothalamus pituitary adrenal axis and findings from neuroimaging studies. *Psychoneuroendocrinology, 35*(1), 154–170.

Wingenfeld, K., & Wolf, O. T. (2014). Effects of cortisol on cognition in major depressive disorder, posttraumatic stress disorder and borderline personality disorder. *Psychoneuroendocrinology, 51C*, 282–295.

Winter, D., Krause-Utz, A., Lis, S., Chiu, C. D., Lanius, R., Schriner, F., . . . Schmahl, C. (2015). Dissociation in borderline personality disorder: Disturbed cognitive and emotional inhibition and its neural correlates. *Psychiatry Research, 233*(3), 339–351.

Wolf, E. J., Lunney, C. A., Miller, M. W., Resick, P. A., Friedman, M. J., & Schnurr, P. P. (2012). The dissociative subtype of PTSD: A replication and extension. *Depression and Anxiety, 29*(8), 679–688.

Wolf, R. C., Sambataro, F., Vasic, N., Schmid, M., Thomann, P. A., Bienentreu, S. D., & Wolf, N. D. (2011). Aberrant connectivity of resting-state networks in borderline personality disorder. *Journal of Psychiatry & Neuroscience, 36*(2), 100150.

Woon, F. L., & Hedges, D. W. (2009). Amygdala volume in adults with posttraumatic stress disorder: A meta-analysis. *Journal of Neuropsychiatry and Clinical Neuroscience, 21*(1), 5–12.

Yanowitch, R., & Coccaro, E. F. (2011). The neurochemistry of human aggression. *Advances in Genetics, 75*, 151–169.

Zetzsche, T., Frodl, T., Preuss, U. W., Schmitt, G., Seifert, D., Leinsinger, G., . . . Meisenzahl, E. M. (2006). Amygdala volume and depressive symptoms in patients with borderline personality disorder. *Biological Psychiatry, 60*(3), 302–310.

/// 7 /// Genetic Influences on Borderline Personality Disorder

MARIJN A. DISTEL
AND MARLEEN H. M. DE MOOR

INTRODUCTION

Many behavioral traits and mental disorders "run in families." This also holds for borderline personality disorder (BPD). In first-degree relatives of BPD patients, increased rates of BPD and BPD-related traits are found (Gunderson et al., 2011). The familial resemblance observed for a trait or disorder can represent environmental influences that are shared within a family ("nurture"), or they can represent genetic influences ("nature"). Twin studies can separate genetic sources of resemblance from environmental sources of resemblance between relatives by making use of the different genetic relatedness between monozygotic (MZ) and dizygotic (DZ) twins. If genes are important for a trait, there will be a correlation between phenotypic and genetic resemblance. For example, the chance that both MZ twins have a disorder is larger than in DZ twin pairs. Similarly, the chance that both relatives have a disorder is larger for first-degree relatives as compared to second-degree relatives. We have known for some time now that genes influence most if not all behavioral traits and disorders. Moreover, genes and environment often do not act independently. Although in recent years an increasing number of studies have been published on the etiology of BPD, genetic studies of BPD remain relatively scarce when compared to the number of studies of other disorders in psychiatric genetics such as depression and schizophrenia. This chapter will describe how genetic and environmental effects on complex traits can be studied and how these studies have informed us on the etiology of BPD.

THE CLASSICAL TWIN DESIGN EXPLAINED

Twin studies can directly decompose familial resemblance into genetic and shared environmental influences by comparing the resemblance in a trait or disorder of interest between MZ and DZ twins. When twins are reared together, they share part of their environment and this sharing of the family environment is (assumed to be) the same for MZ and DZ twins. The important difference between MZ and DZ twins is that the former share (close to) all of their genotypes, whereas the latter share on average only half of the genotypes segregating in that family. This distinction is the basis of the classical twin study. If the resemblance in a trait within MZ pairs is larger than in DZ pairs, this suggests that genetic factors influence the trait. If the resemblance in a trait is as large in DZ twins as it is in MZ twins, this points to shared environmental factors as the cause of family resemblance (Boomsma, Busjahn, & Peltonen, 2002).

When studying genetic and environmental influences on a trait, four possible components contribute to the total trait variance: additive genetic factors (A), dominant genetic factors (D), shared environmental factors (C), and unique environmental factors (E). A, D, and C factors, if present for the trait of interest, cause twin resemblance, whereas the extent to which twins do not resemble each other is ascribed to the E factors. These include all unique experiences that have been gained throughout life, like the experience of negative life events; differential treatment by the parents during childhood; the influence of friends or peers who are not shared with the co-twin; or, for example, different job experiences, lifestyle habits, and diseases. In the classical twin design, we can only estimate three components of variance at the same time (A, C, and E, or A, D, and E), and we have to assume that these factors are uncorrelated and do not interact with each other. If one wishes to estimate more than three variance components at the same time or allow for specific forms of gene–environment correlation or interaction, a solution is to add relatives of twins to the design, such as parents or offspring (Keller et al., 2009).

Twin researchers typically use structural equation modeling (SEM) to formally estimate the relative contribution of A, D/C, and E to the individual differences in the trait. In SEM, a path model is drawn that specifies the relationships between several latent unobserved variables (e.g., the genetic and environmental factors) and observed variables (e.g., the phenotypes in twin 1 and twin 2). An example is depicted in Figure 7.1, where BPD features have been measured in MZ and DZ twin pairs. In Figure 7.1, the genetic and environmental variables (A, C or D, and E) have a causal influence on the phenotypes as measured in a twin and his or her co-twin. In addition, the latent A and C/D factors are allowed to be correlated across the twins within pairs. The correlation between A factors in MZ pairs is 1 because they share all their genetic material, and it is 0.5 in DZ pairs because they share on average half of their segregating material. The correlation between C factors in both types of twin pairs is 1 because twin pairs, by definition, share all of their shared environmental factors. The correlation between D factors is 1 in MZ pairs and 0.25 in DZ

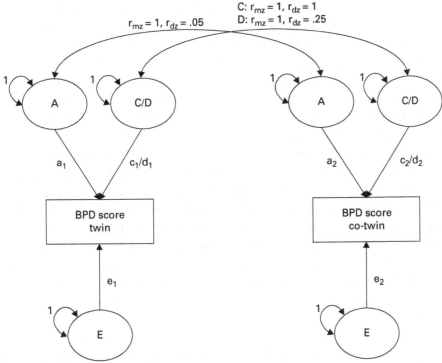

FIGURE 7.1 Path model of the classical twin model for borderline personality disorder (BPD) features. A, additive genetic factors; C, common environmental factors; D, dominant genetic factors; E, unique environmental factors. Pathloadings (a, c/d, and e) are estimated to calculate the relative influence of A, C/D, and E. Either A, C, and E or A, D, and E can be modeled with twin data.

pairs. Based on this path model, it is then possible to specify the expected variance-covariance matrix implied by the model by using matrix algebra. Please note that if the phenotype of interest is a binary rather than continuous variable, such as a BPD diagnosis, a threshold model can be used. For an introduction to the matrix algebra used in SEM see, for example, Plomin et al. (1977).

HERITABILITY OF BORDERLINE PERSONALITY DISORDER

The many twin registries worldwide provide a valuable resource for studies into the genetic and environmental influences on individual differences in traits or disorders (for a selection of worldwide twin registries and their characteristics, see the special issue of *Twin Research and Human Genetics*, February 2013). Several twin registries assessed the presence of BPD, BPD features, and/or related traits in the registered twins and their family members. In clinical practice, BPD is assessed using a structured clinical interview based on the presence of the criteria for BPD as described in the *Diagnostic and Statistical Manual for Mental Disorders* (DSM-IV-R; American Psychiatric Association [APA], 2000). In this categorical classification system, one either has BPD or does not.

For research purposes, this assessment method usually leads to a prevalence rate that is too low to reliably analyze the data categorically. A dimensional representation based on subclinical criteria is often used to assess BPD symptoms in twin studies. Dimensional or quantitative scales provide information about the degree to which symptoms of a disorder are present instead of a sole statement about whether the disorder is present or not. A practical alternative to psychiatric interviews is the use of self-report questionnaires, given that features assessed in the questionnaires have predictive value for the disorder under study (Hopwood et al., 2008).

The first large-scale studies on the heritability of BPD were published in 2008 by study groups from the Netherlands Twin Registry, the East Flanders Prospective Twin Survey, the Australian Twin Registry, and the Norwegian Twin Registry (Distel, Trull et al., 2008; Torgersen et al., 2008). The twin study of Distel et al. was based on questionnaire data (PAI-BOR) from the Netherlands, Belgium, and Australia. Correlations for MZ and DZ male, female, and opposite-sex twin pairs for these three countries are shown in the first columns of Table 7.1. For all three countries, the twin correlations for MZ males and MZ females were not significantly different, as were the twin correlations for DZ males, DZ females, and DZ opposite-sex twins. This indicates that there is no sex difference in the heritability of BPD features and that the same genes influence BPD features in males and females. Torgersen et al. (2008) assessed BPD by a structured clinical interview and analyzed the count of subclinical criteria. MZ and DZ twin correlations are shown in the last column of Table 7.1.

TABLE 7.1 Correlations for monozygotic and dizygotic male, female, and opposite sex twin pairs *(number of twins)*

	The Netherlands	Belgium	Australia	Norway
Monozygotic males	0.46 (*n* = 937)	0.48 (*n* = 281)	0.28 (*n* = 236)	–
Monozygotic females	0.42 (*n* = 2636)	0.43 (*n* = 557)	0.49 (*n* = 363)	–
Dizygotic males	0.27 (*n* = 459)	0.19 (*n* = 97)	0.12 (*n* = 134)	–
Dizygotic females	0.11 (*n* = 1,227)	0.12 (*n* = 231)	0.32 (*n* = 204)	–
Dizygotic opposite sex	0.24 (*n* = 1,193)	0.12 (*n* = 358)	0.16 (*n* = 287)	–
Monozygotic	0.43 (*n* = 3,573)	0.45 (*n* = 838)	0.43 (*n* = 599)	0.34 (*n* = 1,338)
Dizygotic	0.19 (*n* = 2,879)	0.13 (*n* = 686)	0.22 (*n* = 625)	0.18 (*n* = 1,434)

As published in Distel, Trull et al. (2008) and Torgersen et al. (2008).

The heritability estimates were 45% for BPD features in the Dutch, Belgian, and Australian samples and 35% for BPD symptom count in the Norwegian study. There is no evidence that shared environmental factors play a role. Thus, in addition to additive genetic factors influencing variation in BPD features, the remainder of the variance can be explained by individual specific environmental factors.

Livesley (2006) proposed a dimensional model of personality pathology in which personality disorders, including BPD, are not assessed as categorical outcomes (diagnosis yes/no) but that rather distinguishes four higher order factors (emotional dysregulation, dissocial behavior, inhibitedness, compulsivity) and 18 lower order factors. This trait model of personality pathology is operationalized through a self-report questionnaire, the Dimensional Assessment of Personality Pathology – Basic Questionnaire (DAPP-BQ; Livesley, 2006). According to Livesley, the emotional dysregulation factor and its lower order traits resemble, but are broader than, the diagnostic construct of BPD. The heritability for emotional dysregulation has been reported at 53% and, for the lower order traits making up emotional dysregulation, at 44–53% (Jang, Livesley, Vernon, & Jackson, 1996; Livesley, Jang, & Vernon, 1998). These heritability estimates are highly similar to the estimates found for BPD features and symptom counts. This means that approximately half of the variance in BPD seem to be inherited or "genetic."

THE EXTENDED TWIN FAMILY DESIGN: BEYOND HERITABILITY

Twin studies showed that BPD symptom counts and BPD features are moderately heritable. This is an important first step. However, by adding data from siblings, spouses, and parents of twins to the classical twin design some important additional research questions can be answered that go beyond the simple question of whether BPD is heritable.

Adding siblings and parents of twins to the classical twin design considerably increases the power to detect dominant genetic effects. MZ twins are perfectly correlated for all nonadditive genetic effects. DZ twins and siblings share on average one-quarter of the dominant genetic effects. In contrast, whereas the correlation for additive genetic effects in parents and offspring is 0.5, parents and offspring are not correlated for dominant genetic effects. Therefore, if dominance is of importance, the correlation between parents and offspring is expected to be lower than the correlations among DZ twins and siblings. Only one study (Distel, Rebollo-Mesa et al., 2009) investigated the influence of dominant genetic factors in an extended twin family design for BPD. Familial resemblances (Pearson correlations) for pairs of family members in this study with different degrees of genetic relatedness are depicted in Figure 7.2. As can be seen in this figure, the DZ correlations are less than half of the MZ correlations, and the parent–offspring correlations are in turn less than the DZ–sibling correlations. This pattern of correlations suggests that dominant genetic influences are at play. Structural equation modeling confirmed this and found that genetic effects on BPD features were additive (21%) as well as dominant (24%).

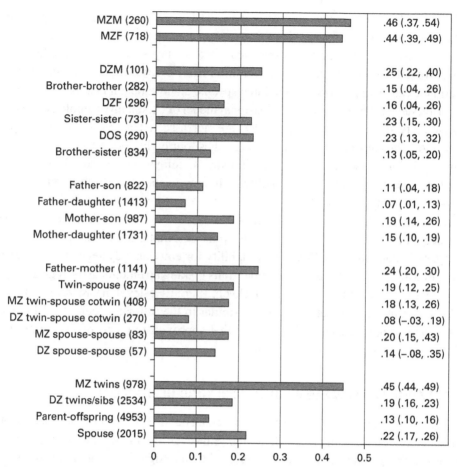

FIGURE 7.2 Correlations for borderline personality disorder (BPD) features between family members of different degrees of relatedness (number of pairs) and 95% confidence intervals. The bottom four bars represent correlations independent of sex or generation. (From Distel et al., 2009a.)

Adding parents to the model also showed that resemblance between parents and their adult offspring in BPD features can be completely explained by the transmission of genes. The influence of parents through the environment (vertical cultural transmission) independent of the genetic transmission did not contribute to the resemblance between parents and their children. In other words, there is no nongenetic influence of parents' BPD features on their adult children.

Assortative mating is the process of nonrandom mating in which individuals select a spouse with specific observable characteristics. For genetic research, it is important to know whether there is nonrandom mating for a trait. If individuals tend to select their spouse based on the spouse's heritable phenotype, this will lead to increased genetic resemblance between family members and thereby may lead to increased heritability estimates. Children of individuals at increased genetic risk for developing BPD who marry someone who is also at increased risk will be more likely to receive risk alleles from both parents rather than from just one parent. The children will therefore be more likely to resemble each other for BPD features (Heath & Eaves, 1985).

Spouse similarity for BPD features is depicted in Figure 7.2. The correlation between the borderline score of an MZ twin and their co-twin's spouse was higher than the correlation between the borderline score of a DZ twin and their co-twin's spouse, suggesting the existence of phenotypic assortative mating for BPD traits. Distel, Rebollo-Mesa et al. (2009) took phenotypic assortment into account in their model and showed that it had only a very small effect on the heritability of BPD (1% of the genetic variance was due to the effects of phenotypic assortment).

COMORBIDITY WITH AXIS I AND II DISORDERS

BPD and Axis I and II disorders are highly comorbid. Individuals with BPD are likely to have a co-occurring mental disorder such as major depression, bipolar I and II disorder, attention deficit hyperactivity disorder (ADHD), anxiety disorders, substance use disorders, and other personality disorders (Ferrer et al., 2010; Tomko et al., 2014). Tomko et al. (2013) reported lifetime comorbidity rates of around 80% for an anxiety disorder, mood disorder, and substance use disorders. Twin and twin family studies have established the heritability of all comorbid disorders. Twin family data can also be used to study the shared etiology between traits. Instead of decomposing the variance of a single trait, the covariance (comorbidity) between two traits can be decomposed into parts that are due to genetic and environmental factors.

Multivariate genetic analysis of all cluster B personality disorders (histrionic, borderline, antisocial, and narcissistic personality disorders) showed that BPD shares almost all of its genetic risk factors with the other cluster B personality disorders. BPD was genetically most closely related to antisocial personality disorder (Torgersen et al., 2008). Multivariate analysis of all the 10 DSM-IV personality disorders showed that they were influenced by three genetic factors. The first genetic factor influenced borderline, paranoid, narcissistic, histrionic, dependent, and obsessive-compulsive personality disorders, reflecting a general vulnerability to personality pathology and/or neuroticism. The second factor had substantial loadings on borderline and antisocial personality disorders, reflecting high impulsivity and low agreeableness and conscientiousness. The third factor had substantial loadings on schizoid and avoidant personality disorders reflecting introversion. The heritability of BPD can be explained 28%, 50%, and 7% by the first, second, and third factor, respectively. The remaining 15% can be explained by a BPD-specific genetic factor. The genetic structure found in this study is inconsistent with the cluster A, B, and C typology for personality disorders as published in the DSM-IV and retained in DSM-5. In the structure of environmental risk factors, however, the cluster A, B, and C typology is well reflected, suggesting that it is due to the environmental risk factors that personality disorders within a cluster tend to co-occur (Kendler et al., 2008).

The association between BPD and Axis I disorders has primarily been investigated at the phenotypic level. At the genetic level, the association has been investigated for BPD and adult ADHD, major depressive disorder (MDD), and substance use (Bornovalova, Hicks, Iacono, & McGue, 2013; Distel, Carlier et al., 2011; Distel et al., 2012; Reichborn-Kjennerud et al., 2010). Distel et al. (Distel, Carlier et al., 2011) performed a genetic analysis to determine the extent to which genetic and environmental risk factors influence the covariation between BPD features and ADHD symptoms (see Figure 7.3) and found that 49% of the phenotypic correlation could be explained by A and 51% by E. This suggests that ADHD symptoms in individuals with BPD emerge in substantial part from the same set of inherited characteristics.

Substantial overlap of genetic risk factors has also been found for a dimensional measure of BPD and MDD. Although the genetic correlation was highest between BPD and MDD (r_g = .56), there was also an overlap in genetic risk factors between MDD and the other DSM-IV personality disorders (Reichborn-Kjennerud et al., 2010). The origin of the association between BPD and substance use measures seems to be dependent on the substance under study. In a sample of twins aged between 21 and 50 years, the correlation with BPD features could be explained by genetic factors for ever-use of cannabis and regular smoking, whereas for high alcohol consumption, the correlation with BPD features was explained by unique environmental

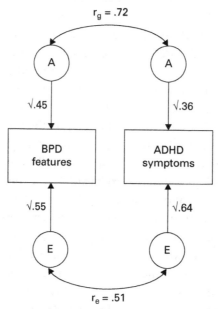

FIGURE 7.3 Graphical representation of the results of the best-fitting bivariate genetic model for borderline personality disorder (BPD) features and attention deficit hyperactivity disorder (ADHD) symptoms. (From Distel et al., 2011a). A, additive genetic factor; E, unique environmental factor. Path coefficients represent the percentage of explained variance in BPD features and ADHD symptoms. r_g, genetic correlation; r_e, environmental correlation.

factors (Distel et al., 2012). In a sample of female twins aged 14–18, the association between BPD features and a composite measure of substance use (cannabis, tobacco, and alcohol use) was explained by shared environmental factors at age 14 and by genetic factors at age 18 (Bornovalova, Hicks, Iacono, & McGue, 2013).

NORMAL PERSONALITY TRAITS AND BORDERLINE PERSONALITY DISORDER

In recent years, the nature of the relationship between normal personality traits and personality disorders has received extensive attention. The fourth version of the DSM (DSM-IV-R; APA, 2000) describes nine criteria for BPD, of which at least five out of nine must be present for a BPD diagnosis to be made. In this categorical classification system, one receives the BPD diagnosis or not. Normal personality traits are assessed on a quantitative scale. In this dimensional representation, the degree to which a personality trait is present is assessed. Figure 7.4 shows a graphical representation of both conceptualizations. Several studies showed that dimensional measures of personality traits correlate with personality disorders (Samuel & Widiger, 2008). Consequently, it has been suggested that personality disorders might represent the extreme ends of normal personality traits (Trull, Widiger, Lynam, & Costa, 2003). The association between BPD and the personality traits from the Five-Factor Model (FFM; i.e., neuroticism, extraversion, openness to experience, agreeableness, and conscientiousness) has been explored at the phenotypic as well as at the genetic level. At the phenotypic level, the DSM diagnosis of BPD can be meaningfully clinically translated into a profile of FFM personality traits. Individuals with BPD tend to score high on all facets of the neuroticism domain (anxiousness, angry hostility, depressiveness, self-consciousness, impulsiveness, vulnerability); low on the extraversion facets of warmth and positive emotions; low on the agreeableness facets of trust, straightforwardness, and compliance; and low on the conscientiousness

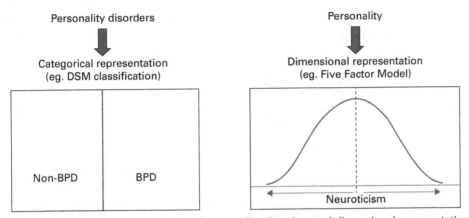

FIGURE 7.4 Categorical representation of personality disorders and dimensional representation of personality traits.

facets of competence, dutifulness, self-discipline, and deliberation (Samuel & Widiger, 2008).

Multivariate twin studies can be conducted to explore whether genetic and environmental influences on "normal" personality traits also play a role in maladaptive personality traits and personality disorders. Jang and Livesley (1999) found substantial genetic correlations between most of the emotional dysregulation factors of the DAPP-BQ and neuroticism, agreeableness, and conscientiousness. Correlations between environmental influences were lower but showed a similar pattern.

Research into the nature of the association between normal personality traits and borderline personality features showed that all genetic variation in borderline personality features was shared with genetic variation in the personality traits of the FFM. Environmental influences on variation in borderline personality features, however, were for a large part specific to borderline personality features. One of the hypotheses is that these environmental influences discriminate between individuals who score high on normal personality traits (e.g., neuroticism) but do not fulfil criteria for a clinical diagnosis, and individuals who do fulfil criteria for a clinical diagnosis.

GENE-FINDING FOR BORDERLINE PERSONALITY DISORDER

It is well-established that genetic factors influence variation in BPD and associated traits, but which genes play a role? Three types of gene-finding studies—genome-wide linkage studies, candidate gene association studies, and genome-wide association (GWA) studies—have been conducted for BPD.

Through linkage analysis, the location of genes involved can be detected. Genetic linkage is the phenomenon that alleles at loci close together on the genome tend to be inherited together because the chance of a recombination event for two loci close together is very small (Ferreira, 2004). Therefore, these close loci are said to be "linked." Genetic linkage studies make use of this fact by studying the degree to which a marker travels together with a trait or disease within families. For example, in pairs of siblings, it can be tested whether an increased sharing of a marker identical-by-descent (IBD) predicts concordance, or resemblance, for the trait under study. To date, only one linkage study has been conducted to identify the genomic region(s) that may contain the quantitative trait loci (QTLs) that influence the manifestation of BPD features. Distel, Hottenga et al. (2008) carried out a linkage study showing suggestive linkage on chromosomes 1q31.1, 4p16.1, and 18q23. Significant genome-wide evidence for linkage was found on chromosome 9p24.1. To determine the importance of chromosomes 1, 4, 9, and 18 in the development of BPD, it is essential that the results are replicated in other samples and that fine-mapping and association studies in these regions are conducted to identify the actual genetic variants.

Candidate-gene association studies assess genetic variants in specific hypothesis-driven candidate genes and can also be performed at the population level instead of at the family level. Case-control studies are the most commonly used type of association studies. Case-control studies compare allele frequencies between a group of unrelated affected individuals (e.g., BPD patients) and a group of unrelated controls. Most candidate genes are functional genes that have biological consequences that are hypothesized to be related to the trait, disorder, or disease. They can be suggested by linkage studies if interesting genes are located under a linkage peak, by animal models for behaviors hypothesized to be linked to the disorder in humans, or by pharmacological studies, or they can be based on theoretical models. Several association studies have been conducted to identify the genetic variants that influence BPD and associated traits. The main focus in these studies has been on genes influencing serotonin dysfunction, dopamine dysfunction, and monoamine oxidase-A (MAOA) deficiency.

Several studies found associations between genes involved in the serotonergic system and BPD. Ni et al. (2006) found an association between a haplotype containing the short allele of the serotonin transporter gene (5-HTT) and BPD, but results were not replicated (Pascual et al., 2008). Wilson et al. (2009) reported an association between BPD and polymorphisms in the tryptophan hydroxylase 1 gene (TPH1). A recent meta-analyses for three serotonergic polymorphisms showed no association (Calati, Gressier, Balestri, & Serretti, 2013). In addition to serotonergic dysfunction, there is some evidence that dopamine dysfunction may be associated with BPD. Dopamine dysfunction is associated with emotional dysregulation, impulsivity, and cognitive-perceptual impairment (for a review, see Friedel, 2004), three important dimensions of BPD. Joyce et al. (2006) found a significant replicated association between the 9-repeat allele of dopamine transporter 1 (DAT1) and BPD in depressed patients. Finally, genes involved in the production of MAOA are suggested to be involved in BPD because it is shown to be associated with impulsive aggression and emotion regulation (Buckholtz & Meyer-Lindenberg, 2008). To test whether MAOA is also associated with the BPD diagnosis, Ni et al. (2007) genotyped two MAOA polymorphisms (promoter VNTR and rs6323) in a group of BPD patients and a group of control subjects. A high frequency of the high activity VNTR alleles and a low frequency of the low activity haplotype were found in BPD patients, suggesting that the high-activity allelic variant may play a role in the etiological development of BPD. Although the studies just described found associations between serotonin dysfunction, dopamine dysfunction, and MAOA deficiency and BPD or related traits, the results could not always be replicated. This suggests that, as is true for most mental disorders, the development of BPD is most likely influenced by many genes with small effects. GWA studies can be conducted to test the polygenic hypothesis of BPD, but only one has been conducted so far. GWA analysis is a method to identify the variations that occur more frequently in people with a particular disorder than in people without the disorder. To detect small effects of genes, extremely large sample sizes are needed, often obtained through meta-analysis by combining the results from many samples. Recently, the first GWA study has been conducted in two Dutch samples ($N = 7,125$) that showed a promising signal in a region on chromosome 5. This result was replicated in an independent third sample ($N = 1,301$) (Lubke et al., 2014).

THE INTERPLAY OF GENES AND ENVIRONMENT

Both genes and environment contribute to the risk of developing BPD, as is true for most psychiatric disorders. The heritability is moderate, and there is a strong relationship between having experienced (one or more) traumatic life events and (the severity of) BPD symptoms. Until now, we assumed that the effects of genes and environment act independently. However, the influence of genes and environment are often interrelated. Parents with an alcohol use disorder may create a family environment in which alcohol is easily available for their children; in addition, they pass on the genes that make them more vulnerable to the development of an alcohol use disorder. Individuals with an inherited impulsive temperament will have more conflicts with others than individuals with a less impulsive temperament. Sensation-seeking individuals will create environments that give them exciting experiences. These examples illustrate the processes of passive, evocative, and active genotype–environment correlation (rGE), respectively. rGE thus refers to the role of genetics in exposure to environments. For BPD, there is evidence for correlated genetic factors with certain stressful life events such as divorce, job loss, and violent assault (Distel, Middeldorp et al., 2011). Genes that are responsible for BPD thus increase the risk of exposure to stressful life events. In addition, genes and environment may interact with each other (gene–environment interaction; G × E). The sensitivity to environmental influences depends on the genetic vulnerability of an individual (Kendler & Eaves, 1986). Carpenter et al. (Carpenter, Tomko, Trull, & Boomsma, 2013) reviewed the literature available on G × E for BPD and domains relevant to BPD. Only three studies are available on G × E for BPD.

Distel, Middeldorp et al. (2011) examined the interactions of environmental influences with latent genetic effects (e.g., the accumulated effect of many genetic variants) and found that having experienced a sexual assault negatively moderated the effect of genetic factors. This strong negative moderating effect made the effect of genes negligible. This might suggest that sexual assault has such a large effect that even in less genetically vulnerable individuals it is associated with more BPD features. However, since there is evidence for rGE as well, the presence of G × E needs further attention before definite conclusions can be drawn.

Wilson et al. (2012) examined whether the association between childhood abuse and BPD in adults was moderated by a specific measured gene, tryptophan hydroxylase I (TPH1). The TPH1 polymorphisms significantly increased the strength of the association between childhood abuse and the risk for developing BPD in later life.

Bornovalova, Huibregtse, Hicks, Keyes, McGue, & Iacono (2013) investigated rGE and G × E as alternative explanations for the often-made assumption that childhood abuse has a causal effect on BPD. More specifically, they investigated whether the interaction between symptoms of childhood internalizing (INT) and externalizing (EXT) disorders, serving as a genetic vulnerability, and childhood abuse (CA; emotional, physical, and/or sexual abuse before age 18), serving as an environmental risk factor, produces BPD traits (at age 24). No evidence was found for any interaction (CA×INT, CA×EXT, CA×INT-EXT [combined childhood INT and EXT psychopathology]). CA does not have an especially strong effect on BPD traits in those with an INT or EXT vulnerability. Bivariate genetic modeling showed that the association between CA and BPD traits can be explained by genetic factors, which can be interpreted as *r*GE (genes for BPD are correlated with CA). In some cases, the genetic factors also overlapped with symptoms of INT and EXT disorders. In conclusion, the interplay between genes and environment most likely plays out through *r*GE. The genes that account for the genetic overlap remain unknown.

CONCLUSION

Several twin- and family studies showed that BPD is heritable, with some evidence that nonadditive genetic influences account for part of the genetic variance. Genetic and environmental influences do not always act independently of each other. Some environmental influences have a direct effect on vulnerability to BPD, whereas others interact with or are correlated with genetic or environmental influences. Consistent with most other Axis I and II psychiatric disorders (Kendler et al., 2008; Shea et al., 2004) and normal personality traits (Keller, Coventry, Heath, & Martin, 2005), shared environmental factors do not seem to contribute to the etiology of BPD in adults. The co-occurrence with other Axis I and II disorders that is often reported for BPD is partly due to genetic associations. Individuals with BPD tend to have a personality structure characterized by high scores on neuroticism and low scores on conscientiousness and agreeableness. This phenotypic association is also present at the genetic level. There is some evidence for the presence of *r*GE and G × E, but results have not yet been replicated. Candidate gene-finding studies for BPD suggest the possible role of genes in the serotonergic and dopaminergic systems; however, more large genome-wide studies need to confirm these associations.

Future Directions

The knowledge summarized here about the genetic influence on BPD has resulted in several directions for future research. First, what does it mean that genetic correlations have been found for BPD and several Axis I and II disorders? The correlation between two sets of genes can reflect genetic "pleiotropy," implying that a single gene has an effect on multiple traits or disorders through (partly) different biological mechanisms. However, an important alternative explanation is that the two traits or disorders are causally related. Does a genetic predisposition toward BPD increase the risk of developing ADHD, or does ADHD increase the risk of developing BPD? A combination of cross-sectional and longitudinal research designs using genetically informative data can be applied to test for causality and, more importantly, whether this causal association is independent of a genetic association (De Moor, Boomsma, Stubbe, Willemsen, & De Geus, 2008).

Second, the effect of environmental factors is not simply additive to the effect of genetic factors on BPD. Genetic influences on BPD are correlated with and moderated by experiencing certain life events. Results of early studies on this topic, however, need to be replicated. Well-designed studies are needed to reliably characterize $G \times E$ effects. Large samples, and possibly even meta-analytic approaches using several samples, are necessary, and the measurement of environmental influences needs to be improved.

Third, future genetic research will aim to further identifying the genes that influence BPD. Genes influencing the serotonergic and dopaminergic systems have been important candidate genes for BPD, but the results could not always be replicated and have not led to identification of one main biological mechanism behind BPD. This suggests that, as is true for most mental disorders, BPD should be considered among the complex traits. It is likely that a large number of genes, all with minor effects, account for the heritability of BPD. To detect such small effects, large numbers of genetic variants across the whole genome need to be examined in large samples. Since the genetic architecture of BPD is similar across cultures, datasets from different countries can readily be combined for these analyses. Another strategy that can be applied for BPD is to test for the accumulated association of genetic variants in gene groups. The hypotheses is that most genes do not operate independently but rather in functional networks that influence biological mechanisms. Evidence for this hypothesis is found in a study that showed that a group of synaptic genes was significantly associated with the risk of schizophrenia (Lips et al., 2012).

Knowledge about the biological basis of BPD and its interaction and correlation with environmental influences holds several implications for the prevention and treatment of BPD.

First, many patients and their family members struggle with feelings of guilt and blame regarding the causes of the disorder. In addition, fear of recurrence in at-risk family members and offspring is often present. Giving the patient and his or her family insight into the etiology of BPD will increase the feeling of control over the illness, which may improve quality of life (Jorm & Griffiths, 2008). Second, a specific profile of scores on the FFM personality traits can be taken as an etiological precursor or a risk factor to develop BPD. By identifying these profiles, more effective prevention and treatment programs can be started. For example, one might suggest that young adults in clinical practice who display a pattern of high neuroticism, low agreeableness, and low conscientiousness should be assigned to interventions that target emotion regulation skills. Also, these individuals who are biologically at risk should be advised and helped to avoid high-risk environments to decrease the risk of developing BPD. Third, the genetic correlation between BPD features and several environmental factors emphasizes the importance of paying attention to relationship problems, anger control, and functioning at work during treatment because the genes that influence BPD features increase the risk of experiencing a divorce/break-up, violent assault, or job loss. Also, exposure to these life events increases the number of BPD features, stressing the importance of preventing these life events even more. Finally, knowledge about genes or gene networks that influence BPD will provide information on the biological processes that are influenced by these genes, which makes it possible to optimize treatment with medication in the future.

REFERENCES

American Psychiatric Association (APA). (2000). *Diagnostic and statistical manual of mental disorders* (4th ed., text rev.). Washington, DC: Author.

Boomsma, D. I., Busjahn, A., & Peltonen, L. (2002). Classical twin studies and beyond. *Nature Reviews Genetics, 3*, 872–882.

Bornovalova, M. A., Hicks, B. M., Iacono, W. G., & McGue, M. (2013). Longitudinal twin study of borderline personality disorder traits and substance use in adolescence: Developmental change, reciprocal effects, and genetic and environmental influences. *Personality Disorders, 4*, 23–32.

Bornovalova, M. A., Huibregtse, B. M., Hicks, B. M., Keyes, M., McGue, M., & Iacono, W. (2013). Tests of a direct effect of childhood abuse on adult borderline personality disorder traits: A longitudinal discordant twin design. *Journal of Abnormal Psychology, 122*, 180–194.

Buckholtz, J. W., & Meyer-Lindenberg, A. (2008). MAOA and the neurogenetic architecture of human aggression. *Trends in Neurosciences, 31*, 120–129.

Calati, R., Gressier, F., Balestri, M., & Serretti, A. (2013). Genetic modulation of borderline personality disorder: Systematic review and meta-analysis. *Journal of Psychiatric Research, 47*(10), 1275–1287.

Carpenter, R. W., Tomko, R. L., Trull, T. J., & Boomsma, D. I. (2013). Gene-environment studies and borderline personality disorder: A review. *Current Psychiatry Reports, 15*, 336.

Distel, M. A., Carlier, A., Middeldorp, C. M., Derom, C. A., Lubke, G. H., & Boomsma, D. I. (2011). Borderline personality traits and adult attention-deficit hyperactivity disorder symptoms: A genetic analysis of comorbidity. *American Journal of Medical Genetics Part B: Neuropsychiatric Genetics, 156*, 817–825.

Distel, M. A., Hottenga, J. J., Trull, T. J., & Boomsma, D. I. (2008). Chromosome 9: Linkage for borderline personality disorder features. *Psychiatric Genetics, 18*, 302–307.

Distel, M. A., Middeldorp, C. M., Trull, T. J., Derom, C. A., Willemsen, G., & Boomsma D. I. (2011). Life events and borderline personality: Gene-environment correlation or gene-environment interaction? *Psychological Medicine, 41*, 849–860.

Distel, M. A., Rebollo-Mesa, I., Willemsen, G., Derom, C. A., Trull, T. J., Martin, N. G., & Boomsma, D. I. (2009). Familial resemblance of borderline personality disorder features: Genetic or cultural transmission? *PloS ONE, 4*, e5334. doi:10.1371/ journal.pone.0005334

Distel, M. A., Trull, T. J., de Moor, M. H. M., Vink, J. M., Geels, L. M., van Beek, J. H. D. A.,. . . Boomsma, D. I. (2012). Borderline personality traits and substance use: Genetic factors underlie the association with marijuana initiation and smoking, but not with alcohol use. *Journal of Personality Disorders, 26*, 867–879.

Distel, M. A., Trull, T. J., Derom, C. A., Thiery, E. W., Grimmer, M. A., Martin, N. G., Willemsen G., & Boomsma, D. I. (2008). Heritability of borderline personality disorder features is similar across three countries. *Psychological Medicine, 38*, 1219–1229.

Distel, M. A., Trull T. J., Willemsen, G., Vink, J. M., Derom, C. A., Lynskey, M.,. . . Boomsma, D. I. (2009). The Five Factor Model of personality and borderline personality disorder: A genetic analysis of comorbidity. *Biological Psychiatry, 66*, 1131–1138.

Ferrer, M., Andion, O., Matali, J., Valero, S., Navarro, J. A., Ramos-Quiroga, J. A.,. . . Casas. M. (2010). Comorbid attention-deficit/hyperactivity disorder in borderline patients defines an impulsive subtype of borderline personality disorder. *Journal of Personality Disorders, 24*, 812–822.

Ferreira, M. A. (2004). Linkage analysis: Principles and methods for the analysis of human quantitative traits. *Twin Research, 7*, 513–530.

Friedel, R. O. (2004). Dopamine dysfunction in borderline personality disorder: A hypothesis. *Neuropsychopharmacology, 29*, 1029–1039.

Gunderson, J. G., Zanarini, M. C., Choi-Kain, L. W., Mitchell, K. S., Jang, K. L., & Hudson, J. I. (2011). Family study of borderline personality disorder and its sectors of psychopathology. *Archives of General Psychiatry, 68*, 753–762.

Heath, A. C., & Eaves, L. J. (1985). Resolving the effects of phenotype and social background on mate selection. *Behavior Genetics, 15*, 15–30.

Hopwood, C. J., Morey, L. C., Edelen, M. O., Shea, M. T., Grilo, C. M., Sanislow, C. A.,. . . Skodol, A. E. (2008). A comparison of interview and self-report methods for the assessment of borderline personality disorder criteria. *Psychological Assessment, 20*, 81–85.

Jang, K. L., & Livesley, W. J. (1999). Why do measures of normal and disordered personality correlate? A study of genetic comorbidity. *Journal of Personality Disorders, 13*, 10–17.

Jang, K. L., Livesley, W. J., Vernon, P. A., & Jackson, D. N. (1996). Heritability of personality disorder traits: A twin study. *Acta Psychiatrica Scandinavica, 94*, 438–444.

Jorm, A. F., & Griffiths, K. M. (2008). The public's stigmatizing attitudes towards people with mental disorders: How important are biomedical conceptualizations? *Acta Psychiatrica Scandinavica, 118*, 315–321.

Joyce, P. R., Mchugh, P. C., McKenzie, J. M., Sullivan, P. F., Mulder, R. T., Luty, S. E.,. . . Kennedy, M. A. (2006). A dopamine transporter polymorphism is a risk factor for borderline personality disorder in depressed patients. *Psychological Medicine, 36*, 807–813.

Keller, M. C., Coventry, W. L., Heath, A. C., & Martin, N. G. (2005). Widespread evidence for nonadditive genetic variation in Cloninger's and Eysenck's personality dimensions using a twin plus sibling design. *Behavior Genetics, 35*, 707–721.

Keller, M. C., Medland, S. E., Duncan, L. E., Hatemi, P. K., Neale, M. C., Maes, H. H., & Eaves, L. J. (2009). Modeling extended twin family data I: Description of the Cascade model. *Twin Research and Human Genetics, 12*, 8–18.

Kendler, K. S., Aggen, S. H., Czajkowski, N., Roysamb, E., Tambs, K., Torgersen, S., . . . Reichborn-Kjennerud, T. (2008). The structure of genetic and environmental risk factors for DSM-IV personality disorders a multivariate twin study. *Archives of General Psychiatry, 65*, 1438–1446.

Kendler, K. S., & Eaves, L. J. (1986). Models for the joint effect of genotype and environment on liability to psychiatric illness. *American Journal of Psychiatry, 143*, 279–289.

Lips, E. S., Cornelisse, L. N., Toonen, R. F., Min, J. L., Hultman, C. M.; the International Schizophrenia Consortium, . . . Posthuma, D. (2012). Functional gene group analysis identifies synaptic gene groups as risk factor for schizophrenia. *Molecular Psychiatry, 17*, 996–1006.

Livesley, W. J. (2006). The dimensional assessment of personality pathology (DAPP) approach to personality disorder. In S. Strack (Ed.), *Differentiating normal and abnormal personality.* (2nd ed., pp. 401–425). New York: Springer.

Livesley, W. J., Jang, K. L., & Vernon, P. A. (1998). Phenotypic and genetic structure of traits delineating personality disorder. *Archives of General Psychiatry, 55*, 941–948.

De Moor, M. H. M., Boomsma, D. I., Stubbe, J. H., Willemsen, G., & De Geus, E. J. C. (2008). Testing causality in the association between regular exercise and symptoms of anxiety and depression. *Archives of General Psychiatry, 65*, 897–905.

Lubke, G. H., Laurin, C., Amin, N., Hottenga, J. J., Willemsen, G., van Grootheest, G., . . . Boomsma, D. I. (2014). Genome-wide analyses of borderline personality features. *Molecular Psychiatry, 19*, 923–929.

Ni, X. Q., Chan, K., Bulgin, N., Sicard, T., Bismil, R., McMain, S., & Kennedy, J. L. (2006). Association between serotonin transporter gene and borderline personality disorder. *Journal of Psychiatric Research, 40*, 448–453.

Ni, X. Q., Sicard, T., Bulgin, N., Bismil, R., Chan, K., McMain, S., & Kennedy, J. L. (2007). Monoamine oxidase A gene is associated with borderline personality disorder. *Psychiatric Genetics, 17*, 153–157.

Pascual, J. C., Soler, J., Barrachina, J., Campins, M. J., Alvarez, E., Perez, V., . . . Baiget, M. (2008). Failure to detect an association between the serotonin transporter gene and borderline personality disorder. *Journal of Psychiatric Research, 42*, 87–88.

Plomin, R., Defries, J. C., & Loehlin, J. C. (1977). Genotype-environment interaction and correlation in analysis of human-behavior. *Psychological Bulletin, 84*, 309–322.

Reichborn-Kjennerud, T., Czajkowski, N., Røysamb, E., Ørstavik, R. E., Neale, M. C., Torgersen, S., . . . Kendler, K. S. (2010). Major depression and dimensional representations of DSM-IV personality disorders: A population-based twin study. *Psychological Medicine, 40*, 1475–1484.

Samuel, D. B., & Widiger, T. A. (2008). A meta-analytic review of the relationships between the five factor model and DSM-IV-TR personality disorders: A facet level analysis. *Clinical Psychology Review, 28*, 1326–1342.

Shea, M. T., Stout, R. L., Yen, S., Pagano, M. E., Skodol, A. E., Morey, L. C., . . . Zanarini, M. C. (2004). Associations in the course of personality disorders and Axis I disorders over time. *Journal of Abnormal Psychology, 113*, 499–508.

Takao, T., Tachikawa, H., Kawanishi, Y., Mizukami, K., & Asada, T. (2007). CLOCK gene T3111C polymorphism is associated with Japanese schizophrenics: A preliminary study. *European Neuropsychopharmacology,17*, 273–276.

Torgersen, S., Czajkowski, N., Jacobson, K., Reichborn-Kjennerud, T., Roysamb, E., Neale, M. C., . . . Kendler, K. S. (2008). Dimensional representations of DSM-IV cluster B personality disorders in a population based sample of Norwegian twins: A multivariate study. *Psychological Medicine, 38*, 1617–1625.

Trull, T. J., Widiger, T. A., Lynam, D. R., & Costa, P. T. (2003). Borderline personality disorder from the perspective of general personality functioning. *Journal of Abnormal Psychology, 112*, 193–202.

Wilson, S. T., Stanley, B., Brent, D. A., Oquendo, M. A., Huang, Y. Y., Haghighi, F., . . . Mann, J. J. (2012). Interaction between tryptophan hydroxylase I (*TPH1*) polymorphisms and childhood abuse is associated with increased risk for borderline personality disorder in adulthood. *Psychiatric Genetics, 22*, 15–24.

Wilson, S. T., Stanley, B., Brent, D. A., Oquendo, M. A., Huang, Y. Y., & Mann, J. J. (2009). The tryptophan hydroxylase-1 A218C polymorphism is associated with diagnosis, but not suicidal behavior, in borderline personality disorder. *American Journal of Medical Genetics Part B: Neuropsychiatric Genetics, 150b*, 202–208.

/// 8 /// Suicidal and Nonsuicidal Self-Injury in Borderline Personality Disorder

MARGARET S. ANDOVER,
HEATHER T. SCHATTEN,
AND BLAIR W. MORRIS

INTRODUCTION

Numerous studies have demonstrated strong associations between a diagnosis of borderline personality disorder (BPD) and self-injurious behaviors, including suicide, attempted suicide, and nonsuicidal self-injury (NSSI). Self-injurious behaviors are common among individuals with BPD (Welch & Linehan, 2002); up to 87% of BPD patients report a history of attempted suicide (e.g., Black, Blum, Pfohl, & Hale, 2004; Soloff, Lis, Kely, Cornelius, & Ulrich, 1994a; Soloff, Lynch, & Kelly, 2002), and research in clinical samples has found that as many as 37% of those who engage in NSSI meet criteria for a diagnosis of BPD (Briere & Gil, 1998). Recurrent self-injury is a diagnostic criterion of BPD (American Psychiatric Association [APA], 2013), and it can be a prominent and concerning symptom for those diagnosed with the disorder. In this chapter, we first discuss the associations between attempted suicide, NSSI, and specific BPD criteria and review the prevalence of self-injurious behaviors in BPD. Next, we review risk factors for and characteristics of attempted suicide and NSSI among individuals with BPD. We then provide a brief overview of treatments that specifically address self-injurious behaviors in BPD. Finally, we present a case example to illustrate the correlates and risk factors discussed in the chapter.

DEFINING NONSUICIDAL SELF-INJURY AND SUICIDAL BEHAVIOR

NSSI, defined as deliberate harm to the body without intent to die (Favazza, 1998), includes behaviors such as cutting, burning, scratching, self-hitting, needle-sticking, and carving words, designs, or symbols (Walsh, 2008). The prevalence of NSSI is alarmingly high in the general population (Muehlenkamp & Gutierrez, 2004; Ross & Heath, 2002), and it is associated with many maladaptive consequences, including medical sequelae such as scarring and infections, psychological symptoms such as anxiety and depression (Andover, Pepper, Ryabchenko, Orrico, & Gibb, 2005; Ross & Heath, 2002), and increased risky behaviors such as illicit drug use and frequent binge drinking (Serras, Saules, Cranford, & Eisenberg, 2010). Important to the treatment of self-injurious behaviors without suicidal intent, research has focused on identifying the functions of NSSI. A functional model of NSSI focuses on the immediate antecedents and consequences of NSSI as opposed to focusing on distal risk factors, vulnerability factors, and psychosocial correlates that may influence behavior (Nock, 2009). Historically, there have been multiple functions proposed for NSSI; however, research indicates that NSSI is most often utilized as a method to reduce or eliminate negative affect (Klonsky, 2009).

NSSI and suicidal behavior, including attempted and completed suicide, both involve deliberate injury to the body, but they differ in suicidal intent, perception of the event, proposed function of the behavior, chronicity, and method (Muehlenkamp, 2005; Suyemoto, 1998). NSSI is performed only without intent to die, whereas suicidal behavior is performed with some degree of intent to die (attempted and completed suicide differ in fatality of the injury). NSSI is a chronic and repetitive behavior, whereas suicide attempts occur more infrequently, and NSSI is usually of lower lethality than attempted suicide (Muehlenkamp, 2005). Furthermore, NSSI is more common than attempted suicide (Muehlenkamp & Gutierrez, 2004; Ross & Heath, 2002). However, the behaviors often co-occur; approximately 55–85% of individuals with an NSSI history report at least one suicide attempt (Stanley, Gameroff, Michalsen, & Mann, 2001), and recent research suggests that NSSI may be an important risk factor for attempted suicide (e.g., Andover, Morris, Wren, & Bruzzese, 2012).

Given their differences, it is essential to consider NSSI and suicidal behavior separately. This can at times be hampered by lack of a standard nomenclature in the self-injury literature. For example, terms such as "parasuicide" and "deliberate self-harm" may be used to describe self-injurious behaviors regardless of suicidal intent (NSSI and attempted suicide; e.g., Welch & Linehan, 2002), or it may be used to describe nonsuicidal behaviors (e.g., Gratz & Gunderson, 2006). This chapter will use the term "nonsuicidal self-injury" to describe harm without suicidal intent, and the term "self-injurious behaviors" when attempted suicide and NSSI are considered together.

PREVALENCE OF SUICIDAL BEHAVIOR AND NSSI IN BPD

Attempted suicide is highly prevalent among individuals with BPD and is associated with poorer outcomes than BPD without attempted suicide (Mehlum, Friis, Vaglum, & Karterud, 1994). Among individuals who died by suicide, between 7% and 38% met criteria for BPD when criteria were assessed on psychological autopsy (Linehan & Dexter-Mazza, 2007), and between 4% and 10% of those with BPD die by suicide (Paris, 2002a; Zanarini, Frankenburg, Hennen, Reich, & Silk, 2005). Studies have shown that more than 80% of BPD patients report a suicide attempt history (Black et al., 2004; Soloff et al., 2002) with an average of 3.4 lifetime attempts (Paris & Zweig-Frank, 2001). One study found that 86.4% of patients with BPD reported a suicide attempt in the 2 years prior to assessment (Soloff et al., 1994a). Researchers have reported that 27.8% of patients with BPD reported a suicide attempt during a 6-year follow-up study, with nearly 25% reporting an attempt within the first 2 years (Soloff & Chiappetta, 2012). A high rate of suicide deaths has also been reported among patients with BPD; over a 27-year follow-up period, Paris and Zweig-Frank (2001) reported that 10.3% of their sample died by suicide, and Zanarini and colleagues (2005) reported suicide deaths in 4% of their sample over a 6-year follow-up. Although the diagnosis of BPD among adolescents is controversial, researchers have documented validity and reliability for the diagnosis in adolescents (Miller, Muehlenkamp, & Jacobson, 2008). A strong association between attempted suicide and a BPD diagnosis has been reported among adolescents as well as adults; Jacobson and colleagues (Jacobson, Muehlenkamp, Miller, & Turner, 2008) reported that 38% of adolescent outpatients with a history of attempted suicide met criteria for BPD. The association between BPD and attempted suicide is also found outside clinical samples. For example, symptoms of BPD have been associated with a history of attempted suicide among adolescent community members and undergraduate students, in addition to adolescent psychiatric inpatients (Klonsky, May, & Glenn, 2013).

Self-injury performed without suicidal intent, NSSI, is often associated with BPD (Nock, Joiner, Gordon, Lloyd-Richardson, & Prinstein, 2006). Nearly 40% of self-injuring individuals in one clinical sample met criteria for a diagnosis of BPD (Briere & Gil, 1998). Nearly 27% of adolescent outpatients and 63% of adolescent inpatients who had engaged in NSSI met criteria for BPD (Ferrara, Terrinoni, & Williams, 2012; Jacobson et al., 2008). However, not all individuals who engage in NSSI meet criteria for BPD. Studies have shown that among individuals with NSSI, rates of BPD can range from 0% to 50% (Andover et al., 2005; Nock et al., 2006). In addition, not all individuals with BPD report a history of NSSI (Zlotnick, Mattia, & Zimmerman, 1999). However, even if a diagnosis of BPD is not present, research has found that individuals with a history of NSSI endorse significantly more symptoms of BPD than those with no NSSI history

(Andover et al., 2005; Briere & Gil, 1998; Klonsky & Olino, 2008; Klonsky, Oltmanns, & Turkheimer, 2003; Stanley et al., 2001). This suggests that even if a diagnosis of BPD is not present, it is important for clinicians and researchers to consider the symptoms of the disorder when self-injurious behaviors—NSSI in particular—are present.

THE SELF-INJURY CRITERION OF BPD

The associations among NSSI, suicide, and BPD are clearly well documented. In fact, one of the nine criteria for a diagnosis of BPD in the DSM (DSM-5; APA, 2013) refers to recurrent suicidal behavior, gestures, or threats, or NSSI, and BPD is the only psychiatric diagnosis in the DSM-5 that includes NSSI as a criterion (nonsuicidal self-injury disorder is included as a condition for further study in the DSM-5; APA, 2013). Because a positive diagnosis of BPD only requires five of nine symptoms, it is important to note that self-injury is neither necessary nor sufficient for a diagnosis of BPD. This is supported by the aforementioned research indicating that not all individuals with a history of NSSI or attempted suicide have a BPD diagnosis. However, some clinicians may inappropriately diagnose an individual who engages in NSSI or recurrent suicidal behaviors as having BPD (Ghaziuddin, Tsai, Naylor, & Ghaziuddin, 1992). The criterion of self-injurious behaviors can also be a confound in research on BPD and self-injury because it represents an overlap of constructs. Researchers should consider statistically controlling for the recurrent self-injury criterion in analyses to better understand the relationship between self-injurious behaviors and BPD.

ATTEMPTED SUICIDE, NSSI, AND SPECIFIC SYMPTOMS OF BPD

Given the rates of self-injurious behaviors in BPD, researchers have begun to explore the associations between specific BPD criteria and suicidal and nonsuicidal self-injury. History of suicide attempts was found to be associated with the criteria of impulsivity and recurrent self-injury in a college sample (Klonsky, 2008). Similarly, when statistically controlling for history of depression, substance abuse, and the BPD criterion of recurrent self-injury, Brodsky and colleagues (Brodsky, Malone, Ellis, Dulit, & Mann, 1997) reported that only the criterion of impulsivity was associated with previous suicide attempts among psychiatric inpatients diagnosed with BPD. However, in a study of individuals diagnosed with a personality disorder, only the affective instability criterion predicted history of suicide attempts, but this was reduced to nonsignificant when statistically controlling for the criterion of recurrent self-injury (Yen et al., 2004). Although these studies suggest that the specific BPD criteria of impulsivity and affective instability are associated with attempted suicide, findings have been mixed and additional research is necessary.

Researchers have also investigated the BPD criteria most strongly associated with other types of self-injurious behaviors, such as completed suicide, suicidal ideation, and self-injury performed with and without suicidal intent. These studies have yielded inconsistent findings, again confirming the need for further investigation. For example, results of a psychological autopsy suggested that, among individuals with BPD, those who died by suicide were significantly less likely to have met the affective instability and paranoid ideation/dissociation criteria of BPD than those who did not die by suicide (McGirr, Paris, Lesage, Renaud, & Turecki, 2009). Suicidal ideation was found to be associated with all criteria of BPD, with the criterion of emptiness most strongly associated after the recurrent self-injury criterion (Klonsky, 2008). Finally, self-injurious behaviors performed with and without intent to die were significantly predicted by the criteria of affective instability, identity disturbance, and impulsivity, although only affective instability remained significant when statistically controlling for the criterion of recurrent self-injury (Yen et al., 2004).

Two studies have investigated differences in BPD criteria associated with self-injury with intent to die (attempted suicide) and without intent to die (NSSI). Andión and colleagues (2013) found that among individuals referred to an outpatient BPD program, patients high in all symptom clusters of BPD were more likely to report suicide attempts and NSSI than were those low in all symptom clusters. In addition, history of attempted suicide was more likely among those high in BPD symptoms reflecting behavioral dysregulation, including impulsivity and self-injurious behaviors. History of NSSI was more likely among those high in symptoms reflecting both behavioral dysregulation and affective dysregulation, which include affective instability, inappropriate anger, and avoidance of abandonment. Interestingly, symptoms reflecting disturbed relatedness, including unstable relationships, emptiness, identity disturbance, and paranoid ideation, were less likely to be associated with self-injurious behaviors than symptoms reflecting behavioral regulation (Andión et al., 2013). However, in this study, the behavioral regulation cluster of symptoms included impulsivity and recurrent self-injury, highlighting the need to account for overlap between the constructs. An understanding of the impulsivity criterion alone would be helpful in evaluating the findings from this study. Among a clinical sample of adolescents, two BPD symptoms distinguished those with NSSI alone and those who had attempted suicide in addition to NSSI. Specifically, less confusion about self and more interpersonal chaos were more strongly associated with engagement in NSSI alone than with engagement in both types of self-injurious behaviors. However, there were no differences between those with a history of NSSI only and a history of suicide attempts only (Muehlenkamp, Ertlet, Miller, & Claes, 2011), suggesting that, in this sample, similar BPD criteria were associated with engagement in one type of self-injury regardless of whether the self-injury was performed with or without suicidal intent. Although research on the specific BPD symptoms associated with self-injurious behaviors has been mixed, these studies indicate that self-injury and BPD are linked by more than simply a shared diagnostic criterion. Further research into BPD criteria, especially with studies that account for the overlap in construct reflected by the recurrent self-injury criterion, will help us to understand the mechanisms underlying the associations.

RISK FACTORS FOR ATTEMPTED SUICIDE IN BPD

Given the high suicide risk among those with BPD, it is important to understand the factors that may contribute to an increased risk of suicide attempts. Risk factors for attempted suicide among individuals with BPD include older age, history of suicide attempts, antisocial personality disorder, history of impulsive behaviors (Soloff, Lis, Kelly, Cornelius, & Ulrich, 1994b), low socioeconomic status, poor psychosocial adjustment, a family history of suicide, previous psychiatric hospitalizations, and the absence of outpatient treatment (Soloff & Chiappetta, 2012). Soloff and colleagues (Soloff, Lynch, Kelly, Malone, & Mann, 2000) found that impulsivity and hopelessness predicted the number of suicide attempts among BPD patients (Soloff et al., 2000). Contrary to expectation, however, severity of BPD has not been shown to be associated with number of suicide attempts (Soloff, Fabio, Kelly, Malone, & Mann, 2005). A 16-year longitudinal study of patients with BPD found that NSSI; having a caretaker who died by suicide; affective instability; dissociation; and diagnoses of MDD, substance use disorder, and post-traumatic stress disorder were unique predictors of attempted suicide after statistically controlling for other related variables (Wedig et al., 2012). A current diagnosis of bulimia nervosa has also been associated with a greater risk of suicide attempts among women with BPD (Chen, Brown, Harned, & Linehan, 2009). Among women with BPD receiving dialectical behavior therapy (DBT), Brown and colleagues (Brown, Linehan, Comtois, Murray, & Chapman, 2009) found that shame may increase the risk of self-injurious behavior; further research is necessary to investigate this variable in a broader sample. Negative stressful life events may be a predictor of attempted suicide among adolescents and young adults (Horesh, Nachshoni, Wolmer, & Toren, 2009). Interestingly, Horesh and colleagues (2009) found that the loss of a first-degree relative during childhood may actually be a protective factor against suicidal behavior. They suggest that if a parent is abusive or neglectful, the loss of that parent may actually be less harmful than if the parent was present.

Although some researchers have noted that comorbid affective and substance use disorders may be risk factors for attempted suicide in those with BPD (Fyer, Frances, Sullivan, Hurt, & Clarkin, 1988), other research has not supported this finding (Soloff et al., 1994b). However, individuals with BPD who have attempted suicide report greater depressive symptoms than do those without a history of suicide attempts (Soloff et al., 1994b). Therefore, clinicians should be aware that increased depressive symptoms, even without a diagnosis of depression, may be a risk factor for attempted suicide.

Longitudinal research of attempted suicide in BPD suggests that risk factors for the behavior may change over time. Soloff and colleagues (Soloff, Feske, & Fabio, 2008; Soloff & Chiappetta, 2012) found that during the first 12 months of a 6-year longitudinal study, attempted suicide was predicted by MDD and poor social adjustment. However, risk of suicide attempt was predicted by psychiatric hospitalization prior to an attempt and poor social adjustment between 18 and 24 months, and by psychiatric hospitalization and medication visits prior to an attempt, an attempt during the first year of follow-up, and low functioning at baseline between the second and fifth year (Soloff & Fabio, 2008). Although risk factors appeared to change over time, poor psychosocial functioning was consistently associated with increased suicide risk, and higher global assessment of functioning (GAF) scores at baseline, indicating better functioning, were associated with decreased risk of suicide attempts over time (Soloff & Chiappetta, 2012). This finding highlights the importance of improving psychosocial functioning among individuals with BPD because this may mitigate risk for suicide attempts.

Researchers have also investigated general risk factors for attempted suicide in BPD and non-BPD samples. Generally, suicide attempters with BPD report increased risk factors for suicidal behaviors than do suicide attempters without a BPD diagnosis. Specifically, Berk and colleagues (Berk, Jeglic, Brown, Henriques, & Beck, 2007) found that, among suicide attempters, those with BPD endorsed more depression, hopelessness, and overall psychopathology than did those without BPD. In addition, suicide attempters with BPD reported greater suicidal ideation and more past suicide attempts than did those without BPD. Consistent with findings of psychosocial functioning as a risk factor for attempted suicide in BPD (Soloff & Chiappetta, 2012; Soloff & Fabio, 2008), suicide attempters with BPD report poorer social problem-solving than do suicide attempters without BPD (Berk et al., 2007). These findings suggest that individuals with BPD may be at greater risk of suicide attempts than individuals with other psychiatric disorders, even with a suicide attempt history.

History of childhood sexual abuse is often associated with suicidal behavior (e.g., Kolla, Eisenberg, & Links, 2008); researchers report that BPD patients with suicide attempt histories report more sexual abuse throughout their lifetimes than their nonsuicidal counterparts. In addition, suicide attempters with BPD report more sexual abuse than suicide attempters with MDD (Horesh et al., 2009). The association between childhood sexual abuse and suicide attempts may not be purely direct, however; Soloff and colleagues (2008) found the association to be partially mediated by psychotic and schizotypal symptoms and poor social adjustment, suggesting that these factors increase the risk of suicidal behavior among BPD patients with a history of childhood sexual abuse.

One important focus of research has been suicide attempts among individuals with comorbid BPD and MDD because both diagnoses are associated with an increased risk of suicide attempts (see also Chapter 11). Individuals with both BPD and MDD report more suicide attempts than do those with MDD alone, and they are more likely to report interpersonal triggers for their attempts (Brodsky, Groves, Oquendo, Mann, & Stanley, 2006). Patients with comorbid BPD and MDD also report first attempting suicide at a younger age than those with MDD alone, and they report greater hostility, aggression, and impulsivity, suggesting that comorbid BPD may be associated with increased risk factors for attempted suicide. Individuals with MDD alone report greater suicidal intent for their most recent suicide attempt than do those with comorbid BPD; however, the lethality of the most recent attempt was comparable between those with MDD alone and those with MDD and BPD (Brodsky et al., 2006). These findings suggest that individuals with comorbid BPD and MDD may report a more extensive suicide history, more risk factors for attempted suicide, and a greater discrepancy between reported suicidal intent and lethality of attempt than those with MDD alone.

Risk Factors for Completed Suicide in BPD

Fewer studies have investigated risk factors for completed suicide in BPD patients than risk factors for attempted suicide. Paris (1990) found that, compared to BPD patients who did not die by suicide, those who did had more years of education and more suicide attempts, decreased psychosis, and fewer separations and losses early in childhood. However, there were no differences between those who did and did not die by suicide in age, gender, marital status, presence of affective disorders, or impulsive actions. Although there may be differences in risk factors for attempted and completed suicide in BPD, it is important to note that one of the strongest predictors for completed suicide is history of attempted suicide (Joiner et al., 2005), thus emphasizing the importance of identifying risk factors for attempted suicide in patients with BPD.

Characteristics of Suicide Attempts Among Individuals with BPD

Research has shown BPD to be a risk factor for multiple suicide attempts (Boisseau et al., 2012). Among patients diagnosed with MDD, those with a comorbid diagnosis of BPD report more suicide attempts than do those without (Brodsky et al., 2006), and BPD patients attempt suicide more often than other psychiatric groups (i.e., Soloff et al., 2000). Researchers have sought to identify factors associated with increased suicide attempts in individuals with BPD. Soloff and colleagues (2000) found that impulsivity and hopelessness predicted the number of suicide attempts among BPD patients (Soloff et al., 2000). Contrary to expectation, however, severity of BPD has not been shown to be associated with number of suicide attempts (Soloff et al., 2005).

By definition, all suicide attempts must involve at least some intent to die, but the injuries themselves can vary greatly in terms of medical severity. Some have suggested that the presence of recurrent suicidal and nonsuicidal behaviors in BPD may lead clinicians to assume that individuals with BPD are more likely to engage in low-intent, low-lethality behaviors (e.g., Brodsky et al., 2006). However, researchers have identified no differences between patients with and without BPD in the medical lethality of suicide attempts (Berk et al., 2007; Brodsky et al., 2006; Soloff et al., 2000). In fact, more than 40% of BPD patients with a suicide attempt history rated their worst attempt as being of high lethality (Soloff et al., 1994b), and longitudinal studies have shown that as many as 10.3% of individuals with BPD die by suicide

(Paris & Zwieg-Frank, 2001). Therefore, predictors of the medical lethality of suicide attempt injuries and suicidal intent have been a focus of research.

Although some researchers have reported that frequency of past suicide attempts does not increase risk for high-lethality attempts (Chesin, Jeglic, & Stanley, 2010), others have shown that BPD patients with high-lethality suicide attempts report greater intent to die and an increased number of suicide attempts than do those with low lethality attempts (Soloff et al., 2005). Shearer and colleagues (Shearer, Peters, Quaytman, & Wadman, 1988) found that much of the variance in suicidal intent among individuals with BPD was accounted for by specific demographic and clinical factors, including age, number of previous suicide attempts, presence of an eating disorder, history of psychotic symptoms, and history of an affective disorder in a parent. Soloff and colleagues (2000) found that hopelessness is an important predictor of lethal intent and planning for a suicide attempt in BPD patients. Interestingly, a diagnosis of generalized anxiety disorder was found to be protective against suicidal intent among individuals with BPD (Shearer et al., 1988).

Among BPD patients, having a suicide attempt that is of high medical lethality is associated with specific demographic characteristics when compared to individuals with low-lethality attempts. Specifically, more medically severe suicide attempts are associated with older age (Shearer et al., 1988; Soloff et al., 2005), having children, having less education, lower socioeconomic status (Soloff et al., 2005), and family history of substance abuse (Shearer et al., 1988; Soloff et al., 2005). Higher medical lethality of attempts among BPD patients is also associated with a number of clinical variables, including impulsivity (Chesin et al., 2010), comorbid eating disorder (Shearer et al., 1988), comorbid MDD or antisocial personality disorder, more psychiatric hospitalizations, longer length of stays during hospitalizations (Soloff et al., 2005), rejection-sensitive dysphoria (Soloff et al., 1994b), and a greater number of lifetime suicide attempts (Shearer et al., 1988; Soloff et al., 1994b). Similar to research findings regarding number of suicide attempts, severity of BPD is not related to medical lethality (Soloff et al., 2005). However, distress tolerance is an important factor to consider in understanding suicidal intent and lethality in BPD. Anestis and colleagues (Anestis, Gratz, Bagge, & Tull, 2012) found that among BPD patients, those with high distress tolerance report more suicide attempts, more attempts with intent to die, and more medically severe suicide attempts than do those with low distress tolerance. Although this finding seems counterintuitive, the authors suggest that a greater ability to tolerate distress would allow individuals to engage in repeated suicidal behaviors despite associated distress and negative consequences.

Patients with BPD are at an elevated risk of suicide attempts and deaths. Research on risk factors for suicide in BPD has focused not only on variables that increase risk for suicide attempts and death, but also on suicide attempt characteristics, such as the number of attempts, suicidal intent, and the objective medical lethality of the attempt. This and future research is important to develop our understanding of the association between BPD and suicide and to better identify patients who are at high risk.

RISK FACTORS FOR NONSUICIDAL SELF-INJURY IN BPD

Both a diagnosis of BPD and borderline personality features have been associated with engagement in NSSI (Andover et al., 2005; Briere & Gil, 1998; Ferrara et al., 2012; Jacobson et al., 2008; Klonsky & Olino, 2008; Klonsky et al., 2003). In addition, Glenn and Klonsky (2011) found that borderline personality features predicted engagement in NSSI at a 1-year follow-up, and NSSI predicted attempted suicide among BPD patients (Wedig et al., 2012). Because of the prevalence of NSSI in BPD and the negative consequences associated with the behavior, it is important to identify factors that are associated with or increase the risk of NSSI among BPD patients.

Increased rates of some comorbid diagnoses have been reported among individuals with BPD who engage in NSSI. Specifically, history of NSSI has been associated with current anorexia nervosa (Chen et al., 2009) and increased obsessive-compulsive symptoms (McKay, Kulchycky, & Danyko, 2000) among BPD patients. In addition, women with BPD who report experiencing dissociative symptoms are more likely to engage in NSSI than those who do not report dissociation (Brodsky et al., 1995). Even in nonclinical samples, BPD may play an important role in explaining the associations between increased levels of psychiatric symptoms among those who engage in NSSI. For example, Andover and colleagues (2005) found that associations between symptoms of anxiety and depression and NSSI were reduced to nonsignificant when statistically controlling for borderline personality features. Further research is needed to better understand if specific comorbid conditions affect the severity, intensity, and frequency of NSSI behaviors among BPD patients in order to inform assessment, prevention, and treatment efforts.

As with attempted suicide, childhood abuse has been suggested as a risk factor for NSSI. Some studies do report an increased rate of childhood abuse among those who self-injure. For example, Zlotnick and colleagues (1996) found that psychiatric inpatients with NSSI were significantly more likely to report childhood sexual abuse than were those without an NSSI history. Among male substance abusers, Evren and colleagues (Evren, Cinar, Evren, & Celik, 2012) found that childhood emotional neglect and severity of borderline personality features statistically predicted a history of NSSI. In addition, the number of NSSI episodes was statistically predicted by childhood physical neglect and severity of borderline personality features. However, research suggests that the association between childhood abuse and NSSI may not be direct. In a meta-analysis investigating the association between childhood sexual abuse and NSSI, Klonsky and Moyer (2008) found that the strength of the association is relatively small, reporting that, in studies that controlled for other psychiatric risk factors, childhood sexual abuse explained little or no unique variance in NSSI. Instead, the authors suggested that childhood sexual abuse and NSSI are related because they are associated with the same psychiatric risk factors. Childhood trauma has also been investigated in association with NSSI in BPD samples specifically. Among women with BPD, those with NSSI reported more childhood sexual abuse and dissociation than those without NSSI, but only a diagnosis of BPD was significantly associated with NSSI when all variables were analyzed together (Zweig-Frank, Paris, & Guzder, 1994a). However, the associations between childhood abuse and NSSI were not found when the study was replicated with a male sample (Zweig-Frank, Paris, & Guzder, 1994b), suggesting a complex association between childhood abuse and NSSI in individuals with BPD.

Limited research has investigated risk factors for NSSI behavior specifically among individuals with BPD. Because NSSI by definition occurs without suicidal intent, some may argue that it is a less important focus of attention than attempted suicide. However, because NSSI is associated with increased psychopathology and is an important risk factor for attempted suicide among individuals with BPD (Wedig et al., 2012), it should be a specific focus of research. Zanarini and colleagues (Zanarini, Laudate, Frankenburg, Reich, & Fitzmaurice, 2011) is the only study to date to prospectively investigate risk factors for NSSI in BPD patients. In their 10-year longitudinal study, the authors found that NSSI behavior was predicted by several demographic and clinical variables. Specifically, female gender, history of childhood sexual abuse, sexual assaults as an adult, MDD, depressive affect and cognitions, and severity of dissociative symptoms were identified as risk factors for NSSI. Overall, additional research is needed to better understand clinical correlates and risk factors that may predict engagement in NSSI among BPD patients in order to better inform clinical assessment, prevention, and treatment efforts. In addition, research comparing the risk factors for NSSI and attempted suicide can develop our understanding of the association between self-injurious behaviors and specific mechanisms for self-injurious behaviors within BPD.

Self-Injurious Behaviors over the Course of BPD

The occurrence of NSSI over the course of BPD has recently become an area of research interest. Sansone and colleagues (Sansone, Gaither, & Songer, 2002) examined the prevalence of self-injurious behaviors with and without intent to die across the life span among individuals with BPD. The mean number of self-injurious behaviors among those with BPD increased dramatically between the ages of 18 and 24 years, and this rate of behavior was sustained through the last time point assessed at ages 50 to 59 years. This pattern of engagement was found for both high- and low-lethality behaviors. Psychiatric inpatients without a BPD diagnosis showed a similar pattern of self-injurious behaviors across the life span, although significantly fewer behaviors were noted. However, Zanarini and colleagues (2005) noted a 65% reduction in NSSI among BPD patients over a 6-year follow-up period. Further research is necessary to understand the pattern of engagement in NSSI and attempted suicide over time and the factors that may be associated with a decrease in behaviors.

EMOTION REGULATION AND SELF-INJURIOUS BEHAVIORS IN BPD

Borderline personality disorder is considered a disorder of pervasive emotion dysregulation (Crowell, Beauchaine, & Linehan, 2009). Linehan's (1993) biosocial theory is the most commonly cited model of emotion dysregulation used to explain self-injurious behavior in BPD. This model proposes that individuals with BPD experience pervasive difficulties with emotion regulation. Individuals with BPD have a high sensitivity to negative emotional stimuli, high emotional intensity, and slow return to baseline (Linehan, 1993). Linehan suggests that the emotional difficulties individuals with BPD experience are rooted in biological vulnerabilities that are then exacerbated by experiences in specific environments that invalidate the expression of private emotional experiences. Self-injurious behaviors, including NSSI and attempted suicide, are maladaptive solutions to the problem of overwhelming, uncontrollable, and intensely painful negative emotions; they are either the outcomes of emotion dysregulation or performed as an attempt to regulate intense affect.

Empirical research supports the association between emotion regulation and self-injurious behaviors. Consistent with Linehan's (1993) model, individuals who engage in NSSI report using it as a strategy to regulate emotions (e.g., Klonsky, 2009). Emotion dysregulation has also been associated with suicidal ideation, single and multiple suicide attempts (e.g., Rajappa, Gallagher, & Miranda, 2012), and NSSI (e.g., Gratz & Chapman, 2007; Gratz & Roemer, 2008). Further investigation into emotion dysregulation and self-injurious behaviors in BPD is necessary because this may be an important focus of intervention for self-injurious behaviors in BPD.

TREATING SUICIDAL AND NONSUICIDAL SELF-INJURY IN BPD

Self-injurious behaviors present an additional challenge in the treatment of BPD. However, interventions have been developed to specifically address these dangerous behaviors. Although treatments for BPD are discussed at length elsewhere, we provide a brief review of the most empirically supported interventions for self-injury in BPD. Perhaps the best-known and most empirically supported example is DBT (Linehan, 1993; Stanley et al., 2007). Developed specifically as a treatment for BPD, DBT incorporates cognitive-behavioral techniques with a focus on dialectical thinking and Eastern philosophy. Self-injurious behaviors are directly addressed in DBT; as part of the first stage of the treatment, therapist and client focus on reducing life-threatening behaviors such as attempted suicide and NSSI.

Given the theoretical and empirical associations between self-injurious behaviors and emotion dysregulation, several treatments, including DBT, focus on the development of emotion regulation skills to address self-injurious behaviors. For example, Gratz and colleagues (Gratz & Gunderson, 2006; Gratz & Tull, 2011) have developed a 14-week acceptance-based emotion regulation group intervention. This intervention, which focuses on decreasing emotion dysregulation and emotional avoidance, has demonstrated decreases in NSSI among women with BPD and subclinical BPD (Gratz & Gunderson, 2006; Gratz & Tull, 2011). Further research is necessary to investigate the acceptance-based emotion regulation group intervention as an empirically supported treatment (EST) for self-injurious behaviors in BPD.

Other interventions have focused on increasing problem-solving skills to decrease self-injurious behaviors. For example, manual assisted cognitive therapy (MACT) is a cognitive-behavioral intervention with a focus on problem-solving developed for the treatment of NSSI. This six-session intervention incorporates elements of DBT, cognitive-behavioral therapy, and bibliotherapy. The intervention is promising for the treatment of self-injurious behaviors. Researchers have recently investigated the intervention specifically among patients with BPD, finding that the addition of MACT to treatment as usual was associated with significantly fewer episodes of NSSI and significantly less NSSI severity 6 months later. No differences in suicidal ideation were reported between the treatment groups (Weinberg, Gunderson, Hennen, & Cutter, 2006).

Research suggests that specialized hospital programs may be appropriate for suicidal individuals with BPD. For example, Berrino and colleagues (2011) found a significant decrease in the number of suicide attempts 3 months after hospital discharge among patients receiving a brief inpatient crisis intervention program, compared with those receiving treatment as usual. Although additional research is necessary, this finding suggests that, for those BPD patients who are admitted to the hospital with suicidality, a tailored intervention may decrease the rate of future attempts.

For many patients with BPD, NSSI and increased levels of suicidality are recurrent and chronic. While hospitalization may at times be the appropriate course of action, experts in the field caution against hospitalization unless necessary (i.e., Linehan, 1993; Paris, 2002b). The suicidality of BPD patients tends not to improve significantly with hospitalization, and hospitalization itself may have reinforcing properties for an individual (e.g., Paris, 2002b). Consistent with established treatments for BPD (i.e., Linehan, 1993), Paris (2002b) suggests focusing on the distress underlying the suicidality rather than the suicidality itself. Similarly, treating the modifiable distal causes of and skills deficits associated with NSSI should be a focus of therapy, while understanding the functions of an individual's NSSI, such as emotion regulation, can provide clinicians and patients with a model to address NSSI itself (i.e., Paris, 2005).

CASE STUDY: NSSI

Ashley is a 26-year-old, single, Caucasian female who presented for treatment following a recent breakup from her boyfriend approximately 1 month ago. Since the breakup, Ashley reported experiencing intense urges to contact her ex-boyfriend and indicated that she had called and text messaged him continuously since their breakup, often calling him up to 10 times per day. She indicated that she had been experiencing depressive symptoms, including sadness, feelings of emptiness, lack of energy, and difficulty sleeping. In addition, Ashley reported experiencing suicidal thoughts approximately once per day for the past few weeks, stating that she considered overdosing on prescribed psychotropic medications that she had in her home; however, she denied suicidal intent.

Ashley endorsed a history of one psychiatric hospitalization at 22 years of age. She reported that she was admitted to the hospital after a suicide attempt in which she took a bottle of Tylenol and drank a bottle of wine. Ashley's roommate found her and called 911, and she was discharged after 2 weeks on an inpatient unit. She reported that she had been feeling increasingly distressed following a series of "blowups" with her close group of female friends and losing her job and that she felt hopeless that things would improve. In addition to this suicide attempt, Ashley reported experiencing transient suicidal ideation since she was 16 years of age, with noticeable increases in the frequency and intensity of suicidal thoughts during periods of increased stress and interpersonal conflict. Ashley also reported a history of NSSI with onset at age 14. Her most frequently used method of self-injury was cutting, typically on her forearms and thighs with a razor, but she reported that she had also burned herself with cigarettes on her thighs numerous times, and she often picked at her skin severely enough to draw blood. Ashley noted that she engaged in NSSI approximately two to three times a month until she was 17 years old, when she stopped until she was 22. She reported that she engaged in NSSI "once in awhile" since then, but that the frequency had increased over the past 2 weeks, when she started cutting daily. Ashley indicated that she has felt extremely "lonely and distressed" since her breakup and that she does not know what else to do to make herself feel better.

In addition to impulsively contacting her ex-boyfriend, Ashley reported a history of impulsive behaviors including alcohol use and promiscuous sex. She stated that she started drinking alcohol in high school and that she typically drinks two to three times per week, often to the point of "blacking out." Ashley reported engaging in sexual activity with men while drunk before she met her ex-boyfriend, including men she did not know very well. Ashley stated that she and her ex-boyfriend would often get into arguments when she would come home intoxicated, which was one of the factors leading to their breakup.

Ashley described a history of tumultuous relationships with friends, family, and romantic partners. She stated that while she made friends easily, she always had a difficult time maintaining relationships because some conflict always arose that would lead to the friendship ending abruptly. Ashley indicated that she had always gotten upset easily, and she recalled engaging in screaming fights with her parents almost daily in her teens and early twenties. In addition, she often argued with ex-boyfriends, once throwing a picture frame against a wall and other times leaving the room in an intense rage and not returning phone calls for days. However, Ashley reported experiencing extreme distress following the end of romantic relationships, which have often precipitated increases in NSSI and suicidal ideation, as well as urges to call and email ex-boyfriends asking them to give her a second chance. Ashley reported that she worries about how sensitive she is, stating that she feels like she's on an emotional roller coaster, feeling happy one moment and sad the next, with no trigger that she can pinpoint.

CONCLUSION

Attempted suicide and NSSI occur at high rates among BPD patients, although it is important to note that self-injurious behaviors also commonly occur among individuals who do not meet criteria for a BPD diagnosis. Given the prevalence of self-injurious behaviors, researchers have investigated factors that may contribute to an increased risk of these behaviors among patients with BPD, as well as factors that may contribute to more lethal suicidal behavior. Specific demographic factors such as age and socioeconomic status and clinical factors such as history of suicide attempts, family history of suicide, specific comorbid diagnoses, and poor psychosocial adjustment have been shown to be risk factors for attempted suicide in BPD patients (e.g., Chen et al., 2009; Soloff & Chiappetta, 2012; Soloff et al., 1994b; Wedig et al., 2012). Few studies have identified risk factors for NSSI among BPD patients, but demographic and clinical factors such as gender, history of sexual abuse and assaults, and comorbid psychiatric diagnoses and symptoms have been shown to predict NSSI over a 10-year period (Zanarini et al., 2011). By understanding risk factors for attempted suicide and NSSI in BPD, we can better identify patients who are at increased risk and focus treatment efforts on addressing modifiable risk factors.

REFERENCES

American Psychiatric Association (APA). (2013). *Diagnostic and statistical manual of mental disorders* (5th ed.). Washington, DC: Author. doi: 10.1176/appi.books.9780890425596.dsm18

Andión, O., Ferrer, M., Calvo, N., Gancedo, B., Barral, C., Di Genova, A., Arbos, M. A., Torrubia, R., & Casas, M. (2013). Exploring the clinical validity of borderline personality disorder components. *Comprehensive Psychiatry, 54*(1), 34–40.

Andover, M. S., Morris, B. W., Wren, A., & Bruzzese, M. E. (2012). The co-occurrence of nonsuicidal self-injury and attempted suicide among adolescents: Distinguishing risk factors and psychosocial correlates. *Child and Adolescent Psychiatry and Mental Health, 6.* doi:10.1186/1753-2000-6-11

Andover, M. S., Pepper, C. M., Ryabchenko, K. A., Orrico, E. G., & Gibb, B. E. (2005). Self-mutilation and symptoms of depression, anxiety, and borderline personality disorder. *Suicide and Life Threatening Behaviors, 35,* 581–591. doi: 10.1521/suli.2005.35.5.581

Anestis, M. D., Gratz, K. L., Bagge, C. L., & Tull, M. T. (2012). The interactive role of distress tolerance and borderline personality disorder in suicide attempts among substance users in residential treatment. *Comprehensive Psychiatry, 53,* 1208–1216. doi: 10.1016/j.comppsych.2012.04.004

Berk, M. S., Jeglic, E., Brown, G. K., Henriques, G. R., & Beck, A. T. (2007). Characteristics of recent suicide attempters with and without borderline personality disorder. *Archives of Suicide Research, 11,* 91–104. doi: 10.1080/13811110600992951

Berrino, A., Ohlendorf, P., Duriaux, S., Burnand, Y., Lorillard, S., & Andreoli, A. (2011). Crisis intervention at the general hospital: An appropriate treatment choice for acutely suicidal borderline patients. *Psychiatry Research, 186,* 287–292. doi: 10.1016/j.psychres.2010.06.018

Black, D. W., Blum, N., Pfohl, B., & Hale, N. (2004). Suicidal behavior in borderline personality disorder: Prevalence, risk factors, prediction, and prevention. *Journal of Personality Disorders, 18,* 226–239. doi: 10.1521/pedi.18.3.226.35445

Boisseau, C. L., Yen, S., Markowitz, J. C., Grilo, C. M., Sanislow, C. A., Shea, M. T., . . . McGlashan, T. H. (2012). Individuals with single versus multiple suicide attempts over 10 years of prospective follow-up. *Comprehensive Psychiatry.* doi: 10.1016/j.comppsych.2012.07.062

Briere, J., & Gil, E. (1998). Self-mutilation in clinical and general population samples: Prevalence, correlates, and functions. *American Journal of Orthopsychiatry, 68,* 609–620. doi: 10.1037/h0080369

Brodsky, B. S., Cloitre, M., & Dulit, R. A. (1995). Relationship of dissociation to self-mutilation and childhood abuse in borderline personality disorder. *American Journal of Psychiatry, 152,* 1788–1792.

Brodsky, B. S., Groves, S. A., Oquendo, M. A., Mann, J. J., & Stanley, B. (2006). Interpersonal precipitants and suicide attempts in borderline personality disorder. *Suicide and Life-Threatening Behavior, 36,* 313–322. doi: 10.1521/suli.2006.36.3.313

Brodsky, B. S., Malone, K. M., Ellis, S. P., Dulit, R. A., & Mann, J. J. (1997). Characteristics of borderline personality disorder associated with suicidal behavior. *American Journal of Psychiatry, 154,* 1715–1719.

Brown, M. Z., Linehan, M. M., Comtois, K. A., Murray, A., & Chapman, A. L. (2009). Shame as a prospective predictor of self-inflicted injury in borderline personality disorder: A multi-modal analysis. *Behavior Research and Therapy, 47,* 815–822. doi: 10.1016.j.brat.2009.06.008

Chen, E. Y., Brown, M. Z., Harned, M. S., & Linehan, M. M. (2009). A comparison of borderline personality disorder with and without eating disorders. *Psychiatry Research, 170,* 86–90. doi: 10.1016/j.psychres.2009.03.006

Chesin, M. S., Jeglic, E. L., & Stanley, B. (2010). Pathways to high-lethality suicide attempts in individuals with borderline personality disorder. *Archives of Suicide Research, 14,* 342–362. doi: 10.1080/13811118.2010.524054

Crowell, S. E., Beauchaine, T. P., & Linehan, M. M. (2009). A biosocial developmental model of borderline personality: Elaborating and extending Linehan's theory. *Psychological Bulletin, 135,* 495–510. doi: 10.1037/a0015616

Evren, C., Cinar, O., Evren, B., & Celik, S. (2012). Relationship of self-mutilative behaviours with severity of borderline personality, childhood trauma, and impulsivity in male substance-dependent inpatients. *Psychiatry Research, 200,* 20–25. doi: 10.1016/j.psychres.2012.03.017

Favazza, A. R. (1998). The coming of age of self-mutilation. *Journal of Nervous and Mental Disease, 186,* 259–268. doi: 10.1097/00005053-199805000-00001

Ferrara, M., Terrinoni, A., & Williams, R. (2012). Non-suicidal self-injury (NSSI) in adolescent inpatients: Assessing personality features and attitude toward death. *Child and Adolescent Psychiatry and Mental Health, 30,* 1–8. doi: 10.1186/1753-2000-6-12

Fyer, M. R., Frances, A. J., Sullivan, T., Hurt, S. W., & Clarkin, J. (1988). Suicide attempts in patients with borderline personality disorder. *American Journal of Psychiatry*, *145*, 737–739.

Ghaziuddin, M., Tsai, L., Naylor, M., & Ghaziuddin, N. (1992). Mood disorder in a group of self-cutting adolescents. *Acta Paedopsychiatrica*, *55*, 103–105.

Glenn, C. R., & Klonsky, E. D. (2011). Prospective prediction of nonsuicidal self-injury: a 1-year longitudinal study in young adults. *Behavior Therapy*, *42*(4), 751–762.

Gratz, K. L., & Chapman, A. L. (2007). The role of emotional responding and childhood maltreatment in the development and maintenance of deliberate self-harm among male undergraduates. *Psychology of Men and Masculinity*, *8*, 1–14. doi: 10.1037/1524-9220.8.1.1

Gratz, K. L., & Gunderson, J. G. (2006). Preliminary data on an acceptance-based emotion regulation group intervention for deliberate self-harm among women with borderline personality disorder. *Behavior Therapy*, *37*, 25–35. doi: 10.1016/j.beth.2005.03.002

Gratz, K. L., & Roemer, L. (2008). The relationship between emotion dysregulation and deliberate self-harm among female undergraduate students at an urban commuter university. *Cognitive Behaviour Therapy*, *37*, 14–25. doi: 10.1080/16506070701819524

Gratz, K. L., & Tull, M. T. (2011). Extending research on the utility of an adjunctive emotion regulation group therapy for deliberate self-harm among women with borderline personality pathology. *Personality Disorders: Theory, Research, and Treatment*, *2*, 316–326. doi: 10.1037/a0022144

Horesh, N., Nachshoni, T., Wolmer, L., & Toren, P. (2009). A comparison of life events in suicidal and nonsuicidal adolescents and young adults with major depression and borderline personality disorder. *Comprehensive Psychiatry*, *50*, 496–502. doi: 10.1016/j.comppsych.2009.01.006

Jacobson, C. M., Muehlenkamp, J. J., Miller, A. L., & Turner, J. B. (2008). Psychiatric impairment among adolescents engaging in different types of deliberate self-harm. *Journal of Clinical Child and Adolescent Psychology*, *37*, 363–375. doi: 10.1080/15374410801955771

Joiner, T. E., Conwell, Y., Fitzpatrick, K. K., Witte, T. K., Schmidt, N. B., Berlim, M. T., . . . Rudd, M. D. (2005). Four studies on how past and current suicidality relate even when "everything by the kitchen sink" is covaried. *Journal of Abnormal Psychology*, *114*, 291–303. doi: 10.1037/0021-843X.114.2.291

Klonsky, E. D. (2008). What is emptiness? Clarifying the 7th criterion for borderline personality disorder. *Journal of Personality Disorders*, *22*, 418–426. doi: 10.1521/pedi.2008.22.4.418

Klonsky, E. D. (2009). The functions of self-injury in young adults who cut themselves: Clarifying the evidence for affect-regulation. *Psychiatry Research*, *166*, 260–268. doi: 10.1016/j.psychres.2008.02.008

Klonsky, E. D., May, A. M., & Glenn, C. R. (2013). The relationship between nonsuicidal self-injury and attempted suicide: Converging evidence from four samples. *Journal of Abnormal Psychology*, *122*, 231–237. doi: 10.1037/a0030278

Klonsky, E. D., & Moyer, A. (2008). Childhood sexual abuse and non-suicidal self-injury: meta-analysis. *British Journal of Psychiatry*, *192*, 166–170. doi: 10.1192/bjp.bp.106.030650

Klonsky, E. D., & Olino, T. M. (2008). Identifying clinically distinct subgroups of self-injurers among young adults: A latent class analysis. *Journal of Consulting and Clinical Psychology*, *76*, 22–27. doi: 10.1037/0022-006X.76.1.22

Klonsky, E. D., Oltmanns, T. F., & Turkheimer, E. (2003). Deliberate self-harm in a nonclinical population: Prevalence and psychological correlates. *American Journal of Psychiatry*, *160*, 1501–1508. doi: 10.1176/appi.ajp.160.8.1501

Kolla, N. J., Eisenberg, H., & Links, P. S. (2008). Epidemiology, risk factors, and psychopharmacological management of suicidal behavior in borderline personality disorder. *Archives of Suicide Research*, *12*, 1–19. doi: 10.1080/13811110701542010

Linehan, M. M. (1993). Cognitive-behavioral treatment of borderline personality disorder. New York: Guilford.

Linehan, M. M., & Dexter-Mazza, E. T. (2007). Dialectical behavior therapy for borderline personality disorder. In D. Barlow (Ed.), *Clinical handbook of psychological disorders: A step-by-step treatment manual* (4th ed., pp. 365–420). New York: Guilford.

McGirr, A., Paris, J., Lesage, A., Renaud, J., & Turecki, G. (2009). An examination of DSM-IV borderline personality disorder symptoms and risk for death by suicide: a psychological autopsy study. *Canadian Journal of Psychiatry, 54*(2), 87–92.

McKay, D., Kulchycky, S., & Danyko, S. (2000). Borderline personality and obsessive-compulsive symptoms. *Journal of Personality Disorders, 14*, 57–63. doi: 10.1521/pedi.2000.14.1.57

Mehlum, L., Friis, S., Vaglum, P., & Karterud, S. (1994). The longitudinal pattern of suicidal behaviour in borderline personality disorder: A prospective follow-up study. *Acta Psychiatrica Scandinavica, 90*, 124–130. doi: 10.111/j.1600-0447.1994.tb01567.x

Miller, A. L., Muehlenkamp, J. J., & Jacobson, C. M. (2008). Fact or fiction: Diagnosing borderline personality disorder in adolescents. *Clinical Psychology Review, 28*, 969–981. doi: 10.1016/j.cpr.2008.02.004

Muehlenkamp, J. J. (2005). Self-injurious behavior as a separate clinical syndrome. *American Journal of Orthopsychiatry, 75*, 324–333. doi: 10.1037/0002-9432.75.2.324

Muehlenkamp, J. J., Ertelt, T. W., Miller, A. L., & Claes, L. (2011). Borderline personality symptoms differentiate non-suicidal and suicidal self-injury in ethnically diverse adolescent outpatients. *Journal of Child Psychology and Psychiatry, 52*, 148–155. doi: 10.1111/j.1469-7610.2010.02305.x

Muehlenkamp, J. J., & Gutierrez, P. M. (2004). An investigation of differences between self-injurious behavior and suicide attempts in a sample of adolescents. *Suicide and Life-Threatening Behavior, 34*, 12–23. doi: 10.1521/suli.34.1.12.27769

Nock, M. K. (2009). Why do people hurt themselves? New insights into the nature and functions of self-injury. *Current Directions in Psychological Science, 18*(2), 78–83.

Nock, M. K., Joiner, T. E., Gordon, K. H., Lloyd-Richardson, E., & Prinstein, M. J. (2006). Non-suicidal self-injury among adolescents: Diagnostic correlates and relation to suicide attempts. *Psychiatry Research, 144*, 65–72. doi: 10.1016/j.psychres.2006.05.010

Paris, J. (1990). Completed suicide in borderline personality disorder. *Psychiatric Annals, 20*, 19–21.

Paris, J. (2002a). Chronic suicidality among patients with borderline personality disorder. *Psychiatric Services, 53*, 738–742. doi: 10.1176/appi.ps.53.6.738

Paris, J. (2002b). Implications of long-term outcome research on the management of patients with borderline personality disorder. *Harvard Review of Psychiatry, 10*, 315–323. doi: 10.1080/10673220216229

Paris, J. (2005). Understanding self-mutilation in borderline personality disorder. *Harvard Review of Psychology, 13*, 179–185. doi: 10.1080/10673220591003614

Paris, J., & Zweig-Frank, H. (2001). A 27-year follow-up of patients with borderline personality disorder. *Comprehensive Psychiatry, 42*, 482–487. doi: 10.1053/comp.2001.26271

Rajappa, K., Gallagher, M., & Miranda, R. (2012). Emotion dysregulation and vulnerability to suicidal ideation and attempts. *Cognitive Therapy and Research, 36*, 833–839. doi: 10.1007/s10608-011-9419-2

Ross, S., & Heath, N. (2002). A study of the frequency of self-mutilation in a community sample of adolescents. *Journal of Youth and Adolescence, 31*, 67–77. doi: 10.1097/01.chi.0000096627.64367.74

Sansone, R. A., Gaither, G. A., & Songer, D. A. (2002). Self-harm behaviors across the life cycle: A pilot study of inpatients with borderline personality disorder. *Comprehensive Psychiatry, 43*, 215–218. doi: 10.1053/comp.2002.32354

Serras, A., Saules, K. K., Cranford, J. A., & Eisenberg, D. (2010). Self-injury, substance use, and associated risk factors in a multi-campus probability sample of college students. *Psychology of Addictive Behaviors, 24*, 119–128. doi: 10.1037/a0017210

Shearer, S. L., Peters, C. P., Quaytman, M. S., & Wadman, B. E. (1988). Intent and lethality of suicide attempts among female borderline inpatients. *American Journal of Psychiatry*, *145*, 1424–1427.

Soloff, P. H., & Chiappetta, L. (2012). Prospective predictors of suicidal behavior in borderline personality disorder at 6-year follow-up. *American Journal of Psychiatry*, *169*, 484–490. doi: 10.1176/appi.ajp.2011.11091378

Soloff, P. H., & Fabio, A. (2008). Prospective predictors of suicide attempts in borderline personality disorder at one, two, and two-to-five year follow-up. *Journal of Personality Disorder*, *22*, 123–134. doi: 10.1521/pedi.2008.22.2.123

Soloff, P. H., Fabio, A., Kelly, T. M., Malone, K. M., & Mann, J. J. (2005). High-lethality status in patients with borderline personality disorder. *Journal of Personality Disorders*, *19*, 386–399. doi: 10.1521/pedi.2005.19.4.386

Soloff, P. H., Feske, U., & Fabio, A. (2008). Mediators of the relationship between childhood sexual abuse and suicidal behavior in borderline personality disorder. *Journal of Personality Disorders*, *22*, 221–232. doi: 10.1521/pedi.2008.22.3.221

Soloff, P. H., Lis, J. A., Kelly, T., Cornelius, J., & Ulrich, R. (1994a). Self-mutilation and suicidal behavior in borderline personality disorder. *Journal of Personality Disorders*, *8*, 257–267. doi: 10.1521/pedi.1994.8.4.257

Soloff, P. H., Lis, J. A., Kelly, T., Cornelius, J., & Ulrich, R. (1994b). Risk factors for suicidal behavior in borderline personality disorder. *American Journal of Psychiatry*, *151*, 1316–1323.

Soloff, P. H., Lynch, K. G., & Kelly, T. M. (2002). Childhood abuse as a risk factor for suicidal behavior in borderline personality disorder. *Journal of Personality Disorder*, *16*, 201–214. doi: 10.1521/pedi.16.3.201.22542

Soloff, P. H., Lynch, K. G., Kelly, T. M., Malone, K. M., & Mann, J. J. (2000). Characteristics of suicide attempts of patients with major depressive episode and borderline personality disorder: A comparative study. *American Journal of Psychiatry*, *157*, 601–608. doi: 10.1176/appi.ajp.157.4.601

Stanley, B., Brodsky, B., Nelson, J. D., & Dulit, R. (2007). Brief dialectical behavior therapy (DBT-B) for suicidal behavior and non-suicidal self-injury. *Archives of Suicide Research*, *11*, 337–341. doi: 10.1080/13811110701542069

Stanley, B., Gameroff, M. J., Michalsen, V., & Mann, J. J. (2001). Are suicide attempters who self-mutilate a unique population? *American Journal of Psychiatry*, *158*(3), 427–432.

Suyemoto, K. L. (1998). The functions of self-mutilation. *Clinical Psychology Review*, *18*, 531–554. doi: 10.1016/S0272-7358(97)00105-0

Walsh, B. (2008). *Treating self-injury: A practical guide* (2nd ed.). New York: The Guilford.

Wedig, M. M., Silverman, M. H., Frankenburg, F. R., Reich, D. B., Fitzmaurice, G., & Zanarini, M. C. (2012). Predictors of suicide attempts in patients with borderline personality disorder over 16 years of prospective followup. *Psychological Medicine*, *42*, 2395–2404. doi: 10.1017/S0033291712000517

Weinberg, I., Gunderson, J. G., Hennen, J., & Cutter, C. J. (2006). Manual assisted cognitive treatment for deliberate self-harm in borderline personality disorder patients. *Journal of Personality Disorders*, *20*, 482–492. doi: 10.1521/pedi.2006.20.5.482

Welch, S. S., & Linehan, M. M. (2002). High-risk situations associated with parasuicide and drug use in borderline personality disorder. *Journal of Personality Disorders*, *16*, 561–569. doi: 10.1521/pedi.16.6.561.22141

Yen, S., Shea, M. T., Sanislow, C. A., Grilo, C. M., Skodol, A. E., Gunderson, J. G., McGlashan, T. H., Zanarini, M. C., & Morey, L. C. (2004). Borderline personality disorder criteria associated with prospectively observed suicidal behavior. *American Journal of Psychiatry*, *161*(7), 1296–1298.

Zanarini, M. C., Frankenburg, F. R., Hennen, J., Reich, B., & Silk, K. R. (2005). The McLean Study of Adult Development (MSAD): Overview and implications of the first six years of prospective follow-up. *Journal of Personality Disorders*, *19*, 505–523. doi: 10.1521/pedi.2005.19.5.505

Zanarini, M. C., Laudate, C. S., Frankenburg, F. R., Reich, D. B., & Fitzmaurice, G. (2011). Predictors of self-mutilation in patients with borderline personality disorder: A 10-year follow-up study. *Psychiatry Research, 45,* 823–828. doi: 10.1016/j.jpsychires.2010.10.015

Zlotnick, C., Mattia, J., & Zimmerman, M. (1999). Clinical correlates of self-mutilation in a sample of general psychiatric patients. *Journal of Nervous and Mental Disease, 187,* 296–301. doi: 10.1097/00005053-199905000-00005

Zlotnick, C., Shea, T. M., Pearlstein, T., Simpson, E. Costello, E., & Begin, A. (1996). The relationship between dissociative symptoms, alexithymia, impulsivity, sexual abuse, and self-mutilation. *Comprehensive Psychiatry, 37,* 12–16. doi: 10.1016/S0010-440X(96)90044-9

Zweig-Frank, H., Paris, J., & Guzder, J. (1994a). Dissociation in female patients with borderline and non-borderline personality disorders. *Journal of Personality Disorders, 8,* 203–209. doi: 10.1521/pedi.1994.8.3.203

Zweig-Frank, H., Paris, J., & Guzder, J. (1994b). Dissociation in male patients with borderline and non-borderline personality disorders. *Journal of Personality Disorders, 8,* 210–218. doi: 10.1521/pedi.1994.8.3.210

/// 9 /// Substance Use Disorder in Borderline Personality Disorder

BETH S. BRODSKY AND LINDA DIMEFF

INTRODUCTION

Individuals diagnosed with borderline personality disorder (BPD) present with multiple, distinct disorders that are often better understood as behavioral constellations driven by the personality disordered pathology (Eaton et al., 2011; Linehan et al., 1999). In particular, substance use disorder (SUD) diagnoses are extremely common among individuals with BPD. The incidence of someone diagnosed with BPD having a comorbid SUD diagnosis (primary and lifetime) ranges from 21% to 23% (Koenigsberg, Kaplan, Gilmore, & Cooper, 1985). Conversely, anywhere from 9% to 65% (community samples vs. treatment samples; Trull, Sher, Minks-Brown, Durbin, & Burr, 2000), of individuals with a SUD have a comorbid diagnosis of BPD. This comorbidity is partially, but not solely, due to the fact that substance abuse can constitute one of the two areas of impulsive behavior required to positively endorse the BPD impulsivity criterion (Sullivan & Frances, 1990).

As with other comorbid mental disorders, it is often difficult to distinguish whether SUDs arise from BPD pathology, whether SUDs exacerbate BPD symptomatology, or both, in comorbid populations (Trull, 2001). Also unclear is whether the nature of SUD in BPD is distinct from SUD in non-BPD clinical populations, although there is considerable evidence indicating that the diagnostic comorbidity results in more complex clinical presentations that involve greater treatment challenges (Lee, Bagge, Schumacher, & Coffey, 2010; Links, Heslegrave, Mitton, & Van Reekum, 1995). For example, individuals with both SUD and BPD, when compared with non-BPD SUD populations, have higher rates of suicide attempts, impulsivity, emotional dysregulation, and social, medical, and legal issues as well as poor treatment adherence (Bornovalova & Daughters, 2007; Bornovalova, Hicks, Iacono, & McGue, 2013; Gregory, DeLucia-Deranja, & Mogle, 2010; Kienast, Stoffers, Bermpohl, & Lieb, 2014; Martínez-Raga, Marshall, Keaney, Ball, & Strang, 2002; Stone, 1990; van den Bosch, Verheul, Schippers, & van den Brink, 2002). They also have an extremely high rate of treatment dropout (Bornovalova et al., 2013) and higher rates of substance use relapse (Pennay et al., 2011). In addition, there is some speculation that individuals with BPD have specific biological vulnerabilities, such as endogenous opiate systems, that drive their substance use. Thus, substance abuse can be conceptualized as an effort, for example, to feel "normal" rather than to escape or feel "high" through the use of opioid-based pain killers or street drugs (Kalivas & Volkow, 2005; Lane, Carpenter, Sher, & Trull, 2016; Trull et al., 2008; Verheul, van den Brink, & Geerlings, 1999).

Clearly, there is a need for greater understanding of the possibly unique etiology and clinical presentation of SUDs in BPD and the ensuing implications for conceptualization and effective approaches to treatment. Along these lines, a number of treatments modify substance abuse "treatment as usual" to address the specific presentation of SUDs in individuals diagnosed with BPD. Specifically, *dialectical behavior therapy* (DBT), an evidence-based psychosocial intervention for the treatment of suicidal and nonsuicidal self-injury (NSSI) in BPD, has been adapted (DBT for substance use disorders [DBT-SUD]) to target substance abuse and dependence behaviors in BPD populations and has been studied in a number of randomized controlled trials (Dimeff & Koerner, 2007; Dimeff & Linehan, 2008; Linehan et al., 2002; Linehan et al., 1999).

In this chapter, we will present what is currently known about the comorbidity of SUD and BPD, outline the ways in which substance use and SUDs have a unique clinical presentation within the context of BPD, and explore how the distinct features of SUDs in BPD inform conceptualization and treatment approach. We will also outline lessons learned at the University of Washington in efforts to adapt DBT for this particularly challenging comorbid population.

SUBSTANCE USE AND SUD IN BPD

Prevalence Rates

As described in Chapter 2, estimates of the prevalence of BPD in the general population ranges from 1.6% to 5.9% (American Psychiatric Association [APA], 2013; Grant et al., 2008), and individuals with BPD are high utilizers of mental health care, with about 6% presenting in primary care settings, 10% in outpatient mental health clinics, and 20% among psychiatric inpatients (APA, 2013). Regarding substance abuse, in 2014, approximately 21.5 million (8.1%) of the general population age

12 years and older reported illicit drug use in the past 30 days, 42.7% of which met criteria for SUD (SAMHSA, 2017). Both BPD and SUDs share a high comorbidity rate with other Axis I and Axis II diagnoses (Sansone & Sansone, 2011), and BPD is the second most prevalent Axis II disorder (after antisocial personality disorder) among SUD populations (Cacciola, Alterman, McKay, & Rutherford, 2001).

The rate of SUD diagnoses among BPD population is high in both clinical and community samples, ranging from 14% current comorbidity to 72% of BPD populations meeting criteria for a lifetime SUD diagnosis (Sansone & Sansone, 2011). In clinical BPD samples, men are more likely than women to meet criteria for a SUD, except in the prevalence of prescription drug abuse (type of drugs unknown), where the gender rates are equal (Sansone, Lam, & Wiederman, 2010*a*). A study comparing three subtypes of BPD found that substance abuse (primarily alcohol, cocaine, and anxiolytics) was more significantly prevalent in the behavioral dysregulation subtype of BPD than in the affective dysregulation or disturbed interpersonal relatedness subtypes (Calvo, Valero, Ferrer, Barral, & Casas, 2016). Thus, SUDs in BPD (BPD-SUD) can be understood as most related to the behavioral impulsivity aspect of the disorder.

Types of Substances

Little is known regarding the types of substances most highly abused among individuals with BPD. In a consecutively admitted sample of 96 inpatients with BPD, among those with a DSM III-R SUD diagnosis, drug choice differed by gender. Males preferred stimulants, whereas alcohol and sedative/hypnotics were the substances of choice for females (Miller, Abrams, Dulit, & Fyer, 1993). In a more recent epidemiological study using a nationally representative sample, controlling for shared variables across the SUD disorders as well as demographic and other psychopathology covariates in a multivariate regression model, alcohol, cocaine, and opiate use disorder were the best SUD predictors of BPD diagnosis, indicating a unique association between BPD and these three SUDs (Carpenter, Wood, & Trull, 2016). There is supporting evidence that these three substances—alcohol (14.3% of BPD abuse alcohol), cocaine (16.8% of BPD with cocaine use disorder), and opiates (18.5% of BPD abuse opiates)—are the most widely abused substances among individuals with BPD (Carpenter et al., 2016). However, cannabis and prescription drugs, mostly in the sedative/hypnotic category, are also widely abused (Sansone, Lam, & Wiederman, 2010*b*).

BPD Vulnerability to SUD

The self-medication hypothesis, a psychoanalytically informed theory of addiction, has been put forth as a possible explanation for the high prevalence of substance abuse in individuals diagnosed with BPD. Although more widely studied in posttraumatic stress disorder (PTSD) populations (Khantzian, 1997; McCauley, Killeen,

Gros, Brady, & Back, 2012), the theory maintains that substance abuse represents an individual's best attempt to cope with and "medicate away" his or her intense emotional experiences, particularly feelings of intense anger, anxiety, and emptiness. Opiates in particular are effective in ameliorating these emotional symptoms, thereby providing a rationale for the popularity of heroin and other opiate-based prescription medications as drugs of choice among BPD individuals (Verheul et al., 1999). Cocaine use, on the other hand, is cited to fill feelings of emptiness and/or to lift depression (Khantzian, 1997). Cannabis may be a drug of choice for medicating anxiety (Eaton et al., 2011).

Relatedly, recent neurobiological studies reveal possible biological vulnerabilities in BPD that might drive substance abuse behaviors. In particular, Bandelow et al. (Bandelow, Schmahl, Falkai, & Wedekind, 2010) propose that many of the impulsive destructive behaviors in individuals with BPD can be understood as attempts to stimulate the endogenous opiate and dopaminergic reward systems, and, consequently, substances used by these individuals often target opiate-related brain receptor systems (Bandelow et al., 2010; Prossin, Love, Koeppe, Zubieta, & Silk, 2010). In addition, there is evidence of a relationship among NSSI behaviors, substance abuse, and the endogenous opiate system (Niaura et al., 1988). NSSI behaviors can, in some individuals, result in a release of endogenous opiates, which not only relieve physical and emotional pain, but also produce an experience of euphoria and therefore provide positive reinforcement that promotes the behavior (Akil et al., 1984). Thus, it is possible that some types of substance use in BPD may be driven by unconscious and uncontrollable motivations to regulate deficits in the endogenous opioid system (Stanley et al., 2010; Zubieta et al., 2001). Substance abuse in BPD can represent an attempt to self-medicate emotional pain and/or neurological vulnerabilities to physiological arousal associated with attachment seeking (Stanley et al., 2010) and intense affective experience (New & Stanley, 2010; Stanley & Siever, 2009).

Clinical Presentation and Treatment Challenges

Clinical Presentation

The comorbidity of BPD with SUDs is associated with a more complex clinical presentation, as well as with negative treatment outcomes (Lee et al., 2010; Links et al., 1995; Skodol, Oldham, & Gallaher, 1999). Studies comparing comorbid BPD/SUD with non-BPD SUD and non-SUD BPD-only populations have found significant differences in symptomatology and course. In particular, BPD/SUD comorbidity heightens suicide risk and tendency to engage in suicidal and self-harm behaviors. In a longitudinal study, Links et al. (1995) found that comorbid BPD/SUD populations, when compared with BPD-only populations, demonstrated higher BPD psychopathology and more self-destructive and suicidal thoughts and behaviors, and they were twice as likely to be diagnosed with BPD on follow-up (Links et al., 1995). Although one study found an independent relationship between deliberate self-harm behaviors and SUDs while controlling for the presence of BPD (Gratz & Tull, 2010), the same study documented among individuals with SUD high levels of three types of emotional dysregulation that are also prevalent in BPD: (1) limited access to effective emotion regulation strategies, (2) difficulties engaging in goal-directed behaviors when distressed, and (3) emotional nonacceptance (Gratz & Tull, 2010) indicating a close relationship among self-harm, emotional dysregulation, and SUD similar to that found in BPD. Also, when compared to SUD-only populations, BPD/SUD groups have been found to have a higher risk of having experienced emotional and physical abuse, neglect, or family violence in childhood (Wapp et al., 2015), and they score higher in certain areas of impulsivity (lower behavioral response inhibition) (Coffey, Schumacher, Baschnagel, Hawk, & Holloman, 2011).

Treatment Challenges

Despite the high utilization of mental health treatment by individuals diagnosed with BPD, these patients are difficult to retain in treatment (Linehan et al., 2002; Martínez-Raga et al., 2002) largely due to exquisite interpersonal sensitivity and inability to tolerate the difficult emotions that arise. Similarly, among individuals who abuse substances, reliance on avoidance and escape behaviors interferes with the ability to maintain motivation for treatment. In one study, substance abusers with BPD were found to engage in more avoidance/escape coping strategies than were substance abusers without BPD (Kruedelbach, McCormick, Schulz, & Grueneich, 1993). In another study focusing explicitly on distress tolerance, individuals with BPD-SUD comorbidity showed elevated levels of distress intolerance compared to those with only a SUD diagnosis (Bornovalova, Gratz, Delany-Brumsey, Paulson, & Lejuez, 2006). Thus, tendency to avoid and escape distress is heightened in BPD-SUD comorbid populations, detracting from the ability to persist in goal-directed behavior and to remain in treatment, which requires tolerance of emotional experiencing (Bornovalova & Daughters, 2007).

Treatment Implications

Individuals with substance use and SUD within the context of BPD constitute a complex, unique, and challenging clinical picture that requires modifications of substance abuse "treatment as usual." First and foremost, this comorbid population presents at even greater risk for suicide and self-harm behaviors. Suicidal and NSSI behaviors are often preceded by some type of substance use, and substances are used as a secondary method to enhance capability to act on suicidal urges (LeGris & van Reekum, 2006; Wilson, Fertuck, Kwitel, Stanley, & Stanley, 2006). And substances are often abused as attempts to regulate emotional distress in the form of nonsuicidal "micro-overdoses." Thus, targeting substance use within BPD requires concurrent attention to suicidal and self-harm impulses and simultaneous focus on substance use reduction along with increase of reasons for living.

Second, impulsivity is a prominent feature in the BPD/SUD comorbidity profile, leading to—in addition to suicide and substance use—numerous destructive behaviors that cause instability in social and vocational functioning. Therefore, making consistent progress on the reduction of substance use is complicated by the need to maintain equal emphasis on the reduction of destructive impulsive behaviors. Any substance use treatment should target impulsivity, such as through distress tolerance behavioral skills training in addition to psychopharmacology.

Another consideration is that individuals who abuse substances rely heavily on avoidance and escape strategies to unskillfully manage distress. Individuals with BPD similarly tend to avoid and escape, and they have difficulties with distress tolerance and emotional dysregulation. They are highly interpersonally sensitive and are quick to interpret and experience blame, emotional invalidation, and rejection. These tendencies compound the difficulty in tolerating and maintaining motivation for treatment in this comorbid population, leading to low treatment adherence and retention. Implications for treatment of SUDs within BPD are to provide explicit emphasis on treatment engagement, motivation enhancement, and attachment strategies. These can be promoted through increased contact between clinician and patient; addressing obstacles for treatment nonadherence, including issues that arise in the therapeutic relationship; and through the teaching of distress tolerance and emotion regulation skills, including graded exposure to emotional experiencing.

Substance abuse relapse rates are higher among individuals with BPD than in non-BPD SUD populations. Given that individuals with BPD struggle with cognitive distortions in terms of black-and-white thinking, it is possible that a modification of the 12-step total abstinence "all-or-nothing" model is warranted to effectively reduce substance abuse in these individuals.

Finally, further research is necessary to identify neurobiological underpinnings and deficits that may be driving substance use in individuals with BPD. This can lead to the more effective use of replacement medications and more specifically targeted psychopharmacological interventions to enhance psychosocial approaches to reducing substance use behaviors.

Observations and Clinical Recommendations from University of Washington Research

DBT, originally designed to treat suicidal and NSSI behaviors in individuals with BPD, is a well-suited psychotherapeutic approach to address the specific challenges of treating substance-dependent individuals with BPD (BPD-SUD). Responding to the need for an efficacious treatment for multidisordered substance-dependent individuals with BPD (BPD-SUD), Linehan, Dimeff, and colleagues evaluated and adapted DBT for this particularly challenging and high-risk population (Linehan & Dimeff, 2000). These adaptations were based on impressions formed from years of National Institute on Drug Abuse (NIDA)-funded clinical research at the University of Washington, with poly-substance dependent individuals with BPD. In earlier pilot phases, the most common primary drugs of abuse included alcohol, opiates, marijuana, and cocaine. Subsequent trials required BPD-SUD patients to meet criteria for opiate dependence, although many also met dependence criteria for a number of other drugs of abuse—most commonly cocaine and marijuana. Only one study included men as well as women with opiate dependence and BPD. In all studies, DBT treatment developer Marsha M. Linehan and Dr. Dimeff, a co-developer of DBT-SUD, served as individual therapists and DBT skills trainers in order to directly observe and understand the special needs of those with BPD-SUD, and directly craft clinical adaptations.

DBT-SUD directly targets substance use with the same approach that standard DBT targets life-threatening suicidal and NSSI behaviors. Additional modifications to the treatment have been made to address high avoidance of cues associated with negative emotions, lack of reinforcement of therapeutic contact, challenges with treatment engagement and adherence, building supportive structure to counteract persistent urges to use, and the involvement of family and social supports when possible.

High Avoidance of Cues Associated with Negative Emotions

Observations of the BPD-SUD research participants over time were instrumental in developing the modified DBT approach. These individuals were observed to be far more avoidant than BPD non-SUD patients of cues likely to elicit negative emotion, particularly earlier in treatment when still using drugs. Common cues include attending therapy, making eye contact during sessions, perceiving disappointment in the therapist, and experiencing physical discomfort associated with withdrawal from drugs. To reduce aversive stimuli related to therapy, sessions can be often conducted in less conventional contexts early on in treatment, with therapists paying even greater attention to their own emotional responses to prevent nonstrategic eliciting of negative emotions in the patient.

Examples of unique adaptations to address the significant avoidance of negative emotions are described here and were particularly important during the initial months of treatment:

- Conducting therapy while taking a walk or driving rather than requiring that therapy be conducted while sitting in an office. For many, the movement was a helpful distraction and functioned to help regulate their emotions. Such activities also functioned to reduce the eye contact that some found aversive.
- Therapeutic efforts to modulate emotional intensity by strategically inserting humor, lightness, and irreverence into therapy sessions and including brief strategic "chit-chat" about neutral, nontriggering topics at the start of sessions.
- Reducing the length of the therapy session, starting with 30 minutes and shaping to the usual 50-minute hour.
- Expanding the session duration from 50 minutes to 120 minutes to allow for greater "warming-up" and "cooling-down" periods to ensure that the patient is fully emotionally regulated before ending the session.

Enhancing the Reinforcing Nature of Therapeutic Contact

Those with BPD-SUD were observed to prefer quick-acting drugs when confronted with emotional distress rather than reliance on or seeking help from people, as is more common in BPD non-SUD populations.

Therefore, for individuals with BPD-SUD, therapeutic contact is more aversive and not reinforcing because it represents an impediment to the natural inclination to resolve crises through the use of quick-acting drugs. This necessitates a modified approach to make therapists (and therapy) as relevant and salient as possible. At the University of Washington, therapists made themselves available in unconventional ways: helped with resumes, provided transportation to court, offered assistance and coaching for interaction with administrative officials (children's protective services, court judges), accompanied patients to emergency room visits, and provided meals. Therapists reached out to patients' social networks, making it a point to know an intimate partner, and they associated themselves with positive stimuli cues, including replacement medications. With opiate-addicted patients, for example, therapists provided opiate replacement medication ("picked up" the medications at the pharmacy on patients' behalf, then personally handed them over to them for their use) and also met patients at the dispensary while taking their dose. Healthy snacks and tea were provided during therapy sessions and groups.

Treatment Nonadherence

Patients with BPD (non-SUD) often have difficulty attaching to therapy and instead act like butterflies, flying into and out of their therapist's hand (Linehan, 1993). For them, the primary therapy-interfering behavior is noninvolvement or inconsistent involvement with their primary therapist: they cancel sessions, don't return calls or texts, are no-shows to sessions after offering assurances they will be there; they repeatedly come to session then miss a string of sessions, come to a session then miss several more weeks of treatment, and so it goes. At the other end of the spectrum are those patients who easily and immediately attach—seemingly with little effort (Linehan, 1993). The "attacher" patient's primary therapy-interfering behavior typically involves difficulty observing limits with respect to phone calls, texts, number and length of session, and the like, and these patients have difficulty tolerating separations from their therapist. The majority of the BPD-SUD patients at the University of Washington were "butterflies" and did not readily attach to the treatment or treatment provider. A strong, positive relationship with BPD clients, however, is often the only factor that keeps these patients in treatment and, in some cases, alive. In DBT, the relationship is used as a means to an end, a way to achieving greater "contact and leverage with the client to cause change and growth" (Linehan, 1993, p. 514). For these reasons, attachment during the early phases of treatment is an important goal in our work.

The challenge to achieve this type of positive therapeutic relationship appears to be more pronounced in BPD-SUD individuals. Thus, engagement of the reluctant patient needs to be a therapeutic task to target. In the beginning phase of treatment, an assessment can be made, based on treatment history, as to where the patient falls on the "attachers–butterfly" spectrum. Any past history of difficulty with treatment engagement and adherence can be framed as presenting a challenge to the current treatment, one that requires problem-solving. In order to enhance treatment engagement, therapists can increase between-session contact with patients via scheduled and spontaneous text or phone contact, conduct sessions in vivo instead of in the clinic office, be flexible regarding session length as needed, and reach out with a nondemanding message to break avoidance patterns when patients don't attend.

One particularly challenging example of the butterfly problem for BPD-SUD patients is the tendency to go missing when using drugs. More so than BPD non-SUD patients, those with comorbid SUD seem to "drop off the grid," so that phone calls go unanswered and even roommates and emergency contacts have no information as to their whereabouts. This behavior of completely "avoiding life" often signals even higher risk for encountering more problems beyond drug use. In the case of one patient who illustrates this point, all was well during a late Friday afternoon appointment. By the evening, the patient had relapsed and didn't resurface for 2 weeks. By the time she did, she had lost her housing, job, and custody of her 3-year-old son—all of which she had only tenuously previously held because of her long history of problems associated with drug use.

Other common problems that occur when patients are lost to contact include stealing, getting arrested, having unprotected sex with a stranger or drug dealer in exchange for drugs, getting raped, and overdosing. Thus, therapeutic steps are necessary to address problems associated with "getting lost." As part of an initial intake evaluation phase, DBT modified for BPD-SUD incorporates a routine inquiry into the places a patient might go if he or she fell off the grid. This inquiry includes recording of addresses, contacts, street corners, and names of bars, and obtaining permission at the very start (while motivation to get off drugs is high) to come looking for them. Guidelines for looking for "missing" patients include a number of principles that reach beyond safety concerns. Clinically, the intervention often requires a light, matter-of-fact, and at times playful touch to avoid eliciting intense negative emotions. Examples of such an approach might include cajoling, generating hope, and reminding them of their most important reasons for getting off drugs. Other outreach efforts can include sending witty gifts with simple notes: a pack of lifesavers ("We're here for you, just grab hold"), a glue stick ("Stick with us. You've made great progress"), delivery of helium balloons ("You're not flying away are you?"), and pizza delivery ("Thinking lots about you"). When patients emerge, the therapy includes a collaborative discussion of what worked and what was less helpful to refine the approach for the future.

Lessons Learned from Developing DBT-SUD

The following are some key lessons learned over the course of conducting DBT-SUD treatment development research.

Choose Your Battles

Like most people, individuals with BPD-SUD can only change so many problematic behaviors at a time if they are to have any success. In the research population, the BPD-SUD patient typically met criteria for no less than four other mental disorders, not including BPD and SUD. Many possessed outstanding warrants for their arrest, had tenuous housing, were unemployed, and were addicted to a number of drugs.

DBT-SUD is an abstinence-based treatment program for the simple reason that patients with severe psychopathology do better with abstinence. Additionally, continued use of drugs, particularly when illegal, simply puts them in high-risk situations and involved in illegal behavior.

Although abstinence from all drugs of abuse may be the goal of DBT-SUD, it is not always the goal of the patient. Seeking complete abstinence from all drugs can alienate these patients from treatment and cause other problems, such as lying about their use. The treatment development team found that many of the patients were willing to give up "hard drugs" (e.g., cocaine, heroin, methamphetamine, etc.), but were reluctant to stop marijuana and alcohol use. This led to a decision to back off from insistence on complete abstinence and to settle (for the moment) on abstinence from the drugs causing the most harm. This "choosing of battles" is accompanied by working to strengthen the commitment to give up the other drugs if they are determined at some point to contribute to higher order treatment targets (e.g., suicidal behaviors, using drugs they agreed to give up).

To illustrate, one patient was perfectly content to give up heroin, cocaine, and suicidal behaviors, but not alcohol. After several months, a clear pattern emerged where drinking (not always, but often) resulted in using benzodiapizines, which then resulted in drinking alcohol to potentially fatal excess. Although her intent was not to kill herself, she drank and used drugs in a fashion that was potentially lethal. The therapist and patient then revisited the initial lack of commitment to giving up alcohol and decided that if she drinks in a potentially life-threatening fashion and/ or it leads to using drugs she decided to give up, she would stop drinking. From that moment on, the patient made the commitment to give up alcohol, and alcohol use was then added to the list of problem behaviors to treat.

In the absence of a commitment to abstain from the use of a particular drug, the treatment nonetheless tracks the use of that substance and the amount, frequency, context, and consequence of use. The therapist can then use this information to notice patterns and highlight anything of clinical relevance related to the patient's use of that substance (e.g., pattern of use going up or down; drug use was interfering with using new skills to manage emotion, etc.). This provides a good therapeutic opportunity to highlight ways in which continued use of the substance is interfering with the achievement of important goals. To illustrate, one BPD-SUD patient with opiate and marijuana dependence as well as alcohol dependence (in remission) had no interest in quitting pot. She did agree, however, to give it up if it interfered with other problems—which it did not. Early on in treatment, she reported wanting a stable, meaningful romantic relationship with someone who would love her faithfully and lovingly. We highlighted how her ongoing pot use may get in the way of finding that person: most people who were like the person she sought would not want to partner with someone who smoked pot daily. Over time, her use significantly dropped and she eventually gave it up—on her terms.

Establish Structure

Unlike suicidal behaviors and NSSI, use of drugs is a 24/7 affair, requiring "work" to pay for drugs (e.g., steal and/or sell off items, trade sex, etc.), use drugs, and recover from drug use. The flow of a BPD-SUD's daily activities, including with whom they interact and where they go, are all associated with drug use in one way or another. Deciding to become and stay abstinent requires substituting the structure once created by substance use with alternative activities and social contacts.

This problem is certainly not unique to BPD-SUD individuals. Indeed, recognizing this common problem as addicts and alcoholics transition from using to recovery, 12-step programs encourage 90 meetings in 90 days. By attending at least one meeting a day, particularly during the initial period of abstinence, those struggling with addictive behaviors have a place to go that is drug-free, a community of people to interact with who share a common goal to stop using drugs, and an activity to structure their time. To further strengthen their engagement with this new community, newcomers are often assigned roles such as the meeting's greeter, coffee maker, or the like—all functioning to help the newly "clean" member form a new set of "people, places, and things" that support recovery.

Not all BPD-SUD patients are willing to attend 12-step meetings. They can be particularly sensitive about "fitting in" to "normal" non–drug using culture. Interpersonal problems that challenge chronically suicidal people with BPD also compromise the ease of making and sustaining friends for those with BPD-SUD, functioning to further reinforce the notion that it is only with other addicts and alcoholics that they belong.

There is no right answer or approach to building structure. Just as a therapist might help a depressed patient schedule up reinforcing activities throughout the week, so should those treating BPD-SUD. Creative brainstorming and problem-solving are essential, as is great willingness on the patient's part—replacing the ideal or even preferred activity with one that is possible and safe (i.e., low risk of contact with cues to use). Some suggestions are to get a job (part-time, full-time), volunteer for meaningful causes, join clubs and church groups, and find local opportunities for meeting up with groups via Internet posts.

Help Them Get and Keep a Job

There is probably no better way to structure up one's time, have a place to go, meet new people, and (re)engage in nonaddict culture than through paid work. Except for a few, not working places individuals outside the mainstream. Employment provides a rich context to practice newly acquired, effective behavioral responses and provides financial resources to increase stability.

There is increasing recognition of the importance of vocational functioning as a psychotherapeutic target. From a DBT-SUD perspective, the goal of obtaining and maintaining employment is an essential therapeutic task because (1) getting/keeping a job helps prevent relapse; (2) patients will commonly avoid job-seeking tasks to avoid self-loathing and intense negative emotions that arise; (3) preparing for job interviews, including explaining legal problems and/or significant gaps in employment, is quite aversive and demoralizing, requiring rehearsal and support; and (4) these individuals need guidance to know where and how to take steps to re-enter the workforce. The primary therapist is often best able to determine what the patient is capable of (shaping)—aiming not too high nor too low. While the ultimate goal is full-time employment with opportunities for advancement, a first step for some may involve providing day-labor or other temporary positions

Teaching Patients to Fail Well, when Needed

"Failing well," the ability to pick oneself up after a fall, slip, or transgression; learning from one's mistakes; and getting back up and going at it again is an important life skill for all people who endeavor to anything difficult or great. When it comes to treatment of drug addiction, failing well is of paramount importance when slips do occur to avert a full-blown relapse. G. Alan Marlatt first described what happens when people striving for abstinence slip and do not fail well. His "abstinence violation effect" (AVE; Marlatt & Gordon, 1985) describes the overwhelming negative emotion, self-recrimination, and belief that the event is simply more proof that the person is fundamentally flawed (versus the view that it is just a usual, to-be-expected outcome in an anything-but-linear process of habit change). The more important abstinence is to the person, the harder the fall. While we know of no studies comparing the AVE in BPD-SUD patients compared to those without BPD, it is reasonable to assume that those with BPD are far more sensitive to its effect.

DBT-SUD incorporates teaching "failing well" before a relapse occurs and following an episode of use. Extending Marlatt's concept of "prolapse," DBT-SUD highlights (1) that relapses can help catapult a person into enduring change so long as the person learns from the event and resumes effort; (2) that habit change is inherently hard for everyone and is typically accompanied by making many mistakes—of all sizes—before getting it right; and (3) reframing failing in a positive light, noting that technology firms (e.g., Amazon, Google, and Microsoft) routinely ask applicants about their experiences of failing because all great innovators and inventors fail first before they achieve great success. Success requires resilience and the ability to continue problem-solving despite feelings of demoralization in order to reach the goal.

Stringing Together a Drug-Free Life a Moment at a Time

Considering total abstinence and never using drugs ever again can be overwhelming and can lead to a range of negative emotions and thoughts. In order to enhance self-efficacy, DBT-SUD therefore focuses on maintaining abstinence for only a period a person knows with 100% certainty he or she can achieve. Focus just on that period—whether it's a day, 3 weeks, or 5 minutes. Key to this cognitive strategy is renewal of the commitment to abstain for the next doable period of time once you reach the end of that period.

One patient with a long history of methamphetamine abuse remarked that when her urges and cravings to use were particularly high, she wisely held on for 5 minutes—just 5 minutes: "I knew I could make it for 5 minutes." Then, after reaching the end of that period, she recommitted to another 5 minutes, then to another. She later shared: "In my mind, I managed each 5 minutes like it was a little pearl, and I was stringing together a beautiful pearl necklace, pearl by pearl, 5 minutes at a time."

Targeting Lying

The assumptions of standard DBT are that patients are doing the best they can, but they need to do better (Linehan, 1993). This leads to a very trusting therapeutic stance toward BPD patients, in which therapists do not regularly take dishonesty on the part of the patient into account. For those with BPD-SUD, the therapist conducting standard DBT may be too gullible and quick to assume innocence. Feedback from the University of Washington research participants was that the treatment needed to more directly address lying behaviors. Indeed, it is difficult to imagine developing drug addiction without simultaneously developing a habit of lying and other deceitful actions. It is difficult to help someone solve a problem behavior that they are lying about. Just as lying is required to sustain drug dependence, honesty is incompatible with drug use.

DBT-SUD strategies to address lying include having patients record the number of lies told on a daily basis; asking patients if they are lying (without insisting on knowing what they may be lying about); weekly drug screens; and talking openly and nonjudgmentally about lying as an old, deeply ingrained behavior. DBT-SUD encourages taking a matter-of-fact approach in asking for "proof" of important aspects of the treatment plan, whether it means directly observing a patient take an opiate replacement medication or have them send daily videos (with date/time stamps) showing them taking Antabuse. Any uncovered lies are subjected to a behavioral analysis in an effort to understand the conditions that gave rise to the lying and to engage in problem-solving.

Involving the Family and Social Supports

The National Collaborating Centre for Mental Health's (2009) expansive best-practice findings point to the importance of family involvement in the care of treatment for BPD. This may be particularly important for families and loved ones of those with BPD-SUD who have endured, in many cases, endless disappointment and heartbreak as they have provided money for food and shelter, or a room in their own home only to have their valued possessions stolen for drug money. Families endure months of silence, not knowing if their loved one is alive or dead from drug overdose. Although these types of experiences often fray family relationships, many families want to help and need guidance regarding how to be more effective in providing support.

DBT-SUD includes assessment as to whether a bridge back to the family remains and to consider how the family may help their loved one achieve his or her goal. Family members can help in a variety of important ways: they can assist with transportation to and from treatment; hold, distribute, and observe their loved one taking replacement medications or Antabuse during early recovery; provide drug screens and communicate results to primary treatment provider; coach loved one on skills; and offer up encouragement. During particularly difficult periods where urges to use are unusually high, families can provide additional support by doing activities together, having a get-together, and providing extra childcare to provide brief respite. In one extreme case, a parent "locked" her son into her apartment for 30 days while he transitioned off heroin and onto an opiate replacement medication. When asked later about his views of being under his mom's watchful "house arrest," he reported feeling extremely cared about by her and said "I always knew I could get out if I wanted to, through the window. I just didn't want to." As the haze of drug use lifted over the course of 30 days, he returned to writing and recording music.

CONCLUSION

The high comorbidity of SUD in individuals diagnosed with BPD adds to the complexity of clinical presentation, symptom severity, and obstacles to treatment engagement and effectiveness. In developing DBT, Linehan originally introduced the concept of modifications to "treatment as usual" for individuals with BPD, for whom traditional approaches were ineffective in terms of symptom reduction, treatment engagement, and retention. In this chapter, we reviewed the increased risks, challenges, and obstacles to treatment presented by SUD-BPD comorbidity, which necessitate "modifications within modifications" to "DBT as usual." Efforts to adapt DBT to this challenging comorbid population have resulted in new interventions for treatment engagement, behavioral goal setting, and expansion of the standard frame of conducting psychotherapy that more directly target the specific challenges of treating SUD-BPD.

REFERENCES

Akil, H., Watson, S. J., Young, E., Lewis, M. E., Khachaturian, H., & Walker, J. M. (1984). Endogenous opioids: Biology and function. *Annual Review of Neuroscience, 7*(1), 223–255.

American Psychiatric Association (APA). (2013). *Diagnostice and statistical manual of mental disorders* (5th ed.). Washington, DC: Author.

Bandelow, B., Schmahl, C., Falkai, P., & Wedekind, D. (2010). Borderline personality disorder: A dysregulation of the endogenous opioid system? *Psychological Review, 117*(2), 623.

Bornovalova, M. A., & Daughters, S. B. (2007). How does dialectical behavior therapy facilitate treatment retention among individuals with comorbid borderline personality disorder and substance use disorders? *Clinical Psychology Review, 27*(8), 923–943.

Bornovalova, M. A., Gratz, K. L., Delany-Brumsey, A., Paulson, A., & Lejuez, C. (2006). Temperamental and environmental risk factors for borderline personality disorder among inner-city substance users in residential treatment. *Journal of Personality Disorders, 20*(3), 218–231.

Bornovalova, M. A., Hicks, B. M., Iacono, W. G., & McGue, M. (2013). Longitudinal-twin study of borderline personality disorder traits and substance use in adolescence: Developmental change, reciprocal effects, and genetic and environmental influences. *Personality Disorders, 4*(1), 23–32. doi:10.1037/a0027178

Cacciola, J. S., Alterman, A. I., McKay, J. R., & Rutherford, M. J. (2001). Psychiatric comorbidity in patients with substance use disorders: Do not forget Axis II disorders. *Psychiatric Annals, 31*(5), 321–331.

Calvo, N., Valero, S., Ferrer, M., Barral, C., & Casas, M. (2016). Impulsive clinical profile of borderline personality disorder with comorbid substance use disorder. *Actas españolas de psiquiatría, 44*(4), 145.

Carpenter, R. W., Wood, P. K., & Trull, T. J. (2016). Comorbidity of borderline personality disorder and lifetime substance use disorders in a nationally representative sample. *Journal of Personality Disorders, 30*(3), 336–350.

Coffey, S. F., Schumacher, J. A., Baschnagel, J. S., Hawk, L. W., & Holloman, G. (2011). Impulsivity and risk-taking in borderline personality disorder with and without substance use disorders. *Personality Disorders: Theory, Research, and Treatment, 2*(2), 128.

Dimeff, L. A., & Koerner, K. E. (2007). *Dialectical behavior therapy in clinical practice: Applications across disorders and settings.* New York: Guilford.

Dimeff, L. A., & Linehan, M. M. (2008). Dialectical behavior therapy for substance abusers. *Addiction Science and Clinical Practice, 4*(2), 39–47.

Eaton, N. R., Krueger, R. F., Keyes, K. M., Skodol, A. E., Markon, K. E., Grant, B. F., & Hasin, D. S. (2011). Borderline personality disorder co-morbidity: Relationship to the internalizing–externalizing structure of common mental disorders. *Psychological medicine, 41*(05), 1041–1050.

Grant, B. F., Chou, S. P., Goldstein, R. B., Huang, B., Stinson, F. S., Saha, T. D., . . . Pickering, R. P. (2008). Prevalence, correlates, disability, and comorbidity of DSM-IV borderline personality disorder: Results from the Wave 2 National Epidemiologic Survey on Alcohol and Related Conditions. *Journal of Clinical Psychiatry, 69*(4), 533.

Gratz, K. L., & Tull, M. T. (2010). The relationship between emotion dysregulation and deliberate self-harm among inpatients with substance use disorders. *Cognitive Therapy and Research, 34*(6), 544–553.

Gregory, R. J., DeLucia-Deranja, E., & Mogle, J. A. (2010). Dynamic deconstructive psychotherapy versus optimized community care for borderline personality disorder co-occurring with alcohol use disorders: A 30-month follow-up. *Journal of Nervous and Mental Disease, 198*(4), 292–298.

Kalivas, P. W., & Volkow, N. D. (2005). The neural basis of addiction: A pathology of motivation and choice. *American Journal of Psychiatry, 162*(8), 1403–1413.

Khantzian, E. J. (1997). The self-medication hypothesis of substance use disorders: A reconsideration and recent applications. *Harvard Review of Psychiatry, 4*(5), 231–244.

Kienast, T., Stoffers, J., Bermpohl, F., & Lieb, K. (2014). Borderline personality disorder and comorbid addiction: Epidemiology and treatment. *Deutsches Ärzteblatt International, 111*(16), 280–286. doi:10.3238/arztebl.2014.0280

Koenigsberg, H. W., Kaplan, R. D., Gilmore, M. M., & Cooper, A. M. (1985). The relationship between syndrome and personality disorder in DSM-III: Experience with 2,462 patients. *American Journal of Psychiatry, 142*(2), 207–212.

Kruedelbach, N., McCormick, R. A., Schulz, S. C., & Grueneich, R. (1993). Impulsivity, coping styles, and triggers for craving in substance abusers with borderline personality disorder. *Journal of Personality Disorders, 7*(3), 214–222. doi:10.1521/pedi.1993.7.3.214

Lane, S. P., Carpenter, R. W., Sher, K. J., & Trull, T. J. (2016). Alcohol craving and consumption in borderline personality disorder: When, where, and with whom. *Clinical Psychological Science.* doi:10.1177/2167702615616132

Lee, H. -J., Bagge, C. L., Schumacher, J. A., & Coffey, S. F. (2010). Does comorbid substance use disorder exacerbate borderline personality features? A comparison of borderline personality disorder individuals with vs. without current substance dependence. *Personality Disorders: Theory, Research, and Treatment, 1*(4), 239.

LeGris, J., & van Reekum, R. (2006). The neuropsychological correlates of borderline personality disorder and suicidal behaviour. *Canadian Journal of Psychiatry, 51*(3), 131–142.

Linehan, M. M. (1993). *Cognitive behavioral treatment for borderline personality disorder.* New York: Guilford.

Linehan, M. M., & Dimeff, L. A. (2000). *DBT for substance abusers: An extension of standard DBT.* Unpublished manuscript.

Linehan, M. M., Dimeff, L. A., Reynolds, S. K., Comtois, K. A., Welch, S. S., Heagerty, P., & Kivlahan, D. R. (2002). Dialectical behavior therapy versus comprehensive validation therapy plus 12-step for the treatment of opioid dependent women meeting criteria for borderline personality disorder. *Drug and Alcohol Dependence, 67*(1), 13–26.

Linehan, M. M., Schmidt, H., Dimeff, L. A., Craft, J. C., Kanter, J., & Comtois, K. A. (1999). Dialectical behavior therapy for patients with borderline personality disorder and drug-dependence. *American Journal on Addictions, 8*(4), 279–292.

Links, P. S., Heslegrave, R. J., Mitton, J. E., & Van Reekum, R. (1995). Borderline personality disorder and substance abuse: Consequences of comorbidity. *Canadian Journal of Psychiatry.*

Marlatt, G. A., & Gordon, J. R. (1985). *Relapse prevention: Maintenance strategies in the treatment of addictive behaviors.* New York: Guilford.

Martínez-Raga, J., Marshall, E. J., Keaney, F., Ball, D., & Strang, J. (2002). Unplanned versus planned discharges from in-patient alcohol detoxification: Retrospective analysis of 470 first-episode admissions. *Alcohol and Alcoholism, 37*(3), 277–281.

McCauley, J. L., Killeen, T., Gros, D. F., Brady, K. T., & Back, S. E. (2012). Posttraumatic stress disorder and co-occurring substance use disorders: Advances in assessment and treatment. *Clinical Psychology: Science and Practice, 19*(3), 283–304.

Miller, F. T., Abrams, T., Dulit, R., & Fyer, M. (1993). Substance abuse in borderline personality disorder. *American Journal of Drug and Alcohol Abuse, 19*(4), 491–497.

National Collaborating Centre for Mental Health. (2009). *Borderline personality disorder: Recognition and management.* London: National Institute for Health and Care Excellence.

New, A. S., & Stanley, B. (2010). An opioid deficit in borderline personality disorder: Self-cutting, substance abuse, and social dysfunction. *American Journal of Psychiatry, 167*(8), 882–885.

Niaura, R. S., Rohsenow, D. J., Binkoff, J. A., Monti, P. M., Pedraza, M., & Abrams, D. B. (1988). Relevance of cue reactivity to understanding alcohol and smoking relapse. *Journal of Abnormal Psychology, 97*(2), 133.

Pennay, A., Cameron, J., Reichert, T., Strickland, H., Lee, N. K., Hall, K., & Lubman, D. I. (2011). A systematic review of interventions for co-occurring substance use disorder and borderline personality disorder. *Journal of Substance Abuse Treatment, 41*(4), 363–373.

Prossin, A. R., Love, T. M., Koeppe, R. A., Zubieta, J. -K., & Silk, K. R. (2010). Dysregulation of regional endogenous opioid function in borderline personality disorder. *American Journal of Psychiatry, 167*(8), 925–933.

Sansone, R., Lam, C., & Wiederman, M. (2010b). The abuse of prescription medications: A relationship with borderline personality? *Journal of Opioid Management, 6*(3), 159.

Sansone, R. A., Lam, C., & Wiederman, M. W. (2010a). The abuse of prescription medications in borderline personality disorder: A gender comparison. *Primary Care Companion to the Journal of Clinical Psychiatry, 12*(6).

Sansone, R. A., & Sansone, L. A. (2011). Substance use disorders and borderline personality: Common bedfellows. *Innovations in Clinical Neuroscience, 8*(9).

Skodol, A. E., Oldham, J. M., & Gallaher, P. E. (1999). Axis II comorbidity of substance use disorders among patients referred for treatment of personality disorders. *American Journal of Psychiatry.*

Stanley, B., Sher, L., Wilson, S., Ekman, R., Huang, Y. -Y., & Mann, J. J. (2010). Non-suicidal self-injurious behavior, endogenous opioids and monoamine neurotransmitters. *Journal of Affective Disorders, 124*(1), 134–140.

Stanley, B., & Siever, L. J. (2009). The interpersonal dimension of borderline personality disorder: Toward a neuropeptide model. *American Journal of Psychiatry, 167*(1), 24–39.

Stone, M. H. (1990). *The fate of borderline patients: Successful outcome and psychiatric practice.* New York: Guilford.

Substance Abuse and Mental Health Services Administration (2017). Mental and substance use disorders. https://www.samhsa.gov/disorders.

Sullivan, T., & Frances, J. (1990). Substance use in borderline personality disorder. *American Journal of Psychiatry, 147*, 1002–1007.

Trull, T. J. (2001). Structural relations between borderline personality disorder features and putative etiological correlates. *Journal of Abnormal Psychology, 110*(3), 471.

Trull, T. J., Sher, K. J., Minks-Brown, C., Durbin, J., & Burr, R. (2000). Borderline personality disorder and substance use disorders: A review and integration. *Clinical Psychology Review, 20*(2), 235–253.

Trull, T. J., Solhan, M. B., Tragesser, S. L., Jahng, S., Wood, P. K., Piasecki, T. M., & Watson, D. (2008). Affective instability: Measuring a core feature of borderline personality disorder with ecological momentary assessment. *Journal of Abnormal Psychology, 117*(3), 647.

van den Bosch, L. M., Verheul, R., Schippers, G. M., & van den Brink, W. (2002). Dialectical behavior therapy of borderline patients with and without substance use problems: Implementation and long-term effects. *Addictive Behaviors, 27*(6), 911–923.

Verheul, R., van den Brink, W., & Geerlings, P. (1999). A three-pathway psychobiological model of craving for alcohol. *Alcohol and Alcoholism, 34*(2), 197–222.

Wapp, M., van de Glind, G., van Emmerik-van Oortmerssen, K., Dom, G., Verspreet, S., Carpentier, P. J., . . . Franck, J. (2015). Risk factors for borderline personality disorder in treatment seeking patients with a substance use disorder: An international multicenter study. *European Addiction Research, 21*(4), 188–194.

Wilson, S. T., Fertuck, E. A., Kwitel, A., Stanley, M. C., & Stanley, B. (2006). Impulsivity, suicidality and alcohol use disorders in adolescents and young adults with borderline personality disorder. *International Journal of Adolescent Medicine and Health, 18*(1), 189–196.

Zubieta, J. -K., Smith, Y. R., Bueller, J. A., Xu, Y., Kilbourn, M. R., Jewett, D. M., . . . Stohler, C. S. (2001). Regional mu opioid receptor regulation of sensory and affective dimensions of pain. *Science, 293*(5528), 311–315.

Eating Disorders in Borderline
Personality Disorder

EUNICE CHEN

INTRODUCTION

Eating disorders (EDs) often arise from a complex interplay of biological, psychological, and social processes in which there is a dialectical tension between the overabundance of food and an obsession with thinness. The *Diagnostic and Statistical Manual of Mental Disorders* (DSM-5; American Psychiatric Association [APA], 2013), recognizes three specific types of EDs that are common in BPD: anorexia nervosa (AN), bulimia nervosa (BN), and binge eating disorder (BED). The essential features of AN include persistent energy intake restriction; intense fear of gaining weight or of becoming fat, or persistent behavior that interferes with weight gain; and a disturbance in self-perceived weight or shape (APA, 2013). Moreover, individuals with AN may be classified by either a refusal to eat and excessive exercise (restricting type) or an inclination to engage in bingeing and purging behaviors (binge eating/purge type). BN is characterized by recurrent episodes of binge eating, inappropriate compensatory methods to prevent weight gain, and an overvaluation of body weight and shape (APA, 2013). The binge eating and compensatory behaviors must occur, on average, at least once per week over a 3-month period to qualify for the diagnosis. Binge eating is defined as consuming an objectively large amount of food (e.g., more than what most individuals would eat during a discrete period of time under similar circumstances) accompanied by a feeling of loss of control. The compensatory behaviors, collectively referred to as *purge behaviors* or *purging*, typically include self-induced vomiting, laxative misuse, or diuretic misuse. Individuals with BN may also fast for a day or more or exercise excessively in an attempt to prevent weight gain. This disorder also affects young women who may or may not have had AN because those with BN also demonstrate a fear of weight gain, and, although weight is commonly within the normal range, it may be greater than normal. There are some instances in which an individual may engage in binge eating and purging but also be unwilling to maintain a normal body weight. In this case, the individual may be diagnosed with AN, binge eating/purging type.

BED is characterized by eating, in a discrete period of time, an amount of food that is larger than what most people would eat in a similar period of time under similar circumstances and a sense of lack of control over eating during the episode (APA, 2013). Furthermore, in BED, binge eating episodes are associated with three or more of the following: (1) eating much more rapidly than normal; (2) eating until feeling uncomfortably full; (3) eating large amounts of food when not feeling physically hungry; (4) eating alone because of feeling embarrassed by how much one is eating; or (5) feeling disgusted with oneself, depressed, or very guilty after eating. Moreover, episodes of binge eating must occur, on average, at least once per week for 3 months and are associated with marked distress. These episodes must not occur exclusively during the course of AN or BN.

EPIDEMIOLOGY

AN is a rare ED with symptoms typically appearing in adolescence or young adulthood. The onset of this disorder is often associated with a stressful life event, such as leaving home for college. The 12-month prevalence of AN among young females is approximately 0.4% (Stice, Marti, & Rohde, 2013) and is far less common in males, with clinical populations generally reflecting approximately a 10:1 female-to-male ratio (APA, 2013). Although an estimated 3 in 10 individuals with AN are male, many males do not present for treatment, and, consequently, about 90% of patients diagnosed are female (Smink, Hoeken, Oldehinkel, & Hoek, 2014). Higher prevalence rates (of 0.9% for females and 0.3% for males) were reported by Hudson, Hiripi, Pope, and Kessler (2007) utilizing a nationally representative sample. Results suggest that the incidence of AN has been substantially underestimated in previous studies due to a large proportion of true cases remaining undetected. Lifetime prevalence rates for AN tend to be higher among women than men and more common among white women than black women. In terms of trends, AN demonstrates an increased incidence (i.e., registered cases) since the 1950s, which is most pronounced in females aged 15–24 (Allen, Byrne, Oddy, & Crosby, 2013; van Hoeken, Seidell, & Hoek, 2005). The disorder has been recognized throughout history and across cultures (Keel & McCormick, 2010). The possibility exists that differences in rates over time could be due to improved case detection, increased public awareness leading to earlier detection, and wider availability of treatment services rather than to a true increase in occurrence. There are considerable physical and psychological morbidities with AN. The mortality rate of AN is estimated at roughly 5–20% lifetime mortality (Neumarker, 1997) and is primarily a result of cardiac problems and suicide. In a meta-analysis of medical mortality, AN was associated with the highest rate of mortality among all mental disorders (Harris & Barraclough, 1998).

Prevalence estimates for BN among young females range from 1% to 1.5% (Stice et al., 2013). Women in late adolescence or early adulthood appear to be at the highest risk for onset of BN, and the female-to-male ratio is approximately 10:1 (APA, 2013). The lifetime prevalence of BN is 1.5% among females and 0.5% among males (Smink et al., 2014). Mortality rates of up to 3.9% have been reported for BN due to medical complications and increased risk of suicide (Arcelus, Mitchell, Wales, & Nelson, 2011; Crow et al., 2009). Diagnostic crossover from initial BN to AN occurs in a minority of cases (10–15%). It is common for individuals who experience crossover to revert back or have multiple occurrences of crossovers between BN and AN (Allen et al., 2013). A subset of individuals with BN continues to binge but no longer engage in compensatory behaviors, and therefore their symptoms meet criteria for BED or other specified eating disorders (APA, 2013).

BED occurs in normal-weight/overweight and obese individuals (APA, 2013). The disorder is the most prevalent ED, with lifetime prevalence estimates of 3.5% in women and 2.0% in men (Hudson et al., 2007). Prevalence estimates among obese individuals are even higher, ranging from 4% to 8% in community samples. The majority of patients presenting for treatment with BED are women; however, in community samples the rates of BED are similar for males and females (e.g., Grucza, Przybeck, & Cloninger, 2007). BED is as prevalent among females from racial or ethnic minority groups as has been reported for white females. The disorder is more prevalent among individuals seeking weight loss treatment than in the general population (APA, 2013). BED is associated with a range of functional consequences, including social role adjustment problems, impaired health-related quality of life and life satisfaction, increased medical morbidity and mortality, and associated health care utilization (APA, 2013).

ASSOCIATED FEATURES AND COMORBIDITY

When seriously underweight, many individuals with AN often display disturbances in affect, including depressed mood and anxiety, and this may be explained or exacerbated by the effects of starvation in AN. Studies of starvation such as that by Keys, Brozek, Henschel, Mickelsen, and Taylor (1950) demonstrate that malnutrition leads to depressed mood, anhedonia, and anxiety.

Given this, a diagnosis of a mood or anxiety disorder should be made when the symptoms do not appear to be explained by starvation and do not appear to be related to the primary diagnosis of AN. Symptoms of mood disturbance may therefore be reassessed after partial or complete weight restoration. Obsessive-compulsive features, both related and unrelated to food, are often prominent in AN as well.

Ritualistic behaviors include cutting food into tiny pieces, eating unusual food combinations, refusing to eat in public, or needing to repeatedly calculate caloric intake and expenditure. Obsessions and compulsions related to food may be caused or exacerbated by starvation. An additional diagnosis of obsessive-compulsive disorder (OCD) may be warranted only when individuals with AN exhibit obsessions and compulsions that are not related to food, body shape, or weight.

BN and BED both overlap with several other forms of psychopathology, including mood, anxiety, and substance use (O'Brien & Vincent, 2003). Mood disorders, especially major depression and dysthymia, are common, with estimates ranging from 36% to 50% (O'Brien & Vincent, 2003).

Lifetime prevalence of anxiety disorders among those with BN ranges from 41% to 75% (Godart, Flament, Perdereau, & Jeammet, 2002). Post-traumatic stress disorder (PTSD) was the only anxiety disorder that occurred significantly (three times) more often in BN than AN (Kaye et al., 2005). There is also a strong relationship—in the range of 30% overlap—between substance abuse and binge or purge behaviors, regardless of whether the behaviors occur within the context of AN or BN (O'Brien & Vincent, 2003) or in the context of BED (Eldredge & Agras, 1996).

CULTURAL INFLUENCES

EDs are, in fact, more prevalent within various cultural groups than previously acknowledged, both within American ethnic minorities and ethnic minorities in other countries. A number of studies have demonstrated that African Americans have different attitudes about weight, body size, and attractiveness than do Caucasians, with less drive for thinness and greater acceptance of larger body proportions (Taylor, Caldwell, Baser, Faison, & Jackson, 2007).

Although EDs were initially thought to be more prevalent among white females from higher income families, recent studies have found that binge eating and purging were equally common among white (Caucasian) females compared to minority females. However, dieting behaviors were reported to be more common in the white sample (Crago & Shisslak, 2003). This report reflects a growing body of literature suggesting that disordered eating and diagnosable EDs have increased in recent years among non-white races and ethnicities and among young women in all social classes and within all religions (Walcott, Pratt, & Patel, 2003). Evidence does suggest that living in (or moving to) a Western culture puts one at increased risk for the development of BN (Keel & Klump, 2003).

COURSE AND OUTCOME

AN is a serious illness known to be associated with a chronic course and high mortality (Centers for Disease Control, 1995). Longer term follow-up studies (>20 years) have shown that although greater than 50% of patients with AN recover, 20% have a relapsing course and 10–15% remain chronically ill (Zipfel, Lowe, Reas, Deter, & Herzog, 2000). Rates of recovery, improvement, and chronicity appear to be more favorable in individuals diagnosed at a younger age and who thereby experience a shorter delay between onset of illness and initiation of treatment (Steinhausen, 2002).

Aside from longer illness duration prior to the first hospitalization, other factors that predict outcome in AN include very low body mass index (BMI) and inadequate weight gain during first hospitalization, physical symptoms, and severe psychological or social problems as factors associated with worse outcomes (Deter, Schellberg, Kopp, Friederich, & Herzog, 2005). Long-term outcomes seem to be more favorable in the AN restricting subtype than in those classified as binge eating/purging type (Deter et al., 2005).

Typical age of onset for BN is late adolescence or early adulthood (APA, 2013). Due to the high levels of distress that accompany binge/purge symptoms in addition to fears about weight, individuals with bulimia are more likely to seek treatment voluntarily than are women with AN (Klein & Walsh, 2004). BN and BED both tend to run a chronic course (APA, 2013).

MEDICAL EVALUATION

A thorough medical evaluation is advisable to assess the physical problems that may result from weight loss, vomiting, and laxative abuse. Other than height and weight measurements suggested by medical guidelines (Yager et al., 2006), basic tests should include physical and mental status evaluation, complete blood cell count, a metabolic panel, urinalysis, a pregnancy test in females of childbearing age, and an electrocardiogram (EKG) to evaluate cardiac problems. Other tests include checking amylase levels, BUN/creatinine, and liver and kidney function, as well as thyroid function. A chemistry panel is also suggested for hypokalemia (low potassium levels in the blood serum), which often results from diuretic and laxative use as well as prolonged fasting and starvation (Kreipe & Birndorf, 2000).

The dehydration and starvation that occurs with AN can reduce fluid and mineral levels leading to electrolyte imbalances (Winston, 2012). Electrolyte disturbances, most often in the form of severely low potassium levels, can cause a wide variety of symptoms ranging from muscle weakness, constipation, lack of mental clarity, and difficulty processing information, to, in severe cases, cardiac arrhythmias that can cause sudden death. It is not uncommon for eating-disordered patients to report a misleading sense of well-being despite dangerously low potassium levels. Some individuals drink excessive volumes of water prior to weigh-ins, which can lead to hyponatremia (low serum sodium level), increasing vulnerability to seizures. In order to detect water loading, an individual's urine can be tested for specific gravity. Finally, another danger is refeeding syndrome, which consists of metabolic disturbances that occur as a result of reinstitution of nutrition to patients who are starved or severely malnourished, and which often has a potentially adverse effect on the heart, lungs, kidneys, and other organs (Higa, Okura, Imai, & Yoshida, 2013). Semi-starvation tends to impede the ability of the bone marrow to generate new blood cells, leading to anemia and/or leukopenia (low white blood cell count) and/ or thrombocytopenia (reduced platelet count) (Caregaro, et al., 2012). Patients may also show evidence of osteopenia, which indicates early signs of bone density loss that can turn into osteoporosis.

Complications of AN can affect nearly every organ system. However, laboratory findings might be completely normal in many individuals, especially early in the disorder. It is important to explain to individuals and their families that a normal physical examination does not rule out an ED. In cases of unstable vital signs and EKG abnormalities or other signs of medical instability, it is appropriate to consider hospitalization to achieve medical stability. Inpatient treatment is also warranted in order to achieve weight restoration or interrupt steady weight loss in individuals who are emaciated and in medical danger (Kreipe & Birndorf, 2000).

The most common medical symptoms of BN are lethargy, irregular menses, abdominal pain, electrolyte complications, and constipation (Westmoreland, Krantz, & Mehler, 2016). Other common signs include tachycardia, hypotension, dry skin, parotid gland swelling, erosion of dental enamel, and Russell's sign (scars on knuckles from inducing vomiting). Use of ipecac to induce vomiting can lead to extreme muscle weakness, including heart muscle weakness. Within the context of a complete physical examination, key components include weight and height measurements, vital signs, oropharyngeal damage assessment, and a comprehensive serum metabolic profile, including electrolyte screening (Academy for Eating Disorders, 2012).

Patients with BED often describe somatic symptoms and dissatisfaction with health. However, there is little evidence of medical complications that can be directly attributed to binge eating symptoms (Wilson, Nonas, & Rosenblum, 1993) although there are medical problems that may be associated with the obesity seen to co-occur with BED. For instance, hypercholesterolemia has been found to occur significantly more often in patients with BED, therefore cholesterol testing is routinely done after a diagnosis of BED (Bulik, Sullivan, & Kendler, 2002).

TREATMENT APPROACHES

Different forms of psychotherapy, including individual, group, and family-based, have been employed for AN. Currently, the only evidence-based treatment identified for AN is a specific form of family-based therapy based on the "Maudsley model," which has demonstrated efficacy in the treatment of children and adolescents (Campbell & Peebles, 2014). Indicative of the difficulty of treating adult AN, possibly due to the ego-syntonic nature of the disorder, the largest adult AN randomized controlled trial ($N = 122$) showed a 60% dropout rate, making it difficult to draw conclusions about treatment efficacy in an older age group (Halmi, 2005). The clinical trials for adults with AN are notable in their paucity and small sample size (Hay, Claudino, Touyz, & Abd Elbaky, 2015). The lack of treatment for adults with AN is a serious problem given the severity of the disorder.

A substantial number of clinical trials for BN have been reported (Wilson, Grilo, & Vitousek, 2007). These studies have established cognitive-behavioral therapy (CBT) (Fairburn, 1995) as the first-line treatment for adults with BN. Additionally, a meta-analysis conducted by the UK National Institute for Health and Clinical Excellence (NICE) suggests that CBT, given the evidence, should be the front-line treatment for BN in adults. There are three phases of treatment when utilizing CBT for BN treatment. The first phase is to normalize eating behavior using psychoeducation and behavioral strategies such as self-monitoring eating, planning and eating regularly, and using stimulus control methods and alternative strategies to prevent binge eating. The second phase is to teach clients to identify, monitor, and challenge the cognitions that maintain the disorder, and the final phase is to teach strategies to prevent relapse. The course of CBT for BN normally consists of 16–20 sessions over 4–5 months. CBT has proved effective at lessening the frequency of binge eating behaviors and compensatory responses and normalizing cognitions in individuals with BN (Agras, Walsh, Fairburn, Wilson, & Kraemer, 2000). This version of CBT results in approximately half of the patients reaching abstinence from their ED behavior (Mitchell et al., 2011).

Given that CBT for BN may not lead to recovery for some clients with BN and that this treatment only addresses individuals with BN, a more comprehensive form of CBT has been developed.

"Enhanced" CBT (CBT-E) is based on a transdiagnostic view of EDs and is designed to treat ED behaviors and common maintaining factors rather than a particular ED diagnosis. It is described as "enhanced" because it uses a variety of new strategies and procedures to improve outcome, and it includes modules to address certain maintaining factors to change that are "external" to the core ED, namely, clinical perfectionism, low self-esteem, and interpersonal difficulties. There are two forms of CBT-E. The first is the "focused" form that exclusively addresses ED psychopathology. The second, "broader" form addresses external obstacles to change in addition to the core ED psychopathology. There are also two intensities of CBT-E. With patients who are not significantly underweight (BMI above 17.5), it consists of 20 sessions over 20 weeks. This version is suitable for the majority of adult outpatients. For patients who have a BMI below 17.5, treatment involves 40 sessions over 40 weeks. Clinical trials have been almost exclusively done with young adult women, but what is known about treatment for males or older women suggests that the CBT treatment effect is robust, and there is evidence that CBT can be successfully adapted for adolescents (Lock & LeGrange, 2005).

Interpersonal psychotherapy (IPT) is regarded as a second-line well-evidenced treatment option for BN. The research findings suggest that although initial outcome in IPT is not as positive as CBT, there is continued improvement in IPT over the course of follow-up so that by 1 year follow-up those individuals are not significantly different from those who received CBT (Wilfley, Wilson, & Agras, 2003). IPT helps patients identify and resolve interpersonal difficulties, without focusing on treating ED symptoms. Given the emphasis of IPT on current relationships, it appears helpful for youth, for whom the social network is of heightened importance (Wilfley, Kolko, & Kass, 2011).

Although IPT has proved to be effective in certain groups, it may take up to a year longer than CBT-BN to achieve a comparable effect (Murphy, Straebler, Cooper, & Fairburn, 2010).

Antidepressant medication (e.g., fluoxetine at a dose of 60 mg daily) has also been found to have a beneficial effect on binge eating in BN but appears less effective than CBT-BN (Mitchell, Agras, & Wonderlich, 2007). An even smaller proportion of individuals (20%) achieve abstinence by the end of treatment, and relapse following medication withdrawal is a significant problem (Mitchell et al., 2007). Combining CBT-BN with antidepressant medication does not appear to offer any clear advantage over CBT-BN alone (Murphy et al., 2010).

Most of the treatments that have been used to treat BN have also been applied to BED (Brownley, Berkman, Sedway, Lohr, & Bulik, 2007). CBT is also the most established psychological treatment for BED (Wilson et al., 2007). To date, the largest randomized controlled trial (RCT) for BED treatment (Wilson, Wilfley, Agras, & Bryson, 2010) has shown that IPT and CBT-guided self-help are the most effective treatments for adults with BED when compared to behavioral weight loss, showing remission rates of more than 60% after 2 years. Arguably, the leading first-line treatment is a form of guided cognitive behavioral self-help that typically involves psychoeducation and teaching behavioral strategies of the standard CBT program over six to eight 25-minute sessions over a 12-week period. CBT for BED places a primary emphasis on binge eating reduction and a secondary emphasis on weight loss. CBT for BED treatment in a group format has been found to have a sustained and marked effect on binge eating but does not produce clinically significant weight loss (Wilfley et al., 2011).

Dialectical behavior therapy (DBT) is a potentially promising treatment for BN and BED. This treatment was originally developed for individuals with borderline personality disorder (BPD) wherein emotional dysregulation is considered an influencing factor for the ED and symptomatic behaviors to be maladaptive coping skills. A number of RCTs suggest that DBT holds potential for decreasing binge eating and purging symptoms in BN and BED (Safer & Joyce, 2011).

As in BN, antidepressants have also proved effective in BED. Recent work investigating the effects of topiramate suggest that it decreases binge eating by moderating general tendencies toward impulsivity. Initial studies on BED with comorbid obesity reported topiramate was associated with modest weight loss in addition to significant reduction of binge eating (about 58% abstinence), but rates of medication discontinuation were 30% (McElroy et al., 2007).

ED AND BPD COMORBIDITY

Available research has generally reported high rates of diagnostic co-occurrence between EDs and personality disorders (PD). Studies show that 25–54% of individuals with an ED also meet diagnostic criteria for BPD (Sansone & Sansone, 2011). Such comorbidity may reflect expressions of underlying personality pathology. Similarly, empirical studies point to a common genetic or environmental diathesis underlying both EDs and PD (Sansone & Sansone, 2011). Research conducted over the past two decades has resulted in numerous general trends in terms of possible associations, including BPD with BN and with AN-binge-purge type, and cluster C PD (e.g., obsessive-compulsive PD) with AN-restrictor type. The co-occurrence of BPD and EDs tends to be higher among those who exhibit more impulsive behaviors, such as binge eating and purging. More recently, research has reported significant associations for cluster C, but not clusters A or B PD, with BED. Specifically, BPD has been found to be present in approximately 25% of individuals with AN, binge-purging type, and in 28% of individuals with BN (Sansone & Sansone, 2011). Roughly 11% of those with restricting type AN suffer from BPD (Sansone & Sansone, 2011).

Among those with BED, the empirical data indicate prevalence rates around 12% (Sansone & Sansone, 2011). Prevalence rates for EDs among individuals with BPD are cited to be even higher, and the rates of ED not otherwise specified (EDNOS) in BPD are higher than are those of BN and AN (Zanarini, Frankenburg, Hennen, Reich, & Silk, 2004).

Bornstein (2001) conducted a meta-analysis of 13 BN studies and found BN had significant correlations with BPD (31%). A recent review by Cassin and von Ranson (2005), which reviewed 10 studies since 1992 (but not including clinical trial samples), found roughly 21% of BN participants met BPD criteria based on a diagnostic interview to assess BPD. It is most likely that approximately one in three BPD clients suffer from BN, as found in the studies of Marino and Zanarini (2001) and Zanarini et al. (Zanarini, Reichman, Frankenburg, Reich, & Fitzmaurice, 2010) that have employed the largest BPD samples ($N = 279$ and $N = 379$, respectively).

Personality pathology may have negative effects on ED outcome and treatment response (Keel & Mitchell, 1997). For instance, cluster B diagnosis predicted significantly greater binge eating 1 year after CBT and IPT ($N = 162$) (Wilfley, Schwartz, Spurrell, & Fairburn, 2000). BN with BPD had less bulimic remission than BN alone (62% vs. 21%) after 1 year of treatment (Johnson, Tobin, & Dennis, 1990), and cluster B disorders or impulsivity predict worse outcome (Agras et al., 2000; Steiger et al., 2004; Thompson-Brenner & Westen, 2005).

HOW BPD AND EATING DISORDERS MIGHT BE RELATED

Understanding the relationship between PDs and EDs has important treatment implications because individuals with an ED and PD may have poorer treatment outcomes than those with PDs alone. A longitudinal study by Zanarini and colleagues (2004) in a sample of individuals with BPD found that absence of an ED improves the odds of BPD remission. A longitudinal study by Harned et al. (2009) also found that although BPD can improve in treatment, co-occurring EDs in this sample may not. It does appear, however, that patients characterized more by impulsive behaviors, such as BN or BED, tend to more frequently present with PD like BPD (Zanarini et al., 2010). Indeed, comorbid BN has been found to be associated with a history of recurrent suicide attempts among treatment-seeking women with BPD although co-occurring AN was found to be associated with increased risk of recurrent non-suicidal self-injury in this BPD sample (Chen, Brown, Harned, & Linehan, 2009). However, the relationship between BPD and EDs is unclear, although there is some evidence for common biological correlates, stressors, traits, and emotion regulation deficits.

Common biological systems that have been implicated in both EDs and BPD include the serotonin system, which has been well-investigated in BPD (New, Goodman, Triebwasser, & Siever, 2008). In humans, suicide, violence, and BPD have all been linked with decreased serotonin (5-hydroxytryptamine [5HT]) in the brain. Likewise, impulsive suicidal ideation and behavior and aggression have been linked to low platelet 5HT contents and reduced response to 5HT agonists in an eating-disordered population (Claes, Vandereycken, & Vertommen, 2005). In patients with BN (Carrasco JL, Díaz-Marsá M, Hollander E, César J, Saiz-Ruiz J, 2000) observed reduced 5HT activity in those with impulsive or "borderline" traits. These findings suggest that hypoactivity of the 5HT system in BN may be linked to self-aggressive impulsivity, a defining characteristic of BPD. In addition to increased impulsivity, alterations in 5HT function are thought to contribute to diverse aspects of EDs, including binge eating, perfectionism, and mood-regulation problems (Steiger, 2004).

In individuals with EDs and BPD, 5HT abnormalities are thought to result from secondary effects of their nutritional status, inherited genetics, and, possibly, long-term neurobiological developmental stressors, such as childhood abuse. One possible explanation for the comorbidity seen between BPD and EDs (particularly BN) is the fact the two may share common risk factors: for instance, both are associated with histories of childhood trauma, such as physical, sexual, and emotional abuse. There also may be common behaviors in both EDs and BPD resulting from abuse, such as insecure attachment, or shared genetically determined traits, such as sensation-seeking, both of which are, on average, elevated in 5HTTLPR S-allele carriers with bulimic syndromes who report prior physical or sexual maltreatment (Steiger et al., 2000). These results add to a diathesis–stress model that may underlie both EDs and BPD, which suggests that the conjoint effects of stress and the 5HTTLPR polymorphism may lead to both impulsive ED and BPD behaviors. Furthermore, when exacerbated by effects of dieting, such susceptibilities could cause certain people to become especially impulsive or prone to further restriction (Steiger, 2004).

The literature has also examined possible commonalities between EDs and BPD with regards to difficulties in regulating emotions. Emotion regulation, the processes by which individuals consciously or without awareness modify their emotions (Gross & Thompson, 2007), has been examined in BPD (Linehan, 1993; Linehan, Bohus, & Lynch, 2007) and also in EDs (Overton, Selway, Strongman, & Houston, 2005). Increasing evidence suggests that ED symptoms, such as bingeing, purging, and/or restricting, serve as dysfunctional attempts to regulate or suppress negative emotions (Fairburn, Cooper, & Shafran, 2003). Negative mood predicts bingeing and purging in BN (Smyth et al., 2007) as well as binge episodes in BED (Hilbert & Tuschen-Caffier, 2007). ED behaviors tend to work to regulate affect in the short term, and, as a result, other more adaptive strategies are not employed. Similarly, self-injurious behavior and dissociation in the context of BPD may be like ED behaviors in serving to regulate emotions.

CASE STUDY: BULIMIA AND BPD

Ms. P has a long history of self-destructive behaviors that began as a teenager and included drugs and alcohol, suicide attempts, cutting herself, and outbursts of temper, particularly with boyfriends. Ms. P first began seeing a psychiatrist at age 13 for these difficulties. According to Ms. P, she was distraught over her parents' decision to divorce. She sought counseling to address symptoms of depression and "suicidal tendencies." Ms. P was often moody and experienced several episodes of depression, but more prominent was her emotional volatility, rapidly shifting from feelings of abandonment to rage. Her outbursts of temper made her personal relationships stormy and interfered with her effectiveness at school.

Ms. P reported the first time in her life that she attempted to harm herself was when she was 11 years of age, when she attempted to jump out of a moving car. She reported she was upset at learning she would be moving in with her mother. At age 23, Ms. P had begun cutting herself with razor knives.

Three years later, Ms. P reported punching a wall, injuring her arm and requiring medical attention, during an argument with her live-in boyfriend. In her episodes of despair, usually after a relationship ended, she would abuse sedatives and alcohol. On some of these occasions, overwhelmed with self-hatred, she cut her body with razor blades until she felt a sense of relief. This was not the first time such behaviors had led to admission to the hospital. Ms. P had two inpatient visits that occurred at ages 25 and 28, one admission the result of suicidal ideation and the other after an overdose.

At 25, Ms. P reported her initial issues with disordered eating followed an episode of depression.

Having learned that her boyfriend of 2 years was ending their relationship, Ms. P began to feel hopeless and discouraged. She reported being depressed and experiencing a reduced appetite, enabling her to lose a significant amount of weight. This may have also been partially due to the weight-loss medication she had secured from her primary care physician. At this time, Ms. P's weight was 140 pounds, normal for her age and height of 5'7", and her diet was not unusual. She reported that she began to increase her exercise to maintain her new shape. Shortly thereafter, she started to prepare her own meals, omitting some of the more calorie-laden foods she had been accustomed to enjoying with her parents. Within weeks, Ms. P had embarked on a rigorous program of exercise and dieting, sometimes choosing to skip meals altogether. In addition to daily 2-hour, brisk walks in her neighborhood, Ms. P attended an aerobics class 5 days a week. Within 6 months, Ms. P had lost 30 pounds, causing menstruation to cease. Despite losing a significant amount of weight, primarily through restriction, Ms. P continued to display an obsessive fear of weight gain. Because of the time-consuming nature of these activities, Ms. P grew distant from her friends, and her performance at work suffered. Ms. P's parents grew concerned about her sudden weight loss and insisted that she see her primary physician who, in turn, recommended she see a psychologist to begin outpatient treatment. During this time, however, Ms. P's eating habits began to change. Although Ms. P tried to maintain the dieting program she had begun months earlier, she found herself struggling to control her appetite and, on several occasions, ate a pint of ice cream and cake late at night before she went to sleep. That summer, Ms. P continued to intermittently overeat and eventually developed a pattern of dieting during the day and overeating late at night. Ms. P also reported her binge eating resulted in a decrease in negative affect immediately following a binge episode. The problem, Ms. P maintained, was that she quickly grew distressed over the calories consumed; vomiting seemed to serve an anxiety-reducing function. Although she continued to walk outside in the evening, she was unable to maintain the rigorous exercise program she initiated that winter. Her weight gradually rose to 138 pounds, and her menses resumed after 6 months of amenorrhea. Her weight continued to rise and reached a high of 160 pounds. Soon she found herself unable to stop eating cookies and cakes often found in the house. Fearful that her late-night bingeing would cause her to gain more weight, Ms. P decided she would induce vomiting after eating. She quickly began a pattern of overeating and then inducing vomiting several times a week; this pattern persisted for over a year.

Ms. P continues to struggle with BN and occasional thoughts of suicide. She currently is a 45-year-old unemployed shop assistant living at home with her parents until she secures employment. When depressed about her situation, Ms. P typically purchases a pint of ice cream and a box of cookies on her way over to a friend's house after exercising. After arriving at the home of her parents, she consumes the dessert over the course of an hour while she watches television in her room.

She then induces vomiting, a habit she reported as "embarrassing and disgusting." When she is not overeating, Ms. P attempts to diet regularly. Ms. P attempts to control her shape and weight through restricting food intake, as well as employing the compensatory methods of self-induced vomiting and fasting. Her weight has stabilized at 145 pounds. Ms. P reported her social life has been impaired by her concern about her eating, shape, and weight. This case highlights the movement between different ED diagnoses and how the co-occurrence of BPD and EDs may present.

CONCLUSION

EDs are multidetermined psychological disorders that may be influenced by personality pathology. BPD co-occurs with some frequency among those with EDs, most often among those with binge eating and purging behaviors. Recent advances in neuroscience have resulted in great understanding of the brain mechanisms and processes that control behavior associated with EDs and BPD. Research has supported the idea that the co-occurrence of both disorders may be caused by an inability to tolerate and skillfully manage negative or unpleasant emotions. Other possible commonalities between EDs and BPD involve shared risk factors, such as a history of childhood trauma.

The impulsive, self-destructive tendencies of those with BPD may also make them particularly vulnerable to developing an ED. Only further research can clarify and increase our understanding of the various relationships between and treatment approaches to these challenging disorders.

REFERENCES

Academy for Eating Disorders. (2012). A Comprehensive assessment. In *Eating Disorders* (2nd ed., pp 8–11). Deerfield, IL: Author. https://www.aedweb.org/downloads/Guide-English.pdf

Agras, W. S., Walsh, B. T., Fairburn, C. G., Wilson, G. T., & Kraemer, H. C. (2000). A multicenter comparison of cognitive-behavioural therapy and interpersonal psychotherapy for bulimia nervosa. *Archives of General Psychiatry, 57*, 459–466. doi:10.1002/eat.20333

Allen, K. L., Byrne, S. M., Oddy, W. H., & Crosby, R. D. (2013). DSM–IV–TR and DSM-5 eating disorders in adolescents: Prevalence, stability, and psychosocial correlates in a population-based sample of male and female adolescents. *Journal of Abnormal Psychology, 122*(3), 720.

American Psychiatric Association (APA). (2013). *Diagnostic and statistical manual of mental disorders* (5th ed.). Washington, DC: Author.

Arcelus, J., Mitchell, A. J., Wales, J., & Nielsen, S. (2011). Mortality rates in patients with anorexia nervosa and other eating disorders: A meta-analysis of 36 studies. *Archives of General Psychiatry, 68*(7), 724–731.

Bornstein, R. F. (2001). A meta-analysis of the dependency–eating-disorders relationship: Strength, specificity, and temporal stability. *Journal of Psychopathology and Behavioral Assessment, 23*(3), 151–162. doi:10.1016/j.cpr.2005.04.012

Brownley, K. A., Berkman, N. D., Sedway, J. A., Lohr, K. N., & Bulik, C. M. (2007). Binge eating disorder treatment: A systematic review of randomized controlled trials. *International Journal of Eating Disorders, 40*, 337–348. doi:10.1002/eat.20370

Bulik, C. M., Sullivan, P. F., & Kendler, K. S. (2002). Medical and psychiatric morbidity in obese women with and without binge eating. *International Journal of Eating Disorders, 32*(1), 72–78. doi:10.1002/eat.10072

Campbell, K., & Peebles, R. (2014). Eating disorders in children and adolescents: State of the art review. *Pediatrics, 134*(3): 582–592. doi:510.1542/peds.2014-0194

Caregaro, L., Di Pascoli, L., Nardi, M., Santonastaso, P., Boffo, Camozzi, V., & Favaro, A. (2006). Osteopenia and osteoporosis in adult patients with anorexia nervosa. Role of nutritional factors. *Nutritional Therapy & Metabolism, 24*(4), 194–202.

Carrasco, J. L., Díaz-Marsá, M., Hollander, E., César, J., & Saiz-Ruiz, J. (2000). Decreased platelet monoamine oxidase activity in female bulimia nervosa. *European Neuropsychopharmacology, 10*(2), 113–117.

Cassin, S. E., & von Ranson, K. M. (2005). Personality and eating disorders: A decade in review. *Clinical Psychology Review, 25*(7), 895–916. doi:10.1016/j.cpr.2005.04.012

Centers for Disease Control. (1995). Case-control study of HIV seroconversion in health care workers after percutaneous exposure to HIV-infected blood: France, United Kingdom and United States, 1988–August 1994. *MMWR Morbidity and Mortality Weekly Report, 44*, 929–933. doi:10.1001/jama.275.4.274

Chen, E. Y., Brown, M. Z., Harned, M., & Linehan, M. (2009). A comparison of borderline personality disorder with and without eating disorders. *Psychiatry Research, 170*(1), 86–90. doi:10.1016/j.psychres.2009.03.006

Claes, L., Vandereycken, W., & Vertommen, H. (2005). Impulsivity-related traits in eating disorder patients. *Personality and Individual Differences, 39*(4), 739–749. doi:10.1016/j.pid.2005.02.022

Crago, M., & Shisslak, C. M. (2003). Ethnic differences in dieting, binge eating, and purging behaviors among American females: A review. *Eating Disorders, 11*(4), 289–304.doi:10.1080/10640260390242515

Crow, S. J., Mitchell, J. E., Crosby, R. D., Swanson, S. A., Wonderlich, S., & Lancanster, K. (2009). The cost effectiveness of cognitive behavioral therapy for bulimia nervosa delivered via telemedicine versus face-to-face. *Behaviour Research and Therapy, 47*(6), 451–453. doi:10.1016/j.brat.2009.02.006

Deter, H. C., Schellberg, D., Kopp, W., Friederich, H. C., & Herzog, W. (2005). Predictability of a favorable outcome in anorexia nervosa. *European Psychiatry, 20*(2), 165–172. doi:10.1016/j.eurpsy.2004.09.006

Eldredge, K. L., & Agras, W. S. (1996). Weight and shape overconcern and emotional eating in binge eating disorder. *International Journal of Eating Disorders, 19*(1), 73–82. doi:10.1002/(SICI)1098-108X(199601)19:1<73::AID-EAT9>3.0.CO;2-T

Fairburn, C. G. (1995). *Overcoming binge eating.* New York: Guilford.

Fairburn, C. G., Cooper, Z., & Shafran, R. (2003). Cognitive behaviour therapy for eating disorders: a "transdiagnostic" theory and treatment. Behavioral Researcher Therapy, *41*(5), 509–528.

Godart, N. T., Flament, M. F., Perdereau, F., & Jeammet, P. (2002). Comorbidity between eating disorders and anxiety disorders: A review. *International Journal of Eating Disorders, 32*(3), 253–270. doi:10.1002/eat.10096

Gross, J. J., & Thompson, R. A. (2007). Emotion regulation: Conceptual foundations. In J. Gross (Ed.), *Handbook of emotion regulation* (pp. 3–24). New York: Guilford.

Grucza, R. A., Przybeck, T. R., & Cloninger, C. R. (2007). Prevalence and correlates of binge eating disorder in a community sample. *Comprehensive Psychiatry, 48*(2), 124–131.

Halmi, K. (2005). Psychopathology of anorexia nervosa. *International Journal of Eating Disorders, 37*(S1), S20–S21. doi:10.1002/eat.20110

Harned, M. S., Chapman, A. L., Dexter-Mazza, E. T., Murray, A., Comtois, K. A., & Linehan, M. M. (2009). Treating co-occurring Axis I disorders in recurrently suicidal women with borderline personality disorder. *Personality Disorders: Theory, Research, and Treatment, 1*, 35–45. doi:10.1037/1949-2715.S.1.35

Harris, E. C., & Barraclough, B. (1998). Excess mortality of mental disorder. *British Journal of Psychiatry, 173*, 11–53. doi:10.1192/bjp.173.1.11

Hay, P. J., Claudino, A. M., Touyz, S., & Abd Elbaky, G. (2015). Individual psychological therapy in the outpatient treatment of adults with anorexia nervosa. *Cochrane Database of Systematic Reviews, 7*, CD003909. doi:10.1002/14651858.CD003909.pub2

Higa, T., Okura, H., Imai, K., & Yoshida, K. (2013). Refeeding syndrome in a patient with anorexia nervosa. *Journal of the American College of Cardiology, 62*(19), 1810.

Hilbert, A., & Tuschen-Caffier, B. (2007). Maintenance of binge eating through negative mood: A naturalistic comparison of binge eating disorder and bulimia nervosa. *International Journal of Eating Disorders, 40*, 521–530. doi:10.1002/eat.20401

Hudson, J. I., Hiripi, E., Pope, H. G., & Kessler, R. C. (2007). The prevalence and correlates of Eating disorders in the National Comorbidity Survey Replication. *Biological Psychiatry, 61*(3), 348–358. doi:10.1016/j.biopsych.2006.03.040

Johnson, C., Tobin, D. L., & Dennis, A. (1990). Differences in treatment outcome between borderline and nonborderline bulimics at one year follow up. *International Journal of Eating Disorders, 9*(6), 617–627. doi:10.1002/1098-108X(199011)9:6<617

Kaye, W. H., Frank, G. K., Bailer, U. F., Henry, S. E., Meltzer, C. C., Price, J. C., . . . Wagner, A. (2005). Serotonin alterations in anorexia and bulimia nervosa: New insights from imaging studies. *Physiology & Behavior, 85*(1), 73–81. doi:10.1016/j.physbeh.2005.04.013

Keel, P. K., & Klump, K. L. (2003). Are eating disorders culture-bound syndromes? Implications for conceptualizing their etiology. *Psychological Bulletin, 129*, 747–769. doi:10.1037/ 0033-2909.129.5.747

Keel, P. K., & McCormick, L. (2010). Diagnosis, assessment, and treatment planning for anorexia nervosa. In C. M. Grilo & J. E. Mitchell (Eds.), *The treatment of eating disorders: A clinical handbook* (pp. 3–27). New York: Guilford.

Keel, P. K., & Mitchell, J. E. (1997). Outcome in bulimia nervosa. *American Journal of Psychiatry.* doi:10.1001/archpsyc.56.1.63

Keys, A., Brozek, J., Henschel, A., Mickelson, O., & Taylor, H. L. (1950). *The biology of human starvation.* Minneapolis: University of Minneapolis Press.

Klein, D. A., & Walsh, B. T. (2004). Eating disorders: Clinical features and pathophysiology. *Physiology & behavior, 81*(2), 359–374. doi:10.1016/j.physbeh.2004.02.009

Kreipe, R. E., & Birndorf, S. A. (2000). Eating disorders in adolescents and young adults. *Medical Clinics of North America, 84*(4), 1027–1049, viii-ix. doi:10.1016/S0025-7125(05)70272-8

Linehan M. (1993). *Cognitive-behavioral treatment of borderline personality disorder.* New York: Guilford.

Linehan, M. M., Bohus, M., & Lynch, T. R. (2007). Dialectical behavior therapy for pervasive emotion dysregulation: Theoretical and practical underpinnings. In J. J. Gross (Ed.), *Handbook of emotion regulation* (pp. 581–606). New York: Guilford.

Lock, J., & le Grange, D. (2005). Family-based treatment of eating disorders. *International Journal of Eating Disorders, 37*(S1), S64–S67.

Marino, M. F., & Zanarini, M. C. (2001). Relationship between EDNOS and its subtypes and borderline personality disorder. *International Journal of Eating Disorders, 29*(3), 349–353. doi:10.1002/eat.1029

McElroy, S. L., Frye, M. A., Altshuler, L. L., Suppes, T., Hellemann, G., Black, D., . . . Keck, P. E. (2007). A 24-week, randomized, controlled trial of adjunctive sibutramine versus topiramate in the treatment of weight gain in overweight or obese patients with bipolar disorders. *Bipolar Disorders, 9*(4), 426–434. doi:10.1111/j.1399-5618.2007.00488.x

Mitchell, J. E., Agras, S., Crow, S., Halmi, K., Fairburn, C. G., Bryson, S., & Kraemer, H. (2011). Stepped care and cognitive–behavioural therapy for bulimia nervosa: Randomised trial. *British Journal of Psychiatry, 198*(5), 391–397. doi:10.1192/bjp.bp.110.082172

Mitchell, J. E., Agras, S., & Wonderlich, S. (2007). Treatment of bulimia nervosa: Where are we and where are we going? *International Journal of Eating Disorders, 40*(2), 95–101. doi:10.1002/ eat.20343

Murphy, R., Straebler, S., Cooper, Z., & Fairburn, C. G. (2010). Cognitive behavioral therapy for eating disorders. *Psychiatric Clinics of North America, 33*(3), 611.

Neumarker, K. J. (1997). Mortality and sudden death in anorexia nervosa. *International Journal of Eating Disorders, 2*(1)205–212. doi:10.1002/ (SICI)1098-108X(199704)21:3<205::AID-EAT1>3.0.CO;2-O

New, A. S., Goodman, M., Triebwasser, J., & Siever, L. J. (2008). Recent advances in the biological study of personality disorders. *Psychiatric Clinics of North America, 31*(3), 441–461. doi:10.1016/j.bbr.2011.03.031

O'Brien, K. M., & Vincent, N. K. (2003). Psychiatric comorbidity in anorexia and bulimia nervosa: Nature, prevalence, and causal relationships. *Clinical Psychology Review, 23*(1), 57–74. doi:10.1016/S0272-7358(02)00201-5

Overton, A., Selway, S., Strongman, K., & Houston, M. (2005). Eating disorders—The regulation of positive as well as negative emotion experience. *Journal of Clinical Psychology in Medical Settings, 12*(1), 39–56.

Safer, D. L., & Joyce, E. E. (2011). Does rapid response to two group psychotherapies for binge eating disorder predict abstinence? *Behaviour research and therapy, 49*(5), 339–345. doi:10.1016/j.brat.2011.03.001

Sansone, R. A., & Sansone, L. A. (2011). Personality pathology and its influence on eating disorders. *Innovations in Clinical Neuroscience, 8*(3), 14. doi: PMC3074200

Smink, F. R., Hoeken, D., Oldehinkel, A. J., & Hoek, H. W. (2014). Prevalence and severity of DSM-5 eating disorders in a community cohort of adolescents. *International Journal of Eating Disorders, 47*(6), 610–619.

Smyth, J. M., Wonderlich, S. A., Heron, K. E., Sliwinski, M. J., Crosby, R. D., Mitchell, J. E., & Engel, S. G. (2007). Daily and momentary mood and stress are associated with binge eating and vomiting in bulimia nervosa patients in the natural environment. *Journal of Consulting and Clinical Psychology, 75*(4), 629–638.

Steiger, H. (2004). Eating disorders and the serotonin connection: State, trait and developmental effects. *Journal of Psychiatry and Neuroscience, 29*(1), 20.

Steiger, H., Leonard, S., Ng Ying Kin, N. M, Ladouceur, C., Ramdoyal, D., & Young, S. N. (2000). Childhood abuse and platelet tritiated paroxetine binding in bulimia nervosa: Implications of borderline personality disorder. *Journal of Clinical Psychiatry, 61*,428–435.

Steinhausen, H. C. (2002). The outcome of anorexia nervosa in the 20th century. *American Journal of Psychiatry, 159*, 1284–1293. doi:10.1176/appi.ajp.159.8.1284

Stice, E., Marti, C. N., & Rohde, P. (2013). Prevalence, incidence, impairment, and course of the proposed DSM-5 eating disorder diagnoses in an 8-year prospective community study of young women. *Journal of Abnormal Psychology, 122*(2), 445.

Taylor, J. Y., Caldwell, C. H., Baser, R. E., Faison, N., & Jackson, J. S. (2007). Prevalence of eating disorders among Blacks in the National Survey of American Life. *International Journal of Eating Disorders, 40*, Suppl, S10–4. doi:10.1002/eat.20451

Thompson-Brenner, H., & Westen, D. (2005). Personality subtypes in eating disorders: Validation of a classification in a naturalistic sample. *British Journal of Psychiatry, 186*(6), 516–524. doi:10.1192/bjp.186.6.516

van Hoeken, D., Seidell, J., & Hoek, H. W. (2005). Epidemiology. In J. Treasure, U. Schmidt, & E. van Furth (Eds.), *The Essential handbook of eating disorders* (pp. 11–34). Hoboken, NJ: John Wiley & Son.

Walcott, D. D., Pratt, H. D., & Patel, D. R. (2003). Adolescents and eating disorders: Gender, racial, ethnic, sociocultural, and socioeconomic issues. *Journal of Adolescent Research, 18*(3), 223–243. doi:10.1177/0743558403018003003

Westmoreland, P., Krantz, M. J., & Mehler, P. S. (2016). Medical complications of anorexia nervosa and bulimia. *American Journal of Medicine, 129*(1), 30–37.

Wilfley, D. E., Kolko, R. P., & Kass, A. E. (2011). Cognitive behavioral therapy for weight management and eating disorders in children and adolescents. *Child and Adolescent Psychiatric Clinics of North America, 20*(2), 271–285.

Wilfley, D. E., Schwartz, M. B., Spurrell, E. B., & Fairburn, C. G. (2000). Using the eating disorder examination to identify the specific psychopathology of binge eating disorder. *International Journal of Eating Disorders, 27*(3), 259–269. doi:10.1002/(SICI)1098-108X(200004)27:3<259::AID-EAT2>3.0.CO;2-G

Wilfley, D. E., Wilson, G. T., & Agras, W. S. (2003). The clinical significance of binge eating disorder. *International Journal of Eating Disorders, 34*(S1), S96–S106.doi:10.1002/eat.10209

Wilson, G. T., Grilo, C. M., & Vitousek, K. M. (2007). Psychological treatment of eating disorders. *American Psychologist, 62*(3), 199.

Wilson, G. T., Nonas, C. A., & Rosenblum, G. D. (1993). Assessment of binge eating in obese patients. *International Journal of Eating Disorders, 13*(1), 25–33. doi:10.1002/1098-108X(199301)13:1

Wilson, G. T., Wilfley, D. E., Agras, W. S., & Bryson, S. W. (2010). Psychological treatments of binge eating disorder. *Archives of General Psychiatry, 67*(1), 94. doi.org/10.1001/archgenpsychiatry.2009.170

Winston, A. P. (2012). The clinical biochemistry of anorexia nervosa. *Annals of Clinical Biochemistry, 49*(2), 132–143.

Yager, J., Devlin, M. J., Halmi, K. A., Herzog, D. B., Mitchell, J. E. III, Powers, P., & Zerbe, K. J. (2006). *Practice guideline for the treatment of patients with eating disorders* (3rd ed.). Washington, DC: American Psychiatric Association.

Zanarini, M. C., Frankenburg, F. R., Hennen, J., Reich, D. B., & Silk, K. R. (2004). Axis I comorbidity in patients with borderline personality disorder: 6-year follow-up and prediction of time to remission. *American Journal of Psychiatry, 161*(11), 2108–2114. doi.org/10.1176/appi.ajp.161.11.2108

Zanarini, M. C., Reichman, C. A., Frankenburg, F. R., Reich, D. B., & Fitzmaurice, G. (2010). The course of eating disorders in patients with borderline personality disorder: A 10-year follow-up study. *International Journal of Eating Disorders, 43*(3), 226–232. doi:10.1002/eat.20689

Zipfel, S., Lowe, B., Reas, D. L., Deter, H. C., & Herzog, W. (2000). Longterm prognosis in anorexia nervosa: Lessons from a 21-year follow-up study. *Lancet, 355*(9205), 721–722. doi:10.1016/S0140-6736(99)05363-5

/// 11 /// Borderline Personality Disorder and Mood Disorders

ERIC A. FERTUCK, MEGAN S. CHESIN, AND BRIAN JOHNSTON

INTRODUCTION

Assessing and treating mood disorders (MD), such as major depression, dysthymia, or bipolar disorder (BD) in the context of borderline personality disorder (BPD) can be a difficult task. However, the differential diagnosis of MD and BPD is essential in making effective treatment recommendations and managing suicide risk. In the clinical assessment process, mood symptoms can be conceptualized as analogous to the presence of fever symptoms in a medical diagnosis. A fever is an important diagnostic sign that an illness is present, but the presence of the fever itself does not provide enough information to make a differential diagnosis among various diseases. Without a thorough differential diagnosis, the physician cannot provide the most effective treatment of the underlying cause of the fever. Just as with a fever in medical diagnosis, mood symptoms in mental health care require further assessment for accurate diagnosis and the most effective treatment plan.

BPD is commonly neglected or misdiagnosed when it co-occurs with MDs, and, conversely, individuals diagnosed with BPD with co-occurring MD are often treated only for BPD and not the mood disorder (Kernberg & Yeomans, 2013; Silk, 2010). Incomplete or deferred differential diagnosis between BPD and MD can lead to several troubling yet preventable consequences. These include ineffective or even countertherapeutic medication trials and polypharmacy (Paris, 2011; Silk, 2011), inadequate or nontherapeutic courses of treatment (Bongar, Peterson, Golann, & Hardiman, 1990; Chiesa & Fonagy, 2000), preventable suicide attempts and completions (Fertuck, Makhija, & Stanley, 2007; Oldham, 2006), and poor public health outcomes (John & Sharma, 2009). In addressing these clinically important co-occurring diagnoses, this chapter highlights the most salient aspects of the assessment and treatment of MDs, including major depression (MDD), dysthymia, and bipolar I and II disorders (BD) in the context of individuals who also have a BPD diagnosis.

CO-OCCURRING BPD AND DEPRESSIVE DISORDERS

The most frequently co-occurring psychiatric disorders with BPD are depressive disorders, predominantly MDD and dysthymia. Between 70% and 90% of individuals with BPD go through at least one major depressive episode or exhibit another depressive disorder in their lifetime (Gunderson et al., 2004; Skodol et al., 2011; Zanarini, Frankenburg, Hennen, & Silk, 2003; Zimmerman & Mattia, 1999). At the same time, BPD co-occurs for 25% of those with MDD (Pfohl, Stangl, & Zimmerman, 1984) or dysthymia (Pepper et al., 1995).

This high degree of overlap between BPD and MD has contributed to considerable research and debate over whether BPD is, in fact, a mood disorder and not a personality disorder. Since the 1980s, some have proposed that BPD symptoms, such as sensitivity to interpersonal loss and intense self-criticism, are expressions of a depressive disorder (Davis & Akiskal, 1986). Indeed, these clinical researchers proposed that effective psychopharmacological treatment of depressed mood in BPD would result in a full resolution of BPD symptoms as well. This argument led to a prohibition against diagnosing BPD when the individual was also in a major depressive episode because the BPD symptoms may reflect the untreated MDD and thus resolve as mood improves.

The consensus of most recent studies that have addressed this MDD and BPD hypothesis has generally not supported the assertion that BPD is reducible to an expression of a depressive disorder. An early review of the literature (Gunderson & Phillips, 1991) documented that MDD and BPD exhibit a different phenomenology, course of illness, familial aggregation, treatment response, and biomarkers. This earlier review has been reinforced by an update of the literature (New, Triebwasser, & Charney, 2008), which also argued that BPD was a distinct disorder, although it shares some features of mood disorders in terms of familial aggregation and symptom profiles. Longitudinally, the presence of co-occurring MDD with BPD has little impact on the stability of BPD symptoms and traits over time. Those with BPD and other personality disorders have the same number of BPD symptoms after a depressive episode remits as those with BPD without MDD (Morey et al., 2010). Relatedly, improvements in MDD symptoms in those with BPD are predicted by improvements in BPD criteria, not MDD symptoms (Gunderson et al., 2004). These findings undermine the hypothesis that the symptoms of BPD can be fully explained as episodic manifestations of a major depressive disorder.

Impact on Prognosis

There are pronounced clinical risks when both MDD and BPD are part of the clinical picture. Consequently, clarification of this co-occurrence promotes the identification of prognostic factors that will influence the treatment plan and course of illness for both disorders. Individuals with both an MDD and a BPD diagnosis are more likely to attempt suicide those with MDD without BPD (Corbitt, Malone, Haas, & Mann, 1996). This increased risk for suicidal behavior is most apparent when the individual with BPD is in a depressive episode. Additionally, a diagnosis of BPD is associated with longer major depressive episodes when both MDD and BPD are present (Skodol et al., 2011). Furthermore, among those with BPD whose MDD is in remission, the length of time to the next major depressive episode is shorter relative to those with MDD without BPD (Grilo et al., 2010). The negative impact of BPD on MDD course is reflected in the finding that co-occurring BPD was present in more than half of the cases of nonremitting major depression over a 3-year period (Skodol et al., 2011). In sum, BPD and MDD have a mutually negative impact on each other, and those with both are at very high risk for suicidal behavior and a poorer prognosis.

The Experience of Depression

The symptom picture of BPD can be particularly confusing in the differential diagnosis between MDD-only and dysphoric experience in BPD due to the following features of BPD that can be mistaken for MDD: (1) emotional instability with intense and rapidly fluctuating negative emotions, (2) extreme negative self-evaluation and self-criticism, (3) aversive emotional tension or "mental pain," (3) suicidality and nonsuicidal self-injury (NSSI) that is expressed within *and* outside of depressive episodes, and (4) chronic feelings of emptiness that are also not only manifested in an major depressive episode, but instead are also a chronic part of inner experience in BPD (see Table 11.1).

When assessing depressive moods and emotions in individuals with BPD, it is important to determine if negative mood states are relatively transient and therefore part of affective instability, or whether depressed mood episodes are sustained consistently for most of the day nearly every day, a presentation more consistent in major depressive episodes and MD. Even if an individual with BPD endorses sustained, depressed mood, it is important to inquire if she has moments during the day when she is not depressed because there is the potential to recall only the most dysphoric moments of the day or week. In this context, a mood diary that tracks emotions several times a day can be a very helpful diagnostic aid. Another complicating factor arises from the finding that clinicians assess severity of depression in BPD and MDD individuals comparably using standardized rating scales such as the Hamilton Depression Rating Scale (Hamilton, 1960). However, individuals with co-occurring BPD report a subjective intensification of depressive psychological experiences relative to MDD alone (Beck & Steer, 1993; Stanley & Wilson, 2006). Moreover, in the cognitive domain of depressive symptoms (e.g., guilt, self-criticism, feelings of worthlessness) on the Beck Depression Inventory, those with BPD tend to self-report higher symptoms scores than do those with MDD alone (Beck & Steer, 1993). The heightened subjective intensity of depressive experiences and cognitions in BPD

TABLE 11.1 Distinguishing features of depressed and dysphoric mood symptoms in major depressive disorder (MDD) compared to borderline personality disorder (BPD)

	MDD	BPD
Depressed mood: Duration	Sustained and consistent depressed mood over weeks	Unstable, rapidly fluctuating negative emotions (sadness, anger, anxiety, mental anguish) that is part of affective instability, not a depressive episode
Depressed mood: Quality	Episodic sadness and low mood with prominent neurovegetative symptoms; euthymic mood when not in major depressive episode (MDE); intensification of guilt and worthlessness feelings during the MDE	Trait-like feelings of emptiness or mental pain; intense self-criticism ("badness") and/or feelings of shame, in *and* out of MDE
Suicide and nonsuicidal self-injurious behavior (NSSI)	Planned, after sustained period of MDE; occur at older age on average; lower ratio of attempts to completions; prompted by prolonged feelings of failure, of guilt, and/or worthlessness	Impulsive; occur at younger age on average; high ratio of attempts to completions; NSSI is prominent and prompted by interpersonal stress, conflict, loss; can occur both in *and* outside of MDE

may be a reflection of the emotional sensitivity and instability characteristic of this population. Those with BPD are impaired in their ability to regulate intense, mostly negative emotions (Linehan, 1993; Stiglmayr et al., 2005; Westen, Muderrisoglu, Fowler, Shedler, & Koren, 1997). In BPD, these emotions are readily aroused, very intense, extreme, and, when activated, are delayed in returning to a homeostatic baseline (Coifman, Berenson, Rafaeli, & Downey, 2012; Koenigsberg et al., 2002).

Those with both BPD and MDD exhibit more ruminative thoughts, hopelessness, proneness to depressive affects, and poorer self-esteem than do those with MDD alone (Abela, Payne, & Moussaly, 2003). Of note, depressed adolescents with BPD are at a heightened propensity to self-critical thoughts and negative self-concept relative to adolescents with MDD alone (Rogers, Widiger, & Krupp, 1995). Last, although BPD may share some symptoms with atypical depression, such as rejection sensitivity, severe social anxiety, and atypical neurovegetative symptoms (i.e., increased appetite, weight, sleep, or libido), these depressive symptoms are also present *outside* of an episode of major depression in BPD (Bassett, 2012; Morey et al., 2010). Thus, BPD is characterized by a unique quality of depressive mood and experience that is distinctive, pervasive, and multifaceted.

Mental Pain in BPD

A trait-like, negative emotional experience labeled "mental pain" has recently been proposed as a core feature of BPD that is distinct from the symptoms of a major depressive episode (Pazzagli & Monti, 2000; Zanarini & Frankenburg, 2007; Zanarini et al., 1998; Zittel Conklin, Bradley, & Westen, 2006; Zittel Conklin & Westen, 2005). Mental pain features an extreme, multifaceted inner pain with both emotional and cognitive dimensions. Whereas, superficially, mental pain sounds like depressed mood, it can be distinguished from depressed mood. In a study comparing mental pain with self-reported depression and anxiety scales, mental pain was only moderately correlated with depressive and anxious symptoms (Orbach, Mikulincer, Sirota, & Gilboa-Schechtman, 2003). There was also evidence that mental pain was elevated in psychiatric illness and in suicide risk (Orbach, Mikulincer, Gilboa-Schechtman, & Sirota, 2003).

A series of related studies have found that individuals with BPD experience elevated dysphoric affect in BPD that is distinct from MD. Mental pain in BPD is associated with turbulent affects, negative core beliefs (i.e., that one is "bad" and "worthless"), incoherence of inner experience, and feelings of chronic resentment (Zanarini & Frankenburg, 2007; Zittel Conklin et al., 2006; Zittel Conklin & Westen, 2005). Dysphoria in BPD is uniquely characterized by pervasive aversive mental states, a sense of aloneness, and emptiness (Westen et al., 1992). This qualitatively distinct dysphoria may influence the relational and high-risk behavior of BPD (Pazzagli & Monti, 2000; Stanley & Siever, 2010). Many of the diagnostic criteria in the *Diagnostic and Statistical Manual of Mental Disorders* (DSM-IV-TR; American Psychiatric Association [APA], 2000)—including affective instability, chronic feelings of emptiness, intense anger, and recurrent suicidal behavior—may be symptomatic manifestations of mental pain. These criteria emphasize the behavioral and emotional consequences rather than the equally important subjective experiences of chronic internal anguish (Zittel Conklin et al., 2006; Zittel Conklin & Westen, 2005). Interpersonal dysfunction and self-destructive behaviors may be maladaptive strategies to avoid or attempt to suppress emotional anguish in BPD.

Suicidal and Nonsuicidal Self-Injurious Behaviors

Concordant with differences in depressive and dysphoric affects and moods, suicidal behavior in BPD and MDD exhibits unique behavioral constellations as well. Compared to those with BPD alone, suicide attempters with BPD and MDD execute more suicide attempts in their lives, make their initial attempt at an earlier age, experience more interpersonal precipitants prior to suicide attempts, and exhibit heightened aggressive behaviors, hostility, and impulsivity during their lives (Brodsky,

Groves, Oquendo, Mann, & Stanley, 2006). In BPD, dysphoric affects are triggered by social loss and other interpersonal stressors and are usually more transient than in MDD. By contrast, in MDD, the severity of depression and suicidal feelings build up more gradually and can persist for weeks or even months. As a result, suicide attempts in MDD with BPD can be more planful and are often executed after a longer period of constantly depressed mood (Soloff, Lynch, Kelly, Malone, & Mann, 2000). Another distinction is the perception that the *only* choice one has is to end one's life prompts suicide attempts in MDD alone more than in BPD, where suicidal ideation can be more transient and situational (Oldham, 2006).

The predictive power of the severity of depression for suicidal behavior can be more opaque in BPD relative to MDD (Kernberg, 2001). In a prospective study, for instance, affective instability rather than depression severity was the most robust predictor of suicidality in BPD (Yen, Zlotnick, & Costello, 2002). At the same time, depression severity is a prognostic indicator of increased likelihood of a larger number of suicide attempts (Kelly, Soloff, Lynch, Haas, & Mann, 2000) and greater medical severity of suicide attempts in BPD (Runeson & Beskow, 1991; Soloff et al., 2000). Moreover, the individual with BPD does not need to experience severe depressive symptoms to be at increased risk for suicide attempts. Moderate symptoms are enough to increase risk, and suicide attempts and NSSI can occur outside of a depressive episode. Consequently, assessment of the severity of depressive symptoms in BPD is crucial even when the depressed mood is mild to moderate because these increase risk of the frequency of suicide attempts in BPD.

Finally, in accord with the hypersensitivity to interpersonal loss and conflict typical of BPD, these features can trigger highly lethal suicide attempts among those with both BPD and MDD compared to MDD alone (Brodsky et al., 2006). Concurrently, the medical severity of suicide attempts in BPD is similar to MDD alone, highlighting that the type precipitant is not predictive of the medical seriousness of the suicidal behavior. It is essential, then, for clinicians to assess environmental precipitants when evaluating suicidality in BPD and not to assume that suicide attempts are less risk in BPD compared to MD.

TREATMENT OF CO-OCCURRING DEPRESSIVE DISORDERS AND BPD

There is compelling evidence that MDD in BPD responds less robustly to standard treatments for MDD (Binks et al., 2006; Feske et al., 2004; Feurino Iii & Silk, 2011; Joyce et al., 2003; New et al., 2008; Silk, 2011; Soloff, 2000). However, a strong evidence base is not present to guide clinicians regarding the treatment of BPD with a co-occurring MDD diagnosis. While there are several psychotherapeutic approaches for individuals with BPD that have some empirical support (Stoffers et al., 2012), these psychotherapies on the whole have not focused on the impact of depressed mood episodes and depression severity on the course and outcome of these treatments. One of the few such studies that focused on depression severity compared 1 year of dialectical behavior therapy (DBT) to community treatment by experts for the management of co-occurring Axis I disorders among suicidal individuals with BPD. There was not a significant difference found between groups for improvement in co-occurring MDD (Harned et al., 2008). Interpersonal psychotherapy (IPT) was originally developed to treat major depression, however preliminary studies suggest that it may be a promising therapy for BPD with a co-occurring depressive disorder (Klerman, Weissman, Rounsaville, & Chevron, 1984). A rationale for this indication is that the therapy was designed to improve depressed individual's interpersonal functioning, and disturbances in interpersonal relations are a core dysfunction in BPD. One study compared the impact of 6 months of IPT combined with the selective serotonin reuptake inhibitor (SSRI) fluoxetine to fluoxetine alone for individuals diagnosed with co-occurring BPD and MDD (Bellino, Zizza, Camilla, & Filippo, 2006). Compared to the SSRI-only group, the combination treatment was more effective in treating MDD in BPD. The combined IPT-fluoxetine condition also demonstrated more significant improvements in interpersonal functioning than the fluoxetine-alone group. Another investigation compared IPT and fluoxetine to cognitive therapy with fluoxetine and found no significant differences between treatments on depression in BPD (Bellino et al., 2006). More recently, IPT was modified to treat individuals with BPD. A randomized control trial (RCT) compared the adapted IPT psychotherapy with fluoxetine to standard clinical management with fluoxetine. The IPT-fluoxetine group showed more significant improvement in psychological and social functioning (Bellino, Zizza, Rinaldi, & Bogetto, 2007). However, individuals with BPD and co-occurring MDD were excluded from the study; therefore, it remains unknown whether a modified version of IPT will be efficacious when extended to BPD with a co-occurring MDD.

Pharmacotherapy often plays a valuable adjunctive role in symptom management of BPD (Binks et al., 2006; Paris, 2011; Silk, 2011). Specifically, fluoxetine may reduce co-occurring depression in BPD; however, other SSRIs do not demonstrate clear benefits relative to placebos in RCTs for BPD (Biskin & Paris, 2012). Additionally, the benefit of SSRIs for BPD is limited in terms of both duration and symptom reduction because it only appears to be therapeutic in reducing externally expressed anger (Biskin & Paris, 2012). The lack of efficacy of these agents in BPD, and the tendency to misdiagnose BPD for MD, contributes to the frequent but dubious practice of polypharmacy for depressed mood in BPD. In polypharmacy, the psychopharmacologist progressively adds medications in an attempt to improve unremitting depressive or other MD symptoms. These MD symptoms may in fact be the affective instability of BPD rather than mood symptoms of MDD. By not diagnosing and treating BPD in MDD, individuals with BPD can be prescribed a "cocktail" of multiple, largely ineffective medications (Zanarini, Frankenburg, Hennen, Reich, & Silk, 2004). No research exists on these multiple medication combinations for BPD, yet there are often pressures on the prescribing clinician for medication-only treatments in lieu of the more clinically sound, cautious, and simple psychopharmacology and comprehensive and specialized psychotherapy for BPD (Paris, 2011).

CASE STUDY: MDD AND BPD

Ms. M was a 25-year-old, single, Caucasian female who was a college graduate with honors, but was unable to support herself financially. Ms. M was able to find employment, but she was frequently late to work, would engage in arguments with co-workers and supervisors, and quit jobs or got fired repeatedly. After her most recent job loss, Ms. M became increasingly despondent and self-critical toward herself for her employment instability and inability to find social acceptance from others. In a moment of intense dysphoria and self-criticism, she took an overdose of acetaminophen without forethought. She quickly became frightened, called her father, and informed him of the overdose. He responded by promptly taking her to the nearest Emergency Department. She stated during her clinical assessment at the ED that her motivation for overdosing was that, "It was just too hard to go on." During the assessment, Ms. M was tearful and agitated, and she described intensifying symptoms of depressed mood over the prior 2 months, including insomnia and increased hostility and argumentativeness. Ms. M also reported that she had engaged in several low-lethality overdoses in the past, with recurrent suicidal ideation, although she had not told anyone about these overdoses. She stated that for this most recent attempt she took more pills than these prior attempts, and only after the overdose became fearful for her life. During her childhood, she was viewed as a difficult, "high strung" child who had difficulty maintaining friendships and had frequent periods of dysphoria and loneliness. She met criteria for current MDD, but also BPD because BPD symptoms were evident even when she was not in a depressive episode.

As this case illustrates, individuals with BPD and MDD exhibit frequent, low-lethality suicide attempts, particularly when severity of depression worsens, in the context of interpersonal instability and high levels of self-directed aggression.

CO-OCCURRING BIPOLAR DISORDERS AND BPD

Rates of co-occurrence of BD and BPD range from 5% to 30% (Azorin et al., 2013; Gunderson et al., 2006; Paris, Gunderson, & Weinberg, 2007, for a review), which are appreciably lower than the BPD co-occurrence with unipolar depressive disorders. When bipolar symptoms are expanded beyond current DSM criteria to include very rapid mood cycling, up to 50% of BPD individuals can be categorized in the "bipolar spectrum" (Deltito et al., 2001; Perugi, Angst, Azorin, Bowden, Vieta, Young et al., 2013). The moderate co-occurrence of BPD and BD, combined with the similarity of certain core features of the disorders (i.e., impulsivity, mood instability) have led some to propose that BPD is a bipolar spectrum disorder (Akiskal, 2004; Perugi, Angst, Azorin, Bowden, Vieta, & Young, 2013). However, bipolar spectrum is a controversial diagnostic entity and can mistakenly be conflated with affective instability in BPD.

Early longitudinal studies suggested that BD develops more often among BPD individuals than individuals with other personality disorders (Akiskal et al., 1985; Gunderson et al., 2006). Moreover, these early studies suggested significant familial co-aggregation of both BD and BPD (Akiskal et al., 1985). More recent and rigorous studies indicate that mood instability in BPD has only a superficial similarity to manic and hypomanic mood episodes in BD and that BD is not more common among family members of BD individuals than non–psychiatrically ill probands (Bassett, 2012; Magill, 2004; New et al., 2008; Paris et al., 2007; Paris, Silk, Gunderson, Links, & Zanarini, 2009; Riso, Klein, Anderson, & Ouimette, 2000). Prospective studies highlight that BD is no more likely to emerge in the course of illness of BPD individuals than in other psychiatric disorders (Links, Mitton, & Patrick, 1995; Zanarini, Frankenburg, et al., 2004). BD and BPD individuals also seem to exhibit distinctive neural correlates, suggesting divergent pathophysiology (Rossi et al., 2012).

Although distinctions between BD and BPD are now established in the literature, in practice, the apparent overlap in symptom presentation and pathophysiology of BPD and BD makes assessment difficult and can result in misdiagnosis. BPD is routinely misdiagnosed as BD, in particular BD-II (Coulston, Tanious, Mulder, Porter, & Malhi, 2012). One study documented that 40% of individuals rigorously diagnosed with BPD had previously been misdiagnosed as BD (Ruggero, Zimmerman, Chelminski, & Young, 2010). This misdiagnosis of BPD as BD leaves BPD individuals with unrealistic expectations for largely ineffective mono-psychopharmacological treatment with mood stabilizers and unnecessary delays in the initiation of evidence-based treatment for BPD (Gunderson et al., 2006; Ruggero et al., 2010).

The Impact on Prognosis

The combination of BPD and BD is associated with several important clinical phenomena in the course of illness. The most high-risk behavior associated with co-occurring BPD and BD is suicidality. Individuals with co-occurring BPD and BD are more likely to attempt suicide, make more lifetime suicide attempts, and make more violent attempts than are individuals with BD alone (Gonda et al., 2012; Perugi, Angst, Azorin, Bowden, Vieta, Young et al., 2013). A study of individuals with co-occurring BD and cluster B personality disorder, the majority of whom had BPD, found that individuals with BD and co-occurring personality disorder had more lifetime suicide attempts than BD individuals without cluster B co-occurrence (Garno, 2005). Compared to individuals with BD alone, individuals with BD and BPD have higher rates of co-occurring substance abuse and anxiety disorders as well as more psychotic features, mood episodes, and an earlier age of onset of psychopathology (Perugi, Angst, Azorin, Bowden, Vieta, Young, et al., 2013). Individuals with co-occurring BD and other cluster B personality disorders, compared to BD individuals without such diagnoses, also have greater impulsivity and less cooperativeness and self-directedness (Sayın, Kuruoğlu, Yazıcı Güleç, & Aslan, 2007; Swann, Lijffijt, Lane, Steinberg, & Moeller, 2012). Co-occurring BPD and BD has also been associated with prolonged unemployment, defined as 2 or more years unemployed in a 5-year period (Zimmerman et al., 2010). Meanwhile, the impact of BD on the course of BPD is less clear. Only one study (Gunderson et al., 2006) has compared the functioning of BPD individuals with and without BD. Individuals with co-occurring BD and BPD were no more functionally impaired than individuals with BPD and no BD. Taken together, these findings suggest a more severe course for individuals with co-occurring BD and BPD compared to BD individuals. Whether co-occurring BD impacts the course of BPD is not yet determined.

FACETS OF IMPULSIVITY AND AFFECTIVE INSTABILITY IN BD COMPARED TO BPD

Affective Instability

As noted previously, the affective instability of BPD is commonly mistaken for bipolar mood episodes (Zanarini & Frankenburg, 2007). However, distinct types of affective instability have been identified in the two disorders. Affective instability involving shifts from anger to and from anxiety is more common among BPD individuals, whereas shifts between depression and positive and elevated emotions are more often observed among BD individuals (Coulston et al., 2012; Henry et al., 2001; Reich, Zanarini, & Fitzmaurice, 2012). Individuals with BPD display more intense emotional reactivity to negative and neutral stimuli and to interpersonal events than do BD individuals (Renaud, Corbalan, & Beaulieu, 2012). Mood episodes in BD, on the other hand, are often triggered by other stressful life events (e.g., death of a family member) and disruptions in social or biological rhythms (e.g., sleep disturbance) (Grandin, Alloy, & Abramson, 2006). The duration of affective shifts is also different in BD and BPD. As noted earlier, emotions shift rapidly—within minutes to hours—in BPD, whereas moods must remain elevated or depressed for several days in BD. Specifically, in BD, moods are characterized by consistent elevation, sadness, irritability, or euthymia all day nearly every day for weeks (Henry et al., 2001; Koenigsberg et al., 2002).

Impulsivity

Impulsivity is also part of the clinical picture of both BD and BPD (Benazzi, 2008). Again, however, qualitative differences in the impulsivity of BD and BPD have been found (Table 11.2). When depressed, BD individuals report more cognitive impulsivity (e.g., distractibility), whereas BPD individuals report greater nonplanning impulsiveness (e.g., a short-term rather than long-term orientation problem) (Wilson et al., 2007). Motor impulsivity (e.g., unplanned action), meanwhile, is linked to both mania and BPD (APA, 2000; Swann, Steinberg, Lijffijt, & Moeller, 2008). Impulsivity may wane somewhat among BD individuals between mood episodes, whereas impulsivity is commonly a stable trait in BPD (Dougherty et al., 1999). Suicidal behavior among

TABLE 11.2 Features of impulsivity and unstable mood in bipolar disorder (BD) compared to borderline personality disorder (BPD)

	BD Without BPD	BPD
Duration of elevated and unstable moods	Sustained and consistent over weeks or days	Unstable emotions fluctuate over hours or days
Valence of elevated and unstable moods	Positive, negative, or mixed	Often shift to negative emotions, especially anger and anxiety
Precipitants to affective instability	Stressful life events and/ or disruption of biological rhythms	Interpersonal conflict and disruption of relationships
Type of impulsivity	Distractibility and impulsive behavior within manic episodes	Present orientation and trait-like (not mood dependent)
Presentation of impulsivity	Impulsivity elevated during mood episodes	Impulsivity often in and out of mood episodes
Precipitants of suicide attempts	Suicide ideation with anxiety or agitation	Interpersonal difficulties such as an argument with a significant other or feeling abandoned or rejected

individuals with BPD is often characterized as more impulsive than in those without BPD (Brodsky et al., 2006), likely due to the impulsivity characteristic of BPD individuals. However, BPD individuals can and do plan many suicide attempts, with recent studies showing equal rates of BPD among impulsive suicide attempters and those who planned their attempt (Brodsky et al., 2006; Chesin, Jeglic, & Stanley, 2010; Spokas, Wenzel, Brown, & Beck, 2012). Triggers for suicidal behavior may differ between BD and BPD. Suicidal ideation with anxiety and agitation may more commonly trigger suicide behavior among BD individuals (Begley, 2001; Harris & Barraclough, 1997). Interpersonal triggers, such as breakup of an important relationship or the perception that a partner has done something untrustworthy, are common in individuals with BPD (Brodsky et al., 2006). More study, however, is needed to determine differential triggers for suicidal behavior among those with BPD and BD (Chesin & Stanley, in press.).

TREATMENT OF BD AND BPD

Concordant with the course of illness literature, there are several considerations in the treatment of co-occurring BPD and BD. Individuals with co-occurring BPD and

BD are less likely to stabilize than BD individuals without co-occurring BPD receiving psychotherapy and psychopharmacotherapy (Rosenbluth, MacQueen, McIntyre, Beaulieu, & Schaffer, 2012). Furthermore, co-occurring BPD and BD individuals who recover require more mood-stabilizing medications and a longer treatment course than BD individuals without co-occurring BPD (Garno, 2005; Swartz, Pilkonis, Frank, Proietti, & Scott, 2005). Similarly, treatment response to lithium is poorer among BD individuals with co-occurring personality disorder (Bowden & Maier, 2003). Moreover, there is greater mood instability and irritability with antidepressant treatment as well as greater resistance to antidepressant medication and poorer response to mood stabilizers and psychotherapy in co-occurring BD and BPD compared to BD-alone individuals (Garno, 2005; Perugi, Angst, Azorin, Bowden, Vieta, Young et al., 2013; Swartz et al., 2005). Contrary to findings suggesting a deleterious effect of co-occurring BPD on treatment response among individuals with BD, co-occurring BD does not predict treatment response or treatment utilization among individuals with BPD (Gunderson et al., 2006).

Few studies have tested treatments for individuals with co-occurring BD and a personality disorder. One evaluated a psychoeducation treatment for co-occurring BD and BPD. In this study, psychoeducation was compared to a nonstructured intervention. Both treatment conditions also included adjunctive pharmacotherapy. For BD individuals with a personality disorder, psychoeducation treatment was found to reduce the likelihood and frequency of recurrent mood episodes and inpatient days and increase the time to relapse for 2 years post-intervention (Colom et al., 2004). While a few promising approaches exist for treating co-occurring BPD and BD, evidence in this area is preliminary (Bowden & Maier, 2003). Taken together, these results suggest that co-occurring BD and BPD is a particularly challenging combination to treat effectively.

The following clinical vignette illustrates the difficulty in diagnosing co-occurring BPD and BD and the complicated clinical picture presented by co-occurring BD and BPD, as well as the consequences of misdiagnosis on treatment.

CASE STUDY: BD AND BPD

Ms. E was a 25-year-old black, Hispanic female college student. She presented with limited prior contact with the mental health system. As an adolescent, she saw a therapist for a few sessions after her father was imprisoned and she was, as a result, placed in foster care. A few months prior to evaluation in a clinic, she was hospitalized for suicidal thoughts and depression. At assessment, Ms. E was diagnosed with BPD based on her history of NSSI, paranoid stress-related ideation, difficulty managing intense anger, and significant sensitivity to interpersonal triggers, and she was motivated to work on these difficulties. She also readily reported past depressive episodes, sleep disturbance, and significant marijuana use mainly to manage anxiety. Ms. E also exhibited a number of strengths: she was an extremely resilient and resourceful young woman who maintained a job; she was a full-time scholar-ship student; and she was in a committed, intimate relationship for most of her late adolescence and young adulthood. Three weeks after assessment, Ms. E called to say she had not slept in 3 days and, upon questioning, endorsed an increase in both goal-directed and pleasurable but problematic activities (i.e., increased spending and risky sexual behavior with someone in addition to her partner) and a decreased need for sleep (e.g., she felt rested after only 3 hours of sleep). She also endorsed increased distractibility and presented with pressured speech. Ms. E acknowledged that such sleep and behavior patterns were not unfamiliar to her and that they had posed employment and relationship difficulties for her in the past. Ms. E was then re-evaluated by a team of psychiatrists and psychologists and given the additional diagnosis of BD because she currently met criteria for hypomania and had a history of depressive episodes. Ms. E had difficulty accepting this diagnosis and was resistant to continuing in psychotherapy and to initiating mood stabilizers to treat her BD. She missed her next few treatment appointments and did not fill her prescriptions. For a number of weeks, her psychotherapist focused on validation of her sad and angry feelings surrounding the BD diagnosis that Ms. E found unacceptable and viewed as a major and debilitating mental illness. After discussing these attitudes, Ms. E eventually recommitted to continuing in treatment and to following the treatment team's new recommendations. She began taking her mood stabilizers and attending individual and group therapy as well as medication management appointments with a psychiatrist. After 6 months of DBT plus medication, Ms. E reported a reduction in suicidal ideation, NSSI, and urges for NSSI, and her mood became more stable. She reported that for the first time in her adult life she did not feel miserable.

This case illustrates the importance of establishing the co-occurring BPD and BD diagnosis, which was difficult to diagnose until the emergence of a hypomanic episode. Treatment for BD was recommended, but several weeks of a specialized therapy for BPD were needed to help the patient accept the BD diagnosis and treatment, exemplifying the need for comprehensive, cooperative, and multimodal treatment for these individuals.

CONCLUSION

There are two primary and, regrettably, common pitfalls in the assessment of MD and BPD. The most common problem is diagnosing a MD while neglecting to consider a co-occurring BPD diagnosis when it is, in fact, present. One study found that approximately 40% of individuals rigorously assessed for BPD had been given a prior misdiagnosis of BD, not BPD. Neglect of this differential diagnosis can lead to a multiplication of medications for BD that are of dubious effectiveness in BPD and leave the BPD untreated. Preventable suicidality and hospitalization is common in this scenario, as evidenced by the high frequency of individuals with BPD present-ing recurrently to the ED (Bender et al., 2001; Bongar et al., 1990). Furthermore, when both BPD and MD are present, treating the symptoms of BPD first leads to improvement in the mood disorder rather than the reverse (Gunderson et al., 2004). The second problem is diagnosing BPD but neglecting a co-occurring MD. This can lead to delays in the effective adjunctive treatment of the MD and the worsening of a mood episode. In BPD, severe depressive episodes can render specialized psychotherapies for BPD less effective and increase risk of suicidality and hospitalization. Thus, ongoing assessment and adjunctive treatment of MD in BPD is key for successful treatment of BPD. In sum, although there have been impressive strides in the assessment and treatment of BPD over the past three decades, the impact of MD on BPD creates several complications that, when carefully assessed and treated, can lead to better outcomes for those with both BPD and MD.

REFERENCES

Abela, J. R., Payne, A. V., & Moussaly, N. (2003). Cognitive vulnerability to depression in individuals with borderline personality disorder. *Journal of Personality Disorders, 17*(4), 319–329.

Akiskal, H. (2004). Demystifying borderline personality: Critique of the concept and unorthodox reflections on its natural kinship with the bipolar spectrum. *Acta Psychiatrica Scandinavica, 110*(6), 401–407. doi: 10.1111/j.1600-0447.2004.00461.x

Akiskal, H., Chen, S. E., Davis, G. C., Puzantian, V. R., Kashgarian, M., & Bolinger, J. M. (1985). Borderline: An adjective in search of a noun. *Journal of Clinical Psychiatry, 46*, 7.

American Psychiatric Association (APA). (2000). *(DSM-IV-TR) Diagnostic and statistical manual of mental disorders* (4th ed.). Washington DC: Author.

Azorin, J. M., Kaladjian, A., Adida, M., Fakra, E., Belzeaux, R., Hantouche, E., & Lancrenon, S. (2013). Factors associated with borderline personality disorder in major depressive patients and their relationship to bipolarity. *European Psychiatry*(0). Retrieved from: http://dx.doi.org/10.1016/j.eurpsy.2012.11.007

Bassett, D. (2012). Borderline personality disorder and bipolar affective disorder. Spectra or spectre? A review. *Australian and New Zealand Journal of Psychiatry, 46*(4), 327–339. doi: 10.1177/0004867411435289

Beck, A. T., & Steer, R. A. (1993). *Beck depression inventory manual.* San Antonio, TX: Psychological Corporation.

Begley, C. E. (2001). The lifetime cost of bipolar disorder in the US: An estimate for new cases in 1998. *PharmacoEconomics, 19*(parts 1 and 2), 483–495. doi: 10.2165/00019053-200119050-00004

Bellino, S., Zizza, M., Camilla, R., & Filippo, B. (2006). Combined treatment of major depression in patients with borderline personality disorder: A comparison with pharmacotherapy. *Canadian Journal of Psychiatry, 51*(7), 453–460.

Bellino, S., Zizza, M., Rinaldi, C., & Bogetto, F. (2007). Combined therapy of major depression with concomitant borderline personality disorder: Comparison of interpersonal and cognitive psychotherapy. *Canadian Journal of Psychiatry, 52*(11), 718–725.

Benazzi, F. (2008). A relationship between bipolar II disorder and borderline personality disorder? *Progress in Neuro-Psychopharmacology and Biological Psychiatry, 32*(4), 1022–1029. doi: 10.1016/j.pnpbp.2008.01.015

Bender, D. S., Dolan, R. T., Skodol, A. E., Sanislow, C. A., Dyck, I. R., McGlashan, T. H., . . . Gunderson, J. G. (2001). Treatment utilization by patients with personality disorders. *American Journal of Psychiatry, 158*(2), 295–302.

Binks, C. A., Fenton, M., McCarthy, L., Lee, T., Adams, C. E., & Duggan, C. (2006). Pharmacological interventions for people with borderline personality disorder. *Cochrane Database of Systematic Reviews, 25*(1).

Biskin, R. S., & Paris, J. (2012). Management of borderline personality disorder. *Canadian Medical Association Journal, 184*(17), 1897–1902. doi: 10.1503/cmaj.112055

Bongar, B., Peterson, L. G., Golann, S., & Hardiman, J. J. (1990). Self-mutilation and the chronically suicidal patient: An examination of the frequent visitor to the psychiatric emergency room. *Annals of Clinical Psychiatry, 2,* 217–222.

Bowden, C., & Maier, W. (2003). Bipolar disorder and personality disorder. *European Psychiatry, 18,* 3.

Brodsky, B. S., Groves, S. A., Oquendo, M. A., Mann, J. J., & Stanley, B. (2006). Interpersonal precipitants and suicide attempts in borderline personality disorder. *Suicide and Life-Threatening Behavior, 36,* 313–322.

Chesin, M., Jeglic, E. L., & Stanley, B. (2010). Pathways to high-lethality suicide attempts in individuals with borderline personality disorder. *Archives of Suicide Research, 14*(4), 342–362. doi: 10.1080/13811118.2010.524054

Chesin, M., & Stanley, B. (2013). Risk assessment and psychosocial interventions for suicidal patients. *Bipolar Disorders, 15*(5), 584–593.

Chiesa, M., & Fonagy, P. (2000). Cassel personality disorder study. Methodology and treatment effects. *British Journal of Psychiatry, 176*(MAY), 485–491.

Coifman, K. G., Berenson, K. R., Rafaeli, E., & Downey, G. (2012). From negative to positive and back again: Polarized affective and relational experience in borderline personality disorder. *Journal of Abnormal Psychology, 121*(3), 668–679. doi: 10.1037/a0028502

Colom, F., Vieta, E., Sanchez-Moreno, J., Martinez-Aran, A., Torrent, C., Reinares, M., . . . Comes, M. (2004). Psychoeducation in bipolar patients with comorbid personality disorders. *Bipolar Disorders, 6,* 4.

Corbitt, E. M., Malone, K. M., Haas, G. L., & Mann, J. J. (1996). Suicidal behavior in patients with major depression and comorbid personality disorders. *Journal of Affective Disorders, 39*(1), 61–72. doi: 0165032796000237 [pii]

Coulston, C. M., Tanious, M., Mulder, R. T., Porter, R. J., & Malhi, G. S. (2012). Bordering on bipolar: The overlap between borderline personality and bipolarity. *Australian and New Zealand Journal of Psychiatry, 46*(6), 506–521. doi: 10.1177/0004867412445528

Davis, G. C., & Akiskal, H. S. (1986). Descriptive, biological, and theoretical aspects of borderline personality disorder. *Hospital and Community Psychiatry, 37*(7), 685–692.

Deltito, J., Martin, L., Riefkohl, J., Austria, B., Kissilenko, A., & Corless, C. M. P. (2001). Do patients with borderline personality disorder belong to the bipolar spectrum? *Journal of Affective Disorders, 67*(1-3), 221–228.

Dougherty, D. M., Bjork, J. M., Huckabee, H. C., Moeller, F. G., & Swann, A. C. (1999). Laboratory measures of aggression and impulsivity in women with borderline personality disorder. *Psychiatry Research, 85*(3), 315–326.

Fertuck, E. A., Makhija, N., & Stanley, B. (2007). The nature of suicidality in borderline personality disorder. *Primary Psychiatry, 14*(12), 40–47.

Feske, U., Mulsant, B. H., Pilkonis, P. A., Soloff, P., Dolata, D., Sackeim, H. A., & Haskett, R. F. (2004). Clinical outcome of ECT in patients with major depression and comorbid borderline personality disorder. *American Journal of Psychiatry, 161*(11), 2073–2080.

Feurino I., L., & Silk, K. R. (2011). State of the art in the pharmacologic treatment of borderline personality disorder. *Current Psychiatry Reports, 13*(1), 69–75.

Garno, J. L. (2005). Bipolar disorder with comorbid cluster B personality disorder features: Impact on suicidality. *Journal of Clinical Psychiatry, 66*(3), 339.

Gonda, X., Pompili, M., Serafini, G., Montebovi, F., Campi, S., Dome, P., . . . Rihmer, Z. (2012). Suicidal behavior in bipolar disorder: Epidemiology, characteristics and major risk factors. *Journal of Affective Disorders, 143*(1-3), 16–26. Retrieved from: http://dx.doi.org/10.1016/j.jad.2012.04.041

Grandin, L. D., Alloy, L. B., & Abramson, L. Y. (2006). The social zeitgeber theory, circadian rhythms, and mood disorders: Review and evaluation. *Clinical Psychology Review, 26*(6), 679–694. Retrieved from: http://dx.doi.org/10.1016/j.cpr.2006.07.001

Grilo, C. M., Stout, R. L., Markowitz, J. C., Sanislow, C. A., Ansell, E. B., Skodol, A. E., ... McGlashan, T. H. (2010). Personality disorders predict relapse after remission from an episode of major depressive disorder: A 6-year prospective study. *Journal of Clinical Psychiatry, 71*(12), 1629–1635.

Gunderson, J. G., Morey, L. C., Stout, R. L., Skodol, A. E., Shea, M. T., McGlashan, T. H., ... Bender, D. S. (2004). Major depressive disorder and borderline personality disorder revisited: Longitudinal interactions. *Journal of Clinical Psychiatry, 65*(8), 1049–1056.

Gunderson, J. G., & Phillips, K. A. (1991). A current view of the interface between borderline personality disorder and depression. *American Journal of Psychiatry, 148*(8), 967–975.

Gunderson, J. G., Weinberg, I., Daversa, M. T., Kueppenbender, K. D., Zanarini, M. C., Shea, M. T., ... Dyck, I. (2006). Descriptive and longitudinal observations on the relationship of borderline personality disorder and bipolar disorder. *American Journal of Psychiatry, 163*(7), 1173–1178.

Hamilton, M. (1960). A rating scale for depression. *Journal of Neurology, Neurosurgery, and Psychiatry, 23*, 56–62.

Harned, M. S., Chapman, A. L., Dexter-Mazza, E. T., Murray, A., Comtois, K. A., & Linehan, M. M. (2008). Treating co-occurring Axis I disorders in recurrently suicidal women with borderline personality disorder. *Journal of Consult Clinical Psychology, 76*(6), 1068–1075.

Harris, E. C., & Barraclough, B. (1997). Suicide as an outcome for mental disorders. A meta-analysis. *British Journal of Psychiatry, 170*(3), 205–228. doi: 10.1192/bjp.170.3.205

Henry, C., Mitropoulou, V., New, A., Koenigsberg, H. W., Silverman, J., & Seiver, L. J. (2001). Affective instability and impulsivity in borderline personality and bipolar II disorders: Similarities and differences. *Journal of Psychiatric Research, 35*, 5.

John, H., & Sharma, V. (2009). Misdiagnosis of bipolar disorder as borderline personality disorder: Clinical and economic consequences. *World Journal of Biological Psychiatry, 10*(4 Pt 2), 612–615. doi:10.1080/15622970701816522

Joyce, P. R., Mulder, R. T., Luty, S. E., McKenzie, J. M., Sullivan, P. F., & Cloninger, R. C. (2003). Borderline personality disorder in major depression: Symptomatology, temperament, character, differential drug response, and 6-month outcome. *Comprehensive Psychiatry, 44*(1), 35–43.

Kelly, T. M., Soloff, P., Lynch, K. G., Haas, G. L., & Mann, J. J. (2000). Recent life events, social adjustment, and suicide attempts in patients with major depression and borderline personality disorder. *Journal of Personality Disorders, 14*(4), 316–326.

Kernberg, O. F. (2001). The suicidal risk in severe personality disorders: Differential diagnosis and treatment. *Journal of Personality Disorders, 15*(3), 195–208; discussion 209–115.

Kernberg, O. F., & Yeomans, F. E. (2013). Borderline personality disorder, bipolar disorder, depression, attention deficit/hyperactivity disorder, and narcissistic personality disorder: Practical differential diagnosis. *Bulletin of the Menninger Clinic, 77*(1), 1–22. doi: 10.1521/bumc.2013.77.1.1

Klerman, G. L., Weissman, M. M., Rounsaville, B. J., & Chevron, E. S. (1984). *Interpersonal psychotherapy of depression.* New York: Basic Books.

Koenigsberg, H. W., Harvey, P. D., Mitropoulou, V., Schmeidler, J., New, A. S., Goodman, M., ... Siever, L. J. (2002). Characterizing affective instability in borderline personality disorder. *American Journal of Psychiatry, 159*(5), 784–788.

Linehan, M. M. (1993). *Cognitive-behavioral treatment of borderline personality disorder.* New York: Guilford.

Links, P. S., Mitton, J. E., & Patrick, J. (1995). Borderline personality disorder and the family environment. *Canadian Journal of Psychiatry, 40*(4), 218–219.

Magill, C. A. (2004). The boundary between borderline personality disorder and bipolar disorder: Current concepts and challenges. *Canadian Journal of Psychiatry, 49*(8), 551.

Morey, L. C., Shea, M. T., Markowitz, J. C., Stout, R. L., Hopwood, C. J., Gunderson, J. G., ... Skodol, A. E. (2010). State effects of major depression on the assessment of personality and personality disorder. *American Journal of Psychiatry, 167*(5), 528–535.

New, A. S., Triebwasser, J., & Charney, D. S. (2008). The case for shifting borderline personality disorder to Axis I. *Biological Psychiatry, 64*(8), 653–659.

Oldham, J. M. (2006). Borderline personality disorder and suicidality. *American Journal of Psychiatry, 163*(1), 20–25.

Orbach, I., Mikulincer, M., Gilboa-Schechtman, E., & Sirota, P. (2003). Mental pain and its relationship to suicidality and life meaning. *Suicide and Life-Threatening Behavior, 33*(3), 231–241.

Orbach, I., Mikulincer, M., Sirota, P., & Gilboa-Schechtman, E. (2003). Mental pain: A multidimensional operationalization and definition. *Suicide and Life-Threatening Behavior, 33*(3), 219–230.

Paris, J. (2011). Pharmacological treatments for personality disorders. *International Review of Psychiatry, 23*, 303–309.

Paris, J., Gunderson, J., & Weinberg, I. (2007). The interface between borderline personality disorder and bipolar spectrum disorders. *Comprehensive Psychiatry, 48*(2), 145–154. doi: S0010-440X(06)00107-6 [pii]10.1016/j.comppsych.2006.10.001

Paris, J., Silk, K. R., Gunderson, J., Links, P. S., & Zanarini, M. C. (2009). The case for retaining borderline personality disorder as a psychiatric diagnosis. *Personality and Mental Health, 3*(2), 96–100. doi: 10.1002/pmh.73

Pazzagli, A., & Monti, M. R. (2000). Dysphoria and aloneness in borderline personality disorder. *Psychopathology, 33*(4), 220–226.

Pepper, C. M., Klein, D. N., Anderson, R. L., Riso, L. P., Ouimette, P. C., & Lizardi, H. (1995). DSM-III-R axis II comorbidity in dysthymia and major depression. *American Journal of Psychiatry, 152*(2), 239–247.

Perugi, G., Angst, J., Azorin, J., Bowden, C., Vieta, E., & Young, A. H. (2013). Is comorbid borderline personality disorder in patients with major depressive episode and bipolarity a developmental subtype? Findings from the international BRIDGE study. *Journal of Affective Disorders, 144*(1–2), 72–78. Retrieved from: http://dx.doi.org/10.1016/j.jad.2012.06.008

Perugi, G., Angst, J., Azorin, J. M., Bowden, C., Vieta, E., Young, A. H.; Bridge Study Group. (2013). The bipolar–borderline personality disorders connection in major depressive patients. *Acta Psychiatrica Scandinavica, 128*, 376–383. doi: 10.1111/acps.12083

Pfohl, B., Stangl, D., & Zimmerman, M. (1984). The implications of DSM-III personality disorders for patients with major depression. *Journal of Affective Disorders, 7*(3-4), 309–318.

Reich, D. B., Zanarini, M., & Fitzmaurice, G. (2012). Affective lability in bipolar disorder and borderline personality disorder. *Comprehensive Psychiatry, 53*(3), 230–237. Retrieved from: http://dx.doi.org/10.1016/j.comppsych.2011.04.003

Renaud, S., Corbalan, F., & Beaulieu, S. (2012). Differential diagnosis of bipolar affective disorder type II and borderline personality disorder: Analysis of the affective dimension. *Comprehensive Psychiatry, 53*(7), 952–961. Retrieved from: http://dx.doi.org/10.1016/j.comppsych.2012.03.004

Riso, L. P., Klein, D. N., Anderson, R. L., & Ouimette, P. C. (2000). A family study of outpatients with borderline personality disorder and no history of mood disorder. *Journal of Personality Disorders, 14*(3), 208–217.

Rogers, J. H., Widiger, T. A., & Krupp, A. (1995). Aspects of depression associated with borderline personality disorder. *American Journal of Psychiatry, 152*(2), 268–270.

Rosenbluth, M., MacQueen, G., McIntyre, R. S., Beaulieu, S., & Schaffer, A. (2012). The Canadian Network for Mood and Anxiety Treatments (CANMAT) task force recommendations for the management of patients with mood disorders and comorbid personality disorders. *Annals of Clinical Psychiatry, 24*(1), 56–68.

Rossi, R., Lanfredi, M., Pievani, M., Boccardi, M., Beneduce, R., Rillosi, L., . . . Frisoni, G. B. (2012). Volumetric and topographic differences in hippocampal subdivisions in borderline personality and bipolar disorders. *Psychiatry Research: Neuroimaging, 203*(2–3), 132–138. Retrieved from: http://dx.doi.org/10.1016/j.pscychresns.2011.12.004

Ruggero, C. J., Zimmerman, Chelminski, I., & Young, D. (2010). Borderline personality disorder and the misdiagnosis of bipolar disorder. *Journal of Psychiatric Research*, *44*(6), 405–408. Retrieved from: http://dx.doi.org/10.1016/j.jpsychires.2009.09.011

Runeson, B., & Beskow, J. (1991). Borderline personality disorder in young Swedish suicides. *Journal of Nervous and Mental Disease*, *179*(3), 153–156.

Sayın, A., Kuruoğlu, A., Yazıcı Güleç, M., & Aslan, S. (2007). Relation of temperament and character properties with clinical presentation of bipolar disorder. *Comprehensive Psychiatry*, *48*(5), 446–451. Retrieved from: http://dx.doi.org/10.1016/j.comppsych.2007.04.004

Silk, K. R. (2010). The quality of depression in borderline personality disorder and the diagnostic process. *Journal of Personality Disorders*, *24*(1), 25–37. doi: 10.1521/pedi.2010.24.1.25

Silk, K. R. (2011). The process of managing medications in patients with borderline personality disorder. *Journal of Psychiatric Practice*, *17*(5), 311–319.

Skodol, A. E., Grilo, C. M., Keyes, K. M., Geier, T., Grant, B. F., & Hasin, D. S. (2011). Relationship of personality disorders to the course of major depressive disorder in a nationally representative sample. *American Journal of Psychiatry*, *168*(3), 257–264.

Soloff, P. (2000). Psychopharmacology of borderline personality disorder *Psychiatric Clinics of North America*, *23*, 169–192.

Soloff, P., Lynch, K. G., Kelly, T. M., Malone, K. M., & Mann, J. J. (2000). Characteristics of suicide attempts of patients with major depressive episode and borderline personality disorder: A comparative study. *American Journal of Psychiatry*, *157*(4), 601–608.

Spokas, M., Wenzel, A., Brown, G. K., & Beck, A. T. (2012). Characteristics of individuals who make impulsive suicide attempts. *Journal of Affective Disorders*, *136*(3), 1121–1125. Retrieved from: http://dx.doi.org/10.1016/j.jad.2011.10.034

Stanley, B., & Siever, L. J. (2010). The interpersonal dimension of borderline personality disorder: Toward a neuropeptide model. *American Journal of Psychiatry*, *167*(1), 24–39. doi: 10.1176/appi.ajp.2009.09050744

Stanley, B., & Wilson, S. T. (2006). Heightened subjective experience of depression in borderline personality disorder. *Journal of Personal Disorders*, *20*(4), 307–318.

Stiglmayr, C. E., Grathwol, T., Linehan, M. M., Ihorst, G., Fahrenberg, J., & Bohus, M. (2005). Aversive tension in patients with borderline personality disorder: A computer-based controlled field study. *Acta Psychiatrica Scandinavia*, *111*, 372–379.

Stoffers, J. M., Völlm, B. A., Rücker, G., Timmer, A., Huband, N., & Lieb, K. (2012). Psychological therapies for people with borderline personality disorder. *Cochrane Database of Systematic Reviews*, *15*(8), CD005652.

Swann, A. C., Lijffijt, M., Lane, S. D., Steinberg, J. L., & Moeller, F. G. (2012). Antisocial personality disorder and borderline symptoms are differentially related to impulsivity and course of illness in bipolar disorder. *Journal of Affective Disorders*(0). Retrieved from: http://dx.doi.org/10.1016/j.jad.2012.06.027

Swann, A. C., Steinberg, J. L., Lijffijt, M., & Moeller, F. G. (2008). Impulsivity: Differential relationship to depression and mania in bipolar disorder. *Journal of Affective Disorders*, *106*(3), 241–248. Retrieved from: http://dx.doi.org/10.1016/j.jad.2007.07.011

Swartz, H. A., Pilkonis, P. A., Frank, E., Proietti, J. M., & Scott, J. (2005). Acute treatment outcomes in patients with bipolar I disorder and co-morbid borderline personality disorder receiving medication and psychotherapy. *Bipolar Disorders*, *7*(2), 192–197.

Westen, D., Moses, M. J., Silk, K. R., Lohr, N. E., Cohen, R., & Segal, H. (1992). Quality of depressive experience in borderline personality disorder and major depression: When depression is not just depression. *Journal of Personality Disorders*, *6*(4), 382–393.

Westen, D., Muderrisoglu, S., Fowler, C., Shedler, J., & Koren, D. (1997). Affect regulation and affective experience: Individual differences, group differences, and measurement using a Q-sort procedure. *Journal of Consulting and Clinical Psychology*, *65*(3), 429–439.

Wilson, S. T., Stanley, B., Oquendo, M. A., Goldberg, P., Zalsman, G., & Mann, J. J. (2007). Comparing impulsiveness, hostility, and depression in borderline personality disorder and bipolar II disorder. *Journal of Clinical Psychiatry, 68*(10), 1533.

Yen, S., Zlotnick, C., & Costello, E. (2002). Affect regulation in women with borderline personality disorder traits. *Journal of Nervous and Mental Disease, 190*(10), 693–696.

Zanarini, M., & Frankenburg, F. R. (2007). The essential nature of borderline psychopathology. *Journal of Personality Disorders, 21*(5), 518–535.

Zanarini, M., Frankenburg, F. R., DeLuca, C. J., Hennen, J., Khera, G. S., & Gunderson, J. G. (1998). The pain of being borderline: Dysphoric states specific to borderline personality disorder. *Harvard Review of Psychiatry, 6*(4), 201–207.

Zanarini, M., Frankenburg, F. R., Hennen, J., Reich, D. B., & Silk, K. R. (2004). Axis I comorbidity in patients with borderline personality disorder: 6-year follow-up and prediction of time to remission. *American Journal of Psychiatry, 161*(11), 2108–2114.

Zanarini, M., Frankenburg, F. R., Hennen, J., & Silk, K. R. (2003). The longitudinal course of borderline psychopathology: 6-year prospective follow-up of the phenomenology of borderline personality disorder. *American Journal of Psychiatry, 160*(2), 274–283.

Zimmerman, M., Galione, J. N., Chelminski, I., Young, D., Dalrymple, K., & Ruggero, C. J. (2010). Sustained unemployment in psychiatric outpatients with bipolar disorder: Frequency and association with demographic variables and comorbid disorders. [10.1111/j.1399-5618.2010.00869.x]. *Bipolar Disorders, 12*(7), 720–726.

Zimmerman, M., & Mattia, J. I. (1999). Axis I diagnostic comorbidity and borderline personality disorder. *Comprehensive Psychiatry, 40*(4), 245–252.

Zittel Conklin, C., Bradley, R., & Westen, D. (2006). Affect regulation in borderline personality disorder. *Journal of Nervous and Mental Disease, 194*(2), 69–77.

Zittel Conklin, C., & Westen, D. (2005). Borderline personality disorder in clinical practice. *American Journal of Psychiatry, 162*(5), 867–875.

Aggressive Behavior and
Interpersonal Difficulties in
Borderline Personality Disorder

LORI N. SCOTT AND PAUL A. PILKONIS

INTERPERSONAL DIFFICULTIES AND AGGRESSIVE BEHAVIOR

Interpersonal dysfunction, including aggression, is one of the most impairing, chronic, and difficult to manage aspects of borderline personality disorder (BPD). Three out of the nine diagnostic criteria for BPD directly reference interpersonal difficulties, including criterion 1 ("frantic efforts to avoid real or imagined abandonment"), criterion 2 ("a pattern of unstable and intense interpersonal relationships characterized by alternating between extremes of idealization and devaluation"), and criterion 8 ("inappropriate, intense anger or difficulty controlling anger" (American Psychiatric Association [APA], 2013). However, the other six diagnostic criteria often function as either catalysts or consequences of interpersonal dysfunction. For example, both clinical impressions and empirical evidence suggest that emotion dysregulation, impulsive behaviors, recurrent suicidal or self-injurious behaviors, and transient stress-related paranoid ideation or dissociation are often triggered by aversive interpersonal events or perceptions (for review, see Gunderson & Lyons-Ruth, 2008). The reverse is also true: affective, cognitive, and behavioral dyscontrol have undeniable effects on the quality of patients' relationships and behavior in relation to others. Furthermore, in factor analytic studies of BPD criteria, identity disturbance and chronic feelings of emptiness have been shown to load on a factor representing interpersonal dysfunction (e.g., Sanislow et al., 2002), which is consistent with theoretical conceptualizations of a disrupted self in relation to others as a core area of dysfunction in BPD.

Interpersonal difficulties, particularly those related to dependency and intolerance of aloneness, are also among the most intransigent symptoms of BPD over long-term follow-up, enduring even after other BPD symptoms have remitted (e.g., Choi-Kain, Zanarini, Frankenburg, Fitzmaurice, & Reich, 2010). Longitudinal studies suggest that improved general functioning and symptom reduction in those with BPD is usually associated with the formation of positive and stable relationships (Links & Heslegrave, 2000), whereas exacerbation of symptoms typically follows from the dissolution or loss of important relationships (Pagano et al., 2004). These observations corroborate clinical impressions that chronic interpersonal dysfunction is a defining feature of BPD and represents one of the best overall markers for the disorder (Gunderson & Lyons-Ruth, 2008).

Intense emotional reactions can develop rapidly in the psychotherapeutic relationships with this group of patients, consistent with their characteristically intense and chaotic interpersonal relationships outside of treatment. The appearance and intensity of such dynamics are often diagnostic but can also quickly lead to various difficulties in treatment, including perceived empathic failures, ruptures in therapeutic alliance, provider burnout, and premature termination of treatment (Gunderson et al., 1989). Hence, the interpersonal difficulties that plague these individuals' personal and professional lives are often the very same ones that create obstacles to treatment continuation and success. Careful assessment frequently reveals an extensive history of failed treatment attempts and problematic relationships with previous providers. Such signs can be daunting to clinicians, pointing to a road ahead fraught with difficulties in forming and maintaining an effective therapeutic relationship. As many experienced clinicians can attest, it is frequently the formation of a positive working relationship and bond with the therapist that constitutes the first major goal of therapy with this patient population, one that can take a year or more to accomplish (Gabbard et al., 1988). A strong attachment with the therapist is one of the most powerful tools for reducing problem behaviors, establishing healthier relational patterns, helping patients to productively use therapeutic interventions, and keeping them motivated "when the going gets tough."

Considering the central role of interpersonal dysfunction in BPD and the potential for these difficulties to derail even the most expertly delivered treatment, it becomes essential for clinicians to be acquainted with ways of understanding, assessing, tolerating, and responding to these behaviors. In addition, even though efficacious treatments for BPD now exist, there is still considerable variability in treatment response and high rates of premature dropout (Levy, 2008). This suggests that there is a need to explore patient characteristics, especially interpersonal behaviors, that predict differential treatment outcomes and to work toward tailoring interventions more effectively to individuals in the treatment planning stage. Therefore, the primary goal of this chapter is to review the various manifestations and potential determinants of interpersonal difficulties and aggression in those with BPD, drawing on both theory and empirical evidence. Furthermore, we will discuss the clinical utility of assessing interpersonal problems and risk for aggressive behavior and present a clinical case to illustrate how interpersonal patterns might manifest in the course of treatment with BPD patients.

INTERPERSONAL THEMES IN BPD

Characterization of BPD in terms of a coherent interpersonal style is a difficult endeavor, in large part because the interpersonal behaviors of those with BPD are by definition "unstable" and "vacillating," as described in the diagnostic criteria. In addition, even though research has shown that the diagnostic criteria for BPD tend to cohere into a unitary pathology, evidence also suggests considerable interpersonal heterogeneity both within and across BPD samples (Wright et al., 2013). Most research on interpersonal styles in BPD has used the interpersonal circumplex to characterize interpersonal functioning around the broad domains of Agency (dominance to submission) and Communion (coldness to affiliation). Unlike most other disorders, BPD has not been consistently associated with any particular interpersonal profile according to the circumplex; rather, studies have variously shown BPD to be associated with a variety of interpersonal themes that are often contradictory.

Some of the interpersonal inconsistencies of BPD may be attributable to intra-individual variability (i.e., the tendency for those with this disorder to fluctuate between opposing interpersonal styles). Prominent clinical theories of BPD emphasize vacillations in interpersonal behavior and mental states as central to the disorder (Kernberg, 1984; Linehan, 1993). These vacillations might manifest in markedly contradictory verbalizations, views of self and others, morals and values, and behavioral patterns, which often occur outside of patients' conscious awareness and in tandem with rapid shifts in affective experiences. Accordingly, one study found that individuals with BPD were not only more submissive, less dominant, and more quarrelsome than healthy controls in their everyday social interactions, but that they also showed more intraindividual variability in dominance, quarrelsomeness, and agreeableness, reflecting the tendency to oscillate between hostility and friendliness and between high and low levels of controlling behavior (Russell, Moskowitz, Zuroff, Sookman, & Paris, 2007). Those with BPD also showed disparate interpersonal behaviors, suggesting the use of a variety of interpersonal strategies and a greater tendency to switch between various interpersonal styles over time. A more recent study found that the social interactions of individuals with BPD were characterized by more ambivalence as well as greater disagreements, anger, sadness, and emptiness, compared to those with other personality disorders or no personality disorder (Stepp, Pilkonis, Yaggi, Morse, & Feske, 2009). Hence, the interpersonal universe of BPD might best be conceptualized as a constellation of distinct patterns that may differentially be activated or deactivated at various times based on the vicissitudes of mood and relational events.

In addition to this within-individual variability, however, is the significant inter-individual variation among groups of individuals with BPD in terms of interpersonal predilections. Clinical theorists have proposed a subtype of BPD patients who demonstrate more dependent and submissive interpersonal patterns and another subtype who tend to be more autonomous and hostile. For instance, Linehan (1993) has discussed two types: "butterfly-like" patients who flutter in and out of treatment and have difficulties attaching and "attached" patients who quickly form intense, dependent, and stormy relationships. Likewise, Kernberg (1984) has discussed heterogeneity within BPD patients on the basis of aggression, with some patients demonstrating lower aggression and higher internalizing symptom expression and a more severely impaired subgroup with high levels of aggression and more externalizing (e.g., antisocial) features.

One recent study used latent class analysis to reveal six homogeneous subgroups with distinct interpersonal themes in a sample of 255 patients with significant BPD symptoms (Wright et al., 2013). These classes were labeled as Intrusive, Vindictive, Avoidant, Nonassertive, Moderate Exploitable, and Severe Exploitable. Consistent with previous findings of high submissiveness in those with BPD (Russell et al., 2007), the majority of the sample demonstrated a tendency toward a nonassertive/submissive interpersonal style, and these individuals tended to show more identity-related pathology (e.g., identity disturbance and emptiness) and self-injurious behaviors. However, the relatively smaller Vindictive class (representing a blend of hostility and dominance, and comprising 22% of the sample), was characterized by greater antisocial features, anger, and aggression directed toward others. Thus, as a group, patients with BPD demonstrate clinically meaningful heterogeneity of interpersonal patterns, which are likely to predict differential symptom profiles and response to treatment.

Despite these complexities in capturing a prototypical BPD-related interpersonal style, clinical and empirical observations point to at least two important relational themes in this patient population: (1) interpersonal hypersensitivity, linked with insecure attachment, rejection sensitivity, and social cognitive distortions or deficits; and (2) angry, hostile, and/or aggressive behavior. Importantly, these manifestations of interpersonal behavior are not mutually exclusive and are, in many patients, integrally related, as demonstrated in the tendency for those with BPD to oscillate between extremes of dependency and angry withdrawal (Levy, 2005) and to respond to perceived interpersonal rejection with intense rage (Berenson, Downey, Rafiaeli, Coifman, & Paquin, 2011).

INTERPERSONAL HYPERSENSITIVITY

Most clinicians who have worked with patients with BPD have experienced first-hand their exquisite sensitivity to subtle interpersonal cues. An example is the patient who greets her therapist in the waiting room with the statement, "you look moody." Whether such perceptions represent enhanced sensitivity to others' emotional expressions, impaired social information processing, or defensive processes (e.g., projection) is still an open question, and each possibility may have relevance depending on the context. However, evidence abounds that BPD is related to high levels of interpersonal stress, heightened affective responses to social events or cues, and enhanced amygdala activation in response to socially relevant stimuli (for reviews, see Dinsdale & Crespi, 2013; Gunderson & Lyons-Ruth, 2008). Such observations, combined with evidence for the familiality and heritability of interpersonal dysfunction in BPD, have led Gunderson and colleagues to propose that the prototypical relational difficulties in BPD evolve from an interaction between a genetically based hypersensitivity to interpersonal interactions and an adverse early environment (Gunderson & Lyons-Ruth, 2008). Although other etiological theories of BPD also emphasize a diathesis between constitutional vulnerabilities to emotion dysregulation or aggression and environmental stress (e.g., invalidating environment or adverse early experiences with caregivers; Kernberg, 1984; Linehan, 1993), Gunderson and Lyons-Ruth (2008) propose a constitutional vulnerability to heightened reactivity *particularly in relational contexts*, manifesting in heightened distress proneness (especially on separation from caregivers), difficulty being soothed, and enhanced reactivity to maternal affective communications. Although such temperamental disposition does not in and of itself lead to BPD or any form of psychopathology, this innate hypersensitivity to interpersonal stress is seen as a general risk factor that increases vulnerability to BPD, particularly in the context of inconsistent, neglectful, and/or abusive caregiving. The interaction between this constitutional interpersonal hypersensitivity and an inadequate caregiving environment is hypothesized to evolve into interpersonal endophenotypes associated with BPD: namely, disturbed attachment, rejection sensitivity, and social cognitive abnormalities.

The Attachment System

According to Bowlby (1969), the innate tendency for human infants to seek proximity to caregivers is part of an evolutionary biological system (i.e., the *attachment behavioral system*), the purpose of which is to maintain proximity to caregivers in order to ensure safety, comfort, and survival. The attachment system is at rest (i.e., deactivated) when attachment figures are perceived as available and responsive. At these times, the infant happily plays and explores. Thus, a deactivated attachment system results in explorative behavior and is accompanied by low anxiety. However, the attachment system becomes activated in times of distress, especially when an attachment figure's availability is uncertain or threat is perceived. Activation of the attachment system results in behaviors aimed to maintain or reestablish proximity to the caregiver (i.e., proximity-seeking behaviors), which might include crying, clinging, and following.

Bowlby (1969) further hypothesized that the affective bond between child and caretaker influences the child's emerging self-concept and worldview, forming the basis for later personality development and adjustment. From repeated interactions between child and caretaker, mental representations (or *internal working models*) of self and others are formed, which are social cognitive schemata that contain beliefs about the self as well as expectations about others. Repeated experiences with responsive and loving attachment figures contribute to the development of predominantly positive representations of self and others and a sense of *secure attachment*. Such individuals come to view the world as a safe place, expect that others will be available in times of need, and view themselves as worthy of love and attention. Research suggests that these attachment-related representations persist into adulthood as general representations with respect to close relationships, acting as prototypes in social situations and serving important self-regulatory functions (Shaver & Mikulincer, 2007). Adults with a sense of secure attachment are often better able to sustain effective emotion regulation through such strategies as reappraisal, problem-solving, and other self-soothing tactics. They are also able to effectively seek and obtain support from important others and are less likely to feel the need to defensively suppress, deny, or distort their emotional experiences.

Disturbed Attachment and Rejection Sensitivity in BPD

A large clinical literature discusses the important role of disturbed attachment processes in the development and maintenance of BPD (Levy, 2005). Not surprisingly, few individuals (<10%) with BPD demonstrate secure attachment patterns (Agrawal, Gunderson, Holmes, & Lyons-Ruth, 2004). Although there is no single attachment style that is specific to BPD and findings vary depending on the method used to assess attachment, reviews of the literature suggest that the most commonly observed attachment patterns in those with BPD are preoccupied, fearful, and "unresolved" (Agrawal et al., 2004; Levy, 2005). What these attachment patterns share in common are intense needs for closeness and dependency along with equally intense fears of rejection or abandonment. Such individuals value close relationships, but they are acutely sensitive to interpersonal slights, devaluation, rejection, or threats of desertion. Hence, their relationships are often infused with negative emotions, ambivalence, and instability. This acute sensitivity to rejection, exclusion, or abandonment has also been referred to as "rejection sensitivity," a construct closely akin to preoccupied and fearful attachment styles (Berenson et al., 2011).

These attachment styles are also marked by hyperactivation of the attachment system in the face of emotional distress or threat of abandonment. Because they tend to believe that they are unable to manage distress on their own, these individuals are hypervigilant to the possibility that attachment figures may be unavailable in times of need (Shaver & Mikulincer, 2007). Hence, in the context of upsetting events or perceived threats of rejection or abandonment, negative emotions are intensified and exaggerated to ensure the proximity and availability of attachment figures. Hyperactivation interferes with the ability to access adaptive emotion regulation strategies and is associated with distress-intensifying appraisals (i.e., perceiving threats as more serious than they are and perceiving oneself as unable to cope), emotion-focused coping strategies, excessive rumination, and other maladaptive behaviors that exacerbate distress, such as impulsive self-destructive behaviors and frantic attempts to maintain proximity to attachment figures. Such difficulties parallel the difficulties commonly observed in patients with BPD in their ability to self soothe and modulate negative emotions, as well as in their excessive dependency on others to reduce their distress and frantic efforts to avoid abandonment.

Impaired Social Cognitive Processes in BPD

Several theories hypothesize that interpersonal dysfunction and many other symptoms of BPD result from impaired social cognitive and representational processes. Kernberg (1984) conceptualizes borderline pathology as a broad level of personality organization (within which BPD is one of many severe personality disorders) characterized by intensely negative and poorly articulated mental representations of self and others. Similarly, according to attachment theory, the interpersonal difficulties in those with BPD can be understood as stemming from negative internal working models of self and others (Levy, 2005). Cognitive theories of BPD also emphasize the role of rigid and maladaptive cognitive schemata, or *core dysfunctional beliefs*, which are cognitive structures that are largely automatic and serve to organize and process incoming information (Beck, Freeman, & Davis, 2006). These schemata are seen as underlying the attributional biases and irrational thinking patterns (e.g., *black-and-white* or *all-or-none thinking*) about self and others that are often observed clinically in patients with this disorder. Consistent with these theoretical views, studies have demonstrated that those with BPD tend to hold views of others as untrustworthy, rejecting, abandoning, and neglectful, and of themselves as unlovable, inherently evil or bad, dependent, and helpless (e.g., Butler, Brown, Beck, & Grisham, 2002). Social cognition research suggests that those with predominantly negative representations of self and others are likely to selectively attend to emotional and social information that is consistent with these beliefs, misinterpret or misperceive social cues, and engage in maladaptive social behaviors that evoke responses from others that confirm and perpetuate their worldview (Dodge, Bates, & Pettit, 1990).

A common thread across theoretical accounts of BPD is that these individuals have difficulties accurately processing and appraising emotional information, especially in social contexts (Fonagy & Bateman, 2008; Kernberg, 1984; Levy, 2005). Fonagy and Bateman (2008) hypothesize that BPD is characterized by deficits in the capacity for *mentalization*, or the ability to reflect on one's own mental experience and the mental experiences of others in terms of underlying emotional states. Linehan (1993) has discussed deficits in *mindfulness*, which involves nonjudgmentally observing, reflecting on, and describing mental, emotional, and perceptual experiences. Similarly, Kernberg (1984) suggests that negative and polarized representations of self and others may interfere with reality testing in social domains, manifesting in distorted perceptions and misinterpretations of others' feeling states, intentions, and motivations.

Despite these various theoretical accounts that emphasize social cognitive impairments in BPD, clinicians often describe individuals with BPD as exquisitely sensitive to picking up on emotions in others. In fact, this phenomenon was first described by Krohn (1974) as the "BPD empathy paradox." A growing body of research attempts to reconcile this discrepancy by studying social cognitive processes in those with BPD, most often using facial emotion perception paradigms. This work has yielded mixed results regarding BPD patients' overall accuracy and sensitivity in attributing emotions to others (for review, see Daros, Zakzanis, & Ruocco, 2013). However, several studies have found that individuals with BPD or elevated BPD symptoms show a bias for attributing negative emotions or intentions to benign, neutral, or even positive social stimuli. Recent evidence suggests that adolescents with BPD may not necessarily show failures or impairments per se in mentalization or emotion recognition abilities, but rather tend to engage in a process of *hypermentalization* (i.e., the overinterpretation or overattribution of overly complex intentions or mental states), leading to inaccuracies (Sharp et al., 2011). Taken together, these findings corroborate clinical observations that patients with BPD show, at times, an uncanny ability for perceiving negative mental states in others but that they might also be prone to "reading into situations" and misattributing negative emotions or intentions to others in some social contexts (Dinsdale & Crespi, 2013).

AGGRESSIVE BEHAVIOR

Aggression, defined broadly as hostile, harmful, injurious, or destructive behavior, is arguably the most functionally debilitating and life-threatening of interpersonal problems among individuals with BPD, interfering with virtually every domain of patients' lives. Although self-directed aggression (e.g., suicide attempts and self-injurious behavior) is a cardinal feature of BPD, evidence suggests that BPD also increases risk for aggression directed toward others (Sansone & Sansone, 2012). Not only does externalized aggression pose dangers for patients, their loved ones, and society at large, but it also places intensive demands on close relationships (including with therapists) that are distinct from the demands of internalizing problems such as anxiety and depression. Hostility and aggression also contribute to the stigma associated with BPD and the reluctance of many clinicians to treat these patients. However, in comparison to affective instability and self-harm, there is a relative paucity of research on externalized aggression in those with BPD, leaving little guidance to clinicians regarding how to understand and manage aggressive behavior in these individuals.

Aggression is a heterogeneous construct that can be defined in terms of form (i.e., indirect/covert forms such as relational aggression or direct/overt forms such as psychological/verbal or physical aggression) and function (i.e., reactive/impulsive or proactive/instrumental/premeditated aggression). These distinctions are clinically useful because they may imply distinct causal mechanisms and approaches to prevention and treatment. Relational forms of aggression are typically defined as behaviors intended to damage another person's relationships or social status, such as spreading malicious rumors, gossiping, or intentionally excluding someone from a group. Psychological aggression can include verbal insults or other behaviors designed to harm someone emotionally (e.g., intentionally destroying another person's belongings, giving someone the "silent treatment," etc.). Physical aggression is the most commonly recognized manifestation of direct aggression and can range in severity from shoving/pushing to attacking another person with a weapon.

Among both men and women, BPD has been shown to be associated with heightened risk for the perpetration of both direct and indirect forms of aggression, including intimate partner violence, nonintimate physical assaults, psychological and relational aggression, child maltreatment, and property damage (Sansone & Sansone, 2012). In addition, high rates of BPD are observed in violent criminal populations, suggesting associations between BPD and severe physically aggressive behavior. Nonetheless, even more subtle forms of aggression, such as relational and psychological aggression, are impairing to relationships and often lead to direct physical assault perpetration and heightened risk for victimization.

The function of aggression is an even more clinically valuable distinction than its form. BPD is most consistently associated with reactive aggression, which is impulsive rather than planned, often evoked by perceived insult or injury, and usually accompanied by intense negative emotions, especially anger (Siever, 2008). BPD has been associated with reactive aggression toward others as assessed by various methods including self-reports (Fossati et al., 2004; Ostrov & Houston, 2008), informant or official reports (Newhill, Eack, & Mulvey, 2009, 2012; Walsh et al., 2010), and measurable behavioral reactions in the laboratory (McCloskey et al., 2009; New et al., 2009). On the other hand, BPD is less consistently associated with proactive or instrumental aggression, which is premeditated and goal-oriented and may or may not be associated with negative emotions. Several studies suggest that proactive/instrumental aggression is more strongly associated with antisocial or psychopathic features than with BPD (Gilbert & Daffern, 2011; Ostrov & Houston, 2008). This distinction is important because differences in the function of a behavior imply that it may be mediated by distinct processes. In the case of BPD, reactive aggression is likely mediated by emotion dysregulation and sensitivity to rejection or abandonment.

Some have suggested that aggressive behavior among those with BPD is secondary to comorbid antisocial personality disorder (ASPD) features (Allen & Links, 2012), but empirical evidence to support this position is equivocal. In a large sample of 801 individuals recruited from inpatient units (28% of whom were diagnosed with BPD and 22% with ASPD), Newhill and colleagues (2009) found that a substantial proportion (66%) of those with BPD who did not also have a comorbid ASPD diagnosis engaged in violent behavior over the course of a year. Although associations between a diagnosis of BPD and violent behavior in this sample were diminished after controlling for both psychopathic features and a diagnosis of ASPD, further path analyses suggested that the shared variance between these constructs was most predictive of violence. Hence, the characteristics that BPD, ASPD, and psychopathy share in common (e.g., impulsivity, irritability, and uncontrolled anger) rather than features that are unique to ASPD or psychopathy were most predictive of violent behavior, suggesting that BPD is not irrelevant in predicting violence. Furthermore, in a study of late middle-age adults (ages 55–64), only BPD symptoms, and not ASPD symptoms, were associated with aggression against romantic partners (Weinstein, Gleason, & Oltmanns, 2012). It is possible that BPD is less associated with severe violent crimes against strangers, which may increase as a function of general impulsivity, hostility, or comorbid ASPD symptoms, than it is with emotionally mediated conflict and aggression in close personal relationships, such as with romantic partners.

Thus, although it is likely that comorbid ASPD further increases risk for severely violent behavior in those with BPD, it also appears that BPD may be independently associated with various forms of externalized aggression due to factors that are unique to BPD. Beyond the temperamental aspects that BPD and ASPD share in common, emotion dysregulation could be a unique feature of BPD that mediates externalized aggression along with the interpersonal context (e.g., rejection sensitivity) and specific emotions that accompany interpersonal interactions (e.g., shame and anger). Associations between these characteristics and aggression in patients with BPD have not yet been extensively studied; however, we will review preliminary evidence of these features as they relate to aggression and BPD.

Role of Emotion Dysregulation

Emotion dysregulation has been defined in various ways throughout the literature on BPD but generally refers to difficulties managing and flexibly responding to emotions (Carpenter & Trull, 2013). According to Linehan's (1993) biosocial theory, emotion dysregulation is defined as heightened emotional reactivity and intensity, and prolonged affective arousal. Emotion dysregulation is widely viewed as a core feature of BPD that is not as frequently observed in those with ASPD (Paris, Chenard-Poirier, & Biskin, 2012). It has been suggested that difficulties regulating emotions are key mechanisms in the link between BPD and aggression (Newhill et al., 2009). Few prospective studies of these processes have been conducted thus far, but one longitudinal study demonstrated that increases in emotion dysregulation over the course of a year fully mediated the association between a baseline BPD diagnosis and future violence, even after accounting for comorbid ASPD (Newhill et al., 2012). Our recent work with a mixed sample of psychiatric outpatients and community participants suggests that emotion dysregulation may be a specific mechanism underlying aggression (i.e., both psychological and physical aggression in close personal relationships) in those with BPD. Using prospective data, we found that the association between BPD symptoms and aggressive behavior over the course of a year was fully mediated by emotion dysregulation, even after controlling for

ASPD symptoms and trait impulsivity (Scott, Stepp, & Pilkonis, 2014). Thus, an emerging line of evidence suggests that aggression, defined broadly in terms of both psychological aggression and physical assaults, in outpatients with BPD might be best understood in the context of emotion dysregulation and not as merely an epiphenomenon of general impulsivity or comorbid ASPD symptoms.

Role of the Interpersonal Context and Rejection Sensitivity

The centrality of emotion dysregulation for understanding aggressive behavior in BPD is consistent with Linehan's (1993) biosocial theory, which conceptualizes emotion dysregulation as the driving force of all other BPD symptoms. However, it is important to note that affect does have context, and we propose that the interpersonal context of emotion dysregulation is key for understanding aggression and interpersonal dysfunction in those with BPD. Cognitive, behavioral, and modern psychodynamic theories all discuss the importance of relational contexts (e.g., invalidating environment, inconsistent caregiving, etc.) for exacerbating emotion dysregulation in both the development and maintenance of BPD (Beck et al., 2006; Fonagy & Bateman, 2008; Kernberg, 1984; Linehan, 1993).

Consistent with theoretical views on the relational context of emotion dysregulation and aggression in those with BPD, empirical studies suggest that intense and unmodulated affective responses and their behavioral concomitants among individuals with BPD are frequently preceded or accompanied by perceived rejection, abandonment, or criticism (e.g., Chapman, Dixon-Gordon, Butler, & Walters, 2015; Sadikaj, Moskowitz, Russell, Zuroff, & Paris, 2013). In fact, a recent study found that although individuals with BPD and community controls reported similar amounts of quarrelsome behavior in response to negative affect in daily life, the BPD group reported significantly more quarrelsome behavior and greater negative affective reactivity specifically to perceptions of others as cold and quarrelsome (Sadikaj et al., 2013). These findings underscore the importance of the relational context and social perceptions relevant to perceived rejection for understanding emotional arousal and aggression in those with BPD.

Role of Specific Emotions

Shame and anger appear to be particularly problematic emotions for these individuals, especially in response to perceived negative evaluation or rejection (Berenson et al., 2011; Gratz, Rosenthal, Tull, Lejuez, & Gunderson, 2010; Rivzi et al., 2011). Berenson and colleagues (2011) have shown that those with BPD are exquisitely sensitive to interpersonal rejection and react to perceived rejection in daily life with more intense anger than those without BPD. In addition, one study found that patients with BPD react to negative evaluation in the laboratory with greater increases in shame relative to a clinical group without personality disorder (Gratz et al., 2010). A number of theorists and researchers have discussed shame as a central emotion in

BPD (e.g., Crowe, 2004; Linehan, 1993; Rizvi, Brown, Bohus, & Linehan, 2011). In our own experience as therapists and as members of consultation teams for clinicians working with BPD patients, intense shame is a common experience among BPD patients that often serves as both a trigger and a consequence of self-injurious and angry or aggressive behavior.

Although speculative, it is possible that shame, a self-conscious emotion characterized by feeling that one is inherently bad or defective, may be the primary emotion triggered in the context of perceived rejection or criticism among those with BPD, with anger and aggression being secondary as defensive strategies designed to deflect attention away from the humiliated self and retaliate against those perceived to have evoked these feelings (Schoenleber & Berenbaum, 2012). This conjecture is based not only on our own clinical experience, but also on evidence that shame is associated with anger, hostility, and self-harm among those with BPD (Brodsky, Groves, Oquendo, Mann, & Stanley, 2006; Brown, Linehan, Comtois, Murray, & Chapman, 2009; Rusch et al., 2007). Beyond the BPD literature, social psychologists have written extensively on the potential for rejection to evoke intense shame and for shame to lead to anger, aggression, and violence (e.g., Gilligan, 1997; Lutwak, Panish, Ferrari, & Razzino, 2001). Furthermore, both shame and hostility are associated with poor outcomes and higher likelihood of future self-harm and suicide attempts among those with BPD (Brodsky et al., 2006; Brown et al., 2009; Rusch et al., 2008; Welch & Linehan, 2002). Such shame- and affective reactivity-based processes are antithetical to those who have been traditionally implicated in aggression among those with more antisocial or psychopathic features (e.g., blunted affective arousal and lack of remorse) and would likely require different intervention approaches.

TREATMENT IMPLICATIONS

Assessment of Interpersonal Problems

Given the relevance of interpersonal contexts for understanding emotional and behavioral dysregulation in those with BPD, as well as the evidence that specific interpersonal characteristics adversely affect therapeutic outcome (Ruiz et al., 2004), we join several others in advocating the explicit assessment of interpersonal dysfunction in clinical settings (Hopwood, 2010). Although some information about interpersonal problems may be gleaned from clinical interviews and history-taking at intake, we recommend augmenting these standard procedures with tools designed specifically to assess interpersonal problems and aggression. Characterizing patients' interpersonal patterns is particularly important considering that certain interpersonal behaviors are likely to pull for complementary interpersonal behaviors from others, including the therapist, which may perpetuate problematic interactional cycles. In order to move a client out of habitual maladaptive patterns, the clinician may wish to deliberately adopt an *anti-complementary* stance in response to the client's problematic interpersonal behaviors (Pincus, 2005).

One of the most commonly used and clinically relevant instruments is the Inventory of Interpersonal Problems (IIP; Horowitz, Rosenberg, Baer, Ureno, & Villasenor, 1988), a 127-item self-report measure derived from recurrent interpersonal themes that emerged in the intake interviews of patients seeking outpatient therapy. Briefer versions of the IIP, which may be more easily administered at intake and periodically throughout treatment to monitor progress in specific interpersonal problem domains, include the 64-item IIP-Circumplex scales (IIP-C; Alden, Wiggins, & Pincus, 1990) and the 32-item version (IIP-32; Barkham, Hardy, & Startup, 1996). The IIP produces scores on a range of interpersonal problems along the dimensions of dominance (i.e., domineering to nonassertive/submissive) and affiliation (i.e., cold/hostile to self-sacrificing/friendly) within the interpersonal circumplex. These domains have been shown to be predictive of psychotherapy outcome and sensitive to client change as a function of treatment (for a review, see Ruiz et al., 2004). Other clinically useful scales that can be calculated from the IIP include the Personality Disorder scales, which were empirically derived to assess five distinct types of interpersonal problems that are relevant to personality disorders: Interpersonal Sensitivity (strong affectivity and reactivity in relational contexts), Interpersonal Ambivalence (struggling against others and difficulties with cooperation and collaboration), Aggression (hostile and verbally aggressive behavior), Need for Social Approval (chronic anxiety about evaluation), and Lack of Sociability (social anxiety and avoidance; Pilkonis, Kim, Proietti, & Barkham, 1996). Importantly, studies have shown that the Interpersonal Sensitivity scale predicts greater risk for suicide attempts and self-injury and less risk for aggression directed toward others, whereas the Interpersonal Aggression scale predicts less risk for suicide attempts and self-injury and greater risk for psychological and physical aggression (Stepp et al., 2008; Stepp, Smith, Morse, Hallquist, & Pilkonis, 2012).

Attachment-related patterns constitute another clinically relevant interpersonal domain for which multiple brief measures exist that can be utilized in therapy. Brief self-report measures such as the 36-item Revised Experiences in Close Relationships Scale (ECR-R; Fraley, Waller, & Brennan, 2000) may be used to characterize adult clients' attachment tendencies in close (e.g., romantic) relationships along two orthogonal dimensions: attachment anxiety, which refers to fears of separation and abandonment, and attachment avoidance, which refers to discomfort with intimacy and dependency. Although the measure focuses on attachment patterns within intimate relationships, these dimensions have been shown to predict therapeutic alliance and outcome. A recent meta-analysis of 14 studies concluded that attachment anxiety was related to worse outcome in psychotherapy with an effect size (*d*) of .46, which is similar in magnitude to associations between therapeutic alliance and psychotherapy outcome (Levy, Ellison, Scott, & Bernecker, 2011). Other resources provide more extensive coverage of how assessment of attachment can be used therapeutically (Levy et al., 2011; Meyer & Pilkonis, 2002).

Assessing Risk for Aggression

Although aggression in those with BPD is often impulsive in nature and therefore somewhat difficult to predict, there are several risk factors that may signal greater potential for violence. It is crucial to assess for risk factors at the outset of treatment and take necessary precautions with high-risk clients to ensure the safety of the clinician as well as of staff and other patients. Based on empirical studies, some factors associated with greater risk for violence include younger age (especially late teens and young adults), low socioeconomic status, past exposure to violence in the home or neighborhood, experiences of childhood abuse, low intellectual ability or neurologic impairment, substance abuse, antisocial or psychopathic features, violent thoughts or fantasies, expectations that aggressive behavior will be rewarded, and, perhaps most importantly, a history of aggressive and impulsive behavior (for a review, see Otto, 2000). Manic states and certain acute psychotic symptoms may further increase risk for violent behavior, particularly paranoid or persecutory delusions and/or command hallucinations to commit violent acts (especially if command hallucinations are of a familiar voice and/or consistent with co-existing persecutory delusions). Although studies in the general population have shown that males are more likely to be physically violent than females, evidence suggests that this gender difference may not exist in clinical populations. Thus, it may be erroneous for clinicians to assume that female BPD patients are less likely to become violent than males. Likewise, despite racial differences in rates of violent crimes and incarceration, studies suggest that race no longer predicts aggressive behavior after controlling for low socioeconomic status.

Past violent behavior is one of the best predictors of future violence (for review, see Otto, 2000); therefore, intake assessment should include a thorough history of difficulties controlling anger, conflict with others, violent behavior, and history of arrests. Evidence also suggests that those whose violent behavior began early (i.e., prior to age 12) are at greater risk for continued violence in adulthood. Assessment of past episodes of aggressive behavior should be as specific and descriptive as possible, including not only what was done and to whom but also the antecedents, exacerbating factors (e.g., alcohol intoxication at the time), concomitant physiological sensations or changes (e.g., racing heart, clenching fists), assumptions or expectations, and consequences attached to the behaviors. During the course of such assessment, the clinician should take an attitude of concerned curiosity because these sensitive questions may evoke shame and defensiveness. Clinical interviews may be supplemented by collateral information from other sources (e.g., criminal and hospital records, interviews with parents or intimate partners, etc.) as well as self-report measures of past and current aggressive thoughts and behaviors. Some clients may be more likely to report problems with anger and aggression on a form rather than in a face-to-face interview. We refer the reader to some excellent resources for further advice regarding the assessment, management, and treatment of patients who are at high risk for severe violence (Alpert & Spillmann, 1997; Berg, Bell, & Tupin, 2000; Otto, 2000).

CASE STUDY: INTERPERSONAL DIFFICULTIES

Ms. A began engaging in disordered eating, self-injury, and suicide-related behaviors in her teens. As a young adult, her attempts to further her education beyond high school were interrupted by frequent hospitalizations for suicide attempts or dangerously low weight. By her mid-twenties she was living with her parents and working a low-level part-time job that she disliked. Ms. A was still exceptionally close with her mother and was highly dependent on her for emotional and instrumental support. When emotionally regulated, she was affectionate, kind, and playful with her mother. Other times, her mother was the target of Ms. A's angry outbursts, which occurred several times a week. These episodes were usually triggered by upsetting interpersonal events (e.g., feeling rejected or criticized) and were expressed by screaming, throwing objects, or even hitting or kicking. Ms. A's other personal relationships were equally tumultuous. She had several brief affairs with older men who expressed little interest in her other than sexually but to whom she became strongly attached nonetheless. These relationships were fraught with conflict over Ms. A's demands for attention and reassurance, fits of rage, and suspicions of infidelity or disloyalty.

Ms. A began seeing a new therapist after her most recent hospitalization. She reported that she had numerous therapists over the years, but she perceived none of them as helpful and said that they all "gave up" on her. Although she had not engaged in suicide-related or self-injurious behaviors in several months, her low weight (85% of her ideal body weight) and continued intermittent engagement in disordered eating and other impulsive behaviors remained concerning. Ms. A was ambivalent about stopping these behaviors, and she was intensely focused on trying to rekindle a relationship with an ex-boyfriend who had indicated to her that he wanted no further contact. With every failed attempt to contact him, she became more filled with shame and rage, which often led to angry outbursts and/or urges to engage in other mood-dependent behaviors such as purging or binging on alcohol.

In therapy sessions, Ms. A alternated between hostile and controlling behaviors at some times and withdrawing into a fetal position while refusing to speak or make eye contact at other times. When she was able to express her emotions verbally, she spoke of feeling worthless, unlovable, and repulsive. She called her therapist frequently between sessions for help managing her emotions and self-destructive urges. Although she sometimes perceived these contacts as helpful and was able to use them effectively, she was less receptive to intervention when she was feeling particularly shameful and hopeless. At these times, she directed her rage at her therapist for being unhelpful and not "getting it." When her therapist set limits (e.g., on between-session contact or demands for increased session time), Ms. A berated her for "not caring" and predicted that she would "dump" her, "just like everyone else." The therapist began to feel exhausted and trapped, noticing urges to transfer Ms. A to another clinician, which would have confirmed and perpetuated the patient's fears of being rejected and abandoned.

The therapist's recognition of her decreasing motivation to work with the client combined with support and consultation from colleagues were crucial to the continuation of therapy with Ms. A. Instead of transferring her to a new therapist only to begin the same cycle again, the therapist made the interpersonal behaviors that were interfering with treatment the primary focus of their work, with the exception of addressing any life-threatening behaviors should they reoccur. For several months, their work focused primarily on helping Ms. A to respect her therapist's limits and interact more effectively in sessions and during between-session contacts while also building Ms. A's ability to tolerate and modulate her distress and work toward greater autonomy. Over time, the therapist's firm but warm stance helped Ms. A to contain strong affects with less angry attacks on others and to feel more secure that she was not going to be abandoned as she predicted. Although progress was gradual, the interpersonal behaviors which initially interfered with treatment began to stabilize, and the focus shifted toward increasing Ms. A's sense of self-worth and competency in relationships and work.

CONCLUSION

The case in this chapter illustrates the importance of interpersonal/attachment-related contexts for understanding strong affect and mood-dependent behaviors in those with BPD. The patient demonstrates the two general interpersonal themes reviewed in this chapter: interpersonal hypersensitivity and aggression, as well as the way these patterns emerge in the therapeutic relationship and how closely linked these are to difficulties regulating emotions and behavior. This case also illustrates how these problematic interpersonal dynamics can evoke intense emotional reactions in both patient and therapist that, if left unattended, can be treatment-destroying and can perpetuate dysfunctional interpersonal cycles. Thus, interpersonally focused approaches to treatment are likely to be especially helpful for patients with BPD. Careful assessment of aggressive behavior and other interpersonal problems in those with BPD is helpful for risk evaluation, case formulation, treatment planning, and monitoring treatment progress and outcome.

REFERENCES

Agrawal, H. R., Gunderson, J., Holmes, B. M., & Lyons-Ruth, K. (2004). Attachment studies with borderline patients: A review. *Harvard Review of Psychiatry*, *12*(2), 94–104. doi: 10.1080/10673220490447218

Alden, L. E., Wiggins, J. S., & Pincus, A. L. (1990). Construction of circumplex scales for the Inventory of Interpersonal Problems. *Journal of Personality Assessment*, *55*(3-4), 521–536. doi: 10.1080/00223891.1990.9674088

Allen, A., & Links, P. S. (2012). Aggression in borderline personality disorder: Evidence for increased risk and clinical predictors. *Current Psychiatry Reports*, *14*(1), 62–69. doi: 10.1007/s11920-011-0244-9

Alpert, J. E., & Spillmann, M. K. (1997). Psychotherapeutic approaches to aggressive and violent patients. *Psychiatric Clinics of North America, 20*(2), 453–472. Retrieved from: http://dx.doi.org/10.1016/S0193-953X(05)70322-1

American Psychiatric Association (APA). (2013). *Diagnostic and statistical manual of mental disorders DSM-5* (5th ed.). Washington, DC: Author.

Barkham, M., Hardy, G. E., & Startup, M. (1996). The IIP-32: A short version of the Inventory of Interpersonal Problems. *British Journal of Clinical Psychology, 35*(1), 21–35.

Beck, A. T., Freeman, A., & Davis, D. D. (2006). *Cognitive therapy of personality disorders*. New York: Guilford.

Berenson, K. R., Downey, G., Rafiaeli, E., Coifman, K. G., & Paquin, N. L. (2011). The rejection-rage contingency in borderline personality disorder. *Journal of Abnormal Psychology, 120*(3), 681–690.

Berg, A. Z., Bell, C. C., & Tupin, J. (2000). Clinician safety: Assessing and managing the violent patient. *New Directions for Mental Health Services, 2000*(86), 9–29. doi: 10.1002/yd.23320008604

Bowlby, J. (1969). *Attachment and loss*. New York: Basic Books.

Brodsky, B. S., Groves, S. A., Oquendo, M. A., Mann, J. J., & Stanley, B. (2006). Interpersonal precipitants and suicide attempts in borderline personality disorder. *Suicide and Life-Threatening Behavior, 36*(3), 313–322. doi: 10.1521/suli.2006.36.3.313 16805659

Brown, M. Z., Linehan, M. M., Comtois, K. A., Murray, A., & Chapman, A. L. (2009). Shame as a prospective predictor of self-inflicted injury in borderline personality disorder: A multi-modal analysis. *Behaviour Research and Therapy, 47*(10), 815–822. doi: 10.1016/j.brat.2009.06.008 19596223

Butler, A. C., Brown, G. K., Beck, A. T., & Grisham, J. R. (2002). Assessment of dysfunctional beliefs in borderline personality disorder. *Behaviour Research and Therapy, 40*(10), 1231–1240.

Carpenter, R. W., & Trull, T. J. (2013). Components of emotion dysregulation in borderline personality disorder: A review. *Current Psychiatry Reports, 15*(1), 335. doi: 10.1007/s11920-012-0335-2

Chapman, A. L., Dixon-Gordon, K. L., Butler, S. M., & Walters, K. N. (2015). Emotional reactivity to social rejection versus a frustration induction among persons with borderline personality features. *Personality Disorders, 6*(1), 88–96. doi: 10.1037/per0000101

Choi-Kain, L. W., Zanarini, M. C., Frankenburg, F. R., Fitzmaurice, G. M., & Reich, D. B. (2010). A longitudinal study of the 10-year course of interpersonal features in borderline personality disorder. *Journal of Personality Disorders, 24*(3), 365–376. doi: 10.1521/pedi.2010.24.3.365

Crowe, M. (2004). Never good enough—part 1: Shame or borderline personality disorder? *Journal of Psychiatric and Mental Health Nursing, 11*(3), 327–334. doi: 10.1111/j.1365-2850.2004.00732.x

Daros, A. R., Zakzanis, K. K., & Ruocco, A. C. (2013). Facial emotion recognition in borderline personality disorder. *Psychological Medicine, 43*(9), 1953–1963. doi: 10.1017/S0033291712002607

Dinsdale, N., & Crespi, B. J. (2013). The borderline empathy paradox: Evidence and conceptual models for empathic enhancements in borderline personality disorder. *Journal of Personality Disorders, 27*(2), 172–195. doi: 10.1521/pedi.2013.27.2.172

Dodge, K. A., Bates, J. E., & Pettit, G. S. (1990). Mechanisms in the cycle of violence. *Science, 250*(4988), 1678–1683. doi: 10.1126/science.2270481

Fonagy, P., & Bateman, A. (2008). The development of borderline personality disorder: A mentalizing model. *Journal of Personality Disorders, 22*(1), 4–21. doi: 10.1521/pedi.2008.22.1.4

Fossati, A., Barratt, E. S., Carretta, I., Leonardi, B., Grazioli, F., & Maffei, C. (2004). Predicting borderline and antisocial personality disorder features in nonclinical subjects using measures of impulsivity and aggressiveness. *Psychiatry Research, 125*(2), 161–170. doi: 10.1016/j.psychres.2003.12.001

Fraley, R. C., Waller, N. G., & Brennan, K. A. (2000). An item response theory analysis of self-report measures of adult attachment. *Journal of Personality & Social Psychology, 78*(2), 350–365.

Gabbard, G. O., Horwitz, L., Frieswyk, S., Allen, J. G., Colson, D. B., Newsom, G., & Coyne, L. (1988). The effect of therapist interventions on the therapeutic alliance with borderline patients. *Journal of the American Psychoanalytic Association*, *36*(3), 697–727.

Gilbert, F., & Daffern, M. (2011). Illuminating the relationship between personality disorder and violence: Contributions of the General Aggression Model. *Psychology of Violence*, *1*(3), 230–244. doi: 10.1037/a0024089

Gilligan, J. (1997). *Violence: Reflections on a national epidemic* (1st Vintage Books ed.). New York: Vintage Books.

Gratz, K L., Rosenthal, M. Z., Tull, M. T., Lejuez, C. W., & Gunderson, J. G. (2010). An experimental investigation of emotional reactivity and delayed emotional recovery in borderline personality disorder: The role of shame. *Comprehensive Psychiatry*, *51*(3), 272–285. doi: 10.1016/j.comppsych.2009.08.005 20399337

Gunderson, J. G., Frank, A. F., Ronningstam, E. F., Wachter, S., Lynch, V. J., & Wolf, P. J. (1989). Early discontinuance of borderline patients from psychotherapy. *Journal of Nervous and Mental Disease*, *177*(1), 38–42.

Gunderson, J. G., & Lyons-Ruth, K. (2008). BPD's interpersonal hypersensitivity phenotype: A gene-environment-developmental model. *Journal of Personality Disorders*, *22*(1), 22–41. doi: 10.1521/pedi.2008.22.1.22

Hopwood, C. J. (2010). An interpersonal perspective on the personality assessment process. *Journal of Personality Assessment*, *92*(6), 471–479. doi: 10.1080/00223891.2010.513284

Horowitz, L. M., Rosenberg, S. E., Baer, B. A., Ureno, G., & Villasenor, V. S. (1988). Inventory of interpersonal problems: Psychometric properties and clinical applications. *Journal of Consulting and Clinical Psychology*, *56*(6), 885–892.

Kernberg, O. F. (1984). *Severe personality disorders: Psychotherapeutic strategies*. New Haven, CT: Yale University Press.

Krohn A. (1974). Borderline "empathy" and differentiation of object representations: a contribution to the psychology of object relations. *International Journal of Psychoanalytic Psychotheraphy*, *3*(2), 14265.

Levy, K. N. (2005). The implications of attachment theory and research for understanding borderline personality disorder. *Development and Psychopathology*, *17*(4), 959–986.

Levy, K. N. (2008). Psychotherapies and lasting change. *American Journal of Psychiatry*, *165*(5), 556–559. doi: 10.1176/appi.ajp.2008.08020299

Levy, K. N., Ellison, W. D., Scott, L. N., & Bernecker, S. L. (2011). Attachment style. In J. C. Norcross (Ed.), *Psychotherapy relationships that work: Evidence-based responsiveness* (2nd ed., pp. 377–401). New York: Oxford University Press.

Linehan, M. M. (1993). *Cognitive-behavioral treatment of borderline personality disorder*. New York: Guilford.

Links, P. S., & Heslegrave, R. J. (2000). Prospective studies of outcome: Understanding mechanisms of change in patients with borderline personality disorder. *Psychiatric Clinics of North America*, *23*(1), 137–150. Retrieved from: http://dx.doi.org/10.1016/S0193-953X(05)70148-9

Lutwak, N., Panish, J. B., Ferrari, J. R., & Razzino, B. E. (2001). Shame and guilt and their relationship to positive expectations and anger expressiveness. *Adolescence*, *36*(144), 641–653.

McCloskey, M. S., New, A. S., Siever, L. J., Goodman, M., Koenigsberg, H. W., Flory, J. D., & Coccaro, E. F. (2009). Evaluation of behavioral impulsivity and aggression tasks as endophenotypes for borderline personality disorder. *Journal of Psychiatric Research*, *43*(12), 1036–1048. doi: 10.1016/j.jpsychires.2009.01.002 19232640

Meyer, B., & Pilkonis, P. A. (2002). Attachment style. In J. C. Norcross (Ed.), *Psychotherapy relationships that work: Therapist contributions and responsiveness to patients* (pp. 367–382). London: Oxford University Press.

New, A. S., Hazlett, E. A., Newmark, R. E., Zhang, J., Triebwasser, J., Meyerson, D., . . . Buchsbaum, M. S. (2009). Laboratory induced aggression: A positron emission tomography study of aggressive individuals with borderline personality disorder. *Biological Psychiatry*, *66*(12), 1107–1114. doi: 10.1016/j.biopsych.2009.07.015

Newhill, C. E., Eack, S. M., & Mulvey, E. P. (2009). Violent behavior in borderline personality. *Journal of Personality Disorders*, *23*(6), 541–554.

Newhill, C. E., Eack, S. M., & Mulvey, E. P. (2012). A growth curve analysis of emotion dysregulation as a mediator for violence in individuals with and without borderline personality disorder. *Journal of Personality Disorders*, *26*(3), 452–467. doi: 10.1521/pedi.2012.26.3.452 22686232

Ostrov, J., & Houston, R. (2008). The utility of forms and functions of aggression in emerging adulthood: Association with personality disorder symptomatology. *Journal of Youth and Adolescence*, *37*(9), 1147–1158. doi: 10.1007/s10964-008-9289-4

Otto, R. K. (2000). Assessing and managing violence risk in outpatient settings. *Journal of Clinical Psychology*, *56*(10), 1239–1262. doi: 10.1002/1097-4679(200010)56:10<1239::aid-jclp2>3.0.co;2-j

Pagano, M. E., Skodol, A. E., Stout, R. L., Shea, M. T., Yen, S., Grilo, C. M., . . . Gunderson, J. G. (2004). Stressful life events as predictors of functioning: Findings from the collaborative longitudinal personality disorders study. *Acta Psychiatrica Scandinavica*, *110*(6), 421–429. doi: 10.1111/j.1600-0447.2004.00398.x

Paris, J., Chenard-Poirier, M. P., & Biskin, R. (2013). Antisocial and borderline personality disorders revisited. *Comprehensive Psychiatry*, *54*(4), 321–325.

Pilkonis, P. A., Kim, Y., Proietti, J. M., & Barkham, M. (1996). Scales for personality disorders developed from the inventory of interpersonal problems. *Journal of Personality Disorders*, *10*(4), 355–369.

Pincus, A. L. (2005). A contemporary integrative interpersonal theory of personality disorders. In M. F. Lenzenweger & J. F. Clarkin (Eds.), *Major theories of personality disorder* (Vol. 2, pp. 282–331). New York: Guilford.

Rizvi, S. L., Brown, M. Z., Bohus, M., & Linehan, M. M. (2011). The role of shame in the development and treatment of borderline personality disorder. In R. L. Dearing & J. P. Tangney (Eds.), *Shame in the therapy hour* (pp. 237–260). Washington, DC: American Psychological Association.

Ruiz, M. A., Pincus, A. L., Borkovec, T. D., Echemendia, R. J., Castonguay, L. G., & Ragusea, S. A. (2004). Validity of the Inventory of Interpersonal Problems for predicting treatment outcome: An investigation with the Pennsylvania Practice Research Network. *Journal of Personality Assessment*, *83*(3), 213–222.

Rusch, N., Lieb, K., Gottler, I., Hermann, C., Schramm, E., Richter, H., . . . Bohus, M. (2007). Shame and implicit self-concept in women with borderline personality disorder. *American Journal of Psychiatry*, *164*(3), 500–508. doi: 10.1176/appi.ajp.164.3.500 17329476

Rusch, N., Schiel, S., Corrigan, P. W., Leihener, F., Jacob, G. A., Olschewski, M., . . . Bohus, M. (2008). Predictors of dropout from inpatient dialectical behavior therapy among women with borderline personality disorder. *Journal of Behavior Therapy and Experimental Psychiatry*, *39*(4), 497–503. doi: 10.1016/j.jbtep.2007.11.006 18299116

Russell, J. J., Moskowitz, D. S., Zuroff, D. C., Sookman, D., & Paris, J. (2007). Stability and variability of affective experience and interpersonal behavior in borderline personality disorder. *Journal of Abnormal Psychology*, *116*(3), 578–588.

Sadikaj, G., Moskowitz, D. S., Russell, J. J., Zuroff, D. C., & Paris, J. (2013). Quarrelsome behavior in borderline personality disorder: Influence of behavioral and affective reactivity to perceptions of others. *Journal of Abnormal Psychology*, *122*(1), 195–207.

Sanislow, C. A., Grilo, C. M., Morey, L. C., Bender, D. S., Skodol, A. E., Gunderson, J. G., . . . McGlashan, T. H. (2002). Confirmatory factor analysis of DSM-IV criteria for borderline personality disorder: Findings from the collaborative longitudinal personality disorders study. *American Journal of Psychiatry*, *159*(2), 284–290.

Sansone, R. A., & Sansone, L. A. (2012). Borderline personality and externalized aggression. *Innovations in Clinical Neuroscience*, *9*(3), 23.

Schoenleber, M., & Berenbaum, H. (2012). Shame regulation in personality pathology. *Journal of Abnormal Psychology, 121*(2), 433–446. doi: 10.1037/a0025281

Scott, L. N., Stepp, S. D., & Pilkonis, P. A. (2014). Prospective associations between features of borderline personality disorder, emotion dysregulation, and aggression. *Personality Disorders: Theory, Research, and Treatment, 5*(3), 278–288.

Sharp, C., Pane, H., Ha, C., Venta, A., Patel, A. B., Sturek, J., & Fonagy, P. (2011). Theory of mind and emotion regulation difficulties in adolescents with borderline traits. *Journal of the American Academy of Child and Adolescent Psychiatry, 50*(6), 563–573.

Shaver, P. R., & Mikulincer, M. (2007). Adult attachment strategies and the regulation of emotion. In J. J. Gross (Ed.), *Handbook of emotion regulation* (pp. 446–465). New York: Guilford.

Siever, L. J. (2008). Neurobiology of aggression and violence. *American Journal of Psychiatry, 165*(4), 429–442. doi: 10.1176/appi.ajp.2008.07111774 18346997

Stepp, S. D., Morse, J. Q., Yaggi, K. E., Reynolds, S. K., Reed, L. I., & Pilkonis, P. A. (2008). The role of attachment styles and interpersonal problems in self-injurious behaviors. *Suicide and Life-Threatening Behavior, 38*, 592–607.

Stepp, S. D., Pilkonis, P. A., Yaggi, K. E., Morse, J. Q., & Feske, U. (2009). Interpersonal and emotional experiences of social interactions in borderline personality disorder. *Journal of Nervous and Mental Disease, 197*, 484–491.

Stepp, S. D., Smith, T. D., Morse, J. Q., Hallquist, M. N., & Pilkonis, P. A. (2012). Prospective associations among borderline personality disorder symptoms, interpersonal problems, and aggressive behaviors. *Journal of Interpersonal Violence, 27*(1), 103–124. doi: 10.1177/0886260511416468

Walsh, Z., Swogger, M. T., O'Connor, B. P., Chatav Schonbrun, Y., Shea, M. T., & Stuart, G. L. (2010). Subtypes of partner violence perpetrators among male and female psychiatric patients. *Journal of Abnormal Psychology, 119*(3), 563.

Weinstein, Y., Gleason, M. E., & Oltmanns, T. F. (2012). Borderline but not antisocial personality disorder symptoms are related to self-reported partner aggression in late middle-age. *Journal of Abnormal Psychology, 121*(3), 692–698. doi: 10.1037/a0028994

Welch, S. S., & Linehan, M. M. (2002). High-risk situations associated with parasuicide and drug use in borderline personality disorder. *Journal of Personality Disorders, 16*(6), 561–569.

Wright, A. G. C., Hallquist, M. N., Morse, J. Q., Scott, L. N., Stepp, S. D., Nolf, K. A., & Pilkonis, P. A. (2013). Clarifying interpersonal heterogeneity in borderline personality disorder using latent mixture modeling. *Journal of Personality Disorders, 27*(2), 125–143. doi: 10.1521/pedi.2013.27.2.125

/// 13 /// Pharmacological Interventions for Borderline Personality Disorder

KENNETH R. SILK

INTRODUCTION

Patients with borderline personality disorder (BPD) comprise a substantial percentage of the patients whom we see in outpatient treatment and clinics, especially in clinics where patients with tertiary problems in psychiatry or "treatment resistance" are encountered (Zimmerman, Rothschild, & Chelminski 2005). They may be people who present only with BPD although that would be more rare than common. More often they have a comorbid Axis I disorder (Zanarini et al., 1998) (although note that in the fifth edition of the *Diagnostic and Statistical Manual of Mental Disorders* [DSM-5], there is no longer separate axes [American Psychiatric Association (APA), 2013]). If the patient has previously been identified as an Axis II patient, in most academic institutions, unless there is a formal dialectical behavior therapy (DBT), mentalization-based therapy (MBT), or some other specifically defined treatment program for BPD, the patient will, more often than not, be assigned to trainees in a clinic setting. Thus, while it may seem more logical for these very difficult and at times recalcitrant patients to be treated by experienced clinicians who can tease apart the subtle and perhaps not so subtle intricacies of the presentation to determine how best to intervene clinically, it is because these patients are viewed as difficult and time-consuming that they are often assigned to clinicians who are on the broadly trainee level (i.e., residents, interns, fellows, and beginning faculty).

This does not imply that these are patients who are impossible to treat and that, no matter what is done, they (and the clinician) will be stuck in their clinical quagmire forever. There is growing evidence from two fine follow-along studies to support the fact that the majority of these patients improve, and, while true sustained recovery remains less frequent than we would hope, remissions, even those sustained for many years, are not uncommon (Zanarini, Frankenburg, Reich, & Fitzmaurice, 2012). What is intriguing about the data from these follow-along studies is that they were not treatment studies. They were studies that followed these patients in their "natural" environment. While a large percentage of them were in some treatment (either psychotherapy or psychopharmacology or both) throughout or for a substantial portion of the follow-along period, the treatment that they received was not controlled or standardized. There was no treatment protocol that was followed or assessed at the time of follow-up data collection in either of the studies. The mythology that these patients never get better and never leave those who treat them may have developed because we selectively remember those who do not improve and do not leave. And those who do not leave or improve seem to cause therapists constant angst and countertransference feelings, distorting the therapists' recall that most patients with BPD get better in some sense of the word and move on and out of treatment.

Major interventions for BPD include both psychotherapy and psychopharmacology. The most well-known guidelines for treatment of BPD, including the American Psychiatric Association (APA) Guidelines (APA, 2001) and the National Institute for Health and Clinical Excellence (NICE) Guidelines (National Institute for Health and Clinical Excellence, 2009) (as well as the recently published Australian guidelines) suggest much greater effectiveness for psychotherapeutic treatment of BPD than for pharmacologic treatment. Over the past 20 years, there have been a number of well-tested psychotherapeutic treatments that have earned the "evidence-based" designation (Zanarini, 2009). No such strong evidence or endorsement exists for the pharmacologic treatment (Silk & Feurino III, 2012). Nonetheless, patients with BPD are treated with psychopharmacologic agents (Bender et al., 2001), and Zanarini and colleagues determined in their large follow-along cohort that at least 75% of patients with BPD had been treated with psychopharmacologic agents for at least 75% of the time over the 6 years of follow-up (Zanarini, Frankenburg, Hennen, & Silk, 2004).

THEORY (RATIONALE) FOR THE PHARMACOLOGIC TREATMENT

Although there is no specific theory underlying the treatment of patients with BPD with psychopharmacologic agents, there are many reasons why it is included as one of the modalities of treatment for these patients. While some experts (see Paris, 2009) and some guidelines suggest insufficient evidence to support pharmacologic intervention (see NICE, 2009), a number of issues converge to support at least a trial of medication with these patients. The issues that converge are historical, diagnostic, biological, and pragmatic. Each of these will be reviewed briefly.

HISTORICAL PERSPECTIVE

The first mention or at least the use of the adjective "borderline" in a diagnostic sense occurred in 1938 (Stern, 1938). From 1938 until at least the mid to late 1960s, BPD was thought to be a disorder close to the border of psychosis (Knight, 1953). Thus, it makes clinical sense that the earliest pharmacologic intervention(s) in patients who were thought to lie in the borderline "realm" were treated primarily with anti-psychotic (at that time, the typicals) medication. This idea of borderline patients sitting on the border of psychosis was to shift to the idea that perhaps they sat on the border of affective disorders, suffering primarily from a dysregulation of affect. The "stable instability" of Schmideberg (1947), Kernberg's writings in the mid-1960s (1967), and Roy Grinker's (Grinker, Werble, & Dry, 1968) study of borderline types supported this idea, but it was not until 1975, with Gunderson and Singer's paper on "Defining Borderline Patients" (Gunderson & Singer, 1975), followed by the studies developing the Diagnostic Interview for Borderlines (Gunderson, Kolb, & Austin, 1981), and culminating in the inclusion of BPD into DSM-III (APA, 1980) that BPD achieved the status of an official diagnostic category. Then, the "on the border of psychosis" concept became more strongly associated with the diagnosis of schizotypal personality disorder (STPD) (Spitzer, Endicott & Gibbon, 1979), rather than with BPD.

DIAGNOSTIC PERSPECTIVE

Although the idea of BPD or at least of patients displaying the clinical characteristics that we currently associate with BPD had existed before DSM-III, it was the inclusion of BPD in DSM III that established it as a bona fide diagnosis within the official DSM nomenclature. In 1980, at the same time that BPD was incorporated into the new DSM (DSM-III), a major shift was happening in psychiatry. Major academic departments of psychiatry that previously had been led by individuals firmly rooted in the psychoanalytic/psychodynamic persuasion now were led by individuals more interested in the biological underpinnings of all psychiatric disorders, including BPD (Shorter, 1997). The development of the selective serotonin reuptake inhibitors (SSRIs), as well as the introduction of a broader range of mood stabilizers and "atypical" antipsychotic medications, led to more psychiatric patients being treated with psychotropic medication (Healy, 1997). The idea that BPD might respond to medications, an idea that was not previously considered because patients with BPD were thought to belong in the consulting rooms of psychodynamic clinicians, now seemed more plausible.

Furthermore, there were two diagnostic confounds, as it were, that also led to a greater readiness to treat these people pharmacologically. First, there was the growing knowledge that many if not most of these patients had Axis I diagnostic comorbidity (Zanarini et al., 1998). Then, even if there was no specific medication to which the specific symptoms of BPD might respond, there certainly were symptoms that borderline patients complained of that could be found either in Axis I disorders or that were exacerbated (so it seemed) by the comorbid presence of an Axis I disorder. Thus, it made logical sense to target those specific symptoms with medications that had been found to be effective in the Axis I disorder even though they were co-occurring in patients who also had BPD.

Second, there was the contention of many clinicians and researchers that BPD was not a "real" disorder but rather was an abnormal presentation of an affective disorder, either depression or bipolar disorder (Akiskal, 1981; Perugi, Fornaro, & Akiskal, 2011), or was a manifestation of early trauma. In these instances, then, we might think it beneficial to treat these people in a pharmacological manner similar to these others patients with whom they seemed to share a number of clinical features.

BIOLOGICAL PERSPECTIVE

As BPD was finally achieving "diagnostic legitimacy," there was the strong belief that all psychiatric symptoms—in fact, all psychological experiences—are mediated through biological mechanisms, an idea that has only grown stronger over time (Kandel, 1998). A key paper applying these ideas to personality disorders appeared in the *American Journal of Psychiatry* in 1991 (Siever & Davis, 1991). Siever and Davis argued that if we are to understand better how biology plays a role in the personality disorders, we should be looking at biological irregularities not within a single personality disorder diagnosis but rather across the personality disorders (i.e., biological dimensions that apply to some or all the personality disorders). In this way, we might be able to identify more clearly biological systems and irregularities to those systems that span a number of personality disorders and are related to specific clinical presentations (phenotypes). No longer would it be sufficient for there to be purely environmental explanations for personality disorder pathology; instead, we needed to appreciate better what dimensions of psychopathology are driven by which biological systems. This would then naturally lead to trying to understand how to modify those biological abnormalities through psychopharmacology.

PRAGMATIC ISSUES

In the simplest terms, patients with BPD not only experience a great deal of psychological pain but also appear to have a knack for being able to convey the extent and depth of that pain most profoundly to us. We always feel (and are regularly reminded by the patient) that, for them, life is too hard, too painful, too disappointing, and too hopeless for us not to try every possible way to make their lives less overwhelming. Thus, even though the evidence for pharmacologic intervention is not as strong in this disorder as is the evidence for psychotherapeutic treatment, if we use the medications judiciously with careful attention to side effects, medication lethality, polypharmacy, and psychopharmacologic overenthusiasm, there might be some benefit that accrues to the patient that can make his or her life a little more worth living.

THE PHARMACOLOGIC TREATMENT OF BPD: WHAT TO CHOOSE AND HOW TO PROCEED

The process of prescribing medication to patients with BPD may be as, if not more, important than what the final decision is on particular medication or medication class chosen to prescribe in a given clinical situation. While this may at first seem to be an overstatement, in many situations, this statement is very relevant, including the overall decision on whether to even prescribe medications (Silk, 2011).

Deciding Whether to Intervene Pharmacologically: The Cost-Benefit Equation

There are no medications that have an indication for treatment in BPD. This applies not only to the pharmacologic treatment of core symptoms of BPD but also to the symptoms that patients with BPD share with other patients who do not have BPD (such as anxiety, reactive mood changes, and transient psychotic or psychotic-like experiences). Although many studies have been performed to appreciate better how a specific medication might relieve or reduce reasonably "common" psychiatric symptoms such as anxiety or depression, when these symptoms occur in patients with BPD, the studies' results are at times contradictory. This lack of clarity or consistency in results may arise from a number of different reasons that include insufficient numbers of studies and insufficient numbers of subjects within the studies that examine the same pharmacologic compound or class across studies (Zanarini et al., 2010). In a 2009 review, it was found that out of 20 studies that compared active drug to placebo, only 3 of those studies had N's that exceeded 100 subjects. Furthermore, although one study might explore the effectiveness of fluoxetine (for depression, anxiety, emotional instability, or impulsivity), a similar study examining those same (or different) clinical symptoms might use the SSRI fluvoxamine or sertraline instead. Another problem occurs when different instruments are used in different studies to examine the same outcome or to measure the severity of symptoms. For example, one study may examine depression via the Hamilton Rating Scale for Depression (HAM-D), another via the Beck Depression Scale, and another via the Montgomery-Asberg Depression Scale (MADRS). How does one translate improvement or lack of improvement from one study to another when the instruments measuring the clinical phenomena differ? Furthermore, sometimes the same instrument, for example the Symptom Checklist (SCL-90) is used to measure more than one outcome (Saunders & Silk, 2009). Most of these studies were short-term. Only one study went beyond 12 weeks, and that study looked at medications we rarely employ today in the pharmacologic treatment of BPD, such as haloperidol and phenelzine (Soloff, Cornelius, George, Nathan, Perel, & Ulrich, 1993).

Confounding the decision of whether to treat is trying to decide whether or not a patient with BPD has an Axis I comorbidity that actually meets full criteria for the comorbid disorder. For example, patients frequently use the term "depression," but, when explored further, the depression does not meet criteria for a major depressive episode. Rather, the patient is often referring to helplessness, loneliness, and transient and reactive sadness that may keep her at home for 2–3 days without a desire to do anything; closer examination reveals that this is not an episode of mood disorder with significant sleep, appetite, and hedonic capacity changes that lasts constantly for 2 weeks or more and is accompanied by guilt and self-recrimination culminating in suicidal ideation that is not present when the patient is not in such an episode (Silk, 2010). Similar conundrums can be found in needing to distinguish between the "anxiety attacks" (often described as being overwhelmed) that these patients repeatedly experience and a classic panic attack (Eaton et al., 2011; Stiglmayr et al., 2008) or between a sleepless night with increased dysphoric physical anxiety that leads to cleaning house in order to diffuse tension from an episode of no or very little sleep because there are too many things to discover, to plan, to expand upon and sleep is merely a bother to the manic or hypomanic patient. In each of these instances, what we are trying to distinguish clinically are the behavioral manifestations of emotional dysregulation and heightened clinical reactivity as part of the BPD criteria from a bona fide comorbid Axis I disorder. If it is determined that the person, in addition to their personality disorder is indeed in a bona fide Axis I episode or meets full criteria for a comorbid Axis I disorder, then the pharmacologic decision, at least initially, should follow the recommended pharmacologic treatment for that Axis I or mental state disorder.

Given the uncertainties just described, it behooves the clinician to have a series of discussions before deciding to initiate psychopharmacologic treatment. The first would, of course, be with the patient and would entail, beyond the usual history of symptoms and previous trials of and successes or failures with medications, exploring what it is that the patient expects from the medication. This discussion is necessary so that if the patient (or the referring therapist/physician) has unrealistic expectations for the medication's effectiveness, these expectations can hopefully be modified and brought more in line with reality. In this same vein, then, it is important to discuss these same issues with the patient's therapist if the patient is in some ongoing psychotherapeutic treatment (Schlesinger & Silk, 2005). Also, it is helpful to discuss with the therapist why the patient has been referred for consideration of initiation of psychotropic medication or consideration of change in the patient's ongoing treatment regimen at this particular time. These conversations are essential to put into focus how beneficial (if at all) medications might be in this patient. It is important to recall that specific expectations are frequently beyond the capacity of the medications to meet, especially for patients who experience substantial pain and who often have few coping strategies and for therapists who are appropriately and empathically concerned while also experiencing the desperate demands of patients who often have constant suicidal thoughts or self-destructive behaviors.

The major discussions, of course, take place between the potential prescriber and the patient. It is helpful if the patient has been told that she or he has the diagnosis of BPD (LeQuesne & Hersh, 2004). If the patient is unaware of that, and if the prescriber believes that the diagnosis is actually BPD, then it is useful to have the diagnostic discussion before even getting into the details of prescribing and the prescribing process. Often, if the loneliness, emptiness, and depressive reactions of the patient have been diagnosed as major depressive episodes, then it may be assumed by the patient that she or he has a treatment-resistant depression. If that is so, then the patient may have already been prescribed a number of medications, either alone or in combination, and the failure to respond has led to the "treatment-resistant" label and may be experienced by the patient as another way in which she has "failed."

The discussion with the patient at this time should touch on a number of topics: (1) what the actual diagnosis is and why perhaps she has been viewed as having major depressive, bipolar II, or post-traumatic stress disorder (PTSD) when in fact BPD probably most accurately describes the complicated clinical picture; (2) what might be the reason(s) that the patient has been given an Axis I diagnosis in the face of what is probably a primary Axis II diagnosis for which medications have not been very effective; (3) the realistic expectation that medications in BPD have at best modest impacts on many of the issues/symptoms that the patient is struggling with; (4) that, because of the limitations of the effectiveness of the medication, it is important to remain in some psychological/psychotherapeutic treatment; (5) that the patient is expected to be compliant with the medication as prescribed (although one cannot be certain that the medication will be effective, it is a certainty that if it is not taken, it has no chance at being effective.); (6) that it may be a number of weeks (perhaps up to 12–16) before we can determine if the medication is effective, as well as the extent of its effectiveness; and (7) that the prescribing of medications will probably be a trial-and-error process (Silk, 2011). It might be useful at this point, especially if the patient is using substances, to discuss how the concomitant use of alcohol or other illicit substances will merely confuse and probably reduce the ability to judge the prescribed medication's effectiveness.

What is important to emphasize is that medications seem to be less effective in patients with BPD than they would be in patients with a similar clinical picture who do not have BPD. In addition, patients with BPD seem to be quite sensitive to the side effects of these medications. Thus, we have a situation of less effectiveness and greater proneness to side effects culminating in a shift in the cost-benefit equation from what would apply for pharmacologic treatment of an Axis I disorder without BPD (i.e., a shift to greater side effects [cost] and less therapeutic effects [benefit]). This shift then entails rethinking whether to use the medication that is thought to be effective in the Axis I disorder without BPD in the patient who also has BPD.

The idea of trial and error should be expanded upon. The patient should be informed that the process will hopefully be that a medication is tried for a period of time sufficient to allow the impact of the medication to be revealed clinically and that, if the medication proves ineffective, then it will be stopped and a new medication tried rather than augmenting one medication with another. Although this is not a hard and fast rule, it nonetheless is often the wisest course since we have no single medication or combination of medications that stand out as being significantly more effective for any clinical symptom or combination of symptoms in BPD (NICE,

2009). Thus, by adding one medication to another, we more often than not increase the chance of troublesome side effects, especially weight gain, which is not a welcome side effect in a patient population that is often young and female (Zanarini et al., 2012). And the weight gained while on a psychotropic medication does not magically fade away after the medication has been discontinued. It is useful to urge the patient to stay in contact either via email or patient portal messages (if available), particularly if there are questions about the medication or if there are physical symptoms that are being attributed to the medication.

It is often useful to ask patients to name the one thing about their symptoms or their behaviors that they wish they could change. This question is important because even though the chief complaint may be depression and it is that symptom for which the referral was made, the patient may say that what she would most like to better control is how she reacted to things (depression perhaps being only one of those reactions), or how she quickly becomes angry with other people, or to diminish her propensity for self-damaging acts. These answers can help direct you to choosing one class of medication over another and also allow you to discuss the possibility and limitations of the medication in the treatment of that particular symptom or symptom complex. It also allows you to discuss the fact that there might not be any medication or certainly no evidence for a medication's effectiveness in the particular behavior or affect that the patient is describing as so troublesome.

Choosing the Medication

The next issue is which medication or medication class to use for which symptom, symptom complexes, or behaviors in the patient with BPD. Table 13.1 provides a summary of the classes of psychotropic medication that have the greatest evidence for effectiveness within specific dimensions of psychopathology (e.g., emotion dysregulation, cognitive problems, impulsivity and aggression, and anxiety). This table was derived from reviewing not individual studies of randomized controlled trials (RCTs) of pharmacologic treatment in BPD, but rather from taking the findings from either meta-analyses or systematic reviews of placebo-controlled double-blinded RCTs of pharmacologic treatment in BPD. These systematic reviews and/or meta-analyses review some subset of 23 RCTs that are the most frequently cited placebo-controlled double-blinded RCTs of psychopharmacologic treatment of BPD. These studies compare a single active medication against placebo and not against another medication. The 23 studies and the class of psychotropic medication examined in those studies are listed in Table 13.2, as well as which of those 23 studies are considered in each of the eight systematic reviews or meta-analyses listed in Table 13.1. It is interesting that these eight reviews and meta-analyses do not come to the same conclusion with respect to a medication or medication class for a given set or subset of symptoms in BPD, despite the fact that most are using the same data or a subset of these 23 studies.

TABLE 13.1 Summary of evidence of effectiveness from 8 meta-analyses/systematic reviews of randomized controlled trials of psychopharmacologic agents in borderline personality disorder

Dimensions of Psychopathology: Perceptual Distortions	Anxiety	Affective Instability	Aggression/ Impulsivity	Cognitive
Binks et al., 2006	NA	(AD)	(AD)	AP
Lieb et al., 2010	NA	MS (AP)	MS (AP)	AP
Nosè et al., 2006	NA	AD/MS	AP	NA
WFSBP (Herpertz et al., 2007)	AD	AD[a]	AP/MS	AP
Duggan et al., 2008	NA	NA	MS	AP
Mercer et al., 2009	–	AP/MS	MS	–
Ingenhoven et al., 2010	MS	MS	MS/AP	AP
Vita et al., 2011	–	MS (AD)	MS (AP)	AP
SUMMARY	(AD/MS)	MS (AD[a])	MS/AP	AP

[a]If concurrently depressed.

AD, Antidepressants; MS, Mood stabilizers; AP, Antipsychotics

The parentheses () implies that the evidence for this category of medication being effective is weaker or more marginal than those medication classes that do not have a ().

Adapted from Silk, K. R., & Feurino III, L. (2012). Psychopharmacology of personality disorders. In T. Widiger (Ed.), *The Oxford handbook of personality disorders* (p. 721). Oxford: Oxford University Press.

In choosing a medication for a patient with BPD, the final line of Table 13.1 presents a summary of medication classes one might consider. The consideration process can involve a series of steps. The first would be to decide which of the many symptoms or behaviors with which the patient presents is most disruptive for the patient. When that symptom is decided on, it is important to determine which of the four dimensions of psychopathology the symptom or behavior fit into most appropriately. (See Box 13.1 and Saunders & Silk, 2009.) In Box 13.1, both suicidality and anger are underlined because they can easily be placed in a different dimension. One can appreciate that suicidality can fit as well under impulsivity as it does under affective instability, and anger can fit as well under affective instability as it does under impulsivity. One might then be able to make a reasonable judgment as to which of the four dimensions one might wish to target through a pharmacological intervention.

It is important to try to target only one dimension at this juncture and to target it by using only a single drug. Because there is always a propensity to polypharmacy in these patients, it is best to choose only one dimension. As one can see from Table 13.1, some classes of medication might be useful in more than one dimension, but one should try to focus on one dimension and one medication. If, after an adequate trial period and at an adequate dose level there is no response, the suggestion is made to switch to a different medication (and perhaps a different medication class) rather

TABLE 13.2 Listing of the double-blind placebo-controlled studies of the psychopharmacology of borderline personality disorder that are considered in at least three of the systematic reviews or meta-analyses

	Class of Medication									
Bogenschutz & Nurnberg, 2004	ATY	Dug	WF	ING	NOSE		COCHL	TOR	NICE	VITA
Coccaro & Kavoussi, 1997	SSRI	Dug	WF	ING	NOSE			TOR		VITA
Cowdry et al., 1998	MIX	WF	ING					TOR	NICE	VITA
De la Fuente et al., 1994	MS	Dug	WF	ING	NOSE	COCH	COCHL	NICE	NICE	
Frankenburg & Zanarini, 2002	MS	Dug	WF	ING			COCHL	TOR	NICE	VITA
Goldberg et al., 1986	TYP	Dug	WF	ING	NOSE	COCH	COCHL	NICE		
Hollander et al., 2001	MS	Dug	WF	ING	NOSE	COCH	COCHL	TOR	NICE	VITA
Hollander et al., 2005	MS	Dug	WF	ING	NOSE		COCHL	TOR	NICE	VITA
Leone, 1982	TYP	Dug				COCH	COCHL			
Loew et al., 2006	MS	Dug	WF	ING				TOR	NICE	
Montgomery & Montgomery, 1982	ADEP	Dug	WF	ING		COCH	COCHL			
Nickel et al., 2004	MS	Dug	WF	ING	NOSE		COCHL	TOR	NICE	VITA
Nickel et al., 2005	MS	Dug	WF	ING	NOSE		COCHL	TOR	NICE	VITA
Nickel et al., 2006	ATY	Dug	WF	ING	NOSE		COCHL	TOR	NICE	VITA
Pascual et al., 2008	ATY						COCHL	TOR	NICE	VITA
Rinne et al., 2002	SSRI	Dug WF	ING	NOSE			COCHL	TOR	NICE	VITA
Salzman et al., 1995	SSRI	Dug	WF	ING	NOSE	COCH	COCHL	TOR	NICE	VITA
Simpson et al., 2004	ATY	Dug	WF	ING	NOSE		COCHL	TOR	NICE	VITA
Soler et al., 2005	ATY	Dug	WF	ING	NOSE		COCHL	TOR		VITA

Study										
Soloff et al., 1993	MAOI, TCA	Dug	WF	ING	NOSE	COCH	COCHL	TOR	NICE	VITA
Soloff et al., 1989	MAOI, TCA	Dug	WF	ING	NOSE	COCH	COCHL	TOR	NICE	VITA
Tritt et al., 2005	MS	Dug	WF	ING	NOSE		COCHL	TOR	NICE	VITA
Zanarini & Frankenburg, 2001	ATY	Dug	WF	ING	NOSE	COCH	COCHL	TOR	NICE	

Adapted from Silk, K. R., & Feurino III, L. (2012). Psychopharmacology of personality disorders. In T. Widiger (Ed.), *The Oxford handbook of personality disorders* (p. 718). Oxford: Oxford University Press.

Antidepressants: MAOI, monoamine oxide inhibitors;TCA, tricyclic antidepressant; SSRI, selective serotonin reuptake inhibitors; ADEP, other antidepressants; ATY, antipsychotics both typical and atypical; MS, mood stabilizers

Numbers here represent how many of the 23 studies were included in the review/meta-analysis:

Dug, Duggan et al., 22; WF, Herpertz et al., 21; ING, Ingenhoven et al., 21; Nosè et al., 22; COCH, Binks et al., 10; COCHL, Lieb et al., 25 (2 Omega-3s);TOR, Mercer et al., 18; NICE, National Institute of Health and Clinical Excellence, 18; and Vita, Vita et al., 17

BOX 13.1
SIEVER AND DAVIS OUTCOME MEASURES

Outcome measures from 20 double-blind placebo-controlled studies of the psycho-pharmacology of borderline personality disorder (BPD) categorized into the dimensions of Siever and Davis (1991)

- Affective Instability: abandonment, affective instability, capacity for pleasure, depression, emptiness, euphoria/mania, identify disturbance, interpersonal sensitivity, irritability, rejection sensitivity, *suicidality*[a]
- Anxiety inhibition: general anxiety, anxiety—intropunitiveness, obsessive-compulsive score, phobic anxiety, somatization
- Cognitive perceptual: paranoid ideation, perceptual distortion, psychoticism-schizotypy
- Impulsivity/Aggression: aggression, *anger*[b], hostility, impulsiveness

---

[a] *Suicidality can be categorized in either the affective instability or the impulsivity/aggression dimension.*

[b] *Anger can be categorized in either the impulsivity/aggression or the affective instability dimension.*

Adapted from Saunders, E. F. H., & Silk, K. R. (2009). Personality trait dimensions and the pharmacologic treatment of borderline personality disorder. Journal of Clinical Psychopharmacology 29, 267-461.

than to augment with another medication, again to restrict the tendency toward polypharmacy. These patients have so many symptoms and complaints that it is very easy to end up prescribing four or five medications simultaneously, and there is no evidence that polypharmacy has effectiveness among this population, even though the effectiveness of any medication is quite limited.

Next, we look at each dimension and summarize both the medication choice as well as the dosing recommendations.

Affective Instability

In the dimension of affective instability, which often is seen clinically as rapid and transient changes in mood and intensity of mood especially in response to environmental triggers, the current data appear to support the use of mood stabilizers. There is no substantial evidence that the antidepressants, particularly the SSRIs that were the most studied drug class in the 1990s, have any effect on affective instability, but they do appear to have some impact on depression in BPD when that depression occurs as part of a bona fide major depressive episode (MDE) (Herpertz et al., 2007; Silk & Feurino III, 2012). There is little evidence that antidepressants impact the type of depression that those with BPD often complain about: the chronic emptiness, loneliness, and dysphoria that is so prevalent in their lives and in their clinical history (Silk, 2010). It is often these complaints that are so draining to mental health professionals because their moods and mood changes appear to be so resistant to medication. The prescriber needs to refrain from the tendency to become overenthusiastic pharmacologically by prescribing unusual (or perhaps usual) combinations of drugs in an attempt to augment antidepressant effects. In too many instances, the "depression" we are trying to treat with an antidepressant unfortunately is not very responsive to antidepressants.

Although there are many different mood stabilizers to choose from, the best data appears to support the use of topiramate (Loew et al., 2006; Nickel et al., 2004, 2005), although this comes from only a single group of researchers. There is also some support for lamotrigine (Reich, Zanarini, & Bieri, 2009; Tritt et al., 2005), and that support also comes from a pair of double-blind studies. Valproate has support from at least two groups of researchers (Frankenburg & Zanarini, 2002; Hollander et al., 2001, 2005) and might be the preferred medication at this juncture. What is intriguing about the use of topiramate in these patients is that the target population is often young women who have self-image and self-esteem issues. Topiramate often does not lead to weight gain or certainly not to the type of weight gain associated with other psychotropic medications (Gupta, Masand, Frank, Lockwood, & Keller, 2000). However, patients on topiramate can experience word-finding difficulties and/ or paresthesias (Loring, Williamson, Meador, Wiegand, & Hulihan, 2011) even at the 200 mg/day thought to be the target dose for psychiatric patients. Data for effectiveness of lithium are weak (Links, Steiner, Boiago, & Irwin, 1990).

Aggression/Impulsivity

The aggression/impulsivity dimension reveals itself clinically in poor impulse control with subsequent impulsive behavior often of an aggressive nature. The individual appears unable to inhibit action even if the action is not in the persona's own best interests. It often shows up as impulsive sexual behavior, impulsive self-destructive acts, and impulsive substance use. Here, the mood stabilizers appear to have the most support, followed closely by the atypical antipsychotics. The dosing goal should be about 200 mg of either topiramate or lamotrigine (although there is no hard data to support this particular dosing). The appropriate blood levels for valproate and lithium are no different than blood levels one might wish to achieve in the treatment of bipolar disorder. In treating patients with antipsychotic medication, the rule of thumb in BPD patients is to treat them at the lower end of the therapeutic dose range. Again, there are no hard data on this "rule," but if there is one thing that has been consistent in recommendations on pharmacotherapy of BPD, it is that the antipsychotic medications should be used in low doses. (See the recent study by Black and colleagues [2014] that suggested 150 mg quetiapine may be more effective with less side effects than 300 mg quetiapine.)

Depending on the patient, one might begin with either a mood stabilizer or an antipsychotic. If, after a reasonable length of time, there has been no noticeable response, one could switch either to another medication in the same class or switch classes, although I would not at an early phase in treatment choose to augment one class with another class. While there is some evidence, as stated earlier, for effectiveness with most of the mood stabilizers (including some old data for carbamazepine [Cowdry & Gardner, 1988]), the situation is different for the atypical antipsychotics. There has been some data to support the use of aripiprazole (Nickel et al., 2006) or quetiapine (in open-label studies and recently in a double-blind study [Black et al., 2014), olanzapine (for which there might be the most data among the atypicals [Schulz et al., 2008; Zanarini & Frankenburg, 2001), or some of the typicals such as haloperidol (Soloff et al., 1986) or trifluoperazine (Cowdry & Gardner, 1988). Some atypical antipsychotic medications have no evidence of effectiveness in BPD. While risperidone has been shown to be effective in schizotypal personality disorder (Koenigsberg et al., 2003), it has not been shown to be effective in BPD. There are no data with respect to iloperidone or lurasidone. Although there is little data-driven guidance here, it is useful to keep a patient on this class of medication for 1–2 months (assuming there are minimal or tolerable side effects) before deciding that there has been no response.

Although there have been no systematic studies of this specific phenomenon or clinical outcome, patients who take mood stabilizers sometimes report developing a "reflective delay" when taking this class of medications. Reflective delay is described as being able to experience or being aware of a sequence of steps from the initial provocation to the behavior. Before taking a mood stabilizer, a patient may report that she had an argument and then, the next thing she knew was that she had cut her arm. The patient experienced no time passing or was unaware of time passing between the insult and the action. After taking a mood stabilizer, some (but clearly not all) patients might describe the argument and then remember going into the kitchen, getting a knife, and then cutting. These mood stabilizers thus do not prevent the impulsive act from taking place, but they can in some people induce an awareness of time passing. This may provide the "time" that could permit other learned strategies such as mentalization or DBT skills to come into play to move the patient away from (in this instance self-destructive) unwise behaviors or actions.

Cognitive/Perceptual Symptoms

Cognitive-perceptual symptoms are eccentric behaviors, strange speech or thought patterns, and social detachment, as well as outright blatant cognitive distortions extending all the way to outright psychotic thinking. Almost uniformly, the antipsychotic medications have been shown to be effective when symptoms in this dimension appear to be the most disruptive (Silk & Feurino III, 2012). (Refer to the earlier discussion on how to use this class of medications in these patients.) However, there should be at least two important considerations in using these medications. The first has to do with the side effects. Many of the atypical antipsychotics have been known to cause significant weight gain in patients and can lead to a metabolic syndrome (McEvoy et al., 2005). The potential to gain weight among patients with BPD is no different than among other patients, but we also need to consider that often the target population consists of young women who are already struggling with substantial identity and self-esteem issues. Weight gain can only make those issues stronger and more troublesome. Thus, a cost-benefit analysis of the possible benefits of the medications versus their possible costs needs to be considered on an individual basis for every patient we prescribe any medication to (not just those with BPD). The second consideration, somewhat related to the first, is that, in most instances, patients with BPD do not have chronic cognitive distortions; these seem to occur only when the patient is under significant stress. There is little evidence that these medications need to be prescribed chronically for these cognitive distortions. They can probably be used short term (even perhaps prophylactically short term) and should be stopped as soon as the increased stress or stressor is reduced.

However, if one is using antipsychotic medication to treat affective instability and/or impulsivity, then use of these medications might be for a longer period. The goal here, no matter what the dimension of psychopathology being addressed, is eventually to replace the medications with skills and strategies and increased self- and cognitive awareness involving mindfulness or mentalization that can assist in improving overall coping (Zanarini, 2009).

Anxiety/Inhibition

These patients seem to have a low tolerance for anxiety, with accompanying high arousal when faced with a potentially (in the patient's mind) fearful situation. And many situations seem to engender fear. They seem ready to respond with panic that seems to go on for hours or to live in a chronic state of moderate fear and arousal. The data for use of pharmacologic agents in this dimension is quite weak and disappointing. As can be seen from Table 13.1, of the eight systematic reviews or meta-analyses, six concluded that no medication class had effectiveness here. One review (Ingenhoven, Lafay, Rinne, Passchier, & Duivenvoorden, 2010) suggested that mood stabilizers and one study suggested that antidepressants from the SSRI class (Herpertz et al., 2007) might have some effectiveness. While the evidence for effectiveness for either of these classes of medications is very weak, if one chooses to prescribe SSRIs, one might wish to prescribe them at dose levels and for the period of time recommended in the treatment of an anxiety disorder (i.e., higher doses and up to 12–16 weeks before deciding that they were not effective).

There is a potential pitfall here in trying to treat patients with BPD and significant anxiety. The pitfall is that these patients seek and often get immediate relief from benzodiazepines. Yet these are people who are also prone to misuse substances, often seeking the immediate relief from dysphoric affects that benzodiazepines can initially appear to provide. However, studies have also shown that when the immediate effects of the benzodiazepines begin to wear off, more impulsive and dysregulated behavior can occur (Gardner & Cowdry, 1985). Thus, while it is not suggested that benzodiazepines never be used in these patients, they should be used for very short periods of time (say, less than a week) before they are discontinued and hopefully replaced by other psychotropic medication or, more preferentially, by skills learned in CBT or DBT work.

CONCLUSION

The evidence for the pharmacologic treatment of the symptoms or behaviors found in BPD remains quite weak. Nonetheless, they are frequently used, and hopefully this chapter can provide some guidance for their use. But the most recent guidelines from both the United Kingdom and Australia see the use of medications as adjunctive or secondary to psychotherapeutic interventions. This was true even in the 2001 APA Guidelines (which could use updating particularly because the recommendations for which class of medication to use in which dimension involved only 7 of the 23 studies that are now considered in evaluating the effectiveness of medications among these patients). Furthermore, of those seven studies, six involved antidepressants, and two each involved mood stabilizers. (The sum here is more than seven because some studies looked at more than one class of psychotropic medication.) This may reflect why the APA Guidelines emphasized so heavily the use of antidepressants in both the affective instability and well as the impulse/aggression dimensions. Studies that came too late to be considered in the APA Guidelines involved seven instances where antipsychotics were studied, seven instances where mood stabilizers were studied, and only one additional study of antidepressants.

Thus, one must use caution in considering even the conclusions put forth in Table 13.1. Do the conclusions represent true deductions as to which medication class is most effective in which dimension, or do they merely reflect biased conclusions based upon the frequency of studies of each of the different classes of medications? Further systematic studies with much larger N's and groups of researchers agreeing to choose a prototypic medication in each drug class might lead to a better database from which more rational medication decisions can be made for patients with BPD (Saunders & Silk, 2009; Zanarini et al., 2010).

There will be, I am certain, better pharmacologic strategies for patients with BPD in the future. As we appreciate the genetic predispositions that contribute to the behavioral and symptomatic responses that these patients display, as we narrow in on pharmacogenetic underpinnings of pharmacologic responses among various individual patients and patient groups, and as we better appreciate through neuroimaging the pathways in the brain that are involved in these behaviors and symptoms, we should be able to develop more precise pharmacologic interventions to help relieve at least some of the chronic misery and painful behaviors with which these patients appear to struggle continuously.

CASE STUDY: PHARMACOLOGICAL INTERVENTIONS

A is a 21-year-old undergraduate who was referred to the clinic because of frequent visits to the local emergency room with cutting behavior and suicidal threats and ideation. She had been seeing for the past 8 months and continues to see an outpatient therapist once or twice weekly, and, while in some ways the therapy has been helpful, A continues to feel overwhelmed at times and complains of chronic depression and a wish to cut herself when overwhelmed, something that she did frequently during early adolescence and resumed during her first year at college. Her therapist as well as the local emergency room has referred her for consideration for treatment with psychotropic medication.

After a thorough history, it turns out that A was treated briefly in middle school with fluoxetine. She says that this was because her parents did not like the fact that she seemed to become angry easily, although A still feels that most of her anger at her parents was justified. She says she continues to get angry easily, but mostly she says she has to fight depression all the time. Then she gets overwhelmed by how depressed she usually is, and this impacts both her interpersonal relationships as well as her schoolwork. The psychiatrist then asks her a number of questions that involve her use of substances (she drinks 7–8 drinks one or two nights every other weekend but denies blacking out), her relationships with her friends (she gets into quarrels with them but they are really supportive of her and support her going to therapy and taking medications to help her to feel better), her relationships to her parents (she does better when she does not have too much contact with them), her school performance (OK, but some semesters she has done more poorly than she would like), and what she thinks her diagnosis is. She says that her therapist has suggested that she has BPD, and, in exploring what that means with her therapist and through the Internet, she agrees that this is probably the correct diagnosis.

She says she is willing to take medications because, although the therapy has been somewhat helpful, it nonetheless has not been able to control these periods of emotional turmoil as well as depression. But she also warns the psychiatrist that she is quite sensitive to medications and often easily gets side effects. The psychiatrist suggests that she seems to be a person who reacts quite easily—perhaps too easily—to many things, such as life and medications. The psychiatrist wonders: if there was only one medication that could be chosen, would she choose a medication that treats her depression or one that helps her to better control her emotions so that she does not overreact to so many things? She chooses the latter.

The psychiatrist says that A needs to know that medications, when used with people with BPD, probably have modest effects at best. Nonetheless, the psychiatrist believes that it is worth a trial of medications and discusses both mood stabilizers as well as atypical antipsychotic medication. The decision is made to try lamotrigine. The side effects, including the potential dermatologic problems, are explained, and the dosing schedule is presented carefully to her. The psychiatrist lets the patient know that he can be contacted either by phone or email or through the patient portal of the electronic health record and emphasizes that he would like to hear from her, especially when she thinks she is having some negative responses from or reactions to the medication. He also talks about her drinking behavior and says that he wishes that she could moderate the number of drinks she is having because the degree to which she is drinking can confuse what her real feelings are in any given situation as well as whether she is getting any benefit from the medication. If she is trying to control her emotional reactions, alcohol simply facilitates the inability to control those reactions and can lead to more commotion in her feelings and in her life.

The psychiatrist explains that he usually likes to prescribe only one medication at a time and to prescribe it for a long enough period to evaluate whether that particular medication is having any impact. It is important that they agree on the symptom they are targeting with that medication, and both agree that they are trying to have her feelings bounce around less frequently and less dramatically (which they define as emotional instability). The psychiatrist says that he is sure that she will have periods when she is focused on problems other than on how much her emotions are bouncing around, but it would be important not to begin to add other medications for these other problems until they have a clear sense of whether the mood stabilizer is doing any good. If it is not doing any good, then they will discuss whether to continue to target the mood instability. If so, the psychiatrist says he usually likes to stop the current medication and try a different one rather than add a medication. He also says that, if that should occur, they might want to discuss whether to stay within the same class of medications (mood stabilizer) or switch to an atypical antipsychotic. He also says that if they should switch to the atypical, it is not because she is psychotic but that the atypicals are sometimes referred to as major tranquilizers (in contrast to the minor tranquilizers such as alprazolam or clonazepam) and that, at times, he thought that she needed to become more "majorally" tranquil. She agrees, and the lamotrigine is prescribed.

REFERENCES

Akiskal, H. S. (1981). Subaffective disorders: Dysthymic, cyclothymic and bipolar II disorders in the "borderline" realm. *Psychiatric Clinics of North America*, *4*(1), 25–46.

American Psychiatric Association (APA). (1980). *Diagnostic and statistical manual of mental disorders* (3rd ed.). Washington, DC: Author.

American Psychiatric Association (APA). (2001). Practice guidelines for the treatment of patients with borderline personality disorder. *American Journal of Psychiatry*, *158*(10, Suppl), 1–52.

American Psychiatric Association (APA). (2013). *Diagnostic and statistical manual of mental disorders* (5th ed.). Arlington, VA: Author.

Bender, D. S., Dolan, R. T., Skodol, A. E., Sanislow, C. A., Dyck, I. R., McGlashan, T. H., . . . Gunderson, J. G. (2001). Treatment utilization by patients with personality disorders. *American Journal of Psychiatry*, *158*, 295–302.

Binks, C. A., Fenton, M., McCarthy, L., Lee, T., Adams, C. E., & Duggan, C. (2006). Pharmacological interventions for people with borderline personality disorder. *Cochrane Database of Systematic Reviews, 1,* CD005653.

Black, D. W., Zanarini, M. C., Romine, A., Shaw, M., Allen, J., & Schulz, S. C. (2014). Comparison of low and moderate dosages of extended-release quetiapine in borderline personality disorder: A randomized, double-blind, placebo-controlled trial. *American Journal of Psychiatry 171,* 1174–1182.

Bogenschutz, M. P., & Nurnberg, H. G. (2004). Olanzapine versus placebo in the treatment of borderline personality disorder. *Journal of Clinical Psychiatry, 65,* 104–109.

Coccaro, E. F., & Kavoussi, R. J. (1997). Fluoxetine and impulsive aggressive behavior in personality-disordered subjects. *Archives of General Psychiatry, 54,* 1081–1088.

Cowdry, R. W., & Gardner, D. L. (1988). Pharmacotherapy of borderline personality disorder. Alprazolam, carbamazepine, trifluoperazine, and tranylcypromine. *Archives of General Psychiatry, 45,* 111–119.

Duggan, C., Huband, N., Smailagic, N., Ferriter, M., & Adams, C. (2008). The use of pharmacological treatments for people with personality disorder: A systematic review of randomized controlled trials. *Personality and Mental Health, 2,* 119–170.

Eaton, N. R., Krueger, R. F., Keyes, K. M., Skodol, A. E., Markon, K. E., Grant, B. F., & Hasin, D. S. (2011). Borderline personality disorder co-morbidity: Relationship to the internalizing-externalizing structure of common mental disorders. *Psychological Medicine, 41*(5), 1041–1050.

Frankenburg, F. R., & Zanarini, M. C. (2002). Divalproex sodium treatment of women with borderline personality disorder and bipolar II disorder: A double-blind, placebo-controlled pilot study. *Journal of Clinical Psychiatry, 63,* 443–446.

Gardner, D. L., & Cowdry, R. W. (1985). Alprazolam-induced dyscontrol in borderline personality disorder. *American Journal of Psychiatry, 142,* 98–100.

Goldberg, S. C., Schulz, S. C., Schulz, P. M., Resnick, R. J., Hamer, R. M., & Friedel, R. O. (1986). Borderline and schizotypal personality disorders treated with low-dose thiothixene vs placebo. *Archives of General Psychiatry, 43,* 680–686.

Grinker, R. R., Werble, G., & Drye, R. C. (1968). *The borderline syndrome. A behavioral study of ego functions.* New York: Basic Books.

Gunderson, J. G., Kolb, J. E., & Austin V. (1981). The diagnostic interview for borderline patients. *American Journal of Psychiatry, 138,* 896–903.

Gunderson, J. G., & Singer, M. T. (1975). Defining borderline patients: An overview. *American Journal of Psychiatry, 132,* 1–10.

Gupta, S., Masand, P. S., Frank, B. L., Lockwood, K. L., & Keller, P. L. (2000). Topiramate in bipolar and schizoaffective disorders: Weight loss and efficacy. *Primary Care Companion, Journal of Clinical Psychiatry, 2*(3), 96–100.

Healy, D. (1997). *The antidepressant era.* Cambridge, MA. Harvard University Press.

Herpertz, S. C., Zanarini, M., Schulz, C. S., Siever, L., Lieb, K., Möller, H. J., & WFSBP Task Force on Personality Disorders. (2007). World Federation of Societies of Biological Psychiatry (WFSBP) guidelines for biological treatment of personality disorders. *World Journal of Biological Psychiatry, 8,* 212–244.

Hollander, E., Allen, A. Lopez, R. P., Bienstock, C. A., Grossman, R., Siever, L. J., . . . Stein, D. J. (2001). A preliminary double-blind, placebo-controlled trial of divalproex sodium in borderline personality disorder. *Journal of Clinical Psychiatry, 62,* 199–203.

Hollander, E., Swann, A. C., Coccaro, E. F., Jiang, P., & Smith, T. B. (2005). Impact of trait impulsivity and state aggression on divalproex versus placebo response in borderline personality disorder. *American Journal of Psychiatry, 162,* 621–624.

Ingenhoven, T., Lafay, P., Rinne, T., Passchier, J., & Duivenvoorden, H. (2010). Effectiveness of pharmacotherapy for severe personality disorders: Meta-analyses of randomized controlled trials. *Journal of Clinical Psychiatry, 71,* 14–25.

Kandel, E. R. (1998). A new intellectual framework for psychiatry. *American Journal of Psychiatry*, *155*, 457–469.

Kernberg, O. F. (1967). Borderline personality organization. *Journal of the American Psychoanalytic Association*, *15*, 641–685.

Knight, R. P. (1953). Borderline states. *Bulletin of the Menninger Clinic*, *17*, 1–12.

Koenigsberg, H. W., Reynolds. D., Goodman, M., New, A. S., Mitropoulou, V., Trestman, R., . . . Siever, L. J. (2003). Risperidone in the treatment of schizotypal personality disorder. *Journal of Clinical Psychiatry, 64*, 628–634.

Leone, N. F. (1982). Response of borderline patients to loxapine and chlorpromazine. *Journal of Clinical Psychiatry*, *43*, 148–150.

LeQuesne, E. R., & Hersh, R. G. (2004). Disclosure of a diagnosis of borderline personality disorder. *Journal of Psychiatric Practice*, *10*, 170–176.

Lieb, K., Völlm, B., Rücker, G., Timmer, A., & Stoffers J. M. (2010). Pharmacotherapy for borderline personality disorder: Cochrane systematic review of randomised trials. *British Journal of Psychiatry*, *196*, 4–12.

Links, P. S., Steiner, M., Boiago, I., & Irwin D. (1990). Lithium therapy for borderline patients: Preliminary findings. *Journal of Personality Disorders*, *4*, 173–181.

Loew, T. H., Nickel, M. K., Muehlbacher, M., Kaplan, P., Nickel, C., Kettler, C., . . . Egger, C. (2006). Topiramate treatment for women with borderline personality disorder: A double-blind, placebo-controlled study. *Journal of Clinical Psychopharmacology*, *26*, 61–66.

Loring, D. W., Williamson, D. J., Meador, K. J., Wiegand, F., & Hulihan, J. (2011). Topiramate dose effects on cognition: A randomized double-blind study. *Neurology*, *76*, 131–137.

McEvoy, J. P., Meyer, J. M., Goff, D. C., Nasrallah, H. A., Davis, S. M., Sullivan, L., . . . Leiberman, J. A. (2005). Prevalence of the metabolic syndrome in patients with schizophrenia: Baseline results from the Clinical Antipsychotic Trials of Intervention Effectiveness (CATIE) schizophrenia trial and comparison with national estimates from NHANES III. *Schizophrenia Research*, *80*, 19–32.

Mercer, D., Douglass, A. B., & Links, P. S. (2009). Meta-analyses of mood stabilizers, antidepressants and antipsychotics in the treatment of borderline personality disorder: Effectiveness for depression and anger symptoms. *Journal of Personality Disorders*, *23*, 156–174.

Montgomery, S. A., & Montgomery, D. (1982). Pharmacological prevention of suicidal behavior. *Journal of Affective Disorders*, *4*, 291–298.

National Institute for Health and Clinical Excellence (NICE). (2009). *Borderline personality disorder, treatment and management*. London: The British Psychological Society and The Royal College of Psychiatrists. Retrieved from NICE website: http://www.nice.org.uk/CG78

Nickel, M. K., Muehlbacher, M., Nickel, C., Kettler, C., Pedrosa Gil, F., Bachler, E., . . . Kaplan, P. (2006). Aripiprazole in the treatment of patients with borderline personality disorder: A double-blind, placebo-controlled study. *American Journal of Psychiatry*, *163*, 833–838.

Nickel, M. K., Nickel, C., Kaplan, P., Lahmann, C., Muehlbacher, M., Tritt, K., . . . Loew, T. H. (2005). Treatment of aggression with topiramate in male borderline patients: A double-blind, placebo-controlled study. *Biological Psychiatry*, *57*, 495–499.

Nickel, M. K., Nickel, C., Mitterlehner, F. O., Tritt, K. Lahmann, C., Leiberich. P. K., . . . Loew, T. H. (2004). Topiramate treatment of aggression in female borderline personality disorder patients: A double-blind, placebo-controlled study. *Journal of Clinical Psychiatry*, *65*, 1515–1519.

Nosè, M., Cipriani, A., Biancosino, B., Grassi, L., & Barbui C. (2006). Efficacy of pharmacotherapy against core traits of borderline personality disorder: Metaanalysis of randomized controlled trials. *International Clinical Psychopharmacology*, *21*, 345–353.

Paris, J. (2009). The treatment of borderline personality disorder: Implications of research on diagnosis, etiology, and outcome. *Annual Review of Clinical Psychology*, *5*, 277–290.

Pascual, J. C., Soler, J., Puigdemont, D., Pérez-Egea, R., Tiana, T., Alvarez, E., & Pérez, V. (2008). Ziprasidone in the treatment of borderline personality disorder: A double-blind, placebo-controlled, randomized study. *Journal of Clinical Psychiatry, 69*, 603–608.

Perugi, G., Fornaro, M., & Akiskal, H. S. (2011). Are atypical depression, borderline personality disorder and bipolar II disorder overlapping manifestations of a common cyclothymic diathesis? *World Psychiatry, 10*(1), 45–51.

Reich, D. B., Zanarini, M. C., & Bieri, K. A. (2009). A preliminary study of lamotrigine in the treatment of affective instability in borderline personality disorder. *International Clinical Psychopharmacology, 24*(5), 270–275.

Rinne, T., van den Brink, W., Wouters, L., & van Dyck, R. (2002). SSRI treatment of borderline personality disorder: A randomized, placebo-controlled clinical trial for female patients with borderline personality disorder. *American Journal of Psychiatry, 159*, 2048–2054.

Salzman, C., Wolfson, A. N., Schatzberg, A., Looper, J., Henke, R., Albanese, M., . . . Mayawaki, E. (1995). Effect of fluoxetine on anger in symptomatic volunteers with borderline personality disorder. *Journal of Clinical Psychopharmacology, 15*, 23–29.

Saunders, E. F. H., & Silk, K. R. (2009). Personality trait dimensions and the pharmacologic treatment of borderline personality disorder. *Journal of Clinical Psychopharmacology, 29*, 461–467.

Schlesinger, A. B., & Silk, K. R. (2005). Collaborative treatment. In J. M. Oldham, A. S. Skodol, & D. S. Bender (Eds.), *The American psychiatric textbook of personality disorders* (pp. 431–446). Washington, DC: American Psychiatric Publishing.

Schmideberg, M. (1947). The treatment of psychopaths and borderline patients. *American Journal of Psychotherapy, 1*, 145–155.

Schulz, S. C., Zanarini, M. C., Bateman, A., Bohus, M., Detke, H. C., Trzaskoma, Q., . . . Corya, S. (2008). Olanzapine for the treatment of borderline personality disorder: A variable-dose, 12-week, randomized, double-blind, placebo-controlled study. *British Journal of Psychiatry, 193*, 485–492.

Shorter, E. (1997). *A history of psychiatry.* New York: Wiley and Sons.

Siever, L. J., & Davis, K. L. (1991). A psychobiological perspective on the personality disorders. *American Journal of Psychiatry, 148*, 1647–1658.

Silk, K. R. (2010). The quality of depression in borderline personality disorder and the diagnostic process. *Journal of Personality Disorders, 24*, 25–37.

Silk, K. R. (2011). The process of managing medications in patients with borderline personality disorder. *Journal of Psychiatric Practice, 17*, 311–319.

Silk, K. R., & Feurino III, L. (2012). Psychopharmacology of personality disorders. In T. Widiger (Ed.), *The Oxford handbook of personality disorders* (pp. 713–724). Oxford, UK: Oxford University Press.

Simpson, E. B., Yen, S., Costello, E., Rosen, K. Begin, A., Pistorello, J., & Pearlstein, T. (2004). Combined dialectical behavioral therapy and fluoxetine in the treatment of borderline personality disorder. *Journal of Clinical Psychiatry, 65*, 379–385.

Soler, J., Pascual, J. C., Campins, J., Barrachina, J., Puigdemont, D., Alvarez, E., & Pérez, V. (2005). Double-blind, placebo-controlled study of dialectical behavior therapy plus olanzapine for borderline personality disorder. *American Journal of Psychiatry, 162*, 1221–1224.

Soloff, P. H., Cornelius, J., George, A., Nathan, S., Perel, J. M., & Ulrich, R. F. (1993). Efficacy of phenelzine and haloperidol in borderline personality disorder. *Archives of General Psychiatry, 50*, 377–385.

Soloff, P. H., George, A., Nathan, R. S., Schulz, P. M., Cornelius, J. R., Herring, J., & Perel, J. M. (1989). Amitriptyline versus haloperidol in borderlines: Final outcomes and predictors of response. *Journal of Clinical Psychopharmacology, 9*, 238–246.

Soloff, P. H., George, A., Nathan, R. S., Schulz, P. M., Ulrich, R. F., & Perel, J. M. (1986). Progress in pharmacotherapy of borderline disorders. A double-blind study of amitriptyline, haloperidol, and placebo. *Archives of General Psychiatry, 43*, 691–697.

Spitzer, R. L., Endicott, J., & Gibbon, M. (1979). Crossing the border into borderline personality and borderline schizophrenia. *Archives of General Psychiatry, 36,* 17–24.

Stern, A. (1938). Psychoanalytic investigation of and therapy in the borderline group of neuroses. *Psychoanalytic Quarterly, 7,* 467–489.

Stiglmayr, C. E., Ebner-Priemer, U. W., Bretz, J., Behm, R., Mohse, M., Lammers, C. -H., ... Bohus, M. (2008). Dissociative symptoms are positively related to stress in borderline personality disorder. *Acta Psychiatrica Scandinavica, 117*(2), 139–147.

Tritt, K., Nickel, C., Lahmann, C., Leiberich, P. K., Rother, W. K., Loew, T. H., & Nickel, M. K. (2005). Lamotrigine treatment of aggression in female borderline-patients: A randomized, double-blind, placebo-controlled study. *Journal of Psychopharmacology, 19,* 287–291.

Vita, A., De Peri, L., & Sacchetti, E. (2011). Antipsychotics, antidepressants, anticonvulsants, and placebo on the symptom dimensions of borderline personality disorder: A meta-analysis of randomized controlled and open-label trials. *Journal of Clinical Psychopharmacology, 31*(5), 613–624.

Zanarini, M. C. (2009). Psychotherapy of borderline personality disorder. *Acta Psychiatrica Scandinavia, 120*(5), 373–737.

Zanarini, M. C., & Frankenburg, F. R. (2001). Olanzapine treatment of female borderline personality disorder patients: A double-blind, placebo-controlled pilot study. *Journal of Clinical Psychiatry, 62,* 849–854.

Zanarini, M. C., Frankenburg, F. R., Dubo, E. D., Sickel, A. E., Trikha, A., Levin, A., & Reynolds, V. (1998). Axis I comorbidity of borderline personality disorder. *American Journal of Psychiatry, 155,* 1733–1739.

Zanarini, M. C., Frankenburg, F. R., Hennen, J., & Silk, K. R. (2004). Mental health service utilization by borderline personality disorder patients and Axis II comparison subjects followed prospectively for 6 years. *Journal of Clinical Psychiatry, 65,* 28–36.

Zanarini, M. C., Frankenburg, F. R., Reich, D. B., & Fitzmaurice, G. (2012). Attainment and stability of sustained symptomatic remission and recovery among patients with borderline personality disorder and axis II comparison subjects: A 16-year prospective follow-up study. *American Journal of Psychiatry, 169,* 476–483.

Zanarini, M. C., Schulz, S. C., Detke, H., Zhao, F., Lin, D., Pritchard, M., ... Corya, S. (2012). Open-label treatment with olanzapine for patients with borderline personality disorder. *Journal of Clinical Psychopharmacology, 32*(3), 398–402.

Zanarini, M. C., Stanley, B., Black, D. W., Markowitz, J. C., Goodman, M., Pilkonis, P., ... Sanislow, C. A. (2010). Methodological considerations for treatment trials for persons with borderline personality disorder. *Annals of Clinical Psychiatry, 22,* 75–83.

Zimmerman, M., Rothschild, L., & Chelminski, I. (2005). The prevalence of DSM-IV personality disorders in psychiatric outpatients. *American Journal of Psychiatry, 162,* 1911–1918.

/// 14 /// Mentalization-Based Treatment

LOIS W. CHOI-KAIN

INTRODUCTION

Mentalization is a fancy word describing the common psychological process that people use to understand mental states (i.e., emotions, beliefs, desires, intentions) within one's self and others. Mentalization broadly encompasses a wide territory of mental activities by which people understand themselves and their identity, manage their emotions and thoughts meaningfully and effectively, respond to their own experience and others in behavior, and maintain secure and productive relationships. These are basic socioemotional tasks that everyone encounters in daily life. The stability, flexibility, benevolence, and honesty with which people mentalize determines how their psychology works or how their personality functions. Conversely, when mentalization dysfunctions, personalities become disordered.

Mentalization as a concept integrates ideas from both traditional psychoanalytic theory to modern-day neuroscience. It involves a complex set of networks between numerous aspects of the brain and the endocrine system. Its universality makes mentalization relevant to a wide scope of psychological problems and also psychotherapeutic approaches. At the same time, its complexity confers a dynamic, evolving interface with emerging scientific ideas and evidence. The bridging of theories from the psychoanalytic tradition with current neuroscientific discovery makes mentalization-based treatment (MBT) a broadly appealing intellectual framework with which to relate clinical theory, empirical evidence, and psychotherapeutic technique in the treatment of borderline personality disorder (BPD).

When Anthony Bateman and Peter Fonagy published the outcomes for the randomized controlled trial (RCT) of MBT in a partial day hospital program for BPD (Bateman & Fonagy, 1999), MBT became the second manualized evidence-based treatment for BPD (Stoffers et al., 2012) and contributed to a major paradigm shift in the treatment of BPD. Bateman and Fonagy's MBT study demonstrated that a psychoanalytically oriented structured therapy for BPD could be effective, which in its open-ended unstructured intense formats proved not only ineffective but some-times harmful to BPD patients (Gunderson, 1996; Waldinger & Gunderson, 1984). MBT's simple, common sense approach, found effective in a public health setting with clinical teams of limited formal therapy training (Bateman & Fonagy, 2003), has practical advantages in its simplicity and limited demands on practitioners and patients (Choi-Kain, Albert, & Gunderson, 2016).

This chapter reviews the formulation of BPD as a disorder of mentalization, the MBT technique and treatment framework, and the empirical literature that provides the evidentiary basis for MBT's theories and efficacy. In its conclusion, this chapter also discusses some limitations to its application and claims.

FORMULATING BPD IN MBT: DEVELOPMENTAL THEORY AND NEUROBIOLOGICAL EVIDENCE

In 1991, the same year that Linehan published her first randomized controlled trial of DBT, Fonagy published both the first major clinical paper describing BPD in terms of failed mentalization, as well as an empirical report of the first prospective study showing that the attachment classification of pregnant women on the Adult Attachment Interview (AAI) predicted the attachment classification of their infants at 12 months. Later, Fonagy (Fonagy et al., 1996) and others (Barone, 2003; Patrick et al., 2004) reported that disorganized and preoccupied styles characterized the attachment of individuals with BPD on the AAI. This empirical evidence confirmed existing clinical theories that posed interpersonal functioning, and insecure attach-ment specifically, as the central mechanism of BPD (Benjamin, 1993; Gunderson, 1996). While DBT formulates BPD as a problem of emotional dysregulation and lack of skills to manage distress and relationships, MBT centralizes instability of attachment and its developmental byproduct, mentalization, as the core dysfunction underlying the syndrome of BPD (Fonagy, Target, & Gergely, 2000).

Attachment theory posits that infants activate attachment through a bid to caretak-ers when emotionally distressed and that the caretaker optimally responds in a way that re-regulates the infant, first soothing and then reinstating confidence to explore the environment (i.e., via a secure base). Ultimately, secure attachment facilitates self-regulation in terms of emotions, attentional control, and behavior. Early attach-ment also provides a template, called an *internal working model* (IWM), for expec-tations of oneself and others in relationships. In optimal circumstances, an infant's caretaker manages to reasonably imagine and interpret the mental states of the child, responding in a way that helps the child understand and manage his own distress. According to Fonagy et al. (Fonagy, Gergeley, Jurist, & Target, 2002), this is the process by which secure attachment facilitates the development of mentalization as depicted in Figure 14.1. A child in distress enacts a nonverbal signal to the caretaker, who then must interpret the child's mental state and respond in a way that is both contingent (i.e., resonant) as well as marked (i.e., differentiated as a metabolized),

Clingy, angry, passive, oscillatory (preoccupied)
Confused, dissociated, conflicted, controlling (disorganized)

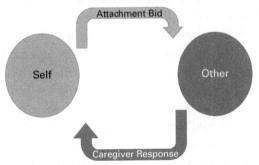

Involving, overprotective, inconsistent (preoccupied)
Hostile, helpless, fearful, frightening (disorganized)

FIGURE 14.1 Attachment Interactions in BPD.

re-presenting a version of what the caretaker imagines as the child's experience. (Note that if the mirroring was only contingent and literal, e.g., a caregiver crying when the child is crying, this would be neither soothing nor encouraging of mentalization.) If the caretaker is able to provide this type of marked and contingent mirroring when the child is emotionally distressed, the child then begins to develop a coherent sense of his own experience. This kindles the child's ability to mentalize his own internal experience and eventually also orients him to the mind of another, allowing him to begin to understand the relationship between actions and mental states in an interpersonal interaction. Several scientific reports have documented a relationship between attachment and social cognitive development (see Bateman & Fonagy, 2012, for review), thus supporting this model of how mentalizing emerges through attachment interactions.

Considering the features of stress sensitivity, emotional and behavioral dysregulation, and interpersonal instabilities characteristic of the disorder, the idea that attachment problems underlie the multiple dimensions of BPD makes clear sense. Numerous investigations have confirmed a relationship between insecure attachment and BPD (see Agrawal, Gunderson, Holmes, & Lyons-Ruth, 2004, and Levy, 2005, for comprehensive review). The attachment styles most common in BPD include preoccupied, fearful, and disorganized types. Preoccupied attachment is characterized by enmeshed, oscillatory, and dependent relationships with caretakers. Fearful attachment is distinguished by mistrust and social avoidance. Disorganized attachment is marked by confused, conflicted, and dissociated states of mind where there is both a need for attachment but also a concomitant fear that leads to mental disorganization with regard to the relationship with the caretaker. Over time, individuals with disorganized attachment adapt by developing controlling behavioral strategies to manage the instability, or disorganization, of the attachment (Gunderson & Lyons-Ruth, 2008; Lyons-Ruth & Jacobvitz, 1999). The combination of dependency, mistrust, and disorganization leads to a tendency to be embroiled in interpersonal struggles in which caretakers are needed but engaged in demanding, suspicious, and confusing ways. The individual with BPD has a tendency to engage (or make attachment bids to) the caretaker with disorganized, dependent, and controlling strategies; elicits disorganized, confusing, controlling tendencies in the caretaker; and vice versa (Figure 14.2). This attachment transaction not only fails to regulate and re-establish a sense of safety, but also creates additional distress, increasing both the vulnerability and need within the child as well as risk for burnout or dysregulation in the caretaker. This vicious cycle of distress and ineffective attachment functioning leads to a "hyperactivated" attachment in which mentalizing in both child and caretaker is likely to be overwhelmed in favor of behavioral means of communication and problem-solving. Individuals with BPD are more likely to have histories of both abuse and neglect than are those without the disorder (Johnson, Cohen, Brown, Smailes, & Bernstein, 1999; Zanarini et al., 2000) (see Chapter 5). Trauma causes a hyperactivation of attachments and undermines the development of mentalizing capacities. However, trauma is not necessary or sufficient as an etiological factor for the development of BPD (Bandelow et al., 2005; Gunderson & Sabo, 1993).

Biological factors such as neurocognitive and neuroendocrine functions can promote attachment problems and the development of BPD, both independently of and in interaction with traumatic events. Neuroimaging research has identified dysfunction in prefrontal and frontolimbic circuits, with impaired top-down regulation, as a mechanism underlying symptoms of dysregulation in BPD (Minzenberg, Fan, New, Tang, & Siever, 2007; Ruocco, Medaglia, Ayaz, & Chute, 2010; Silbersweig et al., 2007). Differences in the functioning of anterior cingulate and insula, which are positioned at the interface of the frontal and limbic systems, are implicated in processing of emotions, pain, and social information and show different patterns of

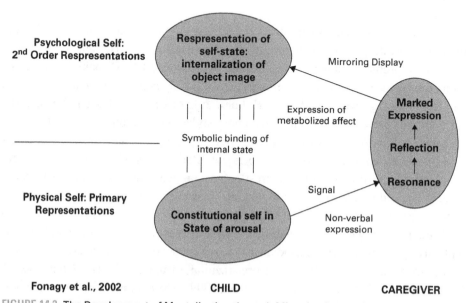

FIGURE 14.2 The Development of Mentalization through Mirroring Interactions.

activation in individuals with BPD when engaged in social cognitive tasks (King-Casas et al., 2008; Ruocco et al., 2013). These findings elucidate how the deficits in both processing and organizing effective responses to emotional and social information observed in individuals with BPD map onto neurocircuitry.

Arnsten's *dual arousal systems* model (Arnsten, 2000) explains how functioning between the frontal and posterior aspects of the brain can switch between controlled and automatic modes at different levels of arousal, resulting in shifts in quality of mentalizing in response to different levels of stress. Under mild to moderate levels of arousal, stress responsive neurohormones (i.e., catecholamines) enhance prefrontal functions such as effortful control, planning, and working memory to coordinate mentalizing processes in a way that flexibly responds to in-the-moment contexts. In contrast, under higher levels of arousal, in the presence of excessive catecholamines, prefrontal functions are inhibited and more subcortical functions take over, leading to more rigid and stress-reactive fight-or-flight responses that derive from instinct and memory (rather than an appraisal of the most current and relative contexts). Arnsten's model explains why, under some conditions, individuals with BPD are quite robust in their mentalizing capacities and may be very attuned to their own and other's internal experiences, whereas under stress, they may resort to overreactive, irrational, unmodulated responses because the balance of prefrontal and subcortical activity in the brain takes mentalizing offline (Bateman & Fonagy, 2012).

The way the brain responds to emotional and social stimuli also interacts with neuropeptide systems in ways that influence attachment and mentalization. Clinically, symptoms of BPD appear stress reactive and are associated with dysfunction of the hypothalamic pituitary adrenal (HPA) axis (Zimmerman & Choi-Kain, 2009). Opioids and oxytocin also effect stress responses and affiliative tendencies (Stanley & Siever, 2010). Oxytocin administration is associated with enhanced performance on "mind-reading" from social cues and collaboration in social exchange tasks in normal subjects (Bartz et al., 2011; Domes, Heinrichs, Michel, Berger, & Herpertz, 2007). However, the administration of oxytocin to subjects with BPD is associated with increased mistrust and decreased cooperation in a social exchange paradigm (Bartz et al., 2011). This suggests that the BPD's oxytocin system may produce a paradoxical tendency toward mistrust that undermines rather than promotes attachment. These scientific findings point to biological factors that dysregulate an individual's stress response system, making him or her more vulnerable and perhaps more prone to activate and ultimately hyperactivate his or her attachment system. The tendencies to high levels of arousal and a switch to automatic mentalizing combined with a paradoxically mistrustful oxytocin response may converge to destabilize both attachment and mentalizing in individuals with BPD.

Phenomenologically, the disorganization of attachment is associated with disorganization of mental states such that the connections between internal experiences and external reality, self and other, and feelings and behaviors become either undifferentiated or completely dissociated. This leads to the emergence of prementalistic states (Table 14.1) that signify failures to mentalize. The extreme and volatile

TABLE 14.1 Prementalistic states

Prementalistic State	Description	Example	Relevant Features of BPD	Typical Countertransference or Reactions by Clinicians
Psychic Equivalence	Concrete, rigid thought processes paired with an unfounded certainty that renders a person's position impenetrable to new information and immovable despite inaccuracy. Internal imagination becomes undifferentiated from external reality.	Patient does not receive a return call from a psychiatrist, believes the psychiatrist is angry with her. She shows up at her next appointment angry, stating "I know you hate me," leaving the psychiatrist completely perplexed. *Action (not returning call) is equated with mental state (anger) and worry about psychiatrist's anger is equated with reality and prompts angry confrontation with absolute certainty of her interpretation of events.*	Paranoia Black-and-white thinking Frantic efforts to avoid abandonment/rejection sensitivity Grandiosity Idealization and devaluation	Confusion Frustration Lack of curiosity and increase in therapist sense of certainty and authority
Pretend Mode	Disconnected sometimes complex and pseudo-psychological thought processes that have no basis in actual experience or external reality. In contrast to psychic equivalence, there is a complete decoupling of internal and external realities, of what is thought and felt and what is conveyed. Referred to as pseudomentalization.	Patient attends treatment dutifully and can talk the talk, appearing to be a "good patient" in sessions but engaging in a secret double life of self-destructiveness and increasing dysfunction. *Patient's reality of psychic and behavior dysfunction is walled off and disconnected from what she says to the therapist and does in treatment. This can result in years of intensive seemingly meaningful therapy without change.*	Dissociation Self-harm and suicidality Splitting Secretive or "dishonest" behavior Emptiness Identity diffusion	Boredom Feelings of disconnection or exclusion Feeling like one is on autopilot Tendency for therapist to try harder or do more work making sense of confused disconnected material patient brings to sessions

| *Teleological Mode* | Belief that mental states are only real if they are expressed in actions that are contingent with patient's aims or ends. Different from but overlapping with psychic equivalence in the sense that actions are equated with mental states that match the patient's wishes, giving them a sense of being in control of the actions of others. | Patient demands proof that a therapist is dedicated by requesting special treatment such as double sessions and rides home. When therapist refuses, patient self-harms to communicate distress and elicit rescuing by the therapist.

Boundary crossings become an index of caring and self-harm an index of pain, which functions to control or provoke predictable responses in therapist. | Self-harm
Suicidality
"Manipulative" reputation
Promiscuity
Frantic efforts to avoid abandonment | Feeling compelled to act or respond to patient in behavioral ways (boundary crossings, hospitalization, and medication when in crisis)
Offering direction |

emotions and behaviors exhibited in BPD occur when mentalization fails. The MBT approach aims to therefore reinstate mentalizing as a mechanism to reduce symptoms. Ultimately, enhanced mentalizing can stabilize attachments, which can reduce vulnerability to stress so that more controlled mentalization processes can stay online.

DESCRIPTION OF TREATMENT: THE MBT TECHNIQUE

While the clinical theories and neuroscientific evidence integrated in MBT's formulation of BPD is sophisticated, the techniques involved in MBT are simple and humble. Its unpretentious approach renders it relatable to early-stage clinicians, front-line staff, patients, and family members but also make it sometimes challenging to adopt for more experienced clinicians trained in other formal psychotherapeutic approaches where authority and certainty (or confidence) may be encouraged. At the basis of the mentalizing stance is a position of curiosity, of expressly not knowing but being interested in exploring different perspectives on the patient's experience both in relationships outside treatment and with the therapist. The job of the therapist is to encourage the patient to mentalize rather than do it for them by providing interpretations or by instructing them on how to manage behavior or distress. There is no agenda to arrive at any particular insights or behavioral changes, but rather to sustain the mentalizing process so that the patient's capacity to arrive at whatever insight or behavioral change remains optimized.

As discussed in the previous section, Bateman and Fonagy formulate the problem of BPD as arising from *unstable*, not absent, mentalization capacities. In contrast to autism, where social cognitive deficits are more fixed, mentalization is prone to go offline in situations of stressful arousal (e.g., intense emotion) and hyperactivated attachment. The MBT therapist intervenes when mentalizing becomes compromised. Therefore, the assessment of mentalizing—in others words the detection of prementalistic states or imbalanced mentalizing—prompts the clinician to recognize that the patient is unlikely to be able to understand her or others' mental states realistically, benevolently, or flexibly and to use MBT techniques to broaden and thereby stabilize her capacity. According to this model, a common mistake in psychotherapeutic practice with BPD patients is to assume that the patient can mentalize when emotionally activated and offer complex interpretations or behavioral plans when the patient may be too vulnerable in her psychological and interpersonal capacities to either trust the therapist or make use of the offered interventions.

One way to assess mentalizing is by detecting prementalistic states and noting features of good and bad mentalizing. Robust mentalizing is characterized by a sense of curiosity, uncertainty, and balance between considerations of self and others, cognitive and affective mental states, and internal mental states and overt, external behaviors. Impaired mentalizing involves the converse: absolute certainty and imbalance in attention to selective aspects of experience to the exclusion of other relevant perspectives. When patients are overly self-focused, the MBT therapist may encourage curiosity about the other person involved in a situation. Similarly, when patients are overly fixated on what they or others are doing, the MBT therapist attempts to enlarge appreciation of what may be going on internally in terms of mental states underlying behavior. Yet, when patients are overly intellectualized, the MBT therapist encourages attention to how something feels or may be experienced and vice versa; when patients are too consumed by intense emotions, the therapist attempts to counterbalance this with attention to what the patients think. Here, the therapist first determines the imbalance or lack of integration in perspectives; then, he encourages patients to consider alternative perspectives to strengthen mentalization. These are called *contrary moves* in MBT. Contrary moves promote broadening of perspectives, allowing integration of different aspects of the patient's and others' experience. Simply put, these moves aim to expand reflection where a patient's tendency to collapse into action or dissociation would lead to symptoms of BPD.

The therapist is also charged with the task of monitoring attachment. Given the vulnerabilities BPD patients have toward hyperactivating attachment and shifting to automatic rather than controlled modes of mentalization, the MBT therapist is instructed to both activate attachment enough to facilitate the development of mentalization while not overly activating it to a point of switching the patient into a mode of heightened arousal. Specifically, the MBT therapist engages patients in interchange characterized by marked and contingent mirroring, where the therapist shows warmth, sympathy, and interest in them, thus showing contingency by making a genuine effort to really understand, relate to, and reflect back their perspective while also reflecting alternative or marked perspective. For example, if a patient comes to the office stating that she slapped her boss and got fired, the MBT therapist, having noted this as a manifestation of mentalizing gone wrong, would start with a curious inquiry of what happened and elucidation of what the patient was thinking or feeling that could have prompted such as reaction. Once the patient described her mental state, rewinding to and identifying the trigger for the loss of mentalization, the therapist can then point to what he understands in the reaction but also note the aspects of the situation he still cannot comprehend, so that the patient and therapist together can orient to further exploration of what makes sense and does not make sense within the situation. Ultimately, the therapist may disclose what he would think or feel in the same situation to provide an alternative perspective without condemning the patient's position or indicating that the therapist's perspective is right or superior (which would be marking without contingency). This is done with tentativeness and humility, rather than authority and judgment. The therapist should mark his own perspective as belonging to him rather than an absolute or abstract (e.g., "I am surprised you felt X because when I imagine it, I might feel Y. I wonder how you arrived at that?"). If the patient can consider the therapist's alternative perspective, she has already begun to more flexibly mentalize, perhaps out of psychic equivalence or another state of certainty, which may reduce stress and improve in-the-moment appraisal of the situation, thereby reinstating controlled mentalizing. This shift toward more flexible mentalization also facilitates the attachment by mutual responsiveness to each other's perspectives and positions.

When there are signs of poor or absent mentalizing, the therapist's effort to engage and explore the mind of the patient may be experienced as intrusive and confusing; if this is unknown to the therapist, attempting to engage more deeply and become solicitous may hyperactivate the attachment. Considering the association between BPD and disorganized attachment driven by both need and fear, the therapist's effort to lean in emotionally and interpersonally may have the effect of further intensifying the patient's distress, thus undermining their mentalization. Here, the MBT therapist steps back, acknowledge his possible contribution to making matters worse, and cools off the intensity of the interaction to help reduce arousal thereby increasing conditions for mentalizing.

Apart from monitoring and modulating both mentalizing and attachment, the MBT therapist follows a stepwise process of (1) supportive and empathic clarification, (2) challenge, (3) affect focus, and (4) mentalizing the transference. The first step, already described in the discussion of providing marked contingent mirroring, involves the therapist's effort to acknowledge problems and difficulties that the patient presents before encouraging further explication of the situation at hand. This provides an opportunity for the therapist and patient to attend jointly to considering the problems at hand and allows the patient to see how the therapist understands her point of view before generating alternative perspectives. Sometimes, when efforts to re-establish mentalization fail, the therapist might try to challenge the patient in a way that "surprises" the mind rather than strong-arms the patient into compliance. This is accomplished by introducing something unexpected into the interaction. For example, say a patient is fixated on a view that nobody would ever love her. After a fruitless back and forth in which a therapist inquires why she thinks that and the patient remains convinced it is true, the therapist may challenge the patient with a counterfactual that changes up the approach by instead asking "What would it look like if someone did love you? How would you know?" More intense challenges may be required in more heated, rigid, and escalating moments of nonmentalizing; then, the therapist may resort to a radically frank statement about something the patient is saying or doing to insert his own mental process and disrupt the patient's. These may be high stakes methods, but they can be balanced with both a reorientation to the patient's problem or an exploration of the in-the-moment difficulty between the therapist and patient. Either way, when a patient is rigidly fixed in a point of view that is excessively self-oriented, the radically frank or surprising insertion of the therapist's state of mind may abruptly shift the mentalizing balance from self to therapist (the other mind in the session); then the therapist can repair any problems this challenge created by owning his own contribution to the difficulty at hand. This will allow the discourse to be more interpersonally interactive and spontaneous rather than stuck in the patient's mental representation of a past event.

The last few steps of the MBT approach remain focused on the interpersonally interactive process generated between the patient and therapist. Once the patient is able to mentalize to some degree, the MBT therapist orients to the *affect focus*, which refers not only to the patient's emotional experience and expression, but also to the affects generated in both the patient and the therapist in the transactions between the two. This part seeks to explicitly attend to and clarify those emotions generated that may be less obvious, unexpressed, or outright avoided in the interaction, which renders the attachment vulnerable to old schemas on which the patient's most problematic interpersonal functioning is rooted. This naturally can fold into mentalizing the transference, which refers to the relationship between the therapist and patient in the moment or here and now, rather than as related to the patient's early history. Specifically, the MBT therapist must first validate the patient's experience of the therapist—however much this may be surprising or confusing to him—and himself accept his contribution to any enactments within the therapeutic process. After the patient and therapist collaboratively develop a view of what is happening, alternative perspective are generated, along with curiosity to see how the shift in perspectives might be experienced. At this point, metacognitive processes regarding the self and other in an in vivo transactional relationship can be engaged, allowing the patient to practice and strengthen her capacity for good mentalizing.

These steps in the mentalizing process do not happen linearly and neatly. The MBT approach does not seek to fix the therapeutic interaction into a rigid mold or preconception of what it should be, but it instead provides a technical guideline to structure a simple and flexible means by which to explore unmentalized territory with the borderline patient.

EMPIRICAL EVIDENCE SUPPORTING MBT IN PARTIAL HOSPITALIZATION AND OUTPATIENT SETTINGS

The evidence base supporting the effectiveness of MBT includes studies by its developers Bateman and Fonagy (1999, 2001, 2003, 2008a, 2008b, 2009), as well as replication studies done at both partial hospitalization (Bales et al., 2012) and outpatient levels of care (Jorgensen et al., 2013). In addition, there is one study reporting on MBT-A, an adaptation of MBT for adolescents (Rossouw & Fonagy, 2012). All these studies demonstrate that MBT effectively reduces self-harm, suicidal behavior and ideation, depression, symptoms of BPD, reliance on medications, and use of intensive hospital-based mental health services while increasing functioning (Bales et al., 2012; Bateman & Fonagy, 1999, 2001, 2003, 2008a, 2009; Jorgensen et al., 2013; Roussouw & Fonagy, 2012). The results of these studies are summarized in Table 14.2.

Results from Bateman and Fonagy's original partial hospitalization study were published in four reports (Bateman & Fonagy, 1999, 2001, 2003, 2008a). The study, carried out at a personality disorders specialty service within the National Health Service (NHS), involved 44 subjects with the usual comorbidity profiles of BPD patients and low levels of functioning. Notably, of all studies, Bateman and Fonagy's

TABLE 14.2 Outcomes studies for mentalization-based therapy (MBT)

Year of Publication Length and Setting of Treatment	Patients	MBT Treatment	Comparison Treatment	Outcomes	Methodologic Strengths & Limitations
ORIGINAL MBT RCTS: BATEMAN & FONAGY					
1999 18 months Partial Hospitalization Program, public National Health Service, London	44 adult males and females with BPD randomized 38 subjects included in statistical analysis => 19 in MBT 19 in general TAU Patients in both groups matched in age, DIB-R score, trauma exposure, substance abuse.	Psychoanalytically oriented day hospital Individual therapy 1×/week Group therapy 3×/week Expressive therapy/psychodrama 1×/week Community meeting 1×/week Case administrator meeting 1×/month Medication review by a resident psychiatrist with polypharmacy discouraged 1×/month	General psychiatric treatment/TAU Psychiatric review by senior psychiatrist on average 2×/month Inpatient admission (90% admitted, average LOS = 11.6 days) Problem-solving focused partial day hospitalization (72% admitted, average LOS = 6 months) Outpatient visits in community with psychiatric nurse 2×/month *No formal psychotherapy was offered to patients in this group*	MBT >TAU in ⇓ 1) self-harm 2) suicide attempts 3) need for medication 4) inpatient hospitalization 5) anxiety 6) depression AND ⇑ in social functioning	*Strengths:* 1) Rigorous diagnostic screening for BPD 2) Therapist were psychiatrically trained nurses with no formal psychotherapy training 3) Dropouts low ($n = 3$ or 12%) *Limitations:* 1) No adherence monitoring 2) No assessment of changes in mentalizing as the operative factor in the difference in change

| 2001 | 18-month follow-up study of same patients as reported in 1999 RCT

3 patients from the comparison group crossed over to the MBT group | Follow-up program offered to all MBT patients attended by all but 3 who had prematurely terminated treatment. This program consisted of:

Group therapy 2×/week

Psychiatric review by Anthony Bateman as requested 1–3× monthly | Continued use and access to general psychiatric services.

No subjects in this group received any formal psychotherapy. | Gains from MBT treatment were not only maintained but also continued to improve over the period of follow-up. Subjects in TAU also improved but to a lesser degree in fewer areas of assessment. | Same as in 1999 study |
|---|---|---|---|---|---|
| 2003 | Study of health service utilization on same RCT reported in 1999, 2001 | | | 6 months prior to RCT=> mean annual health care utilization costs: MBT = $44,967 versus TAU = $52,563.

During trial => MBT= $27,303 versus TAU = $30,960

At 18-month follow-up=> MBT = $3,183 versus TAU = $15,490 | *Strengths:*

1) Mental health services easy to track by medical records in the public health service where care is organized by locale

2) Analysis spans 3 years, tracking substantial changes in cost for all patients from pretreatment

Limitations:

1) Small study size

(continued) |

TABLE 14.2 Continued

Year of Publication Length and Setting of Treatment	Patients	MBT Treatment	Comparison Treatment	Outcomes	Methodologic Strengths & Limitations
2008	8-year follow-up of patients in RCT reported in 1999, 2001, 2003			MBT < TAU in 1) suicide attempts 2) hospitalizations 3) use of emergency room 4) BPD symptoms MBT > TAU in 1) GAF score 2) Years of employment	*Strengths:* 1) Length of follow-up greater than for any other treatment for BPD 2) Reliable medical records as part of NHS 3) High study retention rate over 8 years *Limitations:* 1) Not clear mentalizing was the operative factor in differences

OUTPATIENT MBT TRIAL: BATEMAN & FONAGY

Year of Publication Length and Setting of Treatment	Patients	MBT Treatment	Comparison Treatment	Outcomes	Methodologic Strengths & Limitations
2009 Outpatient Clinic, National Public Health Service, London	134 adult males and females with BPD randomized 71 subjects in MBT 63 subjects in SCM	Outpatient MBT Individual Therapy 1×/week Group Therapy 1×/week	Structured Clinical Management (SCM) Supportive and problem-solving focus in:	MBT < SCM in number of patients attempting suicide at 6 months. No difference at 12 months.	*Strengths:* 1) Larger representative sample with few exclusions

Crisis calls focus
reinstating mentalizing
Psychopharmacology/
General psychiatric
review 1–3× monthly

Individual
psychotherapy
Group therapy
Crisis calls- focus,
problem-solving, and
support
Psychopharmacology/
General psychiatric
review 1–3× monthly

SCM < MBT in number
of patients self-harming
at 6 months, MBT < SCM
at 12 months, MBT >
SCM in rate of decline of
self-harm.

MBT < SCM in days in
hospital throughout study.

MBT > SCM in rate of
decline in symptoms
of depression, social
function, and use of
medications

2) Both treatments
based on a structured
approach with better
matched treatments

3) Level of experience by
clinicians also matched
between groups

4) Adherence monitored

Limitations:

1) Both groups improve
significantly, leading
to the question of
whether the additional
specialization is
cost-effective

2) No post-treatment
follow-up

3) Not clear that change
in mentalizing confers
the difference
in change

4) Need for replication
outside treatment
originators

(continued)

TABLE 14.2 Continued

Year of Publication Length and Setting of Treatment	Patients	MBT Treatment	Comparison Treatment	Outcomes	Methodologic Strengths & Limitations
REPLICATION STUDIES					
Bales et al., 2012 18 month PHP at Personality Disorder Specialty Center in Netherlands	45 adult mostly female (71%) with BPD in MBT No comparison group	Individual therapy 1×/week Group therapy >10/ week Community meeting 1×/week Meeting with psychiatrist 1×/week		84.5% retention in MBT ⇓ Suicide attempts and self-harm, depression, interpersonal problems, BPD symptoms, use of additional acute psychiatric services ⇑ Quality of life, sense of self-control, identity integration, responsibility, relational functioning	*Strengths:* 1) "Naturalistic" treatment setting with severely disordered multiply comorbid BPD patients 2) Independent clinical group to originators of MBT 3) Adherence monitored by Bateman *Limitations:* 1) No comparison group 2) Partial hospitalization program involves more than 20 hours of treatment per week 3) No measure of change in mentalization as relevant factor for change

Jorgensen et al., 2013 24 months of Outpatient Therapy at Outpatient BPD Specialty Clinic in Danish Public Healthcare System	85 adult mostly female (95%) with BPD, patients with antisocial and paranoid personality disorder or severe substance abuse excluded 74 in MBT 37 in supportive treatment	Individual therapy 1×/week Group therapy 1×/week Psychoeducational group 1×/month × 6 months Medication treatment in accordance with APA guidelines	Group Therapy 2×/month Psychoeducational group 1×/month × 6 months Medication treatment in accordance with APA guidelines	Dropout rate 43% => 58 patients completed 24 months of treatment (no difference between treatment arms) In **both** groups: ⇓ Symptom count and severity of depression, anxiety, and BPD; medication use ⇑ social/interpersonal functioning, social adjustment MBT > Supportive only on therapist-rated GAF	*Strengths:* 1) Large study comparing two coherent treatments 2) Independent clinical group to originators of MBT 3) Use of experienced clinicians in both treatment arms *Limitations:* 1) Outcome measures all self-reported 2) In GAF ratings, assessors not blinded to treatment condition 3) High attrition rate

ADOLESCENT OUTPATIENT MBT-A: ROSSOUW & FONAGY

2012 12 months outpatient community based adolescent mental health service in the National Health Service, London	80 adolescent mostly female (85%) aged 12–17 years with self-harm 40 subjects randomized to MBT-A and TAU	Individual therapy 1×/week MBT-F Family therapy 1×/month Supervision of clinicians 1×/week	Based on UK National Institute for Health and Clinical Evidence guidelines	Both MBT-A and TAU groups =>⇓ self-harm, and depression MBT-A < TAU in odds of reporting self-harm and self-harm at end of treatment	*Strengths:* 1) First treatment study to demonstrate significant reduction in both self-harm and depression with a manualized treatment compared to TAU in adolescents

(continued)

TABLE 14.2 Continued

Year of Publication Length and Setting of Treatment	Patients	MBT Treatment	Comparison Treatment	Outcomes	Methodologic Strengths & Limitations
			Variable and nonmanualized, including a range of services including psychiatric review as well as individual and family therapy from cognitive behavioral, psychodynamic, and generic supportive approaches	MBT-A ⇑ mentalizing measure scores and ⇓ attachment avoidance. TAU no change in both measures	2) Demonstrated change in putative mechanisms of psychopathology (mentalization and attachment as related to a difference in outcomes *Limitations:* 1) Adherence monitoring was informal through supervision. No report on statistics regarding adherence 2) Large proportion of sample did not complete either treatment, and sample sizes are small 3) TAU was nonmanualized, and no supervision was offered to clinicians

MBT, mentalization-based treatment; RCT, randomized controlled trial; BPD, borderline personality disorder; LOS, length of stay; DIB-R, Diagnostic Interview for Borderlines; PHP, partial hospitalization program, SCM, structured clinical management; GAF, global assessment of functioning, TAU, treatment as usual.

studies included the highest proportion of men in its trials, which suggests effectiveness of MBT is generalizable to patients of both genders.

The partial hospitalization format in the MBT condition involved about 6–7 hours of treatment with individual and group psychotherapy as well as case management and medication management by a psychiatrist in training. The comparison condition, treatment as usual (TAU), employed senior psychiatrists administering psychiatric review twice monthly with access to acute psychiatric treatment but no psychotherapeutic interventions. Importantly, patients in both treatment conditions improved over the period of treatment and 8 years of follow-up. Bateman and Fonagy's original study established that MBT administered in a partial hospitalization program is more effective in reducing symptoms despite its use of more expensive mental health resources than what most socioeconomically disadvantaged patients get accessing public health services. While the MBT arm involved a long-term, structured partial hospitalization and team-based psychotherapy program, it consistently saved costs of acute services that may temporize but do not actively treat the problems of BPD. Moreover, the clinical staffing employed in the MBT were trained nurses and resident physicians as opposed to the senior psychiatric staff employed in the TAU arm. This aspect of the methodology, along with the public health setting, suggest that MBT is a cost-effective, easily exportable, economically efficient public health measure that can be taught to teams of nonexpert front-line staff.

Longitudinal studies of BPD demonstrate that the disorder remits at dramatic levels with few relapses without specialized treatments (Gunderson et al., 2011; Zanarini, Frankenburg, Hennen, Reich, & Silk, 2006). The TAU group in this study reflects this tendency because both groups improved in most outcomes. However, by the end of 8 years of follow-up, the MBT groups' improvements are both more symptomatically and functionally robust (Bateman & Fonagy, 2008a). Only 13% of the MBT group met diagnostic criteria for BPD at the end of the follow-up, whereas 87% of the TAU group still did. These symptomatic improvement differences are matched by functional improvements. While both groups showed improvement, the majority of the MBT group remitted, and many also engaged in sustained employment (Bateman & Fonagy, 1999).

Bateman and Fonagy followed up their partial hospitalization trial of MBT with an outpatient trial, which examined the effectiveness of MBT applied in a much more pared-down ambulatory treatment consisting of weekly MBT individual and group therapy (Bateman & Fonagy, 2009). The outpatient trial compared MBT to structured clinical management (SCM), which constituted a much more equivalent treatment package. Both treatments were structured with stable teams guided by National Institute for Healthcare Excellence (NICE) guidelines, with crisis on-call availability, crisis planning, medication management, and regular individual and group therapy. The SCM therapy was supportive and problem-solving–oriented, providing the kind of advocacy relationship for patients missing in the prior TAU condition in the partial hospitalization trial. Both teams of therapists consisted of nurses, licensed counselors, or resident psychiatrists with minimal and equivalent amounts of training and exposure to personality-disordered patients. This advance in the intervention protocols controlled more comprehensively to distill differences in treatments, such that it was clearer that the structure, support, consistent contact, longitudinal relationships, generic psychotherapy exposure, clinician's experience with personality disorders, and treatment coherence and standardization could not be implicated as major factors in the differences in outcomes.

Subjects in both arms improved significantly, suggesting that treatments organized and informed by consensus guidelines for BPD are effective. The MBT group showed better improvement in suicide attempts, severe incidents of self-harm, hospitalizations, and self-reported ratings of symptoms. Still, the authors concede they could not empirically demonstrate a link between these improvements and mentalizing. However, this study shows that with relatively modest outpatient treatment plans, patients with BPD could make significant improvements in both a specialized treatment using MBT and a generalist but BPD-informed supportive management approach.

Two other clinical teams in Europe completed trials testing MBT. The first trial, published by Bales and her collaborators at a specialty center in the Netherlands for the treatment of personality disorders, reported on the improvement of patients over the course of 18 months of an MBT-based partial hospitalization program. While this study did not have a comparison group, it did show that, administered outside the hands of the main authors of MBT, MBT was effective in reducing suicidality, self-harm, and utilization of acute psychiatric services. As in Bateman and Fonagy's original partial hospitalization study, the MBT program offered involved significant clinical contact with more than 20 hours of treatment per week. The second trial, published by Jorgensen and collaborators (2013) at a public specialty center in Denmark for personality disorders, compared outpatient MBT in an RCT to a supportive treatment administered by senior experienced clinicians. The MBT group had individual therapy and group therapy weekly while the comparison group only received group therapy every other week. Both groups received medication management and psychoeducation groups. Patients in both groups improved significantly and only differed in changes in therapist-rated Global Assessment of Functioning (GAF). This more equalized outcome in the only RCT replication of MBT to date suggests that, in a specialty personality disorders clinic and administered by experienced clinicians, both MBT and supportive psychotherapy are fairly comparable in efficacy. These replication trials demonstrated that MBT could be administered by clinical teams other than Bateman's in both partial hospitalization and outpatient settings with significant improvement in suicidality, self, harm, psychiatric symptoms, and functioning.

One outpatient adolescent trial of an adapted version of MBT called MBT-A has shown a relationship between reductions of self-harm and changes in attachment and mentalization. The MBT-A treatment included individual MBT weekly sessions and monthly MBT-Family (MBT-F) sessions. The comparison was TAU in the public health system in London and was conducted according to NICE guidelines.

Rossouw and Fonagy (2012) report that theirs is the first published study showing a significant reduction in self-harm and depression in adolescents in a manualized treatment. In addition, these investigators measured changes in attachment using a validated measure called the Experiences in Close Relationships (ECR; Brennan, Clark, & Shaver, 1998) and in mentalizing using a scale called How I Feel (HIF; unpublished, 2008), which measures a proxy of mentalizing, emotional intelligence, and is not validated. Rossouw and Fonagy report a relationship between the changes observed in only the MBT-A group in attachment avoidance and mentalization and reductions in self-harm, suggesting that the core mechanisms of MBT are the operative target in MBT-A that render it effective.

LIMITATIONS

The studies reviewed here did not employ stringent exclusion criteria in recruitment, resulting in patient groups reflective of actual BPD patients in the community. MBT may be well-suited in these scenarios, and Bateman and Fonagy encourage integration of MBT ideas and technique with other treatments, so there is no limiting imperative to practice it in its purely manualized form.

This suggests fairly wide generalizability in terms of types of patients. There is no scientific study to date that identifies particular types of patients who cannot benefit from MBT, but there are some patients and clinicians in whom sufficient interest or capacity to engage in MBT may be lacking. Patients with a mixed borderline and narcissistic personality, where the attachment style and patterns of self-destructive acts are more centrally rooted in a narcissistic core, often have attachment styles that are more dismissing rather than dependent, resulting in a tendency to not activate attachment under stress. In these cases, it may be difficult to engage attachment enough to sufficiently stimulate mentalizing in the treatment. Narcissistic symptoms triggered by dysregulations of self-esteem may be exacerbated when an MBT therapist asks a patient to do something he or she is not skilled in. The patient may characteristically modulate his position vis á vis his sense of competence and the therapist by engaging in pseudomentalizing that appears to mimic the framework of therapy without any connection to the patient's actual experience or life (Ronningstam, 2005).

In terms of therapists, the empirical literature suggests that MBT can be administered effectively by clinicians with little formal psychotherapy training. The outpatient replication trial (Jorgensen et al., 2013) suggests that in a setting with heavily experienced, extensively formally trained therapists, MBT shows limited superiority over a supportive a pared-down approach. It may be that MBT is more difficult to administer effectively when the attitude of "not knowing" is conveyed in a way that is more technical and less than genuine. Therapists who prefer taking a directive, interpretative, or more authoritative approach may have difficulty adhering to the basic MBT stance. Specifically, therapist who themselves have difficulty maintaining uncertainty and curiosity in the face of severe self-destructive behavior or other intense forms of dysfunction inherent to BPD may not be well suited for MBT. In general, MBT asks therapists to be humble, admit to not knowing or to making mistakes, and participate equally in the task of sustaining their own mentalizing process. Those who find difficulty with any aspects of this therapist stance will struggle to deliver MBT in a natural and effective way.

REFERENCES

Agrawal, H. R., Gunderson, J., Holmes, B. M., & Lyons-Ruth, K. (2004). Attachment studies with borderline patients: A review. *Harvard Review of Psychiatry, 12*(2), 94–104.

Arnsten, A. F. (2000). Stress impairs prefrontal cortical function in rats and monkeys: Role of dopamine D1 and norepinephrine alpha-1 receptor mechanisms. *Progress in Brain Research, 126,* 183–192.

Bales, D., van Beek, N., Smits, M., Willemsen, S., Busschbach, J. J., Verheul, R., & Andrea, H. (2012). Treatment outcome of 18-month, day hospital mentalization-based treatment (MBT) in patients with severe borderline personality disorder in the Netherlands. *Journal of Personality Disorders, 26*(4), 568–582.

Bandelow, B., Krause, J., Wedekind, D., Broocks, A., Hajak, G., & Rüther, E. (2005). Early traumatic life events, parental attitudes, family history, and birth risk factors in patients with borderline personality disorder and healthy controls. *Psychiatry Research, 134*(2),169–179.

Barone, L. (2003). Developmental protective and risk factors in borderline personality disorder: A study using the Adult Attachment Interview. *Attachment and Human Development, 5*(1), 64–77.

Bartz, J., Simeon, D., Hamilton, H., Kim, S., Crystal, S., Braun, A., ... Hollander, E. (2011). Oxytocin can hinder trust and cooperation in borderline personality disorder. *Social Cognitive and Affective Neuroscience, 6*(5), 556–563.

Bateman, A., & Fonagy, P. (1999). Effectiveness of partial hospitalization in the treatment of borderline personality disorder: A randomized controlled trial. *American Journal of Psychiatry, 156*(10), 1563–1569.

Bateman, A., & Fonagy, P. (2001). Treatment of borderline personality disorder with psychoanalytically oriented partial hospitalization: An 18-month follow-up. *American Journal of Psychiatry, 158*(1), 36–42.

Bateman, A., & Fonagy, P. (2003). Health service utilization costs for borderline personality disorder patients treated with psychoanalytically oriented partial hospitalization versus general psychiatric care. *American Journal of Psychiatry, 160*(1), 169–171.

Bateman, A., & Fonagy, P. (2008a). 8-year follow-up of patients treated for borderline personality disorder: Mentalization-based treatment versus treatment as usual. *American Journal of Psychiatry, 165*(5), 631–638.

Bateman, A., & Fonagy, P. (2008b). Comorbid antisocial and borderline personality disorders: Mentalization-based treatment. *Journal of Clinical Psychology, 64*(2), 181–194.

Bateman, A., & Fonagy, P. (2009). Randomized controlled trial of outpatient mentalization-based treatment versus structured clinical management for borderline personality disorder. *American Journal of Psychiatry, 166*(12), 1355–1364.

Bateman, A., & Fonagy, P. (2012). *Handbook of mentalizing in mental health practice.* Washington, DC: APPI.

Benjamin, L. S. (1993). *Interpersonal diagnosis and treatment of personality disorders.* New York: Guilford.

Brennan, K. A., Clark, C. L., & Shaver, P. R. (1998). Self-report measurement of adult romantic attachment: An integrative overview. In J. A. Simpson & W. S. Rholes (Eds.), *Attachment theory and close relationships* (pp. 46–76). New York; Guilford.

Choi-Kain, L. W., Albert, E. A., & Gunderson, J. G. (2016). Evidence-based treatments for borderline personality disorder: Implementation, integration, and stepped care. *Harvard Review of Psychiatry, 24*(5), 342–356.

Domes, G., Heinrichs, M., Michel, A., Berger, C., & Herpertz, S. C. (2007). Oxytocin improves "mind-reading" in humans. *Biological Psychiatry, 61*(6), 731–733.

Fonagy, P. (1991). Thinking about thinking: Some clinical and theoretical considerations in the treatment of a borderline patient. *International Journal of Psychoanalysis, 72*, 639–656.

Fonagy, P., Gergeley, G., Jurist, E., & Target, M. (2002). *Affect regulation, mentalization, and the development of the self.* New York: Other Press.

Fonagy, P., Leigh, T., Steele, M., Steele, H., Kennedy, R., Mattoon, G., . . . Gerber, A. (1996). The relation of attachment status, psychiatric classification, and response to psychotherapy. *Journal of Consulting and Clinical Psychology, 64*(1), 22–31.

Fonagy, P., Target, M., & Gergely, G. (2000). Attachment and borderline personality disorder. A theory and some evidence. *Psychiatric Clinics of North America, 23*(1), 103–122, vii-viii.

Gunderson, J. G. (1996). The borderline patient's intolerance of aloneness: Insecure attachments and therapist availability. *American Journal of Psychiatry, 153*(6), 752–758.

Gunderson, J. G., & Lyons-Ruth, K. (2008). BPD's interpersonal hypersensitivity phenotype: A gene-environment-developmental model. *Journal of Personality Disorders, 22*(1), 22–41.

Gunderson, J. G., & Sabo, A. N. (1993). The phenomenological and conceptual interface between borderline personality disorder and PTSD. *American Journal of Psychiatry, 150*(1), 19–27.

Gunderson, J. G., Stout, R. L., McGlashan, T. H., Shea, M. T., Morey, L. C., Grilo, C. M., . . . Skodol, A. E. (2011). Ten-year course of borderline personality disorder: Psychopathology and function from the Collaborative Longitudinal Personality Disorders study. *Archives of General Psychiatry, 68*(8), 827–837.

Johnson, J. G., Cohen, P., Brown, J., Smailes, E. M., & Bernstein, D. P. (1999). Childhood maltreatment increases risk for personality disorders during early adulthood. *Archives of General Psychiatry, 56*(7), 600–606.

Jorgensen, C. R., Freund, C., Boye, R., Jordet, H., Andersen, D., & Kjolbye, M. (2013). Outcome of mentalization-based and supportive psychotherapy in patients with borderline personality disorder: A randomized trial. *Acta Psychiatrica Scandinavica, 127*(4), 305–317.

King-Casas, B., Sharp, C., Lomax-Bream, L., Lohrenz, T., Fonagy, P., & Montague, P. R. (2008). The rupture and repair of cooperation in borderline personality disorder. *Science, 321*(5890), 806–810.

Levy, K. N. (2005). The implications of attachment theory and research for understanding borderline personality disorder. *Development and Psychopathology, 17*(4), 959–986.

Minzenberg, M. J., Fan, J., New, A. S., Tang, C. Y., & Siever, L. J. (2007). Fronto-limbic dysfunction in response to facial emotion in borderline personality disorder: An event-related fMRI study. *Psychiatry Research, 155*(3), 231–243.

Patrick, M., Hobson, R. P., Castle, D., Howard, R., & Maughan, B. (1994). Personality disorder and the mental representation of early social experience. *Development and Psychopathology, 6*, 375–388.

Ronningstam, E. F. (2005). *Identifying and understanding narcissistic personality.* Oxford, UK: Oxford University Press.

Rossouw, T. I. (2013). Mentalization-based treatment: Can it be translated into practice in clinical settings and teams? *Journal of the American Academy of Child and Adolescent Psychiatry, 52*(3), 220–222.

Rossouw, T. I., & Fonagy, P. (2012). Mentalization-based treatment for self-harm in adolescents: A randomized controlled trial. *Journal of the American Academy of Child and Adolescent Psychiatry, 51*(12), 1304–1313; e1303.

Ruocco, A. C., Amirthavasagam, S., Choi-Kain, L. W., & McMain, S. F. (2013). Neural correlates of negative emotionality in borderline personality disorder: An activation-likelihood-estimation meta-analysis. *Biological Psychiatry, 73*(2), 153–160.

Ruocco, A. C., Medaglia, J. D., Ayaz, H., & Chute, D. L. (2010). Abnormal prefrontal cortical response during affective processing in borderline personality disorder. *Psychiatry Research, 182*(2), 117–122.

Silbersweig, D., Clarkin, J. F., Goldstein, M., Kernberg, O. F., Tuescher, O., Levy, K. N., . . . Stern, E. (2007). Failure of frontolimbic inhibitory function in the context of negative emotion in borderline personality disorder. *American Journal of Psychiatry, 164*(12), 1832–1841.

Stanley, B., & Siever, L. J. (2010). The interpersonal dimension of borderline personality disorder: Toward a neuropeptide model. *American Journal of Psychiatry, 167*(1), 24–39.

Stoffers, J. M., Völlm, B. A., Rücker, G., Timmer, A., Huband, N., & Lieb, K. (2012). Psychological therapies for people with borderline personality disorder. *Cochrane Database of Systematic Reviews, 2.*

Waldinger, R. J., & Gunderson, J. G. (1984). Completed psychotherapies with borderline patients. *American Journal of Psychotheraphy, 38*(2), 190–202.

Zanarini, M. C., Frankenburg, F. R., Hennen, J., Reich, D. B., & Silk, K. R. (2006). Prediction of the 10-year course of borderline personality disorder. *American Journal of Psychiatry, 163*(5), 827–832.

Zanarini, M. C., Frankenburg, F. R., Reich, D. B., Marino, M. F., Lewis, R. E., Williams, A. A., & Khera, G. S. (2000). Biparental failure in the childhood experiences of borderline patients. *Journal of Personality Disorders, 14*(3), 264–273.

Zimmerman, D. J., & Choi-Kain, L. W. (2009). The hypothalamic-pituitary-adrenal axis in borderline personality disorder: A review. *Harvard Review of Psychiatry, 17*(3), 167–183.

Transference-Focused
Psychotherapy

A Psychodynamic Treatment
of Personality Disorders

FRANK E. YEOMANS AND JILL C. DELANEY

INTRODUCTION

Transference-focused psychotherapy (TFP) has taken psychoanalytic principles and
techniques and modified them to address the needs of people with personality disorders. It is rooted in the branch of psychoanalysis known as *object relations theory*, which conceptualizes the specific symptoms of borderline personality disorder
(BPD) as originating in the patient's internal experience of "self" in interaction/rela-
tionship with an "other" (object). Building on the work of Jacobson (1964), Fairbairn
(1944, 1952), and other earlier object relations theorists, Kernberg expanded the
theory to emphasize the role of affects in the development of normal and pathological personality (Kernberg, 1975, 1984, 2004).

Object relations theory focuses on the developmental importance of an infant's
subjective experience as it interacts with its environment and caregivers. This theory posits the progression of psychological development on the achievement of
object constancy, a realistic and stable sense of the other; relinquishment of *infan-
tile omnipotence,* the feeling that one can control the environment; and tolerance
of *ambivalence*, the co-existence of positive and negative affects. In essence, the
developing child comes to integrate a sense of "me" that is built up over time in
interaction with the environment. Object relations always refer to representations
(internal models) of one's self in relation to another. We call the unit composed of a
representation of a particular self state in relation to a specific image of the other as

"dyads" to denote that there is an experience of self in interaction with the internal image of someone else. Furthermore, self/other representations are initially linked by the original emotional valence in which they were experienced. So, for example, a baby who is being fed while looking into the loving gaze of mother is a happy, loved baby (Good Self) in relationship to a good and loving mother/caretaker (Good Other). This dyad is embedded in the emotional experience of pleasure. However, a baby's painful experience of, for example, hunger (unhappy, abandoned, frightened self) in relation to a mother/caretaker who is not immediately available imprints the experience of mother/caretaker as uncaring, even persecutory, and bad. We then have an internal object representation of Neglected Self in relation to an Uncaring Other. These events, both pleasurable and unpleasurable, repeat countless times in the development and maturation of the growing child. Assuming that the caregiving and environment are "good enough," the child will develop a healthy, stable sense of self that permits a loving, trusting, flexible understanding of the other person in spite of the latter's shortcomings. The integration of both good and bad aspects of self and others is the hallmark of identity integration, a consolidated and coherent sense of self, and is the foundation of healthy interpersonal functioning. The process of identity consolidation is subject to the many influences that contribute to personality; temperament, genetic loading, and environment are chief among them.

In Kernberg's paradigm of BPD, the core element of disturbance lies in the failure of the developing child to achieve internal stability and coherence of self. We call this disturbance *identity diffusion*. Identity diffusion occurs under conditions of a biological predisposition to negative affects/aggression, of early childhood trauma, and/or of neglectful or misattuned caregiving. It is hypothesized that when negative experiences predominate in the early life of the child, there results a defensive sequestration (also known as *splitting*) of idealized (all good) and persecutory (all bad) representations of self and others. Splitting, a psychological make-up that underlies BPD symptoms, is a primitive response to aversive conditions—it serves to protect the good self and good other from the threat of the painful and persecutory images. It is believed that this is a normal developmental strategy in early infancy that is usually resolved as the infant matures. The problems of BPD and other personality disorders arise when splitting does not resolve due to either a temperamental predisposition to aggressive affect and/or aversive conditions that overwhelm the normal developmental trajectory.

Every developing individual has multiple sets of internal dyads, each a representation of self and other linked by the emotional valence in which they were embedded in the personality. Affects (emotions), via early bodily experiences of pleasure or pain, shape the formation of these primary internal representations. As described earlier, emotions become linked with self and object representations in the infant's mind as either highly pleasurable or intensely unpleasureable experiences. These positive and negative affective experiences accrue in the course of early development and become the building blocks for libidinal (loving) and aggressive (hostile, angry) drives (Kernberg, 2004; Sandler & Sandler, 1987). Thus, early affects constitute a primary motivational system (seek pleasurable experiences and avoid painful ones), cognitively framed to comprehend momentary experiences of self and other. These internalized self and other representations overlap with "internal working models" of interpersonal relationships posited by attachment theory (Main, Kaplan, & Cassidy, 1985).

In BPD, intense reactions can be activated by even minor experiences (triggers), flooding the patient with intense thoughts and emotions that are amplified beyond the objective reality of the situation. In short, the perception of everyday events, in particular those involving stress or emotion, is influenced by a person's repertoire of internal representations (Kernberg, 1975, 1984) that act as a lens through which he or she perceives the surrounding world. Object relations theory posits that people with borderline personality have a predominance of negative experience that overwhelms the developing personality such that good and bad representations of self and others remain separate (any proximity of the bad to the good representations would threaten them) and become fixed caricatures that populate the individual's internal world. This is the primitive coping mechanism known as "splitting." Good and bad aspects of self and other are mentally and emotionally sequestered from one another and do not become integrated into a more complex whole that provides a sense of coherence, continuity, richness, and context in the individual's experience of self and others (Clarkin, Yeomans, & Kernberg, 2006). So, for example, normal maturation, under good enough conditions, leads to a nuanced, realistic comprehension of the complexity of self and others, of the mental states and intentionality of the other. In this scenario, the mother who frustrates the baby's needs is also the same mother who, at other times, gratifies those needs; a balanced temperament and sufficient libidinal (loving) supplies foster the integration of those opposing experiences. In contrast, when the temperament of the child and the experiences with early caregivers are excessively negative, frustrating experiences (the "bad object") must be kept apart from good ones so that the "good/ideal object" is not overwhelmed and destroyed by the power of the emotions related to the bad one. Such unidimensional stereotypes interfere with the accurate perception and appropriate response to the social environment and lead to a vicious cycle of misperception and disruption in the intrapsychic and interpersonal realms. This chronic defensive splitting leads to and perpetuates identity diffusion. The extreme polarization of internal representations continues through the life course and results in the affective instability, interpersonal difficulties, anxiety, depression, and failure in work and love that we see in our patients with BPD. In short, there is no continuous, grounded, integrated sense of self to help individuals with intense temperaments navigate life's challenges.

TFP is designed to address what we consider to be the core problem of *identity diffusion,* which is characterized by a fragmented and unclear sense of both self and others. Recent research lends support to this perspective. Attachment research has linked BPD to classifications of insecure attachment—Anxious/Preoccupied and/or Disorganized/Unresolved—that presuppose a maladaptive internalized sense of self and attachment figures (Diamond, Stovall-McClough, Clarkin, & Levy, 2003; Main,

1999; Fonagy et al., 1996). Studies of mentalization have shown deficits in that capacity which render the individual unable to accurately assess the contents of one's own mind or the mind of the other (Bateman & Fonagy, 2004; Fonagy et al., 1996). Neurocognitive research with individuals with BPD has identified impairment in information processing and social cognition under the stress of negative affect states (Fertuck, Lenzenweger, Clarkin, Hoermann, & Stanley, 2006; Silbersweig et al., 2007). Kernberg (1975, 1984) and Gabbard et al. (Gabbard, Miller, & Martinez, 2006) have found support for the widely held observation that individuals with BPD are likely to form precipitous and negative, even hypervigilant, paranoid reactions in therapy. In the social recognition realm, there is some evidence for a "paradox" (Krohn, 1974) in which individuals with BPD show enhanced sensitivity to the emotional and mental states of others in the moment, but tend to attribute untrustworthiness to neutral human faces of strangers (Donegan et al., 2003; Fertuck, Grinband, Hirsch, Mann, & Stanley, 2009).

Brain imaging studies have identified the neural correlates of these social and cognitive processes that underlie the preponderance of negative affect and the inability to regulate aggression (Silbersweig et al., 2007) that have long been hypothesized to be a crucial aspect of BPD (Kernberg, 1975, 2004). Specifically, Silbersweig et al. (2007) found that hyperreactivity of the amygdala, particularly the left hemisphere, may predispose individuals with BPD to misinterpret neutral facial expressions, in or out of the treatment situation, as malevolent. Furthermore, this study revealed diminished function and reduced volume in the prefrontal regions, which impairs the ability to regulate or modulate affect and, hence, to mentalize; hyperresponsiveness of the HPA axis leading to a chronic state of hypervigilance and affective arousal (Rinne et al., 2002); reduced hippocampal volume leading to the tendency to automatically recapitulate self-object-affect schemas that are encoded as implicit (unconscious) procedural memories and to impaired capacity to generate autobiographical narratives based on both implicit and explicit memories (Gabbard et al., 2006); and reward circuitry associated with the nucleus accumbens, which, driven by dopamine secretion, strengthens the gratification from maladaptive relational patterns and the quest to repeat them (Gabbard et al., 2006, 2009). Although the majority of these factors are particularly evident in patients who have suffered childhood abuse, which encompasses many but not all borderline patients, Gabbard (2006) makes the interesting observation that distortions in the internal world of self and object may themselves catalyze overactivation of the amygdala. Consequently, interventions focused on those elements in the mind that determine the processing of affectively charged perceptions, especially in the social interpersonal sphere, are crucial in achieving symptom reduction, in enhancing the patient's sense of self and the quality of his interpersonal relations, and in improving work, love, and creative endeavors.

Before we go into a description of TFP, it should be noted that there is much debate within the field and among psychotherapy researchers about what, indeed, is at the heart of the disorder and how to best target the treatment. For example, dialectical behavior therapy (DBT) sees constitutional emotional dysregulation and deficits in mindfulness as the core of the disorder (Linehan, 1993; Wupperman, Neumann, & Axelrod, 2008). Mentalization-based therapy (MBT) sees a developmental deficit in the capacity to mentalize the emotional states and intentions of others as the core issue (Bateman & Fonagy, 2004). Gunderson and Lyons-Ruth (2008) consider the primary problem as interpersonal hypersensitivity and insecure working models of attachment. Each of these positions has articulated a model of treatment that targets its respective core issues. There is, of course, wisdom in each of these models. In our experience with treating BPD patients with TFP we have found that the greatest therapeutic gains can be made in focusing on the individual's experience of self and others in the setting of a biological predisposition to experiencing affects intensely and with diminished control.

Summary of Research Findings on the Efficacy of TFP

A number of studies have now demonstrated the effectiveness and efficacy of TFP for borderline pathologies. A full description of the method and findings from the two RCTs can be found elsewhere (Clarkin, Levy, Lenzenweger, & Kernberg, 2007; Doering et al., 2010; Fisher-Kern et al., 2008; Levy., Clarkin, Yeomans., Scott, Wasserman, & Kernberg, 2006; Levy, Meehan, Kelly, Reynoso, Weber, Clarkin, & Kernberg, 2006). In one study, 90 patients diagnosed with BPD were randomly assigned for 1 year to one of the three manualized outpatient treatments: twice-weekly TFP, DBT (Linehan, 1993), and supportive psychodynamic therapy (SPT; Appelbaum, 2005). All three groups had significant improvement in both global and social functioning and significant decreases in depression and anxiety. Patients treated in TFP and DBT, but not SPT, showed significant improvement in suicidality, depression, anger, and global functioning. Only the TFP-treated group demonstrated significant improvements in verbal assault, direct assault, and irritability; attachment style (to a more secure attachment); narrative coherence; and reflective function (Clarkin et al., 2007; Levy et al., 2006). The findings were replicated in a study comparing TFP to treatment delivered by experienced therapists in the community (Buchheim, Horz, Rentrop, Doering, & Fischer-Kern, 2012; Doering et al., 2010). In that study, TFP was superior in reducing suicidality, suicide attempts, BPD symptomatology, Structured Clinical Interview for DSM Disorders (SCID-II) data, inpatient hospitalizations, and dropouts, and in increasing global and personality functioning (Clarkin, Caligor, Stern, & Kernberg, 2004) and attachment (Buchheim et al., 2012).

TRANSFERENCE-FOCUSED PSYCHOTHERAPY: THE TREATMENT MODEL

TFP is a psychodynamic psychotherapy that draws heavily on standard psychoanalytic techniques but with certain modifications to accommodate borderline psychopathology. It is a twice-weekly individual therapy that allows for ancillary therapies (e.g., 12-step meetings) as needed. As suggested by the name, we attempt to focus very much on the transference. "Transference" is the term used to describe a very common experience in which an individual perceives a current situation through a prism of a past experience, usually with early caregivers, that has been internalized in the dyadic representation pairs of self and other described earlier. It is important to note that the representations internalized in the mind of an individual are not exact representations of past experience but are representations that have been modified, and often exaggerated, by the forces of the mind: fears, wishes, anxieties, and the like. When these internal representations are activate by a current experience, we unconsciously attribute (transfer) certain preconceptions, with their attendant emotions, to the present interaction that more appropriately belong to the internal reality. Transference is not a good or bad thing; it just is, and we all experience it in our everyday lives. In the therapeutic situation, the transference can be very useful in understanding the patient's internal representations of past experiences. The phenomenon is useful in understanding a patient's dynamics when made available for the patient's reflection—it leads to an awareness of internal representations of self and others that might not have been present before. The transference of healthier patients to the therapist is generally quite subtle and nuanced, and it is useful in understanding the patient's dynamics and is available for the patient's reflection. However, due to the predominance of splitting-based defenses in borderline patients, transference to the therapist is usually much more prominent and dramatic. The patient is more likely to see the therapist in extremes of all good or all bad, as indeed, they see themselves and others in the same way. Unlike better integrated patients, borderline patients rely to a great extent on projection (as a defense) of unwanted or disassociated aspects of themselves. Thus, they are likely to attribute to the therapist an aspect of their own internal world without being aware of it. For defensive purposes—to avoid awareness of elements of their own mind—they may have an unconscious need to see the therapist as an idealized or persecutory figure from their past. These transferences may shift rapidly within the session. This makes for a dizzying and chaotic presentation and can be difficult for the therapist to sort out.

Another complication in the treatment of borderline patients is that they may rely on "action" to discharge and avoid awareness of difficult emotions. This behavorial, rather than verbal, expression of emotion is what is known as "acting out." So, for example, self-harming behavior, missed sessions, and impulsivity of one sort or another are ways of acting out one's feelings. Treatment, therefore, must first be structured in such a way as to anticipate and limit acting out and provide a framework within which the patient can experience, observe, and reflect on what he or she is feeling. Only when a stable treatment setting framework, called a *frame*, has been achieved, can the self–other dyads that comprise the internal world of the patient emerge in the transference to the therapist in a way that can be reflected on helpfully and achieve change in the patient. As the treatment progresses, focusing on the patient's transference to the therapist (how the patient experiences the therapist at any given moment) gradually allows the patient to realize that there are a variety of distortions in the ways he or she is experiencing interactions with others and that these different ways can include distortions. The patient may be predisposed to seeing him- or herself as a perennial victim of uncaring and exploitive others. Or, at another point, the patient may idealize the therapist out of a need for a perfect caregiver who protects him or her from harm. At another moment, a patient may actively attempt to defeat the therapist as a defense against feelings of inferiority and neediness. These are all different examples of transferences that could occur in the course of a therapy.

Another way to think about this process in terms of attachment theory, is to consider that the treatment situation in TFP activates the primary internal working models of attachment, which in the case of more severely disturbed patients are likely to be insecure, multiple, contradictory, and conflictual in nature (Diamond et al., 2003; Fonagy & Bateman, 2005; Main, 1999). One of the treatment goals is to move the patient toward increased attachment security by fostering identity integration.

THE TREATMENT CONTRACT

To provide the conditions necessary to facilitate a safe and stable space in which to conduct therapy, both patient and therapist must be protected from acting on powerful emotions that may arise. A "pre-therapy" phase of treatment involves assessing the patient, discussing the diagnosis, and establishing this safe and stable space. After the therapist has completed the evaluation, he or she discusses the diagnostic impression and treatment options. If TFP is the recommended treatment, the therapist moves on to the issue of the contract, which establishes the parameters and responsibilities of both parties. The contract is established through discussion with the patient of the nature of the patient's problems as psychological; that is, as a core identity disturbance contributing to rapidly shifting intense affect activation, expressed primarily through behaviors. The guidelines involved in the contract include a description of the responsibilities of both patient and therapist, including recommendations for how to manage the acting out behaviors that allow the patient to bypass conscious experience of unwanted thoughts and feelings and that thereby represent a threat to the exploration of the patient's mind that is at the heart of the treatment. Typical parameters include agreement on scheduling, fee payment, the extent of contact between sessions, and honest and open communication. In addition, agreement must be reached on how to manage any self-harm, suicidality, drugs, or alcohol and eating disorders that have been identified during the evaluation. It is vital that the patient is willing to take a measure of responsibility for managing these issues, using ancillary resources if necessary, so that the therapist is not put in the position of crisis manager. It is not possible to manage crises and explore the patient's internal world simultaneously; they are two different roles. The goal of the contract is to provide a stable environment so that the patient's conscious and unconscious feelings can be explored without interference from external crises.

THE THERAPEUTIC PROCESS

Because TFP focuses on the patient's repertoire of impulses and defenses as expressed primarily through interpersonal interactions, the continuity provided by twice weekly sessions allows these dynamics to surface in the interaction with the therapist. As this occurs, the therapist focuses on *clarifying* with the patient the relationship between their perceptions and feelings. In attending to the patient's material, the therapist relies on three channels of communication: (1) what the patient is saying verbally, (2) how the patient is communicating the material (i.e., tone, facial expressions, body language), and (3) close attention by the therapist to his or her own internal reactions to the patient's material. This last item is what is meant by the term "countertransference reactions." Different dissociated aspects of the patient's internal world of object relations will be conveyed alternately through each of these channels. Taken together, the verbal, nonverbal, and one's countertransference help the therapist to reflect on what is being activated within the patient.

Exploring the patient's internal world inevitably reveals internal conflicts between competing wishes (loving and hating feelings) and between wishes and internal or external prohibitions to the wishes. The therapist adopts a stance of *neutrality* in relation to the forces involved in the patient's conflicts—both intrapsychic and interpersonal. Technical neutrality should not be confused with the stereotype of Freudian analytic silence. We no longer think of the therapist as a blank slate onto which the patient projects. A warm interest in the patient is conveyed at all times, but the therapist does not side with the patient's urges to act or with the patient's urges to inhibit an action (keeping in mind that BPD pathology can present as both excessive action and excessive inhibition), except in situations where there is undue risk of harm. Rather, the therapist takes the position of observing the patient's conflict and engaging the patient to observe it as well, so that the patient will be better able to resolve it him- or herself and thus gain more autonomy. A focus on delineating conflicts as residing *within* the patient, rather than *between* the patient and the therapist, is essential since patients often experience intense anxiety from their conflicts without a clear awareness of the internal conflict itself due to their tendency to project aspects of self onto others. The therapist's avoiding siding with one or the other side of the conflict helps the patient to recognize and reflect on conflicts, thereby enhancing the ability to successfully deal with feelings rather than be at the mercy of them. So, to sum up, the therapist's neutrality assists both in the reactivation of the patient's characteristic object relations dyads and helps the patient to see, accept, and eventually integrate parts of the self that previously were not consciously tolerated and therefore were behaviorally enacted or projected. By fostering reflection and containment through the identification of self–object dyads and their linking affects, the repetitive re-enactment of these dyads is short-circuited as the patient becomes increasingly capable of cognitively reframing his or her emotional states. Rigid and chaotic reactions become more flexible and nuanced.

Although every treatment has its own trajectory, TFP generally progresses along the following lines: during the initial phases of therapy, the primary task is to tolerate the affective chaos and confusion in the patient. The early phase of treatment may be marked by testing the limits of the therapist and various acting-out behaviors. We have found that the sessions settle down over time as the patient is more able to contain feelings and impulses and discuss rather than act on difficult feelings. The twice-weekly frame provides a structure that patients find helpful. The next phase involves making sense of the chaos and formulating a hypothesis of self–other representations that are manifest in the patient's affect states in the here and now. The same applies to the type of patient with BPD who presents with an affective deadness: this, too, represents a window into the patient's internal world of object relations.

Subsequent phases involve exploring role reversals in the transference as the patient alternates between the self and object poles of the dyadic constellations evoked in the sessions. Again, because self and object representations are embedded and elaborated in the developing personality in the context of heightened affect states, dyads are likely to express prototypical affiliative/loving or aggressive strivings and prohibitions, but the chronic influence of primitive defensive splitting mechanisms results in extreme, highly caricatured representations of self and other (all good/all bad, victim/persecutor) and in distortions of the interpersonal field.

As the patient's repertoire of object relational dyads emerge in the transference, it is important to be alert to role oscillations: the patient alternately identifies with each pole of a dyad. For instance, a patient may be complaining that the therapist is not doing enough to help them with their suffering. This suggests that the patient is having, in this moment, an experience of a self that is being neglected and uncared for. This logically, then, attributes to the therapist/other the characteristics of being callous, uncaring, self-involved, withholding. If, when the therapist points out the dynamics that seem to be implied in the patient's comments so that they can be reflected upon, the patient reacts in a hostile withdrawal or an angry outburst. The power to withhold, dismiss, and devalue, which a moment ago was being attributed to the therapist, now resides within the patient, and the roles have reversed. The patient is now treating the therapist as she had been feeling treated a minute ago. Such oscillations generally occur outside of the patient's (and, sometimes, the therapist's) awareness as the patient attempts to project or dissociate from unwanted aspects of self (anger, helplessness, self-pity, neediness, etc.). Such oscillation of polarized experience in the transference (i.e., who is doing what to whom) is very characteristic of primitive splitting mechanisms and identity diffusion. Through numerous iterations of these developments in the transference, the patient is gradually able to recognize the characteristic ways in which he or she manages difficult affect states and how that might be contributing to his or her difficulties.

In the more advanced phase of treatment, once a greater tolerance and capacity to reflect has been achieved, it is time to begin to explore with the patient the ways in which different opposite dyads may be defending against each other. The systematic interpretation of defensively split-off dyads, as they are lived out in the transference,

can gradually lead to an understanding of the underlying motivation that unconsciously keeps these opposite sides of internal experience radically separated from
each other. Although this separation of positive and negative affects may not correspond to the complexity of the world, it can feel like the safest option to protect
oneself against the danger that the internal aggressive affects pose to the mental
representations of ideal caretaking and nurturing. These phases of treatment should
serve as a guideline only since no treatment unfolds in a purely linear fashion. Under
stress, patients may temporarily retreat from previously attained integrated states to
a period of regression.

THE INTERPRETATIVE PROCESS

This movement through the phases of TFP is effected predominantly through a stepwise process of interpretation that roughly corresponds to the sequences of treatment. Clarification, confrontation, and interpretation of the patient's dominant object
relational worlds, as they are experienced with the therapist as well as with external
figures, help the patient to expand his reflective capacities and move toward identity
consolidation as the need to rely on projective mechanisms to deal with feelings
dissipates. The therapist appeals to the patient's capacity to reflect on internal states
with the goal of increasing the ability to cognitively and coherently contextualize
affects and the intentional states of others in interpersonal interactions. By engaging
the patient in identifying and observing various scenarios as they are experienced in
the transference, the patient comes to understand his or her experiences as construc-
tions rather than as veridical images of self and others. The therapist then helps the
patient to understand the anxieties that make it difficult to integrate primitive posi-
tive/affiliative/libidinal and negative/aggressive affects.

Initially, the capacity of the patient with BPD to "hold onto" a clear distinction
between self and other is defective because of a predominance of splitting and projective mechanisms that prevent the attainment of an integrated sense of self and
other. The ability to perceive the intentionality (motivations) of others as separate
from one's own motivations (which, as well, may not be understood) is severely
compromised. Therefore, our interpretative process begins with an effort to clarify how the patient experiences an affect or an action expression of an affect in
the here-and-now representations of self and other. These representations are frequently characterized by affects and impulses that are "unacceptable," whether they
be aggressive or libidinal in nature. Bringing these underlying representations to
conscious awareness allows the patient to develop awareness and empathy for the
motivation that lies beneath such unwanted feelings; in turn, it fosters further elabo-
ration of the accuracy of one's perceptions and responses. When successfully carried out, this increased understanding of self and other in the momentary experience
with the therapist helps the patient to tolerate difficult thoughts and feelings without having to project, dissociate, or discharge them through action or somatization.
Most importantly, increased tolerance and contextualization of experience leads to a

decrease in self-condemnation of one's feelings and a more benign apprehension of the complexity and intentions of others.

Thus, the interpretative process begins with clarification, which invites the patient to say more about what is being felt and to ensure that both parties understand the patient's experience. In this sense, clarification is similar to the concept of mentalization in that the goal is to help the patient accurately perceive his or her own internal state and that of the person with whom the interaction is occurring. This pertains to any communication from the patient but is especially relevant when the patient is referring to a reaction to the therapist since this provides an opportunity to jointly explore a shared experience, one in which the affect is immediately accessible for observation and reflection.

The second step of interpretation is confrontation, by which we invite the patient to reflect on contradictions that appear to represent split-off elements of the patient's internal world. Contradictions may arise between what is being verbally communicated and what is, simultaneously, being behaviorally communicated. For instance, the patient is speaking about a conversation with a boss that went well while drumming her fingers or biting her lip. Contradictions may arise, seemingly out of awareness, with what the patient has communicated on other occasions or when content and affect are not congruent. The technique of confrontation tactfully presents the patient with these contradictions, of which he or she is often unaware. As patients can begin to reflect (nondefensively) on these disparities, they develop an awareness and appreciation of their own complexity.

The third level of the interpretative process helps the patient become aware of how the understanding of a particular affect in relation to an object could be related to other conflicting affects that exist within themselves. For example, the therapist might say: "It may be that the reason you talk about dropping out of treatment after each session where we have experienced a positive contact is because a part of you is convinced that the positive feeling isn't real, could not last, or might even be a trick that will lead to my hurting you. If this were true, it would make sense that you would want to protect yourself and get away from me, and explain that you seem to be more comfortable in hostile relations." A later stage of interpretation might focus on the patient's split-off and projected identification with an aggressive part of him- or herself that makes it impossible to escape from relations that take on a negative tone and that, once understood, could be integrated, so that the awareness of the aggressive part both removes it as an obstacle to more successful libidinal fulfillment and allows for adaptive uses of aggression, such as striving for higher achievement.

Interpretations in TFP are largely based on an appreciation of the psychological structure of the patient as observed in the here and now of the patient's life. The traditional psychoanalytic focus on historical antecedents is helpful insofar as those antecedents help contextualize the patient's present life. Early childhood experience is incorporated in the process of addressing how the patient's expectation of the other may be largely determined by the makeup of her own mind: "Your fear that if you allow yourself to feel close to me is understandable, given that your early experience in life was to be humiliated when you tried to get close [an interpretation of the past]. It could also be that you are afraid of feeling close to me because you assume that I could react to you as you often do to others. . . . One false move and they are out of your life forever [an interpretation of current psychological structure]."

The interpretive process and the phases of TFP are overlapping but not synonymous in that, at almost any point in the process, one might go through each step of interpretation in one session or stay in one phase of interpretation for many sessions, depending on the patient's progress.

CLINICAL ILLUSTRATION

We are aware that the TFP strategy of helping the patient resolve the externalization of unbearable self-states is a difficult challenge that may temporarily increase the patient's anxiety by questioning his defensive system. However, TFP advises the therapist and the patient to work actively in the transference (usually the transference relates to how the patient is experiencing and relating to the therapist) to identify aspects of the patient that cannot be tolerated and therefore tend be projected onto others, notably, the therapist. In addition, representations (often unconscious) of others as persecutory objects (Gabbard, 2009; Gabbard et al., 2006; Kernberg, 2004), or what Fonagy refers to as the "alien self" (Fonagy, Gergely, Jurist, & Target, 2002), also interfere with nuanced and realistic interactions with significant others. The therapist's consistent attention to and authentic interest in the patient, combined with the therapist's ability to contain (sit with) intense affects in the interaction, help the patient tolerate the process of becoming aware of previously unacceptable internal states. This process ultimately leads the negative affects associated with the unacceptable internal representations to be modulated and the internal world to be enriched with a fuller, more nuanced range of affective coloring. All of this, in turn, helps to diminish the intensity of negative affects, particularly aggression, that interfere with the healthy experience of an expression of loving affects, leading to improved interpersonal functioning in addition to symptom change. The following clinical vignette illustrates our approach and many of the key elements of TFP. The material is a composite and all identifying elements have been disguised.

CASE STUDY: TRANSFERENCE-FOCUSED PSYCHOTHERAPY

Jennifer was 39 years old at the time she was referred for TFP treatment. She had recently been discharged from a 3-week inpatient hospitalization and was currently in a partial day hospitalization program, attending groups 5 days a week. She had been admitted for inpatient treatment by her therapist for severe depression and unremitting suicidal ideation subsequent to the break-up of a 3-year relationship. Although she had been in treatment since her college days, this was her first hospitalization. She had never made an actual suicide attempt and had no history of cutting or self-injury, with the exception of severe nail biting.

Jennifer had been in numerous short-term and several long-term relationships, but she had never married and had no children. She was the oldest of four children and grew up in a rather remote area of a southern state. She described her childhood as unhappy and lonely. She was significantly affected by her discovery, at age 7, of her mother's affair with a family friend—a secret that she kept to herself, but one which fostered an intense curiosity and mistrust in her interactions with others. She herself was markedly secretive and guarded in her interactions with others. Also of note was the fact that her father was the undertaker in the small, remote town in which she grew up. This, too, seemed to stimulate an intense, dark curiosity in her. She was highly intelligent and exceptionally artistically talented, which served as protective barriers against a part of her that was very self-destructive.

Jennifer described her mother as loud, intrusive, demanding, and embarrassing. For many years she lived in fear that her mother would run off with the other man, leaving her with her father, whom she described as quiet and inscrutable, but with an unpredictable anger. There was no notable psychiatric history in her family.

The pre-therapy assessment of Jennifer established a diagnosis of BPD with narcissistic and masochistic features. She had a history, dating back to latency, of depression, fear of abandonment as evidenced by a clinging dependency despite chronic anxiety and paranoia in interpersonal interactions, identity diffusion, impulsivity, and alcohol abuse. Prominent narcissistic features were noted in the patient's report of grandiose and omnipotent fantasies concerning success, fame, and uniqueness.

The contract with Jennifer established, with the usual details of scheduling, fees, missed sessions, lateness, and free association of her thoughts and feelings, particularly her suicidal ideation. She had already stopped drinking before she came to TFP, and continued abstinence was addressed as one of her responsibilities to the treatment.

Although she had been in two previous treatments of many years' duration in which she had intense dependent and erotic transferences, the supportive nature of these treatments made no impact on her underlying personality organization and, indeed, seemed to facilitate chronic regression/dependent behaviors.

The initial treatment course was marked by the patient's intense dislike of the therapist. This was expressed by a haughty, derogatory attitude, alternating with a hostile silence and avoidance of eye contact. Attempts to clarify the patient's experience revealed that the patient felt the therapist was someone she could not relate to in terms of common interests, style of dress (the therapist was too "preppy"), or life experience. In short, she didn't think the therapist was "hip" enough to understand her. However, the patient never missed a session or came late. During sessions, while avoiding eye contact, she drummed her fingers, jiggled her leg, and shifted in her chair as far away from the therapist as she could get, as if in the presence of a mortal danger. She frequently cleared her throat in an almost theatrical way and often brought her fingers to her mouth when she was speaking. The therapist confronted (brought the patient's attention to) the patient with these behavioral mannerisms, which seemed to be at odds with the patient's stated devaluation of her, and asked the patient to reflect on the possibility that her surface attitude of fear and contempt might be protecting her from her own anxieties about how she was being perceived by the therapist. The therapist's formulation of the transference, given the contradicting material, was that of a self who was defective and dismissed in relation to another who was imperious and rejecting. Furthermore, it seemed that these roles oscillated, so that in some moments the patient seemed to identify with a waif-like child who could be abandoned at any moment, whereas at other moments she was the haughtily dismissive one holding the power to cast out her inferiors, with the therapist cast in the complementary roles. This clearly resonated with Jennifer, although it would be repeated many times before the patient could tolerate the idea that her expressed hatred defended against an intense longing for a special place in the mind and heart of the therapist/mother. The patient was eventually able to reveal that her mother was always telling her to go outside so that she could be alone in the house with her lover. The patient related how she would peep through the windows to see what was going on with her mother. The waif-like child, always on the outside looking in, became a working metaphor for the patient's split-off libidinal longings.

However, that is only half the picture. Through repeated interpretation of the transference enactments, the patient was gradually able to see that the self-representation of the rejected child, ego syntonic in that the bad was in the other person who was mistreating her, protected her from awareness of her own aggression and capacity to be critical and even sadistic at times, which was undeniably present in the transference. So, here we have an example of the first and second stages of interpretation. Clarification of what is in the patient's mind, confrontation of the apparent contradictions between what the patient is saying ("You are inferior and not worth my time"), and the nonverbal cues that were saying "I'm a helpless, defenseless child who is at the mercy of a malevolent other." The therapist's countertransference was particularly useful in that the patient was frequently silent and unresponsive, refusing eye contact, while appearing bored or, alternately, highly anxious (fingers drumming). When the patient did speak it was in a halting, disjointed manner that trailed off without an evident point, inducing the therapist to pull from the patient in an effort to make meaning of the patient's communication, only to have these efforts thwarted by the patient's seeming refusal or inability to link her thoughts together to some conclusion that would allow both patient and therapist to understand what the patient was trying to say. These "attacks on linking" (Bion, 1967), resulted in a muddle of confusion and frustration for both parties. Although the therapist often felt deskilled and tortured by these apparent impasses, they were, nonetheless, important clues to what was being activated in the transference. Gradually, over the course of many months, the therapist was able to interpret the disavowed aggression and sadistic pleasure that the patient got from being so omnipotently withholding and controlling while remaining consciously identified with a self-state of the defenseless victim of a bad object. As the patient was able to recognize and reflect on her own aggression and sadism, the stage was set for next level of interpretation. It was significant that this patient was rarely able to be reflective during the sessions but clearly was so once out of the office. And despite the sullen withholding and haughty dismissal of the therapist's offerings, she was intensely curious about the therapist's personal life, doing repeated and extensive research on the Internet in an attempt to learn any detail she could. She located the home address of the therapist and drove a considerable distance to see where she lived, a reenactment of peeping through the window at mother. Invitations to elaborate her fantasies often revealed a projection onto the therapist of social differences that would preclude commonality and closeness (most of them wrong). The therapist used this information to hypothesize that the surface dyad of victim–persecutor, was defending against a deep longing for love and protection that could not be risked for fear of being humiliated and spurned. The patient responded to this by saying: "Chosen. I wanted to be the one she chose instead of him." This proved to be a turning point in the treatment because the patient was then able to see how this longing to be chosen above all others had destroyed many relationships in her past and, very importantly, how this played out in her treatment as she actively worked to destroy the therapist whom she desperately wanted to choose only her. Many aspects of her self-defeating behavior decreased as the patient was more able to tolerate her aggression, envy, and grandiosity. She was able to establish a "real" dependency on the therapist as, over time, she no longer had to deny or discharge her more loving feelings and longings.

CONCLUSION

TFP is a specialized treatment that has been shown to be effective with persons with a range of personality disorders. We believe that, together with a treatment contract that establishes with the patient the conditions necessary to conduct this type of intensive treatment, close attention to the transference and the interpretation of transferential developments are what facilitate integration of different and often contradictory aspects of experience. Interpretation is simply a hypothesis offered by the therapist for the patient's consideration on why a certain thing may be happening or why the patient may be feeling a certain way. As patients learn more about how they perceive themselves and others by discussing how they experience the interaction with the therapist, they begin to recognize deeply embedded patterns in interpersonal interactions that have caused considerable difficulty and unhappiness in their lives. We discussed earlier how these patients have a tendency toward black-or-white, all-or-nothing thinking. Coming to understand and accept themselves in more nuanced, complex ways also allows them to see others as whole (and separate) people who operate out of their own set of impulses, defenses, conflicts, wishes, and intentions. The need to maintain splits between all-good and all-bad experience is reduced, as is extreme, action-oriented defense against what once felt intolerable. Assisted by interpretation of internal conflicts, the patient becomes able to reflect, to think about his or her thinking, and to take perspective on the actions and motivations of others. This leads to a more stable sense of self and others across time and situations, or what we call *identity integration*. The patient becomes more able to tolerate frustration, anxiety, and disappointment and, perhaps more importantly, able to allow positive, loving feelings to emerge. As internal chaos is reduced, investment in work, love, friendship, and creativity becomes possible.

REFERENCES

Appelbaum, A. H. (2005). Supportive psychotherapy. In J. M. Oldham, A. E. Skodol, & D. S. Bender (Eds.), *The American Psychiatric Publishing textbook of personality disorders* (pp. 335–346). Washington, DC: American Psychiatric Publishing.

Bateman, A., & Fonagy, P. (2004). *Psychotherapy for borderline personality disorder: Mentalization-based treatment.* New York: Oxford University Press.

Bion, W. R. (1967). *Second thoughts.* Northvale, NJ: Aronson.

Buchheim, A., Horz, S., Rentrop, M., Doering, S., & Fischer-Kern, M. (2012). *Attachment status before and after one year of transference-focused psychotherapy (TFP) versus therapy as usual (TAU) in patients with borderline personality disorder.* Paper presented at the 2nd International Congress on Borderline Personality Disorder and Allied Disorders, The Netherlands.

Clarkin, J. F., Caligor, E., Stern, B. L., & Kernberg, O. F. (2004). *The structured interview of personality organization.* Unpublished manuscript, Personality Disorders Institute, Weill Medical College of Cornell Univ., White Plains, NY.

Clarkin, J. F., Levy, K. N., Lenzenweger, M. F., & Kernberg, O. F. (2007). Evaluating three treatments for borderline personality disorder: A multiwave study. *American Journal of Psychiatry, 164,* 922–928.

Clarkin, J. F., Yeomans, F. E., & Kernberg, O. F. (2006). *Psychotherapy for borderline personality: Focusing on object relations.* Washington, DC: American Psychiatric Publishing.

Diamond, D., Stovall-McClough, C., Clarkin, J. F., & Levy, K. N. (2003). Patient–therapist attachment in the treatment of borderline personality disorder. *Bulletin of the Menninger Clinic, 67*(3), 224–257.

Doering, S., Hörz, S., Rentrop, M., . . . Buchheim, P. (2010). Transference-focused psychotherapy v. treatment by community psychotherapists for borderline personality disorder: A randomized controlled trial. *British Journal of Psychiatry, 196,* 389–395.

Donegan, N. H., Sanislow, C. A., Blumberg, H. P., Fulbright, R. K., Lacadie, C., Skudlarski, P., . . . Wexler, B. E. (2003). Amygdala hyperreactivity in borderline personality disorder: Implications for emotional dysregulation. *Biological Psychiatry, 54,* 1284–1293.

Fairbairn, W. R. D. (1944). *Endopsychic structure considered in terms of object-relationships. An object-relations theory of the personality.* New York: Basic Books.

Fairbairn, W. R. D. (1952). *A synopsis of the development of the author's views regarding the structure of the personality. An object-relations theory of the personality.* New York: Basic Books.

Fertuck, E. A., Grinband, J., Hirsch, J., Mann, J. J., & Stanley, B. (2009, January). *Convergence of psychoanalytic and social neuroscience approaches to borderline personality disorder.* Presented at the meeting of the American Psychoanalytic Association, New York.

Fertuck, E. A., Lenzenweger, M. F., Clarkin, J. F., Hoermann, S., & Stanley, B. (2006). Executive neurocognition, memory systems, and borderline personality disorder. *Clinical Psychology Review, 26*, 346–375.

Fonagy, P., & Bateman, A. (2005). Attachment theory and mentalization-oriented model of borderline personality disorder. In J. M. Oldham, A. E. Skodol, & D. S. Bender (Eds.), *The American Psychiatric Publishing textbook of personality disorders* (pp. 187–207). Arlington, VA: American Psychiatric Publishing.

Fonagy, P., Gergely, G., Jurist, E. L., & Target, M. (2002). *Affect regulation, mentalization, and the development of the self.* New York: Other Press.

Fonagy, P., Leigh, T., Steele, M., Steele, H., Kennedy, R., Mattoon, G., ... Gerber, A. (1996). The relation of attachment status, psychiatric classification and response to psychotherapy. *Journal of Consulting and Clinical Psychology, 64*, 22–31.

Gabbard, G. O. (2009, January). *The interface of neurobiology and psychoanalytic thinking in borderline personality disorders.* Presented at the meeting of the American Psychoanalytic Association, New York.

Gabbard, G. O., Miller, L., & Martinez, M. (2006). A neurobiological perspective on mentalizing and internal object relations in traumatized patients with borderline personality disorder. In J. G. Allen & P. Fonagy (Eds.), *Handbook of mentalization-based treatment* (pp. 123–140). Chichester, UK: John Wiley & Sons.

Gunderson, J. G., & Lyons-Ruth, K. (2008). BPD's interpersonal hypersensitivity phenotype: A gene-environment-developmental model. *Journal Personal Disorders, 22*(1), 22–41.

Jacobson, E. (1964). *The self and the object world.* New York: International Universities Press.

Kernberg, O. F. (1975). *Borderline conditions and pathological narcissism.* New York: Jason Aronson.

Kernberg, O. F. (1984). *Severe personality disorders: Psychotherapeutic strategies.* New Haven, CT: Yale University Press.

Kernberg, O. F. (2004). *Aggressivity, narcissism, and self-destructiveness in the psychotherapeutic relationship: New developments in the psychopathology and psychotherapy of severe personality disorders.* New Haven, CT: Yale University Press.

Krohn, A. J. (1974). Borderline "empathy" and differentiation of object representations: A contribution to the psychology of object relations. *International Journal of Psychiatry, 3*,142–165.

Levy, K. N., Clarkin, J. F., Yeomans, F. E., Scott, L. N., Wasserman, R. H., & Kernberg, O. F. (2006). The mechanisms of change in the treatment of borderline personality disorder with transference-focused psychotherapy. *Journal of Clinical Psychology, 62*(4), 481–502.

Levy, K. N., Meehan, K. N., Kelly, K. M., Reynoso, J. S., Weber, M., Clarkin, J. F., & Kerberg, O. F. (2006). Change in attachment patterns and reflective function in a randomized control trial of Transference Focused Psychotherapy for borderline personality disorder. *Journal of Consulting and Clinical Psychology, 74*, 6,1027–1040.

Linehan, M. M. (1993). *Cognitive-behavioral treatment of borderline personality disorder.* New York: Guilford.

Main, M. (1999). Attachment theory: Eighteen points with suggestions for future studies. In J. Cassidy & P. Shaver (Eds.), *Handbook of attachment: Theory, research, and clinical applications* (pp. 845–887). New York: Guilford.

Main, M., & Goldwyn, R. (1998). *Adult attachment scoring and classification system.* Unpublished scoring manual, Department of Psychology, University of California, Berkeley.

Main, M., Kaplan, N., & Cassidy, J. (1985). Security in infancy, childhood, and adulthood: A move to the level of representation. *Monographs of the Society for Research in Child Development, 50*(1–2, Serial No. 209), 66–104.

Rinne, T., de Kloet, E. R., Wouters, L., ... van den Brink, W. (2002). Hyperresponsiveness of hypothalamic-pituitary-adrenal axis to combined dexamethasone/corticotrophin-releasing hormone challenge in female borderline personality disorder subjects with a history of sustained childhood abuse. *Biological Psychiatry, 52*, 1102–1112.

Sandler, J., & Sandler, A. M. (1987). The past unconscious, the present unconscious, and the vicissitudes of guilt. *International Journal of Psycho-Analysis, 8*, 331–341.

Silbersweig, D., Clarkin, J., Goldstein, M., Kernberg, O. F., Tuescher, O., . . . Stern, E. (2007). Failure of frontolimbic inhibitory function in the context of negative emotion in borderline personality disorder. *American Journal of Psychiatry, 164*(12), 1832–1841.

Wupperman, P., Neumann, C. S., & Axelrod, S. R. (2008). Do deficits in mindfulness underlie borderline personality features and core difficulties ? *Journal of Personality Disorders, 22*, 466–482.

/// 16 /// Dialectical Behavior Therapy

SHIREEN L. RIZVI AND KRISTEN M. ROMAN

INTRODUCTION

Dialectical behavior therapy (DBT), originally developed by Marsha Linehan for individuals with borderline personality disorder (BPD) who engaged in suicidal and nonsuicidal self-injurious behaviors, has become the most well-known and widely practiced psychosocial treatment for BPD. DBT is a cognitive-behavioral treatment (CBT) described fully in the treatment manuals by Linehan (1993a, 1993b) and summarized in this chapter. Despite its origins as an outpatient treatment for suicidal individuals with BPD, it has since been adapted across multiple settings, disorders, and populations (for a review, see Rizvi, Steffel, & Carson Wong, 2013).

DBT is informed by three overarching sets of theories and strategies: dialectics, change, and acceptance. In DBT, *dialectics* refers to both a set of therapeutic strategies as well as to a particular worldview that the therapist and client are encouraged to adopt. With regard to the latter, dialectical theory states that reality is interrelated and connected, made of opposing forces, and constantly changing or in flux. According to the philosophy, opposite views can exist in one person at the same time (e.g., "I want to die" and "I want to live," or "I wish to be alone" and "I want to be with others"), leading to tension and conflict, and yet this conflict may be what is necessary to bring about change. In the treatment, these opposite views are often expressed via the fundamental dialectic—that between acceptance and change. Specifically, the treatment team is charged with accepting the clients as they currently are while simultaneously working to help them change to reduce problem behaviors, achieve their goals, and develop a life worth living.

Change is best exemplified in DBT through the use of cognitive-behavioral techniques. At its core, DBT is a behavioral treatment, and much of the treatment strategies employed in any given session draw from behavioral theory and research. Behavioral theory suggests that all behavior, adaptive and maladaptive, can be conceptualized according to the principles of classical and operant conditioning and observational learning (modeling). To change behavior, one must look to the behavioral factors that contribute to the development and/or maintenance of the behavior. These factors include skills deficits, problematic contingencies, deficiencies in emotional processing, and/or cognitive factors. Thus, DBT focuses on skills training, contingency management, exposure, and cognitive restructuring in order to effectively modify behavior.

The third overarching component of DBT involves active acceptance of the client and the nature of reality exactly as they are. Acceptance of the client is best communicated through the use of specific therapeutic strategies designed to validate clients (i.e., communicate understanding of clients exactly as they are and their inherent capacity to change; Linehan, 1993a, 1997). Linehan (1997) has outlined six levels of validation, which include being awake and attentive in the session; accurately reflecting a client's thoughts and feelings; reflecting thoughts and feelings with an added level of accurate interpretation; validating the client's behavior based on learning history, biology, and/or normative behavior; and validating the person as an individual of equal status rather than an individual with a disorder. These validation strategies often help a client become more emotionally regulated which, in turn, leads to greater capacity for effective problem-solving.

Despite the existence of other psychosocial treatments for BPD, DBT was the first treatment to be subjected to rigorous research trials to determine its efficacy. Perhaps due to its behavioral foundations, Linehan developed DBT in ways to encourage behavioral specificity and empiricism. As such, clinical decision-making is guided by existing research data or, in the absence of such data, done in a way that promotes the capacity to objectively measure success or failure.

CONCEPTUALIZATION OF BPD WITHIN DBT

BPD is a disorder often associated with extreme stigma. Clinical writings on BPD, especially those published prior to the emergence of DBT, are often filled with judgmental statements about the nature of individuals with BPD. In contrast, Linehan specifically conceptualizes BPD in a nonpejorative manner. The presumption is that removing judgments will allow for a more accurate assessment of problems (and thus lead to more effective and efficient solutions) as well as enable the therapist to be more compassionate and helpful, rather than dismissive or critical. This nonpejorative and empathic conceptualization is evidenced in Linehan's biosocial theory on the development of BPD, client and therapist assumptions of treatment, and intended nature of the therapeutic relationship.

Biosocial Theory

The biosocial theory of BPD that informs DBT (Linehan, 1993a) suggests that pervasive emotion dysregulation is the core feature of BPD and that this dysregulation evolves from a transaction over time between two factors: a biological dysfunction in the "emotion regulation system" and an invalidating environment. The biological dysfunction is presumed to be characterized by a heightened emotional sensitivity, greater emotional reactivity, and slower return to emotional baseline. Based on empirical research that has been conducted since Linehan's original formulation, an update to the biosocial theory suggests that an early biological vulnerability expressed in childhood as impulsivity is also an important contributer to the development of BPD (Crowell, Beauchaine, & Linehan, 2009).

The second factor, the invalidating environment, is defined as an environment that chronically and pervasively invalidates an individual's communication of internal experiences, including emotions. Or, emotions expressed by the individual may be intermittently attended to, such that communication of emotion (e.g., "I'm feeling sad") may be ignored or invalidated until they reach a high enough level (e.g., uncontrollable sobbing, statements about wanting to die) that someone in the environment finally attends to them. When this happens, the individual learns, often without conscious awareness, that intense emotional expressions are necessary in order to get appropriate attention from others. Another characteristic of the invalidating environment is that it doesn't model or otherwise teach effective emotion regulation strategies so that the individual does not learn how to understand or regulate emotional experience. It is important to note that the invalidating environment can refer to the client's early family life or could refer to other environments that were impactful such as school environment, early military experiences, or peer network. That is, DBT does not assume that the client's early caregivers were part of the invalidating environment in the absence of assessment.

A key aspect of the biosocial theory is that the relationship between the biological vulnerability and invalidating environment is presumed to be *transactional*. That is, each factor is proposed to affect and influence the other, such that the more "emotional" the individual is, the greater the likelihood of receiving invalidation from the environment, which leads to greater emotionality, and so forth. This transactional aspect of the biosocial theory highlights how a disorder can become more severe over time. In addition, in order for change to occur, both emotion dysregulation and invalidation (by self or others) need to be addressed.

Client and Therapist Assumptions

Linehan further outlined basic assumptions about clients and therapists that contribute to the nonpejorative and accepting approach to treating BPD (Linehan, 1993a). Assumptions about clients include that clients are doing the best they can and want to improve, the lives of suicidal clients with BPD are unbearable as they are currently being lived, and clients need to try harder and be more motivated to change. Perhaps the most important assumption about clients is that clients cannot fail in DBT. However, the treatment itself, therapists, and the consultation team can fail (see Rizvi, 2011). This assumption places the responsibility on the treatment team to determine those factors most likely to lead to a client's success in DBT. It also reminds therapists that DBT as a treatment is fallible and might not be the best treatment for all clients at all times.

Similarly, there is a set of assumptions about therapists and therapy in DBT. These assumptions include that the most caring thing a therapist can do is to help clients change in ways that bring them closer to their long-term goals; the therapeutic relationship is a real relationship between equals; principles of behavior are universal, meaning that they also affect therapists, not just clients; and therapists treating clients with multiple, severe problems need support. This last assumption highlights the consultation team as an essential component of treatment. These assumptions guide therapists to implement DBT as effectively as possible and attempt to prevent some of the common traps that therapists working with BPD clients may encounter, such as becoming burned-out or being afraid to push clients in a way that could be beneficial to them.

The Therapeutic Relationship

Although the therapeutic relationship is considered important in any treatment, it is particularly emphasized in DBT. Many individuals with BPD have few close social connections; therefore, the therapist may quickly become an important figure in their lives. The DBT therapist focuses on establishing a trusting, mutually agreed upon, and reinforcing relationship with the client so that the therapist can use him- or herself as a major contingency. For example, the therapist can use (or not use) warmth, attention, and natural responses to help clients change toward their long-term goals. If clients do not feel a strong connection to their therapists and do not care what their therapists think of them, it is sometimes more challenging to keep clients in treatment and push them in therapeutic ways.

FUNCTIONS AND MODES OF TREATMENT

Standard DBT is defined by its attention to addressing the five functions of comprehensive treatment. These functions are to enhance client capabilities, improve client motivation, generalize to the natural environment, enhance therapist capabilities, and structure the environment so that positive change is more likely than maladaptive behavior to be reinforced and strengthened. The four modes of DBT that are designed to address these five functions are skills training, individual therapy, phone consultation, and consultation team.

Skills Training

The function of enhancing client capabilities is most clearly addressed by skills training, which is typically conducted in a group format with two therapist co-leaders.

The four sets of skills covered in skills training are mindfulness, distress tolerance, interpersonal effectiveness, and emotion regulation (Linehan, 1993*b*).

Mindfulness skills, influenced by Zen Buddhism, are designed to teach clients how to increase their capacity to attend to the present rather than ruminating about the past or the future. Clients learn how to find and activate their "Wise Mind," which is the integration of emotion and reason to make decisions from a centered place. Mindfulness exercises encourage clients to attend to their breath, observe what is around them and in their bodies and minds at the level of direct sensation, describe things without adding judgments or assumptions, and throw themselves into activities without self-consciousness. The mindfulness skills are considered "core" and are referred to frequently throughout the other modules.

The distress tolerance module is divided into crisis survival skills and reality acceptance skills. Crisis survival skills are intended to get a client through a crisis or difficult situation without engaging in ineffective behaviors such as self-injury, drug abuse, or physical fighting, which temporarily relieve some emotional pain but typically cause even more problems for the client. Reality acceptance skills provide ways to begin to completely and totally accept situations, people, and characteristics about themselves that they cannot change. Radical acceptance involves actively working to stop fighting reality and increasing acceptance that every event and situation has a cause. By radically accepting a painful situation that cannot be changed, clients may experience the feeling of a burden being lifted or the freedom to move on with their lives, which in turn may make it easier to tolerate the situation.

Interpersonal effectiveness skills cover how to ask for things from other people and how to effectively say no to others' requests. The module includes discussions about barriers to effective communication, how to rank priorities within a conversation, and how to determine the appropriate intensity of asking or saying no. The acronym "DEAR MAN GIVE FAST" gives clients concrete steps for being interpersonally effective and factors to keep in mind when self-respect and preserving the relationship become important priorities. There is a heavy focus on role play practice in the interpersonal effectiveness module.

The emotion regulation module provides clients with a foundation of knowledge about emotions, ways to decrease their vulnerability to mood-dependent behaviors, and skills to change emotions when they want to change them. Clients learn how to "Check the Facts" of a situation to determine whether their thoughts and assumptions about a situation are justified and effective. Clients think of other possible explanations of people's behavior to reduce rigidity of thinking. If emotions are found to be unjustified and/or ineffective for meeting a client's goals, the client learns to act opposite to the action urge associated with the emotion in order to change or decrease the intensity of the emotion. Step-by-step problem-solving skills are taught to increase clients' ability to regulate emotions when the facts of the situation are the problem. In addition to changing negative emotions, clients learn how to increase positive emotions in the short and long term to buffer themselves against the inevitable painful moments of life.

Individual Therapy

The function of increasing client motivation is largely addressed by the second mode of DBT, the individual therapy. While clients are learning DBT skills in skills training, individual therapy is often the place where clients get more individualized attention on how the skills apply to them and can be used in their lives. Individual therapists are responsible for carefully assessing with the client what is interfering with them changing in positive ways. When clients want to drop out of treatment or give up on accepting or changing, it is the role of the individual therapist to use commitment strategies to help a client get reinvested in DBT.

Phone Consultation

Phone consultation is included as part of DBT in order to generalize skills training to clients' natural environment. Phone consultation includes outside-of-therapy phone, email, or text contact with a client's individual therapist with the specific intention of getting help using skills within clients' day-to-day experiences. For example, a client working on using distress tolerance skills to ride out urges to engage in problematic drinking might call the therapist from a social gathering on a Saturday when friends are offering him drinks and the client is having trouble implementing the distress tolerance plan discussed in individual therapy. The therapist might help the client brainstorm some interpersonal effectiveness skills to use in the moment and guide him through troubleshooting potential problems. Phone consultation is meant to be brief and is not intended to be individual therapy over the phone. Therapists take special care to discuss their personal limits about phone consultation in order to preserve the function of consultation and maintain the therapists' desire to help the client.

Consultation Team

Very important to DBT, although often not given much emphasis in the published literature, is the therapist consultation team mode of DBT, which serves the function of enhancing therapist capabilities and reducing therapist burnout. In DBT, the team is viewed as a community of therapists treating each client, rather than each individual therapist being the sole person responsible for each client. The primary focus of the consultation team is on the therapists rather than on the clients being treated. The team asks this question, or something similar, at each meeting: "How can this therapist's skills and motivation be improved in order to most effectively help the client(s)?" The team process embodies all the principles of the treatment itself, including dialectics and mindfulness practice. It is the team's job to point out what a therapist may be missing from a conceptualization of the client, highlight places where a therapist may be straying from adherence to DBT, and notice when a therapist is on the verge of becoming burned out. The team may help a therapist find compassion for a client who is behaving in a way that decreases the therapist's motivation. Team members balance validation and change to support therapists at the same time that they encourage them to improve.

STAGES AND TARGETS OF DBT

The overall goal of DBT is to build a life worth living. From the very first session, the therapist and client work to understand what would make life worth living for the client. To organize steps toward this goal, DBT outlines stages of treatment and treatment targets within each stage of treatment. These targets help therapists stay focused and structured in treatment when treating clients with many comorbid problems. What follows is a brief summary of these stages and targets as they relate to individual therapy.

Pretreatment Stage

The goal of the pretreatment stage is to obtain the client's commitment to treatment and to working on the treatment targets (e.g., commitment to not commit suicide or self-injure). This stage can last from one session to several months, depending on the nature of the client's willingness to work on these goals and the level of crisis with which the client presents to treatment. The therapist makes ample use of the commitment strategies as specified by Linehan (1993a) to elicit and strengthen commitment. In this stage, the therapist and client also agree to work with each other for a specified period of time, at which point there will be re-evaluation as to whether additional treatment is necessary and/or likely to be effective.

Stage I

Most clients with BPD enter DBT in Stage I, which is characterized by behavioral dyscontrol. The overarching goal of Stage I is to increase behavioral control. In individual therapy sessions, the top priority is decreasing life-threatening behaviors, including suicide attempts, thoughts, and plans; nonsuicidal self-injury; potentially lethal drug use; and homicidal thoughts and behaviors. Following decreasing life-threatening behaviors in priority is decreasing therapy-interfering behaviors, which includes behaviors that clients or therapists engage in that prevent effective therapy from occurring. Therapy-interfering behaviors are discussed in a nonjudgmental, matter-of-fact way. There are no "good" or "bad" reasons for a client being late to session or a therapist continually showing up unprepared; regardless of the reason, the important piece is that these behaviors interfere with effective treatment and should be framed as problems to be solved.

Once life-threatening and therapy-interfering behaviors have been addressed, the next target is decreasing quality-of-life–interfering behaviors. This is a broad category of behaviors including moderate to severe Axis I disorders such as eating disorders, social anxiety, and substance abuse. It also includes general problems that interfere with quality of life such as unemployment, interpersonal chaos, and not going to work or school. Simultaneous with working on decreasing these three top targets of Stage I treatment, the therapist also works to increase the client's skills acquisition and generalization. DBT skills are frequently presented as solutions to problems. The therapist works actively to incorporate DBT skills and skills language into treatment plans for addressing the target behaviors.

Beyond Stage I

The targets of the stages following Stage I have to date been less formally studied and defined. Stage II focuses on decreasing post-traumatic stress for clients with comorbid post-traumatic stress disorder (PTSD), but it also targets inhibited grieving more generally (Wagner & Linehan, 2006). Stage III focuses on increasing self-respect and solving ordinary life problems, whereas Stage IV focuses on developing the capacity for joy and freedom. It is important to note that clients can move in and out of the various stages. For example, a client may experience a high level of behavioral dyscontrol, such as frequent suicidal threats and substance abuse (Stage I); reach a level of relatively high behavioral control after several months of treatment (potentially Stage II); and then shift back to the previous behavioral dyscontrol behaviors (Stage I) after a new traumatic event. Most of the existing research on DBT has studied Stage I problems, although there is increasing attention being paid to treating PTSD within Stage I and Stage II of DBT (Harned, Korslund, Foa, & Linehan, 2012; Wagner, Rizvi, & Harned, 2007).

STRUCTURE OF AN INDIVIDUAL THERAPY SESSION

Since DBT is a principle-based rather than a protocol-based treatment, individual therapy sessions may look drastically different for different clients based on the particular targets the clients are working on. Like in other CBT treatments, DBT therapists often set agendas, work collaboratively with clients on a mutually agreed upon set of targets, and assign homework. There are, however, several key structural components and stylistic strategies that are more unique to DBT. These components include the use of the DBT diary card, incorporation of chain analyses, and reciprocal and irreverent communication strategies.

Diary Card

The diary card is a form completed daily by the client and is used to record, in Stage I, ratings of emotions, drug and alcohol urges and use, self-injury urges and actions, level of suicidal ideation, and information about use of DBT skills. The diary card format may vary across clients and programs, but the function of tracking relevant emotions, urges, and behaviors on a daily basis must be preserved. Each week, the diary card is used in individual therapy to monitor progress on treatment targets and to determine what should be addressed in that week's session. Not completing the diary card or completing the diary card infrequently is considered a therapy-interfering behavior and is addressed as such in session.

Chain Analyses

After the therapist has scanned the diary card and selected targets to focus on in session with the client, a chain analysis is typically conducted on the highest priority target (Rizvi & Ritschel, 2013). A chain analysis involves assessing all the thoughts, sensations, emotions, and behaviors leading up to, during, and following a problematic behavior. These thoughts, sensations, emotions, and behaviors are referred to as the "links" in the chain. Using one specific instance of the behavior (e.g., the client cutting himself with a razor blade three times on Thursday evening), the therapist asks a series of questions to discover the links and the prompting event that started the chain of events. Special focus is also given to the client's vulnerability to the problematic behavior in that instance as well as the short- and long-term consequences of the behavior.

Once both the client and therapist have a thorough understanding of what happened, solution analyses are carried out. Each link in the chain is thought of as a potential place of intervention and thus a potential solution for preventing the dysfunctional behavior in the future. For the example of the client who cut himself with the razor blade, possible points of intervention might be to prevent him from drinking at dinner, which makes him more vulnerable to loneliness, which in turn makes him more vulnerable to cutting; to provide him with skills to manage his intense loneliness without having to engage in cutting; or to eliminate the positive consequence of extra attention from his sister that typically follows his incidents of cutting. Once a link or several links have been selected for intervention, the therapist helps the client practice the needed behavioral skills and develop a plan for next time he has an urge to cut.

Therapist Stylistic Strategies

At first glance, the use of a diary card and chain analyses might seem to paint a picture of DBT as being a rigid, inflexible treatment, when in fact this is far from the truth. The advanced DBT therapist is aware of the necessary components but is able to create a session characterized by movement, speed, and flow. Most beginner DBT therapists are tempted to come into a session with a fixed agenda, but this often is discarded in order to respond fluidly to the style or content of a client's presentation. Part of what creates movement, speed, and flow within a session is the therapist's balance of two types of stylistic strategies: reciprocal communication and irreverent communication. Reciprocal strategies resemble typical therapist skills such as reflective listening and a warm, validating style.

Irreverent stylistic strategies are used when therapists feel as if they are becoming polarized with clients, want to shift clients toward action, or just want to shake things up in a session to create some movement. Irreverent comments may be off-beat, blunt, or contrary to the expected. Irreverence might involve using a deadpan or highly intense style—whichever is opposite to the client's current style, "calling a spade a spade," or reframing something in an unorthodox manner. For example, when a client rattles off a bunch of things she dislikes about the therapist's style, a therapist might respond irreverently by saying, "You know what I like about you? You always tell me just what you're thinking."

STRUCTURE OF A SKILLS TRAINING GROUP

The group is conducted much like a class, with behavioral skills homework review in the first half and teaching of new DBT skills in the second half. Group is intended to be conversational, with frequent opportunities to engage clients and have them participate in discussions about the skills. The main leader is responsible for teaching skills, while the co-leader manages other group-related responsibilities, such as monitoring clients' attendance and, at times, acting as the "voice" of the group when something the leader says is in need of clarification. Just as in individual therapy, DBT outlines a hierarchy of targets for skills training; these are, in order of importance: decreasing therapy-destroying behaviors, increasing skills acquisition, and decreasing therapy-interfering behaviors (Linehan, 1993b).

Crisis Management

In DBT, there is a preference for keeping actively suicidal clients in their own environment rather than routinely using inpatient hospitalization. The rationale for this preference is twofold: one, DBT therapists believe that the best way to decrease suicidal behavior is for the client to get practice dealing with urges skillfully in his or her normal context, and, two, there are little data to suggest that hospitalizations are effective for reducing suicidal behavior (Paris, 2004). It is also believed that some suicidal clients may experience positive reinforcement from going to the hospital, such as extra attention, social activity, and feelings of safety. This positive reinforcement makes it much more difficult for the client to become more skillful and effective outside of the hospital.

This is not to say that DBT therapists do not engage in crisis management. All DBT programs should have a crisis and risk assessment protocol in place. The diary card and regularly assessing suicidal thoughts and behaviors in a straightforward way keep DBT therapists tuned in to their clients' level of risk. DBT therapists are careful to not respond with more warmth or phone consultation time when the severity of clients' suicidal behaviors increases, but rather to coach them on being more skillful and to reinforce successful implementation of skills. Warmth and extra time over the phone and in session are reserved as contingencies for skillful, effective behavior rather than dysfunctional behavior.

CASE STUDY: DIALECTICAL BEHAVIOR THERAPY

Background Information

Anna was a 28-year-old unmarried, unemployed Caucasian female living at home with her father. She was the middle child of three siblings, and her mother passed away when she was a teenager as the result of a car accident. Anna reported having several acquaintances but only two close friends, all of whom she had met through Narcotics Anonymous meetings, which she attended multiple times a week. She was working toward her undergraduate degree at a local community college. She had been on disability for the past 2 years for BPD and her history of hospitalizations for suicide attempts. Her suicide attempts occurred at ages 16 and 26, both of which involved her taking alcohol and prescription pills and her family members finding her and bringing her to the hospital. Anna began burning her wrists and arms with cigarettes at age 16. At the start of treatment, she was burning herself approximately one time per week. Anna was 1 year sober from drugs and alcohol, but continued to report urges to drink. Anna's treatment goals were to stop her self-injury, decrease her feelings of depression and worthlessness, and get continued help with maintaining her sobriety. In addition to hospitalizations, she had an extensive history of prior therapy since her mother's death. After completing a structured diagnostic interview, it was confirmed that Anna currently met the *Diagnostic and Statistical Manual for Mental Disorders* (DSM-IV) criteria for BPD, exhibiting eight out of the nine criteria (all criteria except stress-related paranoia and dissociation). She also met diagnostic criteria for current major depressive disorder and a past history of alcohol and substance abuse.

Biosocial Theory

Since childhood, Anna reported feeling more emotionally sensitive and reactive than other people, and she described feeling as though her bad moods would never end once they started. Growing up, Anna was the only one of her siblings who experienced heightened emotional vulnerability. The rest of her family had fairly well-regulated emotions and preferred not to discuss emotional experiences. Her parents did not model the skills she needed to regulate her intense emotions. When Anna reacted strongly to negative events as a child, her parents would respond by saying things such as "Don't be a cry-baby, you'll be fine" and "Why can't you be more like your sister and brother?" Anna felt alone and confused about how to deal with her emotions. She started not to trust her own evaluation of how she was feeling.

At the time of her mother's death, Anna was overwhelmed with grief and desperately wanted to talk about it with her family members. Her father and siblings often responded to these attempts by ignoring them or leaving the house. This led Anna's expressions of emotion to escalate so that she would burn herself or get drunk and high. Out of her awareness, these behaviors got her attention from her family. Her family ignored her lower intensity emotional expressions such as sleeping excessively and crying openly, but when she told them that she had burned herself, they would stop what they were doing immediately and comfort her. Her father, typically stoic and tough, would take days off from work and dedicate all of his time to Anna each time she returned from the hospital after a suicide attempt.

Stage and Target Hierarchy

Anna entered treatment in Stage I, characterized by behavioral dyscontrol. This dyscontrol was evidenced by Anna's current self-injury, suicidal ideation, and continued urges to abuse drugs and alcohol. These behaviors were conceptualized as dysfunctional attempts to regulate her depression and intense emotions.

According to the target hierarchy, Anna's top treatment targets were decreasing her life-threatening behaviors. Specifically, the top priority of treatment was to decrease Anna's suicidal ideation and behaviors and her vulnerability to abusing drugs or alcohol in a dangerous way. Next on her target hierarchy was to decrease any therapy-interfering behaviors that arose during treatment from Anna or her therapist. For the category of quality-of-life–interfering behaviors, Anna's goals included decreasing her feelings of depression, increasing her number of close social relationships (including being in a romantic relationship), decreasing her financial dependence on disability payments and her father, and decreasing time spent playing video games. Anna's main targets for increasing behavioral skills were to increase interpersonal effectiveness with her family members and increase use of distress tolerance to cope with her urges to self-injure and drink.

Summary of Treatment

Anna underwent 6 months of comprehensive DBT, including weekly individual therapy, group skills training, and phone consultation. At the start of treatment, Anna's individual therapist used commitment strategies to increase her engagement in treatment and to obtain commitment to stopping all suicidal behaviors, self-injury, and dangerous drug and alcohol use. Anna readily committed, although she expressed doubts about how she would do so. In skills group, Anna attended regularly, but was at first very quiet unless called upon. After about a month of group, she started participating more actively.

The majority of Anna's treatment was spent getting her suicidal ideation and self-injury behavior under control. When Anna self-injured during her tenth week of treatment, she came in to session crying and not wanting to make eye contact with her therapist due to intense feelings of shame. As per DBT protocol, Anna's therapist conducted an in-depth chain analysis of the dysfunctional behavior (Linehan, 1993a; Rizvi & Ritschel, 2013) cushioned with a great amount of validation for the shame Anna was feeling. After several chains had been conducted on self-injury incidents over the course of therapy, it became evident that Anna was particularly vulnerable to engaging in self-injury when she negatively compared herself to other people and when other people made comments that implied that her experience of emotions and psychological problems was invalid. These experiences typically led to intense feelings of shame and sadness accompanied by harsh judgments about herself. For example, once when she arrived at a friend's birthday party and discovered that the location was a bar, she immediately felt embarrassed that she could not attend the party for risk of breaking her sobriety. She had thoughts like "What is wrong with me? Why can't I be normal like everyone else?" Her shame led her to hide herself from others and get back in her car immediately so no one would see her. Once in the car, she started crying uncontrollably and felt her heart pounding. She began smoking a cigarette to try and calm herself down, but thought "I can't handle this pain." She instantly put out her cigarette on the inside of her wrist. She felt relief from the overwhelming emotion she had been experiencing and felt ready to drive back home. An hour later, she felt another wave of shame about her behavior and breaking the commitment she had made to her therapist. She called her father, who was out to dinner with a friend, to tell him what happened. Her father immediately came home to comfort her.

This example of a chain analysis speaks to the degree of specificity sought by the therapist in order to gain a better understanding of problematic behavior so that effective solutions could be implemented. Based on chain analyses, the focus of treatment became decreasing Anna's judgments toward herself about being inferior to others, use of distress tolerance skills such as self-soothing herself with relaxing music and squeezing a stress ball when she had urges to self-injure, and helping her effectively communicate to her father that the extra attention he gave her after she engaged in self-injury was inadvertently reinforcing her behavior and making it more challenging for her to stop. Anna's therapist also worked with her on developing the skill of being mindful of her current emotion, which required her to increase her willingness to sit with uncomfortable emotions without engaging in escape behaviors such as self-injury or fantasizing about suicide. Over the course of treatment, Anna had one incident of drinking during the third month of treatment, which the therapist treated similarly to Anna's self-injury example by conducting an in-depth chain analysis and developing potential solutions to prevent the behavior in the future.

After Anna had stopped self-injury altogether and was having only low-level urges to drink, her therapist began a behavioral activation protocol to treat Anna's depression. She worked with her to establish a routine of activities that provided Anna with pleasure and mastery, which gradually helped improve her mood. By the end of 6 months, Anna reported no suicidal ideation or urges to self-injure, had started a 1-day-a-week volunteer position in her community, and had begun applying for part-time jobs. She had joined a dating website and had gone on several dates. While she was still single at the end of treatment, she felt proud of herself for taking steps toward her relationship goals and more confident about how she would act on a date. Although not directly targeted during treatment, Anna's time spent playing video games had decreased as she worked toward becoming more active to improve her mood and increase her sense of mastery.

EMPIRICAL SUPPORT FOR DBT

To date, there are numerous published randomized control trials on the use of DBT with various client groups, although most of the populations that have been studied include predominantly female clients. DBT is officially recognized by the Cochrane Review as the treatment of choice for BPD characteristics including impulsivity, interpersonal difficulties, emotion dysregulation, and self-harm and suicidal behaviors (Stoffers et al., 2012). In the practice guidelines for BPD, the American Psychiatric Association lists DBT as a recommended treatment (American Psychiatric Association, 2001). The UK National Institute for Health and Clinical Excellence (the "NICE guidelines") recognizes DBT as an evidence-based approach for BPD (National Institute for Health and Clinical Excellence, 2009).

The first randomized controlled trial on DBT was published in 1991 and demonstrated that, compared to those receiving treatment as usual, chronically suicidal women receiving 12 months of outpatient DBT showed significantly greater reductions in suicidal and nonsuicidal self-harm behaviors, had fewer inpatient hospital stays, and were more likely to start and complete treatment (Linehan, Armstrong, Suarez, Allmon, & Heard, 1991). Another early study looked at DBT in comparison to community-based treatment as usual for substance-dependent women with BPD. This study found significantly greater reductions in substance use, lower rates of dropout, and greater social and global adjustment scores at follow-up in the DBT group as compared to treatment as usual (Linehan et al., 1999). Whereas these studies examined the effects of 12 months of DBT, others have examined the effects of 6 months of DBT. One comparison of 6 months of DBT to treatment as usual utilized a population of BPD women from the Veterans Administration (not necessarily suicidal) and found that clients in the DBT condition showed greater improvement in the areas of suicidal ideation, anger, depression, and hopelessness than did clients in the treatment as usual condition (Koons et al., 2001). This study gave evidence for the clinical utility of less than 1 year of DBT.

In addition to studies comparing DBT to treatment as usual, some trials have compared DBT to more active treatment comparison groups. One study of opiate-addicted women with BPD compared standard outpatient DBT to comprehensive validation therapy (CVT) plus a 12-step program (Linehan et al., 2002). CVT is a protocol-based treatment developed specifically for this study, and it focuses on validating the client in a warm, reciprocal way with little direction on the part of the therapist. Essentially, CVT incorporates DBT validation strategies and prohibits the use of DBT change-oriented strategies. This study found equally significant reductions in opiate use and psychopathology in both groups. Another important finding was that CVT had a remarkably high treatment retention rate of 100%, as compared to 64% in the DBT condition. This study provides some evidence for which components of DBT may be essential; however, more component-analysis research needs to be conducted on this topic to make any firm conclusions.

Another study that used a more active comparison group compared DBT to non-behavioral community treatment by experts (CTBE) for suicidal women with BPD (Linehan et al., 2006). The findings of this study were that, for most target variables, DBT performed better than CTBE. Clients in the DBT condition were less likely to make suicide attempts, less likely to be hospitalized for suicidal ideation, had lower medical risk for self-harm and suicide attempts, and were less likely to drop out of treatment, among other advantages. This study was crucial because it demonstrated that DBT is effective for reasons beyond its inclusion of treatment by expert psychotherapists. When compared to another treatment by experts, differential effects of DBT remained.

Research has suggested that DBT skills use mediates the relationship between time in treatment and reductions in suicide attempts, depressive symptoms, and dyscontrol of anger (Neacsiu, Rizvi, & Linehan, 2010), and some studies have looked at the utility of skills training only (e.g., Soler et al., 2009). In general, these studies suggest that DBT skills alone may be effective for some populations, depending on the severity and nature of their clinical problems. Individual therapy is primarily included as part of DBT to increase clients' engagement in treatment and manage suicidal behaviors. For less severe clients without the need for crisis management, skills group alone may be sufficient. For example, there is evidence that skills training only is effective for reducing binge eating episodes (Telch, Agras, & Linehan, 2001); reducing behavioral problems of juvenile female offenders in correctional facilities (Trupin, Stewart, Beach, & Boesky, 2002); and reducing depression, hopelessness, and overall psychopathology in females with a history of domestic violence victimization (Iverson, Shenk, & Fruzzetti, 2009). Current research is investigating whether skills training alone may be effective for people with BPD.

LIMITATIONS OF DBT

Despite DBT's widespread popularity, it is important to note that the treatment is not a panacea, and there are a number of potential limitations that need attention and further treatment development efforts. Although research studies generally support the efficacy of DBT compared to control groups, a significant minority of individuals do not make gains in treatment (Rizvi, 2011). Thus, there remains a need to determine ways in which DBT can be improved, which can be partially achieved by research that identifies the essential components of the treatment as well as research that identifies who is most likely to benefit from DBT.

First, although there is ample research to suggest that the "full package" of comprehensive DBT is effective, the field has only recently begun to research whether individual modes of DBT (such as skills training alone) may also be effective. Furthermore, there has yet to be any research conducted on which particular treatment strategies within DBT are necessary conditions for effective outcomes. Although skills use has been identified as a mechanism of change within DBT (Neacsiu et al., 2010), more work is clearly needed to determine other important mechanisms.

Second, there has yet to be very much research published on how to most effectively train clinicians in DBT and which therapist characteristics may be related to outcome. Currently, the gold standard for training in DBT is "intensive training," which is typically 2 full weeks of didactic workshops separated by 6 months of team-based study and assignments. This high-intensity type of training may not be feasible for some therapists, and there are questions as to how easy it is to disseminate DBT at an adherent level. Recent research suggests that online training may be an effective alternative (Dimeff et al., 2009) to in-person training. More research in this area is necessary in order to reach the broadest possible audience of clinicians and thus clients.

Third, DBT can be a relatively expensive treatment to implement. Since comprehensive therapy includes weekly individual therapy, skills training groups for approximately 2 hours per week led by two therapists, weekly consultation team for all therapists (1–2 hours/week typically), and as-needed phone consultation outside of session, the number of clinical hours per client that need to be accounted for each week is quite high. This cost can make some settings or institutions less likely to implement a DBT program. Yet, despite the apparent high cost of DBT, it is important to note that DBT can actually be cost-effective in that multiples studies have shown that individuals in DBT make use of inpatient stays and ER visits at much lower rates than do individuals in control conditions. Given the expense of these crisis services, savings to the system are substantial in favor of DBT (Linehan & Heard, 1999).

Thus, although we now have a significant body of research to support DBT's efficacy, there still remains much to be learned about (1) how to make it even more efficacious for more clients, (2) which aspects of the treatment are most responsible for positive client change (and thus potential ways to be make the treatment more parsimonious), (3) how to provide evidence-based training in DBT and which components of training are necessary/effective, and (4) ways in which to make the implementation of DBT more cost-effective for individual agencies as well as broader systems of care.

CONCLUSION

In the past 20 years since the publication of the DBT treatment manuals (Linehan, 1993a, 1993b), there has been a surge of DBT dissemination and research. The research on DBT's effectiveness is largely compelling and was the first to empirically demonstrate that individuals with BPD and severe emotional dysregulation and/or suicidal behavior could be effectively treated with a psychosocial therapy. In this chapter, we described the foundation and theoretical underpinnings of DBT, provided details about the structure of DBT in all its components, demonstrated the treatment through the use of a detailed case example, and summarized some of the existing research. As the research literature on DBT continues to grow, it will be important to move beyond randomized clinical trials comparing DBT to a control treatment and instead focus on identifying important predictors and mediators of change. Such research will allow for treatment development efforts to aid in making DBT even more effective for a larger group of individuals with BPD and associated problems.

REFERENCES

American Psychiatric Association. (2001). Practice guideline for the treatment of patients with borderline personality disorder. *American Journal of Psychiatry, 158*, 1–52.

Crowell, S. E., Beauchaine, T. P., & Linehan, M. M. (2009). A biosocial developmental model of borderline personality: Elaborating and extending Linehan's theory. *Psychological Bulletin, 135*(3), 495.

Dimeff, L. A., Koerner, K., Woodcock, E. A., Beadnell, B., Brown, M. Z., Skutch, J. M., . . . Harned, M. S. (2009). Which training method works best? A randomized controlled trial comparing three methods of training clinicians in dialectical behavior therapy skills. *Behaviour Research and Therapy, 47*(11), 921–930.

Koons, C. R., Robins, C. J., Tweed, J. L., Lynch, T. R., Gonzalez, A. M., Morse, J. Q., . . . Bastian, L. A. (2001). Efficacy of dialectical behavior therapy in women veterans with borderline personality disorder. *Behavior Therapy, 32*(2), 371–390.

Harned, M. S., Korslund, K. E., Foa, E. B., & Linehan, M. M. (2012). Treating PTSD in suicidal and self-injuring women with borderline personality disorder: Development and preliminary evaluation of a dialectical behavior therapy prolonged exposure protocol. *Behaviour Research and Therapy, 50*, 381–386.

Iverson, K. M., Shenk, C., & Fruzzetti, A. E. (2009). Dialectical behavior therapy for women victims of domestic abuse: A pilot study. *Professional Psychology: Research and Practice, 40*(3), 242.

Linehan, M. M. (1993a). *Cognitive-behavioral treatment of borderline personality disorder.* New York: Guilford.

Linehan, M. M. (1993b). *Skills training manual for treating borderline personality disorder.* New York: Guilford.

Linehan, M. M. (1997). Validation and psychotherapy. In A. Bohart & L. Greenberg (Eds.), *Empathy reconsidered: New directions in psychotherapy* (p. 353–392). Washington DC: American Psychological Association.

Linehan, M. M., Armstrong, H. E., Suarez, A., Allmon, D., & Heard, H. L. (1991). Cognitive-behavioral treatment of chronically parasuicidal borderline patients. *Archives of General Psychiatry, 48*, 1060–1064.

Linehan, M. M., Comtois, K. A., Murray, A. M., Brown, M. Z., Gallop, R. J., Heard, H. L., . . . Lindenboim, N. (2006). Two-year randomized controlled trial and follow-up of dialectical behavior therapy vs therapy by experts for suicidal behaviors and borderline personality disorder. *Archives of General Psychiatry, 63*(7), 757.

Linehan, M. M., Dimeff, L. A., Reynolds, S. K., Comtois, K. A., Welch, S. S., Heagerty, P., & Kivlahan, D. R. (2002). Dialectical behavior therapy versus comprehensive validation therapy plus 12-step for the treatment of opioid dependent women meeting criteria for borderline personality disorder. *Drug and Alcohol Dependence, 67*(1), 13–26.

Linehan, M. M., & Heard, H. L. (1999). Borderline personality disorder: Costs, course, and treatment outcomes. In N. Miller & K. M. Magruder (Eds.), *Cost-effectiveness of psychotherapy: A guide for practitioners, researchers, and policy makers* (pp. 291–305). New York: Oxford University Press.

Linehan, M. M., Schmidt, H., Dimeff, L. A., Craft, J. C., Kanter, J., & Comtois, K. A. (1999). Dialectical behavior therapy for patients with borderline personality disorder and drug-dependence. *American Journal on Addictions, 8*(4), 279–292.

National Institute for Health and Clinical Excellence. (2009, January). *Borderline personality disorder: Treatment and management*. Retrieved from http://www.nice.org.uk/nicemedia/pdf/CG78NICEGuideline.pdf

Neacsiu, A. D., Rizvi, S. L., & Linehan, M. M. (2010). Dialectical behavior therapy skills use as a mediator and outcome of treatment for borderline personality disorder. *Behaviour Research and Therapy, 48*(9), 832.

Paris, J. (2004). Is hospitalization useful for suicidal patients with borderline personality disorder? *Journal of Personality Disorders, 18*, 240–247.

Rizvi, S. L. (2011). Treatment failure in dialectical behavior therapy. *Cognitive and Behavioral Practice, 18*(3), 403–412.

Rizvi, S. L., & Ritschel, L. (2013). *Mastering the art of chain analysis in dialectical behavior therapy*. Manuscript submitted for publication.

Rizvi, S. L., Steffel, L. M., & Carson Wong, A. (2013). An overview of dialectical behavior therapy for professional psychologists. *Professional Psychology: Research and Practice, 44*, 73–80.

Soler, J., Pascual, J. C., Tiana, T., Cebrià, A., Barrachina, J., Campins, M. J., . . . Pérez, V. (2009). Dialectical behaviour therapy skills training compared to standard group therapy in borderline personality disorder: A 3-month randomised controlled clinical trial. *Behaviour Research and Therapy, 47*(5), 353–358.

Stoffers, J. M., Vollm, B. A., Rucker, G., Timmer, A., Huband, N., & Lieb, K. (2012). Psychological therapies for people with borderline personality disorder. *Cochrane Database of Systematic Reviews, 8*, CD005652. doi: 10.1002/14651858.CD005652.pub2

Telch, C. F., Agras, W. S., & Linehan, M. M. (2001). Dialectical behavior therapy for binge eating disorder. *Journal of Consulting and Clinical Psychology, 69*(6), 1061–1064.

Trupin, E. W., Stewart, D. G., Beach, B., & Boesky, L. (2002). Effectiveness of a dialectical behaviour therapy program for incarcerated female juvenile offenders. *Child and Adolescent Mental Health, 7*(3), 121–127.

Wagner, A. W., & Linehan, M. M. (2006). Applications of dialectical behavior therapy to posttraumatic stress disorder and related problems. In V. C. Follette & J. I. Ruzek (Eds.), *Cognitive behavioral therapies for trauma* (p. 117–145). New York: Guilford.

Wagner, A. W., Rizvi, S. L., & Harned, M. S. (2007). Applications of dialectical behavior therapy to the treatment of complex trauma-related problems: When one case formulation does not fit all. *Journal of Traumatic Stress, 20*(4), 391–400.

/// 17 /// Cognitive Therapy for Personality Disorders

KATE M. DAVIDSON

INTRODUCTION

In the 1960s, A. T. Beck began developing cognitive therapy as a form of psychotherapy to help patients overcome their difficulties by changing thinking, behavior, and
emotional responses. Cognitive therapy (CT), or cognitive-behavioral therapy (CBT)
as it is also referred to, has been found to be probably the most effective therapy in
randomized controlled trials (RCTs) for a wide range of health and mental health
disorders. When used in addition to medication, it has also been demonstrated to be
effective for serious mental disorders such as bipolar disorder and schizophrenia.
CBT is used to treat health and mental health problems across all age groups and in
group format as well as individual therapy. Psychological therapies are the treatment
of choice in personality disorders, and there is evidence that CBT is an effective therapy for borderline (Davidson, Norrie, Tyrer, Gumley, Tata, Murray, & Palmer, 2006,
Davidson et al., 2010), avoidant (Emmelkamp et al., 2006), and antisocial personality disorders (Davidson et al., 2009). CBT has developed over the years and been
successful by taking into account the unique aspects of disorders and through developing a cognitive model to fit with specific disorders. CBT for personality disorders
(CBTpd) is one such example of where the model has been adapted to fit specific
disorders, such as borderline and antisocial personality disorders (Davidson, 2007).

The origins of personality problems are recognized as being multifactorial,
involving the interplay between genetic factors, the inherent temperament of the
child, childhood development and experience, and the quality of attachment to caregivers and others in childhood. Any model of the development of personality disorder should take these factors into account, although different psychological models
will emphasize some factors more than others. Child development occurs through a

series of ongoing changes in biological, physiological, cognitive, behavioral, social, and emotional structures, and all of this occurs in a family and social system embedded in a wider cultural context. A model of personality disorder therefore needs to be multifaceted in order to account for these factors (Davidson, 2007).

THEORETICAL ASSUMPTIONS OF THE COGNITIVE MODEL

In CBTpd, emphasis is placed on core beliefs, emotions, and overdeveloped behavioral patterns that have developed as a consequence of the beliefs. The core beliefs are concerned with self-identity and beliefs about other people and are the product of deep schema structures rather than automatic thoughts that occur as a stream of thoughts in response to everyday situations.

A child's first relationship to caregivers is known to have a fundamental influence on development. The way individuals view themselves and other people, the types of relationships that they develop, and their behavioral and emotional responses to experiences are influenced by two main processes that occur in childhood: early attachment to caregivers and the internal working model of relationships that form in childhood. Many individuals with antisocial and borderline personality disorders have been abused, neglected, or treated inconsistently by their caregivers in childhood. These experiences, in turn, form the internal working models that the child develops and applies to other relationships that he or she encounters both in childhood and adulthood. If the type of care received in childhood has been inadequate, inconsistent, or abusive in some way, the child's internal working model that will develop is one of a negative pattern of expectations of others—the child comes to expect that they are not worthy of love and are not able to trust that others will provide them with a sense of security and emotional support. In contrast, a secure attachment to a caregiver is one in which a child's needs for safety and security and help with soothing of distressing emotions are met. Such effective and caring responses from caregivers are thought to be important in helping children develop the ability to self-manage negative emotions such as fear and anger. This ability to regulate emotions and also other aspects of self, such as behavior and thinking, may become problematic and is particularly evident in those with personality disorders. For example, inconsistent or unpredictable experiences with caregivers result in children developing a negative view of themselves and to thinking that they are unworthy of love, described as an anxious attachment style (Ainsworth, Blehar, Waters, & Wall, 1978). If children have had experiences of caregivers as untrustworthy, dismissive, or rejecting they may develop an avoidant attachment style. They may also develop or learn less active coping styles (Rutter & Rutter, 1993). Not everyone who has negative experiences in childhood develops personality disorder or problems. It may be that individuals with borderline and antisocial personality disorders have more frequent, enduring, or extreme negative experiences than others, as well as temperamental dispositions that make them more vulnerable to being overwhelmed by their negative life experiences.

These core beliefs are about self-identity and how others are viewed. They are ways of organizing experience and are attempts at avoiding, compensating, or coping with the negative experiences in childhood. Core beliefs are long-standing, rigid, and activated by a large number of contexts, and they are often expressed in unconditional terms. For example, many individuals with borderline personality disorder (BPD) will hold beliefs such as "I am bad," "others will not like me," and "other people will let me down" (Beck, Freeman, & Davis, 2004; Padesky, 1994). In a sample of 106 people with BPD, the typical themes found were mistrust of others, being undesirable or bad, and being taken advantage of by others, as well as those of failure and emotional deprivation (Davidson, Tyrer, et al., 2006). These core beliefs about self and others shape an individual's sense of identity, emotional well-being, pattern of relationships, and behavior. Individuals develop behavioral strategies to compensate, avoid, or cope with their core dysfunctional beliefs. For example, an individual with BPD believed that she was unattractive and a bad person. She tended to avoid close relationships, fearing that others would find out that she was "bad" and worthless. If people invited her out, she would leave the event early. She found it hard to talk about herself because she believed that others would find her odd, find fault with her opinions, or would dislike her. She tried to cope by agreeing with whatever others said rather than give her own opinion. She would not return phone calls or emails because she was afraid of making a fool of herself or saying something that offended people. Her avoidance of others sometimes led to people acting in a manner she interpreted as rejecting because they often gave up inviting her out or contacting her, and this only served to confirm her negative beliefs about herself. Avoiding close relationships in her case was an overdeveloped behavioral strategy that fitted with her dominant core belief that she was bad and worthless. Figure 17.1 illustrates the cognitive model of personality disorders.

CHARACTERISTICS OF CBTpd

CBTpd is structured, time-limited, and focuses on core beliefs and underdeveloped behavioral patterns. The difficulties that patients experience are due to problems with regulating emotions, behaviors, and thinking. Learning new, more adaptive ways of thinking about self and others is a goal of therapy along with increasing regulation of emotions and behaviors that would be associated with those more adaptive beliefs. Table 17.1 describes the structure and main characteristics of CBTpd. More sessions are needed to change the long-standing behavioral patterns and associated core beliefs than in CBT for other disorders that are episodic and where beliefs and emotional and behavioral patterns are not so ingrained. The therapist utilizes the cognitive formulation to develop a treatment plan that will pay particular attention to the dysfunctional core beliefs that the patient holds about self and others and the behavioral strategies that have become overdeveloped as a way of coping, avoiding, or compensating for these beliefs. Therapy aims to help patients develop behavioral strategies that are underdeveloped and to develop more adaptive beliefs that would

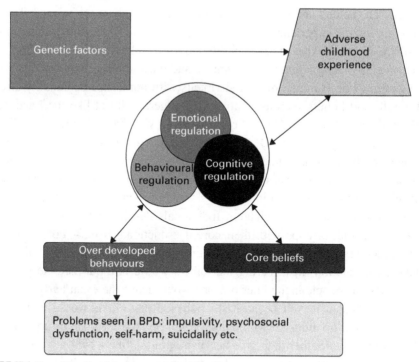

FIGURE 17.1 Cognitive model of personality disorders.

support these new behavioral strategies. In the previous example, the individual had developed a pattern of avoiding close relationships by ignoring or not responding to people who had become friendly toward her. In therapy, she was encouraged to develop behaviors that increased her social competence without avoidance and to develop beliefs that supported the idea that others might like her.

INITIAL PHASE OF THERAPY: DEVELOPING A FORMULATION

CBTpd begins with an assessment phase that aims to develop a coherent psychological understanding of the patient's problems, taking a lifetime perspective through the development of a narrative CBT formulation using the cognitive model. Because the patient's problems are likely to have arisen through childhood experiences and trauma, more sessions are needed at the beginning of therapy to more fully understand the past and how this might relate to the patient's current difficulties. A comprehensive assessment of the patient's life situation and past history is needed. Although the majority of the information may come directly from the patient, a partner, relatives or friends may also provide information with the consent of the patient. Typically, it takes about five or six sessions to develop a CBTpd formulation and to agree on this with the patient before embarking on helping the patient change his or her beliefs and behavioral strategies.

TABLE 17.1 Structure and main strategies of cognitive-behavior therapy for personality disorders (CBTpd)

Structure of therapy 30 sessions over 1 year	Sessions 1–5 (approx.)	Initial phase: Development of formulation through longitudinal assessment
		Explore memories, childhood experiences, daydreams, etc. to help identify core beliefs and schemas that may have formed in childhood and adolescence
		Establish core beliefs and overdeveloped behavioral strategies and their relationship to current problems
	Sessions 6–26	Development of alternative beliefs about self and others.
		Recognition, rehearsal, and repeated practice of underdeveloped behaviors (new skills) in situ.
	Final sessions	Ending phase: Strengthening and generalization of acquisition of new beliefs and skills
		Review of therapy and updating of the narrative formulation in light of new information
		Summary of what has been learned and achieved in therapy.
Therapeutic style	Therapist	Open and collaborative; curious stance taken rather than "all knowing"
		Warm, empathic, genuine, and able to convey a consistently nonjudgmental attitude while not denying the gravity of any problematic behavior
		Able to identify therapeutic ruptures at an early stage and rectify these promptly.
	Patient	The patient is assumed to be being doing the best he or she can at any given point in time
		They are also assumed to want to improve their lives by taking part in therapy and working with the therapist in a collaborative manner

(continued)

TABLE 17.1 Continued

Main therapeutic strategies and techniques	Emotional and cognitive Regulation	Acknowledge and validation of distress
		Understanding context or event that resulted in the distress
		Relate distress to formulation and personal history
		Teach and apply self-soothing techniques where necessary
		Use cognitive and behavioral strategies to reduce distress (e.g., interpretation of situation/interpersonal relationship skills, etc.)
	Behavioral Regulation	Identify specific behavioral problems
		Specify the aim/goal to be reached
		Work with patient to understand determinants of their behavioral response and why it is not optimal response Identify and understand the related emotional and cognitive response
		Decide on what skills or new behaviors are required to meet goal
		Practice new behavior in role play and in situ
		Feedback progress and, if necessary, alter plans and skill set required to meet goals
	Interpersonal problems	Understanding the situation that resulted in relationship problem
		Understand breakdown in relationship in terms of interpersonal patterns already highlighted in the formulation
		Help the client to test the reality of his or her underlying assumptions or beliefs about self and others by using Socratic questioning
		Use cognitive strategies to evaluate the breakdown in relationship
		Utilize behavioral strategies to compensate for any interpersonal skills that need to be strengthened or developed (e.g., assertiveness skills, how to develop and maintain relationships)

Due to the complexity of the patient's history and the links between his or her past history and present day problems, the formulation is often written as a narrative or letter to the patient. It may take some time to write this formulation because it is highly personalized and has to be internally coherent and consistent psychologically. A therapist has to be aware that the patient may show this written explanation of his or her problems to significant others and so it should be written with this in mind. CBT is known to be highly collaborative. It is through the formulation that those with personality disorder become engaged in therapy.

Patients' curiosity about why they have developed the problems they experience is raised in this first phase of therapy and is actively encouraged. They are asked to reflect on how their past may have influenced their problems. Patients' engagement in therapy may well depend on this phase of therapy as the therapist responds compassionately to the early life difficulties that patients may have experienced and the impact that this has on them in their adult lives. At the end of this phase, a written narrative formulation is discussed with patients and can be modified until it gives a full and empathic understanding of why patients have developed the beliefs and behaviors that have brought them into therapy.

Therapists discuss how holding the core beliefs developed through adverse events in childhood has led to emotional and behavioral patterns that are negative and often self-destructive. The patterns may have made sense as a reaction to the adverse events the individual experienced in childhood and adolescence. However, they are now no longer helpful or life-enhancing. Importantly, these patterns can be changed through therapy. Developing new ways of thinking about oneself and new ways of behaving that would fit with a new view of self and others is the aim of therapy.

HELPING WITH REGULATION OF BEHAVIOR AND EMOTIONS

Individuals with BPD have problems regulating emotions and also problems with regulating thinking and behavior. The negative core beliefs that individuals with BPD have about themselves and others come from their early childhood experiences and are maintained by the difficulties they experience in adulthood, especially with being able to develop and maintain relationships. Finding oneself frequently distressed, being unable to keep emotions within comfortable limits, and being hypersensitive or highly reactive to events can lead to a wide range of intrapsychic and interpersonal problems. These can range from extreme fluctuations in mood and emotions, such as anxiety and panic attacks; impulsivity; and suicidal and self-harm behavior as thinking becomes more negative, all of which can be highly disruptive to relationships.

In CBTpd, patients learn to recognize and work with their negative cognitions, particularly core beliefs and associated behaviors, as a means of helping them gain control over their emotional dysregulation. Change in therapy is achieved by practicing, strengthening, and supporting the behavioral patterns that are underdeveloped and by encouraging patients to find new, more adaptive ways of viewing themselves and others. Acknowledging patients' distress and understanding why they are

distressed is validating for patients. Marsha Linehan was one of the first to emphasize the importance of emotional validation because patients with BPD have often
had their distress dismissed or ignored by others (Linehan, 1993).

Work on changing core beliefs is usually accomplished within sessions with the
associated behavioral changes practiced in the time between sessions. Cognitive
techniques are used to examine the validity and usefulness of holding the core
beliefs. Through the work done in developing the formulation, it is often obvious
to patients that these beliefs are a result of their childhood experiences and are now
not adaptive to their adult life. Young's "historical test of schema" (Young, Klosko,
& Weishaar, 2003) can be used to chart examples of where a belief may have arisen
and where it may be fitted with the patient's childhood experiences. A more helpful
and more adaptive form of the same belief is generated by the patient and therapist.
There may have been evidence for a more adaptive way of thinking that was ignored
or distorted at that period in childhood and where this more adaptive belief could
have been applied. For example, a patient may hold core beliefs such as "I am bad"
and "I do not deserved to be loved." Examples of where these beliefs applied may
be very evident to the patient because this belief is dominant and highly salient. So,
he may illustrate times from childhood, such as being punished by a parent for being
messy, as an example of being "bad," or of having his concerns about an upsetting
event at school that led to feelings of rejection by classmates dismissed by a parent
as being unimportant as being an example of "not being worthy" of affection or
love. This highlights the dominance of the core negative belief and illustrates to the
patient how the core belief has colored his view of himself. Patients are encouraged
to keep a log of examples of when a new, more adaptive belief about themselves has
been strengthened or highlighted by experience in the here and now. Therapy aims
to increase prosocial behavior by changing negative beliefs about self and others to
more realistic and adaptive beliefs about self and others, as well as increasing interpersonal skills. More adaptive ways of relating to others are tested out by getting
the patient to experiment with behaving differently and, where possible, can be supported by working with significant others, such as partners. Behavioral experiments
are used to develop these and other more adaptive behaviors.

Because forming and maintaining relationships is often problematic for patients
with personality disorder, the relationship with the therapist can also become problematic. As a result, attention has to be paid to the therapeutic relationship because
the patient's beliefs about the therapist and therapy may interfere with progress.
The formulation of the patient's problems gives the therapist insight into beliefs
that a patient holds about self and others and how these beliefs may impact on the
therapeutic relationship. As these beliefs about self and others are examined over
the course of therapy, they can also be applied to the therapeutic relationship. The
patient can use the experience of the therapeutic relationship as an opportunity to
test if these beliefs are adaptive. Clinical, case-based supervision helps the therapist maintain a healthy relationship with the patient and to keep sessions focused.
A therapist will make the assumption that a patient is willing to work with him

therapeutically and that the patient is doing the best he or she can at any one time. This assumption is helpful for patients whose motivation to change lifelong patterns may fluctuate.

HOW CBTpd DIFFERS FROM CBT

Other differences in the structure and content of therapy arise as a consequence of the major differences between CBT for mental disorders and CBT for personality disorders—CBTpd (Davidson, 2007). For example, it is clear that the therapy is likely to be longer, although we have found that 30 session over the course of 1 year can make significant and lasting changes (Davidson et al., 2010). The process of engaging the client through a historical narrative formulation takes longer because the therapist needs to know much more detail about the patient than he would if the patient had a mental health disorder such as depression. With a disorder such as depression, patients will have experienced times when they are not depressed and will have more capacity through their experience to know the difference between normal and abnormal emotional and behavioral states. Because personality disorder is a disorder that has its origin in childhood, a person who has a personality disorder may have little experience of what it is like to not have the problem. Indeed, they are even likely to find it hard to imagine what it would be like to be without their problems and difficulties.

In CBTpd, the initial phase of therapy is therefore designed to engage the patient by taking an in-depth personal, social, and psychiatric history. This can take up to five or six sessions with someone with BPD. We have found that it takes even more sessions with those who have had less contact with clinical mental health services, such as those with antisocial personality disorder. These patients are not used to "telling their story," describing their problems in a logical order, being questioned systematically, and having to think about how relationships and situations in their childhood and adolescence have had an impact on them as adults. Relationships with parents, siblings, other family members, and peers are explored in considerable depth to understand how these have affected the patient's view of him- or herself and other people. Core beliefs such as "I am unlovable," "I am no good," "other people will hurt me," and "I cannot trust other people" are understood in the context of the patient's life history. The behavioral strategies that have been overdeveloped over the patient's lifetime to cope with these beliefs are charted.

From a developmental perspective and from other historical information, the therapist can develop a formulation of the patients' problems and their development from childhood into adulthood. The way that this is developed and presented to the patient also differs from standard CBT. In CBTpd, we present the formulation as a narrative and write it as a coherent story of the patient's life. This formulation is our psychological understanding, using CBT and our knowledge of developmental psychology, of how the patient has come to hold the beliefs he has about himself and others and the behaviors that are overdeveloped and problematic. This narrative formulation is written either as a letter to the patient or more simply as a two- or three-page account of the patient's life.

POTENTIAL LIMITATIONS OF CBTpd

From our clinical experience and through research examining the efficacy of CBTpd for borderline and antisocial personality disorders, we have found that 30 sessions over the course of 1 year can produce important changes in borderline personality-disordered patients (Davidson, Norrie, et al., 2006, Davidson et al., 2009). We also know that the competence with which the therapy is delivered has an impact on therapy: a more competent therapist will reduce the number of suicidal episodes in patients with BPD more than will a therapist who is less competent by at least a factor of three (Norrie, Davidson, Tata, & Gumley, 2013). This suggests that to be effective at delivering CBTpd, therapists need to be properly trained, knowledgeable about the CBTpd model, and able to apply the therapy skillfully. We have found that regular supervision is important in maintaining the therapist's ability to offer high-quality CBTpd. It helps the therapist reflect on the patient's problems and the content of therapy, as well as on the therapeutic relationship (Davidson et al., 2010).

EMPIRICAL STUDIES SUPPORTING THE TREATMENT

In 2011, there were 28 trials of psychological therapies in BPD (Stoffers et al., 2012); BPD has by far the most trials of all the personality disorders. In the majority of studies, numbers of patients recruited into trials have been low and further larger studies are required that are more methodologically rigorous, such as including blinding assessors to patient treatment groups to decrease investigator bias.

Table 17.2 describes RCTs in which patients with BPD have been treated with CBT. Of note, fewer than 300 patients with BPD in total have been treated in these studies collectively. This relatively small number of people studied means that there is a degree of uncertainty about how effective CBT is overall. The patients and the context of therapy included in the studies may not be similar, and, in addition, the type of CBT intervention varied between the trials.

Davidson's model of CBT (CBTpd) described is an adaptation of Beck's CBT for personality disorder specifically designed to treat antisocial and borderline personality disorders (Davidson, 2007; Davidson et al., 2009). Cottraux et al. (2009) delivered CBT based on Beck's and other CBT colleagues' (e.g., Layden, Newman, Freeman, & Morse, 1993) treatment of people with personality disorders. Bellino et al. (Bellino, Zizza, Rinaldi, & Bogetto, 2007), on the other hand, appears to have utilized standard CBT for depression that would be applied with patients who have an Axis I disorder rather than CBT for personality disorders (Beck & Freeman, 1990). This small study of 35 patients was concerned with the treatment of depression in patients with BPD, not improvement in BPD per se. All patients were outpatients with a diagnosis of BPD and a major depressive episode. They were randomly

TABLE 17.2 Randomized controlled trials of cognitive-behavior therapy (CBT) in borderline personality disorder

	Trial comparison	Participants	N 270	Treatment characteristics	Results	Comments
Davidson et al., 2006; **Davidson et al., 2010**	TAU +CBTpd vs. TAU	All had diagnosis of BPD plus (1) suicidal episode or (2) recent psychiatric admission	106	30 sessions over 52 weeks	TAU + CBTpd >TAU	Average *n* sessions = 16 Follow-up at 6 years gains maintained.
Cottraux et al., 2009	CBT vs. RST	Outpatients with BPD	65	52 weeks plus 1-year follow-up	Difference between groups except CGI: CBT > RST HS: CBT > RST	Only *n* = 38 assessed at year 1 and *n* = 21 in year 2
Bellino, 2007	Combined treatment: fluoxetine + IPT vs. fluoxetine + CT	All had major depressive episode in addition to BPD	35	6 months; no follow-up	ADM+IPT = ADM+CBT for depression	Small study; outcome on BPD not assessed
Evans et al., 1999	MACT vs. TAU	Cluster B suicide attempt in past 12 months	34	6 weekly sessions	MACT > TAU suicide attempts, depression; cost of care less in MACT	Small pilot study
Weinberg et al., 2006	TAU + MACT vs. TAU	Women with nonsuicidal self-harm	30	6 weekly sessions	TAU+MACT >TAU	Small pilot study

BPD, borderline personality disorder; CBT, cognitive-behavioral therapy; IPT, interpersonal therapy; MACT, manual-assisted cognitive therapy; RST, Rogerian supportive psychotherapy; TAU, treatment as usual; ADM, Antidepressant medication, HS, Hopelessness Scale; CGI, Clinical Global Impression Scale.

assigned to one of the two combined treatments and treated for a short period of time (24 weeks). The treatments were fluoxetine plus interpersonal therapy or fluoxetine plus cognitive therapy. The assessments not surprisingly reflected the studies' aim of assessing affective disturbance.

The largest trial of CBT is our own, based in three parts of the United Kingdom and known as the BOSCOT trial (Davidson, Norrie, et al., 2006; Davidson, Tyrer, et al., 2006; Palmer et al., 2006). Therapists, trained in CBTpd, delivered 30, 1-hour sessions over the course of 1 year to 54 of the 106 patients with BPD who had either made a suicide attempt in the previous 12 months or attended accident and emergency services prior to entry into the study or who had received a psychiatric admission. Both groups received the usual treatment they would have received had the study not been undertaken (treatment as usual [TAU]). TAU consisted of a wide variety of resources, such as inpatient and outpatient hospital services, including A&E services; community-based services, such as drop-in centers; and primary and community care services. Both groups improved over the course of the study and at 1-year follow-up. Those who had received CBTpd had less suicidal acts, showed a decrease in dysfunctional beliefs, were less anxious, and were less distressed. The patients in this study were likely to have comorbid diagnoses because we did not rule out comorbid problems such as depression or alcohol and drug abuse that are common in BPD.

One of the strengths of this RCT was that there was very little loss to follow-up with 102 (96%) patients followed-up 2 years post baseline. We also carried out a 6-year follow-up of the BOSCOT patients (Davidson et al., 2010). Follow-up data were obtained for 82% of patients at 6 years. The gains of CBTpd over usual treatment in reduction of suicidal behavior seen after 1-year follow-up were maintained in the longer term. At 6 years, 54% of the sample no longer met diagnostic criteria for BPD: 56% (n = 24/43) of the CBTpd group and 52% (n = 17/33) of the TAU group (Davidson et al., 2010). Like other follow-up studies, self-harm and suicidal behavior had improved, but the affective disturbance that is characteristic of BPD had changed to a lesser degree over time (Plakun, Burkhardt, & Muller, 1995; Zweig-Frank & Paris, 2001). Compared to those who had usual treatment, the length of hospitalization and cost of services were lower in those who had received CBTpd. This study also evaluated the cost effectiveness of therapy (Davidson et al., 2010; Palmer et al., 2006). Those who received usual treatment had approximately three times higher costs than in the CBTpd group: £16,658 vs. £5,015 (mean difference £11,643; 95% confidence interval [CI] £441–29,401) over the follow-up period, indicating that the relatively brief CBTpd is highly cost efficient (see Table 17.2).

The French study by Cottraux and his colleagues (2009) had a modest-sized sample with 33 people randomized to CBT and 32 to Rogerian supportive psychotherapy (RST). Of particular interest in this RCT is the comparison between a directive psychological therapy (CBT) and a nondirective therapy (RST). Therapy was delivered similarly in both groups by the same therapists. Both therapies were delivered in individual 1-hour sessions, over the course of 1 year. However, therapy was delivered in two 6-month phases: an initial phase of weekly sessions of intensive care (24 sessions over the first 6 months) followed by a maintenance phase with a session every fortnight over the course of 6 months (12 sessions). Only 38 participants were evaluated at end of therapy and 21 at a further 1-year follow-up, indicating considerable loss of information and dropout. There were no differences between the two groups on the whole, although there is an indication that CBT did better at retaining patients in treatment. There was some indication at some of the points of assessment that those who received CBT had lower levels of hopelessness (at week 24) and did better on the Clinical Global Impression (CGI) scale at 2-year follow-up.

In an Italian study by Bellino and colleagues (2007), both combined therapies of antidepressant medication plus one of two psychotherapies were found to be efficacious in treating major depression patients with BPD. This small study of 35 patients was concerned with the treatment of depression in patients with BPD, not improvement in BPD per se. All patients were outpatients with a diagnosis of BPD and a major depressive episode. Participants were randomly assigned to one of the two combined treatments and treated for 24 weeks. The treatments were either fluoxetine and interpersonal therapy (IPT) or fluoxetine and cognitive therapy (CT). There were a few differences between the combined interventions. IPT was more effective on a few measures or subscales: social functioning and on the domains domineering or controlling and intrusive or needy in the Inventory of Interpersonal Problems (Horowitz, Alden, & Wiggins, 2000). The combined treatment with CT had greater effects on anxiety and on psychological functioning. However, this was a small study and the findings concentrate on the outcome for depressive symptoms and functioning rather than on BPD per se.

Two studies examining the efficacy of manual-assisted cognitive therapy (MACT) on patients with BPD are included in Table 17.2. MACT (Schmidt & Davidson, 2004) is a brief form of CBT designed to be delivered to patients who are suicidal, many of whom have personality disorder. In MACT, patients receive a 70-page workbook or manual that outlines the therapy and provides self-help. Therapists use the book to guide therapy over six to eight sessions. The book contains some exercises aimed at self-soothing that are found in dialectical behavior therapy (Linehan, 1993). Evans et al. (1999) randomized 34 patients seen after an episode of deliberate self-harm, with personality disturbance within the flamboyant cluster, and who had a previous parasuicidal episode within the past 12 months. Sixteen patients received TAU, and 18 received MACT. Of the 32 patients followed-up at 6 months, 10 patients in each group (56% MACT and 71% TAU) had a further suicidal act. The rate of suicidal acts was lower in the MACT group, and self-rated depression improved more than in the usual treatment group. The observed cost of care was also 46% less with MACT.

Following on from the work of Evans et al. (1999), a larger randomized study of 480 patients was undertaken of MACT (Tyrer et al., 2003). This included a wider range of patients than just BPD patients and is not included in Table 17.2 as a result. In this larger study, MACT was found to be of limited efficacy in reducing self-harm repetition, but when the findings were taken in conjunction with the economic evaluation or assessment of cost effectiveness (Byford et al., 2003), MACT was found to be superior to TAU in terms of cost and effectiveness combined. However, secondary analyses of data from this study found that patients with more personality disorder problems and with BPD did less well than did those with less personality disturbance in that they had a greater incidence of repeat suicidal episodes and showed a shorter time to first repeat episode (Tyrer et al., 2004). There was some evidence that there may have been poor uptake of MACT sessions in this group of patients with repetitious suicidal behavior.

Weinberg et al. (Weinberg, Gunderson, Hennen, Christopher, & Cutter, 2006) modified MACT to focus on deliberate self-harm (DSH) as opposed to suicidal behavior in 30 patients with BPD, all of whom who were also in receipt of usual treatment. Those who received MACT ($n = 15$) had significantly less frequent and less severe DSH at completion of therapy and at 6-months follow-up compared to usual treatment. However, MACT did not affect the level of suicidal ideation or the time to a repeat episode of DSH. Taken together, it would seem that even brief forms of CBT may be cost-effective treatment for patients with personality disturbance who self-harm.

WHO IS BEST SUITED FOR CBTpd?

To date, there are too few studies of any therapy in patients with BPD to make any definitive statement about who would be most likely to benefit and who would not benefit. Davidson et al. (2010) examined some prognostic indicators of good and poor outcome in their 6-year follow-up of patients treated in the BOSCOT trial.

We define poor outcome as any suicide attempt in the follow-up period. Only having special needs at school was specifically associated with the presence of any suicide attempts during the 6-year follow-up. This observation should be treated with caution as only 19 (or 17.9%) of the original sample described problems at school that could be classified as special needs. This group of patients may be particularly vulnerable and may have a variable response to all therapies. It may be the case that other therapies have excluded these patients from their studies and that CBTpd included a sample that is more representative of the general population.

Dropout from therapy can be problematic in studies and may indicate that patients do not engage with therapy. CT retained patients with BPD in therapy longer than RST in one of the trials listed in Table 17.2 (Cottraux et al., 2009). However, determining dropout from treatment can be problematic because it depends on the definition of dropout. We found that, in practice, a minority of patients do not attend therapy at regular intervals, cancelling some appointments and not attending others but nonetheless remaining in therapy. In the BOSCOT trial, patients did not drop out but continued to attend, albeit that some did so rather irregularly (Davidson, Norrie, et al., 2006). Ratings from patients on the Working Alliance Inventory (Andrusyna,

Tan, DeRubeis, & Luborsky, 2001) suggest that both the patients and therapists view the experience of therapy to have been positive.

CONCLUSION

BPD is a disabling condition characterized by emotional instability, interpersonal problems, and impulsive and self-harm behaviors. CBT for personality disorders is one of several evidence-based therapies for those with BPD. The use of a developmental formulation to engage individuals in therapy and increase their psychological understanding of problems is a key characteristic. Of note, this therapy is less intensive than other therapies designed to treat BPD, with 30 sessions over the course of 1 year delivered. When compared to other evidence-based psychological therapies such as MBT and DBT, CBT for personality disorders is also effective in treating those with the more severe levels of problems such as suicidal behavior and severe depression (Davidson & Tran, 2013). The degree of a therapist's competence in delivery of therapy is important in determining outcome, indicating the need for systematic training and supervision of therapy for this challenging group.

REFERENCES

Ainsworth, M. D. S., Blehar, M. C., Waters, E., & Wall, S. (1978). *Patterns of attachment: A psychological study of the Strange situation.* Hillside, NJ: Erlbaum.

Andrusyna, P., Tang, T., DeRubeis, R., & Luborsky, L. (2001). The factor structure of the Working Alliance Inventory in cognitive-behavioral therapy. *Journal of Psychotherapy Practice & Research, 10,* 173–178.

Beck, A. T., & Freeman, A. (1990). *Cognitive therapy of personality disorders.* New York: Guilford.

Beck, A. T., Freeman, A., & Davis, D. D. (2004). *Cognitive therapy of personality disorders* (2nd ed.). New York: Guilford.

Bellino, S., Zizza, M., Rinaldi, C., & Bogetto, F. (2007). Combined therapy of major depression with concomitant borderline personality disorder: Comparison of interpersonal and cognitive psychotherapy. *Canadian Journal of Psychiatry, 52,* 718–725.

Byford, S., Knapp, M., Greenshields, J., Ukoumunne, O. C., Jones, V., Thompson, S., . . . Davidson, K. (2003). Cost-effectiveness of brief cognitive behavior therapy versus treatment as usual in recurrent deliberate self-harm: A rational decision making approach. *Psychological Medicine, 33,* 977–986.

Cottraux, J., Note, I. D., Boutitie, F., Milliery, M., Genouihlac, V., Yao, S., . . . Gueyffieret, F. (2009). Cognitive therapy versus rogerian supportive therapy in borderline personality disorder. *Psychotherapy and Psychosomatics, 78,* 307–316.

Davidson, K., Halford, J., Kirkwood, L., Newton-Howes, G., Sharp, M., & Tata, P. (2010). CBT for violent men with antisocial personality disorder. Reflections on the experience of carrying out therapy in MASCOT, a pilot randomized controlled trial. *Personality and Mental Health, 4,* 86–95.

Davidson K., Norrie J., Tyrer P., Gumley A., Tata P., Murray H., & Palmer S. (2006b). The effectiveness of cognitive behaviour therapy for borderline personality disorder: Results from the Borderline Personality Disorder Study of Cognitive Therapy (BOSCOT) trial. *Journal of Personality Disorders, 20,* 450–465.

Davidson, K. M. (2007). *Cognitive therapy for personality disorders. A guide for clinicians* (2nd ed.). Hove, UK: Routledge.

Davidson, K. M., & Tran, C. F. (2013). Impact of treatment intensity on suicidal behaviour and depression in borderline personality disorder: A critical review. *Journal of Personality Disorders, 27*, 113–130.

Davidson, K. M., Tyrer, P., Gumley, A., Tata, P., Norrie, J., Palmer, S., . . . Macaulay F. (2006a). Rationale, description, and sample characteristics of a randomized controlled trial of cognitive therapy for borderline personality disorder: The BOSCOT study. *Journal of Personality Disorders, 20*, 431–449.

Davidson, K. M, Tyrer, P., Tata, P., Cooke, D., Gumley, A., Ford, I., . . . Crawford, M. J. (2009). Cognitive behaviour therapy for violent men with antisocial personality disorder in the community: An exploratory randomized controlled trial. *Psychological Medicine, 39*, 569–578.

Emmelkamp, P. M. G., Benner, A., Kuipers, A., Feiertag, G. A., Koster, H. C., & van Apeldoorn, F. J. (2006). Comparison of brief dynamic and cognitive-behavioural therapies in avoidant personality disorder. *British Journal of Psychiatry, 189*, 60–64.

Evans, K., Tyrer, P., Catalan, J., Schmidt, U., Davidson, K., Dent, J., . . . Thompson, S. (1999). Manual-assisted cognitive-behaviour therapy (MACT): A randomized controlled trial of a brief intervention with bibliotherapy in the treatment of recurrent deliberate self-harm. *Psychological Medicine, 29*, 19–25.

Horowitz, L. M., Alden, L. E., & Wiggins, J. S. (2000). *Inventory of interpersonal problems*. San Antonio, TX: The Psychological Corporation.

Layden, M. A., Newman, C. F., Freeman, A., & Morse, S. B. (1993). *Cognitive therapy for borderline personality disorder*. Boston: Allyn and Bacon.

Linehan, M. M. (1993). *Cognitive-behavioral treatment of borderline personality disorder*. New York: Guilford.

Norrie, J., Davidson, K., Tata, P., & Gumley, A. (2013). Influence of therapist competence and quantity of CBT on suicidal behaviour and inpatient hospitalisation in a randomized controlled trial in borderline personality disorder. Further analyses of treatment effects in the BOSCOT study. *Psychology and Psychotherapy*.

Padesky, C. A. (1994). Schema change processes in cognitive therapy. *Clinical Psychology and Psychotherapy, 1*, 267–278.

Palmer, S., Davidson, K., Tyrer, P., Gumley, A., Tata, P., Norrie, J., . . . Seivewright, H. (2006). The cost-effectiveness of cognitive behaviour therapy for borderline personality disorder: Results from the BOSCOT trial. *Journal of Personality Disorders, 20*, 466–481.

Plakun, E. M., Burkhardt, P. E., & Muller, J. P. (1995). 14 year follow-up of borderline and schizotypal personality disorders. *Comprehensive Psychiatry, 27*, 443–455.

Rutter, M., & Rutter, M. (1993). *Developing minds: Challenge and continuity across the life span*. New York: Basic Books.

Schmidt, U., & Davidson, K. (2004). *Life after self harm*. Hove, UK: Brunner-Routledge.

Stoffers, J. M., Völlm, B. A., Rücker, G., Timmer, A., Huband, N., & Lieb, K. (2012). Psychological therapies for people with borderline personality disorder. *Cochrane Database of Systematic Reviews, 8*, CD005652. doi:10.1002/14651858.CD005652.pub2

Tyrer, P., Thompson, S., Schmidt, U., Jones, V., Knapp, M., Davidson, K., . . . Wessely, S. (2003). Randomized controlled trial of brief cognitive behavior therapy versus treatment as usual in recurrent deliberate self-harm: The POPMACT study. *Psychological Medicine, 33*, 969–976.

Tyrer P., Tom, B., Byford S., Schmidt U., Jones V., Davidson K., . . . Catalan J. (on behalf of the POPMACT Group). (2004). Differential effects of manual assisted cognitive behaviour therapy in the treatment of recurrent deliberate self-harm and personality disturbance: The POPMACT study. *Journal of Personality Disorder, 18*, 102–116.

Weinberg, I., Gunderson, J. G., Hennen, J., Christopher, J., & Cutter, C. J. (2006). Manual assisted cognitive treatment for deliberate self-harm in borderline personality disorder patients. *Journal of Personality Disorders, 20*, 482–492.

Young, J. E., Klosko, J. S., & Weishaar, M. E. (2003). *Schema therapy: A practitioner's guide.* New York: Guilford.

Zweig-Frank, H., & Paris, J. (2001). Predictors of outcome in a 27-year follow-up of patients with borderline personality disorder. *Comprehensive Psychiatry, 43*, 103–107.

/// 18 /// Supportive Psychotherapy and Case Management

DAVID J. HELLERSTEIN AND RON B. AVIRAM

WHY SUPPORTIVE PSYCHOTHERAPY FOR BORDERLINE PERSONALITY DISORDER?

Supportive psychotherapy (SPT) has been a psychotherapy approach ever since clinicians recognized that a therapeutic relationship is a vital component of the healing process. SPT was developed before structured psychological treatment theories were developed. It can serve as an umbrella approach that is recognizable to most clinicians regardless of their specific theoretical allegiance, as a pragmatic psychotherapeutic modality widely used by clinicians. Unlike cognitive-behavioral therapy (CBT) or dialectical behavior therapy (DBT), there is no school of SPT. In a contemporary context, SPT is not part of a school of psychological theory such as psychoanalysis or CBT. It may be most closely associated with a broad eclectic approach, and yet it has its own unique logic and structure. In describing the foundations of SPT, Novalis, Rojcewicz, and Peele (1993) and Pinsker (1997) have stated that, rather than seeking an underlying theory of SPT, we would be more accurate if we attend to the functional elements of the approach.

Recently, the term "supportive psychotherapy" has been used to describe a broad range of psychotherapy practices. However, when clinicians use the term SPT, it is necessary to clarify the specifics of their particular application. One of the dominant conceptualizations (Brenner, 2012) is a general framework that identifies SPT as embodying the nonspecific factors that comprise all psychotherapies. Another conceptualization views SPT within a general framework of psychodynamic psychotherapies, but functioning primarily as a holding context with minimal interventions to avoid evoking anxiety (Brenner, 2012). According to a third conceptualization of SPT, one that emerged in recent decades within the context of psychotherapy research studies, the psychotherapy control condition is called supportive psychotherapy (Clarkin, Levy, Lenzenweger, & Kemberg, 2007; Kocsis et al., 2009; Markowitz, Kocsis, Christos, Bleiberg, & Carlin, 2008). However, such SPT approaches may actually proscribe certain interventions that are commonly used in clinical treatment, such as reframing or perspective taking. This stand-in SPT is employed to provide a "neutral" psychotherapy control, providing comparable amounts of attention to a putatively more active psychotherapy approach. Discussions of the efficacy of psychotherapy often imply that this attenuated SPT, which is basically being used as an attentional control in psychotherapy studies, is comparable to supportive psychotherapy practiced by skilled clinicians, whereas it clearly lacks many of the basic elements of true supportive psychotherapy (Budge, Baardseth, Wampold, & Flückiger, 2010).

The fourth perspective, as described by Brenner (2012), considers SPT as a uniquely helpful therapeutic modality that incorporates active interventions. When clinicians suggest that SPT is warranted with a particular patient, it often implies that the patient cannot tolerate the more active treatment approach that is usually provided by those clinicians. In contrast, as proponents of this fourth perspective, we (Hellerstein, 1994) have contended that supportive psychotherapy should be the treatment model of choice for most patients seeking psychotherapy.

Pinsker and colleagues (Hellerstein, Pinsker, Rosenthal, & Klee, 1994; Pinsker, 1997) describe SPT as an active therapy with a conversational style that uses direct measures to enhance self-esteem, adaptive skills, and psychological functioning. They indicate that its conversational style is a continuous effort to recognize and enhance adaptive skills and improve psychological functioning, including access to a full range of emotional experience. In the course of an effective SPT, psychological defenses are identified and recognized as adaptive or maladaptive. Defenses are supported unless they are distinctly maladaptive, and reactions to the therapist (transference) are addressed only when they are negative or interfere with the conduct of therapy (Hellerstein et al., 1994). Pinsker et al.'s definition is atheoretical, with the contention that it is an approach comfortably practiced by therapists from a wide range of theoretical backgrounds.

Thus, instead of being a therapy with a unified theoretical underpinning, SPT is a therapeutic approach that is technique-driven with a disciplined interpersonal style. The conversational style of engaging patients is deceptively simple, and yet it seamlessly facilitates underlying shifts in the patient's experience of self in relation to another person. There tends to be agreement about the wide range of interventions that SPT utilizes. Table 18.1, adapted from Aviram et al. (Aviram, Hellerstein, Gerson, & Stanley, 2004) shows the variety of interventions and potential uses of these techniques to address the needs of individuals with a wide variety of mental health difficulties including borderline personality disorder (BPT).

The psychotherapeutic relationship between a patient and therapist is vital in facilitating improvement. It is important to clarify that there is a distinction between a supportive relationship that patients may have with friends or family members and a psychotherapeutic relationship in SPT. One clear difference is that, in SPT, the relationship is intentionally oriented toward change. In contrast, a supportive relationship does not imply that change is intended. Similarly, SPT is conversational in style but differs from a normal conversation in that the intention of talking is for change toward a better life. Rather than giving unconditional support or "handholding," the SPT therapist uses a conversational style and supportive techniques in the pursuit of specific treatment goals (Hellerstein, 2004).

In SPT, the interaction between the therapist and patient is flexible in that it waxes and wanes in the demand placed upon a patient to change. This is not so different from the description provided by DBT, in which change is balanced with acceptance (Lineham, 1987). However, in SPT, the therapist is a collaborator rather than "the expert" seen in DBT. This collaborative therapeutic stance allows for examination of the patient's life without an implicit critical voice that the clinician can unconsciously or sometimes directly convey. There is an effort made to develop and maintain the therapeutic alliance while limiting psychological dependency or regression. SPT's conversational tone creates an important atmosphere in each session: for instance, avoiding prolonged silences may help to decrease the patient's anxiety and avoid regression. As a result, there is a tendency to experience the sessions as not overly emotional or overly intellectual; there is a balance between the thinking and feeling processes. This can enhance the patient's capacity to recognize and temper intense emotions. Alternatively, as obsessive thinking intensifies, it is possible to recognize that there are likely to be particular emotions that can be acknowledged. The atmosphere in SPT helps to facilitate a sense of psychological safety, which many individuals with BPD coming for psychotherapy have rarely had in their lives.

DESCRIPTION OF SUPPORTIVE PSYCHOTHERAPY IN BPD

Because the SPT style is relatively easy to teach and apply, it can be implemented in a wide range of settings by clinicians of various levels of experience. It has been adapted (Aviram et al., 2004; Clarkin, Levy, Lenzenweger, & Kernberg, 2007; Jørgensen et al., 2012) for individuals with BPD, and we believe that it can be used as an active and effective treatment approach with this population.

SPT techniques such as "striking when the iron is cold" and bringing emotionally difficult topics into the discussion are often intuitively recognizable to both clinician and patient, and the demand upon the patient to change is generally tolerable. SPT emphasizes goals within a nondirective therapeutic framework. SPT draws attention to patients' strengths, strengths that have often been overshadowed by repetitive crises and disappointments. In adapting SPT for work with individuals with BPD, SPT therapists are more attentive to modulating the therapeutic relationship than when working with other patients: attending to decreasing patients' anxiety while avoiding excessive regression, emotional dependency, or impulsive behaviors. Since people with BPD are often exquisitely rejection-sensitive, the SPT therapist uses techniques to enhance a patient's self-esteem and avoid taking a critical stance.

TABLE 18.1 Two atheoretical descriptions of supportive psychotherapy

	Novalis, Rojcewicz, & Peele (1993)	Pinsker & Rosenthal (1988)
Conceptual basis and goals	1. Reducing behavioral dysfunction and subjective mental distress 2. Support and enhance patients' strengths/coping skills and capacity to use environmental supports 3. Maximize treatment autonomy and independence from illness	1. Ameliorate symptoms and maintain, restore, or improve self-esteem, adaptive skills, and psychological functioning 2. Examine relationships and patients' emotional response and/or behavior 3. Respect adaptive defenses 4. Emphasize real relationship
Therapeutic relationship	1. Therapist demonstrates involvement, empathy, nonjudgmental acceptance, understanding, respect, interest, liking 2. In response to negative/distorted transference, therapist adjusts without interpreting 3. Therapist regulates distance 4. Therapist utilizes judicious self-disclosure	1. Therapist is conversationally responsive 2. Therapist collaborates in goal-setting 3. Agenda can be set by patient or therapist 4. Therapist frames termination similar to an end of an academic course 5. Therapist demonstrates respect and commitment to stick with patient and not reject because he or she does not get well
Interventions	1. Suggestion 2. Advice and guidance 3. Explicit direction 4. Limit setting 5. Control of affects and impulses 6. Education 7. Cognitive restructuring 8. Modeling	1. Clarification 2. Confrontation 3. Rationalization 4. Reframing 5. Encouragement 6. Advice 7. Modeling 8. Rehearsal and anticipation 9. Listening
Application to borderline personality disorder	1. Clear discussion of expectations and clarification of goals with ST 2. Early efforts to alleviate anxiety and depression 3. Emphasis on leveling emotional roller-coaster 4. Ongoing emphasis on limiting self-destructive behavior: therapist is initially available between sessions by phone; in later stages, self-reliance is supported	

TABLE 18.1 Continued

Novalis, Rojcewicz, & Peele (1993)	Pinsker & Rosenthal (1988)
5. Support of patients' sense of self by providing reality testing, reduction of black-or-white thinking, and acknowledgment of positive qualities	
6. Treatment should progress from early focus on self-injurious behavior, hopelessness, and emotional lability to examination of identity, life goals, and interpersonal satisfaction	
7. Over time, patient addresses his or her sense of being able to sustain positive aspects of life	

Adapted from Aviram et al., 2004.[9]

Psychotherapy with the BPD population needs to focus on their emotional and behavioral reactivity. Individuals with BPD often struggle with significant anger and impulsive behavior, such as self-cutting or impulsive sexual activities. They may have painfully low self-esteem, at times compensated by grandiosity, and entrenched and unforgiving self-criticality. It is important to recognize that BPD is a heterogeneous disorder based on both biological underpinnings and interpersonal learning. BPD manifests along a continuum of functioning that represent a person's effort to self-modulate and self-soothe, particularly in dealing with intense fears of abandonment. Unfortunately, their coping styles are often limited and interpersonally problematic.

For example, when Ms. A's spouse was late coming home from work, her anxiety was associated with the fear that her husband had abandoned her for another woman. Her inability to soothe herself and discuss the incident with her husband led to an extreme emotional reaction when her husband stepped through the door. Supportive psychotherapy addresses such emotional reactivity to stressors and works toward shifting maladaptive impulses to more adaptive strategies. Frequently, the SPT therapist will emphasize the use of the word "and" when dealing with these situations. For example, in work with a patient who repeatedly cuts himself to relieve psychic pain, but who reacts defensively when he is told that he should stop cutting himself, the therapist can offer alternatives: "In the past, when you got upset your go-to strategy to relieve your emotional pain was to cut yourself, and today you can also choose to find new ways of dealing with upset, such as calling a friend or going for a walk, and knowing that you can tolerate your feelings better. Let's see if there is any way you can increase your choices when you are feeling this way." By expanding alternatives in a nonthreatening or challenging way, the SPT therapist works to offer control and to help the patient to increase his or her behavioral choices. Underneath these behavioral improvements, the SPT process intends to facilitate internal shifts in the experience of selfhood that ultimately reinforce the behavioral calm that can become a new normality.

Therapeutic Relationship in SPT

SPT differs from CBT and DBT in that it is nondirective. In comparison with the atmosphere in transference-focused psychotherapy (TFP), the SPT process is less confrontational about interpersonal dynamics that manifest between the patient and therapist. In SPT, the patient and psychotherapist work collaboratively to facilitate a new interpersonal experience. In the course of identifying useful coping strategies and ways to anticipate problem areas, SPT is also, perhaps, facilitating a shift in the experience of self. Holmes (1995) believes that the atmosphere created in an SPT context is healing in and of itself, possibly because it provides a safe and reliable space in which to establish an intimate and caring relationship. This may help the patient internalize the therapist as a real person with whom it is possible to engage safely (Pinsker, 1997; Werman, 1988). Furthermore, there is an active effort to decrease the patient's anxiety by tolerating it together in an interpersonal context, as well as by providing alternative meanings and new perspectives about oneself and situational conditions.

Early in the process of SPT, the therapist is active in establishing a context that is collaborative in tone. This effort at creating an environment for a dialogue between the patient and psychotherapist is instrumental for establishing hope as well as the effort required to alleviate anxiety, depression, and repetitive destructive reactions. As the patient's emotional experience stabilizes, the focus can shift to clarifying and limiting a variety of self-destructive behaviors that impact the patient. The SPT therapist can become a kind of auxiliary ego, offering his or her perspective on events and feelings as a way of providing reality testing. This process can help the patient to recognize the common defensive thinking processes such as splitting or black-and-white thinking. These simplifying thinking processes may have been previously useful for the individual with BPD in dealing with the overwhelming complexity of the world. However, these maladaptive defenses frequently leave them repeatedly disappointed when others react negatively to them.

The underlying goal of SPT in BPD is to support the development of a more secure sense of self. This requires identifying the positive strengths that can easily be overlooked in the context of ongoing life crises. For example, the SPT therapist may use reframing techniques in dealing with angry, overemotional responses. Rather than saying "you are an angry person," the SPT therapist may say, "One way to understand your feelings is to recognize that you are a person of strong passions" and add "You feel things very intensely, and sometimes your strong emotions are helpful and other times these reactions lead to problems." Furthermore, a clinician will ask the patient to identify situations that trigger maladaptive reactions. Ideally, treatment progresses from an early focus on self-injurious behavior, frequent emotional shifts, and hopelessness to helping the patient to discover and value his or her identity and life goals, and to experience a sense of interpersonal satisfaction. As these therapeutic efforts progress, the individual with BPD integrates an underlying self-soothing capacity that is facilitated with the stability and attention of his or her therapist.

Progress in SPT is associated with the patient's ability to tolerate and overcome emotional discomfort as well as finding that intense self-criticism is no longer his or her dominant mental state. Experiences that would have been emotionally overwhelming in the past are worked out with others in new ways. SPT not only attempts to change behavior and thinking, but also to facilitate a shift in the experience of unending misery experienced by individuals with BPD.

Mechanism of Change

Research demonstrates that patients with BPD can benefit from a wide range of treatment options. Bateman (2012) posits that outcomes in treatment studies that examine the efficacy of a therapy approach share some common elements. These include a structured treatment manual and encouraging active efforts to change, including an ongoing effort to process how emotions influence actions. The relationship between the psychotherapist and patient is a mechanism for change as well in all approaches. This alliance provides the value for any effort made to change. Therapeutic interventions become meaningful in a context that has relational meaning. Once a therapeutic alliance is established, one can ask what unique contribution each treatment offers. Each approach has a style that distinguishes it from other approaches. For example, the therapist's stance is very different in a DBT session from TFP (Clarkin et al., 2007), and these two differ from the session climate in SPT. Each of these approaches offers a particular language that is conveyed to patients over time. In DBT, the language learned in sessions includes conceptual use of self-states such as the wise mind or emotional mind framework. Similarly, TFP focuses on the underlying anger that is often present between patient and therapist.

The SPT approach provides its own unique language as well. Individuals with BPD tend to have a harsh self-critical voice. As that is discussed over time, patient and therapist can work collaboratively to identify which environmental conditions trigger those thoughts, and it can be useful to remind the patient that he or she can be kinder to themselves. This perspective may be surprising to a patient but is a clear integration of SPT objectives that involve perspective-taking, emotional patience, and empathy. This is an example of providing a language that a patient can understand and carry forward.

Another language component of SPT offers a way to disassemble the splitting process that is a common cognitive defensive process utilized by individuals with BPD. Patients may repeatedly frame their descriptions of themselves and others in all-or-none terms. Offering an alternative language is very important, and the SPT therapist does this with use of the word "and" during SPT. It is an effort to replace the either/or experience of the world and allow people to recognize the potential of not having to choose one limited option. Patients begin to notice that their interpersonal world can have options. This perspective recognizes that it is also possible to want two disparate choices at the same time. For example, a patient may be very angry at a boyfriend "and" love him and want to be with him simultaneously. A patient may be very anxious in a particular interpersonal environment "and" still want to participate in the activity. This language frees a person from the limits of the spitting defense, which has simplified the world on one hand (which is sometimes helpful) but also diminished its vitality.

The interpersonal experience that the individual with BPD has with the SPT therapist may be a significant contributing factor in improved self-esteem (Pinsker, 1997). However, as noted, the interpersonal experience in SPT goes beyond the supportive relationship that individuals can experience with friends and supportive family members. Identification with the SPT clinician is productive, as Werman (1988) discussed many years ago, because it facilitates an environment of psychological safety. Supportive psychotherapy is fundamentally a flexible approach that paces the work according to the patient's ability to tolerate attending to him- or herself. As the patient recognizes that the intention of the work is not primarily on changing behavior, but rather upon the person who is having the behavioral difficulties, the individual begins to trust the therapist's role and this facilitates his or her sense of safety. In fact, for most individuals with BPD, attention to psychological safety has been missing throughout their lives. Counterintuitively, patients may also have apprehensions about improving. Significant change would require that they relate in new ways to the psychotherapist as well as to individuals in their lives. Understood from a relational standpoint, these individuals know that they at least have some way of relating with others as they have throughout their lives, even with its difficulties. The SPT psychotherapist must be attentive to these anxieties about change and can directly acknowledge that the psychotherapy relationship does not have to end as positive changes develop for the patient.

The emphasis on containing anxiety is an important SPT condition that creates a safe climate during sessions. By considering the level of anxiety that patients manage and by acknowledging its impact on the patient's efforts to soothe in various ways, including maladaptive ways, the SPT clinician draws attention to the patient's actual efforts to manage in life. This normalizes the patient's actual behavior, however maladaptive. In SPT, attending to strengths is vital and so, rather than identifying the patient's behavior as bad and simply needing to change, we can recognize that the behavior began as an effort to manage anxiety and then reorient that same behavior in a positive direction. Even behavior like self-cutting can be recognized as a physical effort to self-soothe. The patient's need to use his or her body to alleviate anxiety might eventually be modified toward exercise or some similar physical activity.

Dealing with Defenses and Transference

In general, positive transference can be enhancing of any treatment, but in SPT it is not imperative that it is overtly acknowledged. In contrast, negative transference will impede progress and does need to be addressed. Psychotherapy with individuals with BPD can be emotionally intense, and patients may expect the therapist to be a disappointing figure similar to many they have known. In an effort to maintain balance between closeness and dependency with distancing and with-drawal, the SPT clinician is alert to the emotional climate during each session. Acknowledging the interpersonal experience in the session can be enhanced by using techniques such as clarification, reframing, limited confrontation, offering alternatives, teaching, or validation. If an adequate rapport has been established, then it is more likely that the patient will recognize that the therapist's perspective is a plausible and fair alternative to his or her experience. However, if it is early in the treatment and the therapeutic alliance is forming, it may be more necessary to accept the patient's perceptions and suggest that "we will see if there is more to say about it as we proceed." The interactions between the therapist and patient include a wide range of topics including self-injury and suicidal ideation. The therapist's ability to tolerate the anxiety that may emerge as these topics are discussed mod-els that need to talk rather than act out the impulses being discussed. As long as the therapist feels secure that actual safety is not compromised, it offers a chance to highlight the patient's strengths and adaptive defenses in dealing with difficult feelings. In contrast to a consistent and ongoing self-awareness about negative attributes and failures, it matters to what extent one's positive qualities are vali-dated. Again, this is a counter to the entrenched splitting process that dominates the cognitive perception of reality for individuals with BPD and which perpetuates their dysphoria and hopelessness.

Addressing Core Symptoms of BPD

SPT interventions that specifically address core DSM symptoms of BPD are dis-cussed in Table18.2.

Based on Pinsker et al.'s (Herllerstein et al., 1994; Pinsker, 1997; Winston, Rosenthal, & Pinsker, 2004) definition, SPT addresses three dimensions in treat-ment: self-esteem, adaptive skills, and psychological functions. These dimensions of self-functioning are interrelated and are ways to guide the focus of treatment. Figure 18.1 shows these components and importantly includes the relational experi-ence with the therapist.

It is vital to attend to the patient's description of emotional pain. Initially, the work is on learning to tolerate these feelings without taking action. This is the "slowing down" effort that can be quite helpful for these individuals. Simultaneously, it is necessary to uncover how interpersonal relationships are intertwined in a maladaptive pattern. As efforts are made in these areas, the treat-ment is likely to be infused with continuous negative self-descriptors associated with self-loathing and negative self-worth. This area is a long-term focus and is crucial if the therapist and patient are to begin to challenge the entrenched quality of these experiences.

TABLE 18.2 Examples of interventions used for patient issues related to core borderline personality disorder (BPD) criteria as set by the *Diagnostic and Statistical Manual of Mental Disorders* (DSM-IV)

BPD Symptom/Criteria	Type of Intervention	Example of ST Intervention
Recurrent suicidal threats or self-injurious behavior	Warning comment	"I want to bring something up, you may be upset, or it may be a difficult topic for you to speak about."
Chronic feelings of emptiness and boredom	Naming feelings	Help identify feelings based on nonverbal behavior or tone of voice when patient is unable to label how he or she feels.
Frantic efforts to avoid real or imagined abandonment	Normalize	"You were trying to hold on to someone that you care about. That is very normal, but it sounds like it backfired. Let's try to understand why."
Pattern of unstable and intense interpersonal relationships	Anticipatory comment	Predicting emotion based on life situation or what was talked about during session.
Affective instability	Alleviate anxiety	"You're telling me that you had a range of emotions in the past week, not just the bad ones. What was going on when you were feeling good about things?"
Inappropriate intense anger or lack of control of anger	Offering control	"If it is too hard, just say you don't want to speak about it anymore, and we'll stop."
Impulsiveness	Strike when the iron is cold	Discuss anxiety-provoking experiences or behaviors later in a session or come back to something, by saying, "You know, let's go back a little. You mentioned that you were so angry at your girlfriend when she was distant. What did you do that helped you stay in control?"

TABLE 18.2 Continued

BPD Symptom/Criteria	Type of Intervention	Example of ST Intervention
Marked and persistent identity disturbance	Realness of therapist to patient	Therapist uses a conversational style that is consistent and displays responsiveness and interest that help the patient develop self-image and establish life goals.

Adapted from Aviram et al., 2004.

How SPT Approaches Suicidal Behavior

Working with a population with BPD can challenge the clinician's ability to stay engaged when suicidal ideation or attempts occur. Behaviors that emerge over the course of treatment can reinforce the stigmatization of individuals with BPD as "difficult patients." The literature has noted that 75% of all patients with BPD make a suicide attempt (Zanarini, Gunderson, Frankenburg, & Chauncey, 1990); as many as 9% eventually die by suicide (Pompili, Girardi, Ruberto, & Tatarelli, 2005). These statistics can contribute to the negative perception of individuals with BPD held by clinicians (Aviram, Brodsky, & Stanley, 2006). As self-injurious behavior occurs in the course of treatment, the clinician may subtly withdraw an emotional investment in the patient. Individuals with BPD are sensitive to these subtle interpersonal shifts, which can trigger severe anxiety associated with abandonment fears. This intensifies a vicious cycle in which the patient may have even more severe reactions, which can lead to further withdrawal by the clinician, and so on. For example, after several months of apparently productive SPT, a patient comes to a session and reports that she had cut her arms 3 days earlier. She shows the therapist the cuts, which are deep but already scabbing. Once the therapist has assessed the medical risk and told the patient that the cuts will need to be looked at by a physician, he notices that he feels angry at the patient and disappointed that she did not call him before cutting, as they had discussed. The therapist must overcome these feelings to stay present and find a way to be productive with his patient. The patient apologizes, sensing her therapist's disappointment. He responds that he knows she feels bad about this, as he does, but together they will try to understand what happened. How the therapist handles his emotional reaction in this session can make a difference in the treatment. The patient will see that she will still be accepted and cared about even when things do not go well. As a way of combating potential therapist-induced exacerbation of a crisis and risk to the patient's safety, the SPT therapist can remain attentive to his or her negative reactions and emotional withdrawal. In doing so, the therapist can address the mutual desire for safety and how sensitivity to closeness and distance can influence safety.

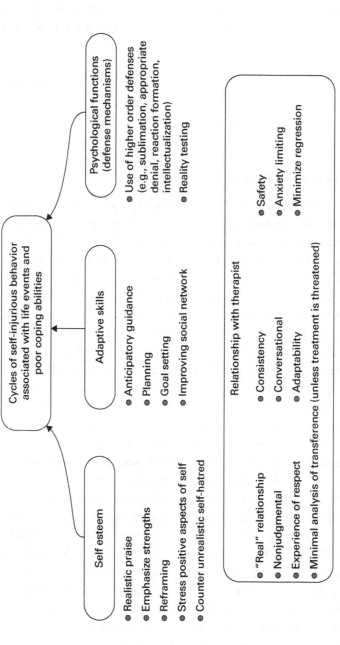

FIGURE 18.1 Components of supportive therapy adapted for patients with borderline personality disorder (BPD) and suicidal behavior. (Adapted from Aviram et al., 2004.)

The SPT therapist must be attentive to ensuring safety during crises, doing good clinical management, and appropriately using emergency room, crisis management services, and hospitalization when needed. The intent of SPT, as of all treatments, is to minimize the continuation of these crisis states and discover more adaptive possibilities. Rockland (1992) suggested that this may be the vital work with this patient group. If the clinician can assess and feel there is enough of a rapport to continue to work in an outpatient setting during crises, it can be a tremendously healing process for a person with BPD.

During these phases, beyond addressing acute safety issues, psychotherapy is oriented toward expanding the range of coping abilities, which can increase awareness about more adaptive options. The therapist must remain attentive to the positive qualities and strengths inherent in the individual to counter self-blaming instincts and impulsive and planned self-injurious behavior. Tangible solutions are often necessary to reduce strong emotions. These include planning activities, anticipating difficulties, normalizing feelings and reactions, and perhaps scheduling additional sessions during a crisis phase. The risk of self-harm is assessed in an ongoing process, and efforts are made to slow down the urgency of reacting to and of seeking reactions from others. This creates a buffer between the emotional crisis and the response.

By reframing the intention of self-injury as a maladaptive effort to get the necessary relief from psychic pain, patients may start to recognize that there can be more effective and healthy ways to resolve difficulties. The SPT method recognizes that patients can choose to harm themselves and that there are also alternatives that are less dangerous and self-destructive. Over a longer treatment process, this validation can have significant benefits. For example, a patient may report that, following a recent argument with a girlfriend, he became increasingly angry and fearful that she would leave him, triggering suicidal ideation. In-session interventions may involve praising his ability to tolerate the discomfort, not lashing out either at himself or his girlfriend, and reframing the experience as an opportunity for learning. Adaptive skills could emphasize planning strategies to manage such experiences more effectively in the future, recognizing his emotional signals, and anticipating situations in which such occurrences may happen. Finally, psychological functions involving higher order defense mechanisms, such as intellectualization or rationalization, would be supported if they minimize negative emotions.

Addressing Anger and Aggression

Supportive psychotherapy makes direct efforts to minimize destructive interpersonal difficulties that are overt, and many times covert, between the therapist and patient. An underlying hostile context between patient and therapist leads to poor outcomes[22] (Henry, Schacht, & Strupp, 1986). A subgroup of patients with BPD experience ongoing anger and impulsive aggression during interpersonal situations. These patients may present as hostile and devaluing or as overtly angry with the therapist. It is vital that the therapist emphasizes the affiliative dimensions of the therapeutic relationship by maintaining a conversational style and focusing on the aspects of the hostility related to self-esteem (Rosenthal, Muran, Pinsker, Hellerstein, & Winston, 1999). Without attacking the patient, the therapist can acknowledge the legitimate parts of the patient's anger. This often helps to defuse some of the emotion. During such moments, the therapist and patient could work together to recognize several features of the emotional reaction.

For example, the therapist may remind the patient that anger is often a signal of some familiar interpersonal situation in which he or she feels mistreated, thus identifying the legitimacy of the patient's feelings. The patient and therapist can also collaborate to figure out what elements of the relationship with the therapist or others are reflected in the current hostility. Although often difficult, the therapist's effort to talk about the hostility is important. If avoided or neglected, it will more than likely interfere with therapy, as it has in the patient's other interpersonal relationships. If the therapist and patient can identify the source of the hostility through a collaborative effort, it not only models that such feelings do not necessarily destroy a relationship, but also illustrates that they can be addressed interpersonally. Unfortunately, if the therapy dyad is unable to move beyond a help-rejecting, hostile, dominant adversarial position, treatment is unlikely to be successful with weekly SPT. In these cases, the individual may require more intensive interventions that include multiple times per week sessions, day treatment, a different psychotherapeutic approach, and/or medication.

EMPIRICAL STUDIES SUPPORTING THE USE OF SPT IN BPD

In the early 1990s, Conte (Conte & Plutchik, 1986) noted that research about SPT has been limited, relative to its widespread implementation in a wide range of clinical settings. Two decades later, this observation remains largely true. Furthermore, as described by Budge et al. (2010), studies of the efficacy of SPT are confounded by a number of factors, including nonecological definitions of supportive psychotherapy, unbalanced study design (more therapy time/training/supervision for comparator treatments), and researcher allegiance to putatively more potent forms of psychotherapy, such as CBT, DBT, and interpersonal psychotherapy (IPT). In 1953, Sullivan described supportive psychotherapy as a "Cinderella" of therapies, stuck at home while her "more glamorous psychotherapeutic sisters are away at the ball" (Budge et al., 2010; Holmes, 1995, p. 167). Budge et al. contend that despite an influx of quantitative outcome literature about the efficacy of SPT, "the empirical research conducted in the past two decades has used supportive therapy as a straw man to which to compare treatments rather than as a treatment of interest" (Budge et al., 2010; Hellerstein, 2011). Nevertheless, despite these caveats, numerous studies have shown that SPT has significant efficacy.

In the 1970s and 1980s, initial empirical data suggested the efficacy of SPT with phobic patients and among individuals with schizophrenia. Stanton et al., 1984; Zitrin, Klein, &Woerner, 1978). In the 1990s, Hellerstein et al. (1998) reported that SPT was equally effective in a population of patients with primarily cluster B and C Axis II disorders in providing relief from symptoms and improvement of interpersonal problems. Their results indicated that the therapeutic alliance remained stable with patients receiving SPT, suggesting that the alliance promoted by SPT might offer an important foundation for the treatment. These results were further supported by preliminary data in which patients participating in SPT completed a measure of interpersonal behavior at intake, the 40th session, and at 6-month follow-up. Results with a small sample suggested that significant and lasting improvement was achieved by subjects participating in SPT (also see Rosenthal et al., 1999).

Recently, Meyer, Hautzinger, and colleagues (2012) compared CBT with SPT for treatment of bipolar disorder, providing 20 sessions of psychotherapy over the course of 9 months in 76 subjects. Patients were randomly allocated to CBT or SPT ($N = 38$ in each condition) and treated weekly for 12 weeks, followed by biweekly then monthly sessions. Both conditions provided information about bipolar disorder, along with daily mood monitoring; in SPT, therapists "adopted a client-centered focus, meaning that whatever problems the patient presented were dealt with by providing emotional support and general advice." In contrast to more active forms of SPT, in Meyer and Hautzinger's SPT treatment, "no efforts were made to specifically link this information to the individual's biography or experience." Despite this hobbled SPT approach, depression decreased and psychosocial functioning improved in both treatments, and depression or mania recurrence did not differ between CBT and SPT. The authors concluded that both CT and SPT improved depressive symptoms, social functioning, and subjects' sense of internal locus of control.

Kocsis et al. (2009) studied cognitive behavioral analysis system of psychotherapy (CBASP) versus supportive therapy for augmentation of antidepressant nonresponse in chronic depression. As defined in that study, brief supportive psychotherapy (BSP) "emphasizes the nonspecific or 'common' factors assumed to be important ingredients across psychotherapies"(Frank, 1971; Rogers, 1951), including reflective listening, empathy, evoking affect, therapeutic optimism, and acknowledgment of patients' assets. Of note, this research SPT intervention strictly proscribed specific interpersonal, cognitive, behavioral, and psychodynamic interventions—types of interventions that might be used by supportive psychotherapists in clinical practice.

Recently, two meta-analyses have compared the efficacy of SPT to other forms of treatment, including psychotherapy and pharmacotherapy. In a 2010 meta-analysis, Tolin (2010) compared the efficacy of CBT to other forms of psychotherapy and concluded that there was no evidence of superiority of CBT to interpersonal or supportive psychotherapy. In a 2012 meta-analysis of the efficacy of "nondirective supportive psychotherapy for adult depression" (NDST), which reviewed 31 studies in which NDST was compared to other psychological or psychopharmacological treatments, Cuijpers et al. (2012) found that NDST was effective in the treatment of depression in adults. Furthermore, although it was less effective than other psychological treatments, "these differences were no longer present after controlling for researcher allegiance." Cuijpers et al. concluded that "NDST has a considerable effect on symptoms of depression."

Empirical Support for SPT in BPD

Data for the efficacy (or lack of efficacy) of SPT in BPD is limited, both in the number of studies performed and by the other factors noted by Budge et al. (2010). Two particularly relevant issues in studies of BPD are (1) whether a robust form of SPT is being tested and (2) the importance of allegiance effects among investigators and study clinicians, whether to DBT, TFP, or other treatment approaches.

We are aware of two large studies comparing SPT to other therapies. Clarkin et al. (2007) compared three treatments for BPD: DBT, TFP, and a dynamic supportive psychotherapy. Enrolling 90 patients who were randomly assigned to treatment, the study's main outcomes were suicidal behavior, aggression, impulsivity, anxiety, depression, and social adjustment, with a multiwave study design. Participants were predominantly female (92%) and Caucasian (68%); prior suicidal behavior was present in 57% and parasuicidal behavior in 62%.

Results indicated that patients in all three treatments showed significant improvement in depression, anxiety, global social functioning, and social adjustment over 1 year of treatment. Overall, patients treated with TFP showed improvement in 10 of 12 domains, whereas those treated with SPT and DBT improved in 6 and 5 of 12 domains, respectively. While some differences were found between treatments on individual domains (TFP and DBT were associated with improvements in suicidality; TFP and SPT were associated with improvements in anger, etc.), the authors stated that there was "general equivalence of outcome across the three treatments" (Clarkin et al., 2007, p. 927).

Jorgensen et al.'s recent study [13] enrolled 111 subjects with BPD into weekly mentalization-based individual psychotherapy (MBT) (plus weekly group therapy) or bi-monthly supportive therapy (SPT). SPT was delivered in a group format, and participants were encouraged to verbalize and understand interpersonal behavior and to reflect on each others' problems; therapists focused on problem-solving and relational problems outside the group and encouraged group members to develop more adaptive behavioral strategies. Therapists avoided making interpretations of transference and defenses. Results demonstrated similar levels of retention and improvement in both treatment groups. Symptom measures improved equally in both MBT and SPT, including on self-rated Beck Depression Inventory (BDI) and global symptom (BSI) items, as well as in the number of BPD diagnostic criteria listed in the *Diagnostic and Statistical Manual of Mental Disorders* (DSM-IV). The authors concluded that both treatment approaches were effective in treating

BPD when conducted by well-trained and experienced staff in a well-organized clinical setting.

In addition to studies of SPT in the treatment of BPD, recently there have been studies of what has been called "general psychiatric management (GPM)" or "structured clinical management (SCM)" (see next section), approaches that appear to contain elements commonly associated with SPT.

LIMITATIONS OF SPT

SPT has limitations in at least 3 areas:

1. *Acute and chronic severity issues*: While most patients with BPD are suitable for treatment using SPT, some patients present in states of extreme crisis, whether acute, subacute, or chronic. They may require clinical management in controlled settings, such as requiring inpatient hospital units, detoxification facilities, or acute medical wards. These patients often have significant comorbid psychiatric disorders (e.g., bipolar disorder), medical illnesses, or substance dependence, or they may be demonstrating high acute suicide risk using lethal means. Such patients may, however, become amenable to SPT interventions once their acute crises have been managed.

2. *Patients who require (or do best) with specific psychotherapy approaches that are not part of the core SPT intervention.* Some patients with BPD have ingrained behavioral patterns (whether impulsive acting out or behavioral inhibition or extreme avoidance) that may require the intensive behavioral approaches used in DBT or CBT. Other patients may have strong repeated transference reactions that repeatedly disrupt SPT treatment, which may need to be addressed in an intensive TFP. Still other patients may have social, interpersonal, or cognitive skill deficits and may do better with skill training or cognitive remediation.

3. *Functional impairment*: Perhaps most difficult for SPT (and other psychotherapy approaches) is the functional impairment associated with BPD over the long-term course. Numerous researchers (e.g., Stone, Hurt, & Stone, 1987) have demonstrated that individuals with BPD have difficulties with multiple areas of life functioning on an ongoing basis, including intimate relationships and work functioning. These areas of impairment persist even given the more positive longitudinal prognosis of BPD that has become evident in recent studies (Zanarini, Frankenburg, Hennen, & Silk, 2003). It is not clear to what degree these long-term impairments can be amenable to psychotherapies, including SPT and other approaches. Clinically, patients with BPD are often improved after a course of SPT, with less depression and suicidality, but a significant level of impairment may remain. Clearly, there is a need for further development of therapeutic interventions to address these common persistent deficits.

WHO IS BEST SUITED FOR SPT?

Given the relative paucity of high-quality SPT psychotherapy outcome research, it is premature to draw definitive conclusions about which patients with BPD are best suited for SPT versus other psychotherapy approaches. In a previous paper (Hellerstein et al., 1994), we contended that supportive psychotherapy should be the default therapy option for *all* individuals seeking psychotherapy; although that paper was not referring specifically to BPD, one could also entertain the possibility that SPT might be the default psychotherapy approach for those individuals as well. Patients not benefiting from SPT as a first treatment approach might then be referred for more specific and intensive treatment approaches, such as DBT or TFP. SPT has the advantages of being widely practiced by a broad range of psychotherapists, of being generally acceptable to patients, and of being adaptable for treatment of BPD (particularly to address impulsive, self-destructive, and suicidal behavior). Furthermore, SPT can be implemented in a variety of settings, including inpatient, outpatient, and residential, as well as in crisis management programs. Furthermore, SPT may provide factors that were shown to be important for good long-term outcome in Stone et al.'s long-term longitudinal study of outcome in BPD, in which positive outcome was associated with a "comfortable working relationship" with a clinician or clinicians and a continuous treatment relationship during periods of maximal suicide risk, rather than "exploration of preexisting dynamic factors" (Stone et al., 1987). Supportive psychotherapy, with its focus on a disciplined yet flexible treatment frame, may allow many patients with BPD to form and maintain such relationships over time.

However, it may be unrealistically optimistic to assume that SPT will become the default treatment option for BPD, particularly given the appeal of more specific and putatively more active treatment approaches to clinicians, researchers, funding agencies, and perhaps insurance companies as well. Even though SPT and structured clinical management have shown positive outcomes in research settings, more specific treatment approaches appear to promise to provide patients with better outcomes and hence have greater "curb appeal." Thus, while well-conducted SPT may achieve equivalent outcomes to DBT, CBT, TFP or other approaches, unfortunately SPT may still be perceived as a treatment option for patients who appear to lack the motivation for keeping behavioral logs, practicing mindfulness exercises, and following instructions in workbooks. What remains unclear at present, however, is whether more highly motivated patients with BPD would do just as well with SPT as with these other approaches.

Regardless of clinical fashion, as Jørgensen et al. (2012) state, given the heterogeneity of BPD, it appears unlikely that any one treatment "will be equally useful for all patients and future studies should examine the possible interaction between patient, treatment, therapist characteristics and treatment intensity." It is possible that not all patients with BPD require intensive long-term psychotherapy. Some patients may do best with TFP or mindfulness-based therapies. Many may benefit most from less intensive long-term (or possibly intermittent) supportive psychotherapy.

CASE MANAGEMENT, STRUCTURED CLINICAL MANAGEMENT, GENERAL PSYCHIATRIC MANAGEMENT IN BPD

Recent studies that examined the efficacy of empirically validated treatments for BPD have used comparison groups that have been labeled *general psychiatric management* (GPM; McMain et al., 2009) and *structured clinical management* (SCM; Bateman & Fonagy, 2009), which incorporate principles of good care of BPD. These two interventions seem to be similar and may overlap with SPT.

THEORY FOR CM, SCM, GPM IN BPD

Case management (CM) has been effective in a wide variety of medical and psychiatric disorders (Elkin et al., 1989). Individuals with BPD may particularly benefit from the continuity of care provided by case managers who can help coordinate care across different settings and providers (psychiatrists, psychologists, and social workers) and can facilitate social supports such as housing and food stamps. Case managers can use SPT techniques to enhance rapport and offer new perspectives on a patient's life.

DESCRIPTION OF CM, SCM, GPM IN BPD

Schiavone and Links (2012) identified key nonspecific variables that can be integrated into a clinical management approach of BPD, including an active stance in which the therapist is emotionally engaged with patients, that can foster hope while problem-solving strategies are developed.

Bateman and Fonagy (2009) utilized SCM as the comparison group for their MBT target treatment. The SCM approach incorporated generic best practices for BPD offered by nonspecialists in United Kingdom's psychiatric services, including individual and group psychotherapy with periodic psychiatric review. The psychotherapy was identified as resembling SPT with the addition of case management, advocacy support, and problem-focused interventions.

The treatment structure in McMain et al.'s study (McMain et al., 2009; McMain, Guimond, Streiner, Cardish, & Links, 2012) included 1-hour individual weekly sessions, including medication management based on a structured drug algorithm. In contrast to DBT, the McMain et al. approach expands the focus away from self-harm and suicidal behavior. The primary treatment strategies include psychoeducation about BPD, a helping relationship, a here-and-now focus, validation and empathy, and "active attention to signs of negative transference."

EMPIRICAL STUDIES SUPPORTING CM, SCM, GPM IN BPD

In 2001, the American Psychiatric Association issued treatment guidelines for BPD, which describe principles and specific best practices for the care of such individuals

(American Psychiatric Association, 2001). Recently, Bateman and Fonagy (2009) compared MBT versus SCM for treatment of 134 individuals with BPD. Therapists were experienced clinicians with equivalent levels of training. Positive outcomes were found in both treatment groups, with substantial improvement, although those assigned to MBT showed "a steeper decline of both self-reported and clinically significant problems, including suicide attempts and hospitalization" (Bateman & Fonagy, 2009). Although MBT showed greater improvements in most primary and secondary outcomes, SCM-treated subjects also improved significantly. For instance, 6-month periods free of suicidal behavior, severe self-injury, and hospitalization increased in both treatment groups. The authors concluded that "the rate of improvement in both groups was higher than spontaneous remission of symptoms" of BPD (Skodol et al., 2005; Zanarini, Frankenburg, Hennen, & Silk, 2003).

McMain et al. (2009) compared DBT with GPM, a combination of psychodynamically informed therapy and symptom-targeted medication management derived from specific recommendations in APA guidelines for BPD (American Psychiatric Association, 2001). Their study enrolled 180 patients diagnosed with BPD who had at least two suicidal episodes or nonsuicidal self-injurious episodes in the prior 5 years.

After 1 year of treatment, both groups showed significant improvement, with decreased frequency and severity of suicidal behavior and nonsuicidal self-injury, as well as fewer ER visits and decreased BPD symptoms. No significant differences were seen between groups. Improvement persisted at 2-year follow-up (McMain et al., 2012). Effects of GPM appeared to be long-lasting and significant. However, participants continued to show high levels of functional impairment, with fewer than 50% working or in school, and 39% receiving disability payments after 3 years.

Schiavone and Links (2012) similarly have concluded that effective psychotherapies for SIB in the context of BPD "contain generic common elements which are responsible for their success." They identify seven common elements: a coherent model to understand SIB, an active therapeutic stance, validation balanced with change-oriented techniques, encouragement of self-agency, establishment of a connection between actions and feelings, a method for assessing lethality; and access to supervision.

Similarly, Bateman concludes that McMain et al.'s study "adds persuasive evidence that well-structured general psychiatric treatment, which targets the acute symptoms of borderline personality disorder and bears little resemblance to the earlier unstructured treatment as usual, is as effective as branded specialized treatments," such as DBT (Bateman, 2012).

Bateman identifies common factors in effective treatments of BPD: "All ... share certain characteristics, and these elements rather than the specific techniques of treatment may be responsible for their effectiveness. These therapies 1) provide a structured manual that supports the therapist and provides recommendations for common clinical problems; 2) are structured so that they encourage increased activity, proactivity, and self-agency for the patients; 3) focus on emotion processing, particularly on creating robust connections between acts and feelings; 4) increase cognitive coherence in relation to subjective experience in the early phase of treatment by including a model of pathology that is carefully explained to the patient; and 5) encourage an active stance by the therapist, which invariably includes an explicit intent to validate and demonstrate empathy and generate a strong attachment relationship to create a foundation of alliance."

LIMITATIONS OF CM, SCM, GPM IN BPD

CM most likely has limitations with the population of patients with BPD. Individuals who are clinically referred to a case manager have significant limitations in their functioning at the onset. The challenge for the case manager is to maintain a working rapport with patients who may automatically limit their reliance on anyone. By the time a case manager is integrated into a treatment team, the patient may be presenting with impulsive behavior, including suicidality, as well as significant comorbidities.

WHO IS BEST SUITED FOR CM, SCM, OR GPM IN BPD?

Studies have not clearly delineated the clinical characteristics of patients most likely to benefit from CM, SCM, or GPM. Individuals with the fewest social supports may be most likely to benefit from traditional CM. They may benefit from having a coordinator who has an overview of their needs (such as housing, financial, and social supports). Often, treatment providers who are addressing problems in any one domain have little ongoing contact with providers in other life domains. One way to consider who is suited for CM is to assess if the patient can manage his or her own coordination of care and self-advocacy. When these skills are lacking or severely limited, then CM may provide significant benefits.

CONCLUSION

Emerging evidence suggests that SPT and various forms of clinical management (SCM, GPM) may be helpful for many, if not most, patients with BPD. Such integrated approaches should form the comparison group to test the efficacy of putatively more powerful interventions, such as DBT, TFP, MBT, and the like—a much higher bar than the "attentional control" often used in psychotherapy research As Schiavone and Links (2012) and Bateman (2012) suggest, well-structured and supervised evidence-based care of patients with this disorder may lead to good outcomes, even without high-intensity specialized interventions.

Livesley (2012) recently advocated for the importance of integrated treatment of BPD, moving beyond specialized treatments, "based on evidence that specialized treatments for borderline personality disorder do not differ significantly from each and that they are not more effective than good structured care designed to meet the needs of patients with the disorder." It is possible to see both SPT and SCM/GPM as playing very significant roles in such an integrated treatment approach because each can provide structured care that meets the needs of patients with BPD and can be adapted to diverse needs of heterogeneous populations.

REFERENCES

American Psychiatric Association. (2001). *Practice guideline for the treatment of patients with borderline personality disorder* (Vol. 158). Arlington, VA: Author.

Aviram, R. B., Brodsky, B. S., & Stanley, B. (2006). Borderline personality disorder, stigma, and treatment implications. *Harvard Review of Psychiatry, 14*(5), 249–256.

Aviram, R. B., Hellerstein, D. J., Gerson, J., & Stanley, B. (2004). Adapting supportive psychotherapy for individuals with borderline personality disorder who self-injure or attempt suicide. *Journal of Psychiatric Practice, 10*(3), 145–155.

Bateman, A., & Fonagy, P. (2009). Randomized controlled trial of outpatient mentalization-based treatment versus structured clinical management for borderline personality disorder. *American Journal of Psychiatry, 166*(12), 1355–1364.

Bateman, A. W. (2012). Treating borderline personality disorder in clinical practice. *American Journal of Psychiatry, 169*(6), 560–563.

Brenner, A. M. (2012). Teaching supportive psychotherapy in the twenty-first century. *Harvard Review of Psychiatry, 20*(5), 259–267.

Bryan, C. M. (1990). The uses of therapy in case management. *New Directions for Mental Health, 46*(Summer), 19–27.

Budge, S., Baardseth, T. P., Wampold, B. E., & Flückiger, C. (2010). Researcher allegiance and supportive therapy: Pernicious affects on results of randomized clinical trials. *European Journal of Psychotherapy and Counselling, 12*(1), 23–39.

Clarkin, J., Levy, K., Lenzenweger, M., & Kernberg, O. (2007). Evaluating three treatments for borderline personality disorder: A multiwave study. *American Journal of Psychiatry, 164*(6), 922–928.

Clarkin, J. F., Levy, K. N., Lenzenweger, M. F., & Kernberg, O. F. (2007). Evaluating three treatments for borderline personality disorder: A multiwave study. *Am J Psychiatry, 164*, 922–928.

Conte, H. R., & Plutchik, R. (1986). Controlled research in supportive psychotherapy. *Psychiatric Annals.*

Cuijpers, P., Driessen, E., Hollon, S. D., van Oppen, P., Barth, J., & Andersson, G. (2012). The efficacy of non-directive supportive therapy for adult depression: A meta-analysis. *Clinical Psychology Review, 32*(4), 280.

Elkin, I., SMWJT, et al. National institute of mental health treatment of depression collaborative research program: General effectiveness of treatments. *Archives of General Psychiatry, 46*(11), 971–982.

Frank, J. (1971). Therapeutic factors in psychotherapy. *American Journal of Psychotherapy, 25*, 350–361.

Hellerstein, D. (2011). From Cinderella to straw man? Supportive psychotherapy in the 21st century. *Psychiatric Times*, 1–2.

Hellerstein D. J., Pinsker H, Rosenthal R. N., & Klee, S. (1994). Supportive therapy as the treatment model of choice. *Journal of Psychotherapy Practice and Research, 3*(4), 300.

Hellerstein, D. J. (2004). Beyond "handholding": Supportive therapy for patients with borderline personality disorder and self-injurious behavior. *Psychiatric Times, 21*(8), 58–61.

Hellerstein, D. J., Rosenthal, R. N., Pinsker, H., Samstag, L. W., Muran, J. C., & Winston, A. (1998). A randomized prospective study comparing supportive and dynamic therapies. Outcome and alliance. *Journal of Psychotherapy Practice and Research, 7*(4), 261–271.

Henry, W. P., Schacht, T. E., & Strupp, H. H. (1986). Structural analysis of social behavior: Application to a study of interpersonal process in differential psychotherapeutic outcome. *Journal of Consulting and Clinical Psychology, 54*(1), 27–31.

Holmes, J. (1995). Supportive psychotherapy. The search for positive meanings. *British Journal of Psychiatry, 167*(4), 439–445.

Jørgensen, C., Freund, C., Bøye, R., Jordet, H., Andersen, D., & Kjølbye, M. (2012). Outcome of mentalization-based and supportive psychotherapy in patients with borderline personality disorder: A randomized trial. *Acta Psychiatrica Scandinavica.*

Kocsis J. H., Gelenberg A. J., Rothbaum B. O., REVAMP Investigators (2009). Cognitive behavioral analysis system of psychotherapy and brief supportive psychotherapy for augmentation of antidepressant nonresponse in chronic depression: The REVAMP trial. *Archives of General Psychiatry, 66*(11), 1178.

Linehan, M. (1987). Dialectical behavioral therapy for borderline personality disorder: Theory and method. *Bulletin of the Menninger Clinic. 51*(3), 261–276.

Livesley, W. J. (2012). Moving beyond specialized therapies for borderline personality disorder: The importance of integrated domain-focused treatment. *Psychodynamic Psychiatry, 40*(1), 47–74.

Markowitz, J. C., Kocsis, J. H., Christos, P., Bleiberg, K., & Carlin, A. (2008). Pilot study of interpersonal psychotherapy versus supportive psychotherapy for dysthymic patients with secondary alcohol abuse or dependence. *Journal of Nervous and Mental Disease, 196*(6), 468–474.

McMain, S., Links, P., Gnam, W., . . . Streiner, D. L. (2009). A randomized trial of dialectical behavior therapy versus general psychiatric management for borderline personality disorder. *American Journal of Psychiatry, 166*(12), 1365–1374.

McMain, S. F., Guimond, T., Streiner, D. L., Cardish, R. J., & Links, P. S. (2012). Dialectical behavior therapy compared with general psychiatric management for borderline personality disorder: Clinical outcomes and functioning over a 2-year follow-up. *American Journal of Psychiatry, 169*(6), 650–661.

Meyer, T., Hautzinger, M., Alloy, L., et al. Cognitive behaviour therapy and supportive therapy for bipolar disorders: Relapse rates for treatment period and 2-year follow-up. *Psychological Medicine, 42*(7), 1429.

Novalis, P. N., Rojcewicz, S. J., & Peele, R. (1993). *Clinical manual of supportive psychotherapy.* Arlington, VA: American Psychiatric Publishing.

Pinsker, H. (1997). *A primer of supportive psychotherapy.* Hillsdale, NJ: Analytic Press.

Pompili, M., Girardi, P., Ruberto, A., & Tatarelli, R. (2005). Suicide in borderline personality disorder: A meta-analysis. *Nordic Journal of Psychiatry, 59*(5), 319–324.

Rockland, L. (1992). *Supportive therapy for borderline patients: A psychodynamic approach.* New York: Guilford.

Rogers, C. R. (1951). *Client-centered therapy: Its current practice, implications and theory.* Boston: Houghton Mifflin.

Rosenthal, R. N., Muran, J. C., Pinsker, H., Hellerstein, D., & Winston, A. (1999). Interpersonal change in brief supportive psychotherapy. *Journal of Psychotherapy Practice and Research, 8*(1), 55–63.

Schiavone, F. L., & Links, P. S. (2012). Common elements for the psychotherapeutic management of patients with self injurious behavior. *Child Abuse & Neglect*

Skodol, A. E., Pagano, M. E., Bender, D. S., Shea, T. (2005). Stability of functional impairment in patients with schizotypal, borderline, avoidant, or obsessive compulsive personality disorder over two years. *Psychological Medicine, 35*(3), 443–451.

Stanton, A. H., Gunderson, J. C., Knapp, P. H., . . . Rosenthal, R. (1984). Effects of psychotherapy in schizophrenia: I. Design and implementation of a controlled study. *Schizophrenia Bulletin, 10*, 520–563.

Stone, M. H., Hurt, S. W., & Stone, D. K. (1987). The PI 500: Long-term follow-up of borderline inpatients meeting DSM-III criteria I. Global outcome. *Journal of Personality Disorders, 1*(4), 291–298.

Tolin, D. F. (2010). Is cognitive–behavioral therapy more effective than other therapies? A meta-analytic review. *Clinical Psychology Review, 30*(6), 710–720.

Werman, D. (1988). On the mode of therapeutic action of psychoanalytic supportive psychotherapy. In A. Rothstein (Ed.), *How does treatment help? On the modes of therapeutic action of psychoanalytic psychotherapy* (pp. 157–167). Madison, CT: International Universities Press.

Winston, A., Rosenthal, R. N., & Pinsker, H. (2004). *Introduction to supportive psychotherapy [Core Competencies in Psychotherapy Series]*: Washington, DC: American Psychiatric Publishing.

Zanarini, M. C., Frankenburg, F. R., Hennen, J., & Silk, K. R. (2003). The longitudinal course of borderline psychopathology: 6-year prospective follow-up of the phenomenology of borderline personality disorder. *American Journal of Psychiatry, 160*(2), 274–283.

Zanarini, M. C., Frankenburg, F. R., Hennen, J., & Silk, K. R. (2003). The longitudinal course of borderline psychopathology: 6-year prospective follow-up of the phenomenology of borderline personality disorder. *American Journal of Psychiatry, 160*(2), 274–283.

Zanarini M. C., Gunderson J. G., Frankenburg F. R., & Chauncey, D. L. (1990). Discriminating borderline personality disorder from other axis II disorders. *American Journal of Psychiatry, 147*(2), 161–167.

Zitrin, C. M., Klein, D. F., & Woerner, M. G. (1978). Behavior therapy, supportive psychotherapy, imipramine, and phobias. *Archives of General Psychiatry, 35*(3), 307.

/// 19 /// Family Psychoeducation Approaches for Borderline Personality Disorder

VALERIE PORR

INTRODUCTION

This chapter provides a rationale for training family members of individuals with borderline personality disorder (BPD) to help them develop into therapeutic allies and treatment adjuncts. It also describes the experiences of family members in finding help for their loved one with BPD and the family psychoeducation (FPE) programs currently available for BPD and other disorders. Often families, by default, are the only alternative available to handle crisis situations because some individuals with BPD refuse to participate in therapy, have dropped out of therapy, or appropriate BPD services are not available in their communities (Hoffman et al., 2005).

THE IMPORTANCE OF FAMILY PSYCHOEDUCATION

With an understanding of BPD, social support, and appropriate training, families can potentially develop as adjuncts that can help improve treatment outcome. When provided with an in-depth understanding of the disorder and training in effective techniques for helping their loved one, family members can become important resources for helping their family member with BPD manage their problems and move forward, thereby improving the characteristic flat line of their Global Assessment of Functioning scores (Skodol, Johnson, Cohen, Sneed, & Crawford, 2007). A significant percentage of individuals with BPD refuse to engage in treatment or drop out of treatment prematurely (Hoffman, Fruzzetti, & Swenson 1999; Rusch et al., 2008). In these cases, family members can become important resources to motivate the person with BPD to enter or remain in therapy, dissuade them from early dropout, generalize treatment techniques to naturalistic settings, and help the individual maintain treatment gains. Family members generally spend more time with their loved one who has BPD than any therapist or program and are usually available for help or support when the person terminates therapy. Through psychoeducation, they can learn to reinforce skillful adaptive behaviors, treatment goals, and methodology and avoid triggering escalation of crises. They can remind the individual with BPD of past accomplishments, such as obstacles they have overcome in the past.

Appropriate training enables families to become therapeutic allies effective in diffusing conflict, reducing the frequency and intensity of episodes, and reinforcing adaptive coping techniques. FPE can also teach family members how to avoid triggering BPD eruptions. The National Institute for Health and Care Excellence Guidelines (NICE) in the United Kingdom recommend active involvement by families for purposes of improving clinical outcomes and reducing family burden (NICE, 2003).

BPD affects more than the individual who meets criteria for the disorder. For family members, BPD pathology has a significant interpersonal impact on the entire family dynamic. The clinical community has tended to neglect the impact on family members of living or loving someone with BPD. Rather, it has focused on how families contribute to the etiology of BPD. For each BPD sufferer, there are family members—usually a parent, partner/spouse, sibling, or child of the individual with BPD—who are affected by the emotional dysregulation seen in BPD. They struggle to cope with the symptoms of BPD and to find a way to help to prevent disruptive escalations. The side effects of dealing with the maladaptive coping behaviors of their loved one with BPD, such as self-injury, drug abuse, shop lifting, violence, verbal abuse, perceived manipulation, and various pathological regressive defenses, can shatter family harmony and rupture relationships (Porr, 2010). Families search for a way to help the siblings or children in the family, to protect themselves from burn-out and angry accusations, or to just cope with the emotional, financial, and sometimes legal consequences of BPD crisis-generated situations. Individuals with BPD are sometimes dependent on their families for financial support. They may understandably become the focus of family discussions, absorbing enormous amounts of the family's emotional energy as well as substantial financial resources. Conversely, the family may see the individual with BPD as a victim who needs rescuing and will inadvertently stifle their growth and development of competency. This can have a profound effect on other family relationships. Many couples cannot sustain the strain of caring for an adolescent or adult child with BPD, and, as with other illnesses affecting a child, the result can be painful schisms or divorce. Dealing with a partner with BPD, especially when children are involved, can be difficult and result in divorce, an option that is far more difficult when children are involved. The family may drain their financial resources paying for therapy, placing the individual in one residential facility, wilderness program, inpatient hospitalization, or rehabilitation setting after another. Older parents worry about what will become of their child with BPD when they have passed on and are no longer here to help (Porr, 2010).

FAMILY PSYCHOEDUCATION IN SCHIZOPHRENIA AND BIPOLAR DISORDER

FPE programs inform and educate family members of individuals with severe mental illness such as schizophrenia and bipolar disorder so that the family members can assist the person in managing his or her illness (Dixon & Lehman, 1995). These professionally delivered FPE programs have shown that informed and trained family members can function as treatment adjuncts, preventing relapse and hospitalizations, reinforcing recovery, and improving outcomes. The patient's functional outcome improves when families participate in these FPE programs. The Substance Abuse and Mental Health Services Administration (SAMHSA) has declared FPE an evidence-based treatment that qualifies for Medicaid reimbursement (SAMHSA,2010).

The schizophrenia Patient Outcomes Research Team (PORT) study investigated programs for families coping with schizophrenia (Dixon et al., 2011). PORT is an FPE program designed to last 6–9 months; it includes multiple family groups, education in crisis interventions, coping skills training, medication management and emotional support. It is considered the gold standard of FPE programs because it has become a model for development of FPE for other disorders. It is an evidence-based, effective practice endorsed by SAMHSA (Lucksted, Mcfarlane, Downing, & Dixon, 2011). A family focused therapy (FFT) program developed for family members of people with bipolar disorder (Miklowitz & Goldstein, 1997) has been highly successful in developing family members as adjuncts to therapy, reducing relapse, and improving treatment outcomes. The National Alliance for the Mentally Ill (NAMI) has developed an FPE program called Family to Family. It is an educational course for families, caregivers, and friends of individuals living with mental illnesses, primarily schizophrenia and depression. The course consists of 12 sessions and is taught by trained family members. It provides critical information and caregiving strategies and was also designated as an evidence-based treatment by SAMHSA (SAMHSA, 2010).

These FPE programs teach family members skills to manage and cope with their loved one's illness and provide problem-solving strategies, crisis management plans, and ways to optimize natural supports so that they can more effectively address the real-life challenges caused by living with these specific mental illnesses. They also provide participants with much needed social support. The primary goal of each of these programs is to help the individual with the disorder in order to improve treatment outcomes, functional improvement, and personal recovery. Participants in these FPE programs generally are coping with an individual with a disorder who is usually engaged in treatment. One focus of these FPE programs is to help the individual with the disorder maintain medication regimens that have been proved effective in treating schizophrenia, bipolar disorder, depression, and anxiety.

Family strengths, motivation, and overall support as effective adjuncts have the potential to result in cost savings for the mental health system as well as for the family. The goal of these programs is not clinical stabilization because that may not be possible. As effective as these psychoeducation programs may be, they are not a substitute for actual therapy and psychiatric care. These FPE programs were not designed to address decreasing family burden.

Efforts are currently under way to develop FPE programs for people with other disorders such as obsessive compulsive disorder, eating disorders, and dual diagnoses (mental illness and substance abuse disorders). FPE has been successful and extremely helpful in treating disorders such as diabetes, asthma, and many allergies. Diabetes management serves as a good example of a family education program that improves patient outcome without "curing" the underlying disorder. Different methodologies and multiple variations of FPE for BPD have made it difficult to compare results for these programs. Another complication for BPD FPE is that, to date, there is no US Food and Drug Administration (FDA) medication approved for treating BPD as there are in other disorders (Lieb, Vollm, Rucker, Timmer, & Stoffers, 2010).

FAMILY PSYCHOEDUCATION PROGRAMS FOR BPD

BPD differs markedly from other mental disorders; therefore, a unique approach to people with BPD and their families is needed. Families of individuals with BPD have unique experiences and face different problems than do families coping with schizophrenia, bipolar disorder, or depression. Individuals with BPD seem to be "apparently competent"(Linehan, 1993), often exhibiting troublesome behaviors only with those with whom they are very close, such as their parent and/or partners. Some individuals with BPD are either not engaged in treatment or refuse treatment, deny having BPD or any problem, or blame their problems on others. They may also either be estranged from the family or completely dependent on them. Clinicians interacting with the families of individuals with BPD need to be aware that they can be desperate for help and not very trusting based on their past experiences with treatment, diagnosis, and stigma (Porr, 2010).

Most currently available family interventions for BPD have been developed by clinicians and are generally delivered as family therapy, often in a multisystemic family therapy modality or as multifamily dialectic behavior therapy (DBT) groups, especially for adolescents (Miller, Rathus, & Linehan, 2007). These programs are mostly based on DBT and used when the individual with BPD is currently in treatment. The goals, rationale, methods, length and number of sessions, settings, structure, and efficacy of each available family intervention vary. Repairing ruptured family relationships does not seem to be the aim of most of these FPE programs for BPD. Currently, little or no empirical research is available regarding the effectiveness of FPE programs for families of individuals with BPD or that compare different family therapy/psychoeducational models for BPD to determine the efficacy of one approach over another.

Providing family members of individuals with BPD with accurate information about their loved one's disorder should be a primary goal of BPD FPE. This is especially important today because web sites, chat groups, and self-help books provide a plethora of information that the public has no means of evaluating for accuracy or effectiveness. Too often, the information publicly available stigmatizes the individual with BPD. This type of information typically justifies hostile, angry reactions; trivializes the pain experienced by the individual with BPD; and assumes that they are manipulative, lying, or just trying to get attention. Family members, whose frustration often results in anger, are discouraged from responding compassionately and, if they are helping, are told that they are "enabling" their loved one.

WHAT DO FAMILIES NEED?

Developing an effective program to help family members of individuals with BPD requires consideration of many factors, such as the effect of living over time with someone with BPD on family dynamics, the severity of the person's BPD symptomatology, the impact of maladaptive behaviors, and prior experiences with diagnosis and treatment. In general, the priority of these parents, partners, siblings, or other relatives is most often to learn how to help their loved one with BPD rather than to make themselves feel better.

Clinically, it seems that there are essential ingredients needed to help families cope with BPD. Chief among them is the development of compassion for the pain the person with BPD experiences through understanding the underlying neurobiology of BPD and how the individual may struggle in his or her environment. If families knew how to effectively cope with suicidal ideation and behaviors, they may be able to deal with the fear and helplessness they experience and decrease emergency room visits and hospitalizations, possibly preventing suicide attempts/completions. Families can also motivate participation in evidence-based therapies. Strategies are needed to improve family trust and communication, as well as awareness of what actually triggers dysregulations and how to decrease these triggers. In addition, families may also assist in problem-solving and crisis management, supporting relationship repair and learning how to coach their loved one to use effective therapeutic techniques in their daily lives.

Overall, an effective BPD FPE program needs to provide families with a thorough understanding of the current research findings regarding the underlying neurobiology of BPD and how these findings manifest themselves in various BPD behaviors. This can help relatives reframe how they react to their loved one, decreasing the frustration and confusion the family experiences and hopefully leading to the development of compassion (Sheehan et al., 2016). For example, realization that the individual with BPD is extremely responsive to perceived threats, criticism, judgment, or blame, especially from the persons closest to them, can motivate family members to pay close attention to the language they use and their tone of voice, facial expressions, and body language (Denny et al. 2015); it is not what they say, but how they say it. Also, awareness of how a person with BPD has negative biases in perception, a tendency toward self-referential behavior, and extreme rejection sensitivity can also help deescalate family members' negative reactions and encourage more compassionate, less personalized responses.

In order to head off eruptions or mood shifts before they begin or have a chance to escalate, family members need to develop awareness of what triggers behavior. According to Korzekwa, Dell, Links, Thabane, and Webb (2008), interpersonal interactions are the leading triggers of BPD dysregulated emotions and behaviors. Trained and aware family members can offer contingency management skills so that the person with BPD can cope in advance. For example, it is entirely predictable that a holiday dinner or a separation from a partner will be a difficult experience for an individual with BPD. Families need to anticipate situations that may be stressful and learn methods to reframe and deescalate these triggers. They need to know problem-solving and crisis management skills and how to coach and reinforce effective behaviors. They need to understand how perceived attempts to control or treat their family member as overly fragile can be misinterpreted and will actually incite emotional reactions, possibly leading to crisis situations. It is important for psychoeducation programs for families of individuals with BPD to acknowledge and enhance the family's capacities and motivation to find an effective way to help their loved one. Families need validation for how hard they are trying; how painful it is to see someone they love suffer so much without knowing how to alleviate that suffering; how helpless, hopeless, and impotent they feel when their efforts to help do not work but seem to cause even more distress. All of these factors can result in an overwhelming sense of failure for parents and other loved ones. A patronizing, condescending, or judgmental attitude toward families at these times can be devastating to them and to family dynamics.

FAMILY THERAPY AND COUNSELING PARENTS WHO HAVE CHILDREN WITH BPD SYMPTOMS

Families faced with burgeoning BPD behaviors in a child sometimes look for help by seeking out a family therapist. Many family therapists are generally trained in family systems therapy wherein the whole family is examined for pathology (LaFavor & Randall, 2013). This may not be an effective approach with BPD because these clinicians are not specifically trained in understanding the manifestations of BPD, how it effects family interactions, or how to actually help the family members. It is more useful to view family members as trying to cope with someone with a severe illness or disability that affects the entire family rather than a family with pathology responding to acute stress. Dysfunctional family patterns often develop alongside the family member's illness rather than preceding or causing it (Hooley, Rosen, & Richters, 1995; Laporta & Falloon, 1992). This is seen in the family in which a member has schizophrenia; negative family dynamics observed among families were reported to largely result from the stresses and negative consequences of coping with the illness (Mcfarlane & Cook, 2007).

Individual therapy is an alternative option that family members may seek out in the hopes of finding ways to cope with their difficult family environment and to develop better ways to respond to and help their loved one with BPD. Here again, families may receive well-intentioned but unhelpful advice. They may be counseled to use "tough love" techniques that can often serve to further alienate their loved one with BPD who may misinterprets their intention or may not understand their family member's logical reaction to their often emotional, impulsive behaviors (Porr, 2010). The individual with BPD is often unable to accept the link connecting cause and effect and therefore does not understand why their parents, who they feel do not understand them in the first place, are reacting to their behaviors or are trying to control them (Denny et al., 2014; Koenigsberg et al., 2014). Family members are often told to remain calm and neutral when their loved one is upset and not to react. The individual with BPD may interpret this type of neutral response to mean that they are not being heard or understood, they "don't count or matter." They do not generally recognize that they may have done something to justify the anger or concern felt by others. The individual with BPD may experience the aversive feeling of shame, which may result in intense feelings that may be projected onto the other person and expressed as blame and/or anger (Donegan et al., 2003; Rusch et al., 2008). Alternatively, the feelings of shame can induce self-harming behavior, avoidance, or withdrawal (Nathanson, 1992). Hooley and Hoffman (1999) found that high levels of emotional involvement by family members resulted in better outcomes for individuals with BPD. In contrast to the opposite reaction in people with schizophrenia (Mcfarlane & Cook, 2007), this may be due to the inability of people with BPD to deal with ambiguity. Expressed emotion is easier to interpret for someone with BPD.

Alternatively, the family may be advised to send their child to a residential treatment center, a therapeutic boarding school, or a wilderness program where the "problematic" behavior can be addressed in a structured environment where the family feels the person is "safe." Often, the person with BPD may do well while in the program, especially when it is highly structured and restrictive; however, regression may occur not long after returning home, especially if the skills and practice using appropriate coping behaviors at home were not well learned and reinforced. For example, in a sequestered environment where individuals are not tempted, it may be easier to deal with restraining from drugs and alcohol use. It will be far more difficult for them to restrain themselves when illicit drugs and alcohol are readily available. Families ultimately may do the wrong thing for the right reasons and are confused and frustrated by their failure to help their loved one or to ameliorate the situation despite the best of intentions.

BPD FAMILY PSYCHOEDUCATION PROGRAMS

Dialectic Behavior Therapy Skills Training

DBT programs endorse teaching families DBT skills in multifamily groups or in parallel or concurrent groups for adolescents and their parents. To date, there are no published trials comparing multifamily DBT groups to separate or parallel DBT groups or demonstrating the advantage of one method over the other. The goal of these programs is not to empower family members to use DBT skills in a therapeutic way or to be a crisis prevention strategy. Family members are taught the same DBT skills as their loved one. Multifamily weekly DBT groups developed by Miller and Rathus (Rathus, Campbell, Miller, & Smith, 2015) were designed for both family members and adolescents meeting criteria for BPD who were already in DBT treatment. The multifamily DBT groups generally include several adolescents and their parents who are learning the skills within the same group. The individual with BPD and his or her parents are learning skills to help them better manage their own emotions, tolerate distress, and interact more effectively with others. Unfortunately, very little help is available for parents of adults with BPD or for BPD individuals who are not in treatment.

Despite a number of randomized control trials currently demonstrating the efficacy of DBT (Koons et al., 2001; Linehan, Tutek, Heard, & Armstrong, 1994; Swenson, Torrey, & Koerner, 2002), data are not yet available to justify teaching DBT skills to families either in multifamily or in concurrent DBT skills groups. Teaching family members DBT skills as they are taught to the identified individual with BPD may inadvertently suggest that the family member meets criteria for BPD, is dealing with the same problems as the person with BPD, and has the same deficits in the same areas. Or it implies that they cannot control their emotions, tolerate distress, be mindful, or have effective interpersonal relationships and therefore would benefit from learning the same DBT skills as the individual with BPD (Miller et al., 2007). This misinterpretation can be addressed by informing the family prior to treatment of the rationale for teaching all members the same DBT skills. It is important that family members "buy in" to the process, that they recognize the need to learn the skills and implement them themselves for DBT to be effective in helping their loved one.

It is possible that family members placed in a public group setting with other family members may want to demonstrate that they are cooperative or that they may be embarrassed in front of these other families that they don't know well. This could result in their holding back true feelings and reactions and being less genuine in the way they participate in the group and in their implementation of the new skills at home. Without an understanding of why they are learning these skills or why it would be effective to implement them, families may only be giving lip service to participation (i.e., giving verbal expression of agreement in public but not practicing or implementing the skills at home). This methodology does not foster development of the parental compassion needed to validate their loved one's painful experience in living with BPD, thus rendering the program a potential "Band-Aid" or temporary solution in the short run and ineffective in the long run as the family faces new problems and situational changes arising in the environment.

Although DBT for adolescents has an evidence base, multifamily skills training on its own has not yet received empirical investigation as compared to other methods. Multifamily DBT skills training may be more effective than individual family therapy because family members and adolescents can see each other struggling with the same issues and can therefore experience modeling and reinforcement of effective behaviors (Miller et al., 2007). Importantly, an overlooked benefit of the multifamily group is that the family, usually for the very first time, has a chance to connect with other families facing the same problems and, consequently, receive social support to help them feel less isolated, frustrated, and responsible (Miller et al., 2007).

An alternative method of delivering family DBT skills training is through participation in parallel groups, one for adolescents or adults with BPD and a separate group for their families. Parents and their adolescents are taught DBT skills concurrently, in separate groups. In addition to teaching DBT skills to the family members, the rationale is that teaching DBT skills to parents will familiarize them with the language and skills of DBT that their adolescents are learning, and they can better implement the skills at home.

Family Psychoeducation in STEPPS

Systems training for emotional predictability and problem solving (STEPPS), developed by Blum and colleagues (Blum, Pfohl, John, Monahan, & Black, 2002), is an evidence-based, cognitive-behavioral, systems-based group treatment combining cognitive-behavioral techniques and skills training with a systems component. It involves people with BPD and their family. Weekly two-hour groups are held over the course of 20 weeks. A manual is used by the facilitator to lead the groups. STEPPS is a supplementary treatment to the primary treatment that the person with BPD is receiving. It focuses on enhancing relationship skills and views the individual's family and friends as a "reinforcement team" to assist in reinforcing the STEPPS skills. The STEPPS curriculum includes awareness of the illness (psychoeducation about BPD, "cognitive filters," and identification of maladaptive schemas), emotion management skills (to predict the course of emotional states, anticipate stressful situations, and develop functional coping strategies), and behavior management skills (goal-setting, daily routine establishment, and interpersonal relationship management). Outcome data on the STEPPS program support it effectiveness in helping patients. Inclusion of the family in a therapy-supportive role is beneficial; however, family inclusion in the STEPPS program is not its primary focus (Blum et al., 2002).

FAMILY CONNECTIONS

Family Connections is a research-based, manualized, 12-week, 6-module, 2-hour interactive manualized education/skills training course for family members with a relative with BPD or symptoms of the disorder. Family Connection classes, developed by Fruzzetti and Hoffman (Hoffman et al., 2005), are co-led by family members who have received 2-day training in the program. The program is divided into six modules: Introduction, Family Education, Relationship Mindfulness Skills, Family Environment Skills, Validation Skills and Problem Management Skills. Each module builds on the prior one. It seeks to provide current information and research on BPD, teach coping skills based on DBT, and develop a support network. The program does not require that the individual be diagnosed with BPD or be in treatment. The goal of Family Connections is to find a way to make relationships healthy and to reduce family burden. Using the biosocial theory developed by Linehan (1993), which postulates that BPD is triggered by innate emotional vulnerability coupled with factors in the environment that may trigger the illness, such as invalidation. The third module teaches relationship mindfulness skills, contrasting the effectiveness of aversive control and judgments with validation. The fourth module covers family and relationship skills. Radical acceptance, benign interpretations, and letting go of assumptions are stressed. Module five encompasses validation skills and observation of one's own limits. The sixth and last module covers defining problems and learning to describe the situation nonjudgmentally. Strong bonds typically develop among group participants as they meet other families sharing the same experiences and who understand their situation. This serves to reinforce the efficacy of the program (Penney, 2008).

Family Connections data demonstrate that family members experience a decrease in depression, burden, and grief and an increase in a sense of empowerment as a result of participation in the program (Hoffman et al., 2005) This program is helpful for those who are motivated to help themselves cope with the stress and burden associated with dealing with a loved one with BPD. At present, many DBT programs are adopting the Family Connection programs because it is manualized, DBT-based, taught over the course of a weekend, and easy to implement while other alternatives are not as easily initiated. Family Connections fits within DBT philosophy and is widely available at multiple sites across the United States, Australia, and Europe (Hoffman reference).

THE TARA METHOD OF FAMILY PSYCHOEDUCATION

Family members at the Treatment and Research Advancements National Association for Personality Disorder (TARA). developed the TARA Method of Family Psychoeducation. The goal of the TARA Method is to teach families how to customize the BPD family environment to make it less stressful for the individual with BPD. It aims to help the individual with BPD by healing and repairing ruptured family relationships, improving communication, increasing trust, and making the environment emotionally safer for the person with BPD. The emphasis is on accepting the person's experience of pain and isolation, realizing how hard they are trying and that they are doing the best they can. TARA is an integrated principle-based program to help family members navigate stressors they face in coping with the capricious and often difficult behaviors of people with BPD. It provides problem-solving strategies, crisis management plans, and creative ways to optimize natural opportunities and abilities. Although it provides participants with much needed social support, it is not specifically designed as a support group. While reducing family burden is not a primary goal of the TARA Method, when family members can actually be effective and help their loved ones, a reduction in family burden will naturally result. The TARA Method acknowledges the crucial role family can play as vital therapeutic partners because they are generally the primary attachment relationships in the life of the individual with BPD. Increasing their repertoire of coping strategies is crucial because, by default, they are often the only alternative available to handle crisis situations, especially when the person refuses to engage in therapy or when appropriate therapy is unavailable in the community.

The TARA Method curriculum is an intense 8-week program that is also offered as a 3-day intensive weekend program (Porr, 2010). Participation does not require the loved one to have received a BPD diagnosis or be involved with treatment. The program was developed by family members who then received clinical training in DBT, MBT, and CFT. The classes are co-led by trained family members who are trained by family leaders over the course of 4 months of meetings and by participating in groups. The program includes eight classes. Class one is "Validating the BPD Family Experience, Neurobiology of BPD" and covers cutting-edge neurobiological findings on brain systems and connections. Class two is "Principles of Cognitive Behavior," which explores understanding the impact of "tough love" and boundaries. Class three is "What Is DBT and Practicing Mindfulness?" Classes four and five deal with validation through acknowledging emotions, generously listening, and speaking emotional language. Class six is "Radical Acceptance and Grief" and explores reframing expectations; in addition, a grieving ritual provides families with the opportunity to grieve the loss they and their loved one with BPD experience. Class seven is "DBT Skills: Implementing DEAR MAN" as a family communication tool, and class eight is "Putting It All Together: Freedom of Choice, Absence of Alternatives."

Overall, the TARA Method data demonstrate a decrease in frequency and intensity of episodes and improvement in family relationships after participation in the program (Porr, Mandelbaum, & Freiigh, 2014). (Poster Biological Psychiatry & NASSPD) Understanding the neurobiology underlying BPD and differences in the brain circuitry between those with BPD and normal controls is a key strategy for shifting family attitude and may help to diminish judgments, stigma, and blaming. It also may jump-start the development of compassion (Sheehan et al., 2016). The TARA Method capitalizes on the love families have for their relative with BPD and their motivation and commitment to find a way to help them.

FUTURE DIRECTIONS

The family is a neglected and underappreciated resource that can help the person with BPD manage his or her disorder and improve his or her life. Informed family members have potential power to aid and assist in the therapeutic process, to model and reinforce skillful behavior, and to offer alternative perspectives by reframing experiences. Families are the repository of memories of positive past experiences and accomplishments and can therefore provide the person with these reminders and help him or her develop an evaluation scale based on prior experiences. These families typically do not give up on the person and will generally persevere when all other alternatives fail (Porr, 2010). Recovery is more difficult for the person with BPD if the family does not have accurate information, understanding, and coping skills. Involving family and healing and repairing family relationships when possible can be a beneficial therapeutic goal. Accurate early diagnosis and BPD treatment with evidence-based treatment can decrease the development of maladaptive coping methods, nonsuicidal self-injury, and suicides. BPD plays a role in many behaviors affecting society, including addictive behaviors such as drug and alcohol abuse, promiscuous sex, gambling, compulsive shopping, eating disorders, violent behaviors resulting in incarceration and hospitalizations, high rates of suicide and nonsuicidal self-injury, and high usage of hospitals and mental health services, both in- and outpatient. The availability of evidence-based BPD treatment is presently not adequate to meet the demand. It is also extremely costly and is often not covered by insurance. By harnessing the family's concerns with skillful psychoeducational training, we can fill in this void and begin to help individuals suffering with BPD.

REFERENCES

Blum, N., Pfohl, B., John, D. S., Monahan, P., & Black, D. W. (2002). STEPPS: A cognitive-behavioral systems-based group treatment for outpatients with borderline personality disorder—a preliminary report. *Comprehensive Psychiatry*, *43*(4), 301–310.

Denny B. T., Inhoff, M. C., Zerubavel, N., Davachi, L., & Ochsner, K. N. (2015). Getting over it: long-lasting effects of emotion regulation on amygdala response. *Psychological Science*, *26*(9), 1377–1388.

Dixon, L., Dickerson, F., Bellack, A., Bennett, M., Goldberg, R., Lehman, A., & Tenhula, W. (2011). The schizophrenia patient outcomes research team psychosocial treatment recommendations USA 2009. *International Clinical Psychopharmacology*, *26*, 61–62.

Dixon, L. B., & Lehman, A. F. (1995). Family interventions for schizophrenia. *Schizophrenia Bulletin*, *21*(4), 631–643.

Donegan, N. H., Sanislow, C. A., Blumberg, H. P., Fulbright, R. K., Lacadie, C., Skudlarski, P., Gore, J. C., Olson, I. R., McGlashan, T. H., & Wexler, B. E. (2003). Amygdala hyperreactivity in borderline personality disorder: implications for emotional dysregulation. *Biological Psychiatry*, *54*(11), 1284–1293.

Hoffman, P. D., Fruzzetti, A., & Swenson, C. (1999). Dialectical behavior therapy—family skills training. *Family Process*, *38*(4), 399–414.

Hoffman, P. D., Fruzzetti, A. E., Buteau, E., Neiditch, E. R., Penney, D., Bruce, M. L., Hellman, F., & Struening, E. (2005). Family connections: A program for relatives of persons with borderline personality disorder. *Family Process*, *44*(2), 217–225.

Hooley, J. M., & Hoffman, P. D. (1999). Expressed emotion and clinical outcome in borderline personality disorder. *American Journal of Psychiatry, 156*(10), 1557–1562.

Hooley, J. M., Rosen, L. R., & Richters, J. E. (1995). Expressed emotion: Toward clarification of a critical construct. In G. R. Miller (Ed.), *The behavioral high-risk paradigm in psychopathology series in psychopathology* (pp. 88–120). New York: Springer.

Koenigsberg, H. W., Denny, B. T., Fan, J., Liu, X., Guerreri, S., Mayson, S. J., Rimsky, L., New, A. S., Goodman, M., & Siever, L. J. (2014). The neural correlates of anomalous habituation to negative emotional pictures in borderline and avoidant personality disorder patients. *American Journal of Psychiatry*, *171*(1), 82–90.

Koons, C. R., Robins, C. J., Tweed, J. L., Lynch, T. R., Gonzalez, A. M., Morse, J. Q., . . . Bastian, L. A. (2001). Efficacy of dialectical behavior therapy in women veterans with borderline personality disorder. *Behavior Therapy*, *32*(2), 371–390.

Korzekwa, M. I., Dell, P. F., Links, P. S., Thabane, L., & Webb, S. P. (2008). Estimating the prevalence of borderline personality disorder in psychiatric outpatients using a two-phase procedure. *Comprehensive Psychiatry, 49*(4), 380–386.

LaFavor, T., & Randall, J. (2013). Multisystemic family therapy. In A. Hearon Rambo, C. West, & A. Schooley (Eds.), *Family therapy review: contrasting contemporary models.* Routledge.

Laporta, M., & Falloon, I. R. H. (1992). Preventive interventions in the community. In D. J. Kavanagh (Ed.), *Schizophrenia* (pp. 439–458). New York: Springer.

Lieb, K., Völlm, B., Rücker G., Timmer A., & Stoffers J. M. (2010). Pharmacotherapy for borderline personality disorder: Cochrane systematic review of randomised trials. *16*(6), CD005653.

Linehan, M. (1993). *Cognitive-behavioral treatment of borderline personality disorder.* Guilford.

Lucksted, A., Mcfarlane, W., Downing, D., & Dixon, L. (2011). Recent developments in family psychoeducation as an evidence-based practice. *Journal of Marital and Family Therapy, 38*(1), 101–121.

Mcfarlane, W. R., & Cook, W. L. (2007). Family expressed emotion prior to onset of psychosis. *Family Process, 46*(2), 185–197.

Miklowitz, D. J., & Goldstein, M. J. (1997). *Bipolar disorder: A family-focused treatment approach.* New York: Guilford.

Miller, A. L., Rathus, J. H., & Linehan, M. (2007). *Dialectical behavior therapy with suicidal adolescents.* New York: Guilford.

Nathanson, D. L. (1992). *Shame and pride: Affect, sex, and the birth of the self.* New York: Norton.

National Institute for Health and Care Excellence (NICE). (2003). *National Institute for Health and Care Excellence: Clinical guidelines.* London: Author.

Penney, D. (2008). Family connections an education and skills training program for family member well being: A leader's perspective. *Social Work in Mental Health, 6*(1-2), 229–241.

Porr, V. (2010). *Overcoming borderline personality disorder: A family guide for healing and change.* Oxford: Oxford University Press.

Porr, V., Mandelbaum, O., & Freiigh, C. (2014). *TARA method of family psychoeducation including neurobiological underpinnings of borderline personality disorder: A promising approach to improving family dynamics.* Poster presented at North American Society for the Study of Personality Disorders (NASSPD), Boston, MA.

Rathus, J., Campbell, B., Miller, A., & Smith, H. (2015). Treatment acceptability study of walking the middle path, a new dbt skills module for adolescents and their families. *American Journal of Psychotheraphy*, *69*(2), 163–178.

Rüsch, N., Schiel, S., Corrigan, P. W., Leihener, F., Jacob, G. A., Olschewski, M., Lieb, K., & Bohus, M. (2008). Predictors of dropout from inpatient dialectical behavior therapy among women with borderline personality disorder. Journal of Behavior Therapy and Experimental Psychiatry, *39*(4), 497–503.

Sheehan, L., Nieweglowski, K., & Corrigan, P. (2016). The stigma of personality disorders. *Current Psychiatry Reports, 18*(1), 11.

Skodol, A. W., Johnson, J. G., Cohen, P., Sneed, J. R., & Crawford, T. N. (2007). Personality disorder and impaired functioning from adolescence to adulthood. *British Journal of Psychiatry*, *190*, 415–420.

Substance Abuse and Mental Health Services Administration. (2010). Family Psychoeducation Evidence-Based Practices (EBP) KIT. http://store.samhsa.gov/product/Family-Psychoeducation-Evidence-Based-Practices-EBP-KIT/SMA09-4423

Swenson, C. R., Torrey, W. C., & Koerner, K. (2002). Implementing dialectical behavior therapy. *Psychiatric Services*, *53*(2), 171–178.

/// 20 /// Meeting the Clinical Challenges of Managing Borderline Personality Disorder

BETH S. BRODSKY

INTRODUCTION

Most mental health providers can easily recollect their most difficult patient. This patient may stand out in their memory as having been quite challenging to treat in a number of ways. The patient may have come regularly and on time to sessions expressing a desperate desire for help, only to then reject every intervention offered. Conversely, the patient may have missed sessions intermittently without explanation, leaving the clinician to wonder and worry about the patient's well-being and making it difficult to stay emotionally engaged with the patient. Well-meaning interventions on the part of the clinician may have been met with extreme hostility, interpreted by the patient as hurtful, invalidating, or rejecting. The patient may have been extremely emotionally labile, behaviorally impulsive and unpredictable, expressing chronic or intermittent suicidal ideation and/or engaging in self-harm behaviors. The patient probably provoked anxiety by threatening self-harm or induced anger and guilt in the clinician by being hostile and critical, making the clinician feel inadequate, unhelpful, or, at worst, hurtful. This patient may have exhibited high levels of academic or vocational competence but an inability to maintain a stable level of functioning, leading to slow or barely noticeable progress in treatment toward life goals.

In all likelihood, this patient was either diagnosed with borderline personality disorder (BPD) or had significant BPD traits underlying any one of a number of commonly comorbid Axis I diagnoses such as major depressive, bipolar, or eating and/or substance use disorders or their symptoms (Eaton et al., 2011).

Due to presenting problems such as these, individuals with BPD are notorious for being extremely difficult to engage and stay engaged with in treatment (Mehlum, 2009). They are high utilizers of mental health services while at the same time exhibiting a high rate of treatment dropout and revolving door hospitalizations (Bender et al., 2001). While clinicians may choose to not work with these patients, this is not always feasible given that individuals with BPD comprise approximately 15–20% of inpatient and 10–15% of outpatient mental health populations (Gunderson, 2001).

These formidable clinical challenges also frequently lead to clinician burnout (Perseius, Kaver, Ekdahl, Asberg, & Samuelsson, 2007). Part of the problem is that traditional training does not equip clinicians to address the specific challenges presented by individuals with BPD. In particular, standard clinical training does not provide instruction on how to distinguish nonsuicidal self-injury (NSSI) from suicidal behavior in these patients or how to treat it. In addition, clinicians are not always prepared to handle the emotional intensity, interpersonal sensitivity, and extreme dependency needs, nor the hostility and anxiety expressed by these patients in response to the most well-intentioned clinical interventions.

Thus, BPD is often considered to be untreatable and has become one of the most stigmatized of the mental disorders. While society places a stigma on mental disorders in general (Link, Phelan, Bresnahan, Stueve, & Pescosolido, 1999), the BPD diagnosis is unique in that it has become stigmatized among mental health professionals (Gallop, Lancee, & Garfinkel, 1989; Nehls, 1998, Aviram, Brodsky, & Stanley, 2006). It is the one disorder in which the diagnosis (and the patient) is blamed for treatment failure rather than the treatment itself.

There are a number of possible explanations, not the least of which are the very real clinical challenges that these patients present. As mentioned, patients with BPD can be extremely hostile/dependent, needy, emotionally labile, behaviorally impulsive, unpredictable, and self-destructive, and they often are unable to show significant progress in treatment. They can provoke feelings of anxiety and hostility, induce feelings of hopelessness, and can challenge the patience and good will of the most dedicated and seasoned clinician.

However, treatment failure for BPD also can be attributed to taking a "one-size-fits-all" treatment approach toward these patients, by applying a standard clinical approach that may not adequately address BPD symptomatology. It is possible that the particular nature of the BPD disorder transacts with certain aspects of the traditional psychotherapeutic treatment frame to contribute to iatrogenic treatment failure in this population.

Certain modifications to traditional psychotherapeutic approaches are necessary to more effectively manage the challenges presented by individuals with BPD in all clinical settings. Recent developments of BPD-specific psychotherapies over the past two decades have indicated (and provided some empirical evidence to demonstrate) that certain modifications to treatment as usual can increase effectiveness in the clinical management of BPD (Bateman, 2012; Bateman & Fonagy 2006, 2009; Brown et al., 2004; Clarkin, Levy, Lenzenweger, & Kernberg, 2007; Clarkin,

Yeomans, & Kernberg, 2006; Giesen-Bloo et al., 2006; Kernberg, Yeomans, Clarkin, & Levy, 2008; Linehan et al., 1991; Wenzel, Brown, & Beck, 2008; Young, Klosko, & Weishaar, 2003). Increased effectiveness is usually empirically measured by the reduction of suicidal and NSSI behaviors, the reduction of hospitalizations, and increased treatment retention (i.e., treatment engagement on the part of the patient). Other clinical measures to consider are increased clinician willingness and ability to stay engaged with and maintain a therapeutic stance toward BPD patients, decreased emotional and behavioral dysregulation, and increased quality of life for these individuals.

This chapter reviews BPD-specific psychotherapeutic conceptualizations and interventions that can facilitate effective management of BPD in outpatient psychotherapy settings specifically, but that can also be extrapolated to various clinical settings such as inpatient units and emergency departments. A composite case example will be presented to aid in illustrating the challenges and the application of these approaches. The aspects of good clinical management of BPD to be reviewed include (1) reducing stigma toward and increasing empathy for BPD patients, (2) increasing treatment engagement of and with BPD patients, (3) both receiving and providing adequate support while maintaining appropriate boundaries, (4) making the most informed decisions regarding when to hospitalize and how to maintain patient safety on an outpatient basis, (5) handling therapeutic separations, (6) setting realistic goals and learning how to measure progress in slow increments, and (7) deciding how and when to end treatment.

CASE STUDY: CLINICAL CHALLENGE OF BPD

Sheryl is a 25-year-old medical student referred for psychotherapy by her school administration because she is struggling to keep up with the demands of the program. She is either late to or missing classes and clinical rounds and has recently revealed to her advisor that she is feeling depressed, anxious, and having trouble sleeping. She is stealing food from her roommate in the middle of the night and binge eating, and she has had several angry outbursts toward her classmates. Most recently, she started superficially cutting herself on her upper arm to relieve intense emotional distress.

Sheryl reports a history of depressed mood, anger outbursts, binge eating and purging, and superficial cutting since the age of 15. She had one brief hospitalization when she was 17 after taking an overdose of about 10 capsules of Benadryl with unclear suicidal intent. Sheryl was always a very good student, and she reports experiencing a lot of pressure to perform well in school from her parents. She has been in psychotherapy on and off during high school and college but has not stayed in treatment with any one clinician for longer than 5 months. She reports that she sometimes feels better after speaking to a clinician, but she has not found therapy to be helpful and has not really felt "connected" to any of her clinicians. She also reports having tried numerous medications, none of which has seemed to help her, although she has not been very adherent in taking the medication as prescribed. She has been diagnosed in the past with bipolar disorder II and bulimia nervosa. One clinician in college suggested the possibility that she might have certain features of BPD.

For the past few months, Sheryl has been attending psychotherapy sessions somewhat regularly, although she has a tendency to miss sessions periodically and does not call to let the clinician know what is happening. When she does attend, she expresses anxiety and panic. She is easily angered and feels misunderstood and criticized when her therapist interprets her "resistance" and suggests that she is experiencing the therapist as having the same expectation for Sheryl to perform as her mother did. Sheryl has been leaving frantic phone messages for her therapist in the middle of the night expressing feelings of panic and hopelessness and thoughts of suicide. The therapist is starting to feel resentful that Sheryl is so needy yet unable to accept help and that Sheryl is seeking attention by making the therapist worried and anxious about her safety. The therapist is also not sure how to determine Sheryl's actual suicide risk and whether she needs to be hospitalized.

STIGMA

As this vignette portrays, one of the greatest challenges for clinicians is to be able to maintain a therapeutic stance toward and remain engaged with their BPD patients. Toward this end, reduction of stigma is the first necessary step. The stigma surrounding BPD often leads clinicians to interpret patients' behaviors to be manipulative, demanding, or provocative (Gallop et al., 1989; Nehls, 1998). As Aviram et al. (2006) noted, certain interpersonal aspects of BPD pathology lead clinicians to attribute deliberate intention to the hostility, neediness, and demands that are actually a manifestation of the illness and not necessarily under the individual's control.

Another reason for misattribution of control might have to do with the fact that individuals with BPD exhibit great variability in their level of functioning. Their moods and behaviors fluctuate wildly and in response to unpredictable precipitants in the environment. When emotionally aroused, they become dysregulated and unable to maintain their highest level of functioning. As Sheryl's case illustrates, individuals with BPD can be extremely high functioning in structured situations in which the expectations are very clear and within their ability to meet. This ability to exhibit emotional and behavioral control and high levels of functioning in certain circumstances leads others to incorrectly assume that they are deliberately choosing not to when they decompensate under more (often interpersonally) stressful conditions.

EMPATHY FOR PATIENTS WITH BPD

Cultivating empathy toward BPD patients can facilitate maintenance of a therapeutic stance. Toward this end, it can be helpful to be aware of the empirical evidence substantiating the role of biological and genetic contributions to and the familial transmission of BPD traits of aggression and impulsivity (Foti et al., 2011; Goodman, New, & Siever, 2004) as well as the role of childhood trauma (Brodsky, Cloitre, & Dulit, 1995; Herman, Perry, & van der Kolk, 1989; Ogata et al., 1990). A deep understanding of the phenomenological experience of having BPD can also increase empathy for a patient's plight. When compared to individuals with other personality disorders, those with BPD are more likely to feel overwhelmed by and out of control of their emotions and to feel worthless, hopeless, helpless, and full of self-hate. They spend a great percentage of time thinking that there is something wrong with them and that they are damaged (Zanarini et al., 1998).

Most BPD-specific interventions place emphasis on explicit validation and encourage clinicians to take pains to highlight the valid aspects of the patients' experience, especially their emotional pain (Bateman & Fonagy, 2006; Beck, Freeman, & Davis, 2003; Linehan, 1997). Thus, rather than becoming angry, Sheryl's therapist might be able to view her emotionally, behaviorally, and interpersonally dysregulated behaviors as a result of biological vulnerabilities and historical environmental experiences that have culminated in unskillful ways of coping. As much as Sheryl is causing the therapist distress, the therapist should realize that Sheryl is experiencing an even higher level of distress on a daily basis. If Sheryl felt understood by her therapist in this way, she might become less defensive, less hostile and avoidant, and possibly more willing and positively responsive to interventions.

Sheryl's case also illustrates how a standard clinical approach may unwittingly exacerbate some of the challenges that individuals with BPD present in treatment. Sheryl is having difficulty utilizing her clinician's well-intentioned interventions, such as interpretation of her "treatment resistance." She also has a history of dropping out of treatment. If the clinical picture stays the same, Sheryl may quit therapy once again, or the clinician might become burned out, determine that Sheryl is "failing" treatment, and give up on her. Rather than blaming the patient for treatment failure, good clinical management of BPD requires a rethinking of treatment as usual and consideration that treatment as we know it may be failing the BPD patient. Certain modifications in case conceptualization and intervention are necessary to more adequately address the clinical challenges presented by BPD patients (Bateman, 2012).

TREATMENT IS FAILING BPD PATIENTS: MODIFICATIONS TO TREATMENT AS USUAL

Seventy-five years ago, psychoanalyst Adolf Stern (1938a, 1938b) first identified a subset of patients who were not responding well to the classical psychoanalytic approach. He termed these treatment-resistant patients as the "borderline group" and proceeded to develop certain modifications to psychoanalysis in order to prepare these patients to be able to eventually tolerate and make use of psychoanalysis.

Stern observed that the "borderline" patients required a more "reality determined" therapeutic relationship and that the therapist needed to provide more support and reassurance to help them experience their painful emotions. Thus, Stern recommended that the patient sit and face the therapist rather than lying on the couch. He discouraged therapists from extended periods of silence, which created too much uncertainty for the patient and led to increased anxiety about what the therapist was thinking. A more "reality determined" relationship also meant that the therapist should not necessarily ascribe the patient's feelings toward the therapist primarily to transference. Stern started to give more credence to the patient's view of what the therapist might be thinking and feeling.

The past two decades have seen the development of at least five BPD-specific psychotherapies (described in Chapters 14–19) that all incorporate certain aspects of the modifications recommended by Stern in 1938. These are transference-focused therapy (TFP; Kernberg et al., 2008), mentalization-based therapy (MBT; Bateman & Fonagy, 2006), schema therapy for BPD (ST; Young et al., 2003), cognitive therapy for BPD (CT; Beck, 2003), and dialectical behavior therapy (DBT; Linehan, 1993a, 1993b). Each of these treatments involves having the therapist take a more directive, supportive, and reassuring stance and encourage a more "reality determined" therapeutic relationship.

As a psychoanalytic psychotherapy, TFP for BPD does emphasize the transference, but it deviates from classical psychoanalysis in that it provides a more highly structured frame within which to address suicidal behaviors. The TFP therapist is more talkative and interactive, and the stance of "technical neutrality" is modified in order to maintain patient engagement (Levy et al., 2007). MBT is also based on psychoanalytic and attachment theory, yet it discourages the use of transference interpretations and aims to arrive at transference interpretations in a collaborative way with the patient. In MBT, there is a strong emphasis placed on validation of the patient, and the MBT clinician maintains a stance of humility and "not knowing" (Bateman & Fonagy, 2006). In ST for BPD, the therapist takes pains to create a safe, stable, and supportive therapeutic environment by providing between-session availability, as well as self-disclosure by the therapist when it is deemed therapeutic (Young et al., 2003). Similarly, the modifications to CT, originally developed by Beck (2011) to treat depression, emphasize a more active clinician role in providing empathy and support for BPD patients. In challenging dysfunctional beliefs, CT therapists are advised to "resist their usual habit of immediately looking for biased interpretations" (Beck, 2011). DBT places a central emphasis on validation (Linehan, 1997) and encourages transparency and self-disclosure on the part of the therapist when clinically appropriate. In DBT, the patient's perspective comes first, and distortions are only addressed after the valid aspects of the patient's experience have been highlighted.

HOW TO PROVIDE SUPPORT AND MAINTAIN BOUNDARIES

Each of these modifications requires a rethinking of the traditional therapeutic "frame" (Cabaniss, Cherry, Douglas, & Schwartz, 2011, pp. 72–83) that clinicians rely on to maintain boundaries. In order to avoid burnout and better tolerate any negative "countertransference" that might be induced by the BPD patient's unskillful communications and behaviors, certain clinical protocols are recommended for both receiving support (supervision), offering more support (being available for between session contact), and learning how to structure the support in a way that feels manageable.

A number of the BPD-specific psychotherapies (TFP and DBT) encourage therapists to participate in a peer supervisory group of some kind. A consultation team for clinician supervision and support is a required component of DBT and is a good example of how clinicians can find support to keep the treatment on track. The team of DBT therapists meets regularly on a weekly basis. Each therapist presents his or her individual psychotherapy patients and receives support and feedback designed to help the therapist maintain a validating stance toward the patient in addition to making sure that the patient is being encouraged to make positive changes and is progressing toward achieving treatment goals (Koerner, 2012, pp. 184–185). This keeps the therapy from getting stuck, which facilitates treatment engagement and effectiveness. The team is also a great support in planning for therapist vacations and other separations since team members become familiar with and can provide coverage based on a nuanced understanding of each other's patients.

A number of the BPD-specific psychotherapies encourage between-session contact for extra support (ST, CT, and DBT). DBT offers a clear protocol for handling between-session phone calls. At the outset of treatment, patients are oriented to the ways in which the therapist will be available for between-session contact. Patients are encouraged—actually expected—to make call for skills coaching, relationship repair, or to report good news, within certain parameters (Linehan, 1993a, pp. 497–503).

When a patient calls for skills coaching, the therapist praises her for reaching out for help and proceeds to collaborate with the patient for about 5–10 minutes to devise a skillful plan for managing the current situation. Skills are taught to the patient in a weekly skills training group and consist of either crisis survival strategies, emotion regulation techniques, skills for being interpersonally effective, or mindfulness skills to help control catastrophic, obsessive, or otherwise dysregulated thinking that leads to emotional dyscontrol (Linehan, 1993b).

The clinician is trained to make these between-session calls time-limited and focused. If the patient is calling to vent and is unwilling to engage in problem-solving, the clinician quickly ends the call and encourages the patient to call back when ready to use skills. When the patient is able to use the phone calls appropriately and therapeutically, the clinician experiences a sense of efficacy and is positively reinforced, rather than burned-out, by the interaction.

Sheryl's clinician could use such a protocol to have time-limited focused phone contact with Sheryl in the evenings to review skills that Sheryl can use to tolerate her distress during the night. This would provide Sheryl with more support than she would otherwise receive by leaving a voice mail message and would help the clinician feel less burdened (less anxious about her safety) and more effective while maintaining therapeutic boundaries and avoiding burnout.

MAKING DECISIONS ABOUT HOSPITALIZATION

The assessment and management of suicide risk within the context of chronic suicidal ideation and seemingly unpredictable impulsive episodes of low-lethality self-harm behaviors performed with ambiguous intent to die poses one of the most stressful aspects of treating BPD. Making decisions regarding when and when not to hospitalize are further complicated by the counterintuitive facts that (1) hospitalization, although an effective intervention to block imminent suicide risk, is nevertheless a risk factor for future suicide attempts in individuals with BPD (Soloff & Fabio, 2008); and (2) BPD individuals often feel better and are therefore at less risk for suicide directly following a low-lethality suicide attempt or episode of NSSI (Klonsky, 2009; Leibenluft, Gardner, & Cowdry, 1987; Nock, 2009). Multiple hospitalizations interrupt the patient's efforts to remain stable and safe on an outpatient basis, leading to demoralization and increased hopelessness over time. And suicidal ideation and NSSI behaviors often serve an emotion regulation function in individuals with BPD and do not necessarily stem from a desire to die. Thus, the bias in treating self-harming patients with BPD should be to avoid unnecessary hospitalizations when at all possible, and NSSI behaviors in and of themselves should not be an indication for hospitalization.

Although comprehensive guidelines for the outpatient management of suicidal behavior in BPD is beyond the scope of this chapter (Brodsky & Stanley, 2013), the BPD-specific psychotherapies have identified some useful tools for effective suicide risk management and for making clinically sound decisions regarding hospitalization.

First, each of the BPD-specific psychotherapies prioritizes the reduction of self-harm behaviors as a target for treatment. This means that at each session the clinician inquires into, monitors, and addresses any spike in suicidal ideation or episode of suicidal or self-harm behavior. Asking about suicidal ideation or behavior at each session does not usually upset the patient. Rather, patients often interpret the clinician *not* asking about or monitoring these behaviors as tacit approval or as a sign of not caring. Careful and consistent monitoring familiarizes both clinician and patient to the patient's "baseline" chronic ideation and makes it easier to recognize an escalation in ideation, urges, or potential to act.

Interventions such as conducting chain analyses (Koerner, 2012, pp. 42–49; Linehan, 1993a, pp. 254–265; Wexler, 2001) or taking an otherwise detailed history of past and recent suicidal and self-harm behaviors can increase clinician and patient awareness of the particular vulnerabilities, environmental precipitants, and thought and behavioral patterns that are associated with the individual's likelihood of engaging in self-harm behavior. Thus, when certain situations arise that appear similar to previous situations in which the patient became actively suicidal, this can alert the clinician to take the risk for acting on suicidal urges more seriously. In Sheryl's case, close monitoring of her suicidal ideation, urges, and NSSI behaviors on a weekly basis; taking a detailed history of Sheryl's previous suicidal behaviors; and becoming familiar with the precipitants and circumstances under which Sheryl's urges, distorted thought processes and behaviors become exacerbated can produce a "risk profile" for Sheryl that will aid in more effective recognition of her suicide risk.

It is often the case that, due to their impulsive nature (Brodsky, Malone, Ellis, Dulit, & Mann, 1997), the suicidal crises experienced by individuals with BPD tend to subside rather quickly and the period of risk for acting on the urges is short. Therefore, the extent to which the patient is willing and able to utilize the support of the clinician and reach out for between-session contact to ride out the urges safely can be a factor in determining whether to hospitalize in a given case. Sheryl currently leaves phone messages in the middle of the night, but perhaps her therapist can work with her to utilize between-session contact more effectively to maintain safety.

When risk assessment, close monitoring, provision of between-session support, and all other efforts to secure safety on an outpatient basis have not adequately reduced the imminent suicide risk, hospitalization is indicated. In these cases, hospitalizations should be as brief as possible to block the behaviors and provide support for individuals to get through crises safely while allowing them to quickly resume their day-to-day functioning outside the hospital with minimal interruption.

HANDLING SEPARATIONS

In addition to being help-rejecting and hostile, individuals with BPD are also extremely rejection-sensitive, quick to feel abandoned, and dependent on significant others for self-definition and for feeling safe (Stanley & Siever, 2010). Therefore, disruptions in the therapeutic relationship due to clinician illness, vacations, or other interruptions can trigger suicidal crises. Whenever possible, therapists should give their patients with BPD advanced notice of planned absences. The time leading up to the separation should be used to both validate the patient's feelings as well as to plan for how to skillfully manage these feelings. Rather than becoming resentful, the therapist can allow the patient to have negative feelings about a separation and highlight the valid aspects of these feelings ("You rely on me to stay stable and I am going away") while not validating a distorted interpretation ("I understand that you are feeling abandoned, but I am not rejecting you by going on vacation"). Therapist and patient can collaborate to both accept the therapist's right to leave along with the patient's need for the therapist to stay. Once validated, the patient is more likely to collaborate with the therapist in devising a safety plan (Stanley & Brown, 2011), a detailed list of skills the patient can use, and the personal and professional supports they can reach out to for help.

As mentioned previously, working with a consultation or supervision team that is familiar with the patient (and the patient's risk profile) can provide extra support for both clinician and patient, as well as decrease the chances of unnecessary hospitalization in the therapist's absence. Or, another adjunct treatment provider who is familiar with the patient's clinical status, such as a psychopharmacologist, nutritionist, substance use counselor or sponsor, or skills group trainer, can be enlisted to provide meaningful support.

MEASURING PROGRESS IN TREATMENT

As in Sheryl's case, a therapist might become demoralized and/or lose interest in working with a patient who seems to make so little progress in therapy. Progress in most psychotherapy treatments, even with higher functioning "neurotic" patients, is slow and can only be measured over time. However, it is often the case with BPD patients that they are in extreme pain and engaging in dangerous and anxiety-provoking behaviors, which adds to a sense of urgency for change to happen quickly. Despite this urgency, breaking large goals down into small, day-to-day steps, and recognizing and highlighting slow but steady progress is more realistic and can be encouraging to the patient and therapist.

The pervasive sense of crisis also makes it difficult to notice small signs of improvement. Thus, for example, Sheryl reports a history of never feeling "connected" with any of her clinicians. Yet, in her current treatment, she is reaching out to and contacting her therapist (albeit unskillfully) for help, something she has not done before. This can be seen as a step forward, and the therapist can reframe the behavior to recognize a possibility for growth and to encourage Sheryl to learn how to ask for help more effectively.

Also, because patients with BPD often demonstrate areas of strength, competence, and achievement, they, their families, and their therapists tend to (understandably) have (sometimes unrealistically) high expectations. The patients' limitations are often interpersonally based, rather than due to depressed mood and lack of motivation, and are therefore difficult to recognize or acknowledge. Sheryl's therapist might view her lack of progress as deliberately willful since she is so bright and accomplished. Sheryl herself may also believe that she is "lazy" and that if she could just "get over herself" she would be able to function more consistently. And Sheryl might interpret her ability to function and achieve in certain situations as proof that she is "choosing" not to when she doesn't.

High expectations for progress need to be balanced with a realistic assessment of the patient's limitations in order to set achievable treatment goals. Sometimes this might require a process of trial and error to determine the pace at which progress can be made. For example, a college student who wants to return to school after a medical leave due to a suicide attempt may be better off seeing how he does taking one class before resuming a full course load.

Even when the therapist is able to recognize and highlight small steps forward, the patient often negates the progress by making comparisons to others or by dwelling on the fact that such a small step should be easy and is therefore not an accomplishment. Therapists can validate that a slow pace may be difficult to tolerate, but also can encourage and teach the patient to recognize and appreciate slow and steady progress.

ENDING TREATMENT

As has been pointed out, psychotherapy treatment with BPD patients often ends badly—either the patient drops out prematurely against medical advice (De Panfilis et al., 2012) or the therapist unilaterally terminates treatment due to feeling overburdened or burned-out.

BPD patients, due to their level of psychopathology and comorbid symptomatology, often require long-term psychotherapeutic support. For those who stay and make progress in treatment, it is not clear whether they can maintain their gains without ongoing support. However, when treatment goals are clearly defined and progress toward reaching these goals is consistently monitored, clinicians and patients can determine when goals have been achieved. They can then decide whether to move on to targeting new goals, enter into a "maintenance" period in which they consolidate their gains, or perhaps take a break from treatment.

Clinicians should be alert to the fact that individuals with BPD may fear losing their therapist or losing a certain amount of emotional support from their therapist (the therapist will stop worrying about them) when they make progress in treatment. This may result in a regression to old, unskillful behaviors in an attempt to keep the therapy going. Therefore, any discussion about the end of treatment should be collaborative, and fears or other possible feelings of rejection should be validated and addressed.

In the case of a mutually agreed upon end to treatment, a clear date for termination should be set, one that allows enough time to review the course of the treatment. Preparation for termination should involve anticipating how it will feel to end the therapy, planning ahead for the possibility of a recurrence of symptoms, and leaving open the possibility of resuming work together in the future. Individuals with BPD may have difficulty tolerating a long goodbye and may preempt the termination by leaving earlier than the set date.

Many therapists end treatment with their patients with BPD after a serious suicide attempt, even though this is the type of behavior that indicates a need for treatment. Therefore, a suicide attempt should *not* be a reason in and of itself to end treatment. Serious attempts might cause an interruption in outpatient psychotherapy due to hospitalization, after which outpatient care should resume once there is no longer the need for a higher level of care.

CONCLUSION

Staying therapeutically engaged with BPD patients while managing anxiety related to suicide risk and tolerating intense affect storms, destructive behaviors, dependency needs, and hostile interactions presents a significant challenge to the most experienced and compassionate clinician. While the BPD diagnosis is objectively difficult to treat, this chapter has reviewed certain modifications to psychotherapy as usual that can increase treatment engagement and effectiveness by destigmatizing the diagnosis, cultivating more empathy for these patients, and providing clinicians and patients with increased support and more effective interventions. These modifications should be taught early on in all mental health professional clinical training programs so that these interventions and ways of conceptualizing the BPD diagnosis are more integral to the clinical approach and no longer considered a "deviation" from treatment as usual.

REFERENCES

Aviram, R. B., Brodsky, B. S., & Stanley, B. (2006). Borderline personality disorder, stigma, and treatment implications. *Harvard Review of Psychiatry*, *14*(5), 249–256.

Bateman, A. (2012). Treating borderline personality disorder in clinical practice. *American Journal of Psychiatry*, *169*, 560–563.

Bateman, A., & Fonagy, P. (2006). *Mentalization-based treatment for borderline personality disorder: A practical guide*. London: Oxford University Press.

Bateman, A., & Fonagy, P. (2009). Randomized controlled trial of outpatient mentalization-based treatment versus structured clinical management for borderline personality disorder. *American Journal of Psychiatry*, *166*, 1355–1364.

Beck, A. T., Freeman, A., & Davis, D. D. (2003). *Cognitive therapy of personality disorders* (2nd ed., pp. 187–215). New York: Guilford.

Beck, J. (2011). *Cognitive behavior therapy: Basics and beyond*. New York: Guilford.

Bender, D. S, Dolan, R. T., Skodol, A. E., Sanislow, C. A., Dyck, I. R., McGlashan,T. H., ... Gunderson, J. G. (2001). Treatment utilization by patients with personality disorders. *American Journal of Psychiatry*, *158*(2), 295–302.

Brodsky, B. S., Cloitre, M., & Dulit, R. A. (1995). Relationship of dissociation and childhood abuse in borderline personality disorder. *American Journal of Psychiatry*, *152*(12), 1788–1792.

Brodsky, B. S., Malone, K. M., Ellis, S. P., Dulit, R. A., & Mann, J. J. (1997). Characteristics of borderline personality disorder associated with suicidal behavior. *American Journal of Psychiatry*, *154*, 1715–1719.

Brodsky B. S., & Stanley B. (2013). *The dialectical behavior therapy primer: How DBT can inform clinical practice*. Oxford: Wiley-Blackwell.

Brown G. K., Newman C. F., Charlesworth S. E., Crits-Christoph, P., & Beck, A. T. (2004). An open clinical trial of cognitive therapy for borderline personality disorder. *Journal of Personality Disorders*, *18*(3), 257–271.

Cabaniss, D. L, Cherry, S., Douglas C. J., & Schwartz, A. R. (2011). *Psychodynamic psychotherapy: A clinical manual*. Oxford: Wiley-Blackwell.

Clarkin, J. F., Levy, K. N., Lenzenweger, M. F., & Kernberg, O. F. (2007). Evaluating three treatments for borderline personality disorder: A multiwave study. *American Journal of Psychiatry*, *164*(6), 922–928.

Clarkin, J. F., Yeomans, F. E., & Kernberg, O. F. (2006). *Psychotherapy for borderline personality disorder. Focusing on object relations* (pp. 33–70). Washington, DC: American Psychiatric Publishing.

De Panfilis, C., Marchesi, C., Cabrino, C., . . . (2012). Patient factors predicting early dropout from psychiatric outpatient care for borderline personality disorder. *Psychiatry Research, 200*(2–3), 422–429.

Eaton, N. R., Krueger, R. F., Keyes, K. M., Skodol, A. E., Markon, K. E., Grant, B. F., & Hasin, D. S. (2011). Borderline personality disorder co-morbidity: Relationship to the internalizing-externalizing structure of common mental disorders. *Psychological Medicine, 41*(5), 1041–1050.

Foti, M. E., Geller, J., Guy, L. S., Gunderson, J. G., Palmer, B. A., & Smith, L. M. (2011). Borderline personality disorder: Considerations for inclusion in the Massachusetts parity list of "biologically-based" disorders. *Psychiatric Quarterly, 82*(2), 95–112.

Gallop R., Lancee, W. J., & Garfinkel, P. (1989). How nursing staff respond to the label "borderline personality disorder." *Hospital and Community Psychiatry,40*(8), 815–819.

Giesen-Bloo, J., van Dyck, R., Spinhoven, P., van Tilburg, W., Dirksen, C., van Asselt, T., . . . Arntz A. (2006). Outpatient psychotherapy for borderline personality disorder: Randomized trial of schema-focused therapy vs transference-focused psychotherapy. *Archives of General Psychiatry, 63*(6), 649–658.

Goodman, M., New, A., & Siever, L. (2004). Trauma, genes, and the neurobiology of personality disorders. *Annals of the New York Academy of Science, 1032*,104–116.

Gunderson, J. G. (2001). *Borderline personality disorder: A clinical guide.* Washington, DC: American Psychiatric Publishing.

Herman, J. L., Perry, J. C., & van der Kolk, B. A. (1989). Childhood trauma in borderline personality disorder. *American Journal of Psychiatry, 146*, 490–495.

Kernberg, O. F., Yeomans, F. E., Clarkin, J. F., & Levy, K. N. (2008). Transference focused psychotherapy: Overview and update. *International Journal of Psychoanalysis, 89*(3), 601–620.

Klonsky, E. D. (2009). The functions of self-injury in young adults who cut themselves: Clarifying the evidence for affect-regulation. *Psychiatry Research, 166*(2–3), 260–268.

Koerner, K. (2012). *Doing dialectical behavior therapy. A practical guide.* New York: Guilford.

Leibenluft, E., Gardner, D. L., & Cowdry, R. W. (1987). The inner experience of the borderline self-mutilator. *Journal of Personality Disorders, 1*(4), 217–324.

Levy, K. N., Yeomans, F. E., & Diamond, D. (2007). Psychodynamic treatments of self-injury. *Journal of Clinical Psychology, 63*(11), 1105–1120.

Linehan, M. M. (1993a). *Cognitive behavior therapy for borderline personality disorder.* New York: Guilford.

Linehan, M. M. (1993b). *Skills training manual for treating borderline personality disorder.* New York: Guilford.

Linehan, M. M. (1997). Validation and psychotherapy. In A. Bohart & L. Greenberg (Eds.), *Empathy reconsidered: New directions in psychotherapy* (pp. 353–392). Washington, DC: American Psychological Association.

Linehan, M. M., Armstrong, H. E., Suarez, A., . . . (1991). Cognitive-behavioral treatment of chronically parasuicidal borderline patients. *Archives of General Psychiatry, 48*, 1060–1064.

Link, B. G., Phelan, J. C., Bresnahan, M., Stueve, A., & Pescosolido, B. A. (1999). Public conceptions of mental illness: Labels, causes, dangerousness, and social distance. *American Journal of Public Health, 89*, 1328–1333.

Mehlum, L. (2009). Clinical challenges in the assessment and management of suicidal behaviour in patients with borderline personality disorder. *Epidemiological Psychiatric Sociology, 18*(3), 184–189.

Nehls, N. (1998). Borderline personality disorder: Gender stereotypes, stigma, and limited system of care. *Issues in Mental Health Nursing, 19*, 97–112

Nock, M. K. (2009). Why do people hurt themselves? New insights into the nature and functions of self-injury. *Current Directions in Psychological Science, 18*(2), 78–83.

Ogata, S. N., Silk, K. R., Goodrich, S., . . . (1990). Childhood sexual and physical abuse in adult patients with borderline personality disorder. *American Journal of Psychiatry, 147,* 1008–1013.

Perseius, K. I., Kaver, A., Ekdahl, S., Asberg, M., & Samuelsson, M. (2007). Stress and burnout in psychiatric professionals when starting to do dialectical behavioural therapy in the work with young self-harming women showing borderline personality symptoms. *Journal of Psychiatric and Mental Health Nursing, 14,* 635–643.

Soloff, P. H., & Fabio, A. (2008). Prospective predictors of suicide attempts in borderline personality disorder at one, two, and two-to-five year follow-up. *Journal of Personality Disorders, 22*(2), 123–134.

Stanley, B., & Brown, G. K. (2011). Safety planning intervention: A brief intervention to mitigate suicide risk. *Cognitive and Behavioral Practice, 19,* 256–264.

Stanley, B., & Siever, L. J. (2010). The interpersonal dimension of borderline personality disorder: Toward a neuropeptide model. *American Journal of Psychiatry, 167,* 24–39.

Stern, A. (1938a). Psychoanalytic therapy in the borderline neuroses. *Psychoanalytic Quarterly, 14,* 190–198.

Stern, A. (1938b). Psychoanalytic investigation and therapy in borderline group of neuroses. *Psychoanalytic Quarterly, 7,* 467–489.

Wenzel, A., Brown, G. K., & Beck, A. T. (2008). *Cognitive therapy for suicidal patients: Scientific and clinical applications.* Washington, DC: American Psychiatric Publishing.

Wexler, D. (2001). *The PRISM workbook.* New York: W. W. Norton & Co.

Young, J. F., Klosko, J. S., & Weishaar, M. E. (2003). *Schema therapy: A practitioner's guide.* New York: Guilford.

Zanarini, M. C., Frankenburg, F. R., DeLuca, C. J., . . . (1998). The pain of being borderline: Dysphoric states specific to borderline personality disorder. *Harvard Review of Psychiatry, 44,* 224–225.

Assessing, Managing, and Resolving Suicide Risk in Borderline Personality Disorder

ADAM CARMEL, JEFFREY SUNG,
AND KATHERINE ANNE COMTOIS

INTRODUCTION

Borderline personality disorder (BPD) is the only psychiatric diagnosis, in addition to major depression, for which suicide attempts and/or nonsuicidal self-injuries (NSSI) are a criterion. Self-injury is thus considered a "hallmark" of BPD. Rates of nonsuicidal self-injury among individuals diagnosed with BPD range from 69% to 80% (Clarkin, Widiger, Frances, Hurt, & Gilmore, 1983; Cowdry, Pickar, & Davies, 1985; Grove & Tellegen, 1991; Gunderson, 1984). The suicide rate is 5–10% and doubles when only those with a previous history of suicide attempts and/or self-injuries are included (Frances, Fyer, & Clarkin, 1986; Linehan, Rizvi, Welch, & Page, 2000; Stone, 1993). See Chapter 8 for a discussion of suicide attempts and NSSI in BPD.

Suicide risk assessment, management, and treatment is clearly indicated with all suicidal individuals, yet typical clinical approaches, such as referral to alternative treatment (including termination of treatment), involuntary hospitalization, or written suicide contracts have no evidence for effectiveness in reducing risk and may even have iatrogenic effects for individuals with BPD (Fowler, 2012; Linehan, Comtois, & Ward-Ciesielski, 2010; Paris, 2002). There is a paucity of research evaluating protocols for assessing and managing risk for suicidal individuals with BPD, which limits the quality of clinical decision making in the treatment of this vulnerable population. However, evidence-based treatments of BPD each conceptualize suicidality as part of BPD and their treatment. And these treatments include specific approaches to assess and manage suicide risk and to resolve suicidality in the course of treatment. While these suicide-specific strategies have not been evaluated independently from the evidence-based treatment overall, consideration of these approaches can help clinicians provide effective care to suicidal patients with BPD.

It should be noted, however, that these approaches apply only to those patients who consent and commit to participate in psychotherapy according to the contract of that treatment. Those who do not consent and commit cannot receive these treatments and are generally referred to standard or crisis care options (case management, supportive care, medication treatment, hospitalization) involving suicide risk management strategies that may not necessarily resolve suicide risk over time. A recent study has suggested that use of a structured protocol for suicide risk assessment management by the treatment team may improve suicide-specific outcomes among patients with BPD at high risk of suicide regardless of participation in a specific type of psychotherapy or in other treatment to manage suicidal thinking and behavior (Linehan et al., 2015). This chapter focuses on those in formal psychotherapy. Myriad strategies for managing suicidal thinking and behavior in other treatments is beyond the scope of this chapter but can be found in reports such as American Psychiatric Association Guidelines for the Assessment and Treatment of Patients with Suicidal Behaviors (APA, 2003), the Department of Defense and Veterans Affairs Clinical Practice Guidelines for the Assessment and Management of Patients at Risk for Suicide (Department of Defense and Veterans Affairs, 2013), and in the Cochrane (Stoffers et al., 2012) and National Institute for Clinical Excellence (NICE, 2004) reviews.

The aim of this chapter is to aid the clinician in managing and resolving suicidality by providing an overview of different theoretical approaches to conceptualizing, assessing, managing, and treating suicidal behaviors in BPD. After a brief introduction to the evidence base for these treatments, the suicide risk management and treatment strategies are examined for five evidence-based psychotherapies designed for BPD. Then, psychotherapies for suicidal patients in general (not specific to BPD) are also considered. Finally, conclusions drawn from comparing and contrasting these psychotherapies will focus on key themes to improve clinicians' approach to patients with BPD at their most difficult time.

BRIEF SUMMARY OF THE EVIDENCE OF TREATMENTS FOR BPD

A number of evidence-based psychotherapies have been used to treat BPD. Among these, dialectical behavior therapy (DBT) is the only treatment for BPD that has been widely disseminated. DBT is the most extensively studied of all approaches to BPD, and several randomized controlled trials have demonstrated the efficacy of DBT in reducing suicidal behaviors (Linehan, Armstrong, Suarez, Allmon, & Heard, 1991; Linehan et al., 2006; Verheul et al., 2003; for a comprehensive review of DBT outcomes, see Lieb, Zanarini, Linehan, & Bohus, 2004, and Robins & Chapman, 2004). Four other psychotherapies also have at least some empirical support. Mentalization-based treatment (MBT) showed decreases in suicidal and NSSI acts, inpatient days, and depressive symptoms and increases in social and interpersonal functioning that were maintained after 18 months of partial hospitalization or outpatient mentalization condition versus two different usual care control conditions (Bateman & Fonagy, 1999, 2001, 2009). Schema-focused therapy (SFT) versus transference-focused psychotherapy (TFP) found more SFT patients showed reliable clinical improvement than did TFP patients (Giesen-Bloo et al., 2006). A randomized comparison of TFP, DBT, and dynamic supportive psychotherapy (SP) found all groups improved. TFP and DBT were more effective for suicidality, TFP and SP for anger and impulsivity, and TFP for irritability and assault (Clarkin, Levy, Lenzenweger, & Kernberg, 2007). Finally, good psychiatric management (GPM) is a year-long psychotherapy plus pharmacotherapy, with the psychotherapy based on the psychodynamic model of Gunderson (Gunderson & Links, 2008) and pharmacotherapy on an algorithm based on the APA Practice Guidelines for BPD (APA, 2001). Preliminary support for GPM is based on a randomized controlled trial (RCT) that randomized 180 participants to either DBT or GPM and found generally similar results between the two treatments, with both treatments significantly improving patient outcomes during treatment, but no between-treatment differences (McMain et al., 2009).

DIALECTICAL BEHAVIOR THERAPY APPROACH TO ASSESSING, MANAGING, AND RESOLVING SUICIDE RISK

DBT (described in detail in Chapter 16) is a behavioral psychotherapy that integrates acceptance and dialectical strategies throughout. DBT assumes that suicidal behaviors are maladaptive problem-solving behaviors. DBT is oriented to two concurrent goals: to help the patient to build a life worth living and to replace maladaptive problem-solving strategies with adaptive, skillful problem-solving behaviors to achieve that life successfully. A critical pre-treatment step in DBT is to obtain a commitment to stay alive and give up suicide as an option. From a DBT perspective, it is critical that this is a top priority because if the patient is dead, it is too late to obtain the commitment. The goal of the therapist is to secure the strongest level of commitment the patient can reasonably provide without lying or becoming overwhelmed. The suicide commitment in DBT is about what the patient wants and intends to do rather than what they can do (because many patients are quite reasonably fearful of making a promise they cannot keep). The key is for the patient to commit to closing the door on suicide as an option and to commit instead to achieving a life worth living using every other strategy the client and his or her therapist (and family or friends) can come up with. Priority in the DBT hierarchically organized therapy structure is given to stopping suicidal behavior and self-inflicted injury (Linehan, 1993). The primary targets of treatment are to reduce and stop suicide crisis behaviors, then suicidal behaviors including attempts and NSSIs, then suicide threats and other communication of suicidal intentions, and, finally, to resolve other suicide-promoting emotions and thoughts. At all times, reducing these primary targets of DBT is balanced by a focus on achieving a life worth living. Thus, a life worth living is the goal of DBT (not suicide prevention per se).

DBT: Managing Suicide Risk

Linehan Risk Assessment and Management Protocol

The Linehan Risk Assessment and Management Protocol (L-RAMP) was developed by Linehan (2009) to operationalize the DBT principles on suicide risk assessment and intervention described in the DBT manual (Linehan, 1993, ch. 15). As with other aspects of DBT, the L-RAMP is a guideline of if-then principles rather than a protocol of ordered steps. The L-RAMP provides clinicians with a structured assessment of risk factors as well as short-term interventions to address these factors during the session. The L-RAMP was designed for specific situations including (1) at the start of treatment, as well as any time that a client (2) makes a suicide attempt, (3) engages in NSSI, (4) makes a suicidal threat, or (5) reports a clinically significant increase in suicide urges. Thus, the L-RAMP is not used in every treatment session (unless these situations continue to be present; Linehan et al., 2010). The L-RAMP assessment starts with a comprehensive risk assessment and then guides the clinician to consider reasonable options as part of the decision-making process for managing risk (Linehan et al., 2010). The L-RAMP prompts the clinician with specific interventions to try (e.g., generating hope, giving advice, mobilizing supports, etc.) and to provide a reason for not intervening (e.g., the risk is negligible, suicidality resolved by the end of the treatment session, or a plan is in place and suicidality is likely to be reinforced by further attention to suicide risk assessment rather than problem-solving and action toward a life worth living). Thus, completion of the L-RAMP addresses not only the steps that were taken to manage risk, but also addresses the reasons why the clinician did not take steps that might be considered the standard of care (e.g., Joiner, Walker, Rudd, & Jobes, 1999). The L-RAMP also prompts for documentation of consultation with other clinicians and social supports when appropriate. Documentation of clinical decision-making is emotionally and legally protective in the unfortunate case of a patient's death by suicide (Linehan et al., 2010). In a study examining suicide-related outcomes among women with BPD at high risk of suicide (Linehan et al., 2015), the L-RAMP was used across three study arms, including groups assigned to case management and DBT skills group, individual DBT and an activities group, and standard DBT with individual psychotherapy and skills group. All three groups were noted to have similar improvements in suicide-related outcomes, suggesting that clinician use of a structured suicide risk assessment and management protocol may improve outcomes regardless of the type of psychotherapy.

Linehan and Comtois have also developed the University of Washington Risk Assessment Protocol (UWRAP) for assessing and managing risk in research assessments (Linehan & Comtois, 2009). The UWRAP is designed on the premise that a research assessor cannot take clinical responsibility or implement management strategies, and thus the focus is on gathering sufficient data to determine the level of risk and then linking the individual to appropriate providers who can intervene. The UWRAP assesses overall distress and suicidal ideation and urges to self-injure or use drugs or alcohol on a 1–7 scale both before and after the assessment. Based on these ratings, the assessor can determine if a more extensive assessment of suicide risk is needed and what level of intervention is appropriate. The suicide risk assessment and a range of intervention options are provided to standardize this process (Linehan et al., 2010). The UWRAP may therefore also be useful for peer or family support providers, milieu staff, or others who encounter suicidal individuals but are not expected to take clinical responsibility.

DBT: Resolving Suicidality

DBT resolves suicidality by monitoring for suicidal behavior or urges, analyzing these behaviors using a chain analysis and generating alternatives to suicidal behavior using a solution analysis. Whenever suicidal or self-injurious urges or actions emerge, the therapist is responsible for prioritizing these in treatment until they are resolved. Overlooking suicidal behaviors, conducting an incomplete chain analysis, or implying acceptance of suicide as a viable option are considered DBT therapeutic errors. The DBT therapist will focus on specific instances suicidal behavior and conduct an analysis of the seconds to minutes to hours before and after these incidents occur. This method of conducting what is called a chain analysis is an adaption of functional analysis specific for DBT based on the importance of unbearable emotions in creating and maintaining suicidality. The time frame of emotions is seconds to minutes to hours, and thus the assessment must examine a comparable time frame. This is in contrast to assessing the systemic context of the patient, historical factors, or cognitive patterns. Chain analysis is conducted on the most recent and severe suicidal behaviors at the beginning of treatment and then for any suicidal urges or behavior occurring during treatment.

Solution analyses are an active attempt to generate adaptive alternatives to the links in the chain considered to be controlling variables (i.e., what caused the patient to choose suicidal behavior) and a plan for regulation and tolerance of the emotions specific to that chain of events. In the face of high risk of future suicidal behavior or self-injury, proximal variables (i.e., what occurred immediately before or after the suicidal behavior) are prioritized over distal ones to ensure the suicidal urges or behavior are stopped as quickly as possible. Other controlling variables, such as lack of sleep, interpersonal conflict, loss, hopeless thinking, lack of skills, rumination and judgmental thinking, become the focus once the suicidal behavior is under immediate control.

Another focus of the DBT approach to suicide is to maintain the dialectical balance between acceptance and change. The therapist holds the acceptance-based stance that assumes the lives of suicidal patients with BPD are intolerable as they are currently being lived and thereby empathizes with the suicidal wish to escape. At the same time, the therapist presses for change by helping the patient appreciate that suicide and suicidal behaviors have negative consequences such as the fact that use of suicidal behavior as a solution prevents the development of emotion regulation and problem-solving skills that would make their life worth living. It is not considered helpful in DBT to view the patient as "manipulative" or "acting out" because such a perspective negates the subjective perception of the patient, can repeat their pathogenic experience, and interferes with collaboratively and creatively solving the problems that make the patient suicidal. Whenever possible, the suicidal crisis should be used to improve the patient's problem-solving capacities by using the DBT skills taught in skills training groups. Only in situations where the situation significantly exceeds the skills of the patient and appears to be imminently life-threatening will the DBT therapist actively intervene, through hospitalization for instance. The DBT strategies allow most suicidal patients with BPD to resolve their suicidality on an outpatient basis with out-of-session coaching. In addition, there are DBT models for use in residential and acute and long-term inpatient settings.

It cannot be emphasized enough that the treatment strategies and skills in DBT are linked to the client's goals for a life worth living. Skillful alternatives to suicidal behaviors are linked to goals in order to facilitate the client's commitment to try to persist with them. Once suicidal behavior and urges stop, the focus of treatment is to other behaviors that decrease the client's quality of life to assure that they achieve a life worth living and have no reason for suicidal coping or wishing to be dead.

MENTALIZATION-BASED TREATMENT APPROACH TO ASSESSING, MANAGING, AND RESOLVING SUICIDE RISK

MBT (described in detail in Chapter 14) posits that a fundamental deficit in the ability to mentalize accounts for the manifestations of BPD, including suicidal behavior. Mentalization is defined as "the mental process by which an individual implicitly and explicitly interprets the actions of himself and others as meaningful on the basis of intentional mental states such personal desires, needs, feelings, beliefs, and reasons" (Bateman & Fonagy, 2004). The ability to mentalize promotes a coherent sense of self-as-agent—that is, a feeling of stability from knowledge that mental states, rather than physical phenomena, motivate behavior in the self and others. In MBT, a suicide attempt represents a desperate effort to restore a sense of coherence to the self after the loss or threatened loss of an external other who had functioned as a repository for alien parts of the self. When an external other is functioning in this manner (i.e., as an interpersonal regulator of unbearable emotions), the loss is experienced at the level of catastrophic abandonment that threatens to destroy the self. Loss of the external other results in a return of the alien parts of the self and is experienced as unbearable emotions. Without an external other functioning as a repository for these alien parts of the self, MBT suggests that the body itself becomes the repository. For example, during an angry conflict, an individual with BPD may pressure his partner to behave as he demands. In this manner, the individual with BPD attempts to regulate his anger by controlling his partner. It is as if a part of himself (the alien self) is located in his partner, and if he can induce a change in this part of himself, he will gain relief from emotional pain. If his partner leaves, he is left alone with unbearable emotional pain (a return of the alien self). Without the option of inducing a change in his partner to regulate his emotion, he engages in self-injury to restore a feeling of agency and control over unbearable emotional pain.

NSSI is understood along the same lines as representing a psychic equivalence mode of unconsciously experiencing body parts as a manifestation of alien parts of the self that must be acted upon with destructive behavior in order to restore coherence in the self in response to unbearable emotions. MBT uses a deficit-based understanding of suicidal behavior and states that only rarely do suicidal threats or behavior represent an attempt to attack, manipulate, or control others.

MBT: Managing Suicide Risk

Suicide risk assessment in MBT includes a review of the patient's history of suicidal behavior and holding a case conference to agree on overall level of risk and distinguish between acute and chronic risk. The initial evaluation in MBT includes a detailed review of suicide attempts and instances of self-harm using the suicide and self-harm inventory (Bateman & Fonagy, 2004). This inventory assesses for the presence of suicide attempts and self-harm and details the frequency, methods, planning, interpersonal contexts, emotional and cognitive contexts, presence of alcohol or drugs, medical consequences, and interpersonal consequences. In MBT, the individual therapist elicits and compares at least three instances of suicidal behavior with three instances of successful coping with similar interpersonal and emotional circumstances and impulses for self-harm. This comparison helps to identify existing capabilities that may help to judge overall risk as well as guide therapeutic interventions. After the initial assessment and first few individual and group meetings, all staff members engaged in the patient's care meet with the patient in a case conference to present a formulation of the patient's suicidal behavior and to reach consensus regarding the overall level of chronic suicide risk. Chronic suicide risk is defined as the risk over a 2-year period and is stratified into high, medium, or low risk depending on how frequently or infrequently the patient engages in suicidal behavior in response to setbacks, rejection, or obstacles to wishes and desires. The initial assessment process also identifies individual acute risk factors that suggest that suicidal behavior may be imminent. MBT distinguishes between chronic and acute risk in order to avoid responding to chronic suicide risk with interventions that are more effective in managing acute risk (hospitalization, increased therapist contact, changing medications). MBT recognizes that, in BPD, these acute risk interventions may result in iatrogenic harm by maintaining or exacerbating long-term risk of suicide. MBT states that chronic risk must be tolerated and treated using psychotherapy and that only a high level of acute risk warrants taking over responsibility for the patient's safety.

Suicide risk management in MBT is facilitated by a crisis protocol to assist when the primary therapist is not available and a crisis response that facilitates a meeting with the patient when suicide risk is judged to be high. The crisis protocol details the role of the therapist and patient in managing a crisis. MBT emphasizes that the patient, not the therapist, is ultimately responsible for the patient's behavior. The therapist is responsible for helping the patient establish a reflective stance whereby the patient can make decisions regarding crisis management. The therapist is also responsible for helping the patient access inpatient treatment if this is deemed necessary. On weekends and between sessions, the patient is given responsibility for managing suicide urges or seeking emergency care. When a patient reports a crisis, the treatment team reviews the circumstances and may arrange for a meeting with a team member who is not the patient's individual therapist (in order to reduce risk of exacerbating suicide risk by responding with increased time with the individual therapist). The team member assesses the current situation in terms of affective experience, interpersonal circumstances, treatment circumstances and historical instances of suicidal behavior. The treatment team meets to reach consensus regarding how to respond in a manner that reduces suicide risk. Any structural interventions (i.e., inpatient hospitalization) must be agreed upon by at least two team members, again to reduce risk of using acute interventions that exacerbate long-term risk. Psychiatric hospitalization is used only in settings of acute suicide risk not contained by other means, homicidal risk, comorbid psychiatric disorder, uncontrollable impulsivity, or treatment team anxiety that cannot be contained with the patient in nonrestrictive care. Psychiatric hospitalization is meant to be brief and voluntary with clearly defined goals and a clearly defined discharge date regardless of clinical deterioration.

MBT: Resolving Suicidality

MBT treats suicide by attempting to restore the ability to mentalize under the conditions of affective arousal that prompt suicidal behavior. Mentalizing restores the coherent psychic experience of self-as-agent and reduces the need to engage in impulsive, self-destructive physical acts to restore coherence. MBT addresses issues in treatment according to a hierarchy that begins with engagement in treatment followed by self-damaging, threatening, or suicidal behavior. All instances of suicidal behavior are framed as problems to be discussed in individual and group sessions. In initial sessions, the individual therapist conducts a detailed, collaborative assessment with the patient of historical instances of suicidal behavior to identify antecedents, interpersonal contexts, concurrent mental states, and outcomes of behavior. Subsequent instances of suicidal behavior are treated similarly. The therapist seeks to determine the affective experiences and precipitants, especially interpersonal and therapy-related experiences that first prompted the patient to think of suicide. In an effort to restore the capacity to mentalize, the therapist adopts the inquisitive stance and asks the patient to identify the mental states (thoughts, feelings, desires) associated with the suicidal behavior while generating hypotheses about these mental states if the patient cannot identify them. The therapist seeks to help the patient replace the prereflective psychic equivalence ("I am worthless and deserve to die") and pretend ("I don't know what happened") modes of experience with mentalized emotional pain: "I felt frightened and angry and thought my life was over when my relationship ended." Discussion of suicidal behavior in group sessions allows patients to observe how their impulses and actions are perceived by others and to gain understanding of how suicidal behavior functions to avoid thinking or feeling or to induce thoughts and feelings in others. Through individual and group sessions, MBT posits that replacing the incoherent alien-self experience of affect in psychic equivalence and pretend modes with a coherent, meaningful experience of emotion in mentalizing mode will reduce impulsivity and suicidal behavior. That is, the ability to identify mental states of thoughts, emotions, and desires as the basis for behavior in the self and others and to link these with antecedent events and historical experiences will protect against the need to regulate overwhelming emotions urgently with suicidal behavior.

TRANSFERENCE-FOCUSED PSYCHOTHERAPY APPROACH TO ASSESSING, MANAGING, AND RESOLVING SUICIDE RISK

TFP is a psychoanalytically based treatment for BPD and other severe personality disorders (Clarkin, Yeomans, & Kernberg, 2006). According to TFP, borderline personality organization is characterized by the syndrome of identity diffusion, described as the chaotic and unstable experience of concepts of self and others with polarized extremes of positive and negative characteristics. Each concept of self is linked to a concept of other by an affect of either positive (idealized) or negative (aggressive) valence to form an affectively charged dyad called an *internal object relation.*

According to TFP, the basis of suicidal behavior in patients with BPD is the expression of aggressively charged internal object relations, especially those involving hatred, at the level of behavior, rather than at the level of coherent emotional experiencing. Unbearable affect that cannot be represented in meaningful patterns of thinking and language will be expressed in action that represents symbolically the object relation associated with the affect. For example, a patient may engage in suicidal behavior after her boyfriend chooses to spend the evening with friends rather than stay home with her after having shared an enjoyable meal. After he leaves, she sends him a series of angry messages. Finally, overwhelmed with shame and anger, the patient cuts herself. In object relations theory, the shame-based aspect of this suicidal behavior may be understood as a symbolic act representing a condemning other punishing a hateful self, and the anger-based aspect of this suicidal behavior may be understood as an enraged self inflicting revenge on an abandoning other. Identity diffusion refers to the fragmented state of these internal self and object representations with alternating, one-dimensional experiences across different moments in time (i.e., "This dinner is perfect. I love you completely" and "You don't care anything about me") rather than an integrated state of simultaneous, multidimensional experiences within one moment in time (i.e., "I'm disappointed that you didn't choose to stay home with me"). Knowledge of this simultaneous identification with the roles of a hateful, scorned self (the feeling of shame) and a hating, sadistic object (the action of cutting) remains outside of awareness and is problematically acted out in self-injurious behavior. Even more fundamentally split-off out of awareness are the identifications with idealized concepts of self and others that could modulate the intensity of negative affect were they not lost to awareness when negative affect is dominant. For example, recalling positive aspects of the self and others while feeling anger and shame could modulate the intensity of the emotions and reduce the impulse to engage in suicidal behavior. TFP seeks to resolve the syndrome of identity diffusion using transference interpretations that clarify the unconscious object relations being activated and then subsequently link them with affectively disparate object relations that exist out of conscious awareness. Resolving identity diffusion modulates the chaotic intensity of negative affect into more bearable painful emotions that can be experienced coherently, without the need for immediate discharge in the form of suicidal behavior.

TFP: Managing Suicidal Risk

The initial, pre-treatment diagnostic assessment focuses on differentiating acute and chronic suicidality and identifying the presence or absence of depression (Kernberg, 1993). TFP suggests that severe depression, especially in the context of psychotic symptoms or a psychotic disorder, is associated with a high risk of acute suicidal behavior. Risk assessment follows with a review of suicide-specific risk factors such as ongoing suicidal wishes, suicide plans and a history of suicide attempts, demographic risk factors, and other clinical factors that relate to suicide risk. If, at this pre-treatment stage, suicide risk is judged to be acute, referral for emergency evaluation and possible hospitalization is indicated. This process of patient selection to differentiate acute from chronic suicidality leaves the diagnostic group of borderline personality organization. Individuals with "characterological" (chronic) suicidality as a manifestation of the syndrome of identity diffusion are then candidates for psychoanalytically oriented psychotherapy as articulated by TFP if a treatment contract can be established. In drawing the distinction between suicidality related to severe depression and characterological suicidality, TFP essentially conceptualizes suicidal behavior as respondent (prompted by severe depression) in depression and operant (maintained by internal and environmental responses) in BPD.

TFP manages suicide risk by establishing a clear treatment contract that describes therapist and patient roles during ongoing treatment and during suicidal crises. Contracting to establish the frame of treatment involves an individualized, collaborative process (rather than a single written document) that establishes roles and responsibilities of the patient and therapist as well as the basic tenants of the therapy (attendance, payment, participation). In TFP, contracting is understood as a crucial element in establishing the conditions necessary for treating the primary drivers of suicide (i.e., the manifestations of identity diffusion as expressed in the treatment relationship). The contract clearly articulates the agreement regarding the responsibilities of the patient in managing suicidal urges and suicidal behavior between and within sessions. In TFP, the correct diagnosis of BPD suggests that the "patient should be able, with effort, to control his or her urges to act out most of the time and to seek help appropriately when he or she cannot" (Clarkin et al., 2006). As such, the treatment contract may state that the patient has responsibility for calling 911 or presenting for emergency evaluation between sessions if suicidal urges are unbearable or, if suicidal urges are bearable, using the following session to discuss the event. The contract may further state that, within a session, the patient agrees to make suicide the highest priority of treatment, and, if urges cannot be managed by the end of the session, the patient must follow the therapist's instructions to seek emergency evaluation (Kernberg, Yeomans, Clarkin, & Levy, 2008). Consistent with TFP's conceptualization of suicidality as problem behavior linked with "secondary gain" and "attempts to dominate, control, or manipulate others" (Clarkin et al., 2006), the treatment contract removes the therapist from emergency decision-making processes regarding suicidal behavior to keep the focus on understanding underlying conflicts and emotions rather than engaging in crisis responses that may maintain patterns of suicidal behavior. The treatment manual emphasizes that the focus of treatment is in-session work to understand the psychodynamics underlying suicide and that "suicidal *behavior* is outside the realm of TFP" (Clarkin et al., 2006, emphasis added). TFP posits that therapist participation at the level of action (crisis management) impedes the ability to promote understanding and reflection (psychotherapeutic treatment), thus risking iatrogenic maintenance of patterns of suicidal behavior. In the treatment contract, the therapist takes responsibility for working with the patient to address the problems that brought the patient to treatment, with suicide being the highest priority. Family and significant others are engaged in the contracting process to clarify that the patient, rather than others, carries responsibility for managing suicidal behavior and that the treatment carries a risk of the patient's death by suicide. A patient with whom a therapeutic contract cannot be reached may be a candidate for supportive treatment that manages the conditions under which suicidal behavior occurs (secondary drivers of suicide). This treatment may include supportive psychotherapy, social rehabilitation, pharmacological management, and establishment of a social support system (Kernberg et al., 2008).

Ongoing suicide risk management in TFP does not follow a standard protocol of structured assessment. Instead, the therapist attends consistently to suicide potential with principles to guide decision-making (Clarkin et al., 2006). These principles mirror those in the initial diagnostic assessment in drawing a distinction between acute and chronic suicidality. In assessing suicide risk, TFP recommends that the therapist first attend to the presence or absence of severe depression. If suicidality occurs with severe depression, hopelessness, affective constriction, and neurovegetative symptoms, TFP recommends more activity on the part of the therapist to manage suicide risk with referrals for medication evaluation or hospitalization. In the absence of severe depressive symptoms, suicidality in BPD is understood to represent a manifestation of underlying character pathology. TFP recommends assessing for suicidal intent with the therapist attending to the state of the transference relationship and therapeutic alliance. If, after this assessment, suicide risk is judged to be high, the patient is reminded of the treatment contract with recommendations to self-manage suicidal impulses or to seek emergency evaluation. Under conditions when the patient does not follow the treatment plan as established in the treatment contract, the therapist is directed to take responsible action to ensure the patient's safety (i.e., calling for immediate emergency assistance) with later discussion regarding whether the treatment can continue given the deviation from the contract. TFP explicitly recommends deviations from technical neutrality when the therapist must act urgently in a crisis to set limits or mobilize emergency services to save the patient's life. An example would be to insist that a patient who is accumulating lethal amounts of medication remove this from the home. The transference consequences of a deviation from neutrality and the underlying reasons that forced it are subsequently analyzed in treatment.

TFP: Resolving Suicidality

Having established a treatment contract that creates the conditions for activation of affectively charged internalized object relations, TFP focuses immediately on clarifying the unconscious meanings of suicidal behavior and how these manifest in the transference. TFP seeks to understand the symbolic meanings of suicidal behavior in attacking the self and others and then replace aggression directed against the patient's body with tolerance of psychic pain and aggression directed against the therapist and the treatment. Thus, TFP treats suicide by seeking first to replace suicidal behavior with suicide-related affect and conflicts expressed in the transference relationship. For example, suicidal behavior as an expression of an envious attack on the self ("When I start to get better, I self-sabotage by trying to kill myself") may be interpreted in terms of the transference implication of aggression directed toward the positive aspects of the treatment. The therapist will seek to replace self-directed aggression with in-session anger and attacks on the therapist as a symbol of hope and change: "Well, I wouldn't keep doing it if you were a better therapist and this treatment were actually helping me."

In TFP, "strategies" refer to overall treatment goals, with the primary goal being the resolution of identity diffusion by integrating positively and negatively invested internal object relations in a process called *identity consolidation* (Caligor, Diamond, Yeomans, & Kernberg, 2009). Other approaches include following a hierarchy of treatment priorities, beginning with suicidal and homicidal behavior followed by problems that threaten the continuation of the treatment, severe acting out that threatens the patient's life or the treatment, dishonesty, trivialization of session content, and "pervasive narcissistic resistances" (Kernberg et al., 2008). "Techniques" refer to the use of the technical interventions of psychoanalysis (with some modification): free association, interpretation, transference analysis, technical neutrality, countertransference analysis, and interpretive linking of dissociated clinical material.

In TFP, the patient is instructed to free associate to problems that brought him or her into treatment following the hierarchy established in the tactics, beginning with a discussion of suicidal behavior if this is relevant. As the patient associates, the therapist observes verbal and nonverbal behavior as well as his or her own reactions to the patient in order to identify the dominant affect. The affect is then used to clarify the dominant internal object relation being expressed in the transference. Because the dominant affect and transference hypotheses will have arisen out of associations to suicidal behavior, TFP may be understood as treating suicide by first observing and describing suicide-related emotional experiences and their associated beliefs and role assignments in regard to the self and others. By maintaining the technically neutral, matter-of-fact interpretive stance regarding these configurations of self and other, the therapist then facilitates non-reinforced exposures to previously intolerable emotions with the intent of reducing affective arousal and integrating previously incompatible positive and negative affective and cognitive states.

TFP recommends that the therapist introduce into the discussion recent suicidal behavior or problems known to relate to suicide if the patient does not include these spontaneously. This recommendation follows the theoretical formulation that the absence of such material in the patient's associations represents the operation of splitting mechanisms that must be addressed in treatment. This deviation from neutrality into directive action functions to maintain the persistent focus on suicidal behavior as the highest treatment priority regardless of whether it represents the affectively dominant topic. Finally, TFP includes participation in regular supervision to ensure fidelity to the treatment and support for the therapist.

GOOD PSYCHIATRIC MANAGEMENT APPROACH TO ASSESSING, MANAGING, AND RESOLVING SUICIDE RISK

GPM (discussed in detail in Chapter 18) is a therapy developed by Links et al. (Links, Bergmans, Novick, & LeGris, 2009) based on a comprehensive set of evidence-based "best practice" recommendations published in the American Psychiatric Association's Clinical Practice Guideline for the Treatment of Patients with BPD (APA, 2001). GPM includes two components of treatment: symptom-targeted medication management based on the APA guidelines and psychotherapy. The psychotherapy is based on the principles developed by Gunderson (2014).

GPM combines Gunderson's (2001) model of BPD with research regarding emotional processing to understand suicidal behavior. Gunderson posits that the core feature of BPD is intolerance of aloneness arising out of insecure attachment relationships. Attachment is thought to function as a means of regulating emotion by restoring a feeling of safety, and insecure attachment leads to problems with emotional processing (Schore, 2000). Dysregulated emotional processing in turn is related to suicidal behavior (Linehan, 1993; Schneidman, 1996). Following this progression from insecure attachment to dysregulated emotional processing to suicidal behavior, GPM views dysregulated emotional processing as a primary driver of suicide in BPD. Consistent with psychodynamic theories of emotion, GPM posits that unconscious experience that cannot be symbolized in coherent patterns of thinking and language is acted out at the level of behavior. Suicidal behavior is thus understood to represent a response to or symbolic acting out of overwhelming and incoherent emotional processes that can be made tolerable and meaningful through treatment.

GPM: Managing Suicidal Risk

GPM uses an "acute-on-chronic" model of suicide risk assessment that creates a distinction between acute and chronic risk of suicidal behavior. Chronic risk of suicidal behavior refers to the long-term, elevated baseline risk of suicide in patients with BPD related to demographic factors and problems with emotional processing. Acute risk refers to an increased risk of self-injury with suicidal intent and higher lethality means based on research that has identified factors associated with this elevated risk in patients with BPD (Links et al., 2009). These factors include worsening of major depressive symptoms or substance use disorders, time period following recent discharge from a psychiatric inpatient service, recent negative life events, and prominent affective instability (Gunderson & Links, 2008; Links & Kolla, 2005). The acute-on-chronic model of risk assessment recognizes the elevated baseline chronic risk of suicide and then monitors for the presence of acute risk superimposed on chronic risk that may indicate a crisis with risk of self-harm with higher suicidal intent and higher lethality means. In GPM, the therapist and patient collaborate to identify relevant acute risk factors for suicidal behavior based on the patient's history. GPM follows the principle of assessing for suicide risk factors without describing a standard protocol for assessment of acute or chronic suicide risk factors.

In GPM, the therapist and patient engage in regular safety monitoring and collaborate to develop an individualized risk management plan based on the patient's acute risk factors. The patient is encouraged to develop awareness of his or her acute risk factors to have these addressed in treatment as they arise. The initial treatment contract for GPM includes a discussion of crisis management with an agreed-upon plan for the patient to contact the therapist if the patient assesses risk of self-injury to be acute. In crisis situations with acute risk of suicidal behavior, GPM recommends identifying the modifiable risk factors related to the crisis and addressing these in treatment (i.e., treating symptoms of depression, actively targeting substance use, problem-solving around a negative life event). Psychiatric hospitalization may be recommended if a crisis cannot be resolved by addressing other risk factors. With chronic risk, GPM recommends that the therapist tolerate the anxiety of baseline suicide risk and adhere to the plan of reducing risk over time using symptom-focused psychopharmacology and psychotherapy focused on emotional processing. GPM recognizes and may explain to the patient that interventions for acute risk (psychiatric hospitalization) are unlikely to be effective for managing chronic risk.

GPM: Resolving Suicidality

The symptom-focused psychopharmacological component of GPM treats suicide risk by targeting mood lability, impulsivity, and aggressiveness because these are thought to relate most closely to preventing suicidal behavior. The psychotherapy component of GPM includes three elements: case management, emotion processing, and relational elements. Each psychotherapy element treats suicide risk in a manner complementary to the others. Case management includes monitoring of suicide risk as described, as well as maintenance of a nonpejorative stance regarding suicidal behavior. Monitoring suicide risk to distinguish acute and chronic risk allows the therapist to determine whether to take a more active stance to modify risk factors associated with acute risk or to engage in emotional processing work to reduce risk over time. To facilitate adherence to and retention in treatment, GPM states that the therapist "must remove the pejorative inferences that are placed on the patient's suicidal behavior" (Links et al., 2009).

The emotional processing element of GPM addresses the dysregulated emotional experiences understood to be the primary basis of suicidal behavior in BPD. Psychotherapy for emotional processing includes identifying feelings, connecting behavior to thoughts and feelings, fostering curiosity about emotions, and clarifying maladaptive responses to feelings. In the initial phase of treatment, priority is given to the identification of feeling states and meanings associated with nonlethal and potentially lethal acts of self-harm. For example, to help clarify the meaning of self-injury, the patient may be given a list of potential meanings for each category of self-injury: relief from overwhelming distress or asking for help in nonlethal self-injury or to end the pain of life or to end extreme self-hate in potentially lethal self-injury. As the patient and therapist collaborate to understand feeling states and meanings associated with risk of nonlethal and lethal self-injury, this process will assist with monitoring suicide risk over time and guiding treatment to address modifiable factors that are associated with risk of lethal self-injury. To address chronic risk of self-injury, the therapist and patient develop a list of early warning signs (EWS) to help the patient recognize that the intensity of a feeling is changing in order to take steps to address this before engaging in suicidal behavior. Over time, through work in emotional processing, the patient develops greater capacity to observe and describe emotional experience in ways that are tolerable and meaningful and to subsequently make choices to reduce unsafe behavior and promote behavior that restores feelings of safety. GPM does not specifically direct the patient to prioritize any particular topic (such as suicidal behavior) in psychotherapy. GPM specifically advises the therapist to expand the focus of psychotherapy beyond a discussion of the chronic risk of suicide in order to address functioning in other aspects of the patient's life. GPM does, however, note that if suicide risk is judged to be high, this becomes the focus of treatment and that the initial step in emotional processing work involves the identification of emotions and meanings associated with high risk of suicidal behavior.

The relational elements of GPM address suicide risk by promoting positive transference, demonstrating empathy and validation, and attending to negative transference and countertransference. The relational elements determine the emotional tone with which the therapist addresses suicidal behavior. Following self-psychology (Kohut, 1971) and intersubjectivity (Stolorow, Brandchaft, & Atwood, 1987), and in contrast to TFP's conflict perspective in object relations theory, suicidal behavior is viewed from a deficit perspective. That is, suicidal behavior is viewed as a result of deficient intrapsychic structures and capabilities arising out of developmental empathic failures and traumatic events rather than as a means of blocking other painful emotional states (i.e., anger as a defense against sadness or guilt). The meaning of a patient's behavior is understood nonpejoratively, first from the patient's perspective as an adaptive response to empathic failure and, second, as having destructive and maladaptive consequences in the present. For example, suicidal behavior arising out of rage may be understood from the patient's perspective as a desperate expression of hopelessness *and* nascent hope that others will understand and respond to emotional needs. With this understanding, the therapist will seek to introduce the maladaptive aspects of this behavior in an effort to replace it with more effective ways of communicating to others. GPM does not utilize direct transference interpretation of aggressive object relations (as in TFP) because these interpretations in a short-term (12 month) treatment are felt to carry the risk of conveying a sense of blame. Negative countertransference arising out of negative transference is managed with supervision groups focused on providing understanding and support for the therapist in maintaining an empathic, validating stance with the patient.

SCHEMA-FOCUSED THERAPY APPROACH TO ASSESSING, MANAGING, AND RESOLVING SUICIDE RISK

SFT (described in detail in Chapter 18) views the inner world of patients with BPD as having five different aspects of self that interact in destructive ways, known as "modes," and it is common for individuals with BPD to flip suddenly from one mode into the other (Kellogg & Young, 2006; Young, Klosko, & Weishaar, 2003). Modes are influenced by genetics but develop in early family environments experienced as unstable, unsafe, depriving, punitive, or subjugating. The major modes that comprise BPD are labeled (1) the abandoned and abused child, (2) the angry and impulsive child, (3) the detached protector, (4) the punitive parent, and (5) the healthy adult (Kellogg & Young, 2006).

SFT views impulsive, self-destructive behaviors such as self-injury or suicide attempts as a form of release from being inundated with unbearable emotions that often become activated when in a particular mode. Coping skills are introduced to increase distress tolerance; however, it is often the case that patients become too overwhelmed to use these skills. Once a patient is able to form an alliance with the therapist and express anger toward the therapist and others, then impulsive and self-destructive behaviors are thought to reduce significantly (Kellogg & Young, 2006; Young et al., 2003).

SFT: Managing Suicidal Risk

The patient is asked to agree that he or she will contact the therapist prior to engaging in suicidal behavior, and this agreement is a condition of therapy. Although patients with BPD can express the wish to die by suicide, a premise in SFT is that they cannot act on this wish and that the therapist must be contacted directly before suicidal behavior takes place so that the therapist has an opportunity to intervene (Young et al., 2003). Access to the therapist via pager or phone is provided for this purpose, and the therapist sets limits if rules around communication are violated.

Patients who receive SFT must agree to follow the hierarchy of rules that are designed to help manage suicidal behaviors. The therapist determines the specific steps to manage suicide risk, the patient must agree to follow the sequence of steps, and warning is given in advance that failure to do so will result in the termination of therapy. In the event that the patient does not adhere to the plan, the therapist sees the patient through the suicidal event and then terminates therapy (Young et al., 2003). The first step to manage suicide risk includes increasing the frequency of contact with the patient, which often results in a decrease of suicidality. Within the contact, the next step is assessing risk on a scale of "high," "medium," and "low," and a response of "high" will result in proceeding to the next steps. The next step is to obtain permission to contact significant others and work to schedule time for the patient to be around others until suicidal urges decrease. Additional steps include arranging consultation with a co-therapist; arranging for consultation with a prescriber of psychotropic medications; considering adjunctive treatments such as day hospitals, crisis lines, or support groups; and, finally, arranging voluntarily hospitalization if necessary (Young et al., 2003).

SFT: Resolving Suicidality

Schema healing is the ultimate goal of schema therapy, and this process involves behavior change as clients work to replace maladaptive coping styles with adaptive patterns of behavior. Schemas that activate suicidal responses are addressed using cognitive, affective, and behavioral interventions (Kellogg & Young, 2006). The therapist works with the patient to create behavioral homework assignments in order to replace maladaptive coping responses with new, more adaptive patterns of behavior (Young et al., 2003). The therapist helps the patient create homework assignments by rehearsing new behaviors using imagery and role-playing, which are practiced during the session, and obstacles to behavioral change are highlighted and addressed using techniques such as flash cards and imagery. After completing assignments, the patient discusses the results with the therapist, evaluating what was learned and identifying the life decisions that perpetuate the schema. The dyad focus is on making healthier choices that break old self-defeating life patterns, including suicidal behavior. As a schema heals, it becomes increasingly more difficult to activate. When schemas do become activated, the experience is less overwhelming, and the patient recovers more quickly (Young et al., 2003).

COMMON THEMES REGARDING SUICIDALITY IN PSYCHOTHERAPIES FOR BPD

Although these treatments vary widely in terms of theory, conceptualization, and approach to managing and treating suicidal behaviors, some common themes arise (Bliss & McCardle, 2014). Weinberg et al. (2010), in their review of manualized treatments for suicidality—four (DBT, TFP, MBT, SFT) of which were specifically for BPD—emphasize the common elements of a clear treatment framework, agreed-upon strategy to manage suicidal crises, attention to affect, active therapist, exploratory interventions, and change-oriented interventions. These themes can be seen in this review as well.

All treatments appear to view unbearable affect as a proximal driver of suicidal behavior while differing in regard to addressing the emotion directly (DBT, GPM) or indirectly by way of exploring underlying causes of the emotion (TFP, MBT, SFT). DBT emphasizes a skills-based approach to managing dysregulated emotion. Similarly, in SFT, clients learning coping strategies is emphasized. In GPM, affect is first observed and described and then used to identify states of danger or safety so that choices can be made to reduce unsafe behavior and promote safe behavior. The psychodynamically oriented approaches to suicide in MBT, TFP, and GPM emphasize the role of transforming unbearable and incoherent feeling states that must be expressed in action into tolerable and meaningful emotional experiences that can be expressed in thinking and language. The meaning of the emotion differs according to theory. In TFP, affect is used to generate hypotheses about configurations of internal object relations. In MBT, affect is used to identify mental states in the self and others. SFT manages affect by focusing on suicide-related modes that underlie unbearable emotional states.

With regard to assessing and managing suicide risk, all treatments emphasize the importance of a clear framework for treatment, risk assessment, and crisis management. The treatments differ in terms of the level of structure in risk assessment and the level of therapist involvement in crisis management, with DBT using the most highly structured risk assessment protocol and highest level of therapist involvement in crisis management. DBT, TFP, MBT, and GPM all make a distinction between acute and chronic suicide risk, considering the potential to intervene with crisis management or hospitalization for acute risk and to treat with outpatient psychotherapy for chronic risk.

With regard to treatment priorities, all treatments recognize suicide risk as the highest priority, with initial steps focused on reducing risk. This is similar to suicide-focused psychotherapies not specific to BPD (Jobes, 2012) and in contrast to many standard pharmacotherapy and psychotherapy treatments not specifically designed for suicidal individuals. Standard treatments are diagnostically and symptomatically focused and implicitly or explicitly assume that suicidality will resolve with the psychiatric symptoms. DBT, TFP, and MBT manuals all adhere to a hierarchy of targets, with suicide as the highest target as well as engagement in treatment. GPM does not explicitly state a hierarchy of targets, although acute risk of suicide must be addressed first if this is present. Also in common among all treatments is the use of a clinician team—a feature also common to most non-BPD–specific suicide prevention treatments.

Some contrasts between treatments were noteworthy. GPM is the only evidence-based treatment for BPD that specifically includes a medication-based approach to treat suicide. GPM and DBT, in contrast to TFP, both explicitly use supportive interventions, skills training (emotion regulation), and a direction to view suicidal behavior nonpejoratively. GPM does not explicitly teach the additional skills seen in DBT, such as mindfulness, interpersonal effectiveness, or distress tolerance. Both DBT and MBT explicitly focus sessions on the function of suicidal behavior—including detailed assessments of key past self-injuries—to develop the case formulation.

In contrast to other treatments, GPM does not engage in a distinct treatment contracting process to detail the roles of therapist and patient in treatment beyond aspects of the frame common to all psychotherapies (attendance, payment, participation, between-session contact). Some therapies—TFP and SFP—have termination of treatment as a potential consequence of violating the contract, whereas DBT does not discharge patients for suicidal behaviors. While TFP and GPM both share a psychoanalytic understanding of BPD and suicidal behavior, GPM uses supportive interventions of problem-solving and psychoeducation and explicitly excludes TFP's use of the exploratory/uncovering intervention of transference interpretation. The meaning of suicidal behavior in GPM is viewed from a deficit perspective as an understandable although maladaptive response to developmental and current empathic failures. This is in contrast to TFP's view of suicidal behavior as representing unconscious internal object relations based on hatred.

OTHER PSYCHOTHERAPEUTIC APPROACHES TO ASSESSING, MANAGING, AND RESOLVING SUICIDE RISK

Several other interventions show promise in the management of suicide risk but are not developed for BPD psychopathology. However, there is reason to believe they would be effective in reducing suicidality in those with BPD.

Cognitive Therapy for Suicidal Patients

Cognitive therapy for suicidal patients (CT-SP; Wenzel, Brown, & Beck, 2009) is a short-term (approximately 10 sessions) psychotherapy. The treatment focuses on developing cognitive and behavioral skills to manage suicide risk and occurs in three phases. The early phase focuses on developing a cognitive conceptualization and immediate safety plan. The intermediate phase focuses on developing cognitive, behavioral, and affective coping skills to manage suicide risk. The later phase focuses on reviewing and consolidating skills as well as planning to prevent a relapse. CT-SP has been shown in a controlled trial to reduce the rate of reattempt by 50% among patients who had attempted suicide (Brown et al., 2005). A similar intervention, brief cognitive behavior therapy (BCBT; Rudd, 2012), has shown a comparable effect.

The overall structural approach to suicide risk in cognitive therapy is consistent with the treatments for BPD reviewed earlier, and the difference from treatments for BPD lies in the short-term nature of cognitive therapy and the greater emphasis placed on emotional processing and interpersonal relationships in treatments for BPD. It is noteworthy, however, that half of the sample in Brown and colleagues study (2005) met criteria for BPD (Brown, personal communication, November 15, 2015). The study of BCBT (Rudd et al., 2015) included 15 participants diagnosed with BPD. Of this subgroup, there were no attempts in BCBT and three attempts in treatment-as-usual (TAU) during the 2-year follow-up—demonstrating the same pattern of response as the full BCBT versus TAU samples (Bryan & Rudd, personal communication, September 1, 2015).

Collaborative Assessment and Management of Suicidality

The collaborative assessment and management of suicidality (CAMS) is a framework for assessing and managing suicide risk in psychotherapy (Jobes, 2006). Instead of being a stand-alone treatment, CAMS provides the structure for a clinician of any theoretical background to work with a suicidal patient in a manner that resolves suicide risk. CAMS distills principles from theoretical and clinical suicidology into a sequenced approach to suicide risk: (1) expressing empathy for the suicidal wish (Orbach, 2001); (2) collaborative assessment of key psychological constructs related to suicide risk such as pain, pressure, agitation, hopelessness, self-hate, reasons for living, and reasons for dying (Baumeister, 1990; Beck, Rush, Shaw, & Emery, 1979; Kovacs & Beck, 1977; Linehan, Goodstein, Nielsen, & Chiles, 1983; Schneidman, 1996); (3) collaborative treatment planning; (4) crisis response planning to manage immediate risk; and (5) collaborative work in psychotherapy to resolve suicide risk.

CAMS (Jobes, 2006) conceptualizes suicidality as a result of direct and indirect drivers. Jobes suggests that individuals considering suicide do so for reasons that make sense to them, and that, in turn, an individual may come to the conclusion that there is no better alternative to coping than suicide. Therapists who seek to influence these reasons must first collaborate with the patient to identify them, and, in the process of doing so, the CAMS therapist and client dyad creates a useful model or theory of the patient's suicidality. Indirect drivers are stressors and background factors that create stress or pain but which are present in many nonsuicidal individuals. Direct drivers are responses to indirect drivers that are derived from suicidology research and theory and link directly to suicidal thoughts and behavior. These include psychological or mental pain, hopelessness, agitation, self-hate, and more reasons for dying than living. The central tenet of CAMS is the single-minded focus on reducing suicidality by reducing or changing these direct drivers that block adaptive responses to the indirect drivers that will lead away from suicide. For example, hopelessness and self-hate about the future prevents actions that will improve the future and promotes destructive behaviors that make the situation worse. Agitation and psychological pain block proactive behavior more generally leading to increased agitation or the sence that psychological pain will be unending.

CAMS uses an assessment tool, the Suicide Status Form (SSF), to prompt the clinician and patient to identify and prioritize the primary drivers of suicide in treatment using any theoretical approach the clinician chooses until suicide risk has resolved. Early sessions emphasize the identification, review, and discussion of the direct and indirect drivers of suicide and breaking the link between direct drivers and suicidality; fostering hope, goals, and dreams for the future; and treatment planning. These tasks are conducted within an explicitly collaborative framework that involves the therapist and patient working together to reduce reliance on nonsuicidal coping options (Jobes, 2012). CAMS clinicians and patients reassess suicide risk at each session and continue to work on changing direct drivers of suicidal thoughts and behaviors until suicidality is resolved for at least three consecutive sessions. At this point, the dyad will either continue to work on remaining indirect drivers or conclude their work. Should suicidality reappear, a full assessment of direct drivers is conducted again because the drivers of relapse are not always those that led to treatment and the CAMS framework is restarted until suicidality again resolves.

As with CT-SP and BCBT, the overall structural approach to suicide risk in CAMS is consistent with the treatments for BPD described, with common elements of a clear treatment framework, a collaborative treatment relationship, and prioritization of suicide risk. CAMS differs from treatments for BPD in that CAMS is meant to resolve acute suicidality while treatments for BPD tend to be longer term, with a focus on resolving long-standing problems with emotional processing and interpersonal relationships. To date, there is evidence that CAMS is feasible with individuals with BPD and had positive results comparable to DBT in an RCT (Andreasson et al., 2014).

Safety Planning Intervention

The safety planning intervention (SPI) (Stanley & Brown, 2012) is brief, evidence-based intervention for suicide risk whereby the clinician and patient collaboratively generate a sequenced safety plan for identifying and managing suicidal crises. The role of brief interventions in preventing suicide is highlighted by the finding that a program of brief intervention and follow-up contacts showed a 10-fold reduction in the rate of suicide death compared to a control condition (Fleischmann et al., 2008). The elements of the safety plan include a specific set of strategies to use to decrease the risk of suicidal behavior, including coping strategies that may be used and individuals or agencies that may be contacted during a crisis (Stanley & Brown, 2012). SPI is a collaborative effort between therapist and a client and takes about 30 minutes to complete. The steps of a safety plan include (1) recognizing the warning signs of an impending suicidal crisis, (2) utilizing coping strategies, (3) contacting others in order to distract from suicidal thoughts, (4) contacting family members or friends who may help to resolve the crisis, (5) contacting mental health professionals or agencies, and (6) restricting access to lethal means (Stanley & Brown, 2012). Guidance is provided to the therapist to maximize the insight and problem-solving of the client into their suicidal process and to facilitate the plan when clients are unable to generate effective ideas for the plan. The SPI is consistent with the use of an agreed-upon plan for management of suicidal crises in all of the treatments for BPD, and the safety plan may serve as a template for this crisis plan. The SPI may also be useful for management of suicide risk for patients who are not enrolled or are awaiting enrollment in psychotherapy for BPD.

CONCLUSION

This chapter reviewed the five psychotherapies for BPD that have been supported by empirical evidence in at least one study. Only DBT and MBT have replicated their results. Three other psychotherapeutic approaches for suicidality that were not developed explicitly for BPD are also reviewed. Clinicians treating individuals with BPD can glean several key themes around which to focus their work. First, all the evidence-based BPD treatments emphasize that suicidality in BPD is caused by intense or out-of-control emotions, although they differ in the etiology of those emotions. Intense emotions can be difficult to treat and are frequently overwhelming, frustrating, tiring, or even frightening to the therapist. This often leads therapists to engage in ineffective behaviors such as avoiding difficult issues, avoiding patient sessions, making rigid and unhelpful therapy rules, and blaming the patient. This may occur because the client's distress causes high emotional arousal in the therapist, thus impairing their cognitive functioning, or because avoidant and blocking behaviors bring relief from the patient's distress in session or by limiting contact with the patient. This thread is also reflected in the general psychotherapies for suicidality, although these do not focus on emotions as a core factor.

In addition to the focus on emotion, it is useful to note four other commonalities across these five BPD psychotherapies. First, all five treatments are long-term, weekly psychotherapies with a specific theoretical and structural model in general and a specific approach to resolving suicidality and not only managing risk. Such a model is key to keeping the therapist's mission clear in the face of a client's emotional or extreme behavior. Second, all treatments explicitly focus on and prioritize suicidal behavior—unlike other treatments that expect suicidality to resolve as psychiatric symptoms resolve. Third, each treatment has a method of distinguishing between acute and chronic suicide risk. Outpatient psychotherapy is used to treat the high level of chronic risk in BPD, and each treatment has varying approaches to managing acute risk. This leads to the fourth commonality: treatments of BPD are done by teams of clinicians who can provide direction and support as well as consultation for decision-making for the case (both for chronic risk and for how suicidality will be resolved) as well as management of acute risk. The combination of the long-term, suicide-focused therapy frame and team consultation allows for both a standard approach that provides structure to the therapist and client to resolve suicidality and BPD as well as the time, ability, and support to make less expected moves when behavior is not responding to standard approaches. In summary, while other psychotherapies for suicidality also prioritize the resolution of suicide risk, treatments for BPD are distinguished by focusing on emotions, expecting longer term treatment, treating chronic as well as managing acute risk, and using a team-based approach. Research does not yet (and may never be able to) inform us on how critical each of these elements is to successful outcomes with suicidal individuals with BPD. In its absence, the development of such similar themes across quite different treatment approaches provides useful direction to the clinician providing treatment to suicidal clients with BPD.

REFERENCES

American Psychiatric Association (APA). (2001). *Practice guidelines for the treatment of patients with borderline personality disorder.* Washington, DC: American Psychiatric Press.

American Psychiatric Association (APA). (2003). *Practice guidelines for the assessment and treatment of patients with suicidal behaviors:* Washington, DC: American Psychiatric Press.

Andreasson, K., Krogh, K., Rosenbaum, B., Gluud, C., Jobes, D., & Nordentoft, M. (2014). The DiaS trial: Dialectical behavior therapy vs. collaborative assessment and management of suicidality on self-harm in patients with a recent suicide attempt and borderline personality disorder traits, study protocol for a randomized controlled trial. *Trials Journal, 15*, 194.

Bateman, A., & Fonagy, P. (1999). Effectiveness of partial hopitalization in the treatment of borderline personality disorder: A randomized controlled trial. *American Journal of Psychiatry, 156*, 1563–1569.

Bateman, A., & Fonagy, P. (2001). Partial hospitalization for borderline personality disorder: In reply to R. Stern. (Letter to the editor). *American Journal of Psychiatry, 158*(11), 1932–1933.

Bateman, A., & Fonagy, P. (2004). *Mentalization-based treatment for borderline personality disorder: A practical guide.* New York: Oxford University Press.

Bateman, A., & Fonagy, P. (2009). Randomized controlled trial of outpatient mentalization-based treatment versus structured clinical management for borderline personality disorder. *American Journal of Psychiatry, 166*(12), 1355–1364.

Baumeister, R. F. (1990). Suicide as escape from self. *Psychological Review, 97*, 90–113.

Beck, A. T., Rush, A. J., Shaw, B. F., & Emery, G. (1979). *Cognitive therapy for depression.* New York: Guilford.

Bliss, S., & McCardle, M. (2014). An exploration of common elements in dialectical behavior therapy, mentalization based treatment and transference focused psychotherapy in the treatment of borderline personality disorder. *Clinical Social Work Journal, 42*(1), 61–79.

Brown, G. K., Ten Have, T., Henriques, G. R., Xie, S. X., Hollander, J. E., & Beck, A. T. (2005). Cognitive therapy for the prevention of suicide attempts. *Journal of the American Medical Association, 294*(5), 563–570.

Caligor, E., Diamond, D., Yeomans, F. E., & Kernberg, O. F. (2009). The interpretive process in the psychoanalytic psychotherapy of borderline personality pathology. *Journal of the American Psychoanalytic Association, 57*(2), 271–301.

Clarkin, J. F., Levy, K. N., Lenzenweger, M. F., & Kernberg, O. F. (2007). Evaluating three treatments for borderline personality disorder: A multiwave study. *American Journal of Psychiatry, 164*(6), 922–928.

Clarkin, J. F., Widiger, T., Frances, A., Hurt, S. W., & Gilmore. (1983). Prototypic typology and the borderline personality disorder. *Journal of Abnormal Psychology, 92,* 263–275.

Clarkin, J. F., Yeomans, F. E., & Kernberg, O. F. (2006). *Psychotherapy for borderline personality focusing on object relations.* Washington, DC: American Psychiatric Publishing.

Cowdry, R. W., Pickar, D., & Davies, R. (1985). Symptoms and EEG findings in the borderline syndrome. *International Journal of Psychiatry in Medicine, 15,* 201–211.

Department of Defense and Veterans Affairs. (2013). *Clinical practice guidelines for the assessment and management of patients at risk for suicide.* https://www.healthquality.va.gov/guidelines/MH/srb/

Fleischmann, A., Bertolote, J. M., Wasserman, D., De Leo, D., Bolhari, J., Botega, N. J., ... Thanh, H. T. T. (2008). Effectiveness of brief intervention and contact for suicide attempters: A randomized controlled trial in five countries. *Bulletin of the World Health Organization, 86,* 703–709.

Fowler, J. C. (2012). Suicidal risk assessment in clinical practice: Pragmatic guidelines for imperfect assessments. *Psychotherapy, 49*(10) 81–90.

Frances, A., Fyer, M., & Clarkin, J. (1986). Personality and suicide. *Annals of the New York Academy of Sciences, 487,* 281–293.

Giesen-Bloo, J., van Dyck, R., Spinhoven, P., van Tilburg, W., Dirksen, C., van Asselt, T., ... Arntz, A. (2006). Outpatient psychotherapy for borderline personality disorder: Randomized trial of schema-focused therapy vs transference-focused psychotherapy. *Archives of General Psychiatry, 63*(6), 649–658.

Grove, W. M., & Tellegen, A. (1991). Problems in the classification of personality disorders. *Journal of Personality Disorders, 5,* 31–41.

Gunderson, J. G. (1984). *Borderline personality disorder.* Washington, DC: American Psychiatric Press.

Gunderson, J. G. (2001). *Borderline personality disorder: A clinical guide.* Washington, DC: American Psychiatric Publishing.

Gunderson, J. G. (2014). *Handbook of good psychiatric management for borderline personality disorder.* Arlington, VA: American Psychiatric Publishing.

Gunderson, J. G., & Links, P. S. (2008). *Borderline personality disorder. A clinical guide* (2nd edition). Washington, DC: American Psychiatric Publishing.

Jobes, D. (2012). *Manual for the collaborative assessment and management of suicidality.* Unpublished.

Jobes, D. A. (2006). *Managing suicidal risk: A collaborative approach.* New York: Guilford.

Joiner, T., Walker, R., Rudd, M. D., & Jobes, D. (1999). Scientizing and routinizing the outpatient assessment of suicidality. *Professional Psychology: Research & Practice, 30,* 447–453.

Joiner, T. E., Brown, J. S., & Wingate, L. R. (2005). The psychology and neurobiology of suicidal behavior. *Annual Review of Psychology, 56,* 287–314.

Kellogg, S. H., & Young, J. E. (2006). Schema therapy for borderline personality disorder. *Journal of Clinical Psychology, 62*(4), 445–458.

Kernberg, O. F. (1993). Suicidal behavior in borderline patients: Diagnosis and Psychotherapeutic Considerations. *American Journal of Psychotherapy, 47*(2), 245–254.

Kernberg, O. F., Yeomans, F. E., Clarkin, J. F., & Levy, K. N. (2008). Transference focused psychotherapy: Overview and update. *International Journal of Psychoanalysis, 89*, 601–620.

Kohut, H. (1971). *The analysis of the self.* New York: International Universities Press.

Kovacs, M., & Beck, A. T. (1977). The wish to die and the wish to live in attempted suicides. *Journal of Clinical Psychology, 33*, 361–365.

Holden, R. R., Kerr, P. S., Mendonca, J. D., & Velamoor, V. R. (1998). Are some motives more linked to suicide proneness than others? *Journal of Clinical Psychology, 54*, 569–576.

Levy, K. N., Wasserman, R. H., Scott, L. N., Yeomans, F. E., Levy, R. A., & Ablon, J. S. (2009). Empirical evidence for transference-focused psychotherapy and other psychodynamic psychotherapy for borderline personality disorder. In R. A. Levy, & J. S. Ablon (Eds.), *Handbook of evidence-based psychodynamic psychotherapy: Bridging the gap between science and practice* (pp. 93–119). Totowa, NJ: Humana.

Lieb, K., Zanarini, M., Linehan, M. M., & Bohus, M. (2004). Seminar section: Borderline personality disorder. *Lancet, 364*, 453–461.

Linehan, M. Linehan risk assessment and management protocol (LRAMP) http://depts.washington.edu/uwbrtc/wp-content/uploads/LSSN-LRAMP-v1.0.pdf.

Linehan, M., Comtois, K., & Ward-Ciesielski, E. (2010). *Assessing and managing risk with suicidal individuals: The UW Risk Assessment Protocol (UWRAP) and UW Risk Assessment and Management Protocol (L-RAMP).* Unpublished Manual. University of Washington.

Linehan, M. M. (1993). *Cognitive-behavioral treatment of borderline personality disorder.* New York: Guilford.

Linehan, M. M., Armstrong, H. E., Suarez, A., Allmon, D., & Heard, H. L. (1991). Cognitive-behavioral treatment of chronically parasuicidal borderline patients. *Archives of General Psychiatry, 48*, 1060–1064.

Linehan, M. M., & Comtois, K. A. (2009). *The UW Risk Assessment and Management Protocol.* University of Washington, Behavioral Research and Therapy Clinics. Retrieved from: http://depts.washington.edu/brtc/files/L-RAMP.pdf

Linehan, M. M., Comtois, K. A., Murray, A. M., Brown, M. Z., Gallop, R. J., Heard, H. L., … Lindenboim, N. (2006). Two-year randomized controlled trial and follow-up of dialectical behavior therapy vs therapy by experts for suicidal behaviors and borderline personality disorder. *Archives of General Psychiatry, 63*(7), 757–766.

Linehan, M. M., Goodstein, J. L., Nielsen, S. L., & Chiles, J. A. (1983). Reasons for staying alive when you are thinking of killing yourself: The Reasons for Living Inventory. *Journal of Consulting and Clinical Psychology, 51*, 276–286.

Linehan, M. M., Korslund, K. E., Harned, M. S., Gallop, R. J., Lungu, A., Neacsiu, A. D., … Murray-Gregory, A. M. (2015). Dialectical behavior therapy for high suicide risk in individuals with borderline personality disorder: A randomized controlled trial and component analysis. *JAMA Psychiatry, 72*(5), 475–482.

Linehan, M. M., Rizvi, S. L., Welch, S. S., & Page, B. (2000). Psychiatric aspects of suicidal beahviour: Personality disorders. In K. Hawton (Ed.), *International handbook of suicide and attempted suicide* (pp. 147–178). Sussex, UK: John Wiley & Sons.

Links, P. S., Bergmans, Y., Novick, J., & LeGris, J. (2009). *General psychiatric management for patients with borderline personality disorder: Clinician's manual.* Unpublished.

Links, P. S., & Kolla, N. (2005). Assessing and managing suicide risk. In J. M. Oldham, A. E. Skodol, & D. S. Bender (Eds.), *Textbook of personality disorders* (pp. 449–462). Washington, DC: American Psychiatric Publishing.

Lynch, T. R., Morse, J. Q., Mendelson, T., & Robins, C. J. (2003). Dialectical behavioral therapy for depressed older adults. A randomized pilot study. *American Journal of Geriatric Psychiatry, 11*, 33–45.

McMain, S. F., Links, P. S., Gnam, W. H., Guimond, T., Cardish, R. J., Korman, L., & Streiner, D. L. (2009). A randomized trial of dialectical behavior therapy versus general psychiatric management for borderline personality disorder. [Comparative Study].Randomized Controlled Trial Research Support, Non-US Gov't. *American Journal of Psychiatry, 166*(12), 1365–1374. doi: 10.1176/appi.ajp.2009.09010039

Moscicki, E. K. (2001). Epidemiology of completed and attempted suicide: Toward a framework for prevention. *Clinical Neuroscience Research, 1*, 310–323.

National Institute for Clinical Excellence. (2004). *The short-term physical and psychological management and secondary prevention of self-harm in primary and secondary care.* National Collaborating Centre for Mental Health (UK). Leicester (UK): British Psychological Society.

Orbach, I. (2001). Therapeutic empathy with the suicidal wish. *American Journal of Psychotherapy, 55*(2), 166–184.

Paris, J. (2002). Implications of long-term outcome research for the management of patients with borderline personality disorder. *Harvard Review of Psychiatry, 10*(6), 315–323.

Robins, C. J., & Chapman, A. L. (2004). Dialectical behavior therapy: Current status, recent developments, and future directions. *Journal of Personality Disorders, 18*(1), 73–89.

Rudd, M. D. (2012). Brief cognitive behavioral therapy (BCBT) for suicidality in military populations. *Military Psychology, 24*(6) 592.

Rudd, M. D., Bryan, C. J., Wertenberger, E. G., Peterson, A. L., Young-McCaughan, S., Mintz, J., ... Bruce, T. O. (2015). Brief cognitive-behavioral therapy effects on post-treatment suicide attempts in a military sample: Results of a randomized clinical trial with 2-year follow-up. *American Journal of Psychiatry, 172*(5), 441–449.

Schneidman, E. S. (1996). *The suicidal mind.* New York: Oxford University Press.

Schore, A. N. (2000). Attachment and the regulation of the right brain. *Attachment and Human Development, 2*, 23–47.

Stanley, B., & Brown, G. K. (2012). Safety planning intervention: A brief intervention to mitigate suicide risk. *Cognitive and Behavioral Practice, 19*, 256–264.

Stoffers, J. M., Vollm, B. A., Rucker, G., Timmer, A., Huband, N., & Lieb, K. (2012). Psychological therapies for people with borderline personality disorder. *Cochrane Database of Systematic Reviews, 8*.

Stolorow, R., Brandchaft, B., & Atwood, G. (1987). *Psychoanalytic treatment: An intersubjective approach.* Hillsdale, NJ: Analytic Press.

Stone, M. H. (1993). Long-term outcome in personality disorders. *British Journal of Psychiatry, 162*, 299–313.

Verheul, R., van den Bosch, L., Louise, M. C., Koeter, M. W., de Ridder, M. A. J., Stijnen, T., & van den Brink, W. (2003). Dialectical behaviour therapy for women with borderline personality disorder: 12-month, randomised clinical trial in the Netherlands. *British Journal of Psychiatry, 182*, 135–140.

Weinberg, I., Ronningstam, E., Goldblatt, M. J., Schechter, M., Wheelis, J., & Maltsberger, J. T. (2010). Strategies in treatment of suicidality: Identification of common and treatment-specific interventions in empirically supported treatment manuals. *Journal of Clinical Psychiatry, 71*(6): 699–706.

Wenzel, A., Brown, G. K., & Beck, A. T. (2009). *Cognitive therapy for suicidal patients: Scientific and clinical applications.* Washington DC: American Psychological Association.

Yeomans, F. E., Diamond, D., Clarkin, J. F., Fonagy, P., & Gabbard, G. O. (2010). Transference-focused psychotherapy and borderline personality disorder. In J. F. Clarkin, P. Fonagy, & G. O. Gabbard (Eds.), *Psychodynamic psychotherapy for personality disorders: A clinical handbook* (pp. 209–238). Arlington, VA: American Psychiatric Publishing.

Young, J. E., Klosko, J. S., & Weishaar, M. E. (2003). *Schema therapy: A practitioner's guide.* New York: Guilford.

/// 22 /// Forensic Issues in Borderline Personality Disorder

ALEXANDER L. CHAPMAN
AND ANDRÉ IVANOFF*

INTRODUCTION

Borderline personality disorder (BPD) is a severe, complex, and costly disorder requiring comprehensive treatment. Characterized by instability in relationships, emotions, identity, and behavior (American Psychiatric Association, 2000, 2013), BPD is prevalent (2–6% of the general population; Grant et al., 2008) and of significant concern for health systems. Despite the emergence of empirically supported treatments over the past 20 years, more work is needed to better understand how best to help subgroups of persons with BPD, particularly those in forensic or correctional settings.

The prevalence of BPD in forensic settings is estimated at from 35% to 57% (Black et al., 2007; Blackburn & Coid, 1999; Chapman, Specht, & Cellucci, 2005; Jordan, Schlenger, Fairbank, & Caddell, 1996; McCann, Ball, & Ivanoff, 2000; Zlotnick, 1999), whereas in the general population it is approximately 1–2% (Grant et al., 2008; Samuels et al., 2002) Correctional settings commonly include mental health treatment and on-site mental health clinicians providing psychosocial and psychopharmacological treatment; however, the mandate of prison settings, in particular, often conflicts directly with providing clinical care to those with complex mental health needs. The necessary emphasis on security, safety, and, in some cases, retribution, can create invalidating environments that both elicit and reinforce the serious behavioral problems often observed among those with BPD, such as self-injury and

* Work on this chapter was supported by a Michael Smith Foundation for Health Research Career Investigator Award to the first author.

suicidal behavior. When effective treatments are available, considerable challenges emerge with regard to the training and preparation of clinical staff to treat and of line staff to manage inmates with BPD. In addition, the research base on the care of BPD in correctional settings and with correctional samples is growing but still relatively sparse. Furthermore, individuals with BPD in correctional settings differ from those in traditional or university outpatient settings (where much of the treatment research has occurred) in ways that have important treatment implications. In this chapter, we discuss these and other issues and provide suggestions for continued work to better understand and treat individuals with BPD in forensic settings.

BPD AMONG FORENSIC PATIENTS

Compared to individuals diagnosed with BPD in more traditional outpatient or inpatient settings, those with BPD in forensic settings differ in important ways. The most obvious differences are the high rate of co-occurring antisocial features, involvement in crime, and problems with drug or alcohol dependence (Chapman et al., 2005; Chapman & Cellucci, 2007). Despite little research on the topic, a corollary of heightened rates of drug and alcohol dependence with antisocial features is an elevated risk for violence toward others (Layden, Chapman, Douglas, & Turner, 2012; Monahan, Steadman, Robbins, Appelbaum, Banks, Grisso, . . . Silver, 2005). In addition to violence toward oneself, which is usually the main focus in standard outpatient treatments of BPD, the combination of BPD with substance use problems in forensic samples likely increases the risk of violence toward others and needs to be targeted in treatment. Recently, an examination of the emotional cascade model (which suggests that rumination mediates emotional and behavioral dysregulation in BPD) in male offenders suggests that rumination may play an important role in both nonsuicidal self-injury (NSSI) and suicidality (Gardner, 2014).

Along with the behavioral and diagnostic characteristics of those with BPD in forensic settings, general personality traits and tendencies also may warrant attention. Researchers have suggested the utility of conceptualizing both child and adulthood psychopathology along dimensions of internalizing (anxiety, behavioral inhibition) versus externalizing (impulsivity, behavioral activation) problems. Internalizing problems tend to be related to behavioral inhibition, neuroticism, and dysphoria, with examples including depression and anxiety disorders. In contrast, externalizing problems tend to be related to impulsivity, sensation- and novelty-seeking, and generally consist of conduct difficulties, anger and aggression, and substance use problems. Individuals with BPD tend to have both internalizing and externalizing problems (Crowell, Beauchaine, & Linehan, 2009), as demonstrated by high rates of depression and anxiety disorders, anger management problems, substance use disorders, and heightened impulsivity. Moreover, a combination of both internalizing and externalizing problems increases risk for suicidal and NSSI (Verona, Sachs-Ericsson, & Joiner, 2004). Research has yet to examine basic differences in personality and temperament among correctional versus community samples of individuals with BPD; however, it is reasonable to hypothesize that those individuals with BPD in forensic or correctional systems arrived there because they are likely higher on the externalizing spectrum compared to their noncriminal counterparts. This may be simply because externalizing behaviors are those more likely to result in arrest than are internalizing behaviors. If accurate, however, this possibility has important implications for both the conceptualization and treatment of those with BPD in forensic settings.

Conceptualization and Theory of BPD

One implication of the prevalence of externalizing characteristics among persons with BPD in forensic settings is that the theories we use to guide treatment may require clearer mapping onto the phenomena under study. Linehan's (1993a) biosocial theory, for example, posits that BPD results from the transaction of an emotionally vulnerable temperament with an invalidating rearing environment (see also Crowell et al., 2009). Individuals poised to develop BPD have a biological disposition toward a low threshold for emotional activation (emotional sensitivity), intense emotional reactions (emotional reactivity), and a delayed return to baseline emotional arousal. The invalidating environment consists of caregivers who (1) indiscriminately reject the child's communication of private experiences (thoughts, preferences, opinions, emotions) by criticizing, trivializing, or punishing the child; (2) oversimplify the ease of problem-solving, when the problem is experienced by the child as overwhelming and painful; and (3) intermittently reinforce the child's periodic excessive emotional expression (thus making such expression resistant to extinction).

Children who are highly emotional require more skilled parenting and may set the occasion for invalidating responses on the part of parents who lack the skills to regulate their own emotions or who do not have the knowledge or skills to respond effectively. At the same time, invalidation increases emotional arousal and can directly lead to emotional dysregulation, both in the short- and long-term. When the invalidating environment is characterized by abuse or trauma or fails to provide adequate support in the face of abuse from other sources, the environment may play a stronger role in the development of BPD.

Although many of these factors likely are applicable to those with BPD in forensic settings, some of the temperament-based vulnerabilities may differ somewhat. Indeed, children with oppositional defiant disorder or conduct disorder, who are at risk to engage in antisocial behavior in adulthood, are likely to experience other vulnerabilities, including irritability, inattentiveness, increased risk of attention-deficit hyperactivity disorder (ADHD), restlessness, and difficulties with impulsivity (Frick & Morris, 2004). These children also are at risk for learning disabilities, peer rejection, and the early development of drug problems. In addition, familial socio-economic problems, drug or alcohol difficulties, and severe neglect may be more common in the histories of those in forensic settings. A challenging temperament, particularly including children who are emotional and impulsive or those who are callous or unemotional, poses unique parenting challenges (Frick, 2012). Difficulties with socioeconomic factors, mental health, and addiction may further reduce the caregivers' resources and leave the child bereft of adequate monitoring, discipline, and care. Essentially, the environment is ill-equipped to manage the child's needs.

The environmental factors contributing to the development of externalizing difficulties also may differ. Reid and Patterson (1991), for example, have posed an influential theory regarding the progression of children from oppositional defiant disorder, to conduct disorder, to adult antisocial behavior. The key environmental factor in this progression is a coercive cycle of caregiver–child interactions whereby the caregiver uses coercive control to modify the child's disruptive behavior by over-emphasizing punishment procedures, often in an erratic and inconsistent manner. The child, in turn, influences the caregivers through aversive and coercive actions, thus escalating the cycle. The caregivers receive negative reinforcement for coercive behavior (the child may temporarily cease unwanted behavior), and the child learns coercive methods to influence others' behavior, initially through modeling and then subsequently through direct experience of these behaviors "working" sporadically with their caregivers. Essentially, this type of environment is excellent training ground for the development of coercive strategies in future situations and relationships and may lead to the child's habituation to and difficulty learning from aversive consequences (Frick, 2012; Frick & Morris, 2004).

CHALLENGES IN MANAGING BPD CHARACTERISTICS IN FORENSIC SETTINGS

The combination of internalizing and externalizing problems, extreme emotional sensitivity, impulsivity, and undercontrolled behaviors in those with BPD are among the most difficult clinical challenges to manage in forensic settings. Self-injury and suicidal behaviors alone exponentially increase the management difficulty, and those with BPD are likely to engage in other problem behaviors, such as introducing contraband, especially alcohol and drugs, and interpersonal altercations, including assaults, property damage, and escape. Along with extreme and impulsive behavior, the interpersonal dysfunction that forms a core feature of BPD can also pose challenges that correctional staff members are not adequately trained to address.

The forensic treatment context in which behaviors characteristic of BPD occur (i.e., correctional or mental health) naturally influences how such behaviors are interpreted, managed, and treated (or not treated). For better or worse, the response is most frequently determined by whether the behavior occurs in a prison or in a hospital. Failing to understand the broader institutional context and function of such behavior (instead relying on explanations of individual pathology) typically results in efforts to control or penalize, which may prove ineffective (Thomas, Leaf, Kazmierczak, & Stone, 2006). Although commonly explained as the tension between security and treatment in these settings, this issue is actually transactional and more complex than is usually recognized. For example, among incarcerated women, self-injury may serve as both a precipitant and a reaction to the conditions of confinements (Dell & Beauchamp, 2006).

Real or perceived decreased security affects both staff and residents and contributes to greater frequency of dysregulation and behavioral incidents on both sides. As incidents increase, so do needs for greater security, interfering with "least restrictive means" mandates for treatment and overall management. Administrators, clinicians, and line staff in forensic settings face particularly high stakes in dealing with suicidal behaviors and self-injury because forensic settings require higher standards of supervision to prevent suicides and other self-injurious behavior than do nonforensic settings. Legal mandate dictates that oversight should be sufficient to prevent harm (including self-injury) to those confined (American Correctional Association, 2003). When these expectations are not met, the consequences of self-injury and suicidal behavior are substantial, and the emotional costs to other residents can be considerable. Anecdotally, the risk for post-traumatic stress disorder symptomatology or other mental disorders increases among other residents in an institutional setting following a completed suicide or serious self-injury incident, as does the risk for other forms of behavioral dysregulation (including self-injury). Research on contagion in the general population also supports this (Gould, Jamieson, & Romer, 2003).

Residents who engage in self-injury demand immediate and scarce resources: expensive emergency medical services, the involvement of highly skilled medical and mental health staff, increased direct observation, and increased documentation requirements. Increased security may also be immediately necessary during incident management to assure effective containment. Other residents may respond to staff focus on the incident as an opportunity to engage in other disruptive or illegal activities. Increased security and monitoring, including one-on-one supervision, regular room checks, and even lockdown may be necessary. This can easily result in other residents losing privileges or being forced to curtail participation in their own program activities or treatment.

Suicidal behaviors and threats, as well as self-injury, have various negative effects on treatment professionals as well, such as loss of drive and motivation; mental, physical, and emotional exhaustion; professional isolation; a sense that continuing to be empathic is a drain and that successes are indeterminable; and "observable decrements in the typical quality and quantity of work performed" (Fox & Cooper, 1998, p. 146). The most extreme stress reported by psychotherapists includes that resulting from patient suicide attempts, threats of suicide attempts, and patient anger (Deutsch, 1984; Farber, 1983; Hellman, Morrison, & Abramowitz, 1987). The training of those staffing most forensic residential programs may or may not include familiarity with BPD as a disorder. Interestingly, staff may find it easier to work with residents suffering from psychosis than with those who engage in behaviors characteristic of BPD. This is not unique to residential forensic settings, applying equally to general psychiatric inpatient hospitals. Staff working in these settings are trained to be on the alert for personality-disordered inmates or patients whose intentions are described as "manipulative" or efforts to "get over" on staff. Staff burden includes the extra vigilance required to monitor and evaluate interactions with BPD patients, the apparent competence of many individuals with BPD, and a tendency to view feeling manipulated as the result of personally directed behavior. Psychotic behavior is simply easier to understand and does not demand personal involvement.

EVIDENCE-BASED CARE FOR BPD IN FORENSIC SETTINGS

The current state of research on disruptive and suicidal behaviors in forensic settings provides a small base for developing effective BPD treatment programs. Again, suicidal behavior and self-injury anchors the discussion. Despite increased attention and resources over the past two decades, the rates of suicidal behavior and self-injury in custody have not decreased. Although there are several reasons for this, the most apparent reason involves the increasing numbers of residents in forensic settings— both prisons and secure hospitals—with severe mental health needs, such as BPD and significant substance use problems (Ditton, 1999; Dvoskin, 2002; Ivanoff, Schmidt, & Finnegan, 2006). Also, efforts to identify other population-based risk factors associated with suicidal behavior and self-injury (e.g., sexual and physical abuse, separation and/or loss of caregiver at early age, and affective quality/security of attachment, cf. Gratz, 2003) fail to meaningfully discriminate individuals at risk for self-injury from the general population, male and female, in custody.

Current prevention and management strategies are summarized elsewhere (Hayes, 2006; Schmidt & Ivanoff, 2007) but generally recommend including screening, provision for timely and appropriate response, environmental structure and accommodation for high-risk individuals, and counseling and peer support (Dvoskin et al., 2002; Eyland, Corben, & Barton, 1997; Gough, 2005). Overall, management is provided via monitoring and staff training. Implementation of these strategies varies widely. Two decades ago, only less than 1% of US departments of correction contained five or more of these elements (Hayes, 1995). Currently, many forensic settings require initial suicide risk assessment and self-report mental health screening within 1–4 hours of incarceration. Based on the rising rates of self-injury and suicide in residential settings, however, the effectiveness or meaningful impact of these management efforts are in question (Hayes, 2013).

Best practices for management and intervention of self-injury and suicidal behaviors in forensic settings are still being defined. The identification of static predictive variables in screening instruments (e.g., gender, previous attempts) offers nothing for clinical focus. The multiple-pathway prediction of self-injury also makes it difficult to identify individuals at higher risk by virtue of specific statistical risk factors; thus, the identification of particular screening tools, procedures, and assessments to identify individuals at high risk is a challenge for administrators. Unfortunately, however, managing without treating the behavioral dysfunction does not decrease the likelihood of future behavior. Even with the best idiographic predictor, recent self-injury, only a small body of literature supporting effective treatments for self-injury in residential or forensic settings exists. Taken together, the magnitude and acute nature of the problem, its consequences, and the state of information available to provide direction create a conundrum for the administrator charged with developing programs to treat BPD criterion behaviors in forensic settings.

Evidence-Based Principles and Practice in Forensic Settings

We will continue this discussion by describing what we know so far about evidence-based care and treatment of those with BPD. Evidence-based practice has been defined broadly as a combination of (1) the use of the best available research evidence with (2) relevant areas of clinical expertise and (3) attention to important individual differences (e.g., culture, preferences, capabilities) that may inform treatment (American Psychological Association, 2007). Although these principles are reasonable on an aspirational level, in forensic settings, this model poses a few key challenges. First, programming must be based on the best available research evidence, but often evidence for treatment of offenders broadly, or BPD in correctional settings more specifically, is sparse or inadequate. Second, regarding clinical expertise, staff often lack the training needed to execute evidence-based practices with challenging, multiproblem clients and often must learn on the job with minimal ongoing training and supervision. Third, a variety of individual differences, such as cultural factors, beliefs, socioeconomic disadvantages, and cognitive limitations, make it difficult to apply empirically supported approaches without significant adaptations.

Beyond evidence-based principles more broadly, there are three best practice treatment principles linked to effective care in forensic settings more specifically: risk, responsivity, and need (Andrews & Bonta, 1998). In terms of risk, more intense treatment is provided for those at higher risk, and typical BPD patients engaging in self-injury are considered high risk and often have multiple co-occurring disorders and problems. With regard to need, treatment works best with those who need it most, and those with BPD are in great need, in no small part because of multiple co-occurring disorders and problems. Responsivity involves matching treatment to the learning styles of intended recipients. As suggested, those with BPD in forensic settings may have a variety of learning styles and capabilities. We have anecdotally observed that one of the biggest challenges for forensic clinicians is to effectively reach those with varying cognitive abilities. For example, in a psychoeducational group comprised of individuals ranging from borderline to superior intellectual functioning, it is very difficult to know at which level to teach the material. Some programs have solved this problem by conducting separate treatment for those with lower cognitive functioning or have diverted these individuals into cognitive rehabilitation programs.

In terms of evidence, meta-analyses and other reviews find cognitive-behavioral or behavioral treatments that actively involve the resident provide the most effective match in custodial settings. Skills training, problem-solving, and emotion regulation strategies are often recommended components (Andrews, 1995; Golder et al., 2005;

Wong & Hare, 2005; Washington State Institute for Public Policy [WSIPP], 2002). If our goal is to treat individuals suffering from BPD while addressing overarching administrative factors, selecting models consistent with known best clinical practice strategies within forensic settings makes good sense. Criminogenic needs, empirically based risk factors associated with recidivism such as substance abuse, and poor self-management and problem-solving, are treated with a variety of cognitive-behavioral interventions. Elsewhere, we and others have explained how cognitive-behavioral approaches address these specific criminogenic needs (McCann, Ivanoff, Schmidt, & Beach, 2007; Wong & Hare, 2005).

Dialectical Behavior Therapy in Forensic Settings

Because DBT has the largest body of evidence for the treatment of BPD and is widely used in forensic settings (compared with other treatments for BPD with empirical support), we will focus here on the use of DBT in forensic and correctional settings. DBT's broad appeal for treating BPD in forensic settings is based on theoretical, structural, and functional elements. DBT includes the skills training, problem-solving, and emotion regulation training identified as effective intervention components in correctional settings (Andrews, 1995; Wong & Hare, 2005) and addresses criminogenic issues, namely severe behavioral dyscontrol, aggression and violence, and poor impulse control.

DBT is particularly compatible with forensic requirements for effectiveness, treatment accountability, and the need for structural elements, such as the identification of specific treatment targets, the ongoing documentation of progress and outcomes, and cost effectiveness (Swenson, Torrey, & Koerner, 2002). DBT identifies a clear target hierarchy that provides guidelines and explicit instructions about the focus of interventions in progressive order. Life-threatening behaviors (to self or others) are given the highest priority, followed by factors interfering with treatment, quality-of-life issues, skills deficits, and other targets (Linehan, 1993a). Because DBT moves from addressing extreme problem behaviors to improving quality of life, new targets emerge as residents' functioning improves (Linehan, 1993a). Explicitly identifying treatment targets helps increase accuracy of problem definition for staff and administration and helps staff to move more quickly from assessment of current risk to intervention. Adapted DBT treatment hierarchies might include a greater emphasis on assault, substance use problems, and disciplinary violations, among other corrections-specific factors; however, the basic structure of the hierarchy remains relevant and practical in forensic settings (Ivanoff et al., 2006; McCann et al., 2007; WSIPP, 2002). Despite the practical appeal of this treatment, however, key challenges make it difficult to implement or sustain DBT or other evidence-based practices in forensic settings.

Unique challenges in correctional settings make it difficult to provide treatment based on the best available evidence. Despite the substantial numbers of residents or patients with BPD, only very few institutions have incorporated DBT-oriented treatment programs. Perhaps the most widespread adoption of DBT services in correctional settings has been in Canadian women's institutions, where DBT services are available at each institution. Even in these institutions, however, DBT services are currently best described as adapted, partial DBT, including primarily DBT skills training and some milieu coaching but not including systematic, individual therapy or the consultation team. Moreover, DBT services are typically provided by individuals with relatively low levels of formal training in mental health assessment or treatment (e.g., post-baccalaureate behavioral counselors). Therefore, comprehensive DBT programs are rare in forensic settings, and, where elements of DBT are in place, treatment is nearly always implemented in an adapted manner for which the empirical support is in question.

This is not a unique problem in correctional settings. Indeed, DBT is already hard to find in general community settings, and the limited funding and resources for mental health services in correctional settings make the problem of treatment accessibility even more pronounced. The implications are that, even if individuals in prison receive DBT services, they are unlikely to continue to receive such services upon their reintegration into community settings.

Many of the barriers to DBT in forensic settings also pose challenges for evidence-based care for BPD more broadly. Through our review of the literature and our work consulting and working in forensic settings, we have identified several barriers to evidence-based care for BPD. The first major challenge involves the balance of security with clinical care. Although forensic settings often involve treatment personnel and programs, the emphasis on security and safety often sets up conditions to reinforce or maintain behavioral problems characteristic of BPD. When it comes to self-injury, often, institutional protocols involve the use of restraints, seclusion, chair restraints, and other punitive safety measures to manage self-injury, without individualizing care or a functional understanding of the factors maintaining self-injury for particular residents. Reviews have suggested that emotion regulation remains a primary function of self-injury in forensic (Dixon-Gordon, Harrison, & Roesch, 2012) and nonforensic populations (Brown, Comtois, & Linehan, 2002); however, staff most often overemphasize instrumental and social gains and functions. Some research has suggested that self-injury increases following entry into custody (up to 44% report such an increase), that the probability of self-injury is the greatest in the first year of imprisonment, and that administrative segregation is associated with lower time between episodes of self-injury in prison (by up to 17 months; Lanes, 2009; Mangnall & Yurkovich, 2010; Smith & Kaminski, 2010). In other cases, residents self-injure and then receive transfer to more desirable treatment centers. While treatment may certainly be necessary, the short-term, episodic, and self-injury–contingent nature of these interventions has the potential to reinforce and maintain self-injury. In addition, in prison settings in particular, emergencies and crises often derail treatment, making it difficult to keep up with regular individual therapy sessions, and rotating schedules and shifts expose residents to a large variety of staff with varying training who may provide inconsistent contingencies and treatment.

A second major barrier is the tension between the need for training and resource limitations. Often, forensic and prison settings generally provide salary and benefit packages that are not adequate to attract highly trained mental health professionals (e.g., licensed psychologists). As a result, treatment is often provided by individuals with much more limited mental health training. In some settings, DBT groups are often run by behavioral counsellors with limited undergraduate university education and little or no formal mental health training. This is a major challenge, considering that the behavioral and mental health problems of forensic residents often are on a different order of magnitude than persons with BPD seen in outpatient settings. Indeed, even highly trained and experienced mental health professionals would find these clients to be clinically challenging. In addition, staffing schedules and turnover and the lack of individuals with expertise both in BPD and forensics make it difficult to schedule and implement consistent, ongoing training.

Research on DBT and Adapted DBT-Based Interventions in Forensic Settings

DBT has been disseminated to and adopted by many forensic institutions in the United States, Canada, and Europe, and the evidence base for this work has been building over the past decade. As early as 1998, DBT was in use at more than two dozen correctional and forensic settings in the United States, Canada, and abroad, although comprehensive DBT was rarely implemented (Ivanoff, 1998). Based on the available studies, however, the development and implementation of DBT in forensic settings and with forensic samples is still in its infancy. In a targeted review of the research supporting DBT for treating mentally disordered incarcerated women, Leschied (2011) identified 13 studies suggesting effectiveness at reducing characteristics of mental disorder most frequent in this population. Of these 13, five were randomized controlled trials (RCTs), five were pre-post design, and the remaining five were uncontrolled and primarily qualitative. We applied these same inclusion criteria to the research cited in Behavioral Tech's 2013 annual Summary of the Data to Date supporting DBT and found more support. A total of 30 published studies, including 11 RCTs, 4 quasi-experimental studies, and 5 uncontrolled studies have reported positive outcomes using DBT to treat behaviors consistent with BPD. A subgroup of 10 studies examined the use of selected DBT components, such as skills training or skills coaching. While this growing database on the application of DBT in forensic settings is promising, the research remains in its infancy, and comprehensive DBT has rarely been examined.

Many of existing studies have examined partial or adapted versions of DBT rather than comprehensive, standard DBT. Telephone consultation, in particular, is difficult or impossible to implement in prison settings; thus, some adaptations have substituted milieu coaching to address the goal of generalizing treatment gains to patients' daily lives. Individual therapy is an essential component of DBT, and yet, forensic settings often involve barriers and challenges to the consistent application of individual therapy. Only a few of the studies we reviewed implemented all four components of standard DBT (weekly individual and group skills training, consult team, and telephone consultation; Nee & Farman, 2005; Rosenfeld et al., 2007; van den Bosch, Hysaj, & Jacobs, 2012), with some of these involving modified or adapted materials or modules (Rosenfeld et al., 2007). The remaining studies utilized either group-only treatment, adapted the content of the DBT modules, or adapted the length of the treatment program. Some of the adaptations have included the use of more visual aids and hands-on exercises to make the material more accessible to those with intellectual disabilities (Sakdalan, Shaw, & Collier, 2010), the renaming of certain DBT modules (e.g., Eccleston & Sorbello, 2002), the inclusion of content specific to offending behavior (e.g., Shelton et al.'s 2009 Corrections Modified DBT), modifications to session length and frequency, and adaptations to the structure and format of skills training or individual therapy (Eccleston & Sorbello, 2002; Sakdalan et al., 2010). In standard DBT, group skills training occurs once weekly and takes approximately 24–26 weeks to complete (Linehan, 1993*b*). In the published research on forensic applications, partial/adapted DBT programs ran group skills training sessions ranging from 13 weeks (Sakdalan et al., 2010) to 18 months (Evershed et al., 2003) in length, with groups commonly occurring 2–3 times per week (e.g., Eccleston & Sorbello). Few studies have included or mentioned the DBT Consultation Team, and only one study included DBT adherence ratings (van den Bosch et al., 2012). In addition, studies generally have not reported inclusion/exclusion criteria, nor have they reported proportions of individuals meeting criteria for BPD.

Despite these limitations, findings have been promising and support the continued exploration of DBT (and other evidence-based approaches to BPD) in forensic settings. DBT-informed treatment has been associated with outcomes relevant to forensic patients, such as reductions in aggressive, impulsive and self-injurious behaviors, as well as stalking behavior, severity of violence, and recidivism (Eccleston & Sorbello, 2002; Evershed et al., 2003; Nee & Farman, 2005; Rosenfeld et al., 2007; Shelton, Sampl, Kesten, Zhang, &Trestman, 2009). Some research has shown reductions in disciplinary infractions at various points during treatment (Shelton et al., 2009).

In terms of broader mental health outcomes, findings are promising as well. Some studies have reported improved global functioning and treatability ratings among lower cognitive functioning inmates (Sakdalan et al., 2010), reduced anxiety and stress (Eccleston & Sorbello, 2002), lower negative affect and improved coping scores, and reduced dissociation and suicidal intent (Low et al., 2001). Moreover, findings also indicated improvements in self-esteem and control of anger (Evershed et al., 2003; Nee & Farman, 2005; Sakdalan et al., 2010; Shelton et al., 2009). A study of DBT-informed programs in Canadian women's institutions ($N = 55$ women) showed medium effect sizes for changes in general psychiatric severity (as measured by the Symptom Checklist-90), anxiety and depression, and self-control (Blanchette, Flight, Verbrugge, Gobeil, & Taylor, 2011). In two other comprehensive residential programs, promising results were reported with juvenile offenders (Trupin, Stewart,

Beach, & Boesky, 2002) and adult forensic patients (McCann et al., 2000). Although these were not randomized trials, both of these studies illustrate the potential for full implementation in highly restricted settings (McCann et al., 2007). These exemplar programs have creatively adapted standard DBT outpatient treatment functions for the milieu of institutional settings; this addresses some of the concerns expressed by administrators and staff that the full model may be too difficult to implement in custodial settings. Notably, DBT was also identified as one of the most cost-effective interventions at reducing felony recidivism in a nonrandomized review of treatments offered to juvenile offenders in the state of Washington (WSIPP, 2002).

Findings are promising, but given various study limitations, the variations in DBT-informed programs, the lack of RCT designs, small sample sizes, and the lack of adherence monitoring, the state of the evidence is rather tentative at present. In addition, although many of the outcomes examined are directly relevant to BPD, it is unclear at present as to whether DBT-informed interventions are effective in the treatment of BPD specifically in forensic settings. BPD often was not mentioned or assessed in the studies we reviewed; thus, the jury is not only out on DBT in general in forensic settings but also on DBT for BPD specifically in forensic settings.

MOVING FORWARD: SURMOUNTING BARRIERS TO EVIDENCE-BASED CARE FOR BPD IN FORENSIC SETTINGS

Although we have focused primarily on barriers and challenges to the treatment of BPD in forensic settings, there are many ways to improve treatment, and forensic/custodial settings provide unique opportunities for intensive interventions to help direct the lives of individuals with BPD onto different trajectories. Because manualized, structured treatments for BPD are often unlikely to be found in forensic settings, one approach to care in forensic settings is to at least ensure that the common principles and components of empirically supported care for BPD occur. Across the treatments with empirical support for BPD, some of the common components include (1) treatment that is based on a clear theory regarding the development and maintenance of BPD and a clear rationale for specific therapeutic interventions; (2) structured treatment focusing on clear and explicit behavioral targets; (3) an emphasis on the therapeutic relationship, validation, and compassionate care; and (4) interventions to improve skills in the areas of self and emotion regulation. In addition, alongside these principles and components, individuals with BPD-related problems in forensic settings need comprehensive treatment. Programs should emphasize the aforementioned five functions of comprehensive treatment, including improving capabilities/skills, enhancing motivation to change, ensuring generalization to the natural environment, enhancing and maintaining clinician skill and motivation, and structuring the environment to ensure adequate treatment and reinforce progress (Linehan, 1993a). Even if the implementation of the nuts and bolts of a specific treatment (DBT) proves to be too resource-intensive or challenging, treatment may still be helpful and successful if the key components of comprehensive evidence-based care for BPD are present (as is reflected by promising data based on the partial DBT programs implemented in the Correctional Services of Canada institutions; Blanchette et al., 2011).

Another recommendation is to avoid rewriting or adapting a treatment before it is found to be inadequate—do not fix it until it is broken. Clinicians and researchers often adapt treatments a priori before trying them out and discovering how or even if they need to be adapted (Berzins & Trestman, 2004). The concern is that the treatment, as it was originally developed, will not effectively address the needs of the clientele or may be mismatched in terms of vocabulary, format, skills, acronyms, and so on. Understanding what level of change to which treatment elements actually constitutes adaptation (structure, modes, treatment length and dose) and what qualifies as adoption (changing examples used to illustrate skills, but still addressing all five functions of treatment) is also important. Although there are unique and unavoidable differences in the service delivery environment of correctional and forensic settings (as compared with the outpatient settings in which DBT has been developed and evaluated), DBT is a flexible, principle-driven treatment. Our recommendation is, where possible, to adopt the treatment (whether it be DBT or another treatment) first, monitor outcomes, collect data, conduct focus groups with staff members and inmates, and then decide how and whether it is working. From there, systematic adaptations might be made, but, if so, it would be ideal to collect further data on the effectiveness, feasibility, and acceptability of these adaptations. This may seem to be a tall order in systems already thin on resources but is a goal to which institutions may aspire.

A final recommendation is to use creative methods to enhance training. As mentioned, one of the major challenges in forensic settings is the lack of training of staff members in how to specifically manage some of the clinical challenges associated with BPD. Limited funding, resources, staffing, time, and availability of individuals to conduct training serve as major barriers. Each institution faces unique challenges, but one way to begin to surmount these barriers would be to form think-tank groups of individuals at different forensic institutions to systematically discuss and solve problems related to training. An international conference, for example, focused on this initiative might bring together persons with diverse expertise and from diverse settings to discuss strategies that have worked, failed, or are promising considerations for the future. In addition, the advent and availability of e-learning opportunities may provide excellent avenues for ongoing training. Ultimately, any initiatives regarding ongoing training will require money and time, and therefore, a degree of lobbying and political action will likely be required. It would be hard to argue, however, that individuals suffering with BPD in forensic settings are not worth the time, money, or effort. We hope that this chapter clarifies many of the key issues unique to persons with BPD in forensic settings and stimulates further work to improve the treatment and, ultimately, the lives of these individuals.

REFERENCES

American Correctional Association. (2003). *Standards for adult correctional institutions* (4th ed.). Laurel, MD: Author.

American Psychiatric Association (APA). (2000). *Diagnostic and statistical manual of mental disorders* (4th ed., text rev.). Washington, DC: Author.

American Psychiatric Association (APA). (2013). *Diagnostic and statistical manual of mental disorders* (5th ed.). Arlington, VA: American Psychiatric Publishing.

American Psychological Association. (2007). Evidence-based practice in psychology. *American Psychologist, 61*, 271–285.

Andrews, D. A. (1995). The psychology of criminal conduct and effective treatment. In J. McGuire (Ed.), *What works? Reducing reoffending, guidelines from research and practice* (pp. 3–34). Chichester, UK: Wiley & Sons.

Andrews, D. A., & Bonta, J. (1998). *The psychology of criminal conduct*. Cincinnati, OH: Anderson.

Berzins, L. G., & Trestman, R. L. (2004). The development and implementation of dialectical behavior therapy in forensic settings. *International Journal of Forensic Mental Health, 3*, 93–103.

Black, D. W., Gunter, T., Allen, J., Blum, N., Arndt, S., Wenman, G., & Sieleni, B. (2007). Borderline personality disorder in male and female offenders newly committed to prison. *Comprehensive Psychiatry, 48*(5), 400–405.

Blackburn, R., & Coid, J. W. (1999). Empirical clusters of DSM-III personality disorders in violent offenders. *Journal of Personality Disorders, 13*(1), 18–34.

Blanchette, K., Flight, J., Verbrugge, P., Gobeil, R., & Taylor, K. (2011). *Dialectical behavior therapy within a women's structured living environment, R-241*. Ottawa, ON: Correctional Services Canada.

Brown, M. Z. Comtois, K. A., & Linehan, M. M. (2002). Reasons for suicide attempts and nonsuicidal self-injury in women with borderline personality disorder. *Journal of Abnormal Psychology, 111*, 198–202.

Chapman, A. L., & Cellucci, A. J. (2007). The role of borderline and antisocial features in substance dependence among incarcerated females. *Addictive Behaviors, 32*, 1131–1145.

Chapman, A. L., Specht, M. W., & Cellucci, A. J. (2005). Factors associated with suicide attempts in female inmates: The hegemony of hopelessness. *Suicide and Life Threatening Behavior, 35*, 558–569.

Crowell, S. E., Beauchaine, T. P., & Linehan, M. M. (2009). A biosocial developmental model of borderline personality: Elaborating and extending Linehan's theory. *Psychological Bulletin, 135*(3), 495–510.

Dell, C. A., & Beauchamp, T. (2006). *Fact sheet: Self-injury among criminalized women*. Ottawa, ON: Canadian Centre on Substance Abuse.

Deutsch, C. J. (1984). Self-reported sources of stress among psychotherapists. *Professional Psychology, 15*, 833–845.

Ditton, P. M. (July, 1999). *Mental health and treatment of inmates and probationers. Bureau of Justice Statistics special report, NCJ 174453*. Washington, DC: US Department of Justice.

Dixon-Gordon, K. L, Harrison, N., & Roesch, R. (2012). Non-suicidal self-injury within offender populations: A systematic review. *International Journal of Forensic Mental Health, 11*, 33–50.

Dvoskin, J. A. (2002). Sticks and stones: The abuse of psychiatric diagnosis in prisons. *Journal of the California Alliance for the Mentally Ill [On-line], 8*(1), www.vachss.com/guest_dispatches/dvoskin.html.

Dvoskin, J. A., Radmonski, S. J., Bennett, C., Onlin, J. A., Hawkins, R. L., Dorson, L. A., & Drewnicky, I. N. (2002). Architectural design of a secure forensic state psychiatric hospital. *Behavioral Sciences and the Law, 20*, 481–493.

Eccleston, L., & Sorbello, L. (2002). The RUSH program—Real Understanding of Self-Help: A suicide and self-harm prevention initiative within a prison setting. *Australian Psychologist, 37*(3), 237–244.

Evershed, S., Tennant, A., Boomer, D., Rees, A., Barkham, M., & Watson, A. (2003). Practice-based outcomes of dialectical behavior therapy (DBT) targeting anger and violence, with male forensic patients: A pragmatic and non-contemporaneous comparison. *Criminal Behavior and Mental Health, 13*(3), 198–213.

Eyland, S., Corben, S., & Barton, J. (1997). Suicide prevention in New South Wales correctional centers. *Crisis, 18*(4), 163–169.

Farber, B. A. (1983). Psychotherapists' perceptions of stressful patient behavior. *Professional Psychology, 14*, 697–705.

Fox, R., & Cooper, M. (1998). The effects of suicide on the private practitioner: A professional and personal perspective. *Clinical Social Work Journal, 26*(2), 143–157.

Frick, P. J. (2012). Developmental pathways to conduct disorder: Implications for future directions in research, assessment, and treatment. *Journal of Clinical Child & Adolescent Psychology, 41*, 378–389.

Frick, P. J., & Morris, A. S. (2004). Developmental pathways to conduct problems. *Journal of Clinical Child & Adolescent Psychology, 33*, 54–68.

Gardner, K. J. (2014). Borderline personality traits, rumination, and self-injurious behavior: An empirical test of the emotional cascade model in adult male offenders. *Journal of Forensic Psychology Practice*, 14, 398–417.

Golder, S., Ivanoff, A., Cloud, R., Besel, K. L., McKernan, P., & Blatt, E. (2005). Evidence-based practice with adults in correctional settings: Strategies, practice and future directions. *Best Practices in Mental Health, 2*, 100–132.

Gough, K. (2005). Guidelines for managing self-harm in a forensic setting. *British Journal of Forensic Practice, 7*, 10–14.

Gould, M., Jamieson, P., & Romer, D. (2003). Media contagion and suicide among the young. *American Behavioral Scientist, 46*, 1269–1284.

Grant, B. F., Chou, S., Goldstein, R. B., Huang, B., Stinson, F. S., Saha, T. D., . . . Ruan, W. (2008). Prevalence, correlates, disability, and comorbidity of DSM-IV borderline personality disorder: Results from the Wave 2 National Epidemiologic Survey on Alcohol and Related Conditions. *Journal of Clinical Psychiatry, 69*(4), 533–545.

Gratz, K. L. (2003). Risk factors for and functions of deliberate self-injury: An empirical and conceptual review. *Clinical Psychology, 10*, 192–205.

Hayes, L. (1995). Prison suicide: An overview and a guide to prevention. *Prison Journal, 75*, 431–457.

Hayes, L. M. (2006). Suicide prevention in correctional facilities: An overview. In M. Puisis (Ed.), *Clinical practice in correctional medicine* (2nd ed., pp. 317–328). Philadelphia, PA: Mosby Elsevier.

Hayes, L. M. (2013). Suicide prevention in correctional facilities: Reflections and next steps. *International Journal of Law and Psychiatry, 36*(3-4), 188–194.

Hellman, I. D., Morrison, T. L., & Abramowitz, S. I. (1987). Therapist flexibility/rigidity and work stress. *Professional Psychology: Research and Practice, 18*, 21–27.

Ivanoff, A. (1998). *Survey of criminal justice and forensic dialectical behaviour therapy in the US and UK* Seattle: Linehan Training Group.

Ivanoff, A., Schmidt, H., III, & Finnegan, D. S. (2006, June). *Addressing DBT treatment functions and modes in criminal justice settings*. Paper presented at the International Association of Forensic Mental Health Service Meeting, Amsterdam, The Netherlands.

Jordan, B., Schlenger, W. E., Fairbank, J. A., & Caddell, J. M. (1996). Prevalence of psychiatric disorders among incarcerated women: Convicted felons entering prison. *Archives of General Psychiatry, 53*(6), 513–519.

Lanes, E. (2009). Identification of risk factors for self-injurious behavior in male prisoners. *Journal of Forensic Sciences, 54*(3), 692–698.

Layden, B. K., Chapman, A. L., Douglas, K., & Turner, B. J. (2012, March). *Factors associated with violence toward others among individuals who engage in self-injury*. Paper presented at the annual meeting of the American Psychology and Law Society Convention, San Juan, Puerto Rico.

Leschied, A. W. (2011). *The treatment of incarcerated mentally disordered women offenders: A synthesis of current research.* Ottawa, ON: Public Safety Canada.

Linehan, M. M. (1993a). *Cognitive-behavioral treatment of borderline personality disorder.* New York: Guilford.

Linehan, M. M. (1993b). *Skills training manual for treating borderline personality disorder.* New York: Guilford.

Low, G., Jones, D., Duggan, C., Power, M., & MacLeod, A. (2001). The treatment of deliberate self-harm in borderline personality disorder using dialectical behavior therapy: A pilot study in a high security hospital. *Behavioral and Cognitive Psychotherapy, 29*, 85–92.

Mangnall, J., & Yurkovich, E. (2010). A grounded theory exploration of deliberate self-harm in incarcerated women. *Journal of Forensic Nursing, 6*(2), 88–95.

McCann, R. A., Ball, E. M., & Ivanoff, A. (2000). DBT with an inpatient forensic population: the CMHIP model. *Cognitive & Behavioral Practice, 7*, 447–456.

McCann, R. A., Ivanoff, A., Schmidt, H., & Beach, B. (2007). Implementing dialectical behavior therapy in residential forensic settings with adults and juveniles. In L. A. Dimeff & K. Koerner (Eds.), *Dialectical behavior therapy in clinical practice: Applications across disorders and settings* (pp. 112–144). New York: Guilford.

Monahan, J., Redlich, A. D., Swanson, J., Robbins, P., Appelbaum, P. S., Petrila, J., . . . McNiel, D. E. (2005). Use of leverage to improve adherence to psychiatric treatment in the community. *Psychiatric Services, 56*, 37–44.

Monahan, J., Steadman, H., Robbins, P., Appelbaum, P., Banks, S., Grisso, T., . . . Silver, E. (2005). An actuarial model of violence risk assessment for persons with mental disorders. *Psychiatric Services, 56*, 810–815.

Nee, C., & Farman, S. (2005). Female prisoners with borderline personality disorder: Some promising treatment developments. *Criminal Behavior and Mental Health, 15*, 2–16.

Reid, J. B., & Patterson, G. R. (1991). Early prevention and intervention with conduct problems: A social interactional model for the integration of research and practice. In G. Stoner, M. R. Shinn, & H. M. Walker (Eds.), *Interventions for achievement and behavior problems* (pp. 715–739). Silver Spring, MD: National Association of School Psychologists.

Rosenfeld, B., Galietta, M., Ivanoff, A., Garcia-Mansilla, A., Martinez, R., Fava, J., . . . Green, D. (2007). Dialectical behavior therapy for the treatment of stalking offenders. *International Journal of Forensic Mental Health, 6*(2), 95–103.

Sakdalan, J. A., Shaw, J. J., & Collier, V. V. (2010). Staying in the here-and-now: A pilot study on the use of dialectical behavior therapy group skills training for forensic clients with intellectual disability. *Journal of Intellectual Disability Research, 54*(6), 568–572.

Samuels, J., Eaton, W. W., Bienvenu III, O. J., Brown, C. H., Costa, P. T., & Nestadt, G. (2002). Prevalence and correlates of personality disorders in a community sample. *British Journal of Psychiatry, 180*, 536–542.

Schmidt III, H., & Ivanoff, A. (2007). Behavioral prescriptions for treating self-injurious behavior in correctional settings. In O. Theinhaus & M. Piasecki (Eds.), *Correctional psychiatry: Practice guidelines and strategies* (pp. 7–23). Kingston, NJ: Civic Research Institute.

Shelton, D., Sampl, S., Kesten, K. L., Zhang, W., & Trestman, R. L. (2009). Treatment of impulsive aggression in correctional settings. *Behavioral Sciences & The Law, 27*(5), 787–800.

Smith, H. P., & Kaminski, R. J. (2010). Inmate self-injurious behaviors: Distinguishing characteristics within a retrospective study. *Criminal Justice and Behavior, 37*(1), 81–96.

Swenson, C. R., Torrey, W. C., & Koerner, K. (February 2002). Implementing dialectical behavior therapy. *Psychiatric Services, 53*(2), 171–177.

Thomas, T., Leaf, M., Kazmierczak, S., & Stone, J. (2006). Self –injury in correctional settings: "pathology" of prisons of prisoners? *Criminology and Public Policy, 38*, 193–202.

Trupin, E. W., Stewart, D. G., Beach, B., & Boesky, L. (2002). Effectiveness of a dialectical behavior therapy program for incarcerated female juvenile offenders. *Child and Adolescent Mental Health, 7*, 121–127.

van den Bosch, L. M. C., Hysaj, M., & Jacobs, P. (2012). DBT in an outpatient forensic setting. *International Journal of Law and Psychiatry, 35*, 311–316.

Verona, E., Sachs-Ericsson, N., & Joiner, T. R. (2004). Suicide attempts associated with externalizing psychopathology in an epidemiological sample. *American Journal of Psychiatry, 161*(3), 444–451.

Washington State Institute for Public Policy (WSIPP). (2002). *Preliminary findings for the Juvenile Rehabilitation Administration's Dialectical Behavior Therapy Program, Document No. 02-07-1203.* Olympia, WA: Washington State Institute for Public Policy.

Wong, S., & Hare, R. D. (2005). *Guidelines for a psychotherapy treatment program.* North Tonawanda, NY: MHS.

Zlotnick, C. C. (1999). Antisocial personality disorder, affect dysregulation and childhood abuse among incarcerated women. *Journal of Personality Disorders, 13*(1), 90–95.

/// 23 /// Borderline Personality Disorder and Advocacy

Individuals and Family Members
Speaking Out for Change

PAULA TUSIANI-ENG
AND BEA TUSIANI

INTRODUCTION

According to the World Health Organization (2003), mental health advocacy developed to promote the human rights of people with mental disorders and to reduce stigma, discrimination, and barriers to recovery. Mental health advocacy formally emerged in the United States with the deinstitutionalization of mental hospitals from the 1950s to the 1970s (Tomes, 2006). Families of people with mental disorders and, later, those with mental disorders themselves, began to speak out publicly and express their concerns about abuses and neglect.

Self-advocacy, the belief that individuals with mental illness could act on their own behalf and have agency over their treatment, became a universally accepted principle (World Health Organization, 2003). This idea was eventually supported by new nonprofit organizations, mental health professional associations, and government agencies that supported reforms.

Advocacy for individuals with borderline personality disorder (BPD), however, is a relatively new concept in the United States. BPD as a diagnosis was barely recognized during the mental health reform movement because those who suffered from BPD had not yet been formally identified (Kernberg, 1975), and it was not entered into the *Diagnostic and Statistical Manual for Mental Disorders* until

1980 (American Psychiatric Association, 1980; Linehan, 1993). While government-funded community-based clinics and social welfare programs developed during this period to fill the needs of those suffering from more recognizable mental illnesses, such as bipolar disorder, schizophrenia, and major depression, BPD was not considered a serious mental illness.

Ongoing controversy in the medical community concerning the characteristic traits of BPD (emotional dysregulation, impulsivity, and suicidality) contributed to its diminished status (Tyrer, 1999). A vast majority of clinicians in the United States did not acknowledge BPD as a legitimate mental disorder, and some fought vehemently against its inclusion in the DSM (Linehan, 1993).

As the mental health advocacy initiative began to grow in the United States, little research existed to help doctors understand the etiology and biology of BPD (Lis, Greenfield, Henry, Guile, & Dougherty, 2007). BPD comprises a multilayered mix of symptoms that are hard to identify as a whole, making diagnosis complex for clinicians without specialty training (Paris, 2007). Thus, individuals with BPD were frequently labeled by clinicians as "difficult," "manipulative," or "hard to handle" due to their lack of medical knowledge, education, and research about BPD (Sulzer, 2015), a stigmatizing practice that continues today.

It was not until the 1990s that new, effective, evidenced-based treatments emerged for individuals in this population. These included transference-focused therapy (Yeomans, Clarkin, & Kernberg, 2005), dialectical behavior therapy (DBT; Linehan, 1993), schema-focused therapy (Young & Swift, 1988), good psychiatric management (Gunderson, 2011), and mentalization (Bateman & Fonagy, 2010). Some were rooted in behavior principles, others in psychoanalytic theory and case management. With the advent of these specialized therapeutic approaches, individuals with BPD could receive specialized treatment with the hope of recovery. Most treatments involved intensive individualized or group therapy, often several times a week.

Now, although research supports the efficacy of these treatments, the cost of such therapies makes it difficult for the majority of those with BPD to access them (Maclean, 2013). Due to the extensive nature of training for evidence-based treatments (Howe, 2013), there are not enough skilled clinicians to meet the demand. The majority of these live near universities or psychiatric research centers on the East or West Coasts of the United States, thus leaving a wide swath of the BPD population in middle America underserved (Lohman, 2016).

Many health insurance companies, designed on short-term mental health model delivery systems, do not code BPD as a billable diagnosis. Thus, many long-term evidence-based treatments to effectively treat BPD are expensive but are not covered by health insurance plans, requiring consumers to pay out of pocket to access them (Lohman, 2016; Maclean, 2013). Thus, significant barriers to treatment remain, including cost, stigma, and discrimination, along with the lack of community resources and scientific research to support recovery.

FAMILY SUPPORT ORGANIZATIONS EMERGE AS EARLY LEADERS IN BPD ADVOCACY MOVEMENT

By necessity, families and caretakers emerged as the first leaders in efforts to raise public awareness about BPD. One of the hallmark characteristics of BPD, resulting from difficulties with emotional regulation and lack of coherent identity, is difficulty with interpersonal relationships. Individuals with BPD suffer from high rejection sensitivity, fears of abandonment, and an intense need for attachment, and they are prone to severe emotional outbursts. The BPD individual's symptoms and behaviors are deeply enmeshed in the family system, affecting all aspects of family communication and interactions. Current research shows that family members of BPD individuals experience more anxiety, stress, and fatigue than do caretakers of those with other mental illnesses (Bailey, 2013).

Early BPD treatments, however, focused solely on the individual–therapist treatment relationship, excluding families as partners in the treatment process. This may be attributed to research linking BPD with an invalidating family environment, neglect, and abuse (Fruzzetti, Shenk, & Hoffman, 2005; Linehan, 1993). Christian Beels (2005) explains, "Until now, therapists have lacked a way of educating both family and patient to see themselves as victimized by the illness, and so they have set up a private 'neutral' relationship with the patient, that, on the psychoanalytic model, excludes and ignores the family" *(page xii)*. Family therapy and psychoeducation were not mandated as the standard of care for BPD by mental health professionals but is more commonly integrated into practice today (Rathus & Miller, 2014).

Because of the fragility of their symptoms, those diagnosed with BPD were unable to advocate for themselves. Many continued to be misdiagnosed, thus inhibiting the progress of their recovery. Frustrated with the lack of progress in their loved ones' lives, family members stepped in to raise awareness about BPD and its impact on individuals, families, and the wider community.

NATIONAL ORGANIZATIONS FOCUS ON PROVIDING DIRECT SUPPORT, RESOURCES, AND ADVOCACY

Treatment and Research Advancements National Association for Personality Disorder (TARA-BPD), a national not-for-profit organization in New York City, was founded in 1994 by Valerie Porr (Porr, n.d.). This organization was the first to gain the public's attention about BPD. Its mission embraced education and providing information on BPD to families, consumers, and providers (www.tara4bpd.org; see Treatment and Research Advances, n.d.). TARA became an advocacy group for the recognition of the BPD diagnosis and to advocate for a focus on research to investigate the neurobiological causes of BPD.

A second national organization founded to meet the needs of family members, the National Education Association for Borderline Personality Disorder

(NEA-BPD, n.d.), was launched in 2001 by Perry Hoffman. It is run by a leadership structure that includes trained clinicians, a scientific advisory board, and trained volunteers. NEA-BPD offers family education, support and advocacy, organizing, and conferences for clinicians as well as family members. According to its website, the NEA-BPD has hosted more than 65 professional conferences for scientists and clinicians to share the latest research on BPD (http://www.borderlinepersonalitydisorder.com).

NEA-BPD was instrumental, through a partnership with the National Alliance for Mental Illness (NAMI), to request a *Congressional Report* on BPD from the Substance Abuse and Mental Health Association (SAMSHA), marking the first time that BPD was entered into the *Congressional Record* as a serious mental illness (Substance Abuse and Mental Health Administration, 2010). Additionally, NEA-BPD work with Representative Tom Davis (R-VA-11) to sponsor House Resolution 1005, Supporting the Goals and Ideals of Borderline Personality Disorder Awareness Month in the 110th Congress in 2008 (https://www.congress.gov/bill/110th-congress/house-resolution/1005/text).

The family of Pamela Ann Tusiani also joined the BPD advocacy movement when their 23-year-old daughter died as a result of a drug interaction between food and the antidepressant tranylcypromine (Parnate). Pamela was being treated for depression and BPD from 1999 to 2001, when her medications were mismanaged at a long-term care facility where she was being treated, causing a brain hemorrhage (Tusiani, Tusiani, & Tusiani-Eng, 2013).

Motivated by their 3-year struggle to find adequate treatment facilities and clinicians trained in BPD, the family used the settlement from wrongful death lawsuits to establish the Borderline Personality Disorder Resource Center (BPDRC) at New York Presbyterian-Hospital's Westchester Division in 2003. Its mission is to promote BPD education and connect those affected by BPD to established resources for treatment and support (http://www.nyp.org/bpdresourcecenter).

The BPDRC is staffed by a social worker who maintains the largest database in the world of clinicians, facilities, and programs specifically involving BPD. Since its inception, the BPDRC has received more than 13,000 calls, averaging 130 a month (Borderline Personality Disorder Resource Center Reports, 2016). A study of the data accumulated by the BPDRC from 2008 to 2015 finds that stigmatization, financial concerns, and comorbid disorders are obstacles for those seeking care for BPD (Lohman, 2016).

NEW REGIONAL ORGANIZATIONS EMPHASIZE EDUCATION AND FAMILY SUPPORT

More recently, new organizations, concentrated in specific regional areas of the United States and Canada, were founded by individuals with a personal or family connection to BPD to raise awareness about BPD and provide family support. One of these, the Florida BPD Association (n.d.), operates as a web-based information service that also hosts support groups and workshops for clinicians, individuals, and family members (www.fbpda.org). Another is the New England Personality Disorders Association (NEPDA, n.d.), which, in addition to a website call-in box, also holds monthly family educational workshops, sometimes partnering with McLean Psychiatric Hospital in Boston, Massachusetts (www.nepda.org).

Outside the United States, Lynn and Mike Menu Courey founded the Sashbear Foundation (n.d.) in Ontario, Canada, in 2011, in honor of their daughter, Sasha, a competitive swimmer and BPD sufferer who took her life at the age of 20. They organize an annual Borderline Walk in her memory, give talks as guest speakers in schools about BPD and suicide prevention, and host conferences for clinicians, with a special focus on early intervention, mindfulness, and DBT at an early age (www.sashbear.org).

New advances are being made to expand outreach exponentially via social media. Founded by parent Frederic Bein in Atlanta, Georgia, in 2012, the Personality Disorder Awareness Network (PDAN, n.d.) promotes early BPD assessment with an emphasis on psychosocial intervention for youngsters at high risk, as well as parent education. PDAN trains volunteers to generate content for its website using social media, blogs, and webinars. The result is a following of 300,000 users, making it the largest social media presence for BPD in the world (www.pdan.org).

FAMILIES AND CLINICIANS TURN ADVOCACY EFFORTS TOWARD RESEARCH

As grassroots family support and education organizations began to grow, clinicians have also recognized the need to organize for the purpose of promoting BPD research. According to the Anatomy of NIMH Funding, from 2009 to 2013, BPD received the least amount of research grants for mental health disorders (http://nimh.nih.gove/funding/funding-strategy-for-research-grants/the-anatomy-of-nimh-funding). Despite its prevalence and devastating impact on both individuals and society, BPD continues to be largely unrecognized by the psychiatric research community as a priority for funding (Zimmerman, 2015).

In 2012, the North American Society for the Study of Personality Disorders (NASSPD, n.d.) was founded as a professional organization for clinicians and scientists devoted to personality disorder research. Its mission emphasized the dissemination of new research pointing to positive treatment outcomes for those with personality disorders to the clinical community and public, as well as advocacy for research funding. Annual NASSPD conferences are held to present new research and cultivate a new generation of young researchers interested in pursuing work in this field (http://www.nasspd.org).

Family members also recognized the lack of funding for BPD research and the small numbers of scientists studying it. Families for Borderline Personality Disorder Research was founded in 2011, to raise and donate funds to the Brain and Behavior Research Foundation (BBRF, 2016) specifically for BPD research (www.

bbrfoundation.org). Since its founding, FBBDR has funded five BPD researchers who have been awarded NARSAD Young Investigator Grants of $70,000 each
from the BBRF (http://www.familiesforbpdresearch.org). BPD advocate and blog-
ger Amanda Wang founded ReThinkBPD (n.d.) in 2016, to promote research and
awareness. Wang hosted a weekly podcast series on topics of treatment and recovery
during Borderline Personality Disorder Awareness Month in May 2016, featuring
clinicians and those affected by the disorder. All funds raised were donated to the
BBRF (http://rethinkbpd.org). She also ran a half-marathon to raise money in support of her mission.

Advocacy for research is a relatively new phenomenon within the BPD movement. However, most individuals and family members in the trenches with this
disorder agree that more research is necessary to understand BPD as a diagnosis
and to develop more effective treatments. In May 2015, a new advocacy nonprofit
called Emotions Matter, Inc. (n.d.) launched an online petition for increased funding for BPD research. In 6 weeks, the organization received more than 5,000 signa-
tures, which were later presented to Dr. Bruce Cuthbert, then Acting Director of the
National Institute of Mental Health (NIMH), during BPD Awareness Month (www.
emotionsmatterbpd.org). People whose lives were impacted by BPD not only signed
the petition, but also left comments imploring NIMH to support their diagnosis. This
mass campaign on social media was among the first to invite citizens to become
self-advocates for BPD. Two months after the campaign ended, the NIMH updated
its BPD webpage, demonstrating that individuals affected by BPD are becoming
empowered to publicly speak out and self-advocate for government policy changes
(http://www.nimh/gov/health/topics/borderline-personality).

INDIVIDUAL VOICES EMERGE TO SHED LIGHT ON THE BPD EXPERIENCE

As families impacted by BPD joined organizations to promote awareness in the
1990s, individuals with BPD remained very much in the closet. The early cultural
references to BPD in films during this period could have been a contributing factor, heavily based as they were on negative stereotypes that caused lack of public
empathy for those who desperately needed support. The one-dimensional portrayal
of BPD in films such as *Fatal Attraction* and *Girl Interrupted* captured many of the
outward negative symptoms of BPD, thus perpetuating public stigma and fear without giving the characters emotional depth to paint a more complete portrait of BPD
(http://www.psychologytoday.com/blog/reel-therapy2012).

During that same period, others began to speak more openly about their personal
struggles with mental illness. Elizabeth Wurtzel's *Prozac Nation* (1994) and Kay
Redfield Jamison's *An Unquiet Mind* (1996) were groundbreaking in that they normalized the role of psychotropic medications in the treatment of mental illness and
gave voice to more authentic experiences of depression and bipolar disorder. This

began to turn the tide toward destigmatizing mental health struggles long considered taboo in a nation that locked up mentally ill patients.

Yet as some mental disorders became safer to discuss in public, BPD remained an enigma. Princess Diana was suspected of having BPD, but this possibility was shrouded in mystery and shame (Smith, 1999). What the public saw were the outwardly negative behaviors that result from BPD—impulsivity, stormy relationships, suicidal thinking—without recognizing that there was a real person, profoundly suffering, on the inside. Public stigma against BPD was too great for the Princess to disclose the true nature of her illness.

MILLENNIALS TURN TIDE IN SELF-DISCLOSURE ABOUT BPD

As evidence-based treatments proved more effective by the end of the 20th century, individuals with BPD began to stabilize with the proper treatment (Zanarini, Frankenburg, & Hennen, 2003). With recovery now possible, the new millennium became a game-changer in terms of public perception. Family members began to write more authentically about the challenges they faced in living with someone who is borderline. *I Hate You—Don't Leave Me* (Kreisman & Straus, 1991) and *Stop Walking on Egg Shells* (Mason & Kreger, 1998) became two groundbreaking books that shed light on what families, particularly spouses and partners, experience.

Similarly, a series of personal memoirs emerged giving more authentic voices to the emotional dimension of the borderline personality. These include Rachel Reiland's *Get Me Out of Here: My Recovery from Borderline Personality Disorder* (2004); Keira Van Gelder's *The Buddha and the Borderline: My Recovery from Borderline Personality Disorder Through Dialectical Behavioral Therapy, Buddhism, and Online Dating* (2010); Merri Lisa Johnson's *Girl in Need of a Tourniquet: Memoir of a Borderline Personality* (2010); and Stacy Pershall's *Loud in the House of Myself: Memoir of a Strange Girl* (2012). These memoirs began to turn the tide, making it safe for others to speak about their experiences.

Hope surfaced when public figures began to publicly disclose their BPD diagnosis to mitigate stigma and spread public awareness. Marsha Linehan, creator of DBT and an expert on mental illness, disclosed in the *New York Times* (Carey, 2011) that the motivation behind her groundbreaking therapy was her own personal struggle with BPD (http://www.nytimes.com/2011/06/23/health). Linehan went on to found the Linehan Institute in support of BPD education, research, and scientifically based treatments, and Behavioral Tech, a training and consulting organization for DBT (http://linehaninsititue.org).

Brandon Marshall, a football player for the New York Jets, revealed his BPD story after years of struggling with anger issues, dealing with law enforcement, and a short-term stay in residential treatment (Klemko, 2011). Marshall later founded Project Borderline to raise awareness for BPD. As the first well-known sports figure to disclose a BPD diagnosis, Marshall made it safe for others, especially men, to become more public about the disorder.

This public exposure set the stage for an explosion of personal narratives, blogs, and peer support groups about BPD and on social media via Facebook, Twitter, and Tumblr. Some of the more popular BPD blogs and webpages with thousands of followers worldwide include www.anythingtostopthepain.com, www.bpdawareness.org, www.facebook.com/bpda1, www.bpdcentral.com., http://bpdawareness.bigcartel.com, www.bpdfamily.com, www.bpddemystified.com. www.hopeforbpd.com, www.mydialecticallife.com, www.thefightwithus.com, www.my-borderline-personality-disorder.com, and http://www.my-borderline-nightmare.tumblr.com/, among many others. While this new development has not been studied, the proliferation of online sites indicates that individuals with BPD find comfort, support, and validation through social media.

Thus, more than 30 years after BPD first became included in the DSM-III, the disorder that was once hidden behind closed doors has emerged in the public domain. Individuals with BPD are finally articulating the depth of their emotional and behavioral struggles, detailing their experiences with addiction, eating disorders, self-harm, and suicidal behaviors as a cry for help, awareness, and support.

ONE EFFORT TO CREATE A NEW MOVEMENT FOR BPD ADVOCACY

In 2013, Bea Tusiani and Paula Tusiani-Eng used their deceased loved one's (Pamela's) personal diaries to write *Remnants of a Life on Paper—A Mother and Daughter's Struggle with Borderline Personality Disorder* (Baroque Press, 2013), chronicling the chaos they lived through during Pamela's 3-year period with BPD. The presentations they gave to clinicians, medical students, and social workers at hospitals and universities, along with the general public, created a groundswell of supporters with strikingly similar experiences.

In May 2015, Tusiani and Tusiani-Eng invited these supporters to participate in a team called Mothers and Others Walk for Borderline Personality Disorder Awareness at the NAMI walk in New York City. More than 50 individuals and family members impacted by BPD participated, discovering a similar passion for advocacy. Focus groups later revealed key interests in changing the way BPD is stigmatized by the medical community, improving health insurance coverage for BPD treatments, increasing government funding for BPD research, and encouraging early diagnosis and prevention.

In August 2015, Rosa Nouvini and Roya Nouvini, who share a sister with BPD, along with Paula Tusiani Eng, launched a new nonprofit organization called Emotions Matter, Inc. to address these concerns. Its mission is to connect and empower those impacted by BPD to raise awareness and advocate for better mental health care (www.emotionsmatterbpd.org). Emotions Matter, Inc. is distinctive in its effort to involve individuals with BPD in its organizational structure, foster leadership development, and offer peer support.

One of the first initiatives of Emotions Matter, Inc. was to reduce the social isolation of individuals with BPD, which they identified as a primary obstacle to their recovery. The organization held face-to-face monthly meetings in New York City, and then, when attendance became difficult due to geography, it additionally formed a closed Facebook group for individuals with BPD. The purpose of this group is to create a private space for individuals with BPD in different phases of treatment and recovery to communicate about advocacy. It is also promotes peer support, empowerment, and the reframing of their BPD narrative.

Narratives are significant because they lend legitimacy to one's personal journey (Nelson, 2008). Many individuals with BPD are initially told by doctors that recovery is difficult, and there is no guarantee that they will get better, creating despair. They internalize public stigma, believing that what others say is true, and this becomes a roadblock to recovery (Roe, Hasson-Ohayon, Mashiach-Eizenberg, Lysaker, & Yanos, 2014). Through the power of narrative, instead of allowing health professionals, stigmatized labels, or grim statistics to define their trajectory, individuals create their own recovery story.

EMPOWERMENT AS REFRAMING THE BPD NARRATIVE FROM DESPAIR TO HOPE

With the plethora of story-telling about BPD that has emerged in the past decade, most especially on social media, common patterns have evolved in the language of empowerment. Individuals with BPD have shifted their personal narratives from despair to hope as they become empowered and participate in broader advocacy.

It is well-documented that individuals with BPD and their family members experience stigma and invalidation by the medical community. Research shows that mental health professionals routinely stigmatize patients with BPD, using negative language and labeling them as manipulative, difficult to manage, attention-seeking, and not worthy of resources (Fallon, 2003; Lewis & Appleby, 1988). Because of this bias, young clinicians often choose not to train and specialize in treating BPD, thereby further diminishing patient access to quality clinical care.

These prejudices are internalized by individuals with BPD who believe they are not worthy of being treated, thus fueling negative self-talk and self-stigma. Some of them reject treatment altogether because clinicians, authority figures in a position to help, make them feel invalidated (Kling, 2014). Clinicians who use stigmatizing language hinder the recovery process because individuals with BPD adopt the clinicians' negative narrative based on the rhetoric of stigma as opposed to owning their own story (Errerger & Foreman, 2016).

It is the experience of Emotions Matter, Inc., through its closed Facebook group and member meetings, that narrative re–story-telling assists individuals with BPD to adopt a more empowering framework that fosters recovery. Through education, treatment, and a supportive environment, individuals with BPD reject the clinician's narrative and develop their own more authentic, validating sense of self through the healing process.

Dominant themes and essential stages have been observed in helping individuals with BPD become empowered as self-advocates and engaged in the process of reframing their personal narratives from victim to survivor, expert to advocate:

1. *Understanding the biological roots of BPD*: "It's all my fault, I caused my BPD," becomes "It's a brain disorder rooted in emotional dysregulation. My brain processes emotions differently, but I can learn skills to retrain my brain to think in a more neutral way."

2. *Wanting others to understand the emotional pain caused by BPD*: "I feel so bad I am hurting everyone around me. I am crazy, pushing them away. . ." becomes "I want them to understand how much I am hurting. Let me share my pain with them, and help them understand how I feel."

3. *Recognizing stigma by family/clinicians*: "I am attention seeking, manipulative, and difficult—that is what the doctor/my family says—so it must be true," becomes "I will find a doctor/friends who listen, understand, and validate my experience with BPD.

4. Recognizing the strengths of one's BPD personality: "You're so borderline," becomes "I am more than my disorder. Being borderline is just one part of me. It makes me sensitive, empathic, creative, and gives me a strong desire to help others. These are great qualities."

5. *Treatment leads to hope and recovery*: "You will never get better," becomes "I see other people get better. I can and will get better, too, if I use my skills and seek support." "I don't need therapy, I can't find or afford a therapist anyone," becomes "treatment is a vital part of my recovery. I can advocate for myself to find doctors, treatment, and support."

6. *Recovery creates a desire for social connection*: "I am the only one suffering from this horrific disorder. I drive people away, nobody wants me. I feel utterly alone and abandoned," becomes "there are other people who have BPD who understand what I am feeling. I am not alone. I have friends that I can call when I am becoming dysregulated. They will not abandon me because they like me for who I am and understand BPD."

7. *Connection leads to BPD advocacy and empowerment*: "I am never going to be able to help anyone except myself," becomes "I can take my experiences and knowledge about BPD and help others. I am not the only one who has experienced invalidation, stigma, and the inability to get treatment. Story-telling is important to my recovery. Raising awareness and advocacy for BPD will make a difference for me and for others who are in my shoes. I can help them recover as part of my own recovery."

In the experience of Emotions Matter, the process of reframing the personal narrative happens best in the context of a peer group. A study on self-stigma and empowerment among women with BPD observed that perceived legitimacy of discrimination and group identification were two critical variables to the empowerment process (Rusch, Lieb, Bohus, & Corrigan, 2006). Women who strongly perceived stigma as unfair felt empowered when the group expressed similar feelings of anger and frustration. Being part of a peer group normalized their experiences of shame, guilt, and isolation. It also empowered them to articulate their anger about those who invalidated their emotions and diagnosis. Articulating stigma is an important part of establishing a new empowerment narrative and serves as a catalyst to their participation in broader advocacy efforts.

CHALLENGES, OBSTACLES, AND OPPORTUNITIES TO PROMOTE FUTURE ADVOCACY

The Individual Level

Although the movement toward BPD self-advocacy, as articulated, is still underdeveloped, understudied, and at an early stage of development, there are some opportunities for future growth. The *New York Times* recently reported a rise in alternative peer-to-peer interventions, such as the Hearing Voices Network, that have proved successful for individuals with schizophrenia and other severe mental illnesses (Carey, 2016). Such approaches rely less on a conventional medical model, emphasizing instead peer-mediated crisis intervention and community support services that have proved effective for those who have not found success otherwise.

Peer-to-peer mediated interventions have long been popular in treating mental illness, particularly for addictions. However, they have not specifically been designed for individuals with BPD. Rachel Kling (2014) reports participation in a successful crisis intervention team in rural Vermont, in which individuals with BPD are trained to participate on the intervention team. However, such interventions have not been studied or developed.

Individuals with BPD at Emotions Matters have expressed an interest in becoming peer counselors, and there is a strong desire for crisis intervention professionals who are knowledgeable about BPD. While there is great potential for peer-to-peer mediated interventions, especially crisis interventions, the high suicide risk among the BPD population would require extensive clinical supervision, a peer leadership training curriculum, and funding for such a program to be effective.

The staff at Emotions Matter has faced organizational challenges in the variability and reliability of its members. The large majority of members who self-disclose as having BPD are also in treatment and have some impaired level of functioning, which may mean that a long-term commitment to peer leadership training could be challenging. However, with the proper clinical oversight and support in place, it could also be an empowering program for the volunteer peer staff in a largely underserved BPD population. This type of program might be more suited for individuals further along the treatment spectrum, as opposed to the newly diagnosed.

The Organizational Level

Presently, there are many obstacles that must be surmounted to bring unity to the wider BPD advocacy movement and effect substantial change. These include increasing communication among existing BPD organizations with the intent of achieving a unified front before governmental agencies and the medical/scientific community, improving connections with BPD social media bloggers and self-advocates across state lines, and expanding financial resources to support efforts to promote BPD advocacy efforts that involve extensive travel, promotion, and educational outreach.

On the plus side, opportunities exist to collaborate with larger established organizations such as Stamp Out Stigma, Bring Change 2 Mind, or the American Foundation for Suicide Prevention, which are already utilizing social media as an ever-expanding meeting place for voices (especially those of young people who are disproportionately impacted by BPD) to be heard and counted worldwide. Various segments of the clinical community have shown that they are passionate about supporting their patients by becoming involved in advocacy. More work needs to be done to connect the efforts of an older generation of clinicians who do not utilize social media with their younger patients who are seeking validation in important, largely unrecognized ways and which may change the way the clinical community perceives BPD.

Advocacy at the Clinical Level

Zimmerman (2015) contends that, compared to other mental disorders, the BPD clinical community lacks an advocacy strategy. BPD as a diagnosis is underfunded, underrecognized, and often misdiagnosed. He attributes this to a lack of an advocacy strategy on the part of clinicians who have largely ignored BPD, and he highlights the public health implications of the disorder (Zimmerman, 2015).

Although the NASSPD has made strides an increasing the dissemination of research about BPD, empowering young researchers, and advocating for new advances in the field, few professional health care organizations have made promoting public awareness and reducing stigma a priority. Future efforts for advocacy at the clinical level include changing the name of BPD to more closely reflect a more positive framework, mandating education about BPD in medical training, developing a comprehensive anti-stigma campaign specifically geared toward clinicians, and advocating for better accounting of prevalence and suicide statistics, among other possible initiatives. It is hopeful that many clinicians are genuinely interested in supporting BPD advocacy and open to collective organizing on behalf of the disorder. However, as Zimmerman (2015) notes, this will take more deliberating planning and strategy on the part of clinicians representing a variety of different treatment modalities and research interests.

Advocacy at the Policy Level

At the policy level, the need for BPD advocacy initiatives filters from the individual client up through the highest government agencies, systems, and health care insurance corporations. Some areas for future growth include the need for more aggressive early intervention for those identified as at-risk for BPD or displaying BPD traits in childhood/early adolescence. Research shows that, on a developmental trajectory, early intervention is a positive mediator for better outcomes, potentially saving lives.

Discrimination by health insurance companies is a macroeconomic issue that has long plagued individuals and families impacted by BPD. More work can be done by advocacy groups and clinicians to lobby for legislation on a state-by-state basis mandating health insurance coverage for evidence-based BPD treatments. Treatment saves lives, and, without treatment, there will be a high cost to society given that untreated BPD contributes to the rising suicide rate and other social problems related to BPD, such as homelessness, children in foster care, incarceration, and unemployment. Further economic and social impact studies of BPD will be necessary to successfully advocate the necessity for health insurance coverage.

A final imperative area for advocacy is for the funding of more research at the NIMH. Paramount to mitigating stigma is legitimizing BPD as a serious mental illness with a devastating impact on public health. While much progress in advocacy has been made in the nearly 80 years since it was first recognized, much remains to be done in various dimensions of brain research to understand BPD as a major mental illness on par with other disorders.

Emphasizing the importance of prevalence studies, more accurate measures of deaths statistics related to BPD, and social and economic impact research will continue to make a case for public awareness. Many studies currently funded by the NIMH examine the effectiveness of BPD interventions. While treatments are essential to recovery, if individuals and family members affected by BPD cannot access such interventions, given their prohibitive cost and limited availability, it is important that the research community strategically examine BPD as a diagnosis to increase access to life-saving treatments, reduce stigma, and enhance general knowledge about BPD.

CONCLUSION

The development of advocacy for BPD in the United States has evolved over time, although, along with clinical understanding, it has lagged behind the mental health reform movement. As better research and interventions became available, individuals and family members experienced recovery and began to advocate for their needs in society, including access to treatment, information, and public validation.

Efforts to empower and mobilize individuals with BPD are still in their infancy, but trends on social media and by BPD organizations demonstrate hopeful new directions for future growth. By reframing their stigmatized narratives and adopting a more empowering framework, individuals with BPD and their family members will continue to evolve as agents of change, affecting a myriad of initiatives at the individual, organizational, clinical, and policy levels of society.

REFERENCES

American Psychiatric Association. (1980). *Diagnostic and statistical manual of mental disorders* (3rd Ed.). Washington, DC: Author.

Bailey, R. C. (2013). Burden and support needs of carers of persons with borderline personality disorder: A systematic review. *Harvard Review Psychiatry, 21*, 248–258.

Bateman, A., & Fonagy, P. (2010). Mentalization based treatment for borderline personality disorder. *World Psychiatry, 9*(1), 11–15.

Beels, C. (2005). Foreword. *Understanding and treating borderline personality disorder.* Arlington VA: American Psychiatric Publishing.

Borderline Personality Disorder Resource Center (BPDRC). (2016). *Reports.* New York-Presbyterian Hospital. Retrieved from: http://www.nyp.org/bpdresourcecenter

The Brain and Behavior Research Foundation (BBRF). https://bbrfoundation.org/

Carey, B. (2011, June 23). Expert on mental illness reveals her own fight. *New York Times.* Retrieved from: http://www.nytimes.com/2011/06/23/health/23lives.html?pagewanted=all&_r=0

Carey, B. (2016, August 8). An alternative form of mental health gains a foothold. *The New York Times.* Retrieved from: https://www.nytimes.com/2016/08/09/health/psychiatrist-holistic mental-health.html

Emotions Matter, Inc. (n.d.) www.emotionsmatterbpd.org

Errerger, S., & Foreman, A. (2016). "That's so borderline"—language matters when talking about BPD. *The New Social Worker.* http://www.socialworker.com

Fallon, P. G. (2003). Traveling through the system: The lived experience of people with BPD in contact with psychiatric services. *Journal of Psychiatric and Mental Health Nursing, 10* (4), 383–401.

Families for Borderline Personality Disorder Research (FBPDR). http://www.familiesforbpdresearch.org

Florida Borderline Personality Disorder Association (FBPDA). (n.d.) www.fbpda.org

Fruzzetti, A. E., Shenk, C., & Hoffman, P. D. (2005). Family interaction and the development of borderline personality disorder: A transactional model. *Development and Psychopathology, 17*, 1007–1030.

Gunderson, J. G., Stout, R. L., McGlashan, T. H., Shea, L. C., Grilo, C. M., Zanarini, M. C., . . . Skodol, A. E. (2011). Ten-year course of borderline personality disorder: Psychopathology and function from the Collaborative Longitudinal Personality Disorders study. *Archives of General Psychiatry, 68*(8), 827–837.

110th Congress. (2007–2008). House Resolution 1005: Supporting the goals and ideals of Borderline Personality Disorder Awareness Month. Rep. Davis, Tom [R-VA-11], Sponsor. Retrieved from: https://www.congress.gov/bill/110th-congress/house-resolution/1005/text

Howe, E. (2013). Five ethical and clinical challenges psychiatrists may face when treating patients with borderline personality disorder who are or may become suicidal. *Innovations in Clinical Neuroscience, 10*(1), 14–19.

Insel, T. (n.d.). *Director's blog: The anatomy of NIMH funding from 2009–2013*. https://www.nimh. nih.gov/funding/funding-strategy-for-research-grants/the-anatomy-of-nimh-funding.shtml

Jamison, K. R. (1996). *An unquiet mind*. New York: Vintage.

Kernberg, O. (1975). *Borderline conditions and pathological narcissism*. New York: Jason Aronson.

Klemko, R. (2011, July 31). Brandon Marshall reveals mental disorder. *USA Today*. Retrieved from: http://content.usatoday.com/communities/thehuddle/post/2011/07/brandon-marshall-reveals-his-borderline-personality-disorder/1.V9NyZforLcs

Kling, R. (2014). Borderline personality disorder, language and stigma. *Ethical human psychology and psychiatry, 16*(2), 114.

Kreisman, M. D., & Straus, H. (1991). *I hate you—Don't leave me*. New York: Avon.

Lewis, G., & Appleby, L. (1988). Personality disorder: The patients psychiatrists dislike. *British Journal of Psychiatry, 153*(1), 44–49.

Linehan Institute. http://linehaninsititue.org

Linehan, M. (1993). *DBT skills training manual*. New York: Guilford.

Lohman, M. C. (2016). Qualitative analysis of resources and barriers for BPD in the US *Psychiatric Services, 68*(2), 167–172.

Maclean, J. C. (2013). *Borderline personality disorder: Insight from economics*. Retrieved from: http://scattergoodfoundation.org/activity/general/borderline-personality-disorder-insight-economics

Mason, P. T., & Kreger, R. (1998). *Stop walking on eggshells*. Oakland, CA: New Harbinger.

National Association for the Study and Advancement of Personality Disorders (NASSPD). (n.d.) http://www.nasspd.org

National Education Alliance for Borderline Personality Disorder (NEA-BPD). (n.d.) http://www.borderlinepersonalitydisorder.com

National Institute of Mental Health. (2016). *Borderline personality disorder*. Retrieved from: https://www.nimh.nih.gov/health/topics/borderline-personality-disorder/index.shtmlpart_145392

Nelson, J. R. (2008). Narratives of recovery: Reducing the stigma of mental illness. *Clergy Journal, 85*(1), 15–16.

New England Personality Disorder Association (NEPDA). (n.d.) www.nepda.org

Paris, J. (2007). Why psychiatrists are reluctant to diagnose borderline personality disorder. *Psychiatry, 4*(1), 25–39.

Pershall, S. (2012). *Loud in the house of myself: Memoir of a strange girl*. New York: W. W. Norton.

Personality Disorder Awareness Network (PDAN). (n.d.) www.pdan.org

Porr, V. (n.d.). *How advocacy is bringing borderline personality disorder into the light*. Retrieved from: http://www.tara4bpd.org/how-advocacy-is-bringing-borderline-personality-disorder-into-the-light

Rathus, J. H., & Miller, A. L. (2014). *DBT skills manual for adolescents*. New York: Guilford.

Reiland, R. (2004). *Get me out of here: My recovery from BPD*. Center City, MN: Hazelden.

Roe, D., Hasson-Ohayon, I., Mashiach-Eizenberg, M., Derhy, O., Lysaker, P. H., & Yanos, P. T. (2014). Narrative Enhancement and Cognitive Therapy (NECT) effectiveness: A quasi-effective study. *Journal of Clinical Psychology, 70*(4), 303–312.

Rüsch, N., Lieb, K., Bohus, M., & Corrigan, P. (2003). Brief reports: Self-stigma, empowerment, and perceived legitimacy of discrimination among women with mental illness. *Psychiatric Services, 57*(3), 399–402.

Sashbear Foundation. (n.d.) www.sashbear.org

Smith, S. B. (1999). *Diana in search of herself*. New York: Times Books.

Substance Abuse and Mental Health Services Administration (SAMSHA). (2010). *Report to congress on borderline personality disorder* (HHS Publication No. SMA-11-4644). Washington, DC: US Department of Health and Human Services.

Sulzer, S. H. (2015). Does "difficult patient" status contribute to de facto demedicalization? The case of borderline personality disorder. *Social Science & Medicine, 142*, 82–89.

Tomes, N. (2006). The patient as a policy factor: A historical case study of the Consumer/Survivor movement in mental health. *Health Affairs, 25*(3), 720–729. Retrieved from: http://libproxy.adelphi.edu:2048/login?url=http://search.proquest.com/docview/204649601?accountid=30971

Treatment and Research Advances National Association for Personality (TARA4BPD). (n.d.) www.tara4bpd.org

Tusiani, B., Tusiani, P., & Tusiani-Eng, P. (2013). *Remnants of a life on paper: A mother and daughter's struggle with borderline personality disorder.* New York: Baroque.

Tyrer, P. (1999). Borderline personality disorder: A motley diagnosis in need of reform. *Lancet, 354*, 2095–2096.

Van Gelder, K. (2010). *The Buddha and the borderline: My recovery from borderline personality disorder through dialectical behavioral therapy, Buddhism, and online dating.* Oakland, CA: New Harbinger.

Wang, A. RethinkBPD. (n.d.) http://rethinkbpd.org

World Health Organization. (2003). *Advocacy and mental health.* Retrieved from: http://www.who.int/mental_health/resources/en/Advocacy.pdf

Wurtzel, E. (1994). *Prozac nation.* New York: Houghton-Mifflin.

Yeomans, F. E., Clarkin, J. F., & Kernberg, O. F. (2005). *A primer of transference-focused psychotherapy for the borderline patient.* New York: Rowman & Littlefield.

Young, J., & Swift, W. (1988). Schema-focused cognitive therapy for personality disorders: Part I. *International Cognitive Therapy Newsletter, 4*, 13–14.

Zanarini, M. C., Frankenburg, F. R., Hennen, J., & Silk, K. (2003). the longitudinal course of borderline psychopathology: 6-year prospective follow-up of the phenomenology of borderline personality disorder. *American Journal of Psychiatry, 160*, 274–283.

Zimmerman, M. (2015). Borderline personality disorder: In search of advocacy. *Journal of Nervous Mental Disease, 203*(1), 8–12.

WEBSITES REFERENCED

www.anythingtostopthepain.com, www.bpdawareness.org, www.facebook.com/bpda1, www.bpd-central.com., http://bpdawareness.bigcartel.com, www.bpdfamily.com, www.bpddemystified.com. www.hopeforbpd.com, www.mydialecticallife.com,www.thefightwithus.com, www.my-borderline-personality-disorder.com, http://www.my-borderline-nightmare.tumblr.com/

INDEX